INDEX OF MODELS

W9-DGE-740

FINITE MATHEMATICS WITH APPLICATIONS

FOR BUSINESS AND SOCIAL SCIENCES

FINITE MATHEMATICS WITH APPLICATIONS

FOR BUSINESS AND SOCIAL SCIENCES
FIFTH EDITION

ABE MIZRAHI
INDIANA UNIVERSITY NORTHWEST

MICHAEL SULLIVAN
CHICAGO STATE UNIVERSITY

JOHN WILEY & SONS
NEW YORK•CHICHESTER•BRISBANE•TORONTO•SINGAPORE

Cover painting by: Crockett Johnson, Smithsonian Institute

Copyright © 1973, 1976, 1979, 1983, 1988, by John Wiley & Sons, Inc.

Library of Congress Cataloging in Publication Data:

Mizrahi, Abe.
    Mathematics for business and social sciences: an applied approach
/ Abe Mizrahi, Michael Sullivan. — 4th ed.
        p.   cm.
    Includes index.
    ISBN 0-471-85291-0
    1. Business mathematics   2. Business Mathematics — Problems,
exercises, etc.   3. Social sciences — Mathematics.   I. Sullivan,
Michael, 1942 –   II. Title.
    HF5691.M59 1988
    513'.93 — dc19   87-31756
                                                                CIP

Printed in the United States of America
10 9 8 7 6 5 4 3 2 1

To Our Parents With Gratitude

PREFACE

The first edition of this book was published in 1973. At that time our purpose was to present a low-level approach to the mathematics required in business and the social sciences, giving emphasis to real-world applications from these fields. In subsequent editions this remained our purpose, as it does in this, the fifth edition. However, in this edition we have enlarged our range of applications to include applications to computers and the field of computer science.

ORGANIZATION

This edition is divided into three independent parts: Linear Algebra, Probability, and Discrete Mathematics. Depending on the interests of the audience, an instructor can start a course at the beginning of any of the three parts.

Part One, Linear Algebra, contains five chapters: Chapter 1 lays the foundation and is considered a review chapter. Chapter 2 presents a discussion of matrices, beginning with systems of linear equations. Chapters 3 and 4 concentrate on linear programming and applications. Chapter 5 contains some of the mathematics found in finance.

Part Two, Probability, contains six chapters. Chapter 6 introduces sets and elementary counting techniques. Chapter 7 deals with probability. Chapter 8 pursues more advanced counting principles, the binomial theorem, and the binomial probability model. Chapter 9 provides an introduction to statistics; Chapter 10 discusses Markov chains; Chapter 11 provides an application to game theory.

Part Three, Discrete Mathematics, contains three chapters. Chapter 12 discusses logic and its application to circuit design. Chapter 13 introduces relations, functions, sequences, and mathematical induction, emphasizing each one's role in computer science. Chapter 14 contains an introduction to graphs and networks.

CHANGES TO THE FIFTH EDITION

Chapter 1: The section on linear inequalities now appears in Chapter 3, where it is needed for the geometric approach to linear programming.

Chapter 2: This chapter has been completely reorganized. Systems of linear equations appear early and are solved using the reduced row-echelon method. An application of the method of least squares has been added.

Chapter 3: The chapter now begins with a section on linear inequalities.

Chapter 4: Rewritten to improve readability, this chapter now has a new section on mixed constraints, using the Phase I/Phase II method of solution.

Chapter 5: New examples and exercises have been added and previous ones updated to reflect current market conditions.

Chapter 6: The Multiplication Principle is given more emphasis. More demanding counting techniques are now found in Chapter 8.

Chapter 7: This chapter now concludes with Bayes' Theorem. The Binomial Probability Model is found in Chapter 8.

Chapter 8: This chapter contains more advanced counting techniques, the Binomial Theorem, and the Binomial Probability Model. New models include error correcting codes and mortgage selection.

Chapter 9: A new result, Chebychev's theorem, is included.

Chapter 10: No significant changes.

Chapter 11: A new model on the stock market is included.

Chapter 12: Rewritten to improve readability, this chapter now contains a full section on circuit design.

Chapters 13 and 14 are completely new to this edition.

The chart on the opposite page illustrates the interaction of the chapters.

FEATURES

* Over 350 illustrative examples.

* Procedures and processes for solving problems are given as a series of steps and are prominantly displayed in boxes. See, for example, page 130 and page 314.

* Over 2000 exercises, ranging from drill to challenging. Many of these are applied-type problems.

* Each chapter contains a review featuring a list of vocabulary from the chapter, True-False and Fill-in-the-blank questions, a collection of Review Exercises, and, when appropriate, Mathematical Questions taken from CPA, CMA, and actuary exams.

* Important Definitions are presented in bold face; formulas and theorems are placed in a box, screened in color.

* Answers to the Odd-Numbered Problems appear in the back of the book.

* Flowcharts are utilized whenever possible to outline procedures. See, for example, page 169.

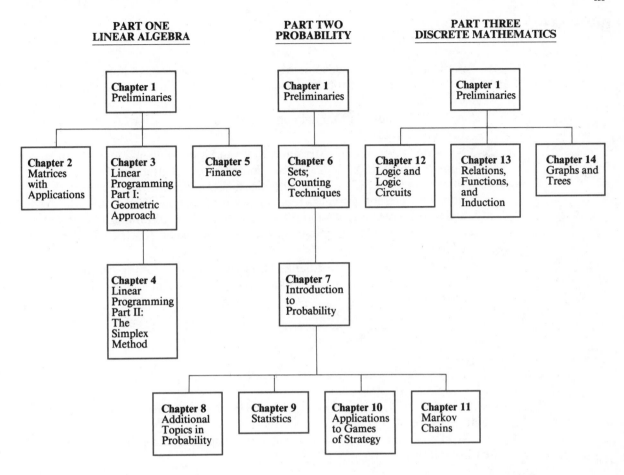

PART ONE
LINEAR ALGEBRA

PART TWO
PROBABILITY

PART THREE
DISCRETE MATHEMATICS

Chapter 1
Preliminaries

Chapter 1
Preliminaries

Chapter 1
Preliminaries

Chapter 2
Matrices
with
Applications

Chapter 3
Linear
Programming
Part I:
Geometric
Approach

Chapter 5
Finance

Chapter 6
Sets;
Counting
Techniques

Chapter 12
Logic and
Logic
Circuits

Chapter 13
Relations,
Functions,
and
Induction

Chapter 14
Graphs and
Trees

Chapter 4
Linear
Programming
Part II:
The
Simplex
Method

Chapter 7
Introduction
to
Probability

Chapter 8
Additional
Topics in
Probability

Chapter 9
Statistics

Chapter 10
Applications
to Games
of Strategy

Chapter 11
Markov
Chains

SUPPLEMENTS

* An Instructor's Manual containing worked-out solutions to both the even and the odd-numbered problems, plus a list of books and articles of interest, is available.

* A Student Solutions Manual contains worked-out solutions to the odd-numbered problems.

* Software to Accompany Mizrahi & Sullivan Finite Mathematics with Applications to Business & Life Science. Computer explorations in Finite/Discrete Math is a series of 12 Software activities that enable the user to perform calculations and present graphical representation of mathematical concepts. These activities serve as an interactive tool for teacher demonstrations, reinforce concepts and promote learning by discovery. Available for IBM PC. Free to adopters.

* Computer-Generated Test Bank. This microcomputer testing system contains questions prepared by the authors and is available for Apple, IBM-PC, and most compatibles.

ACKNOWLEDGMENTS

We thank the many students at Indiana University Northwest and Chicago State University for their comments and criticisms.

We also thank these reviewers for their suggestions and contributions to this and earlier editions:

Professor Judy Barclay	Cuesto College
Professor Charles Barker	DeAnza College
Professor Carole Bernett	William Rainey Harper College
Professor William Blair	Northern Illinois University
Professor W. J. Bonini	Western Wyoming College
Professor Gary G. Cochell	Calver-Stockton College
Professor Portia Cornell	University of Redlands
Professor Milton D. Cox	Miami University
Professor Neale Fadden	Belleville Area College
Professor Eugene Franks	Dyke College
Professor James C. Fraventhal	SUNY at Stony Brook
Professor Dennis Freeman	Montgomery College
Professor Samuel Graff	John Jay College of Criminal Justice
Professor Gerald Hahn	College of St. Thomas
Professor Joseph Hansen	Northeastern University
Professor Herbert Hethcote	University of Iowa
Professor Brian Hickey	First Central College
Professor Wayne Hiles	Kankakee Community College

Institute of Management Accounting of the National Association of Accountants (CMA Exams)

Again we are indebted to the people at John Wiley and at Hudson River Studios, whose talent played a significant part in the publication of this book. We particularly want to single out Ed and Lorraine Burke, Carolyn Moore, and Melissa Van Hise for their assistance.

This is truly a collaborative effort, and the order of authorship signifies alphabetical precedence. We assume equal responsibility for the book's strengths and weaknesses, and welcome comments and suggestions for its improvement.

Abe Mizrahi
Michael Sullivan

ABOUT THE AUTHORS

Abe Mizrahi, received his doctorate in mathematics from the Illinois Institute of Technology in 1986. He is currently Professor of Mathematics at Indiana University Northwest. Professor Mizrahi is the author of other mathematic books and is a member of the Mathematical Association of America. Articles of Professor Mizrahi dealt with topics in math education and the applications of mathematics to economics. Professor Mizrahi served on many CUPM committees, was a panel member on CUPM committee on applied mathematics in the undergraduate curriculum. Professor Mizrahi is a recipient of many NSF grants and served as a consultant to a number of businesses and Federal agencies.

Michael Sullivan, received his Ph.D. degree in mathematics from the Illinois Institute of Technology in 1967. Since 1965 he has been teaching at Chicago State University in the Department of Mathematics and Computer Science, holding the rank of Professor. Professor Sullivan and Professor Mizrahi are co-authors of *Mathematics for Business and Social Science,* 4th Edition, John Wiley and Sons, 1988 as well as *Calculus with Analytic Geometry,* 2nd Edition, Wadsworth Publishing Company, 1986. Professor Sullivan has also written *College Algebra* and *College Algebra and Trigonometry,* Dellen/Macmillan, 1987. Dr. Sullivan is a member of the American Mathematical Society, the Mathematics Association of America, and Sigma Xi. He has served on CUPM Curriculum Committees and is a member of the Illinois Section MAA High School Lecture Committee.

CONTENTS

FINITE MATHEMATICS WITH APPLICATIONS

FOR BUSINESS AND SOCIAL SCIENCES

PART ONE

LINEAR ALGEBRA

PRELIMINARIES

* This section may be omitted without loss of continuity.

1.1 REAL NUMBERS

SETS □ SETS OF NUMBERS □ DECIMALS AND PERCENTS □ PROPERTIES OF REAL NUMBERS □ POSITIVE AND NEGATIVE NUMBERS □ COORDINATES □ VARIABLES □ INEQUALITIES

SETS

Set   We begin with the idea of a *set*. A *set* is a collection of objects considered as a whole. The objects of a set S are called *elements* of S, or *members* of S. The set that has no
Empty Set   elements, called the *empty set* or *null set,* is denoted by the symbol $\varnothing$.

If a is an element of the set S, we write $a \in S$, which is read "a is an element of S" or "a is in S." To indicate that a is not an element of S, we write $a \notin S$, which is read "a is not an element of S" or "a is not in S."

Ordinarily, a set S can be written in either of two ways. These two methods are illustrated by the following example: Consider the set D that has the elements

$$0, 1, 2, 3, 4, 5, 6, 7, 8, 9$$

In this case, we write

$$D = \{0, 1, 2, 3, 4, 5, 6, 7, 8, 9\}$$

This expression is read "D is the set consisting of the elements 0, 1, 2, 3, 4, 5, 6, 7, 8, 9." Here, we list or display the elements of the set D.

Another way of writing this same set D is to write

$$D = \{x \mid x \text{ is a nonnegative integer less than } 10\}$$

This is read "D is the set of all x such that x is a nonnegative integer less than 10." Here, we have described the set D by giving a property that every element of D has and that no element not in D can have.

SETS OF NUMBERS

One of the most frequently used set of numbers in finite mathematics is the set of
Counting Numbers   *counting numbers,* namely

$$\{1, 2, 3, 4, \ldots\}$$

These are sometimes referred to as *positive integers.* As the name *counting numbers* implies, they are used to count things. For example, there are 26 letters in our alphabet, and there are 100 cents in a dollar.
Integers   Another important collection of numbers is the set of *integers,*

$$\{0, 1, -1, 2, -2, \ldots\}$$

which consists of the *nonnegative integers,*

$$\{0, 1, 2, 3, \ldots\}$$

and the *negative integers,*

$$\{-1, -2, -3, \ldots\}$$

Integers enable us to handle certain types of situations. For example, if a company shows a loss of $3 per share, we might decide to denote this loss as a gain of $-$3. Then, if this same company shows a profit of $4 per share next year, the profit over the 2 year period can be obtained by adding -3 to 4, getting a profit of $1.

However, integers do not enable us to solve *all* problems. For example, can we use an integer to answer the question, "What part of a dollar is 49¢?" Or, can we use an integer to represent the length of a city lot (in feet) if we end up with a length more than 125 feet and less than 126 feet?

The answer to both these questions is "No"! We need new or different numbers to handle such situations. These new numbers are called *rational numbers.*

Rational Numbers   Rational numbers are ratios of integers. More specifically, for a rational number $\frac{a}{b}$, the integer a is called the *numerator,* and the integer b, which cannot be zero, is called the *denominator.*

Thus to answer the first question, "What part of a dollar is 49¢?" we can say $\frac{49}{100}$.

Examples of rational numbers are $\frac{3}{4}, \frac{5}{3}, -\frac{2}{7}, \frac{100}{3}, -\frac{8}{3}$. Since the ratio of any integer to 1 is that integer, the integers are also rational numbers. Thus, $\frac{3}{1} = 3, -\frac{2}{1} = -2, \frac{0}{1} = 0$.

In this book, we will always write rational numbers in *lowest terms;* that is, the numerator and the denominator will contain no common factors. Thus, $\frac{4}{6}$, which is not in lowest terms, will be written as $\frac{2}{3}$, which is in lowest terms.

In some situations, even a rational number will not accurately describe the situation. For example, if you have an isosceles right triangle in which the two equal sides are 1 foot long, can the length of the third side be expressed as a rational number? See Figure 1.

Figure 1

And how about the value of π (Greek letter "pi")? The Greeks first learned that no matter what two circles are used, the ratio of the circumference to the diameter of the first circle is always the same as the ratio of the circumference to the diameter of the second one. Can this common value, which we call π, be represented by a rational number? See Figure 2.

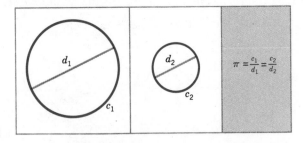

Figure 2

Irrational Numbers

Real Numbers

As it happens, the answer to both these questions is "No." For the first question, by the Pythagorean theorem* the length of the third side is $\sqrt{2}$. However, $\sqrt{2}$ is not a rational number — it is not the ratio of two integers. The well-known symbol assigned to the ratio of the circumference to the diameter of a circle is π, which also cannot be expressed as the ratio of two integers. Such numbers as $\sqrt{2}$, π, $\sqrt[3]{5}$, etc., are called *irrational numbers* — numbers that are not rational.

The irrational numbers and the rational numbers together form the *real numbers*.

DECIMALS AND PERCENTS

Decimals

To represent each real number, we use what is commonly referred to as a *decimal representation,* or simply a *decimal.* The table below lists the decimal equivalents of some frequently encountered rational numbers.

Rational number	$\frac{1}{2}$	$\frac{1}{3}$	$\frac{2}{3}$	$\frac{1}{4}$	$\frac{3}{4}$	$\frac{1}{5}$	$\frac{2}{5}$	$\frac{3}{5}$	$\frac{4}{5}$	$\frac{1}{8}$	$\frac{3}{8}$	$\frac{5}{8}$	$\frac{7}{8}$
Decimal equivalent	0.5	0.333 ...	0.666 ...	0.25	0.75	0.2	0.4	0.6	0.8	0.125	0.375	0.625	0.875

The decimal equivalent of any rational number is obtained by long division: Divide the denominator into the numerator. For example, we find that the decimal equivalent of $\frac{7}{66}$ is 0.10606 . . . as follows:

$$
\begin{array}{r}
0.10606 \\
66\overline{)7.00000} \\
\underline{6\ 6} \\
400 \\
\underline{396} \\
400 \\
\underline{396} \\
\text{etc.}
\end{array}
$$

Observe the following fact: The decimal equivalent of a rational number is always one of two types: *(1)* terminating or ending ($\frac{3}{4}$, $\frac{4}{5}$, etc.) or *(2)* eventually repeating ($\frac{2}{3}$ — the 6's repeat; $\frac{7}{66}$ — eventually the block 06 repeats).

At first, it may appear that these two types account for all possible decimals. However, it is relatively easy to construct a decimal that neither terminates nor

---

* The Pythagorean theorem states that in a right triangle the square of the length of the side opposite the right angle equals the sum of the squares of the lengths of the other two sides. Thus, in the illustration $c^2 = a^2 + b^2$.

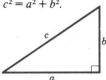

eventually repeats. For example, the decimal

$$0.123456789101112\ldots$$

where we write down the positive integers one after the other, will neither terminate nor eventually repeat.

In fact, there are an infinite number of such decimals, and they represent the irrational numbers. For example, the real numbers

$$\sqrt{2} = 1.414213\ldots \quad \text{and} \quad \pi = 3.14159\ldots$$

are irrational, since they have decimal representations that neither terminate nor eventually repeat.

Thus, *real numbers* and *all possible decimals* are equivalent concepts. It is this feature of real numbers that provides the "practicality" of real numbers.* In the physical world a changing magnitude, such as the length of a heated rod, the velocity of a particle, and so on, is assumed to pass through every possible magnitude from the initial one to the final one. Since the precise measurement of a magnitude is naturally given by a decimal, the logical equivalent of all possible magnitudes is all possible decimals (real numbers).

In practice, it is usually necessary to represent irrational real numbers by approximations. For example, using the symbol ≈, read "approximately equal to," we can write

$$\sqrt{2} \approx 1.4142 \quad \text{and} \quad \pi \approx 3.1416$$

Percents   Many of the problems we shall encounter use *percents* rather than decimals. For example, interest rates and tax rates are almost always expressed as percents. It is easy to convert from a decimal to a percent. Let's look at a few examples.

$$0.15 = 15\% \qquad 0.20 = 20\% \qquad 1.45 = 145\%$$
$$0.08 = 8\% \qquad 0.0525 = 5\tfrac{1}{4}\% \qquad 0.001 = 0.1\%$$

The idea should be clear—to change from a decimal to a percent, move the decimal point two places to the right and add a percent symbol. Reverse this procedure to get from a percent to its decimal equivalent.

□ **Example 1**   A resident of Illinois has base income, after adjustments for deductions, of $18,000. The state income tax on this base income is $2\tfrac{1}{2}\%$. What tax is due?

Solution   We must find $2\tfrac{1}{2}\%$ of $18,000. We convert $2\tfrac{1}{2}\%$ to its decimal equivalent and then multiply by $18,000.

$$2\tfrac{1}{2}\% \text{ of } \$18,000 = (0.025)(\$18,000) = \$450$$

The state income tax is $450.00.   □

---

* Other number systems exist that have many applications (such as the complex numbers). In this book, however, we limit our discussion to problems in which only real numbers are used.

PROPERTIES OF REAL NUMBERS

As an aid to your review of real numbers and their properties, we list several important rules and notations. The letters a, b, c, d represent real numbers; any exceptions will be noted as they occur.

1. *Commutative Laws*
   (a) $a + b = b + a$ (b) $a \cdot b = b \cdot a$
2. *Associative Laws*
   (a) $a + b + c = (a + b) + c = a + (b + c)$
   (b) $a \cdot b \cdot c = (a \cdot b) \cdot c = a \cdot (b \cdot c)$
3. *Distributive Law*
   $a \cdot (b + c) = (a \cdot b) + (a \cdot c)$
4. *Arithmetic of Ratios*

   (a) $\dfrac{a}{b} = a \cdot \dfrac{1}{b}$ $b \neq 0$

   (b) $\dfrac{a}{b} + \dfrac{c}{d} = \dfrac{(a \cdot d) + (b \cdot c)}{b \cdot d}$ $b \neq 0, \quad d \neq 0$

   (c) $\dfrac{a}{b} \cdot \dfrac{c}{d} = \dfrac{a \cdot c}{b \cdot d}$ $b \neq 0, \quad d \neq 0$

   (d) $\dfrac{a}{b} \div \dfrac{c}{d} = \dfrac{a}{b} \cdot \dfrac{d}{c} = \dfrac{a \cdot d}{b \cdot c}$ $b \neq 0, \quad c \neq 0, \quad d \neq 0$

5. *Rules for Division*

   $0 \div a = 0 \quad$ or $\quad \dfrac{0}{a} = 0 \quad$ for any real number a different from 0

   $a \div 0 \quad$ or $\quad \dfrac{a}{0} \quad$ is undefined for any real number a, including 0;

   never divide by zero!
   $a \div a = 1 \quad$ for any real number a different from 0
6. *Cancellation Laws*
   (a) If $a \cdot c = b \cdot c$ and c is not 0, then $a = b$.

   (b) If b and c are not 0, then $\dfrac{a \cdot c}{b \cdot c} = \dfrac{a}{b}$.

7. *Product Law*
   If $a \cdot b = 0$, then either $a = 0$ or $b = 0$.
8. *Rules of Signs*
   (a) $a \cdot (-b) = -(a \cdot b)$ (b) $(-a) \cdot b = -(a \cdot b)$
   (c) $(-a) \cdot (-b) = a \cdot b$ (d) $-(-a) = a$
9. *Agreements: Notations*
   (a) Given $a \cdot b + c$ or $c + a \cdot b$, we agree to multiply $a \cdot b$ first, and then add c.

(b)   A mixed number $3\frac{5}{8}$ means $3 + \frac{5}{8}$; 3 *times* $\frac{5}{8}$ is written as $3(\frac{5}{8})$ or $(3)(\frac{5}{8})$ or $3 \cdot \frac{5}{8}$.

10. *Exponents*

For any positive integer n and any real number x, we define

$$x^1 = x, \quad x^2 = x \cdot x, \quad \ldots, \quad x^n = \underbrace{x \cdot x \cdot \ldots \cdot x}_{n \text{ factors}}$$

For any real number $x \neq 0$, we define

$$x^0 = 1, \quad x^{-1} = \frac{1}{x}, \quad x^{-2} = \frac{1}{x^2}, \quad \ldots, \quad x^{-n} = \frac{1}{x^n}$$

11. *Laws of Exponents* (a, x are real numbers; n, m are integers)

(a) $x^n \cdot x^m = x^{n+m}$ (b) $(x^n)^m = x^{nm}$

(c) $(ax)^n = a^n \cdot x^n$ (d) $\left(\dfrac{x}{a}\right)^n = \dfrac{x^n}{a^n}$ $a \neq 0$

(e) $\dfrac{x^n}{x^m} = x^{n-m}$ $x \neq 0$

12. *Roots*

For a positive integer q, the qth root of x, $\sqrt[q]{x}$, is a symbol for the real number which, when raised to the power q, equals x. If q is even and x is positive, then $\sqrt[q]{x}$ is declared to be positive. For example,

$$\sqrt[3]{8} = 2 \quad \text{since } 2^3 = 8 \qquad \sqrt[2]{64} = 8 \quad \text{since} \quad 8^2 = 64$$

Here $\sqrt[3]{x}$ is called the *cube root* of x and $\sqrt[2]{x}$ is called the *square root* of x. Usually, we abbreviate square roots by $\sqrt{\ }$, dropping the ^{2}. *Be careful! No meaning is assigned to even roots of negative numbers,* since any real number raised to an even power is nonnegative. For example, $\sqrt{4} = 2$, whereas $\sqrt{-4}$ has no meaning in the set of real numbers. On the other hand, $\sqrt[3]{27} = 3$, while $\sqrt[3]{-64} = -4$ since $(-4)^3 = -64$. Thus, meaning is given to odd roots of negative numbers. Finally, following the usual convention, even roots of positive numbers are always positive. Thus, even though $(2)^2 = 4$ and $(-2)^2 = 4$, only the positive root 2 equals $\sqrt{4}$. That is, $\sqrt{4} = 2$.

□ **Example 2**   (a) $\dfrac{2}{3} \cdot \dfrac{9}{4} = \dfrac{18}{12} = \dfrac{6 \cdot 3}{6 \cdot 2} = \dfrac{3}{2}$ (b) $\dfrac{1}{2} + \dfrac{3}{4} = \dfrac{2}{4} + \dfrac{3}{4} = \dfrac{5}{4}$

(c) $(-3)^2 = 9$ (d) $-3^2 = -9$

(e) $3 + 4 \cdot 2 = 3 + 8 = 11$ (f) $(3 + 4)^2 = 7^2 = 49$ □

POSITIVE AND NEGATIVE NUMBERS

The real numbers can be divided into three nonempty sets that have no elements in common: *(1)* the set of positive real numbers; *(2)* the set with just 0 as a member; and *(3)* the set of negative real numbers. We list some familiar properties:

1. Any real number is either positive or negative or equal to zero.

2. The sum and product of two positive numbers is positive.

3. The product of two negative numbers is positive.

4. The product of a positive number and a negative number is negative.

For real numbers a and b, a is less than b ($a < b$) or b is greater than a ($b > a$) if and only if the difference $b - a$ is a positive real number. For example, $2 < 7$ and $-3 > -6$. It is easy to conclude that

$$a \text{ is positive if and only if } a > 0$$

$$a \text{ is negative if and only if } a < 0$$

As a result, if $a < b$ there is a positive number p so that $a + p = b$. If a is less than or equal to b, we write $a \leq b$. If a is greater than or equal to b, we write $a \geq b$. If $a < c$ and $c < b$, we write $a < c < b$. This says that c is between a and b. Similarly, if $a \leq c$ and $c \leq b$, we write $a \leq c \leq b$. The notations $a \leq c < b$ and $a < c \leq b$ are given similar interpretations.

Inequalities obey the following laws:

1. *Addition Law*
   If $a \leq b$, then $a + c \leq b + c$ for any choice of c. That is, the addition of a number to each side of an inequality will not affect the sense or direction of the inequality.

2. *Multiplication Laws*
   (a) If $a \leq b$ and $c > 0$, then $a \cdot c \leq b \cdot c$.

   (b) If $a \leq b$ and $c < 0$, then $a \cdot c \geq b \cdot c$.

   When multiplying each side of an inequality by a number, the sense or direction of the inequality remains the same if we multiply by a positive number; it is reversed if we multiply by a negative number.

3. *Division Laws*
   (a) If $a > 0$, then $\dfrac{1}{a} > 0$. That is, the reciprocal of a positive number is positive.

   (b) If a, b are positive and if $a < b$, then $\dfrac{1}{a} > \dfrac{1}{b}$.

4. *Trichotomy Law*
   For any two real numbers a, b, one and only one of the following is true: $a < b$, $a = b$, or $a > b$.

□ **Example 3** (a) Since $2 < 3$, then $2 + 5 < 3 + 5$, or $7 < 8$.

(b) Since $2 < 3$ and $6 > 0$, then $2 \cdot 6 < 3 \cdot 6$, or $12 < 18$.

(c) Since $2 < 3$ and $-4 < 0$, then $2 \cdot (-4) > 3 \cdot (-4)$, or $-8 > -12$.

(d) Since $3 > 0$, then $\dfrac{1}{3} > 0$.

(e) Since $2 < 3$, then $\dfrac{1}{2} > \dfrac{1}{3}$.   □

COORDINATES

Real numbers can be represented geometrically on a horizontal line. We begin by
Origin   selecting an arbitrary point O, called the *origin,* and associate it with the real number
0. We then establish a scale by marking off line segments of equal length (units) on
each side of 0. By agreeing that the positive direction is to the right of 0 and the
negative direction is to the left of 0, we can successively associate the integers 1, 2,
3, . . . with each mark to the right of 0 and the integers $-1, -2, -3, \ldots$ with each
mark to the left of 0. See Figure 3.

Figure 3

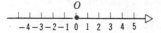

By subdividing these segments, we can locate rational numbers such as $\frac{1}{2}$ and $-\frac{3}{2}$.
The irrational numbers are located by geometric construction (as in the case of $\sqrt{2}$) or
by other means. In this way, every point P on the line is associated with a unique real
Coordinate   number x, called the *coordinate of P* (see Figure 4). Coordinates establish an ordering
for the real numbers; that is, if a and b are coordinates of two points P and Q,
respectively, then $a < b$ means that P lies to the left of Q on the line.

Figure 4

VARIABLES

A *variable* is a symbol (usually a letter x, y, etc.) used to represent any real number.
Equation   An *equation* is a statement involving one or more variables and an "equals" sign (=).
To *solve* an equation means to find all possible numbers that the variables can assume
Solution   to make the statement true. The set of all such numbers is called the *solution.* Two
equations with the same solution are called *equivalent equations.*

□ **Example 4**   Solve the equation: $3x - 8 = x + 4$

Solution   We use the properties of real numbers and proceed as follows:

$$3x - 8 = x + 4$$
$$2x - 8 = 4 \qquad \text{Subtract } x \text{ from both sides}$$
$$2x = 12 \qquad \text{Add 8 to both sides}$$
$$x = 6 \qquad \text{Divide each side by 2}$$

The solution is $x = 6$.   □

□ **Example 5**   Solve the equation: $x^2 + x - 12 = 0$

Solution   We factor the left side, obtaining

$$(x - 3)(x + 4) = 0$$

The Product Law states that either the first factor or the second factor must equal zero. Thus,

$$x - 3 = 0 \quad \text{or} \quad x + 4 = 0$$
$$x = 3 \quad \text{or} \quad x = -4$$

The solutions to the equation are $x = 3$ or $x = -4$.   □

INEQUALITIES

Inequality   An *inequality* is a statement involving one or more variables and one of the inequality symbols ($<, \leq, >, \geq$). To *solve* an inequality means to find all possible numbers that the variables can assume to make the statement true. The set of all such numbers is called the *solution*. Two inequalities with the same solution are called *equivalent inequalities.*

To find the solution of an inequality, we apply the laws for inequalities.

□ **Example 6**   Solve the inequality: $x + 2 \leq 3x - 5$

Solution

$$x + 2 \leq 3x - 5$$

$$-2x \leq -7 \qquad \text{Subtract 2 and then } 3x \text{ from both sides}$$

$$x \geq \frac{7}{2} \qquad \text{Multiply by } -\tfrac{1}{2} \text{ and remember to reverse the inequality because we multiplied by a negative number}$$

The solution is the set of all real numbers to the right of $\frac{7}{2}$, including $\frac{7}{2}$ (see Figure 5).   □

Figure 5

In graphing the solution to an inequality, our practice will be to use a filled-in circle (●) if the number is included (such as $\frac{7}{2}$ in Figure 5) and an open circle (○) if the number is to be excluded.

Exercise 1.1   *Answers to Odd-Numbered Problems begin on page 599.*

In Problems 1–8 represent each rational number as a decimal.

1. $\frac{1}{2}$	**2.** $\frac{3}{4}$	**3.** $\frac{13}{8}$	**4.** $\frac{15}{8}$
5. $\frac{4}{3}$	**6.** $\frac{5}{3}$	**7.** $\frac{1}{6}$	**8.** $\frac{5}{6}$

In Problems 9–16 write each decimal as a percent.

9. 0.45	**10.** 0.85	**11.** 1.12	**12.** 1.25
13. 0.06	**14.** 0.07	**15.** 0.0025	**16.** 0.0015

In Problems 17–24 write each percent as a decimal.

17. 42%	**18.** 7.25%	**19.** 0.2%	**20.** 300%
21. 0.001%	**22.** 4.3%	**23.** 73.4%	**24.** 92%

In Problems 25–28 write each rational number in lowest terms.

25. $\frac{2}{40}$ **26.** $\frac{25}{45}$ **27.** $\frac{6}{8}$ **28.** $\frac{8}{24}$

In Problems 29–32 calculate the indicated quantity.

29. 15% of 1000   **30.** 20% of 500   **31.** 18% of 100   **32.** 10% of 50

In Problems 33–50 find the solution x of each equation.

33. $2x + 5 = 7$ **34.** $x + 6 = 2$

35. $6 - x = 0$ **36.** $6 + x = 0$

37. $3(2 - x) = 9$ **38.** $5(x + 1) = 10$

39. $4x + 3 = 2x - 5$ **40.** $5x - 8 = 2x + 1$

41. $\dfrac{4x}{3} + \dfrac{x}{3} = 5$ **42.** $\dfrac{2x}{5} + \dfrac{x}{5} = 9$

43. $\dfrac{3x - 5}{x - 3} = 1$ **44.** $\dfrac{2x + 1}{x - 1} = 3$

45. $x^2 - x - 12 = 0$ **46.** $x^2 + 7x = 0$

47. $x^2 - 5x + 6 = 0$ **48.** $x^2 - x - 6 = 0$

49. $x^2 - 16 = 0$ **50.** $x^2 - 6x + 9 = 0$

In Problems 51–62 find x.

51. $x = 3^2$ **52.** $x = 2^3$ **53.** $x = 2^{-3}$ **54.** $x = 3^{-2}$

55. $x = -3^2$ **56.** $x = (-3)^2$ **57.** $x^3 = 8$ **58.** $x^5 = -32$

59. $2^x = 4$ **60.** $3^x = 81$ **61.** $4^x = 4^5$ **62.** $2^x = 2^{10}$

In Problems 63–66 replace the * by $<$, $>$, or $=$.

63. $\frac{1}{3} * 0.33$ **64.** $\frac{1}{4} * 0.25$ **65.** $3 * \sqrt{9}$ **66.** $\pi * \frac{22}{7}$

In Problems 67–74 find the solution.

67. $3x + 5 \le 2$ **68.** $14x - 21x + 16 \le 3x - 2$

69. $3x + 5 \ge 2$ **70.** $4 - 5x \ge 3$

71. $-3x + 5 \le 2$ **72.** $8 - 2x \le 5x - 6$

73. $6x - 3 \ge 8x + 5$ **74.** $-3x \le 2x + 5$

In Problems 75–78 graph each inequality.

75. $x + 3 > 4x - 6$ **76.** $2x + 1 < 3x - 2$

77. $2x - 2 \le x + 3$ **78.** $3x - 1 \ge 2x + 5$

1.2 RECTANGULAR COORDINATES

GRAPHS

x-axis
y-axis

Consider two lines, one horizontal and the other vertical. Call the horizontal line the *x-axis* and the vertical line the *y-axis*. Assign coordinates to points on these lines, as described previously, by using their point of intersection as the origin O and using a convenient scale on each. We follow the usual convention that points on the *x*-axis to the right of O are associated with positive real numbers, those to the left of O with negative numbers, those on the *y*-axis above O are associated with positive real numbers, and those below O with negative real numbers. This gives the origin a value of zero on both the *x*-axis and the *y*-axis. See Figure 6.

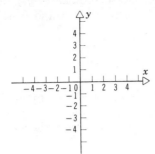

Figure 6

Ordered Pair

Coordinates

Any point P in the plane formed by the *x*-axis and *y*-axis can then be located by using an *ordered pair* of real numbers. Let x denote the signed distance of P from the *y*-axis (signed in the sense that if P is to the right of the *y*-axis, then $x > 0$ and if P is to the left of the *y*-axis, then $x < 0$); and let y denote the signed distance of P from the *x*-axis. The ordered pair (x, y), the *coordinates of P*, then gives us enough information to locate the point P. We can assign ordered pairs of real numbers to every point P, as shown in Figure 7.

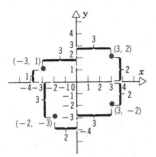

Figure 7

x-coordinate
y-coordinate

If (x, y) are the coordinates of a point P, then x is called the *x-coordinate* of P and y is the *y-coordinate* of P. For example, the coordinates of the origin O are $(0, 0)$. The *x*-coordinate of any point on the *y*-axis is 0; the *y*-coordinate of any point on the *x*-axis is 0.

Rectangular
Coordinate System

The coordinate system described here is a *rectangular* or *cartesian coordinate system* and divides the plane into four sections called *quadrants* (see Figure 8).

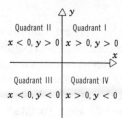

Figure 8

Quadrants

In quadrant I, both the x-coordinate and the y-coordinate of all points are positive; in quadrant II, $x < 0$ and $y > 0$; in quadrant III, both x and y are negative; and in quadrant IV, $x > 0$ and $y < 0$.

GRAPHS

When a specified relationship between x and y is given, its *graph* consists of the set of points (x, y) in the plane that obey the given relationship. To draw a graph, plot a sufficient number of points to see a pattern, and then connect these points.

□ Example 1

Graph the set of points (x, y) given by the equation

$$y = x$$

Solution

We wish to locate all points (x, y) for which the x-coordinate and the y-coordinate are equal. Some of these points are

$$(0, 0), (0.1, 0.1), (1, 1), (1.5, 1.5), (3, 3), (-3, -3), (-0.2, -0.2), (8, 8)$$

The graph is given in Figure 9. Notice that we use an arrow to indicate that the graph keeps going in a certain direction.   □

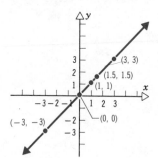

Figure 9

RENÉ DESCARTES (1596–1650), after whom the cartesian coordinate system was named, was born in La Haye, France. After spending several years participating in various wars, he published a treatise introducing analytic geometry. In addition to being a mathematician, he was a respected philosopher and theologian.

□ **Example 2**   Graph the set of points (x, y) given by the equation

$$y = 2x + 5$$

Solution   We want to find all points (x, y) for which the y-coordinate equals twice the x-coordinate plus 5. To locate some of these points (and thus to get an idea of the pattern of the graph), let us *assign* some numbers x and find corresponding values for y. Thus:

$$\text{If } x = 0, \qquad y = 2 \cdot 0 + 5 = 5$$
$$\text{If } x = 1, \qquad y = 2 \cdot 1 + 5 = 7$$
$$\text{If } x = -5, \qquad y = 2 \cdot (-5) + 5 = -5$$
$$\text{If } x = 10 \qquad y = 2 \cdot 10 + 5 = 25$$

We plot the points (x, y), namely $(0, 5)$, $(1, 7)$, $(-5, -5)$, and $(10, 25)$. By connecting these points, we obtain the graph. See Figure 10.   □

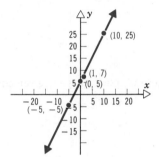

Figure 10

Exercise 1.2   *Answers to Odd-Numbered Problems begin on page* 599.

1. Find the coordinates of each point in Figure 11.
2. Locate the points $(3, -2)$, $(-2, 3)$, $(5, 0)$, $(-3, -4)$, and $(0, 8)$ using Figure 11 as a background.

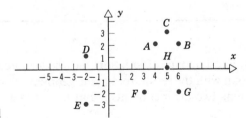

Figure 11

In Problems 3–6 use Figure 11, where $A = (a_1, a_2)$, $B = (b_1, b_2)$, $C = (c_1, c_2)$, and $F = (f_1, f_2)$, to compute each quantity.

3. $\dfrac{f_2 - a_2}{f_1 - a_1}$ 4. $\dfrac{f_2 - c_2}{f_1 - c_1}$ 5. $\dfrac{a_2 - c_2}{a_1 - c_1}$ 6. $\dfrac{a_2 - b_2}{a_1 - b_1}$

In Problems 7–10 copy the tables at the right and fill in the missing values of the given equations. Use these points to graph each equation.

7. $y = x - 3$

x	0		2	-2	4	-4
y		0				

8. $y = -3x + 3$

x	0		2	-2	4	-4
y		0				

9. $2x - y = 6$

x	0		2	-2	4	-4
y		0				

10. $x + 3y = 9$

x	0		2	-2	4	-4
y		0				

In Problems 11–20 graph the set of points (x, y) that obey the given equation.

11. $y = 3x$ **12.** $y = 4x$

13. $y = 2x - 3$ **14.** $y = 2x + 1$

15. $y = 0$ **16.** $x = 0$

17. $y = -2x - 3$ **18.** $y = -2x - 4$

19. $3x + 2y + 6 = 0$ **20.** $2x - 3y + 12 = 0$

21. Graph the equations in Problems 17 and 18 on the same coordinate system. Do you notice anything?

1.3 THE STRAIGHT LINE

EQUATIONS OF LINES ☐ SUMMARY

In this section, we study a certain type of equation, the *linear equation,* and its graph, the *straight line.* We begin with the result from plane geometry that there is one and only one line L containing two distinct points P and Q. See Figure 12.

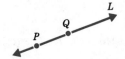

Figure 12

If P and Q are each represented by ordered pairs of real numbers, the following definition can be given:

Slope of a Line Let P and Q be two distinct points with coordinates (x_1, y_1) and (x_2, y_2), respectively. The *slope m* of the line L containing P and Q is defined by the formula*

$$m = \frac{y_2 - y_1}{x_2 - x_1} \quad \text{if} \quad x_1 \neq x_2$$

If $x_1 = x_2$, the slope m of L is *undefined* (since this results in division by zero) and L is a Vertical Line

We can also write the slope m of a nonvertical line as

$$m = \frac{\text{change in } y}{\text{change in } x} = \frac{\Delta y}{\Delta x}$$

That is, the slope m of a nonvertical line L is the ratio of the change in the y-coordinates from P to Q to the change in the x-coordinates from P to Q. In other words, the slope m of a line L equals the "rise over run" of the line. See Figure 13.

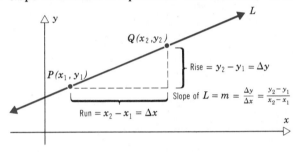

Figure 13

Since

$$\frac{y_2 - y_1}{x_2 - x_1} = \frac{y_1 - y_2}{x_1 - x_2}$$

the result is the same whether the changes are computed from P to Q or from Q to P.

□ **Example 1** The slope m of the line containing the points $(1, 2)$ and $(5, -3)$ may be computed as

$$m = \frac{-3 - 2}{5 - 1} = \frac{-5}{4} \quad \text{or as} \quad m = \frac{2 - (-3)}{1 - 5} = \frac{5}{-4} = \frac{-5}{4} \qquad \square$$

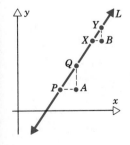

* The following argument, involving similar triangles, shows that the slope of a line L is the same no matter what two distinct points are used: Let L be a nonvertical line joining P and Q and let X and Y be any other two distinct points on L. Construct the triangles depicted in the figure. Since triangle PQA is similar to triangle XYB (why?), it follows that the lengths of the corresponding sides are in proportion. That is, $|AQ|/|BY| = |AP|/|BX|$ or $|AQ|/|AP| = |BY|/|BX|$. But the slope m of L is $|AQ|/|AP|$, and by the foregoing equality, we see that $m = |BY|/|BX|$. In other words, since X and Y are *any* two points, the slope m of a line L is the same no matter what points on L are used to compute m.

To get a better idea of the meaning of the slope of a line L, consider the following example.

☐ **Example 2**   Compute the slopes of the lines $L_1, L_2, L_3,$ and L_4 containing the following pairs of points. Graph each line.

$$L_1: \quad P = (2, 3) \qquad Q_1 = (-1, -2)$$
$$L_2: \quad P = (2, 3) \qquad Q_2 = (3, -1)$$
$$L_3: \quad P = (2, 3) \qquad Q_3 = (5, 3)$$
$$L_4: \quad P = (2, 3) \qquad Q_4 = (2, 5)$$

Solution   Let $m_1, m_2, m_3,$ and m_4 denote the slopes of the lines $L_1, L_2, L_3,$ and L_4, respectively. Then

$$m_1 = \frac{-2 - 3}{-1 - 2} = \frac{-5}{-3} = \frac{5}{3} \qquad \text{A rise of 5 over a run of 3}$$

$$m_2 = \frac{-1 - 3}{3 - 2} = \frac{-4}{1} = -4$$

$$m_3 = \frac{3 - 3}{5 - 2} = \frac{0}{3} = 0$$

m_4 is undefined since $x_1 = x_2 = 2$.

The graphs of these lines are given in Figure 14.

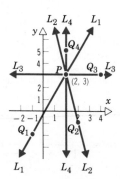

Figure 14

As Figure 14 indicates, when the slope m of a line is positive, the line *slants upward* from left to right (L_1); when the slope m is negative, the line *slants downward* from left to right (L_2); when the slope $m = 0$, the line is horizontal (L_3); and when the slope m is undefined, the line is vertical (L_4). Figure 15 illustrates the slopes of several lines. Note the pattern.

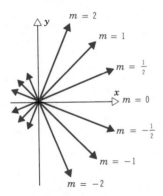

Figure 15

EQUATIONS OF LINES

A vertical line is given by the equation

$$x = a$$

where a is a given real number.

□ **Example 3**   The graph of the equation $x = 3$ is a vertical line (see Figure 16).

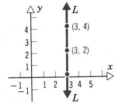

Figure 16

Now let L be a nonvertical line with slope m and containing (x_1, y_1). For (x, y) any other point on L, we have

$$m = \frac{y - y_1}{x - x_1} \qquad \text{or} \qquad y - y_1 = m(x - x_1)$$

Point-Slope Form   An equation of a nonvertical line of slope m that passes through the point (x_1, y_1) is

$$y - y_1 = m(x - x_1)$$

□ **Example 4**   An equation of the line with slope 4 and passing through the point $(1, 2)$ is

$$y - 2 = 4(x - 1)$$
$$y = 4x - 2$$

See Figure 17 on page 20.

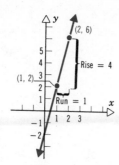

Figure 17

□

□ **Example 5**   Find an equation of the line L passing through the points $(2, 3)$ and $(-4, 5)$. Graph the line L.

Solution   Since two points are given, we first compute the slope of the line:

$$m = \frac{5 - 3}{-4 - 2} = \frac{2}{-6} = \frac{-1}{3}$$

Using the point $(2, 3)$ (we could use the other point instead, if we wished), and the fact that the slope $m = \dfrac{-1}{3}$, the point–slope equation of the line is

$$y - 3 = \frac{-1}{3}(x - 2)$$

See Figure 18 for the graph.

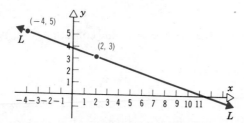

Figure 18

□

Another form of the equation of the line graphed in Example 5 can be obtained by multiplying both sides by 3 and collecting terms.

$$3(y - 3) = 3(-1/3)(x - 2) \qquad \text{Multiply by 3}$$
$$3y - 9 = -1(x - 2)$$
$$3y - 9 = -x + 2$$
$$x + 3y = 11$$

This last form is referred to as the *general form*, because every line has an equation that can be written this way.

General Form The equation of a line L is in *general form* when it is written as

$$Ax + By = C$$

where A, B, C are three real numbers with either $A \neq 0$ or $B \neq 0$.

Intercepts The points at which the graph of a line L crosses the axes are called *intercepts*. The *x-intercept* is the point at which the line crosses the *x*-axis, and the *y-intercept* is the point at which the line crosses the *y*-axis.

For example, the line L in Figure 19 has *x*-intercept $(3, 0)$ and *y*-intercept $(0, -4)$.

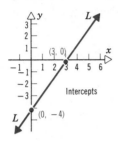

Figure 19

□ **Example 6** Find the intercepts of the line $2x + 3y = 6$. Graph this line.

Solution To find the point at which the graph crosses the *x*-axis — that is, to find the *x*-intercept — we need to find the number x for which $y = 0$. Thus, we set $y = 0$ to get

$$2x + 3(0) = 6$$
$$2x = 6$$
$$x = 3$$

The *x*-intercept is $(3, 0)$. To find the *y*-intercept, we set $x = 0$ and solve for y:

$$2(0) + 3y = 6$$
$$3y = 6$$
$$y = 2$$

The *y*-intercept is $(0, 2)$.
We now know two points on the line: $(3, 0)$ and $(0, 2)$. See Figure 20 for the graph.

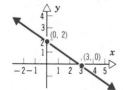

Figure 20   □

Another useful equation of a line is obtained when the slope m and y-intercept $(0, b)$ are known. Since in this event we know both the slope m of the line and a point $(0, b)$ on the line, we may use the point–slope form to obtain the following equation:

$$y - b = m(x - 0) \quad \text{or} \quad y = mx + b$$

> **Slope–Intercept Form** An equation of a line L with slope m and y-intercept $(0, b)$ is
>
> $$y = mx + b$$

When the equation of a line is written in slope–intercept form, it is easy to find the slope m and y-intercept $(0, b)$ of the line. For example, suppose the equation of a line is

$$y = -2x + 3$$

Compare it to $y = mx + b$:

$$y = -2x + 3$$
$$\uparrow \quad \uparrow$$
$$y = \ mx + b$$

The slope of this line is -2 and its y-intercept is $(0, 3)$. Let's look at another example.

☐ **Example 7** Find the slope m and y-intercept $(0, b)$ of the line L given by $2x + 4y = 8$. Graph the line.

Solution To obtain the slope and y-intercept, we transform the equation to its slope–intercept form. Thus, we need to solve for y:

$$2x + 4y = 8$$
$$4y = -2x + 8$$
$$y = \left(\frac{-1}{2}\right)x + 2$$

The coefficient of x, $-\frac{1}{2}$, is the slope, and the y-intercept is $(0, 2)$. To graph this line, we need two points. Normally, the easiest points to locate are the intercepts. The y-intercept is $(0, 2)$. To obtain the x-intercept, set $y = 0$ and solve for x. When $y = 0$, we have

$$2x = 8$$
$$x = 4$$

Thus, the intercepts are $(4, 0)$ and $(0, 2)$, as shown in Figure 21.

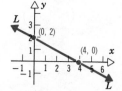

Figure 21

☐

SUMMARY

1. Given the general equation of a line, information can be found about the line:
    (a) Place the equation in slope–intercept form $y = mx + b$ to find the slope m and y-intercept $(0, b)$.
    (b) Let $x = 0$ and solve for y to find the y-intercept.
    (c) Let $y = 0$ and solve for x to find the x-intercept.
2. Given information about a straight line, the equation of the line can be found by using the appropriate form of the equation.

Given	Use	Equation
Point (x_1, y_1) Slope m	Point–slope form	$y - y_1 = m(x - x_1)$
Two points $(x_1, y_1), (x_2, y_2)$	If $x_1 = x_2$, use vertical equation	$x = x_1$
	If $x_1 \neq x_2$, find the slope $m = \dfrac{y_2 - y_1}{x_2 - x_1}$ and use the point–slope form	$y - y_1 = \left(\dfrac{y_2 - y_1}{x_2 - x_1}\right)(x - x_1)$ $= m(x - x_1)$
Slope m, y-intercept $(0, b)$	Slope–intercept form	$y = mx + b$

Exercise 1.3   *Answers to Odd-Numbered Problems begin on page 600.*

In Problems 1–6 find the slope m of the line joining the given pair of points.

1. $P = (2, 3)$ $Q = (0, 1)$
2. $P = (1, 1)$ $Q = (5, -6)$
3. $P = (-3, 0)$ $Q = (-5, -4)$
4. $P = (4, -3)$ $Q = (0, 0)$
5. $P = (0.1, 0.3)$ $Q = (1.5, 4.0)$
6. $P = (-3, -2)$ $Q = (6, -2)$

In Problems 7–18 find a general equation for the line having the given properties.

7. Slope $= 2$; passing through $(-2, 3)$
8. Slope $= 3$; passing through $(4, -3)$
9. Slope $= -\frac{2}{3}$; passing through $(1, -1)$
10. Slope $= \frac{1}{2}$; passing through $(3, 1)$
11. Passing through $(1, 3)$ and $(-1, 2)$
12. Passing through $(-3, 4)$ and $(2, 5)$
13. Slope $= -3$; y-intercept $= (0, 3)$
14. Slope $= -2$; y-intercept $= (0, -2)$
15. x-intercept $= (2, 0)$; y-intercept $= (0, -1)$
16. x-intercept $= (-4, 0)$; y-intercept $= (0, 4)$

17. Slope undefined; passing through $(1, 4)$
18. Slope undefined; passing through $(2, 1)$

In Problems 19–24 find the slope and y-intercept of the given line. Graph each line.

19. $3x - 2y = 6$ **20.** $4x + y = 2$ **21.** $x + 2y = 4$

22. $-x - y = 4$ **23.** $x = 4$ **24.** $y = 3$

In Problems 25–28 find an equation of the line shown in the graphs below.

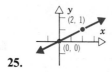

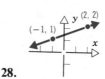

25.   **26.**

27.   **28.**

29. *Temperature Conversion.* The relationship between Celsius (°C) and Fahrenheit (°F) for measuring temperature is linear. Find an equation relating °C and °F if 0°C corresponds to 32°F and 100°C corresponds to 212°F. Use the equation to find the Celsius measure of 70°F.

1.4 PARALLEL AND INTERSECTING LINES

SYSTEMS OF LINEAR EQUATIONS □ METHODS FOR SOLVING A SYSTEM OF EQUATIONS

Let L and M be two lines. Exactly one of the following three relationships must hold for the two lines L and M:

1. All the points on L are the same as the points on M.
2. L and M have no points in common.
3. L and M have exactly one point in common.

Identical Lines   If the first relationship holds, the lines L and M are called *identical lines*. In this case, their slopes and their intercepts will be the same.

Parallel Lines   When two lines (in a plane) have no points in common, they are said to be *parallel*. Look at Figure 22.

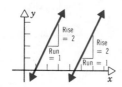

Figure 22

Vertical lines that are distinct are parallel.

For two nonvertical lines that are parallel, equal runs result in equal rises. This suggests the following:

> Two nonvertical lines are parallel if and only if their slopes are equal and their y-intercepts are different.

□ **Example 1**   Show that the lines given by the equations below are parallel:

$$L: \quad 2x + 3y = 6 \qquad M: \quad 4x + 6y = 0$$

Solution   To see if these lines have equal slopes, we put each equation into slope–intercept form:

$$L: \quad 2x + 3y = 6 \qquad\qquad M: \quad 4x + 6y = 0$$
$$3y = -2x + 6 \qquad\qquad 6y = -4x$$
$$y = \frac{-2}{3}x + 2 \qquad\qquad y = \frac{-2}{3}x$$
$$\text{Slope} = -2/3 \qquad\qquad \text{Slope} = -2/3$$
$$y\text{-intercept} = (0, 2) \qquad\qquad y\text{-intercept} = (0, 0)$$

Since each has slope $-\frac{2}{3}$ and different y-intercepts, the lines are parallel. See Figure 23.

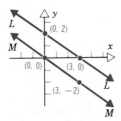

Figure 23

If two lines L and M have exactly one point in common, then L and M are said to intersect, and the common point is called the *point of intersection.*

Intersecting Lines

□ **Example 2**   Find the point of intersection of the two lines:

$$L: \quad x + y = 5 \qquad M: \quad 2x + y = 6$$

Let the coordinates of the point of intersection of L and M be (x_0, y_0). Since (x_0, y_0) is on both L and M, we must have

$$x_0 + y_0 = 5 \qquad \text{and} \qquad 2x_0 + y_0 = 6$$

Solving for y_0 in each equation, we get

$$y_0 = 5 - x_0 \qquad y_0 = 6 - 2x_0$$

Setting these equal, we obtain

$$5 - x_0 = 6 - 2x_0$$
$$x_0 = 1$$

Since $x_0 = 1$, then $y_0 = 5 - x_0 = 4$. Thus, the point of intersection of L and M is $(1, 4)$. To check this result, we verify that $(1, 4)$ is on both L and M:

$$x + y = 5 \qquad 2x + y = 6$$
$$1 + 4 = 5 \qquad 2 \cdot 1 + 4 = 6$$

This verifies that $(1, 4)$ is the point of intersection. The graphs of the lines are given in Figure 24. ◻

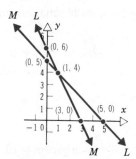

Figure 24

SYSTEMS OF LINEAR EQUATIONS

System of Two Linear Equations in Two Unknowns

A *system of two linear equations in two unknowns* x and y is of the form

$$L: \quad A_1 x + B_1 y = C_1$$
$$M: \quad A_2 x + B_2 y = C_2$$

where $A_1, B_1, C_1, A_2, B_2, C_2$ are real numbers.

Solution of a System of Linear Equations

A *solution* (x, y) of such a system is an ordered pair of real numbers that satisfies both equations. Finding the solution (x, y) of a system of two linear equations in two unknowns is the same as finding the point P of intersection of the two lines determined by the equations. Of course, if the equations of a system represent parallel lines, there will be no solution; if the equations represent identical lines, any point P on the line will be a solution of the system of equations (in this case, there is an infinite number of solutions).

Thus, a system of two linear equations in two unknowns will have:

1. Exactly one solution — the lines intersect.
2. No solution — the lines are parallel.
3. Infinitely many solutions — the lines are identical.

☐ **Example 3** Without solving, determine whether the following systems of equations have one solution, no solution, or infinitely many solutions:

(a) $x + y = -2$ (b) $x + y = -2$ (c) $x + y = -2$

     $4x + 4y = -8$ $2x + 2y = -14$ $2x - y = -4$

Solution   Put each equation in slope–intercept form:

(a) $x + y = -2$ $4x + 4y = -8$

$\quad\quad y = -x - 2$ $\quad\quad 4y = -4x - 8$

$\quad\quad m = -1, b = -2$ $\quad\quad y = -x - 2$

$\quad\quad\quad\quad\quad\quad\quad\quad m = -1, b = -2$

The lines are identical since they have equal slopes, -1, and the same y-intercept $(0, -2)$. The system has infinitely many solutions.

(b) $x + y = -2$ $2x + 2y = -14$

$\quad\quad y = -x - 2$ $\quad\quad 2y = -2x - 14$

$\quad\quad m = -1, b = -2$ $\quad\quad y = -x - 7$

$\quad\quad\quad\quad\quad\quad\quad\quad m = -1, b = -7$

The lines are parallel since they have equal slopes (-1) and different y-intercepts $(0, -2)$ and $(0, -7)$. The system has no solution.

(c) $x + y = -2$ $2x - y = -4$

$\quad\quad y = -x - 2$ $\quad\quad y = 2x + 4$

$\quad\quad m = -1, b = -2$ $\quad\quad m = 2, b = 4$

The lines intersect since they have unequal slopes $(-1$ and $2)$. The system has exactly one solution.   □

METHODS FOR SOLVING A SYSTEM OF EQUATIONS

We can solve systems of equations with exactly one solution by using two basic methods:*

Method 1: Substitution.

Method 2: Add or subtract.

The *substitution method* was used in Example 2. The steps to follow are:

Substitution
Method

> **Step 1:** Pick one of the equations and solve for one of the unknowns in terms of the other.
>
> **Step 2:** Substitute this expression for the same unknown in the other equation.
>
> **Step 3:** Solve this equation.
>
> **Step 4:** Use the solution found in Step 3 in either of the original equations to get the value of the other unknown.

Let's look at an example.

* A third method is given in Chapter 2.

□ **Example 4**   Use the substitution method to find the solution of the system:

$$2x + y = -6$$
$$4x - 2y = -4$$

Solution   **Step 1:** We choose to solve for y in the first equation since this results in the easiest algebra:

$$2x + y = -6$$
$$y = -2x - 6$$

Step 2: We replace y in the second equation by this expression:

$$4x - 2(-2x - 6) = -4$$

Step 3: Simplify and solve this equation:

$$4x + 4x + 12 = -4$$
$$8x = -16$$
$$x = -2$$

Step 4: Replace x by -2 in the first equation:

$$2(-2) + y = -6$$
$$-4 + y = -6$$
$$y = -2$$

The solution of the system is $x = -2$, $y = -2$.   □

The steps used in the *add* or *subtract method* are listed below:

Add or Subtract
Method

> **Step 1:** Multiply each equation by an appropriate nonzero constant so that one of the unknowns drops out when the equations are added (or subtracted).
>
> **Step 2:** Add (or subtract) the equations and solve the resulting equation.
>
> **Step 3:** Use the solution found in Step 2 in either of the original equations to get the value of the other unknown.

Let's redo the system in Example 4, using the add or subtract method.

□ **Example 5**   Use the add or subtract method to solve the system:

$$2x + y = -6$$
$$4x - 2y = -4$$

Solution   **Step 1:** The add or subtract method eliminates one of the variables by adding (or subtracting) the two equations. If we choose to eliminate y, we multiply the first equation by 2, obtaining the equivalent system

$$4x + 2y = -12$$
$$4x - 2y = -4$$

Step 2: Now, when we add these equations, we obtain

$$8x = -16$$
$$x = -2$$

Step 3: To find y, use $x = -2$ in one of the original equations, say the first one:

$$2(-2) + y = -6$$
$$y = -2$$

Thus, the solution of the system is $x = -2$, $y = -2$. Figure 25 illustrates the two lines.   □

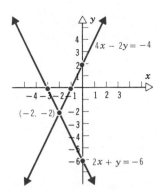

Figure 25

□ **Example 6**   Nutt's Nuts, a store that specializes in selling nuts, sells cashews for $1.50 per pound and peanuts for $0.80 per pound. At the end of the month it is found that the peanuts are not selling well. In order to sell 30 pounds of peanuts more quickly, the store manager decides to mix the 30 pounds of peanuts with some cashews and sell the mixture of peanuts and cashews for $1.00 a pound. How many pounds of cashews should be mixed with the peanuts so that the profit remains the same?

Solution   There are two unknowns: the number of pounds of cashews (call this x) and the number of pounds of the mixture (call this y). Since we know that the number of pounds of cashews plus 30 pounds of peanuts equals the number of pounds of the mixture, we can write

$$y = x + 30$$

Also, in order to keep profits the same, we must have

$$\left(\begin{matrix}\text{Pounds of}\\ \text{cashews}\end{matrix}\right) \cdot \left(\begin{matrix}\text{Price per}\\ \text{pound}\end{matrix}\right) + \left(\begin{matrix}\text{Pounds of}\\ \text{peanuts}\end{matrix}\right) \cdot \left(\begin{matrix}\text{Price per}\\ \text{pound}\end{matrix}\right) = \left(\begin{matrix}\text{Pounds of}\\ \text{mixture}\end{matrix}\right) \cdot \left(\begin{matrix}\text{Price per}\\ \text{pound}\end{matrix}\right)$$

That is,

$$(1.50)x + (0.80)(30) = (1.00)y$$
$$\tfrac{3}{2}x + 24 = y$$

Thus, we have a system of two linear equations in two unknowns to solve, namely,

$$y = x + 30$$
$$y = \tfrac{3}{2}x + 24$$

Using the substitution method, we find

$$\tfrac{3}{2}x + 24 = x + 30$$
$$\tfrac{1}{2}x = 6$$
$$x = 12$$

The store manager should mix 12 pounds of cashews with 30 pounds of peanuts. See Figure 26.

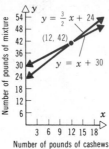

Figure 26   Number of pounds of cashews

Exercise 1.4   *Answers to Odd-Numbered Problems begin on page* 600.

In Problems 1–4 show that the lines are parallel by verifying that the slope of each line is equal and that the y-intercepts are unequal.

1. $x + y = 10$
    $3x + 3y = 1$

2. $x - y = 5$
    $-2x + 2y = 7$

3. $2x - 3y + 8 = 0$
    $6x - 9y + 2 = 0$

4. $4x - 2y + 7 = 0$
    $-2x + y + 2 = 0$

In Problems 5–10 find the point of intersection of each pair of lines. Use the substitution method.

5. $x + y = 5$
    $3x - y = 7$

6. $2x + y = 7$
    $x - y = -4$

7. $3x - 4y = 1$
    $x - 2y = -4$

8. $4x + 3y = 2$
    $2x - y = -1$

9. $3x - 2y + 5 = 0$
    $3x + y - 2 = 0$

10. $4x + y - 6 = 0$
    $4x - 2y = 0$

In Problems 11–18 find the point of intersection of each pair of lines. Use the add and subtract method.

11. $2x - 3y + 4 = 0$
     $3x + 2y - 7 = 0$

12. $3x - 4y - 2 = 0$
     $2x + 5y - 9 = 0$

13. $3x - 4y + 8 = 0$
     $2x + y - 2 = 0$

14. $5x + 2y - 15 = 0$
     $2x - 3y - 6 = 0$

15. $-2x + 3y - 7 = 0$
$\qquad 3x + 2y - 9 = 0$

16. $-3x + 4y - 10 = 0$
$\qquad 2x - 3y + 7 = 0$

17. $\quad 3x + 2y + 6 = 0$
$\qquad 5x - 2y + 10 = 0$

18. $4x + 3y + 1 = 0$
$\qquad 2x + 5y - 3 = 0$

In Problems 19–26 without solving, determine whether the system of equations has one solution, no solution, or infinitely many solutions.

19. L: $2x - 3y + 6 = 0$
$\quad\;\; M$: $4x - 6y + 7 = 0$

20. L: $4x - y + 2 = 0$
$\quad\;\; M$: $\quad 3x + 2y = 0$

21. L: $-2x + 3y + 6 = 0$
$\quad\;\; M$: $\quad 4x - 6y - 12 = 0$

22. L: $2x + 3y - 5 = 0$
$\quad\;\; M$: $•5x - 6y + 1 = 0$

23. L: $3x - 3y + 10 = 0$
$\quad\;\; M$: $\quad x + y - 2 = 0$

24. L: $2x - 5y - 1 = 0$
$\quad\;\; M$: $\quad x - 2y - 1 = 0$

25. L: $\quad 3x - 2y - 4 = 0$
$\quad\;\; M$: $-6x + 4y - 7 = 0$

26. L: $\quad 8x - 2y + 4 = 0$
$\quad\;\; M$: $-4x + y - 2 = 0$

27. Find an equation of the line passing through (1, 2) and parallel to $2x - y = 6$.

28. Find an equation of the line passing through $(-1, 3)$ and parallel to $x + y = 4$.

Applications   **29.** *Mixture Problem.* Sweet Delight Candies, Inc., sells boxes of candy consisting of creams and caramels. Each box sells for $4.00 and holds 50 pieces of candy (all pieces are the same size). If the caramels cost $0.05 to produce and the creams cost $0.10 to produce, how many caramels and creams should be in each box for no profit or loss? Would you increase or decrease the number of caramels in order to obtain a profit?

30. *Mixture Problem.* The manager of Nutt's Nuts regularly sells cashews for $1.50 per pound, pecans for $1.80 per pound, and peanuts for $0.80 per pound. How many pounds of cashews and pecans should be mixed with 40 pounds of peanuts to obtain a mixture of 100 pounds that will sell at $1.25 a pound so that the profit or loss is unchanged?

31. *Investment Problem.* Mr. Nicholson has just retired and needs $6000 per year in income to live on. He has $50,000 to invest and can invest in AA bonds at 15% annual interest or in Savings and Loan Certificates at 7% interest per year. How much money should be invested in each so that he realizes exactly $6000 in income per year?

32. Mr. Nicholson finds after 2 years that because of inflation he now needs $7000 per year to live on. How should he transfer his funds to achieve this amount? (Use the data from Problem 31.)

33. Joan has $1.65 in her piggy bank. She knows she only placed nickels and quarters in the bank and she knows that, in all, she put 13 coins in the bank. Can she find out how many nickels she has without breaking her bank?

34. *Mixture Problem.* A coffee manufacturer wants to market a new blend of coffee that will cost $2.90 per pound by mixing $2.75 per pound coffee and $3 per pound coffee. What amounts of the $2.75 per pound coffee and $3 per pound coffee should be blended to obtain the desired mixture? [*Hint:* Assume the total weight of the desired blend is 100 pounds.]

35. *Mixture Problem.* One solution is 15% acid and another is 5% acid. How many cubic centimeters of each should be mixed to obtain 100 cc of a solution that is 8% acid?

36. *Investment Problem.* A bank loaned $10,000, some at an annual rate of 8% and some at an annual rate of 18%. If the income from these loans was $1000, how much was loaned at 8%? How much at 18%?

37. The Star Theater wants to know whether the majority of its patrons are adults or children. During a week in July, 5200 tickets were sold and the receipts totaled $11,875. The adult admission is $2.75 and the children's admission is $1.50. How many adult patrons were there?

38. After 1 hour of car ride, $\frac{1}{3}$ of the total distance is covered. One hour later, the car is 18 miles past the halfway point. What is the speed of the car (assume it is constant for the entire trip) and what is the total distance to be covered? How long will the trip take? [*Hint:* Distance = Speed · Time.]

1.5 APPLICATIONS*

SIMPLE INTEREST □ BREAK-EVEN POINT □ PREDICTION □ ECONOMICS

SIMPLE INTEREST

A knowledge of interest—whether on money borrowed or on money saved—is of ultimate importance today. The old adage "Neither a lender nor a borrower be" is not true in this age of charge accounts and golden passbook savings plans.

Interest   *Interest* is money paid for the use of money. The total amount of money borrowed (whether by an individual from a bank in the form of a loan or by a bank from an Principal   individual in the form of a savings account) is called the *principal.* The *rate of interest* is the amount charged for the use of the principal for a given period of time (usually Rate of Interest   on a yearly or *per annum* basis). The rate of interest is generally expressed as a *percent.*

Simple Interest   *Simple interest* **is interest computed on the principal for the entire period it is borrowed.**

In general, if a principal of *P* dollars is borrowed at a simple annual rate of interest *r*, expressed as a decimal, for a period of *t* years, the interest *I* charged is

$$I = Prt$$

The amount *A* owed at the end of a period of time is the sum of the principal and the interest. That is,

$$A = P + I = P + Prt$$

□ **Example 1**   If $250 is borrowed for 9 months at a simple interest rate of 8% per annum, what will be the interest charged?

Solution   The actual period the money is borrowed for is 9 months, or $\frac{3}{4}$ of a year. Thus, the interest charged will be the product of the principal ($250) times the annual rate of interest (0.08) times the period of time held expressed in years ($\frac{3}{4}$):

$$\text{Interest charged} = \$(250)(0.08)\left(\frac{3}{4}\right) = \$15$$

□

* This section may be omitted without loss of continuity.

□ **Example 2**   If $500 is borrowed at a simple interest rate of 10% per annum, the amount A due after t years is

$$A = \$500 + \$500(.10)t = \$500 + \$50t$$

Thus, the amount due after 2 years is

$$A = \$500 + \$50(2) = \$600$$

The amount due after 6 months ($\frac{1}{2}$ year) is

$$A = \$500 + \$50(\tfrac{1}{2}) = \$525$$

The equation

$$A = 500 + 50t$$

is a linear equation in which A and t are the variables. If we graph this equation using A for the vertical axis and t for the horizontal axis, we can see how the amount A changes over time (see Figure 27). The slope of the line (50) equals the constant annual interest due on the loan.   □

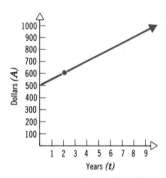

Figure 27

BREAK-EVEN POINT

In many businesses, the cost C of production and the number x of items produced can be expressed as a linear equation. Similarly, sometimes the revenue R obtained from sales and the number x of items produced can be expressed as a linear equation. When the cost C of production exceeds the revenue R from sales, the business is operating at a loss; when the revenue R exceeds the cost C, there is a profit; and when the revenue R and the cost C are equal, there is no profit or loss — the point at which $R = C$ is usually referred to as the *break-even point.*

Break-Even Point

□ **Example 3**   Sweet Delight Candies, Inc., has daily fixed costs from salaries and building operations of $300. Each pound of candy produced costs $1 and is sold for $2 per pound. What is the break-even point — that is, how many pounds of candy must be sold daily to guarantee no loss and no profit?

Solution   The cost C of production is the fixed cost plus the variable cost of producing x pounds of candy at $1 per pound. Thus,

$$C = \$1 \cdot x + \$300 = x + 300$$

The revenue R realized from the sale of x pounds of candy at \$2 per pound is

$$R = \$2 \cdot x = 2x$$

The break-even point is the point where these two lines intersect. Setting $R = C$, we find

$$2x = x + 300$$
$$x = 300$$

That is, 300 pounds of candy must be sold in order to break even.   □

In Figure 28, we see a graphical interpretation of the break-even point for Example 3. Note that for $x > 300$, the revenue R always exceeds the cost C so that a profit results. Similarly, for $x < 300$, the cost exceeds the revenue, resulting in a loss.

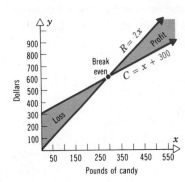

Figure 28

□ **Example 4**
Pricing Candy

After negotiations with employees of Sweet Delight Candies and an increase in the price of chocolate, the daily cost C of production for x pounds of candy is

$$C = \$1.05x + \$330$$

(a)   If each pound of candy is sold for \$2, how many pounds must be sold daily to break even?
(b)   If the selling price is increased to \$2.25 per pound, what is the break-even point?
(c)   If it is known that at least 325 pounds of candy can be sold daily, what price should be charged per pound to guarantee no loss?

Solution   (a)   If each pound is sold for \$2, the revenue R from sales is

$$R = \$2x$$

where x represents the number of pounds sold. When we set $R = C$, we find that the break-even point is the solution of

$$2x = 1.05x + 330$$
$$0.95x = 330$$
$$x = \frac{33{,}000}{95} = 347.37$$

Thus, if 347 pounds of candy are sold, a loss is incurred; if 348 pounds are sold, a profit results.

(b)   If the selling price is increased to $2.25 per pound, the revenue R from sales is

$$R = \$2.25x$$

The break-even point is the solution of

$$2.25x = 1.05x + 330$$
$$1.2x = 330$$
$$x = \frac{3300}{12} = 275$$

With the new selling price, the break-even point is 275 pounds.

(c)   If we know that at least 325 pounds of candy will be sold daily, the price per pound p needed to guarantee no loss (that is, to guarantee at worst a break-even point) is the solution of

$$325p = (1.05)(325) + 330$$
$$325p = 671.25$$
$$p = \$2.07$$

We should charge at least $2.07 per pound to guarantee no loss, provided at least 325 pounds will be sold.   □

□ **Example 5**   A producer sells items for $0.30 each. If the cost for production is

$$C = \$0.15x + \$105$$

where x is the number of items sold, find the break-even point. If the cost can be changed to

$$C = \$0.12x + \$110$$

would it be advantageous?

Solution   The revenue R received is

$$R = \$0.3x$$

The break-even point is the solution of

$$0.3x = 0.15x + 105$$
$$0.15x = 105$$
$$x = 700$$

Thus, for the first cost, the break-even point is 700 items.

To determine the answer to the second part, we find that the break-even point at the new cost is $x = 611.11$. The old break-even point was $x = 700$. Thus, the new cost will require fewer items to be sold in order to break even. Management should probably change over to the new cost. See Figure 29.

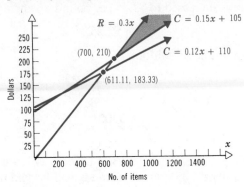

Figure 29

PREDICTION

Linear equations are sometimes used as predictors of future results. Let's look at an example.

☐ **Example 6**   In 1987 the cost of an average home was $60,000. One year later the average home sold for $66,000. Assuming this pattern continues, that is, assuming that the increase will remain at $6000 per year, develop a formula for predicting the cost of an average home in 1991. What will it cost in 1996?

Solution   We agree to let x represent the year and y represent the cost. We seek a relationship between x and y. Two points on the graph of the equation relating x and y are

$$(1987, 60{,}000) \quad \text{and} \quad (1988, 66{,}000)$$

The assumption that the rate of increase remains constant tells us that the equation relating x and y is linear. The slope of this line is

$$\frac{66{,}000 - 60{,}000}{1988 - 1987} = 6000$$

Using this fact and the point $(1987, 60{,}000)$, the point–slope form of the equation of the line is

$$y - 60{,}000 = 6000(x - 1987)$$
$$y = 60{,}000 + 6000(x - 1987)$$

For $x = 1991$, we find the cost of an average home to be

$$y = 60{,}000 + 6000(1991 - 1987)$$
$$= 60{,}000 + 6000(4)$$
$$= \$84{,}000$$

For $x = 1996$, we find

$$y = 60,000 + 6000(9) = \$114,000$$

Figure 30 illustrates the situation.

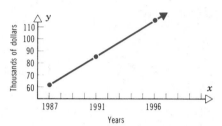

Figure 30

These predictions of future cost are based on the assumption that annual increases remain constant. If this assumption is not accurate, our predictions will be incorrect.

ECONOMICS

Supply Equation   The *supply equation* in economics is used to specify the amount of a particular commodity that sellers have available to offer in the market at various prices. The
Demand Equation   *demand equation* specifies the amount of a particular commodity that buyers are willing to purchase at various prices.

An increase in price p usually causes an increase in the supply S and a decrease in demand D. On the other hand, a decrease in price brings about a decrease in supply
Market Price   and an increase in demand. The *market price* is defined as the price at which supply and demand are equal.

□ **Example 7**   The supply and demand for flour during the period 1920–1935 were estimated as
Market Price of Flour   being given by the equations

$$S = 0.8p + 0.5 \qquad D = -0.4p + 1.5$$

where p is measured in dollars and S and D are measured in 50 pound units of flour. Find the market price and graph the supply and demand equations.

Solution   The market price is the point of intersection of the two lines. Thus, the market price p is the solution of

$$0.8p + 0.5 = -0.4p + 1.5$$
$$1.2p = 1$$
$$p = 0.83$$

The graphs are shown in Figure 31.

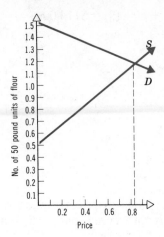

Figure 31

Exercise 1.5   *Answers to Odd-Numbered Problems begin on page* 600.

Simple Interest Problems

1. Suppose you borrow $1000 at a simple interest rate of 18% per annum.
    (a) What is the amount A due after t years?
    (b) How much is due after 6 months?
    (c) How much is due after 1 year?
    (d) How much is due after 2 years?

2. Rework Problem 1 if you borrow $4000 at a simple interest rate of 14%.

Break-Even Problems. In Problems 3–6 find the break-even point for the cost C of production and the revenue R. Graph each result.

3. $C = \$10x + \$600$ $R = \$30x$

4. $C = \$5x + \$200$ $R = \$8x$

5. $C = \$0.2x + \$50$ $R = \$0.3x$

6. $C = \$1800x + \$3000$ $R = \$2500x$

7. A manufacturer produces items at a daily cost of $0.75 per item and sells them for $1 per item. The daily operational overhead is $300. What is the break-even point? Graph your result.

8. If the manufacturer of Problem 7 is able to reduce the cost per item to $0.65, but with a resultant increase to $350 in operational overhead, is it advantageous to do so? Graph your result.

Prediction Problems

9. Suppose the sales of a company are given by

$$S = \$5000x + \$80,000$$

where x is measured in years and $x = 0$ corresponds to the year 1987.
(a) Find S when $x = 0$.
(b) Find S when $x = 3$.
(c) Find the predicted sales in 1992, assuming this trend continues.
(d) Find the predicted sales in 1995, assuming this trend continues.

10. Rework Problem 9 if the sales of the company are given by

$$S = \$3000x + \$60,000$$

Economics Problems. In Problems 11 – 14 find the market price for each pair of supply and demand equations.

11. $S = p + 1$ $D = 3 - p$
12. $S = 2p + 3$ $D = 6 - p$
13. $S = 20p + 500$ $D = 1000 - 30p$
14. $S = 40p + 300$ $D = 1000 - 30p$

15. *Market Price of Sugar.* The supply and demand equations for sugar from 1890 to 1915 were estimated by H. Schulz to be given by

$$S = 0.7p + 0.4 \qquad D = -0.5p + 1.6$$

Find the market price. What quantity of supply is demanded at this market price? Graph both the supply and demand equations. Interpret the point of intersection of the two lines.

16. The market price for a certain product is $5.00 per unit and occurs when 14,000 units are produced. At a price of $1, no units are manufactured and, at a price of $19.00, no units will be purchased. Find the supply and demand equations, assuming they are linear.

CHAPTER REVIEW

Important Terms			
set	inequality	parallel lines
empty set	x-axis	intersecting lines
counting numbers	y-axis	system of two linear equations in two unknowns
integers	rectangular coordinates	
rational numbers	ordered pair	solution of a system of linear equations
numerator	x-coordinate	
denominator	y-coordinate	substitution method
irrational numbers	quadrants	add or subtract method
real numbers	graphs	*simple interest
decimals	linear equation	*principal
percents	straight line	*rate of interest
positive number	slope of a line	*amount
negative number	vertical line	*break-even point

* From optional sections.

origin
coordinate
variable
equation
solution

point–slope form
general form
intercepts
slope–intercept form
identical lines

*prediction
*supply and demand
*market price

(Answers on page 601)

T   F   1. In the slope–intercept equation of a line, $y = mx + b$, m is the slope and b is the
           x-intercept.

T   F   2. The graph of the equation $Ax + By = C$, where A, B, C are real numbers and A, B
           are not both zero, is a straight line.

T   F   3. The y-intercept of the line $2x - 3y + 6 = 0$ is $(0, 2)$.

T   F   4. The slope of the line $2x - 4y + 7 = 0$ is $-\frac{1}{2}$.

(Answers on page 601)

1. If (x, y) are rectangular coordinates of a point, the number x is called the _____
   and y is called the _____ .

2. The decimal equivalent of a rational number is either _____ or
   _____ .

3. The slope of a vertical line is _____ ; the slope of a horizontal line is
   _____ .

4. If a line slants downward as it moves from left to right, its slope will be a _____
   number.

5. If two lines have the same slope but different y-intercepts, they are _____ .

Answers to Odd-Numbered Problems begin on page 601.

In Problems 1–6 find the solution x of each equation.

1. $3x + 6 = 2x - 1$

2. $-3x - 2 = 2x + 8$

3. $-2(x + 3) = x + 5$

4. $2x - 3 = -2(x + 2)$

5. $\dfrac{4x - 1}{x + 2} = 5$

6. $\dfrac{3x + 2}{2x - 1} = 1$

In Problems 7–10 find the solution of each inequality.

7. $2x - 1 \leq 5$

8. $8x + 1 \geq 9$

9. $3x + 7 \geq -2x + 2$

10. $-3x + 4 \leq 2x - 1$

In Problems 11–14 graph each linear equation.

11. $y = -2x + 3$ **12.** $y = 6x - 2$

13. $2y = 3x + 6$ **14.** $3y = 2x + 6$

In Problems 15–18 find a general equation for the line containing each pair of points.

15. $P = (1, 2)$ $Q = (-3, 4)$ **16.** $P = (-1, 3)$ $Q = (1, 1)$

17. $P = (0, 0)$ $Q = (-2, 3)$ **18.** $P = (-2, 3)$ $Q = (0, 0)$

In Problems 19–22 find a general equation for the line.

19. Slope is 2;   **20.** Slope is -1;
     x-intercept is $(-1, 0)$ y-intercept is $(0, 1)$

21. Passing through $(1, 3)$ with slope 1   **22.** Passing through $(2, -1)$ with slope -2

In Problems 23–26 find the slope and y-intercept of each line. Graph each line.

23. $-9x - 2y + 18 = 0$ **24.** $-4x - 5y + 20 = 0$

25. $4x + 2y - 9 = 0$ **26.** $3x + 2y - 8 = 0$

In Problems 27–32, without solving, determine whether the system of equations has one solution, no solution, or infinitely many solutions.

27. $3x - 4y + 12 = 0$ **28.** $2x + 3y + 5 = 0$
     $6x - 8y + 9 = 0$ $4x + 6y + 10 = 0$

29. $x - y + 2 = 0$ **30.** $2x + 3y - 5 = 0$
     $3x - 4y + 12 = 0$ $x + y - 2 = 0$

31. $4x + 6y + 12 = 0$ **32.** $3x - y = 0$
     $2x + 3y + 6 = 0$ $6x - 2y + 5 = 0$

33. *Investment Problem.* Mr. and Mrs. Byrd have just retired and find that they need $10,000 per year to live on. Fortunately, they have a nest egg of $90,000 which they can invest in somewhat risky B-rated bonds at 16% interest per year or in a well-known bank at 6% per year. How much money should they invest in each so that they realize exactly $10,000 in income each year?

34. *Mixture Problem.* One solution is 20% acid and another is 12% acid. How many cubic centimeters of each solution should be mixed to obtain 100 cc of a solution which is 15% acid?

35. The annual sales of Motors, Inc., for the past 5 years are listed in the table.

Year	Units Sold (in thousands)
1982	3400
1983	3200
1984	3100
1985	2800
1986	2200

   (a) Graph this information using the x-axis for years and the y-axis for units sold. (For convenience, use different scales on the axes.)

(b) Draw a line L that passes through two of the points and comes close to passing through the remaining points.

(c) Find the equation of this line L.

(d) Using this equation of the line, what is your estimate for units sold in 1987?

36. *Attendance at a Dance.* A church group is planning a dance in the school auditorium to raise money for its school. The band they will hire charges $500; the advertising costs are estimated at $100; and food is supplied at the rate of $2.00 per person. The church group would like to clear at least $900 after expenses.

(a) Determine how many people need to attend the dance for the group to break even if tickets are sold at $5 each.

(b) Determine how many people need to attend in order to achieve the desired profit if tickets are sold for $5 each.

(c) Answer the above two questions if the tickets are sold for $6 each.

Mathematical Questions

From CPA and CMA Exams (Answers on page 602)

1. **CPA Exam—November 1976**
   The Oliver Company plans to market a new product. Based on its market studies, Oliver estimates that it can sell 5500 units in 1976. The selling price will be $2.00 per unit. Variable costs are estimated to be 40% of the selling price. Fixed costs are estimated to be $6000. What is the break-even point?

   (a) 3750 units (b) 5000 units
   (c) 5500 units (d) 7500 units

2. **CPA Exam—November 1976**
   The Breiden Company sells rodaks for $6.00 per unit. Variable costs are $2.00 per unit. Fixed costs are $37,500. How many rodaks must be sold to realize a profit before income taxes of 15% of sales?

   (a) 9375 units (b) 9740 units
   (c) 11,029 units (d) 12,097 units

3. **CPA Exam—May 1975**
   Given the following notations, what is the break-even sales level in units?

   $$SP = \text{Selling price per unit}$$
   $$FC = \text{Total fixed cost}$$
   $$VC = \text{Variable cost per unit}$$

   (a) $\dfrac{SP}{FC \div VC}$ (b) $\dfrac{FC}{VC \div SP}$ (c) $\dfrac{VC}{SP - FC}$ (d) $\dfrac{FC}{SP - VC}$

4. **CPA Exam—November 1976**
   At a break-even point of 400 units sold, the variable costs were $400 and the fixed costs were $200. What will the 401st unit sold contribute to profit before income taxes?

   (a) $0 (b) $0.50 (c) $1.00 (d) $1.50

Use the following information to answer Problems 5–8:

Akron, Inc. owns 80% of the capital stock of Benson Company and 70% of the capital stock of Cashin, Inc. Benson Company owns 15% of the capital stock of Cashin, Inc. Cashin, Inc., in turn, owns 25% of the capital stock of Akron, Inc. These ownership interrelationships are illustrated in the following diagram:

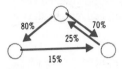

Net income before adjusting for interests in intercompany net income for each corporation follows:

Akron, Inc.	$190,000
Benson Co.	$170,000
Cashin, Inc.	$230,000

The following notations relate to items 5 through 8. Ignore all income tax considerations.

A_e = Akron's consolidated net income; that is, its net income plus its share of the consolidated net income of Benson and Cashin

B_e = Benson's consolidated net income; that is, its net income plus its share of the consolidated net income of Cashin

C_e = Cashin's consolidated net income; that is, its net income plus its share of the consolidated income of Akron

5. *CPA Exam—May 1973*
The equation, in a set of simultaneous equations, which computes A_e is:
(a) $A_e = .75(190,000 + .8B_e + .7C_e)$
(b) $A_e = 190,000 + .8B_e + .7C_e$
(c) $A_e = .75(190,000) + .8(170,000) + .7(230,000)$
(d) $A_e = .75(190,000) + .8B_e + .7C_e$

6. *CPA Exam—May 1973*
The equation, in a set of simultaneous equations, which computes B_e is:
(a) $B_e = 170,000 + .15C_e - .75A_e$
(b) $B_e = 170,000 + .15C_e$
(c) $B_e = .2(170,000) + .15(230,000)$
(d) $B_e = .2(170,000) + .15C_e$

7. *CPA Exam—May 1973*
Cashin's minority interest in consolidated net income is:
(a) .15(230,000)   (b) $230,000 + .25A_e$
(c) .15(230,000) + $.25A_e$ (d) $.15C_e$

8. *CPA Exam—May 1973*
Benson's minority interest in consolidated net income is:
(a) $34,316   (b) $25,500
(c) $45,755   (d) $30,675

9. *CPA Exam—November 1976*

   A graph is set up with "depreciation expense" on the vertical axis and "time" on the horizontal axis. Assuming linear relationships, how would the graphs for straight-line and sum-of-the-years'-digits depreciation, respectively, be drawn?

   (a) Vertically and sloping down to the right
   (b) Vertically and sloping up to the right
   (c) Horizontally and sloping down to the right
   (d) Horizontally and sloping up to the right

The following statement applies to items 10–12:

In analyzing the relationship of total factory overhead with changes in direct labor hours, the following relationship was found to exist: $Y = \$1000 + \$2X$.

10. *CMA Exam—December 1973*

    The relationship as shown above is:

    (a) Parabolic   (b) Curvilinear
    (c) Linear   (d) Probabilistic
    (e) None of the above

11. *CMA Exam—December 1973*

    Y in the above equation is an estimate of:

    (a) Total variable costs   (b) Total factory overhead
    (c) Total fixed costs   (d) Total direct labor hours
    (e) None of the above

12. *CMA Exam—December 1973*

    The $2 in the equation is an estimate of:

    (a) Total fixed costs
    (b) Variable costs per direct labor hour
    (c) Total variable costs
    (d) Fixed costs per direct labor hour
    (e) None of the above

2

MATRICES WITH APPLICATIONS

* This section may be omitted without loss of continuity.

2.1 SYSTEMS OF LINEAR EQUATIONS

MATRIX REPRESENTATION OF A SYSTEM OF LINEAR EQUATIONS □ ROW OPERATIONS □ SUMMARY

In the previous chapter (Section 1.4) we discussed two methods for solving systems of two linear equations in two unknowns. In this section and the next, we present a third method, using matrices, for solving a system of linear equations.

Matrix   A *matrix* can be defined as a rectangular array of numbers that are enclosed by a pair of brackets. Some examples of matrices are

$$
\text{(a)} \begin{bmatrix} 1 & 3 \\ -2 & 4 \end{bmatrix} \quad \text{(b)} \begin{bmatrix} 4 & 1 & -3 \\ 2 & 1 & 2 \end{bmatrix} \quad \text{(c)} \begin{bmatrix} 4 & 3 \end{bmatrix}
$$

Elements   The numbers in a matrix are called *elements* of the matrix. The matrix (a) above
Rows   has two *rows* and two *columns;* the matrix (b) has two rows and three columns; the
Columns   matrix (c) has one row and two columns. For example, in matrix (a), the element 4 is
Diagonal Entries   in row 2 column 2; in matrix (b), the element -3 is in row 1, column 3. The *diagonal entries* of a matrix are those elements for which the row number and column number are equal. Thus, in matrix (a), 1 and 4 are the diagonal entries.

MATRIX REPRESENTATION OF A SYSTEM OF LINEAR EQUATIONS

Consider the following two systems of two linear equations in two unknowns.

$$
\begin{aligned} x + 4y &= 14 \\ 3x - 2y &= 0 \end{aligned} \quad \text{and} \quad \begin{aligned} u + 4v &= 14 \\ 3u - 2v &= 0 \end{aligned}
$$

We make the observation that, except for the symbols used to represent the unknowns, these two systems are identical. That is, it is the coefficients of the unknowns and the numbers that appear to the right of the equal sign that distinguish one system from another. As a result, we can dispense altogether with the letters used to symbolize the unknowns—provided we have some means of keeping track of them. A matrix serves us well in this regard.

The system

$$
\begin{aligned} x + 4y &= 14 \\ 3x - 2y &= 0 \end{aligned}
$$

can be represented by the matrix

	Column one	Column two	Column three
Row one	1	4	14
Row two	3	−2	0

Here it is understood that column one contains the coefficients of the unknown x, column two contains the coefficients of the unknown y, and column three contains the numbers to the right of the equal sign. Each row of the matrix represents an equation of the system. Although not required, it has become customary to place a vertical bar in the matrix as a reminder of the equal sign.

Augmented Matrix   The matrix used to represent a system of linear equations is called the *augmented matrix* of the system.

□ **Example 1**   **System of Linear Equations**   **Augmented Matrix**

(a)
$$5x - 2y = 5$$
$$2x - y = -4$$
$$\begin{bmatrix} 5 & -2 & | & 5 \\ 2 & -1 & | & -4 \end{bmatrix}$$

(b)
$$3x + 4y + 3z = 10$$
$$x + y - z = 1$$
$$x + 6y = 4$$
$$\begin{bmatrix} 3 & 4 & 3 & | & 10 \\ 1 & 1 & -1 & | & 1 \\ 1 & 6 & 0 & | & 4 \end{bmatrix}$$

(c)
$$3x_1 - x_2 + x_3 + x_4 = 5$$
$$2x_1 + 6x_3 = 2$$
$$\begin{bmatrix} 3 & -1 & 1 & 1 & | & 5 \\ 2 & 0 & 6 & 0 & | & 2 \end{bmatrix}$$ □

Given an augmented matrix, we can write the corresponding system of equations.

□ **Example 2**   Write a system of linear equations for each augmented matrix.

(a) $\begin{bmatrix} 4 & -1 & | & 6 \\ 3 & 1 & | & 2 \end{bmatrix}$ (b) $\begin{bmatrix} 3 & 2 & 1 & 1 & | & 5 \\ -1 & 0 & 1 & 4 & | & 0 \end{bmatrix}$

Solution   (a)   If we use x and y as unknowns, the system of equations is:
$$4x - y = 6$$
$$3x + y = 2$$

(b)   If we use x_1, x_2, x_3, and x_4 as unknowns, the systems of equations is:
$$3x_1 + 2x_2 + x_3 + x_4 = 5$$
$$-x_1 + x_3 + 4x_4 = 0$$ □

The use of matrices to solve a system of linear equations requires the use of row operations on the augmented matrix of the system.

ROW OPERATIONS

We begin by going through the solution of a system of two linear equations in two unknowns:

$$x + 4y = 14$$
$$3x - 2y = 0 \tag{1}$$

To find a solution, we multiply the first equation by 3, obtaining $3x + 12y = 42$, and then subtract it from the second:

$$\begin{array}{r} 3x - 2y = 0 \\ \underline{3x + 12y = 42} \\ -14y = -42 \end{array}$$

The original system of equations (1) may now be written as the equivalent system

$$x + 4y = 14$$
$$-14y = -42$$

Dividing the second equation by -14, we get

$$x + 4y = 14$$
$$y = 3$$

To find x, we multiply the second equation by -4 and add it to the first. The result is

$$x = 2$$
$$y = 3 \tag{2}$$

This system of equations has the obvious solution $x = 2$, $y = 3$ and is equivalent to the original system (1), so that the solution of the original system (1) is also $x = 2$, $y = 3$.

We obtained the final system (2) from the original system (1) by a series of operations. Because of its simplicity, the original system could have been solved more quickly by either the substitution method or the add or subtract method (refer to Chapter 1), but we chose the above operations because the *pattern* of the solution shown provides another method for solving a system of equations. The advantages of this third method are:

1. It is algorithmic in character; that is, it consists of repetitive steps so that it can be programmed on a computer.
2. It works on any system of linear equations.

Let's repeat the steps we took to solve this system of equations, except now we will manipulate the augmented matrix instead of the equations. For convenience, the equations are listed next to the augmented matrix.

$$\begin{bmatrix} 1 & 4 & | & 14 \\ 3 & -2 & | & 0 \end{bmatrix} \qquad \begin{matrix} x + 4y = 14 \\ 3x - 2y = 0 \end{matrix}$$

Multiplying the first *equation* by 3 and subtracting it from the second *equation* corresponds to multiplying the first *row* of the matrix by -3 and adding the result to the second *row*. The result is the matrix

$$\begin{bmatrix} 1 & 4 & | & 14 \\ 0 & -14 & | & -42 \end{bmatrix} \qquad \begin{matrix} x + 4y = 14 \\ -14y = -42 \end{matrix}$$

Next, divide the second row of this last matrix by -14 to obtain

$$\begin{bmatrix} 1 & 4 & | & 14 \\ 0 & 1 & | & 3 \end{bmatrix} \qquad \begin{matrix} x + 4y = 14 \\ y = 3 \end{matrix}$$

Finally, multiply the second row of this matrix by -4 and add it to the first row to obtain

$$\begin{bmatrix} 1 & 0 & | & 2 \\ 0 & 1 & | & 3 \end{bmatrix} \qquad \begin{matrix} x = 2 \\ y = 3 \end{matrix}$$

When manipulations such as the above are performed on a matrix, they are called *elementary row operations*. We now list the three basic types of row operations:

Elementary Row
Operations

1. The interchange of any 2 rows of a matrix.

2. The replacement of any row of a matrix by a nonzero multiple of that same row.

3. The replacement of any row of a matrix by the sum of that row and a multiple of some other row.

An example of each elementary row operation is given below.

☐ **Example 3**

$$A = \begin{bmatrix} 3 & 4 & -3 \\ 7 & -\frac{1}{2} & 0 \end{bmatrix}$$

1. The matrix obtained by interchanging the first and second rows of A is

$$\begin{bmatrix} 7 & -\frac{1}{2} & 0 \\ 3 & 4 & -3 \end{bmatrix}$$

2. The matrix obtained by multiplying row 2 of A by 5 is

$$\begin{bmatrix} 3 & 4 & -3 \\ 35 & -\frac{5}{2} & 0 \end{bmatrix}$$

We denote this operation by writing $R_2 = 5r_2$, where r_2 denotes the "old" row 2 and R_2 denotes the "new" row 2.

3. The matrix obtained from A by adding 3 times row 1 to row 2 is

$$\begin{bmatrix} 3 & 4 & -3 \\ 3 \cdot 3 + 7 & 3 \cdot 4 + -\frac{1}{2} & 3 \cdot (-3) + 0 \end{bmatrix} = \begin{bmatrix} 3 & 4 & -3 \\ 16 & \frac{23}{2} & -9 \end{bmatrix}$$

We denote this operation by writing $R_2 = 3r_1 + r_2$. ☐

Let's see how row operations are used to solve a system of equations.

☐ **Example 4**   Solve the system of equations:

$$x - y = 2$$
$$2x - 3y = 2$$

Solution   First, we write the augmented matrix:

$$\begin{bmatrix} 1 & -1 & | & 2 \\ 2 & -3 & | & 2 \end{bmatrix} \qquad \begin{aligned} x - y &= 2 \\ 2x - 3y &= 2 \end{aligned}$$

Perform the row operation

$$R_2 = -2r_1 + r_2$$

(This has the effect of leaving row 1 fixed and getting a 0 in row 2, column 1.)

$$\begin{bmatrix} 1 & -1 & | & 2 \\ 0 & -1 & | & -2 \end{bmatrix} \qquad \begin{array}{l} x - y = 2 \\ -y = -2 \end{array}$$

Perform the row operation

$$R_2 = -r_2$$

(This has the effect of getting a 1 in row 2, column 2.)

$$\begin{bmatrix} 1 & -1 & | & 2 \\ 0 & 1 & | & 2 \end{bmatrix} \qquad \begin{array}{l} x - y = 2 \\ y = 2 \end{array}$$

Perform the row operation

$$R_1 = r_2 + r_1$$

(This has the effect of leaving row 2 fixed and getting a 0 in row 1, column 2.)

$$\begin{bmatrix} 1 & 0 & | & 4 \\ 0 & 1 & | & 2 \end{bmatrix} \qquad \begin{array}{l} x = 4 \\ y = 2 \end{array}$$

The solution of the system is $x = 4$, $y = 2$. $\qquad\qquad\qquad$ □

The pattern of steps used in the previous examples can be followed to solve any system of linear equations. Let's list those steps.

Solving a System of
Equations Using
Matrices

Step 1: Write the augmented matrix corresponding to the system. Remember that the constants must be to the right of the equal sign.

Step 2: Perform row operations to get the entry 1 in row 1, column 1.

Step 3: Perform row operations that leave the entry 1 obtained in Step 2 undisturbed while getting 0's in the rest of column 1.

Step 4: Perform row operations to get a 1 in row 2, column 2 (if possible) without disturbing column 1. If this is not possible, move to the row 2, column 3 position.

Step 5: Perform row operations to get 0's in the rest of column 2 without disturbing the entry 1 obtained in Step 4.

Step 6: Continue in this way up to and including the last row of the matrix.

Here is an example of three linear equations in three unknowns.

□ **Example 5** Solve the system of equations:

$$\begin{array}{l} x + y + z = 6 \\ 3x + 2y - z = 4 \\ 3x + y + 2z = 11 \end{array}$$

Solution   **Step 1:** The augmented matrix corresponding to the system is

$$\begin{bmatrix} 1 & 1 & 1 & 6 \\ 3 & 2 & -1 & 4 \\ 3 & 1 & 2 & 11 \end{bmatrix}$$

Step 2: Since a 1 appears in row 1, column 1, we can skip to step 3.

Step 3: Perform the row operations*

$$R_2 = -3r_1 + r_2$$

Notice that these operations leave row 1 undisturbed, while getting 0's in the rest of column 1:

$$\begin{bmatrix} 1 & 1 & 1 & 6 \\ 0 & -1 & -4 & -14 \\ 0 & -2 & -1 & -7 \end{bmatrix}$$

Step 4: To get a 1 in row 2, column 2, we use

$$R_2 = (-1)r_2$$

Notice that column 1 remains undisturbed:

$$\begin{bmatrix} 1 & 1 & 1 & 6 \\ 0 & 1 & 4 & 14 \\ 0 & -2 & -1 & -7 \end{bmatrix}$$

Step 5: To get 0's in the rest of column 2, we use

$$R_1 = -r_2 + r_1$$
$$R_3 = 2r_2 + r_3$$

Notice that row 2 is left undisturbed:

$$\begin{bmatrix} 1 & 0 & -3 & -8 \\ 0 & 1 & 4 & 14 \\ 0 & 0 & 7 & 21 \end{bmatrix}$$

Step 6: Continuing, we seek a 1 in row 3, column 3, so we use

$$R_3 = \tfrac{1}{7}r_3$$

Notice that this is the only choice available to us, since any other choice would disturb the 0's and 1's already obtained:

$$\begin{bmatrix} 1 & 0 & -3 & -8 \\ 0 & 1 & 4 & 14 \\ 0 & 0 & 1 & 3 \end{bmatrix}$$

---

* You should convince yourself that doing both of these simultaneously is the same as doing the first followed by the second.

To get 0's in the rest of column 3, we use

$$R_1 = \quad 3r_3 + r_1$$
$$R_2 = -4r_3 + r_2$$

The result is

$$\begin{bmatrix} 1 & 0 & 0 & | & 1 \\ 0 & 1 & 0 & | & 2 \\ 0 & 0 & 1 & | & 3 \end{bmatrix}$$

The solution of the system is $x = 1$, $y = 2$, $z = 3$.   ❏

The method outlined here also reveals systems that have no solution or an infinite number of solutions.

❏ **Example 6**   Solve the system

$$3x - 6y = 4$$
$$6x - 12y = 5$$

The augmented matrix representing this system is

$$\begin{bmatrix} 3 & -6 & | & 4 \\ 6 & -12 & | & 5 \end{bmatrix}$$

To get a 1 in row 1, column 1 we use $R_1 = \frac{1}{3}r_1$:

$$\begin{bmatrix} 1 & -2 & | & \frac{4}{3} \\ 6 & -12 & | & 5 \end{bmatrix}$$

To get 0 in row 2, column 1, use $R_2 = -6r_1 + r_2$:

$$\begin{bmatrix} 1 & -2 & | & \frac{4}{3} \\ 0 & 0 & | & -3 \end{bmatrix}$$

Let's stop here to look at the actual system of equations:

$$x - 2y = \frac{4}{3}$$
$$0x + 0y = -3$$

The second equation can never be true—no matter what the choice of x and y. Hence, there are no numbers x and y that can obey both equations. That is, the system has no solution.   ❏

❏ **Example 7**   Solve the system

$$2x - 3y = 5$$
$$4x - 6y = 10$$

Solution   The augmented matrix representing this system is

$$\begin{bmatrix} 2 & -3 & | & 5 \\ 4 & -6 & | & 10 \end{bmatrix}$$

To get a 1 in row 1, column 1, we use $R_1 = \frac{1}{2}r_1$:

$$\begin{bmatrix} 1 & -\frac{3}{2} & | & \frac{5}{2} \\ 4 & -6 & | & 10 \end{bmatrix}$$

To get a 0 in column 1, row 2, we use $R_2 = -4r_1 + r_2$:

$$\begin{bmatrix} 1 & -\frac{3}{2} & | & \frac{5}{2} \\ 0 & 0 & | & 0 \end{bmatrix}$$

The system of equations looks like

$$x - \tfrac{3}{2}y = \tfrac{5}{2}$$
$$0x + 0y = 0$$

The second equation is true for any choice of x and y. Hence, all numbers x and y that obey the first equation are solutions of the system. Since any point on the line $x - \frac{3}{2}y = \frac{5}{2}$ is a solution, there are an infinite number of solutions.

We can list some of these solutions by assigning values to y and then calculating x from the equation $x - \frac{3}{2}y = \frac{5}{2}$.

If $y = 0$, then $x = \frac{5}{2}$. Thus $x = \frac{5}{2}$, $y = 0$ is a solution.

If $y = 1$, then $x = 4$. Thus $x = 4$, $y = 1$ is a solution.

If $y = 5$, then $x = 10$. Thus $x = 10$, $y = 5$ is a solution.

If $y = -3$, then $x = -2$. Thus $x = -2$, $y = -3$ is a solution.

And so on.   □

We close with a capsule summary of what to expect from any system of two equations with two unknowns.

SUMMARY

After completing the steps outlined earlier, one of the following matrices will result for a system of two linear equations with two unknowns:

$$\begin{bmatrix} 1 & 0 & | & c \\ 0 & 1 & | & d \end{bmatrix}$$ **Unique solution:** $x = c, y = d$

$$\begin{bmatrix} a & b & | & c \\ 0 & 0 & | & 0 \end{bmatrix}$$ **Infinite number of solutions:** $ax + by = c$

$$\begin{bmatrix} a & b & | & c \\ 0 & 0 & | & \text{nonzero number} \end{bmatrix}$$ **No solution**

Exercise 2.1 *Answers to Odd-Numbered Problems begin on page* 602 .

In Problems 1–10, write the augmented matrix of each system.

1. $2x - 3y = 5$
   $x - y = 3$

2. $4x + y = 5$
   $2x + y = 5$

3. $2x + y + 6 = 0$
   $x + y = -1$

4. $x - y = -3$
   $4x - y + 2 = 0$

5. $2x - y - z = 0$
   $x - y - z = 1$
   $3x - y = 2$

6. $x + y + z = 3$
   $2x + z = 0$
   $3x - y - z = 1$

7. $2u - 3v + w - 7 = 0$
   $u + v - w = 1$
   $2u + 2v - 3w + 4 = 0$

8. $5r - 3s + 6z + 1 = 0$
   $-r - s + t = 1$
   $2r + 3s + 5 = 0$

9. $4x_1 - x_2 + 2x_3 - x_4 = 4$
   $x_1 + x_2 + 6 = 0$
   $2x_2 - x_3 + x_4 = 5$

10. $3x_1 - 5 = 0$
    $x_1 - x_2 + x_3 = 6$
    $2x_2 + x_3 + 4 = 0$

In Problems 11–14 state the row operation used to transform the matrix on the left to the one on the right.

11. $\begin{bmatrix} 3 & 2 & 1 \\ 2 & 1 & 0 \end{bmatrix}$ $\begin{bmatrix} 2 & 1 & 0 \\ 3 & 2 & 1 \end{bmatrix}$

12. $\begin{bmatrix} 3 & 2 & 1 \\ 2 & 1 & 0 \end{bmatrix}$ $\begin{bmatrix} 1 & 1 & 1 \\ 2 & 1 & 0 \end{bmatrix}$

13. $\begin{bmatrix} 3 & 2 & 1 \\ 2 & 1 & 0 \end{bmatrix}$ $\begin{bmatrix} 12 & 8 & 4 \\ 2 & 1 & 0 \end{bmatrix}$

14. $\begin{bmatrix} 3 & 2 & 1 \\ 2 & 1 & 0 \end{bmatrix}$ $\begin{bmatrix} 3 & 2 & 1 \\ 4 & 2 & 0 \end{bmatrix}$

In Problems 15–20 perform the indicated row operation on the matrix

$$\begin{bmatrix} 3 & 6 & 9 \\ 0 & 1 & 4 \\ 1 & 0 & 2 \end{bmatrix}$$

15. $R_1 = r_3, \quad R_3 = r_1$

16. $R_1 = \frac{1}{3}r_1$

17. $R_1 = (-3)r_3 + r_1$

18. $R_1 = r_2 + r_1$

19. $R_2 = \frac{1}{3}r_1 + r_2$

20. $R_3 = -\frac{1}{3}r_1 + r_3$

In Problems 21–48 solve each system of equations using the method of row operations.

21. $x + y = 6$
    $2x - y = 0$

22. $x - y = 2$
    $2x + y = 1$

23. $2x + y = 5$
    $x - y = 1$

24. $3x + 2y = 7$
    $x + y = 3$

25. $2x + 3y = 7$
    $3x - y = 5$

26. $2x - 3y = 5$
    $3x + y = 2$

27. $5x - 7y = 31$
    $3x + 2y = 0$

28. $2x + 8y = 17$
    $3x - y = 1$

29. $2x - 3y = 0$
    $4x + 9y = 5$

30. $3x - 4y = 3$
    $6x + 2y = 1$

31. $4x - 3y = 4$
    $2x + 6y = 7$

32. $3x - 5y = 3$
    $6x + 10y = 10$

33. $\frac{1}{2}x + \frac{1}{3}y = 2$
    $x + y = 5$

34. $x - \frac{1}{4}y = 0$
    $\frac{1}{2}x + \frac{1}{2}y = \frac{5}{2}$

35. $x + y = 1$
    $3x - 2y = \frac{4}{3}$

36. $4x - y = \frac{11}{4}$
    $3x + y = \frac{5}{2}$

37. $2x + y + z = 6$
    $x - y - z = -3$
    $3x + y + 2z = 7$

38. $x + y + z = 5$
    $2x - y + z = 2$
    $x + 2y - z = 3$

39. $x + y - z = -2$
    $3x + y + z = 0$
    $2x - y + 2z = 1$

40. $2x - y - z = -5$
    $x + y + z = 2$
    $x + 2y + 2z = 5$

41. $2x + y - z = 2$
    $x + 3y + 2z = 1$
    $x + y + z = 2$

42. $2x + 2y + z = 6$
    $x - y - z = -2$
    $x - 2y - 2z = -5$

43. $x + y - z = 0$
    $2x + 4y - 4z = -1$
    $2x + y + z = 2$

44. $x + y - z = 0$
    $4x + 2y - 4z = 0$
    $x + 2y + z = 0$

45. $3x + y - z = \frac{2}{3}$
    $2x - y + z = 1$
    $4x + 2y = \frac{8}{3}$

46. $x + y = 1$
    $2x - y + z = 1$
    $x + 2y + z = \frac{8}{3}$

47. $x_1 + x_2 + x_3 + x_4 = 4$
    $2x_1 - x_2 + x_3 = 0$
    $3x_1 + 2x_2 + x_3 - x_4 = 6$
    $x_1 - 2x_2 - 2x_3 + 2x_4 = -1$

48. $x_1 + x_2 + x_3 + x_4 = 4$
    $-x_1 + 2x_2 + x_3 = 0$
    $2x_1 + 3x_2 + x_3 - x_4 = 6$
    $-2x_1 + x_2 - 2x_3 + 2x_4 = -1$

In Problems 49–60 discuss each system of equations. Determine whether the system has a unique solution, no solution, or infinitely many solutions. Use matrix techniques.

49. $x - y = 5$
    $2x - 2y = 6$

50. $4x + y = 5$
    $8x + 2y = 10$

51. $2x - 3y = 6$
    $4x - 6y = 12$

52. $2x - 3y = 6$
    $4x - 6y = 8$

53. $5x - 6y = 1$
    $-10x + 12y = 0$

54. $3x + 4y = 7$
    $x - y = 2$

55. $2x + 3y = 5$
    $4x + 4y = 8$

56. $2x - y = 0$
    $4x - 2y = 0$

57. $2x - y - z = 0$
    $x - y - z = 1$
    $3x - y - z = 2$

58. $x + y + z = 3$
    $2x + y + z = 0$
    $3x + y + z = 1$

59. $2x_1 - x_2 + x_3 = 6$ **60.** $x_1 - x_2 + x_3 = 2$
           $3x_1 - x_2 + x_3 = 6$ $2x_1 - 3x_2 + x_3 = 0$
           $4x_1 - 2x_2 + 2x_3 = 12$ $3x_1 - 3x_2 + 3x_3 = 6$

61. *Investment Problem.* An amount of $5000 is put into three investments at rates of 6%, 7%, and 8% per annum, respectively. The total annual income is $358. The income from the first two investments is $70 more than the income from the third investment. Find the amount of each investment.

62. *Investment Problem.* An amount of $6500 is placed in three investments at rates of 6%, 8%, and 9% per annum, respectively. The total annual income is $480. If the income from the third investment is $60 more than the income from the second investment, find the amount of each investment.

2.2 SOLVING SYSTEMS OF *m* LINEAR EQUATIONS IN *n* UNKNOWNS

REDUCED ROW-ECHELON FORM □ INFINITE NUMBER OF SOLUTIONS: PARAMETERS □ SUMMARY □ APPLICATION

We learned in Section 1.4 and again in the previous section that a system of two linear equations in two unknowns will have either one solution, no solution, or infinitely many solutions. As it turns out no matter how many equations are in a system and no matter how many unknowns a system has, these are still the only three possibilities that arise.

Thus, for example, the system of three linear equations in four unknowns

$$x_1 + 3x_2 + 5x_3 + x_4 = 2$$
$$2x_1 + 3x_2 + 4x_3 + 2x_4 = 1$$
$$x_1 + 2x_2 + 3x_3 + x_4 = 1$$

will have either one solution, no solution, or infinitely many solutions.

System of *m* Equations in *n* Unknowns

In general, a system of *m* linear equations in the *n* unknowns $x_1, x_2, \ldots, x_n$ is of the form

$$a_{11}x_1 + a_{12}x_2 + \cdots + a_{1n}x_n = b_1$$
$$a_{21}x_1 + a_{22}x_2 + \cdots + a_{2n}x_n = b_2$$
$$a_{31}x_1 + a_{32}x_2 + \cdots + a_{3n}x_n = b_3$$
$$\vdots \qquad \vdots \qquad \qquad \vdots \qquad \vdots$$
$$a_{i1}x_1 + a_{i2}x_2 + \cdots + a_{in}x_n = b_i$$
$$\vdots \qquad \vdots \qquad \qquad \vdots \qquad \vdots$$
$$a_{m1}x_1 + a_{m2}x_2 + \cdots + a_{mn}x_n = b_m$$

where a_{ij} are b_i are real numbers, $i = 1, 2, \ldots, m, j = 1, 2, \ldots, n$.

This is a system of *linear* equations because the unknowns $x_1, x_2, \ldots, x_n$ all appear to the first power and there are no products of unknowns. Finally, if we count the number of equations, we conclude that there are m of them, each containing n unknowns $x_1, x_2, \ldots, x_n$.

Solution A *solution* of a system of m equations in n unknowns $x_1, x_2, \ldots, x_n$ is any ordered set $(x_1, x_2, \ldots, x_n)$ of real numbers for which *each* of the m equations of the system is satisfied.

REDUCED ROW-ECHELON FORM

A system of m linear equations in n unknowns will have either one solution, no solution, or infinitely many solutions. We can determine which of these possibilities occurs and, if solutions exist, find them by performing row operations on the augmented matrix of the system until we arrive at a matrix that has the following configuration:

1. Any rows that consist entirely of zeros are located at the bottom of the matrix.
2. The first nonzero element in each row is 1 and it has 0's above it and below it.
3. The leftmost 1 in any row is to the right of the leftmost 1 in the row above.

Reduced Row-Echelon Form   The matrix having this configuration (there is only one) is called the *reduced row-echelon form* of the augmented matrix.

☐ **Example 1**   The matrix below

$$\left[\begin{array}{ccc|c} 1 & 0 & 0 & 3 \\ 0 & 1 & 0 & 8 \\ 0 & 0 & 1 & -4 \end{array}\right]$$

is the reduced row-echelon form of a system of three linear equations in three unknowns. If the unknowns are x_1, x_2, x_2, this matrix represents the system of equations

$$x_1 = 3$$
$$x_2 = 8$$
$$x_3 = -4$$

Thus, the system has one solution $(3, 8, -4)$.   ☐

☐ **Example 2**   The matrix below

$$\left[\begin{array}{ccc|c} 1 & 0 & 3 & 0 \\ 0 & 1 & 2 & 0 \\ 0 & 0 & 0 & 1 \\ 0 & 0 & 0 & 0 \end{array}\right]$$

is the reduced row-echelon form of a system of four equations in three unknowns. If the unknowns are x_1, x_2, x_3, the equation represented by the third row is

$$0 \cdot x_1 + 0 \cdot x_2 + 0 \cdot x_3 = 1 \qquad \text{or} \qquad 0 = 1$$

Since $0 = 1$ is meaningless, we conclude the system has no solution.   ☐

□ **Example 3** The matrix below

$$\begin{bmatrix} 1 & 0 & 0 & 2 & | & 5 \\ 0 & 1 & 0 & 1 & | & 2 \\ 0 & 0 & 1 & 3 & | & 4 \end{bmatrix}$$

is the reduced row-echelon form of a system of three equations in four unknowns. If x_1, x_2, x_3, x_4 are the unknowns, the system of equations is

$$x_1 + 2x_4 = 5$$
$$x_2 + x_4 = 2$$
$$x_3 + 3x_4 = 4$$

Thus, the system has infinitely many solutions—the unknown x_4 can take on any value from which $x_1, x_2, x_3,$ can be calculated. Some of the possibilities are:

If $x_4 = 0$, then $x_1 = 5$, $x_2 = 2$, $x_3 = 4$
If $x_4 = 1$, then $x_1 = 3$, $x_2 = 1$, $x_3 = 1$
If $x_4 = 2$, then $x_1 = 1$, $x_2 = 0$, $x_3 = -2$

and so on.   □

□ **Example 4** The following matrices are not in reduced row-echelon form:

$$\begin{bmatrix} 1 & 0 & 0 \\ 0 & 0 & 0 \\ 0 & 1 & 0 \end{bmatrix}$$
The second row contains all 0's and the third does not—this violates the rule that states any rows containing all zeroes are at the bottom.

$$\begin{bmatrix} 1 & 0 & 2 & 4 \\ 0 & 0 & 2 & 3 \\ 0 & 0 & 0 & 1 \end{bmatrix}$$
The first nonzero element in row 2 is not a 1.

$$\begin{bmatrix} 1 & 0 & 0 \\ 0 & 0 & 1 \\ 0 & 1 & 0 \end{bmatrix}$$
The leftmost 1 in the third row is not to the right of the leftmost 1 in the row above it.   □

Let's review the procedure for getting the reduced row-echelon form of a matrix.

□ **Example 5** Find the reduced row-echelon form of

$$A = \begin{bmatrix} 1 & -1 & | & 2 \\ 2 & -3 & | & 2 \\ 3 & -5 & | & 2 \end{bmatrix}$$

Solution   The entry in row 1, column 1, namely a_{11}, is 1. Thus, we proceed to obtain a matrix in which all the entries in column 1 except a_{11} are 0. We can obtain such a matrix by performing the row operations

$$R_2 = -2r_1 + r_2$$
$$R_3 = -3r_1 + r_3$$

The new matrix is

$$\left[\begin{array}{rr|r} 1 & -1 & 2 \\ 0 & -1 & -2 \\ 0 & -2 & -4 \end{array}\right]$$

We want the entry in row 2, column 2, namely a_{22}, to be equal to 1. By multiplying row 2 by (-1), we obtain

$$\left[\begin{array}{rr|r} 1 & -1 & 2 \\ 0 & 1 & 2 \\ 0 & -2 & -4 \end{array}\right]$$

Now column 2 should have 0's except for $a_{22} = 1$. This can be accomplished by applying the row operations

$$R_1 = r_2 + r_1$$
$$R_3 = 2r_2 + r_3$$

The new matrix is

$$\left[\begin{array}{rr|r} 1 & 0 & 4 \\ 0 & 1 & 2 \\ 0 & 0 & 0 \end{array}\right]$$

This is the reduced row-echelon form of A.   □

□ **Example 6**   Solve the system

$$x - y = 2$$
$$2x - 3y = 2$$
$$3x - 5y = 2$$

Solution   The augmented matrix of this system is

$$\left[\begin{array}{rr|r} 1 & -1 & 2 \\ 2 & -3 & 2 \\ 3 & -5 & 2 \end{array}\right]$$

Following the solution to Example 5, we place this matrix in reduced row-echelon form.

$$\left[\begin{array}{rr|r} 1 & 0 & 4 \\ 0 & 1 & 2 \\ 0 & 0 & 0 \end{array}\right]$$

We conclude that the system has the solution $x = 4$, $y = 2$.   □

□ **Example 7**   Solve the system

$$x_1 - x_2 + 2x_3 = 2$$
$$2x_1 - 3x_2 + 2x_3 = 1$$
$$3x_1 - 5x_2 + 2x_3 = -3$$
$$-4x_1 + 12x_2 + 8x_3 = 10$$

Solution   We need to find the reduced row-echelon form of the augmented matrix of this system, namely,

$$\begin{bmatrix} 1 & -1 & 2 & | & 2 \\ 2 & -3 & 2 & | & 1 \\ 3 & -5 & 2 & | & -3 \\ -4 & 12 & 8 & | & 10 \end{bmatrix}$$

To obtain 0's in column 1 under $a_{11} = 1$, we use the row operations

$$R_2 = -2r_1 + r_2 \qquad R_3 = -3r_1 + r_3 \qquad R_4 = 4r_1 + r_4$$

The new matrix is

$$\begin{bmatrix} 1 & -1 & 2 & | & 2 \\ 0 & -1 & -2 & | & -3 \\ 0 & -2 & -4 & | & -9 \\ 0 & 8 & 16 & | & 18 \end{bmatrix}$$

To get $a_{22} = 1$, we use $R_2 = -r_2$, obtaining

$$\begin{bmatrix} 1 & -1 & 2 & | & 2 \\ 0 & 1 & 2 & | & 3 \\ 0 & -2 & -4 & | & -9 \\ 0 & 8 & 16 & | & 18 \end{bmatrix}$$

To obtain 0's in column 2 (except for $a_{22} = 1$), we use

$$R_1 = r_2 + r_1 \qquad R_3 = 2r_2 + r_3 \qquad R_4 = -8r_2 + r_4$$

The new matrix is

$$\begin{bmatrix} 1 & 0 & 4 & | & 5 \\ 0 & 1 & 2 & | & 3 \\ 0 & 0 & 0 & | & -3 \\ 0 & 0 & 0 & | & -6 \end{bmatrix} \tag{1}$$

Next, we use $R_3 = -\tfrac{1}{3}r_3$; the result is

$$\begin{bmatrix} 1 & 0 & 4 & | & 5 \\ 0 & 1 & 2 & | & 3 \\ 0 & 0 & 0 & | & 1 \\ 0 & 0 & 0 & | & -6 \end{bmatrix}$$

To obtain 0's in column 4, we use

$$R_1 = -5r_3 + r_1 \qquad R_2 = -3r_3 + r_2 \qquad R_4 = 6r_3 + r_4$$

The result is the matrix

$$\begin{bmatrix} 1 & 0 & 4 & | & 0 \\ 0 & 1 & 2 & | & 0 \\ 0 & 0 & 0 & | & 1 \\ 0 & 0 & 0 & | & 0 \end{bmatrix}$$

Based on the third row, which yields the equation

$$0 \cdot x_1 + 0 \cdot x_2 + 0 \cdot x_3 = 1$$

we conclude the system has no solution.*   □

INFINITE NUMBER OF SOLUTIONS: PARAMETERS

We have seen several examples of systems of linear equations that have an infinite number of solutions. Let's look at a few more examples.

□ **Example 8**   Solve the system

$$x_1 + x_2 + x_3 = 7$$
$$x_1 - x_2 - 3x_3 = 1$$

Solution   The augmented matrix of the system is

$$\begin{bmatrix} 1 & 1 & 1 & | & 7 \\ 1 & -1 & -3 & | & 1 \end{bmatrix}$$

The reduced row-echelon form (as you should verify) is

$$\begin{bmatrix} 1 & 0 & -1 & | & 4 \\ 0 & 1 & 2 & | & 3 \end{bmatrix}$$

The system of equations represented by this matrix are

$$x_1 - x_3 = 4 \tag{2}$$
$$x_2 + 2x_3 = 3$$

We can assign any value to x_3 and use it to compute values of x_1 and x_2. Thus, the system has infinitely many solutions.   □

If we rearrange the equations in (2) in the form

$$x_1 = 4 + x_3$$
$$x_2 = 3 - 2x_3$$

it is easier to see the role the unknown x_3 plays. In fact, because the remaining
Parameter   unknowns are expressed in terms of x_3, we call x_3 a *parameter*.
The next example illustrates a system having an infinite number of solutions with two parameters.

□ **Example 9**   Solve the system

$$x_1 + x_2 + 2x_3 + 2x_4 = 2$$
$$x_1 + x_3 + x_4 = 0$$
$$x_2 + x_3 + x_4 = 2$$

Solution   The augmented matrix of the system is

$$\begin{bmatrix} 1 & 1 & 2 & 2 & | & 2 \\ 1 & 0 & 1 & 1 & | & 0 \\ 0 & 1 & 1 & 1 & | & 2 \end{bmatrix}$$

---

* This conclusion could have been resolved earlier by looking at the equation representing the third row in matrix (1).

The reduced row-echelon form (as you should verify) is

$$\begin{bmatrix} 1 & 0 & 1 & 1 & | & 0 \\ 0 & 1 & 1 & 1 & | & 2 \\ 0 & 0 & 0 & 0 & | & 0 \end{bmatrix}$$

The equations represented by this system are

$$x_1 + x_3 + x_4 = 0$$
$$x_2 + x_3 + x_4 = 2$$

We can rewrite this system in the form

$$x_1 = -x_3 - x_4$$
$$x_2 = 2 - x_3 - x_4 \tag{3}$$

The system has infinitely many solutions, obtained by assigning the two parameters x_3 and x_4 arbitrary values. Some choices are shown in the table.

x_3	x_4	x_1	x_2	Solution (x_1, x_2, x_3, x_4)
0	0	0	2	$(0, 2, 0, 0)$
1	0	-1	1	$(-1, 1, 1, 0)$
0	2	-2	0	$(-2, 0, 0, 2)$

□

Parameters are not unique. We could have chosen x_1 and x_4 as parameters by rewriting the equations (3) in the following manner.

From the first equation

$$x_3 = -x_1 - x_4$$

We can replace the parameter x_3 in the second equation by the above to produce

$$x_2 = 2 - x_3 - x_4 = 2 + x_1 + x_4 - x_4$$

We then get the system

$$x_2 = 2 + x_1$$
$$x_3 = -x_1 - x_4$$

showing the role of x_1 and x_4 as parameters.

SUMMARY

To solve a system of m linear equations in n unknowns

1. Write its augmented matrix.
2. Compute the reduced row-echelon form of the augmented matrix.
3. If this matrix has a row of zeros, except for a nonzero entry in the last column, the system has no solution.
4. Otherwise determine from this matrix whether the system has a unique solution or infinitely many solutions.

APPLICATION

☐ **Example 10**   In a chemistry laboratory one solution is 10% hydrochloric acid (HCl), a second
Mixing Acids   solution contains 20% HCl, and a third contains 40% HCl. How many liters of each
should be mixed to obtain 100 liters of 25% HCl?

Solution   Let x_1, x_2, and x_3 represent the number of liters of 10%, 20%, and 40% solutions of
HCl, respectively. Since we want 100 liters in all and the amount of HCl obtained
from each solution must sum to 25% of 100, or 25 liters, we must have

$$x_1 + x_2 + x_3 = 100$$
$$0.1x_1 + 0.2x_2 + 0.4x_3 = 25$$

Thus, our problem is to solve a system of two equations in three unknowns.
   By matrix techniques, we obtain the solution

$$x_1 = 2x_3 - 50$$
$$x_2 = -3x_3 + 150$$

(4)

where x_3 can represent any real number. Now the practical considerations of this
problem lead us to the conditions that $x_1 \geq 0, x_2 \geq 0, x_3 \geq 0$. From (4) we see that we
must have $x_3 \geq 25$ and $x_3 \leq 50$, since otherwise $x_1 < 0$ or $x_2 < 0$. Some possible
solutions are listed in the table. The final determination by the chemistry laboratory
will more than likely be based on the amount and availability of one acid solution
versus others.   ☐

No. of Liters 10% Solution	No. of Liters 20% Solution	No. of Liters 40% Solution
0	75	25
10	60	30
12	57	31
16	51	33
20	45	35
25	37.5	37.5
26	36	38
30	30	40
36	21	43
38	18	44
46	6	48
50	0	50

Exercise 2.2 *Answers to Odd-Numbered Problems begin on page* 602.

In Problems 1–10, tell whether the given matrix is in reduced row-echelon form.

1. $\begin{bmatrix} 1 & 2 & 3 \\ 0 & 0 & 0 \\ 0 & 0 & 1 \end{bmatrix}$

2. $\begin{bmatrix} 1 & 2 & 3 \\ 0 & 0 & 0 \\ 0 & 0 & 0 \end{bmatrix}$

3. $\begin{bmatrix} 1 & 1 & 0 \\ 0 & 1 & 0 \end{bmatrix}$

4. $\begin{bmatrix} 1 & 0 & 3 \\ 0 & 1 & 0 \end{bmatrix}$

5. $\begin{bmatrix} 0 & 1 \\ 1 & 0 \end{bmatrix}$

6. $\begin{bmatrix} 0 & 1 & 0 \\ 0 & 0 & 1 \\ 0 & 0 & 0 \end{bmatrix}$

7. $\begin{bmatrix} 0 & 0 & 1 \\ 0 & 0 & 0 \end{bmatrix}$

8. $\begin{bmatrix} 0 & 0 \\ 0 & 0 \end{bmatrix}$

9. $\begin{bmatrix} 1 & 0 & 0 & 0 & 0 \\ 0 & 0 & 1 & 2 & 0 \\ 0 & 0 & 0 & 0 & 1 \\ 0 & 0 & 0 & 0 & 0 \end{bmatrix}$

10. $\begin{bmatrix} 1 & 1 & 0 \\ 0 & 0 & 2 \end{bmatrix}$

In Problems 11–20 the reduced row-echelon form of the augmented matrix of a system of equations is given. Tell whether the system has one solution, no solution, or infinitely many solutions.

11. $\left[\begin{array}{cc|c} 1 & 1 & 1 \\ 0 & 0 & 0 \end{array}\right]$

12. $\left[\begin{array}{cc|c} 1 & 0 & 0 \\ 0 & 0 & 1 \end{array}\right]$

13. $\left[\begin{array}{ccc|c} 1 & 0 & 0 & 0 \\ 0 & 1 & 0 & 0 \\ 0 & 0 & 1 & 6 \end{array}\right]$

14. $\left[\begin{array}{ccc|c} 1 & 0 & -2 & 6 \\ 0 & 1 & 3 & 1 \end{array}\right]$

15. $\left[\begin{array}{ccc|c} 1 & 2 & 0 & 1 \\ 0 & 0 & 1 & 2 \\ 0 & 0 & 0 & 0 \end{array}\right]$

16. $\left[\begin{array}{ccc|c} 1 & 2 & 0 & 0 \\ 0 & 0 & 1 & 0 \\ 0 & 0 & 0 & 1 \end{array}\right]$

17. $\left[\begin{array}{cccc|c} 1 & 0 & 1 & -1 & 0 \\ 0 & 1 & 2 & 1 & 1 \\ 0 & 0 & 0 & 0 & 0 \end{array}\right]$

18. $\left[\begin{array}{ccc|c} 1 & 0 & 0 & -1 \\ 0 & 1 & 0 & 3 \\ 0 & 0 & 1 & 4 \\ 0 & 0 & 0 & 0 \end{array}\right]$

19. $\left[\begin{array}{ccc|c} 1 & 0 & -1 & 1 \\ 0 & 1 & 2 & 1 \end{array}\right]$

20. $\left[\begin{array}{cc|c} 1 & 0 & 1 \\ 0 & 1 & 1 \\ 0 & 0 & 0 \end{array}\right]$

In Problems 21–38 solve each system of equations by finding the reduced row-echelon form of the augmented matrix.

21. $x + y = 3$
    $2x - y = 3$

22. $x - y = 5$
    $2x + 3y = 15$

23. $3x - 3y = 12$
    $3x + 2y = -3$

24. $6x + y = 8$
    $x - 3y = -5$

25. $3x_1 - 4x_2 = 1$
    $5x_1 + 2x_2 = 19$

26. $2x_1 + 3x_2 = 8$
    $2x_1 - x_2 = 12$

27. $2x_1 + 3x_2 = 5$
    $2x_1 - x_2 = 7$

28. $3x_1 - 4x_2 = 7$
    $5x_1 + 2x_2 = 3$

29. $\begin{aligned} x_1 - x_2 &= 1 \\ x_2 - x_3 &= 6 \\ x_1 + x_3 &= -1 \end{aligned}$

30. $\begin{aligned} 2x_1 - x_2 + 3x_3 &= 0 \\ x_1 + 2x_2 - x_3 &= 5 \\ 2x_2 + x_3 &= 1 \end{aligned}$

31. $\begin{aligned} x_1 + x_2 &= 7 \\ x_2 - x_3 + x_4 &= 5 \\ x_1 - x_2 + x_3 + x_4 &= 6 \\ x_2 - x_4 &= 10 \end{aligned}$

32. $\begin{aligned} x_1 + x_2 + x_3 + x_4 &= 0 \\ 2x_1 - x_2 - x_3 + x_4 &= 0 \\ x_1 - x_2 - x_3 + x_4 &= 0 \\ x_1 + x_2 - x_3 - x_4 &= 0 \end{aligned}$

33. $\begin{aligned} x_1 + 2x_2 + 3x_3 - x_4 &= 0 \\ 3x_1 - x_4 &= 4 \\ x_2 - x_3 - x_4 &= 2 \end{aligned}$

34. $\begin{aligned} 2x_1 - 3x_2 + 4x_3 &= 7 \\ x_1 - 2x_2 + 3x_3 &= 2 \end{aligned}$

35. $\begin{aligned} x_1 - x_2 + x_3 &= 5 \\ 2x_1 - 2x_2 + 2x_3 &= 8 \end{aligned}$

36. $\begin{aligned} x_1 + x_2 + x_3 &= 3 \\ x_1 - x_2 + x_3 &= 7 \\ x_1 - x_2 - x_3 &= 1 \end{aligned}$

37. $\begin{aligned} 3x_1 - x_2 + 2x_3 &= 3 \\ 3x_1 + 3x_2 + x_3 &= 3 \\ 3x_1 - 5x_2 + 3x_3 &= 12 \end{aligned}$

38. $\begin{aligned} x_1 + x_2 - x_3 &= 12 \\ 3x_1 - x_2 &= 1 \\ 2x_1 - 3x_2 + 4x_3 &= 3 \end{aligned}$

39. A chemistry laboratory has available three kinds of hydrochloric acid (HCl): 10%, 30%, and 50% solutions. How many liters of each should be mixed to obtain 100 liters of 25% HCl? Provide a table showing at least 6 of the possible solutions.

40. Repeat Problem 39 if the mixture is to be 100 liters of 40% HCl.

2.3 MATRIX ALGEBRA

EQUALITY OF MATRICES ☐ ADDITION OF MATRICES ☐ SUBTRACTING MATRICES
☐ MULTIPLYING A MATRIX BY A NUMBER

Matrices can be added, subtracted, and multiplied. They also possess many of the algebraic properties of numbers. Matrix algebra is the study of these properties. Its importance lies in the fact that many situations in both pure and applied mathematics deal with rectangular arrays of numbers. In fact, in many branches of business and the biological and social sciences, it is necessary to express and use a set of numbers in a rectangular array. Let's look at an example.

☐ **Example 1** Motors, Inc., produces three models of cars: a sedan, a hard-top, and a station wagon. If the company wishes to compare the units of raw material and the units of labor involved in 1 month's production of each of these models, the rectangular array displayed below may be used to present the data:

	Sedan Model	Hard-Top Model	Station Wagon Model
Units of Material	23	16	10
Units of Labor	7	9	11

The same information may be written concisely as the matrix

$$\begin{bmatrix} 23 & 16 & 10 \\ 7 & 9 & 11 \end{bmatrix}$$

This matrix, has 2 rows (the units) and 3 columns (the models). The first row represents units of material and the second row represents units of labor. The first, second, and third columns represent the sedan, hard-top, and station wagon models, respectively. □

A formal definition of a matrix as a rectangular array of numbers is given below.

Matrix A *matrix A* is a rectangular array of numbers a_{ij} of the form

$$
A = \begin{bmatrix}
a_{11} & a_{12} & \cdots & a_{1j} & \cdots & a_{1n} \\
a_{21} & a_{22} & \cdots & a_{2j} & \cdots & a_{2n} \\
\vdots & \vdots & & \vdots & & \vdots \\
a_{i1} & a_{i2} & \cdots & a_{ij} & \cdots & a_{in} \\
\vdots & \vdots & & \vdots & & \vdots \\
a_{m1} & a_{m2} & \cdots & a_{mj} & \cdots & a_{mn}
\end{bmatrix}
\begin{matrix} \\ \\ \\ \leftarrow i\text{th row} \\ \\ \\ \end{matrix}
$$

*j*th column ↓

This matrix contains $m \cdot n$ numbers.

Row Index
Column Index

Elements

Each number a_{ij} of the matrix A has two indices: the *row index, i,* and the *column index, j.* The symbols $a_{i1}, a_{i2}, \ldots, a_{in}$ represent the numbers in the *i*th row, and the symbols $a_{1j}, a_{2j}, \ldots, a_{mj}$ represent the numbers in the *j*th column. The numbers a_{ij} of a matrix are sometimes referred to as the *entries* or *components* or *elements* of the matrix. The matrix A above, which has m rows and n columns, can be abbreviated by

$$A = [a_{ij}] \qquad i = 1, 2, \ldots, m; \quad j = 1, 2, \ldots, n$$

Dimension The *dimension of a matrix A* is determined by the number of rows and the number of columns of the matrix. If a matrix A has m rows and n columns, we denote the dimension of A by $m \times n$, read as "*m by n.*"

For a 2×3 matrix, remember that the first number 2 denotes the number of rows and the second number 3 is the number of columns. A matrix with 3 rows and 2 columns is of dimension 3×2.

Square Matrix If a matrix A has the same number of rows as it has columns, it is called a *square matrix.*

Diagonal Entries

In a square matrix $A = [a_{ij}]$ the entries for which $i = j$, namely $a_{11}, a_{22}, a_{33}, a_{44}$, and so on, form the *diagonal of A.*

☐ **Example 2**   In a recent United States census, the following figures were obtained with regard to the city of Glenwood. Each year 7% of city residents move to the suburbs and 1% of the people in the suburbs move to the city. This situation can be represented by the matrix

$$P = \begin{matrix} \text{City} \\ \text{Suburbs} \end{matrix} \begin{array}{cc} \text{City} & \text{Suburbs} \\ \begin{bmatrix} 0.93 & 0.07 \\ 0.01 & 0.99 \end{bmatrix} \end{array}$$

Here, the entry in row 1, column 2, 0.07, indicates that 7% of city residents move to the suburbs. The matrix P is a square matrix and its dimension is 2×2. The diagonal entries are 0.93 and 0.99.   ☐

Row and Column Matrix   A *row matrix* is a matrix with 1 row of elements. A *column matrix* is a matrix with 1 column of elements. Row matrices and column matrices are sometimes referred to as *row vectors* and *column vectors,* respectively.

☐ **Example 3**   The matrices

$$A = \begin{bmatrix} 23 & 16 & 10 \end{bmatrix} \qquad B = \begin{bmatrix} 7 & 9 \end{bmatrix}$$

$$C = \begin{bmatrix} 23 \\ -1 \\ 7 \end{bmatrix} \qquad D = \begin{bmatrix} 16 \\ 9 \end{bmatrix} \qquad E = \begin{bmatrix} 9 \end{bmatrix}$$

have the following dimensions: A, 1×3; B, 1×2; C, 3×1; D, 2×1; E, 1×1. Here A, B, and E are row vectors and C, D, and E are column vectors.   ☐

The matrix $E = [9]$ in Example 3 is a 1×1 matrix and, as such, can be treated simply as a real number.

EQUALITY OF MATRICES

As with most mathematical quantities, we now want to determine various relationships between two matrices. We might ask, "When, if at all, are two matrices equal?"

Let's try to arrive at a sound definition for equality of matrices by requiring equal matrices to have certain desirable properties. First, it would seem necessary that two equal matrices have the same dimension — that is, that they both be $m \times n$ matrices. Next, it would seem necessary that their entries be identical numbers. With these two restrictions, we define equality of matrices.

Equality of Matrices   Two matrices A and B are *equal* if they are of the same dimension and if corresponding entries are equal. In this case, we write $A = B$, read as "matrix A is equal to matrix B."

☐ **Example 4**   In order for the two matrices

$$\begin{bmatrix} p & q \\ 1 & 0 \end{bmatrix} \quad \text{and} \quad \begin{bmatrix} 2 & 4 \\ n & 0 \end{bmatrix}$$

to be equal, we must have $p = 2$, $q = 4$, and $n = 1$.   ☐

□ **Example 5**   Let A and B be two matrices given by

$$A = \begin{bmatrix} x+y & 6 \\ 2x-3 & 2-y \end{bmatrix} \quad B = \begin{bmatrix} 5 & 5x+2 \\ y & x-y \end{bmatrix}$$

Find x and y so that A and B are equal (if possible).

Solution   Both A and B are 2×2 matrices. Thus, $A = B$ if

(a) $x+y=5$ (b) $6 = 5x+2$

(c) $2x-3=y$ (d) $2-y=x-y$

Here we have four equations in the two unknowns x and y. From equation (d), we see that $x = 2$. Using this value in equation (a), we obtain $y = 3$. But $x = 2$, $y = 3$ do not satisfy either (b) or (c). Hence, there are *no* values for x and y satisfying all four equations. This means A and B can never be equal.   □

ADDITION OF MATRICES

Can two matrices be added? And, if so, what is the rule or law for addition of matrices?

Let's return to Example 1. In that example, we recorded 1 month's production of Motors, Inc., by the matrix

$$A = \begin{bmatrix} 23 & 16 & 10 \\ 7 & 9 & 11 \end{bmatrix}$$

Suppose the next month's production is

$$B = \begin{bmatrix} 18 & 12 & 9 \\ 14 & 6 & 8 \end{bmatrix}$$

in which the pattern of recording units and models remains the same.

The total production for the 2 months can be displayed by the matrix

$$C = \begin{bmatrix} 41 & 28 & 19 \\ 21 & 15 & 19 \end{bmatrix}$$

since the number of units of material for sedan models is $41 = 23 + 18$; the number of units of material for hardtop models is $28 = 16 + 12$; and so on.

This leads us to define the sum $A + B$ of two matrices A and B as the matrix consisting of the sum of corresponding entries from A and B.

Addition of Matrices   Let $A = [a_{ij}]$ and $B = [b_{ij}]$ be two $m \times n$ matrices. The *sum* $A + B$ is defined as the $m \times n$ matrix $[a_{ij} + b_{ij}]$.

□ **Example 6**   (a) $\begin{bmatrix} 23 & 16 & 10 \\ 7 & 9 & 11 \end{bmatrix} + \begin{bmatrix} 18 & 12 & 9 \\ 14 & 6 & 8 \end{bmatrix} = \begin{bmatrix} 23+18 & 16+12 & 10+9 \\ 7+14 & 9+6 & 11+8 \end{bmatrix}$

$$= \begin{bmatrix} 41 & 28 & 19 \\ 21 & 15 & 19 \end{bmatrix}$$

(b) $\begin{bmatrix} 0.6 & 0.4 \\ 0.1 & 0.9 \end{bmatrix} + \begin{bmatrix} 2.3 & 0.6 \\ 1.8 & 5.2 \end{bmatrix} = \begin{bmatrix} 0.6+2.3 & 0.4+0.6 \\ 0.1+1.8 & 0.9+5.2 \end{bmatrix}$

$\qquad\qquad\qquad\qquad = \begin{bmatrix} 2.9 & 1.0 \\ 1.9 & 6.1 \end{bmatrix}$ □

Notice that it is possible to add two matrices only if their dimensions are the same. Also, the dimension of the sum of two matrices is the same as that of the two original matrices.

The following pairs of matrices cannot be added since they are of different dimensions:

$$A = \begin{bmatrix} 1 & 2 \\ 7 & 2 \end{bmatrix} \qquad \text{and} \qquad B = \begin{bmatrix} 1 \\ -3 \end{bmatrix}$$

$$A = [2 \quad 3] \qquad \text{and} \qquad B = [1 \quad 1 \quad 1]$$

$$A = \begin{bmatrix} -1 & 7 & 0 \\ 2 & \frac{1}{2} & 0 \end{bmatrix} \qquad \text{and} \qquad B = \begin{bmatrix} -1 & 2 \\ 3 & 0 \\ 1 & 5 \end{bmatrix}$$

It turns out that the usual rules for the addition of real numbers (such as the commutative laws and associative laws) are also valid for matrix addition.

□ **Example 7**   Let

$$A = \begin{bmatrix} 1 & 5 \\ 7 & -3 \end{bmatrix} \qquad \text{and} \qquad B = \begin{bmatrix} 3 & -2 \\ 4 & 1 \end{bmatrix}$$

Then

$$A + B = \begin{bmatrix} 1 & 5 \\ 7 & -3 \end{bmatrix} + \begin{bmatrix} 3 & -2 \\ 4 & 1 \end{bmatrix} = \begin{bmatrix} 1+3 & 5+(-2) \\ 7+4 & -3+1 \end{bmatrix} = \begin{bmatrix} 4 & 3 \\ 11 & -2 \end{bmatrix}$$

$$B + A = \begin{bmatrix} 3 & -2 \\ 4 & 1 \end{bmatrix} + \begin{bmatrix} 1 & 5 \\ 7 & -3 \end{bmatrix} = \begin{bmatrix} 4 & 3 \\ 11 & -2 \end{bmatrix}$$ □

This leads us to formulate the following property:

If A and B are two matrices of the same dimension, then

$$A + B = B + A$$

That is, matrix addition is *commutative.*

The associative law for addition of matrices is also true. Thus:

If A, B, and C, are three matrices of the same dimension, then

$$A + (B + C) = (A + B) + C$$

For a proof of this result, we let

$$A = [a_{ij}] \qquad B = [b_{ij}] \qquad C = [c_{ij}]$$

Then

$$
\begin{aligned}
A + (B + C) &= [a_{ij}] + ([b_{ij}] + [c_{ij}]) = [a_{ij}] + ([b_{ij} + c_{ij}]) \\
&= [a_{ij}] + [b_{ij} + c_{ij}] = [a_{ij} + (b_{ij} + c_{ij})] \\
&= [(a_{ij} + b_{ij}) + c_{ij}] = [a_{ij} + b_{ij}] + [c_{ij}] \\
&= ([a_{ij} + b_{ij}]) + [c_{ij}] = ([a_{ij}] + [b_{ij}]) + [c_{ij}] \\
&= (A + B) + C
\end{aligned}
$$

In the proof, we used the fact that addition of real numbers is associative. Where?

The fact that addition of matrices is associative means that the notation $A + B + C$ is *not* ambiguous, since $(A + B) + C = A + (B + C)$.

Zero Matrix A matrix in which all entries are zero is called a *zero matrix*. We use the symbol **0** to represent a zero matrix of any dimension.

For real numbers, zero has the property that $0 + x = x$ for any x. An important property of a zero matrix is that $A + \mathbf{0} = A$, provided the dimension of **0** is the same as that of A.

□ **Example 8** Let

$$A = \begin{bmatrix} 3 & 4 & -\frac{1}{2} \\ \sqrt{2} & 0 & 3 \end{bmatrix}$$

Then

$$
\begin{aligned}
A + \mathbf{0} &= \begin{bmatrix} 3 & 4 & -\frac{1}{2} \\ \sqrt{2} & 0 & 3 \end{bmatrix} + \begin{bmatrix} 0 & 0 & 0 \\ 0 & 0 & 0 \end{bmatrix} \\
&= \begin{bmatrix} 3+0 & 4+0 & -\frac{1}{2}+0 \\ \sqrt{2}+0 & 0+0 & 3+0 \end{bmatrix} = \begin{bmatrix} 3 & 4 & -\frac{1}{2} \\ \sqrt{2} & 0 & 3 \end{bmatrix} = A
\end{aligned}
$$

□

If A is any matrix, the *negative of A*, denoted by $-A$, is the matrix obtained by replacing each entry in A by its negative.

□ **Example 9** If
$$A = \begin{bmatrix} -3 & 0 \\ 5 & -2 \\ 1 & 3 \end{bmatrix} \qquad \text{then} \qquad -A = \begin{bmatrix} 3 & 0 \\ -5 & 2 \\ -1 & -3 \end{bmatrix}$$
□

For any matrix A, we have the property that
$$A + (-A) = \mathbf{0}$$

SUBTRACTION OF MATRICES

Now that we have defined the sum of two matrices and the negative of a matrix, it is natural to ask about the *difference* of two matrices. As you will see, subtracting matrices and subtracting numbers are much the same kind of process.

Difference of Two Matrices Let $A = [a_{ij}]$ and $B = [b_{ij}]$ be two $m \times n$ matrices. The *difference* $A - B$ is defined as the $m \times n$ matrix $[a_{ij} - b_{ij}]$.

□ **Example 10**

$$A = \begin{bmatrix} 2 & 3 & 4 \\ 1 & 0 & 2 \end{bmatrix} \quad \text{and} \quad B = \begin{bmatrix} -2 & 1 & -1 \\ 3 & 0 & 3 \end{bmatrix}$$

Then

$$A - B = \begin{bmatrix} 2 & 3 & 4 \\ 1 & 0 & 2 \end{bmatrix} - \begin{bmatrix} -2 & 1 & -1 \\ 3 & 0 & 3 \end{bmatrix}$$

$$= \begin{bmatrix} 2 - (-2) & 3 - 1 & 4 - (-1) \\ 1 - 3 & 0 - 0 & 2 - 3 \end{bmatrix} = \begin{bmatrix} 4 & 2 & 5 \\ -2 & 0 & -1 \end{bmatrix}$$ □

Notice that the difference $A - B$ is nothing more than the matrix formed by subtracting the entries in B from the corresponding entries in A.

Using the matrices A and B from Example 10, we find that

$$B - A = \begin{bmatrix} -2 & 1 & -1 \\ 3 & 0 & 3 \end{bmatrix} - \begin{bmatrix} 2 & 3 & 4 \\ 1 & 0 & 2 \end{bmatrix}$$

$$= \begin{bmatrix} -2 - 2 & 1 - 3 & -1 - 4 \\ 3 - 1 & 0 - 0 & 3 - 2 \end{bmatrix} = \begin{bmatrix} -4 & -2 & -5 \\ 2 & 0 & 1 \end{bmatrix}$$

Observe that $A - B \neq B - A$, illustrating that matrix subtraction, like subtraction of real numbers, is not commutative.

MULTIPLYING A MATRIX BY A NUMBER

Let's return to the production of Motors Inc., during the month specified in Example 1. The matrix A describing this production is

$$A = \begin{bmatrix} 23 & 16 & 10 \\ 7 & 9 & 11 \end{bmatrix}$$

Let's assume that for 3 consecutive months, the monthly production remained the same. Then the total production for the 3 months is simply the sum of the matrix A taken 3 times. If we represent the total production by the matrix T, then

$$T = \begin{bmatrix} 23 & 16 & 10 \\ 7 & 9 & 11 \end{bmatrix} + \begin{bmatrix} 23 & 16 & 10 \\ 7 & 9 & 11 \end{bmatrix} + \begin{bmatrix} 23 & 16 & 10 \\ 7 & 9 & 11 \end{bmatrix}$$

$$= \begin{bmatrix} 23 + 23 + 23 & 16 + 16 + 16 & 10 + 10 + 10 \\ 7 + 7 + 7 & 9 + 9 + 9 & 11 + 11 + 11 \end{bmatrix}$$

$$= \begin{bmatrix} 3 \cdot 23 & 3 \cdot 16 & 3 \cdot 10 \\ 3 \cdot 7 & 3 \cdot 9 & 3 \cdot 11 \end{bmatrix} = \begin{bmatrix} 69 & 48 & 30 \\ 21 & 27 & 33 \end{bmatrix}$$

In other words, when we add the matrix A 3 times, we multiply each entry of A by 3. This leads to the following definition.

Scalar Multiplication Let $A = [a_{ij}]$ be an $m \times n$ matrix and let c be a real number, called a *scalar*. The product of the matrix A by the scalar c, called *scalar multiplication*, is the $m \times n$ matrix $cA = [ca_{ij}]$.

When multiplying a matrix by a number, each entry of the matrix is multiplied by the number. Notice that the dimension of A and the dimension of the product cA are the same.

☐ **Example 11**   For

$$A = \begin{bmatrix} 2 \\ 5 \\ -7 \end{bmatrix} \quad \text{and} \quad B = \begin{bmatrix} 20 & 0 \\ 18 & 8 \end{bmatrix}$$

compute: (a) $3A$ (b) $\frac{1}{2}B$

Solution   (a) $3A = 3 \begin{bmatrix} 2 \\ 5 \\ -7 \end{bmatrix} = \begin{bmatrix} 3 \cdot 2 \\ 3 \cdot 5 \\ 3 \cdot (-7) \end{bmatrix} = \begin{bmatrix} 6 \\ 15 \\ -21 \end{bmatrix}$

(b) $\frac{1}{2}B = \frac{1}{2} \begin{bmatrix} 20 & 0 \\ 18 & 8 \end{bmatrix} = \begin{bmatrix} \frac{1}{2} \cdot 20 & \frac{1}{2} \cdot 0 \\ \frac{1}{2} \cdot 18 & \frac{1}{2} \cdot 8 \end{bmatrix} = \begin{bmatrix} 10 & 0 \\ 9 & 4 \end{bmatrix}$ ☐

☐ **Example 12**   For

$$A = \begin{bmatrix} 3 & 1 \\ 4 & 0 \\ 2 & -3 \end{bmatrix} \quad \text{and} \quad B = \begin{bmatrix} 2 & -3 \\ -1 & 1 \\ 1 & 0 \end{bmatrix}$$

compute: (a) $A - B$ (b) $A + (-1) \cdot B$

Solution   (a) $A - B = \begin{bmatrix} 1 & 4 \\ 5 & -1 \\ 1 & -3 \end{bmatrix}$

(b) $A + (-1) \cdot B = \begin{bmatrix} 3 & 1 \\ 4 & 0 \\ 2 & -3 \end{bmatrix} + \begin{bmatrix} -2 & 3 \\ 1 & -1 \\ -1 & 0 \end{bmatrix} = \begin{bmatrix} 1 & 4 \\ 5 & -1 \\ 1 & -3 \end{bmatrix}$ ☐

The above example illustrates the result that

$$A - B = A + (-1) \cdot B = A + (-B)$$

We continue our study of scalar multiplication by listing some of its properties.

Let k and h be two real numbers and let $A = [a_{ij}]$ and $B = [b_{ij}]$, $i = 1, \ldots, m$, $j = 1, \ldots, n$ matrices of dimension $m \times n$. Then

(I) $k(hA) = (kh)A$

(II) $(k + h)A = kA + hA$

(III) $k(A + B) = kA + kB$

We prove (I) and (II) here; the proof of (III) is left as an exercise (Problem 39, Exercise 2.3).

(I)   Here

$$k(hA) = k(h[a_{ij}]) = k([ha_{ij}]) = k[ha_{ij}]$$
$$= [kha_{ij}] = (kh)[a_{ij}] = (kh)A$$

(II)   For this property, we have

$$(k+h)A = (k+h)[a_{ij}] = [(k+h)a_{ij}]$$
$$= [ka_{ij} + ha_{ij}] = [ka_{ij}] + [ha_{ij}]$$
$$= k[a_{ij}] + h[a_{ij}] = kA + hA$$

Properties (I)–(III) are illustrated in the following example.

□ **Example 12**   For

$$A = \begin{bmatrix} 2 & -3 & -1 \\ 5 & 6 & 4 \end{bmatrix} \quad \text{and} \quad B = \begin{bmatrix} -3 & 0 & 4 \\ 2 & -1 & 5 \end{bmatrix}$$

show that:

(a) $5[2A] = 10A$ (b) $(4+3)A = 4A + 3A$ (c) $3[A+B] = 3A + 3B$

Solution   (a) $5[2A] = 5\begin{bmatrix} 4 & -6 & -2 \\ 10 & 12 & 8 \end{bmatrix} = \begin{bmatrix} 20 & -30 & -10 \\ 50 & 60 & 40 \end{bmatrix}$

$$10A = \begin{bmatrix} 20 & -30 & -10 \\ 50 & 60 & 40 \end{bmatrix}$$

(b) $(4+3)A = 7A = \begin{bmatrix} 14 & -21 & -7 \\ 35 & 42 & 28 \end{bmatrix}$

$$4A + 3A = \begin{bmatrix} 8 & -12 & -4 \\ 20 & 24 & 16 \end{bmatrix} + \begin{bmatrix} 6 & -9 & -3 \\ 15 & 18 & 12 \end{bmatrix} = \begin{bmatrix} 14 & -21 & -7 \\ 35 & 42 & 28 \end{bmatrix}$$

(c) $3[A+B] = 3\begin{bmatrix} -1 & -3 & 3 \\ 7 & 5 & 9 \end{bmatrix} = \begin{bmatrix} -3 & -9 & 9 \\ 21 & 15 & 27 \end{bmatrix}$

$$3A + 3B = \begin{bmatrix} 6 & -9 & -3 \\ 15 & 18 & 12 \end{bmatrix} + \begin{bmatrix} -9 & 0 & 12 \\ 6 & -3 & 15 \end{bmatrix} = \begin{bmatrix} -3 & -9 & 9 \\ 21 & 15 & 27 \end{bmatrix}$$ □

Exercise 2.3   *Answers to Odd-Numbered Problems begin on page* 603 .

In Problems 1–8 write the dimension of each matrix.

1. $\begin{bmatrix} 3 & 2 \\ -1 & 3 \end{bmatrix}$ 2. $\begin{bmatrix} -1 & 0 \\ 0 & 5 \end{bmatrix}$ 3. $\begin{bmatrix} 2 & 1 & -3 \\ 1 & 0 & -1 \end{bmatrix}$ 4. $\begin{bmatrix} 1 & 2 \\ 2 & 1 \\ 0 & -3 \end{bmatrix}$

5. $\begin{bmatrix} 4 \\ 1 \end{bmatrix}$ 6. $[2 \quad 1 \quad -3]$ 7. $[2]$ 8. $[0]$

In Problems 9–16 determine whether the given statements are true or false. If false, tell why.

9. $\begin{bmatrix} 0 \\ 1 \end{bmatrix} = [0 \quad 1]$ 10. $\begin{bmatrix} 3 & 2 \\ -1 & 0 \end{bmatrix} = \begin{bmatrix} 3 & 2 \\ -1 & 4 \end{bmatrix}$

11. $\begin{bmatrix} 5 & 0 \\ 0 & 1 \end{bmatrix}$ is square

12. $\begin{bmatrix} 3 & 2 & 1 \\ 4 & -1 & 0 \end{bmatrix}$ is 3×2

13. $\begin{bmatrix} x & 2 \\ 4 & 0 \end{bmatrix} = \begin{bmatrix} 3 & 2 \\ 4 & 0 \end{bmatrix}$ if $x = 3$

14. $\begin{bmatrix} x & y \\ 0 & 0 \end{bmatrix} = [x \quad y]$

15. $\begin{bmatrix} 5 & 0 \\ 1 & 1 \end{bmatrix} = \begin{bmatrix} 2+3 & 0 \\ 1 & 1 \end{bmatrix}$

16. $\begin{bmatrix} 1 & 0 \\ 0 & 1 \end{bmatrix} = \begin{bmatrix} 3-2 & 3-3 \\ 3-3 & 3-2 \end{bmatrix}$

17. Find x and z so that

$$\begin{bmatrix} x \\ z \end{bmatrix} = \begin{bmatrix} 4 \\ 3 \end{bmatrix}$$

18. Find x, y, and z so that

$$\begin{bmatrix} x+y & 2 \\ 4 & 0 \end{bmatrix} = \begin{bmatrix} 6 & x-y \\ 4 & z \end{bmatrix}$$

19. Find x and y so that

$$\begin{bmatrix} x-2y & 0 \\ -2 & 6 \end{bmatrix} = \begin{bmatrix} 3 & 0 \\ -2 & x+y \end{bmatrix}$$

20. Find x, y, and z so that

$$\begin{bmatrix} x-2 & 3 & 2z \\ 6y & x & 2y \end{bmatrix} = \begin{bmatrix} y & z & 6 \\ 18z & y+2 & 6z \end{bmatrix}$$

In Problems 21–30 use the matrices below to find the indicated expression.

$$A = \begin{bmatrix} 2 & -3 & 4 \\ 0 & 2 & 1 \end{bmatrix} \quad B = \begin{bmatrix} 1 & -2 & 0 \\ 5 & 1 & 2 \end{bmatrix} \quad C = \begin{bmatrix} -3 & 0 & 5 \\ 2 & 1 & 3 \end{bmatrix}$$

21. $A + B$
22. $B + C$
23. $2A - 3C$
24. $3C - 4B$
25. $(A + B) - 2C$
26. $4C + (A - B)$
27. $3A + 4(B + C)$
28. $(A + B) + 3C$
29. $2(A - B) - C$
30. $2A - 5(B + C)$

31. Find x, y, and z so that

$$[2 \quad 3 \quad -4] + [x \quad y \quad z] = [6 \quad -8 \quad 2]$$

32. Find x and y so that

$$\begin{bmatrix} 3 & -2 & 2 \\ 1 & 0 & -1 \end{bmatrix} + \begin{bmatrix} x-y & 2 & -2 \\ 4 & x & 6 \end{bmatrix} = \begin{bmatrix} 6 & 0 & 0 \\ 5 & 2x+y & 5 \end{bmatrix}$$

33. Let

$$U = \begin{bmatrix} 2 \\ -1 \\ 3 \end{bmatrix} \quad V = \begin{bmatrix} \frac{1}{2} \\ 0 \\ 1 \end{bmatrix} \quad W = \begin{bmatrix} -3 \\ -7 \\ 0 \end{bmatrix}$$

Compute the following:
(a) $U + V$
(b) $U - V$
(c) $\frac{1}{2}(U + V)$
(d) $U + V - W$
(e) $2U - 7V$
(f) $\frac{1}{4}U - \frac{1}{4}V - \frac{1}{4}W$

34. Find a_1, a_2, a_3 which satisfy the following:

$$\begin{bmatrix} 2 \\ 1 \\ 0 \end{bmatrix} + \begin{bmatrix} a_1 \\ a_2 \\ a_3 \end{bmatrix} = \begin{bmatrix} 2 \\ -1 \\ 3 \end{bmatrix}$$

Applications

35. XYZ Company produces steel and aluminum nails. One week, 25 gross $\frac{1}{2}$-inch steel nails and 45 gross 1-inch steel nails were produced. Suppose 13 gross $\frac{1}{2}$-inch aluminum nails, 20 gross 1-inch aluminum nails, 35 gross 2-inch steel nails, and 23 gross 2-inch aluminum nails were also made. Write a 2 × 3 matrix depicting this. Could you also write a 3 × 2 matrix for this situation?

36. Katy, Mike, and Danny go to the candy store. Katy buys 5 sticks of gum, 2 ice cream cones, and 10 jelly beans. Mike buys 2 sticks of gum, 15 jelly beans, and 2 candy bars. Danny buys 1 stick of gum, 1 ice cream cone, and 4 candy bars. Write a matrix depicting this situation.

37. Use a matrix to display the information given below, which was obtained in a survey of voters. Label the rows and columns.

351	Democrats earning under $15,000
271	Republicans earning under $15,000
73	Independents earning under $15,000
203	Democrats earning over $15,000
215	Republicans earning over $15,000
55	Independents earning over $15,000

38. The sales figures for two car dealers during June showed that Dealer A sold 100 compacts, 50 intermediates, and 40 full-size cars, while Dealer B sold 120 compacts, 40 intermediates, and 35 full-size cars. During July, Dealer A sold 80 compacts, 30 intermediates, and 10 full-size cars, while Dealer B sold 70 compacts, 40 intermediates, and 20 full-size cars. Total sales over the 3-month period of June–August revealed that Dealer A sold 300 compacts, 120 intermediates, and 65 full-size cars. In the same 3-month period, Dealer B sold 250 compacts, 100 intermediates, and 80 full-size cars.

 (a) Write 2 × 3 matrices summarizing sales data for June, July, and the 3-month period for each dealer.

 (b) Use matrix addition to find the sales over the 2-month period for June and July for each dealer.

 (c) Use matrix subtraction to find the sales in August for each dealer.

39. Prove Property III.

2.4 MULTIPLICATION OF MATRICES

PROPERTIES OF MATRIX MULTIPLICATION ☐ IDENTITY MATRIX

While addition of matrices and scalar multiplication are fairly straightforward, defining the *product A · B* of the two matrices A and B requires a bit more detail.

We explain first what we mean by the product of a row vector with a column vector.

If $R = [r_1 r_2 \ldots r_n]$ is a row vector and $C = \begin{bmatrix} c_1 \\ c_2 \\ \vdots \\ c_n \end{bmatrix}$ is a column vector, then by the product of R and C we mean the number

$$r_1c_1 + r_2c_2 + r_3c_3 + \cdots + r_nc_n$$

□ **Example 1** If

$$R = [1 \quad 5 \quad 3] \quad \text{and} \quad C = \begin{bmatrix} 2 \\ -1 \\ 4 \end{bmatrix}$$

then the product of R and C is

$$1 \cdot 2 + 5 \cdot (-1) + 3 \cdot 4 = 9 \qquad \qquad \square$$

Notice that for the $R\ C$ product to make sense, if R is a $1 \times n$ row vector, then C must have dimension $n \times 1$.

□ **Example 2** Let

$$R = [1 \quad 0 \quad 1] \quad \text{and} \quad C = \begin{bmatrix} 0 \\ -11 \\ 0 \end{bmatrix}$$

Then the product of R and C is

$$1 \cdot 0 + 0 \cdot (-11) + 1 \cdot 0 = 0 \qquad \qquad \square$$

Given two matrices A and B the rows of A can be thought of as row vectors, while the columns of B can be thought of as column vectors. This observation will be used in the following main definition.

Matrix Multiplication Let $A = [a_{ij}]$ be a matrix of dimension $m \times r$ and let $B = [b_{ij}]$ be a matrix of dimension $r \times n$. The *product $A \cdot B$* is the matrix of dimension $m \times n$, whose *ij*th entry is the sum of the products of corresponding elements of the *i*th row of A and the *j*th column of B. That is, the *ij*th entry of $A \cdot B$ is

$$a_{i1}b_{1j} + a_{i2}b_{2j} + a_{i3}b_{3j} + \cdots + a_{ir}b_{rj}$$

The rule for multiplication of matrices is best illustrated by an example.

□ **Example 3** Find the product $A \cdot B$ if

$$A = \begin{bmatrix} 1 & 3 & -2 \\ 4 & -1 & 5 \end{bmatrix} \quad \text{and} \quad B = \begin{bmatrix} 2 & -3 & 4 & 1 \\ -1 & 2 & 2 & 0 \\ 4 & 5 & 1 & 1 \end{bmatrix}$$

Solution   Since A is 2×3 and B is 3×4, the product $A \cdot B$ will be 2×4. To get, for example, the entry in row 2, column 3 of $A \cdot B$, we take the product of the second row of A with the third column of B. That is,

$$\begin{bmatrix} 1 & 3 & -2 \\ \boxed{4 & -1 & 5} \end{bmatrix} \quad \begin{bmatrix} 2 & -3 & \boxed{4} & 1 \\ -1 & 2 & \boxed{2} & 0 \\ 4 & 5 & \boxed{1} & 1 \end{bmatrix}$$

We compute

$$4 \cdot 4 + (-1) \cdot 2 + 5 \cdot 1 = 19$$

So far, we have

$$A \cdot B = \begin{bmatrix} \underline{} & \underline{} & \underline{} & \underline{} \\ \underline{} & \underline{} & 19 & \underline{} \end{bmatrix}$$

To obtain the entry in row 1, column 2, we compute

$$1 \cdot (-3) + 3 \cdot 2 + (-2) \cdot 5 = -3 + 6 - 10 = -7$$

The other entries of $A \cdot B$ are obtained in a similar fashion. The final result—and you should verify this—is

$$A \cdot B = \begin{bmatrix} -9 & -7 & 8 & -1 \\ 29 & 11 & 19 & 9 \end{bmatrix} \qquad \square$$

Let's look at some consequences of the definition of matrix multiplication.

If A is a matrix of dimension $m \times r$ (which has r columns) and B is a matrix of dimension $p \times n$ (which has p rows) and if $r \neq p$, the product $A \cdot B$ is not defined. That is, **multiplication of matrices is possible only if the number of columns of the first equals the number of rows of the second.**

If A is of dimension $m \times r$ and B is of dimension $r \times n$, then the product $A \cdot B$ is of dimension $m \times n$. See Figure 1.

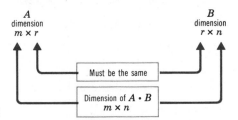

Figure 1

In Example 3, A is of dimension 2×3, B is of dimension 3×4, and we found the product $A \cdot B$ to be of dimension 2×4. Observe that the product $B \cdot A$ is not defined.

□ **Example 4**   For

$$A = \begin{bmatrix} 2 & 0 \\ 1 & 5 \end{bmatrix} \quad \text{and} \quad B = \begin{bmatrix} 3 & 2 \\ 1 & 4 \end{bmatrix}$$

compute $A \cdot B$ and $B \cdot A$.

Solution   We observe that the products $A \cdot B$ and $B \cdot A$ are both defined, and so

$$A \cdot B = \begin{bmatrix} 6 & 4 \\ 8 & 22 \end{bmatrix} \qquad B \cdot A = \begin{bmatrix} 8 & 10 \\ 6 & 20 \end{bmatrix} \qquad \square$$

Note from the above example that even if both $A \cdot B$ and $B \cdot A$ are defined, they may not be equal. We conclude that

matrix multiplication is not commutative.

A natural question to ask is: Why are matrix products so defined? As it turns out, such a definition of product is useful in applications. The following example affords one instance.

□ **Example 5**   Using the data of 1 month's production of Motors, Inc., from Example 1, Section 2.3, we have

$$
\begin{array}{c}
 \begin{array}{ccc} & & \text{Station} \\ \text{Sedan} & \text{Hard-top} & \text{Wagon} \end{array} \\
A = \begin{bmatrix} 23 & 16 & 10 \\ 7 & 9 & 11 \end{bmatrix} \quad \begin{array}{l} \text{Units of material} \\ \text{Units of labor} \end{array}
\end{array}
$$

Suppose that in this month's production, the cost for each unit of material is \$45 and the cost for each unit of labor is \$60. What is the total cost to manufacture the sedans, the hard-tops, and the station wagons?

Solution   For sedans, the cost is 23 units of material at \$45 each, plus 7 units of labor at \$60 each, for a total cost of

$$23 \cdot \$45 + 7 \cdot \$60 = 1035 + 420 = \$1455$$

Similarly, for hard-tops, the total cost is

$$16 \cdot \$45 + 9 \cdot \$60 = 720 + 540 = \$1260$$

Finally, for station wagons, the total cost is

$$10 \cdot \$45 + 11 \cdot \$60 = 450 + 660 = \$1110$$

We can represent the total cost for sedans, hard-tops, and station wagons by the matrix

$$[1455 \quad 1260 \quad 1110]$$

If we represent the cost of units of material and units of labor by the row vector

$$U = [45 \quad 60]$$

the total cost of units for sedans, hard-tops, and station wagons will then be given by the product UA.

$$
\begin{aligned}
U \cdot A &= [45 \quad 60] \begin{bmatrix} 23 & 16 & 10 \\ 7 & 9 & 11 \end{bmatrix} \\
&= [45 \cdot 23 + 60 \cdot 7 \quad 45 \cdot 16 + 60 \cdot 9 \quad 45 \cdot 10 + 60 \cdot 11] \\
&= [1455 \quad 1260 \quad 1110]
\end{aligned}
$$

□

PROPERTIES OF MATRIX MULTIPLICATION

In listing some of the properties of matrix multiplication in this book, we agree to follow the usual convention and write $A \cdot B$ as AB, from now on.

Let A be a matrix of dimension $m \times r$, let B be a matrix of dimension $r \times p$, and let C be a matrix of dimension $p \times n$. Then matrix multiplication is *associative*. That is,

$$A(BC) = (AB)C$$

The resulting matrix ABC is of dimension $m \times n$.

Notice the limitations that are placed on the dimensions of the matrices in order for multiplication to be associative.

Let A be a matrix of dimension $m \times r$. Let B and C be matrices of dimension $r \times n$. Then *matrix multiplication distributes over matrix addition.* That is,

$$A(B + C) = AB + AC$$

The resulting matrix $AB + AC$ is of dimension $m \times n$.

IDENTITY MATRIX

A special type of square matrix is the *identity matrix,* which is denoted by I_n. It has the property that all its diagonal entries are 1's and all other entries are 0's. Thus,

$$I_n = \begin{bmatrix} 1 & 0 & \cdots & 0 & 0 \\ 0 & 1 & \cdots & 0 & 0 \\ \cdot & \cdot & \cdot & & \cdot \\ \cdot & \cdot & & \cdot & \cdot \\ \cdot & \cdot & & \cdot & \cdot \\ 0 & 0 & \cdots & 1 & 0 \\ 0 & 0 & \cdots & 0 & 1 \end{bmatrix}$$

where the subscript n implies that I_n is of dimension $n \times n$.

□ **Example 6** For

$$A = \begin{bmatrix} 3 & 2 \\ -4 & 5 \end{bmatrix}$$

compute: (a) AI_2 (b) $I_2 A$

Solution

(a) $AI_2 = \begin{bmatrix} 3 & 2 \\ -4 & 5 \end{bmatrix} \begin{bmatrix} 1 & 0 \\ 0 & 1 \end{bmatrix} = \begin{bmatrix} 3 & 2 \\ -4 & 5 \end{bmatrix} = A$

(b) $I_2 A = \begin{bmatrix} 1 & 0 \\ 0 & 1 \end{bmatrix} \begin{bmatrix} 3 & 2 \\ -4 & 5 \end{bmatrix} = \begin{bmatrix} 3 & 2 \\ -4 & 5 \end{bmatrix} = A$ □

This example can be generalized as follows:

If A is a matrix of dimension $m \times n$ and if I_n denotes the identity matrix of dimension $n \times n$, and I_m denotes the identity matrix of dimension $m \times m$, then

$$I_m A = A \quad \text{and} \quad AI_n = A$$

The reason for stating two formulas above is that when the matrix A is not square, care must be taken when forming the products AI and IA. For example, if

$$A = \begin{bmatrix} 1 & 2 \\ 3 & 2 \\ 1 & 1 \end{bmatrix}$$

then A is of dimension 3×2 and

$$AI_2 = A \begin{bmatrix} 1 & 0 \\ 0 & 1 \end{bmatrix} = \begin{bmatrix} 1 & 2 \\ 3 & 2 \\ 1 & 1 \end{bmatrix} \begin{bmatrix} 1 & 0 \\ 0 & 1 \end{bmatrix} = \begin{bmatrix} 1 & 2 \\ 3 & 2 \\ 1 & 1 \end{bmatrix} = A$$

Although the product I_2A is not defined, we can calculate the product I_3A as follows:

$$I_3A = \begin{bmatrix} 1 & 0 & 0 \\ 0 & 1 & 0 \\ 0 & 0 & 1 \end{bmatrix} \begin{bmatrix} 1 & 2 \\ 3 & 2 \\ 1 & 1 \end{bmatrix} = \begin{bmatrix} 1 & 2 \\ 3 & 2 \\ 1 & 1 \end{bmatrix} = A$$

In particular if A is a square matrix of dimension $n \times n$, then $AI_n = I_nA = A$. Thus, for square matrices the identity matrix plays the role that the number 1 plays in the set of real numbers.

Exercise 2.4   *Answers to Odd-Numbered Problems begin on page* 603.

In Problems 1–10 let A be of dimension 3×4, let B be of dimension 3×3, let C be of dimension 2×3, and let D be of dimension 3×2. Determine which of the following expressions are defined and, for those that are, give the dimension.

1. BA
2. CD
3. AB
4. DC
5. $(BA)C$
6. $A(CD)$
7. $BA + A$
8. $CD + BA$
9. $DC + B$
10. $CB - A$

In Problems 11–26 use the matrices below to perform the indicated operations.

$$A = \begin{bmatrix} 1 & 2 \\ 0 & 4 \end{bmatrix} \qquad B = \begin{bmatrix} 1 & 2 & 3 \\ -1 & 4 & -2 \end{bmatrix} \qquad C = \begin{bmatrix} 3 & 1 \\ 4 & -1 \\ 0 & 2 \end{bmatrix}$$

$$D = \begin{bmatrix} 1 & 0 & 4 \\ 0 & 1 & 2 \\ 0 & -1 & 1 \end{bmatrix} \qquad E = \begin{bmatrix} 3 & -1 \\ 4 & 2 \end{bmatrix}$$

11. AB
12. DC
13. BC
14. AA
15. $(D + I_3)C$
16. $DC + C$
17. $(DC)B$
18. $D(CB)$
19. EI_2
20. I_3D
21. $(2E)B$
22. $E(2B)$
23. $-5E + A$
24. $3A + 2E$
25. $3CB + 4D$
26. $2EA - 3BC$
27. For

$$A = \begin{bmatrix} 1 & -1 \\ 2 & 0 \end{bmatrix} \quad \text{and} \quad B = \begin{bmatrix} 3 & 2 \\ -1 & 4 \end{bmatrix}$$

find AB and BA. Notice that $AB \neq BA$.

28. Show that, for all values a, b, c, and d, the matrices

$$A = \begin{bmatrix} a & b \\ -b & a \end{bmatrix} \quad \text{and} \quad B = \begin{bmatrix} c & d \\ -d & c \end{bmatrix}$$

are commutative; that is, $AB = BA$.

29. If possible, find a matrix A such that

$$A \begin{bmatrix} 0 & 1 \\ 2 & -1 \end{bmatrix} = \begin{bmatrix} 2 & 1 \\ -1 & 0 \end{bmatrix} \qquad \textit{Hint:} \ \text{Let } A = \begin{bmatrix} a & b \\ c & d \end{bmatrix}.$$

30. For what numbers x will the following be true?

$$\begin{bmatrix} x & 4 & 1 \end{bmatrix} \begin{bmatrix} 2 & 1 & 0 \\ 1 & 0 & 2 \\ 0 & 2 & 4 \end{bmatrix} \begin{bmatrix} x \\ -7 \\ \frac{5}{4} \end{bmatrix} = \mathbf{0}$$

31. Let

$$A = \begin{bmatrix} 1 & 2 & 5 \\ 2 & 4 & 10 \\ -1 & -2 & -5 \end{bmatrix}$$

Show that $A^2 = \mathbf{0}$. Thus, the rule in the real number system that if $a^2 = 0$, then $a = 0$ does not hold for matrices.

32. What must be true about a, b, c, and d, if we demand that $AB = BA$ for the following matrices?

$$A = \begin{bmatrix} a & b \\ c & d \end{bmatrix} \qquad B = \begin{bmatrix} 1 & 1 \\ -1 & 1 \end{bmatrix}$$

Assume that

$$\begin{bmatrix} a & b \\ c & d \end{bmatrix} \neq \begin{bmatrix} 1 & 0 \\ 0 & 1 \end{bmatrix}$$

33. Let

$$A = \begin{bmatrix} a & b \\ b & a \end{bmatrix}$$

Find a and b such that $A^2 + A = \mathbf{0}$, where $A^2 = AA$.

34. For the matrix

$$A = \begin{bmatrix} a & 1-a \\ 1+a & -a \end{bmatrix}$$

show that $A^2 = AA = I_2$.

35. Find the vector $[x_1 \ \ x_2]$ for which

$$[x_1 \ \ x_2] \begin{bmatrix} \frac{1}{2} & \frac{1}{2} \\ \frac{1}{4} & \frac{3}{4} \end{bmatrix} = [x_2 \ \ x_2]$$

under the condition that $x_1 + x_2 = 1$. Here, the vector $[x_1 \ \ x_2]$ is called a *fixed vector* of the matrix

$$\begin{bmatrix} \frac{1}{2} & \frac{1}{2} \\ \frac{1}{4} & \frac{3}{4} \end{bmatrix}$$

36. Mike went to a department store and purchased 6 pairs of pants, 8 shirts, and 2 jackets. Danny purchased 2 pairs of pants, 5 shirts, and 3 jackets. If the pants are $5 each, shirts are $3 each, and jackets are $9 each, use matrix multiplication to find the amounts spent by Mike and Danny.

37. Suppose a factory is asked to produce three types of products, which we will call P_1, P_2, P_3. Suppose the following purchase order was received: $P_1 = 7$, $P_2 = 12$, $P_3 = 5$. Represent this order by a row vector and call it P:

$$P = [7 \quad 12 \quad 5]$$

To produce each of the products, raw material of four kinds is needed. Call the raw material M_1, M_2, M_3, and M_4. The matrix below gives the amount of material needed for each product:

$$Q = \begin{array}{c} \\ P_1 \\ P_2 \\ P_3 \end{array} \begin{array}{cccc} M_1 & M_2 & M_3 & M_4 \\ \begin{bmatrix} 2 & 3 & 1 & 12 \\ 7 & 9 & 5 & 20 \\ 8 & 12 & 6 & 15 \end{bmatrix} \end{array}$$

Suppose the cost for each of the materials M_1, M_2, M_3, and M_4 is $10, $12, $15, and $20, respectively. The cost vector is

$$C = \begin{bmatrix} 10 \\ 12 \\ 15 \\ 20 \end{bmatrix}$$

Compute each of the following and interpret each one:

(a) PQ (b) QC (c) PQC

38. For a square matrix A, it is possible to find $A \cdot A = A^2$. It is also clear that we can compute

$$A^n = \underbrace{A \cdot A \cdot \cdots \cdot A}_{n \text{ times}}$$

Find A^2, A^3, and A^4 for each of the following square matrices:

(a) $A = \begin{bmatrix} 1 & 0 \\ 3 & 2 \end{bmatrix}$

(b) $A = \begin{bmatrix} 3 & 1 \\ -2 & -1 \end{bmatrix}$

(c) $A = \begin{bmatrix} 0 & 1 & 1 \\ 0 & -1 & 2 \\ 6 & 3 & -2 \end{bmatrix}$

(d) $A = \begin{bmatrix} 1 & 0 \\ 0 & 1 \end{bmatrix}$

(e) $A = \begin{bmatrix} \frac{1}{2} & \frac{1}{2} \\ \frac{1}{4} & \frac{3}{4} \end{bmatrix}$

Can you guess what A^n looks like for part (d)? For part (e)?

2.5 INVERSE OF A MATRIX

REDUCED ROW-ECHELON TECHNIQUE
☐ SOLVING A SYSTEM OF n LINEAR EQUATIONS IN n UNKNOWNS USING INVERSES
☐ MATRICES IN PRACTICE

The inverse of a matrix, if it exists, plays the role that the reciprocal of a number plays in the set of real numbers.

Inverse Let A be a matrix of dimension $n \times n$. A matrix B of dimension $n \times n$ is called an *inverse of A* if $AB = BA = I_n$. We denote the inverse of a matrix A, if it exists, by A^{-1}.

□ Example 1 Show that $\begin{bmatrix} \frac{1}{2} & -\frac{1}{2} \\ 0 & 1 \end{bmatrix}$ is the inverse of $\begin{bmatrix} 2 & 1 \\ 0 & 1 \end{bmatrix}$.

Solution   Since

$$\begin{bmatrix} 2 & 1 \\ 0 & 1 \end{bmatrix} \begin{bmatrix} \frac{1}{2} & -\frac{1}{2} \\ 0 & 1 \end{bmatrix} = \begin{bmatrix} 1 & 0 \\ 0 & 1 \end{bmatrix}$$

and

$$\begin{bmatrix} \frac{1}{2} & -\frac{1}{2} \\ 0 & 1 \end{bmatrix} \begin{bmatrix} 2 & 1 \\ 0 & 1 \end{bmatrix} = \begin{bmatrix} 1 & 0 \\ 0 & 1 \end{bmatrix}$$

the required condition is met.   □

The next example provides a technique for finding the inverse of a matrix. Although this technique is not the best, it is illustrative.

□ Example 2 Find the inverse of the matrix: $A = \begin{bmatrix} 2 & 1 \\ 0 & 1 \end{bmatrix}$.

Solution   We begin by assuming that this matrix has an inverse of the form

$$A^{-1} = \begin{bmatrix} a & b \\ c & d \end{bmatrix}$$

Then the product of A and A^{-1} must be the identity matrix:

$$\begin{bmatrix} 2 & 1 \\ 0 & 1 \end{bmatrix} \begin{bmatrix} a & b \\ c & d \end{bmatrix} = \begin{bmatrix} 1 & 0 \\ 0 & 1 \end{bmatrix}$$

Multiplying the matrices on the left side, we get

$$\begin{bmatrix} 2a + c & 2b + d \\ c & d \end{bmatrix} = \begin{bmatrix} 1 & 0 \\ 0 & 1 \end{bmatrix}$$

The condition for equality requires that

$$2a + c = 1 \qquad 2b + d = 0 \qquad c = 0 \qquad d = 1$$

Thus,

$$a = \tfrac{1}{2} \qquad b = -\tfrac{1}{2} \qquad c = 0 \qquad d = 1$$

Hence, the inverse of

$$A = \begin{bmatrix} 2 & 1 \\ 0 & 1 \end{bmatrix} \qquad \text{is} \qquad A^{-1} = \begin{bmatrix} \frac{1}{2} & -\frac{1}{2} \\ 0 & 1 \end{bmatrix}$$

We verify that this is the inverse by computing AA^{-1}:

$$AA^{-1} = \begin{bmatrix} 2 & 1 \\ 0 & 1 \end{bmatrix} \begin{bmatrix} \frac{1}{2} & -\frac{1}{2} \\ 0 & 1 \end{bmatrix} = \begin{bmatrix} 1 & 0 \\ 0 & 1 \end{bmatrix}$$

   □

Sometimes, a square matrix does not have an inverse.

□ **Example 3** Show that the matrix below does not have an inverse.

$$A = \begin{bmatrix} 0 & 1 \\ 0 & 0 \end{bmatrix}$$

Solution We proceed as in Example 2 by assuming that A does have an inverse. It will be of the form

$$A^{-1} = \begin{bmatrix} a & b \\ c & d \end{bmatrix}$$

The product of A and A^{-1} must be the identity matrix. Thus,

$$\begin{bmatrix} 0 & 1 \\ 0 & 0 \end{bmatrix}\begin{bmatrix} a & b \\ c & d \end{bmatrix} = \begin{bmatrix} 1 & 0 \\ 0 & 1 \end{bmatrix}$$

Performing the multiplication on the left side, we have

$$\begin{bmatrix} c & d \\ 0 & 0 \end{bmatrix} = \begin{bmatrix} 1 & 0 \\ 0 & 1 \end{bmatrix}$$

But these two matrices can never be equal. We conclude that our assumption that A has an inverse is false. That is, A does not have an inverse. □

So far, we have shown that a square matrix may or may not have an inverse. The next result tells us that a square matrix will not have more than one inverse.

> A square matrix A has at most one inverse. That is, the inverse of a matrix, if it exists, is *unique*.

To verify this, suppose we have two inverses B and C for a matrix A. Then

$$AB = BA = I_n \quad \text{and} \quad AC = CA = I_n$$

Multiplying both sides of $AC = I_n$ on the left by B, we find

$$B(AC) = BI_n = B$$

Similarly, multiplying both sides of $BA = I_n$ on the right by C, we obtain

$$(BA)C = I_nC = C$$

But $B(AC) = (BA)C$. Hence, $B = C$.

What about nonsquare matrices? Can they have inverses? The answer is "No." By definition, whenever a matrix has an inverse, it will commute with its inverse under multiplication. So if the nonsquare matrix A had the alleged inverse B, then AB would have to be equal to BA. But the fact that A is not square causes AB and BA to have different dimensions and prevents them from being equal. So such a B could not exist.

> A nonsquare matrix has no inverse.

The procedures used above to find the inverse, if it exists, of a square matrix become quite involved as the dimension of the matrix gets larger. A more efficient method is provided next.

REDUCED ROW-ECHELON TECHNIQUE

We will introduce this technique by looking at a specific example.

□ Example 4   Find the inverse of the matrix

$$A = \begin{bmatrix} 2 & 1 \\ 0 & 1 \end{bmatrix}$$

Solution   Assuming A has an inverse, we will denote it by

$$X = \begin{bmatrix} x_1 & x_2 \\ x_3 & x_4 \end{bmatrix}$$

Then the product of A and X is the identity matrix of dimension 2×2. That is,

$$AX = I_2$$

$$\begin{bmatrix} 2 & 1 \\ 0 & 1 \end{bmatrix} \begin{bmatrix} x_1 & x_2 \\ x_3 & x_4 \end{bmatrix} = \begin{bmatrix} 1 & 0 \\ 0 & 1 \end{bmatrix}$$

Performing the multiplication on the left yields

$$\begin{bmatrix} 2x_1 + x_3 & 2x_2 + x_4 \\ x_3 & x_4 \end{bmatrix} = \begin{bmatrix} 1 & 0 \\ 0 & 1 \end{bmatrix}$$

This matrix equation can be written as the following system of four equations in four unknowns:

$$2x_1 + x_3 = 1 \qquad 2x_2 + x_4 = 0$$
$$x_3 = 0 \qquad x_4 = 1$$

By inspection, we find the solution to be

$$x_1 = \tfrac{1}{2} \qquad x_2 = -\tfrac{1}{2} \qquad x_3 = 0 \qquad x_4 = 1$$

Thus, the inverse of A is

$$A^{-1} = \begin{bmatrix} \tfrac{1}{2} & -\tfrac{1}{2} \\ 0 & 1 \end{bmatrix} \qquad\qquad □$$

Let's look at what we did more closely. The system of four equations in four unknowns can be written in two blocks as

(a) $2x_1 + x_3 = 1$ (b) $2x_2 + x_4 = 0$
$x_3 = 0$ $x_4 = 1$

Their augmented matrices are

(a) $\begin{bmatrix} 2 & 1 & | & 1 \\ 0 & 1 & | & 0 \end{bmatrix}$ and   (b) $\begin{bmatrix} 2 & 1 & | & 0 \\ 0 & 1 & | & 1 \end{bmatrix}$

Since the matrix A appears in both (a) and (b), any row operation we perform on (a) and (b) can be performed more easily on the single augmented matrix that combines the two right-hand columns. We denote this matrix by $A|I_2$ and write

$$[A|I_2] = \begin{bmatrix} 2 & 1 & | & 1 & 0 \\ 0 & 1 & | & 0 & 1 \end{bmatrix}$$

If we perform row operations on $[A|I_2]$, just as if we were computing the reduced row-echelon form of A, we get

$$\begin{bmatrix} 1 & 0 & | & \frac{1}{2} & -\frac{1}{2} \\ 0 & 1 & | & 0 & 1 \end{bmatrix}$$

The 2×2 matrix on the right-hand side of the vertical bar is A^{-1}.

This example illustrates the general procedure:

To find the inverse, if it exists, of a square matrix of dimension $n \times n$, follow these steps:

Finding the Inverse
of a Matrix

> **Step 1:** Write the matrix $[A|I_n]$.
>
> **Step 2:** Using row operations, write $[A|I_n]$ in reduced row-echelon form.
>
> **Step 3:** If the resulting matrix is of the form $[I_n|B]$, that is, if the identity matrix appears on the left side of the bar, then B is the inverse of A. Otherwise, A has no inverse.

Let's work another example.

☐ **Example 5**   Find the inverse of

$$A = \begin{bmatrix} 1 & 1 & 2 \\ 2 & 1 & 0 \\ 1 & 2 & 2 \end{bmatrix}$$

Solution   Since A is of dimension 3×3, we use the identity matrix I_3. The matrix $[A|I_3]$ is

$$\begin{bmatrix} 1 & 1 & 2 & | & 1 & 0 & 0 \\ 2 & 1 & 0 & | & 0 & 1 & 0 \\ 1 & 2 & 2 & | & 0 & 0 & 1 \end{bmatrix}$$

We proceed to transform this matrix, using row operations:

Use $\begin{aligned} R_2 &= -2r_1 + r_2 \\ R_3 &= -r_1 + r_3 \end{aligned}$ to get $\begin{bmatrix} 1 & 1 & 2 & | & 1 & 0 & 0 \\ 0 & -1 & -4 & | & -2 & 1 & 0 \\ 0 & 1 & 0 & | & -1 & 0 & 1 \end{bmatrix}$

Use $R_2 = (-1)r_2$ to get $\begin{bmatrix} 1 & 1 & 2 & | & 1 & 0 & 0 \\ 0 & 1 & 4 & | & 2 & -1 & 0 \\ 0 & 1 & 0 & | & -1 & 0 & 1 \end{bmatrix}$

Use $\quad \begin{array}{l} R_1 = -r_2 + r_1 \\ R_3 = -r_2 + r_3 \end{array} \quad$ to get $\quad \left[\begin{array}{ccc|ccc} 1 & 0 & -2 & -1 & 1 & 0 \\ 0 & 1 & 4 & 2 & -1 & 0 \\ 0 & 0 & -4 & -3 & 1 & 1 \end{array}\right]$

Use $\quad R_3 = (-\tfrac{1}{4})r_3 \quad$ to get $\quad \left[\begin{array}{ccc|ccc} 1 & 0 & -2 & -1 & 1 & 0 \\ 0 & 1 & 4 & 2 & -1 & 0 \\ 0 & 0 & 1 & \tfrac{3}{4} & -\tfrac{1}{4} & -\tfrac{1}{4} \end{array}\right]$

Use $\quad \begin{array}{l} R_1 = 2r_3 + r_1 \\ R_2 = -4r_3 + r_2 \end{array} \quad$ to get $\quad \left[\begin{array}{ccc|ccc} 1 & 0 & 0 & \tfrac{1}{2} & \tfrac{1}{2} & -\tfrac{1}{2} \\ 0 & 1 & 0 & -1 & 0 & 1 \\ 0 & 0 & 1 & \tfrac{3}{4} & -\tfrac{1}{4} & -\tfrac{1}{4} \end{array}\right]$

Since the identity matrix I_3 appears on the left side, the matrix appearing on the right is the inverse. That is,

$$A^{-1} = \left[\begin{array}{ccc} \tfrac{1}{2} & \tfrac{1}{2} & -\tfrac{1}{2} \\ -1 & 0 & 1 \\ \tfrac{3}{4} & -\tfrac{1}{4} & -\tfrac{1}{4} \end{array}\right]$$

$\square$

(You should verify that, in fact, $AA^{-1} = I_3$.)

□ **Example 6**   Show that the matrix given below has no inverse.

$$\left[\begin{array}{cc} 3 & 2 \\ 6 & 4 \end{array}\right]$$

Solution   We set up the matrix

$$\left[\begin{array}{cc|cc} 3 & 2 & 1 & 0 \\ 6 & 4 & 0 & 1 \end{array}\right]$$

Use $\quad R_1 = \tfrac{1}{3}r_1 \quad$ to get $\quad \left[\begin{array}{cc|cc} 1 & \tfrac{2}{3} & \tfrac{1}{3} & 0 \\ 6 & 4 & 0 & 1 \end{array}\right]$

Use $\quad R_2 = -6r_1 + r_2 \quad$ to get $\quad \left[\begin{array}{cc|cc} 1 & \tfrac{2}{3} & \tfrac{1}{3} & 0 \\ 0 & 0 & -2 & 1 \end{array}\right]$

The 0's in row 2 tell us we cannot get the identity matrix. This, in turn, tells us the original matrix has no inverse. $\square$

SOLVING A SYSTEM OF n LINEAR EQUATIONS IN n UNKNOWNS USING INVERSES

The inverse of a matrix can also be used to solve a system of n linear equations in n unknowns. Let's look at an example.

□ **Example 7**   Solve the system of equations

$$\begin{aligned} x + y + 2z &= 1 \\ 2x + y &= 2 \\ x + 2y + 2z &= 3 \end{aligned}$$

Solution   If we let

$$A = \begin{bmatrix} 1 & 1 & 2 \\ 2 & 1 & 0 \\ 1 & 2 & 2 \end{bmatrix} \qquad X = \begin{bmatrix} x \\ y \\ z \end{bmatrix} \qquad B = \begin{bmatrix} 1 \\ 2 \\ 3 \end{bmatrix}$$

the above system can be written as

$$AX = B$$

From Example 5, we know A has an inverse, A^{-1}. If we multiply both sides of the equation by A^{-1}, we obtain

$$A^{-1}(AX) = A^{-1}B$$
$$(A^{-1}A)X = A^{-1}B$$
$$I_3 X = A^{-1}B$$
$$X = A^{-1}B$$
$$X = \begin{bmatrix} \frac{1}{2} & \frac{1}{2} & -\frac{1}{2} \\ -1 & 0 & 1 \\ \frac{3}{4} & -\frac{1}{4} & -\frac{1}{4} \end{bmatrix} \begin{bmatrix} 1 \\ 2 \\ 3 \end{bmatrix} = \begin{bmatrix} 0 \\ 2 \\ -\frac{1}{2} \end{bmatrix}$$

Thus, the solution is

$$x = 0 \qquad y = 2 \qquad z = -\tfrac{1}{2} \qquad\qquad \square$$

This method for solving a system of equations is particularly useful for applications in which the constants appearing to the right of the equal sign change while the coefficients of the unknowns on the left side do not. See Problems 47 to 50 for an illustration. See also Section 2.6 on Leontief models for an application.

MATRICES IN PRACTICE

Systems of linear equations arise in business, economics, sociology, chemistry—in fact, in any field that has a quantitative side to it. The systems encountered in practice are often quite large, with 100 equations in 100 unknowns not unusual, making hand calculations with such systems out of the question. Thus computer routines are used to implement work such as row-reducing the augmented matrix. A very popular collection of such routines is the LINPACK package described by Rice.* In more advanced treatments it is shown that solving n equations in n unknowns requires roughly n^3 multiplications and additions. Thus a 100 by 100 system will require 10^6 arithmetic operations. But if we have access to a machine that can perform 100,000 operations per second, the task seems less formidable, since our 100 by 100 system would be solved in 10 seconds. The availability of high speed computing has greatly enhanced the applicability of matrices, since they can now be used in largescale problems. See the article by Kolata in *Science*.†

---

* John R. Rice, *Matrix Computations and Mathematical Software,* McGraw-Hill, New York, 1981.
† Gina Kolata, "Solving Linear Systems Faster," *Science* (June 14, 1985).

There is an aspect of computer-performed matrix calculations that can at times be potentially troublesome in applications. Computers by their nature can perform arithmetic only on decimals that have finitely many nonzero terms. Decimals that are infinite in length are rounded off. For example $\frac{2}{3}$ has the nonterminating decimal expansion .6666. . . . A machine would round this off and store it as, say, .6666667 (the actual number of significant places would vary with the system). This can have consequences for matrix calculations, as we show in the following example.

□ **Example 8**   Suppose we wish to find the row-reduced form of the matrix

$$A = \begin{bmatrix} 1 & \frac{1}{3} \\ 2 & \frac{2}{3} \end{bmatrix}$$

A direct hand calculation shows that the row-reduced form is

$$\begin{bmatrix} 1 & \frac{1}{3} \\ 0 & 0 \end{bmatrix}$$

Now assume we did this on a computer that rounded-off and stored, say, two significant digits.

Our matrix A would then be represented in the machine as

$$A = \begin{bmatrix} 1 & .33 \\ 2 & .67 \end{bmatrix}$$

If a program were now called upon to row-reduce A, the following steps would result:

$$R_2 = r_2 - 2r_1 \qquad \begin{bmatrix} 1 & .33 \\ 0 & .01 \end{bmatrix}$$

$$R_2 = \frac{1}{.01} r_2 \qquad \begin{bmatrix} 1 & .33 \\ 0 & 1 \end{bmatrix}$$

$$R_1 = r_1 - .33r_2 \qquad \begin{bmatrix} 1 & 0 \\ 0 & 1 \end{bmatrix}$$

Note that the end result of the computer calculation differs drastically from our own computed row-reduced form. The problem clearly lies in the rounded representation of the numbers $\frac{1}{3}$ and $\frac{2}{3}$.   □

Though the above example is a bit simplistic, errors in matrix calculations introduced by round-off or truncation can and do occur and can have disastrous consequences. Were the matrix in the example above the coefficient matrix of a system, then the computer program would conclude that the system has a unique solution, while in reality the system has either infinitely many solutions or no solution. The subject of error propagation when doing matrix arithmetic on a computer is of great importance to people who use matrices in practice, since they want to be assured that their results are meaningful. It is also a subject where much current work is being done by computer scientists and mathematicians. The books by Rice and by Noble and Daniel* provide further detail.

* B. Noble and J. Daniel, *Applied Linear Algebra*, Prentice-Hall, Englewood Cliffs, N.J., 1977.

Exercise 2.5 *Answers to Odd-Numbered Problems begin on page* 603.

In Problems 1–6 show that the given matrices are inverses of each other.

1. $\begin{bmatrix} 1 & 2 \\ 2 & 3 \end{bmatrix}\begin{bmatrix} -3 & 2 \\ 2 & -1 \end{bmatrix}$

2. $\begin{bmatrix} 1 & 5 \\ 2 & 0 \end{bmatrix}\begin{bmatrix} 0 & \frac{1}{2} \\ \frac{1}{5} & -\frac{1}{10} \end{bmatrix}$

3. $\begin{bmatrix} -1 & -2 \\ 3 & 4 \end{bmatrix}\begin{bmatrix} 2 & 1 \\ -\frac{3}{2} & -\frac{1}{2} \end{bmatrix}$

4. $\begin{bmatrix} 1 & 3 \\ 2 & -1 \end{bmatrix}\begin{bmatrix} \frac{1}{7} & \frac{3}{7} \\ \frac{2}{7} & -\frac{1}{7} \end{bmatrix}$

5. $\begin{bmatrix} 1 & 2 & 3 \\ 2 & 3 & 4 \\ 1 & 2 & 1 \end{bmatrix}\begin{bmatrix} -\frac{5}{2} & 2 & -\frac{1}{2} \\ 1 & -1 & 1 \\ \frac{1}{2} & 0 & -\frac{1}{2} \end{bmatrix}$

6. $\begin{bmatrix} 1 & 3 & 3 \\ 1 & 4 & 3 \\ 1 & 3 & 4 \end{bmatrix}\begin{bmatrix} 7 & -3 & -3 \\ -1 & 1 & 0 \\ -1 & 0 & 1 \end{bmatrix}$

In Problems 7–20 find the inverse of each matrix using the reduced row-echelon technique.

7. $\begin{bmatrix} 2 & 5 \\ 1 & 3 \end{bmatrix}$

8. $\begin{bmatrix} 4 & 1 \\ 3 & 1 \end{bmatrix}$

9. $\begin{bmatrix} 1 & -1 \\ 3 & -4 \end{bmatrix}$

10. $\begin{bmatrix} 5 & 3 \\ 3 & 2 \end{bmatrix}$

11. $\begin{bmatrix} 2 & 1 \\ 4 & 3 \end{bmatrix}$

12. $\begin{bmatrix} 2 & 3 \\ 2 & -1 \end{bmatrix}$

13. $\begin{bmatrix} 0 & 0 & 1 \\ 0 & 1 & 0 \\ 1 & 0 & 0 \end{bmatrix}$

14. $\begin{bmatrix} -1 & 1 & 0 \\ 1 & 0 & 2 \\ 3 & 1 & 0 \end{bmatrix}$

15. $\begin{bmatrix} 1 & 1 & -1 \\ 3 & -1 & 0 \\ 2 & -3 & 4 \end{bmatrix}$

16. $\begin{bmatrix} 1 & 1 & 1 \\ 2 & 1 & 1 \\ 1 & 1 & 2 \end{bmatrix}$

17. $\begin{bmatrix} 1 & 1 & -1 \\ 2 & 1 & 1 \\ 1 & 0 & 1 \end{bmatrix}$

18. $\begin{bmatrix} 2 & 3 & -1 \\ 1 & 1 & 1 \\ 0 & 2 & -1 \end{bmatrix}$

19. $\begin{bmatrix} 1 & 1 & 0 & 0 \\ 0 & 1 & -1 & 1 \\ 1 & -1 & 1 & 1 \\ 0 & 1 & 0 & -1 \end{bmatrix}$

20. $\begin{bmatrix} 1 & 2 & -3 & -2 \\ 0 & 1 & 4 & -2 \\ 3 & -1 & 4 & 0 \\ 2 & 1 & 0 & 3 \end{bmatrix}$

In Problems 21–26 show that each matrix has no inverse.

21. $\begin{bmatrix} 4 & 6 \\ 2 & 3 \end{bmatrix}$

22. $\begin{bmatrix} -1 & 2 \\ 3 & -6 \end{bmatrix}$

23. $\begin{bmatrix} -8 & 4 \\ -4 & 2 \end{bmatrix}$

24. $\begin{bmatrix} 2 & 10 \\ 1 & 5 \end{bmatrix}$

25. $\begin{bmatrix} 1 & 1 & 1 \\ 3 & -4 & 2 \\ 0 & 0 & 0 \end{bmatrix}$

26. $\begin{bmatrix} -1 & 2 & 3 \\ 5 & 2 & 0 \\ 2 & -4 & -6 \end{bmatrix}$

In Problems 27–32 find the inverse, if it exists, of each matrix.

27. $\begin{bmatrix} 1 & 1 \\ 1 & 2 \end{bmatrix}$

28. $\begin{bmatrix} 2 & 1 \\ 1 & 1 \end{bmatrix}$

29. $\begin{bmatrix} 3 & -2 \\ 0 & 2 \end{bmatrix}$

30. $\begin{bmatrix} 4 & -1 \\ -1 & 0 \end{bmatrix}$

31. $\begin{bmatrix} 3 & 2 \\ 6 & 4 \end{bmatrix}$

32. $\begin{bmatrix} 4 & 2 \\ 2 & 1 \end{bmatrix}$

In Problems 33–46 solve each system of equations by the method of Example 7.

33. $x + y = 6$
$2x - y = 0$

34. $x - y = 2$
$2x + y = 1$

35. $2x + 3y = 7$
$3x - y = 5$

36. $2x - 3y = 5$
$3x + y = 2$

37. $2x - 3y = 0$
$4x + 9y = 5$

38. $3x - 4y = 3$
$6x + 2y = 1$

39. $\frac{1}{2}x + \frac{1}{3}y = 2$
$x + y = 5$

40. $x - \frac{1}{4}y = 0$
$\frac{1}{2}x + \frac{1}{2}y = \frac{5}{2}$

41. $2x + y + z = 6$
$x - y - z = -3$
$3x + y + 2z = 7$

42. $x + y + z = 5$
$2x - y + z = 2$
$x + 2y - z = 3$

43. $2x + y - z = 2$
$x + 3y + 2z = 1$
$x + y + z = 2$

44. $2x + 2y + z = 6$
$x - y - z = -2$
$x - 2y - 2z = -5$

45. $3x + y - z = \frac{2}{3}$
$2x - y + z = 1$
$4x + 2y = \frac{8}{3}$

46. $x + y = 1$
$2x - y + z = 1$
$x + 2y + z = \frac{8}{3}$

In Problems 47–50 solve each system by the method of Example 7, that is, by finding A^{-1}.

47. $3x + 7y = 10$
$2x + 5y = 7$

48. $3x + 7y = -4$
$2x + 5y = -3$

49. $3x + 7y = 13$
$2x + 5y = 9$

50. $3x + 7y = 20$
$2x + 5y = 14$

51. Show that the inverse of

$$A = \begin{bmatrix} a & b \\ c & d \end{bmatrix}$$

is given by the formula

$$A^{-1} = \begin{bmatrix} \dfrac{d}{\Delta} & \dfrac{-b}{\Delta} \\ \dfrac{-c}{\Delta} & \dfrac{a}{\Delta} \end{bmatrix}$$

where $\Delta = ad - bc \neq 0$. The number Δ is called the *determinant of A*.

2.6 APPLICATIONS*

LEONTIEF MODELS □ CRYPTOGRAPHY □ DATA ANALYSIS: METHOD OF LEAST SQUARES □ ACCOUNTING

LEONTIEF MODELS

The Leontief models in economics are named after Wassily Leontief, who received the Nobel prize in economics in 1973. (See the October 29, 1973 issue of *Newsweek*,

---

* This section may be omitted without loss of continuity.

WASSILY LEONTIEF published his first description of the production interdependence of goods and services for an entire economy in 1936. For additional references on Leontief's contributions, see Walter Isard and Phyllis Kaniss, "The 1973 Nobel Prize for Economic Science," *Science* (November 9, 1973) and Wassily W. Leontief, *The Structure of American Economy, 1919–1935,* Oxford University Press, 1951.

p. 94.) These models can be characterized as a description of an economy in which input equals output or, in other words, consumption equals production. That is, the models assume that whatever is produced is always consumed.

Leontief models are of two types: closed, in which the entire production is consumed by those participating in the production; and open, in which some of the production is consumed by those who produce it and the rest of the production is consumed by external bodies.

In the *closed model* we seek the relative income of each participant in the system. In the *open model* we seek the amount of production needed to achieve a forecast demand, when the amount of production needed to achieve current demand is known.

The Closed Model   We begin with an example to illustrate the idea.

□ **Example 1**   Three homeowners, Mike, Dan, and Bob, each with certain skills, agreed to pool their talents to make repairs on their houses. As it turned out, Mike spent 20% of his time on his own house, 40% of his time on Dan's house, and 40% on Bob's house. Dan spent 10% of his time on Mike's house, 50% of his time on his own house, and 40% on Bob's house. Of Bob's time, 60% was spent on Mike's house, 10% on Dan's, and 30% on his own. Now that the projects are finished, they need to figure out how much money each should get for his work, including the work performed on his own house, so that each person comes out even. They agreed in advance that the payment to each one should be approximately $300.00.

Solution   We place the information given in the problem in a 3×3 matrix, as follows:

$$
\begin{array}{c}
\text{Work done by} \\
\begin{array}{ccc}
\text{Mike} & \text{Dan} & \text{Bob}
\end{array}
\end{array}
$$

	Mike	Dan	Bob
Proportion of work done on Mike's house	0.2	0.1	0.6
Proportion of work done on Dan's house	0.4	0.5	0.1
Proportion of work done on Bob's house	0.4	0.4	0.3

Next, we define the unknowns:

$$x_1 = \text{Mike's wages}$$
$$x_2 = \text{Dan's wages}$$
$$x_3 = \text{Bob's wages}$$

For each to come out even will require that the total amount paid out by each one equals the total amount received by each one. Let's analyze this requirement, by looking just at the work done on Mike's house. Mike's wages are x_1. Mike's expenditures for work done on his house are $0.2x_1 + 0.1x_2 + 0.6x_3$. These are required to be equal, so

$$x_1 = 0.2x_1 + 0.1x_2 + 0.6x_3$$

Similarly,

$$x_2 = 0.4x_1 + 0.5x_2 + 0.1x_3$$
$$x_3 = 0.4x_1 + 0.4x_2 + 0.3x_3$$

These three equations can be written compactly as

$$\begin{bmatrix} x_1 \\ x_2 \\ x_3 \end{bmatrix} = \begin{bmatrix} 0.2 & 0.1 & 0.6 \\ 0.4 & 0.5 & 0.1 \\ 0.4 & 0.4 & 0.3 \end{bmatrix} \begin{bmatrix} x_1 \\ x_2 \\ x_3 \end{bmatrix}$$

A simple manipulation reduces the system to

$$0.8x_1 - 0.1x_2 - 0.6x_3 = 0$$
$$-0.4x_1 + 0.5x_2 - 0.1x_3 = 0$$
$$-0.4x_1 - 0.4x_2 + 0.7x_3 = 0$$

Solving for x_1, x_2, x_3, we find that

$$x_1 = \tfrac{31}{36}x_3 \qquad x_2 = \tfrac{32}{36}x_3$$

where x_3 is the parameter. To get solutions that fall close to \$300, we set $x_3 = 360$.*
The wages to be paid out are therefore

$$x_1 = \$310 \qquad x_2 = \$320 \qquad x_3 = \$360 \qquad \square$$

The matrix in Example 1, namely,

$$\begin{bmatrix} 0.2 & 0.1 & 0.6 \\ 0.4 & 0.5 & 0.1 \\ 0.4 & 0.4 & 0.3 \end{bmatrix}$$

Input–Output Matrix is called an *input–output matrix.*
In the general closed model, we have an economy consisting of n components. Each component produces an *output* of some goods or services, which, in turn, is completely used up by the n components. The proportionate use of each component's output by the economy makes up the input–output matrix of the economy. The problem is to find suitable pricing levels for each component so that total income equals total expenditure.

In general, an input–output matrix for a closed Leontief model is of the form

$$A = [a_{ij}] \qquad i, j = 1, 2, \dots, n$$

where the a_{ij} represent the fractional amount of goods or services used by i and produced by j. For a closed model, the sum of each column equals 1 (this is the condition that all production is consumed internally) and $0 \le a_{ij} \le 1$ for all entries (this is the restriction that each entry is a fraction).

If A is the input–output matrix of a closed system with n components and X is a column vector representing the price of each output of the system, then

$$X = AX$$

represents the requirement that total income equal expenditure.

---

* Other choices for x_3 are, of course, possible. The choice of which value to use is up to the homeowners. No matter what choice is made, each homeowner comes out even.

For example, the first entry of the matrix equality $X = AX$ requires that

$$x_1 = a_{11} x_1 + a_{12} x_2 + \cdots + a_{1n} x_n$$

The right side represents the price paid by component 1 for the goods it uses, while x_1 represents the income of component 1; we are requiring they be equal.

We can rewrite the equation $X = AX$ as

$$X - AX = \mathbf{0}$$
$$I_n X - AX = \mathbf{0}$$
$$(I_n - A)X = \mathbf{0}$$

This matrix equation, which represents a system of equations in which the right-hand side is always $\mathbf{0}$, is called a *homogeneous system of equations.* It can be shown that if the entries in the input–output matrix A are positive and if the sum of each column of A equals 1, then this system has a one-parameter solution; that is, we can solve for $n - 1$ of the unknowns in terms of the remaining one, which serves as the parameter. This parameter serves as a "scale factor."

The Open Model For the open model, in addition to internal consumption of goods produced, there is an outside demand for the goods produced. This outside demand may take the form of exportation of goods or may be the goods needed to support consumer demand. Again, however, we make the assumption that whatever is produced is also consumed.

For example, suppose an economy consists of three industries R, S, and T, and suppose each one produces a single product. We assume that a portion of R's production is used by each of the three industries, while the remainder is used up by consumers. The same is true of the production of S and T. To organize our thoughts, we construct a table that describes the interaction of the use of R, S, and T's production over some fixed period of time. See Table 1.

Table 1

	R	**S**	**T**	**Consumer**	**Total**
R	50	20	40	70	180
S	20	30	20	90	160
T	30	20	20	50	120

All entries in the table are in appropriate units, say, in dollars. The first row (row R) represents the production in dollars of industry R (input). Out of the total of \$180 worth of goods produced, R, S, and T use \$50, \$20, and \$40, respectively, for the production of their goods, while consumers purchase the remaining \$70 for their consumption (output). Observe that input equals output since everything produced by R is used up by R, S, T, and consumers.

The second and third rows are interpreted in the same way.

An important observation is that the goal of R's production is to produce \$70 worth of goods, since this is the demand of consumers. In order to meet this demand,

R must produce a total of $180, since the difference $110 is required internally by R, S, and T.

Suppose, however, that consumer demand is expected to change. To effect this change, how much should each industry now produce? For example, in Table 1, **Demand Vector** current demand for R, S, and T can be represented by a *demand vector:*

$$D_0 = \begin{bmatrix} 70 \\ 90 \\ 50 \end{bmatrix}$$

But suppose marketing forecasts predict that in 3 years the demand vector will be

$$D_3 = \begin{bmatrix} 60 \\ 110 \\ 60 \end{bmatrix}$$

Here the demand for item R has decreased; the demand for item S has significantly increased, and the demand for item T is higher. Given the current total output of R, S, and T at 180, 160, and 120, respectively, what must it be in 3 years to meet this projected demand?

In using input–output analysis to obtain a solution to such a forecasting problem, we take into account the fact that the output of any one of these industries is affected by changes in the other two, since the total demand for say, R, in 3 years depends not only on consumer demand for R, but also on consumer demand for S and T. That is, the industries are interrelated.

The solution of this type of forecasting problem is derived from the *open Leontief model* in input–output analysis.

To obtain the solution, we need to determine how much of each of the three products R, S, and T is required to produce 1 unit of R. For example, to obtain 180 units of R requires the use of 50 units of R, 20 units of S, and 30 units of T (the entries in column 1). Forming the ratios, we find that to produce 1 unit of R requires $\frac{50}{180} = 0.278$ of R, $\frac{20}{180} = 0.111$ of S, and $\frac{30}{180} = 0.167$ of T. If we want, say, x_1 units of R, we will require $0.278x_1$ units of R, $0.111x_1$ units of S, and $0.167x_1$ units of T.

Continuing in this way, we can construct the matrix

$$A = \begin{array}{c} \\ R \\ S \\ T \end{array} \begin{array}{ccc} R & S & T \\ \begin{bmatrix} 0.278 & 0.125 & 0.333 \\ 0.111 & 0.188 & 0.167 \\ 0.167 & 0.125 & 0.167 \end{bmatrix} \end{array}$$

Observe that column 1 represents the amounts of R, S, T required for 1 unit of R; column 2 represents the amounts of R, S, and T required for 1 unit of S; and column 3 represents the amounts of R, S, and T required for 1 unit of T. For example, the entry in row 3, column 2 (0.125), represents the amount of T needed to produce 1 unit of S.

As a result of placing the entries this way, if

$$X = \begin{bmatrix} x_1 \\ x_2 \\ x_3 \end{bmatrix}$$

represents the total output required to obtain a given demand, the product AX represents the amounts of R, S, and T required for internal consumption. The condition that production $=$ consumption requires that

Internal consumption $+$ Consumer demand $=$ Total output

In terms of the matrix A, the total output X, and the demand vector D, this requirement is equivalent to the equation

$$AX + D = X$$

In this equation, we seek to find X for a prescribed demand D. The matrix A is calculated as above for some initial production process.*

☐ **Example 2**   For the data given in Table 1, find the total output X required to achieve a future demand of

$$D_3 = \begin{bmatrix} 60 \\ 110 \\ 60 \end{bmatrix}$$

Solution   We need to solve for X in

$$AX + D_3 = X$$

Simplifying, we have

$$[I - A]X = D_3$$

Solving for X, we have

$$X = [I - A]^{-1} \cdot D_3$$

$$= \begin{bmatrix} 0.722 & -0.125 & -0.333 \\ -0.111 & 0.812 & -0.167 \\ -0.167 & -0.125 & 0.833 \end{bmatrix}^{-1} \begin{bmatrix} 60 \\ 110 \\ 60 \end{bmatrix}$$

$$= \begin{bmatrix} 1.6048 & 0.3568 & 0.7131 \\ 0.2946 & 1.3363 & 0.3857 \\ 0.3660 & 0.2721 & 1.4013 \end{bmatrix} \begin{bmatrix} 60 \\ 110 \\ 60 \end{bmatrix}$$

$$= \begin{bmatrix} 178.322 \\ 187.811 \\ 135.969 \end{bmatrix}$$

* The entries in A can be checked by using the requirement that $AX + D = X$, for $D =$ initial demand and $X =$ total output. For our example, it must happen that

Internal consumption $+$ Consumer demand $=$ Total output

$$\underset{AX}{\begin{bmatrix} 0.278 & 0.125 & 0.333 \\ 0.111 & 0.188 & 0.167 \\ 0.167 & 0.125 & 0.167 \end{bmatrix} \begin{bmatrix} 180 \\ 160 \\ 120 \end{bmatrix}} + \underset{D}{\begin{bmatrix} 70 \\ 90 \\ 50 \end{bmatrix}} \overset{=}{\underset{X}{=}} \begin{bmatrix} 180 \\ 160 \\ 120 \end{bmatrix}$$

Thus, the total output of R, S, and T required for the forecast demand D_3 is

$$x_1 = 178.322 \qquad x_2 = 187.811 \qquad x_3 = 135.969 \qquad \square$$

The general open model can be described as follows: Suppose there are n industries in the economy. Each industry produces some goods or services, which are partially consumed by the n industries, while the rest are used to meet a prescribed current demand. Given the output required of each industry to meet current demand, what should the output of each industry be to meet some different future demand?

> The matrix $A = [a_{ij}]$, $i, j = 1, \ldots, n$, of the open model is defined to consist of entries a_{ij}, where a_{ij} is the amount of output of industry j required for one unit of output of industry i. If X is a column vector representing the production of each industry in the system and D is a column vector representing future demand for goods produced in the system, then
>
> $$X = AX + D$$

From the equation above, we find

$$[I_n - A]X = D$$

It can be shown that the matrix $I_n - A$ has an inverse, provided each entry in A is positive and the sum of each column in A is less than 1. Under these conditions, we may solve for X to get

$$X = [I_n - A]^{-1} \cdot D$$

This form of the solution is particularly useful since it allows us to find X for a variety of demands D by doing one calculation: $[I_n - A]^{-1}$.

We conclude by noting that the use of an input–output matrix to solve forecasting problems assumes that each industry produces a single commodity and that no technological advances take place in the period of time under investigation (in other words, the proportions found in the matrix A are fixed).

Exercise 2.6A   *Answers to Odd-Numbered Problems begin on page 604.*

In Problems 1–4 find the relative wages of each person for the given closed input–output matrix. In each case, take the wages of C to be the parameter and use $x_3 = C\text{'s wages} = \$10,000$.

1. $\begin{array}{c} \\ A \\ B \\ C \end{array} \begin{array}{ccc} A & B & C \\ \left[\begin{array}{ccc} \frac{1}{2} & \frac{1}{3} & \frac{1}{4} \\ \frac{1}{4} & \frac{1}{3} & \frac{1}{4} \\ \frac{1}{4} & \frac{1}{3} & \frac{1}{2} \end{array}\right] \end{array}$

2. $\begin{array}{c} \\ A \\ B \\ C \end{array} \begin{array}{ccc} A & B & C \\ \left[\begin{array}{ccc} \frac{1}{4} & \frac{2}{3} & \frac{1}{2} \\ \frac{1}{2} & \frac{1}{6} & \frac{1}{4} \\ \frac{1}{4} & \frac{1}{6} & \frac{1}{4} \end{array}\right] \end{array}$

3. $\begin{array}{c} \\ A \\ B \\ C \end{array} \begin{array}{ccc} A & B & C \\ \left[\begin{array}{ccc} 0.2 & 0.3 & 0.1 \\ 0.6 & 0.4 & 0.2 \\ 0.2 & 0.3 & 0.7 \end{array}\right] \end{array}$

4. $\begin{array}{c} \\ A \\ B \\ C \end{array} \begin{array}{ccc} A & B & C \\ \left[\begin{array}{ccc} 0.4 & 0.3 & 0.2 \\ 0.2 & 0.3 & 0.3 \\ 0.4 & 0.4 & 0.5 \end{array}\right] \end{array}$

5. For the three industries R, S, and T in the open Leontief model of Example 2 on page 96, compute the total output vector X if the forecast demand vector is

$$D_2 = \begin{bmatrix} 80 \\ 90 \\ 60 \end{bmatrix}$$

6. Rework Problem 5 if the forecast demand vector is

$$D_4 = \begin{bmatrix} 100 \\ 80 \\ 60 \end{bmatrix}$$

7. A society consists of four individuals: a farmer, a builder, a tailor, and a rancher (who produces meat products). Of the food produced by the farmer, $\frac{3}{10}$ is used by the farmer, $\frac{2}{10}$ by the builder, $\frac{2}{10}$ by the tailor, and $\frac{3}{10}$ by the rancher. The builder's production is utilized 30% by the farmer, 30% by the builder, 10% by the tailor, and 30% by the rancher. The tailor's production is used in the ratios $\frac{3}{10}$, $\frac{3}{10}$, $\frac{1}{10}$, and $\frac{3}{10}$ by the farmer, builder, tailor, and rancher. Finally, meat products are used 20% by each of the farmer, builder, and tailor, and 40% by the rancher. What are the relative wages of each if the rancher's wages are scaled at $10,000?

8. If in Problem 7 the meat production utilization changes so that it is used equally by all four individuals, while everyone else's production utilization remains the same, what are the relative wages?

9. Suppose the interrelationships between the production of two industries R and S in a given year are given in the table:

	R	S	Current Consumer Demand	Total Output
R	30	40	60	130
S	20	10	40	70

If the forecast demand in 2 years is

$$D_2 = \begin{bmatrix} 80 \\ 40 \end{bmatrix}$$

what should the total output X be?

CRYPTOGRAPHY

Our second application is to *cryptography*, the art of writing or deciphering secret codes. We begin by giving examples of elementary codes.

□ **Example 1**   A message can be encoded by associating each letter of the alphabet with some other letter of the alphabet according to a prescribed pattern. For example, we might have

With the above code, the word *BOMB* would become DQOD.   □

□ **Example 2** Another code may associate numbers with the letters of the alphabet. For example, we might have

A B C D E F G H I J K L M N O P Q R S T U V W X Y Z
↓ ↓
26 25 24 23 22 21 20 19 18 17 16 15 14 13 12 11 10 9 8 7 6 5 4 3 2 1

In this code, the word *PEACE* looks like 11 22 26 24 22.   □

Both the above codes have one important feature in common. The association of letters with the coding symbols is made using a one-to-one correspondence so that no possible ambiguities can arise.

Suppose we want to encode the following message:

BEWARE   THE   IDES   OF   MARCH

If we decide to divide the message into pairs of letters, the message becomes:

BE   WA   RE   TH   EI   DE   SO   FM   AR   CH

(If there is a letter left over, we arbitrarily assign Z to the last position.) Using the correspondence of letters to numbers given in Example 2, and writing each pair of letters as a column vector, we obtain

$$\begin{bmatrix} B \\ E \end{bmatrix} = \begin{bmatrix} 25 \\ 22 \end{bmatrix} \quad \begin{bmatrix} W \\ A \end{bmatrix} = \begin{bmatrix} 4 \\ 26 \end{bmatrix} \quad \begin{bmatrix} R \\ E \end{bmatrix} = \begin{bmatrix} 9 \\ 22 \end{bmatrix} \quad \begin{bmatrix} T \\ H \end{bmatrix} = \begin{bmatrix} 7 \\ 19 \end{bmatrix} \quad \text{etc.}$$

Next, we arbitrarily choose a 2×2 matrix A, which we know has an inverse A^{-1} (the reason for this is seen later). Suppose we choose

$$A = \begin{bmatrix} 2 & 3 \\ 1 & 2 \end{bmatrix}$$

Its inverse is

$$A^{-1} = \begin{bmatrix} 2 & -3 \\ -1 & 2 \end{bmatrix}$$

Now, we transform the column vectors representing the message by multiplying each of them on the left by the matrix A:

$$A \begin{bmatrix} B \\ E \end{bmatrix} = A \begin{bmatrix} 25 \\ 22 \end{bmatrix} = \begin{bmatrix} 116 \\ 69 \end{bmatrix}$$

$$A \begin{bmatrix} W \\ A \end{bmatrix} = A \begin{bmatrix} 4 \\ 26 \end{bmatrix} = \begin{bmatrix} 86 \\ 56 \end{bmatrix}$$

$$A \begin{bmatrix} R \\ E \end{bmatrix} = A \begin{bmatrix} 9 \\ 22 \end{bmatrix} = \begin{bmatrix} 84 \\ 53 \end{bmatrix} \quad \text{etc.}$$

The coded message is

116   69   86   56   84   53   etc.

To decode or unscramble the above message, pair the numbers in 2×1 column vectors. Multiply each of these column vectors by A^{-1} on the left:

$$A^{-1} \begin{bmatrix} 116 \\ 69 \end{bmatrix} = \begin{bmatrix} 25 \\ 22 \end{bmatrix}$$

$$A^{-1} \begin{bmatrix} 86 \\ 56 \end{bmatrix} = \begin{bmatrix} 4 \\ 26 \end{bmatrix}$$

By reassigning letters to these numbers, we obtain the original message.

□ **Example 3** The message to be encoded is

THE   END   IS   NEAR

We agree to associate numbers to letters as follows:

A B C D E F G H I J K L M N O P Q R S T U V W X Y Z
↓ ↓
1 2 3 4 5 6 7 8 9 10 11 12 13 14 15 16 17 18 19 20 21 22 23 24 25 26

The encoded message is to be formed of triplets of numbers.

Solution   This time we must divide the message into triplets of letters, obtaining

THE   END   ISN   EAR

in order for the encoded message to have triplets of numbers. (If the message required additional letters to complete the triplet, we would have used Z or YZ.)

Now we choose a 3×3 matrix such as

$$A = \begin{bmatrix} 1 & 0 & 0 \\ 3 & 1 & 5 \\ -2 & 0 & 1 \end{bmatrix}$$

Its inverse is

$$A^{-1} = \begin{bmatrix} 1 & 0 & 0 \\ -13 & 1 & -5 \\ 2 & 0 & 1 \end{bmatrix}$$

The encoded message is obtained by multiplying the matrix A times each column vector of the original message:

$$A \begin{bmatrix} T \\ H \\ E \end{bmatrix} = \begin{bmatrix} 1 & 0 & 0 \\ 3 & 1 & 5 \\ -2 & 0 & 1 \end{bmatrix} \begin{bmatrix} 20 \\ 8 \\ 5 \end{bmatrix} = \begin{bmatrix} 20 \\ 93 \\ -35 \end{bmatrix}$$

$$A \begin{bmatrix} E \\ N \\ D \end{bmatrix} = \begin{bmatrix} 1 & 0 & 0 \\ 3 & 1 & 5 \\ -2 & 0 & 1 \end{bmatrix} \begin{bmatrix} 5 \\ 14 \\ 4 \end{bmatrix} = \begin{bmatrix} 5 \\ 49 \\ -6 \end{bmatrix}$$

$$A \begin{bmatrix} I \\ S \\ N \end{bmatrix} = \begin{bmatrix} 1 & 0 & 0 \\ 3 & 1 & 5 \\ -2 & 0 & 1 \end{bmatrix} \begin{bmatrix} 9 \\ 19 \\ 14 \end{bmatrix} = \begin{bmatrix} 9 \\ 116 \\ -4 \end{bmatrix}$$

$$A \begin{bmatrix} E \\ A \\ R \end{bmatrix} = \begin{bmatrix} 1 & 0 & 0 \\ 3 & 1 & 5 \\ -2 & 0 & 1 \end{bmatrix} \begin{bmatrix} 5 \\ 1 \\ 18 \end{bmatrix} = \begin{bmatrix} 5 \\ 106 \\ 8 \end{bmatrix}$$

The coded message is

$$20 \quad 93 \quad -35 \quad 5 \quad 49 \quad -6 \quad 9 \quad 116 \quad -4 \quad 5 \quad 106 \quad 8 \qquad \square$$

To decode the message in Example 3, form 3×1 column vectors of the numbers in the coded message and multiply on the left by A^{-1}.

The above are elementary examples of encoding and decoding. Modern-day cryptography uses sophisticated computer-implemented codes that depend on higher level mathematics. For an interesting survey of current cryptographic techniques see the article "The Mathematics of Public-Key Cryptography" in the August 1979 issue of the *Scientific American*.

Exercise 2.6B *Answers to Odd-Numbered Problems begin on page* 604.

1. Using the correspondence

A B C D E F G H I J K L M N O P Q R S T U V W X Y Z
↓ ↓
1 2 3 4 5 6 7 8 9 10 11 12 13 14 15 16 17 18 19 20 21 22 23 24 25 26

and the matrices

$$\text{(I)} \quad A = \begin{bmatrix} 2 & 3 \\ 1 & 2 \end{bmatrix} \qquad \text{(II)} \quad A = \begin{bmatrix} 1 & 0 & 0 \\ 3 & 1 & 5 \\ -2 & 0 & 1 \end{bmatrix}$$

Encode the following messages:

(a) MEET ME AT THE CASBAH
(b) TOMORROW NEVER COMES
(c) THE MISSION IS IMPOSSIBLE

2. Using the correspondence given in Problem 1 and the matrix

$$A = \begin{bmatrix} 2 & 3 \\ 1 & 2 \end{bmatrix}$$

decode the following messages:

(a) 51 30 27 16 75 47 19 10 48 26
(b) 70 45 103 62 58 38 102 61 88 57

3. Using the correspondence given in Problem 1 and the matrix

$$A = \begin{bmatrix} 1 & 0 & 0 \\ 3 & 1 & 5 \\ -2 & 0 & 1 \end{bmatrix}$$

decode the message

$$25 \quad 195 \quad -29 \quad 6 \quad 135 \quad 9 \quad 14 \quad 183 \quad -2$$

DATA ANALYSIS: THE METHOD OF LEAST SQUARES

The method of least squares refers to a technique that is often used in data analysis to find the "best" linear equation that fits a given collection of experimental data. (We shall see a little later just what we mean by the word "best".) It is a technique employed by statisticians, economists, business forecasters, and most all who try to interpret and analyze data. Before we begin our discussion, we will need to define the transpose of a matrix.

Transpose Let A be a matrix of dimension $m \times n$. The *transpose of A,* written A^T, is the $n \times m$ matrix obtained from A by interchanging the rows and columns of A.

Thus, the first row of A^T is the first column of A; the second row of A^T is the second column of A; and so on.

□ **Example 1** If we let

$$A = \begin{bmatrix} 1 & 2 & 3 \\ 0 & -1 & 2 \end{bmatrix}, \qquad B = \begin{bmatrix} 1 & 1 \\ 0 & 1 \\ 2 & 3 \end{bmatrix}, \qquad \text{and} \qquad C = \begin{bmatrix} 1 & 0 & -1 \end{bmatrix}$$

then

$$A^T = \begin{bmatrix} 1 & 0 \\ 2 & -1 \\ 3 & 2 \end{bmatrix}, \qquad B^T = \begin{bmatrix} 1 & 0 & 2 \\ 1 & 1 & 3 \end{bmatrix}, \qquad \text{and} \qquad C^T = \begin{bmatrix} 1 \\ 0 \\ -1 \end{bmatrix} \qquad □$$

Note how dimensions are reversed when computing A^T: A has the dimension 2×3, while A^T has the dimension 3×2, and so on.

We begin our discussion of the method of least squares by an example.

Suppose a product has been sold over time at various prices and that we have some data that shows the demand for the product (in thousands of units) in terms of its price (in dollars). If we use x to represent price and y to represent demand, the data might look like the information in the table below.

Price	x	4	5	9	12
Demand	y	9	8	6	3

Suppose also that we have reason to assume that y and x are *linearly related*. That is, we assume we can write

$$y = ax + b$$

for some, as yet unknown, a and b. In other words we are assuming that when demand is graphed against price the resulting graph will be a straight line. Our belief that y and x are linearly related might be based on past experience or economic theory. However, if we plot the data from the above table (see Figure 2), it seems pretty clear that no single straight line passes through the plotted points.

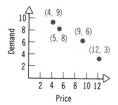

Figure 2

This may be due to several reasons:

1. The reporting of the data may not have been accurate, or
2. Our assumption that $y = ax + b$ may not be totally warranted.

Thus, we are looking for an ideal answer to a question about something in the real world where what happens may only roughly (approximately) fit an ideal design. Refer again to Figure 2. Though no straight line will pass through all the above points, we might still ask: "Is there a straight line that best fits the above points"? Intuitively, we seek a line of the sort in Figure 3 that provides a good straight-line approximation to the data. Finding such a line would give us at least an approximate feel for how the demand y is related to the price x.

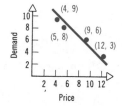

Figure 3

Our Problem Given a set of noncollinear points, find the straight line that "best" fits these points.

In the process we will need to clarify our use of the word "best." First, we label the data points in Figure 2 from left to right as (x_1, y_1), (x_2, y_2), and so on, so that, for example, (x_2, y_2) is (5, 8). Now suppose the equation of the straight line L in Figure 3 is

$$y = ax + b$$

where we do not know what a and b are. If (x_1, y_1) is actually on the line, it would be true that

$$y_1 = ax_1 + b$$

But, since we can't expect (x_1, y_1) to lie on L, the above relation will not be valid or, expressed another way, there will be a nonzero difference between y_1 and $ax_1 + b$. We designate this difference by r_1. That is,

$$r_1 = y_1 - (ax_1 + b)$$

or $$y_1 = ax_1 + b + r_1$$

What we have just said about (x_1, y_1), we can repeat for the other data points (x_i, y_i), $i = 2, 3$ and 4. Therefore, since we can't expect y_i to be equal to $ax_i + b$, we will measure the difference by

$$r_i = y_i - (ax_i + b),$$

or equivalently by

$$y_i = ax_i + b + r_i, \quad i = 1, 2, 3, 4 \tag{1}$$

Geometrically, the r_i's measure the vertical distance between the sought-after line L and the data points (see Figure 4).

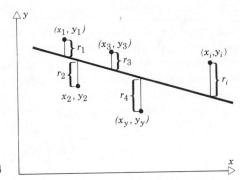

Figure 4

Recall that our problem is to find a line L that "best" fits the data points (x_i, y_i). Intuitively, we would seek a line L for which the r_i's are all simultaneously small. Since some r_i's are positive and some may be negative, it will not do to just add them up. To eliminate the signs, we square each r_i. The method of least squares consists of finding a line L for which the sum of the square of the r_i's is as small as possible. Since finding the line $y = ax + b$ is the same as finding a and b, we restate the least-squares problem for this example:

Least Squares Problem Given the data points (x_i, y_i), $i = 1, 2, 3, 4$, find a and b satisfying the equations (1) so that $r_1^2 + r_2^2 + r_3^2 + r_4^2$ is minimized.

A solution to the problem can be neatly expressed using matrix language.

Solution to Least-Squares Problem The line of best fit

$$y = ax + b \qquad (2)$$

to a set of four points (x_1, y_1), (x_2, y_2), (x_3, y_3), (x_4, y_4) is obtained by solving the system of two equations in two unknowns

$$A^T A X = A^T Y \qquad (3)$$

for a and b, where

$$A = \begin{bmatrix} x_1 & 1 \\ x_2 & 1 \\ x_3 & 1 \\ x_4 & 1 \end{bmatrix}, \qquad X = \begin{bmatrix} a \\ b \end{bmatrix}, \qquad Y = \begin{bmatrix} y_1 \\ y_2 \\ y_3 \\ y_4 \end{bmatrix} \qquad (4)$$

Since a derivation that this, in fact, does give the solution would require either calculus or more advanced linear algebra, we omit it.

□ **Example 2** Use least-squares to find the line of best fit for the points

$$(4, 9), (5, 8), (9, 6), (12, 3)$$

Solution We use equation (4) to set up the matrices A and Y

$$A = \begin{bmatrix} 4 & 1 \\ 5 & 1 \\ 9 & 1 \\ 12 & 1 \end{bmatrix}, \qquad Y = \begin{bmatrix} 9 \\ 8 \\ 6 \\ 3 \end{bmatrix}$$

The equation (3) $A^T A X = A^T Y$ becomes

$$\begin{bmatrix} 4 & 5 & 9 & 12 \\ 1 & 1 & 1 & 1 \end{bmatrix} \begin{bmatrix} 4 & 1 \\ 5 & 1 \\ 9 & 1 \\ 12 & 1 \end{bmatrix} \begin{bmatrix} a \\ b \end{bmatrix} = \begin{bmatrix} 4 & 5 & 9 & 12 \\ 1 & 1 & 1 & 1 \end{bmatrix} \begin{bmatrix} 9 \\ 8 \\ 6 \\ 3 \end{bmatrix}$$

This reduces to a system of two equations in two unknowns:

$$266a + 30b = 166$$
$$30a + 4b = 26$$

The solution, which you can verify, is given by

$$a = \frac{-29}{41}, \qquad b = \frac{484}{41}$$

Hence, the least-squares solution to the problem is given by the straight line

$$y = \frac{-29}{41} x + \frac{484}{41}$$

□

Note, for example, that corresponding to the value $x = 5$, the above line of "best" fit has $y = -29/41 \cdot 5 + 484/41 = 8.27$, while the experimentally observed demand had value 8. Were we to use our computed line to approximate the connection between price and demand, we would predict that a selling price of $x = 6$ would yield a demand of $y = -29/41 \cdot 6 + 484/41 = 7.56$.

The General Least-Squares Problems We presented the method of least squares using a particular example with four data points. It is easy to extend this analysis.

The general least-squares problem consists of finding the best straight line fit to a given set of data points:

$$(x_1, y_1), (x_2, y_2), \ldots, (x_n, y_n) \tag{5}$$

If we let

$$A = \begin{bmatrix} x_1 & 1 \\ x_2 & 1 \\ \cdot & \\ \cdot & \cdot \\ \cdot & \cdot \\ \cdot & \\ x_n & 1 \end{bmatrix}, \quad X = \begin{bmatrix} a \\ b \end{bmatrix}, \quad Y = \begin{bmatrix} y_1 \\ y_2 \\ \cdot \\ \cdot \\ \cdot \\ y_n \end{bmatrix}$$

then the line of best fit to the data points in (5) is

$$y = ax + b$$

where $X = \begin{bmatrix} a \\ b \end{bmatrix}$ is found by solving the system of two equations in two unknowns

$$A^T A X = A^T Y \tag{6}$$

It can be shown that the system given by the equation (6) always has a unique solution provided the data points do not all lie on the same vertical line. The least-squares techniques presented here along with more elaborate variations are frequently used today by statisticians and researchers.

Exercise 2.6C *Answers to Odd-Numbered Problems begin on page* **604**.

In Problems 1–6, compute A^T.

1. $A = \begin{bmatrix} 4 & 1 & 2 \\ 3 & 1 & 0 \end{bmatrix}$

2. $A = \begin{bmatrix} 5 & 2 & -1 \\ 1 & 3 & 6 \\ 1 & -1 & 2 \end{bmatrix}$

3. $A = \begin{bmatrix} 1 & 11 \\ 0 & 12 \\ 1 & 4 \end{bmatrix}$

4. $A = [-1 \quad 6 \quad 4]$

5. $A = \begin{bmatrix} 8 \\ 6 \\ 3 \end{bmatrix}$

6. $A = \begin{bmatrix} 5 & 3 \\ 3 & 7 \end{bmatrix}$

7. The following table shows the supply (in thousands of units) of a product at various prices (in dollars).

Price	x	3	5	6	7
Supply	y	10	13	15	16

(a) Find the least-squares line of best fit to the above data.

(b) Use the equation of this line to estimate the supply of the product at a price of 8 dollars.

8. Data giving the number of hours a person had studied compared to his or her performance on an exam are given below.

Hours Studied x	Exam Score y
0	50
2	74
4	85
6	90
8	92

(a) Find a least-squares line of best fit to the above data.

(b) What prediction would this line make for a student who studied 9 hours?

9. A business would like to determine the relationship between the amount of money spent on advertising and its total weekly sales. Over a period of 5 weeks it gathers the following data.

Amount Spent on Advertising (in thousands) x	Weekly Sales Volume (in thousands) y
10	50
17	61
11	55
18	60
21	70

Find a least-squares line of best fit to the above data.

10. The following data show the connection between the number of hours a drug has been in a person's body and its concentration in the body.

Number of Hours	Drug Concentration (parts per million)
2	2.1
4	1.6
6	1.4
8	1.0

(a)   Fit a least-squares line to the above data.

(b)   Use the equation of the line to estimate the drug concentration after 5 hours.

11.   A matrix is *symmetric* if $A^T = A$. Which of the following matrices are symmetric?

$$(1) \begin{bmatrix} 1 & 1 & 2 \\ 1 & 0 & 1 \\ 3 & 2 & 3 \end{bmatrix} \quad (2) \begin{bmatrix} 0 & 1 & 3 \\ 1 & 4 & 7 \\ 3 & 7 & 5 \end{bmatrix} \quad (3) \begin{bmatrix} 1 & 2 & 3 & 0 \\ 2 & 4 & 5 & 0 \\ 3 & 5 & 1 & 0 \end{bmatrix}$$

Need a symmetric matrix be square?

12.   Show that the matrix $A^T A$ is always symmetric.

ACCOUNTING

Consider a firm that has two types of departments, production and service. The production departments produce goods that can be sold in the market and the service departments provide services to the production departments. A major objective of the cost accounting process is the determination of the full cost of manufactured products on a per unit basis. This requires an allocation of indirect costs, first, from the service department (where they are incurred) to the producing department in which the goods are manufactured and, second, to the specific goods themselves. For example, an accounting department usually provides accounting services for service departments, as well as for the production departments. Thus, the indirect costs of service rendered by a service department must be determined in order to correctly assess the production departments. The total costs of a service department consist of its direct costs (salaries, wages, and materials) and its indirect costs (charges for the services it receives from other service departments). The nature of the problem and its solution are illustrated by the following example.

□ **Example 1**   Consider a firm with two production departments, P_1 and P_2, and three service departments, S_1, S_2, and S_3. These five departments are listed in the leftmost column of Table 3 (on page 109). The total monthly costs of these departments are unknown and are denoted by x_1, x_2, x_3, x_4, x_5. The direct monthly costs of the five departments are shown in the third column of the table. The fourth, fifth, and sixth columns show the allocation of charges for the services of S_1, S_2, and S_3 to the various departments. Since the total cost for each department is its direct costs plus its indirect costs, the first three rows of the table yield the total costs for the three service departments:

$$x_1 = 600 + 0.25x_1 + 0.15x_2 + 0.15x_3$$
$$x_2 = 1100 + 0.35x_1 + 0.20x_2 + 0.25x_3$$
$$x_3 = 600 + 0.10x_1 + 0.10x_2 + 0.35x_3$$

Let X, C, and D denote the following matrices:

$$X = \begin{bmatrix} x_1 \\ x_2 \\ x_3 \end{bmatrix} \qquad C = \begin{bmatrix} 0.25 & 0.15 & 0.15 \\ 0.35 & 0.20 & 0.25 \\ 0.10 & 0.10 & 0.35 \end{bmatrix} \qquad D = \begin{bmatrix} 600 \\ 1100 \\ 600 \end{bmatrix}$$

Then the system of equations above can be written in matrix notation as

$$X = D + CX$$

which is equivalent to

$$[I_3 - C]X = D$$

The total costs of the three service departments can be obtained by solving this matrix equation for X:

$$X = [I_3 - C]^{-1}D$$

Now,

$$[I_3 - C] = \begin{bmatrix} 0.75 & -0.15 & -0.15 \\ -0.35 & 0.80 & -0.25 \\ -0.10 & -0.10 & 0.65 \end{bmatrix}$$

Table 3

Department	Total Costs	Direct Costs, Dollars	Indirect Costs for Services from Departments		
			S_1	S_2	S_3
S_1	x_1	600	$0.25x_1$	$0.15x_2$	$0.15x_3$
S_2	x_2	1100	$0.35x_1$	$0.20x_2$	$0.25x_3$
S_3	x_3	600	$0.10x_1$	$0.10x_2$	$0.35x_3$
P_1	x_4	2100	$0.15x_1$	$0.25x_2$	$0.15x_3$
P_2	x_5	1500	$0.15x_1$	$0.30x_2$	$0.10x_3$
Totals			x_1	x_2	x_3

from which it can be verified that

$$[I_3 - C]^{-1} = \begin{bmatrix} 1.57 & 0.36 & 0.50 \\ 0.79 & 1.49 & 0.76 \\ 0.36 & 0.28 & 1.73 \end{bmatrix}$$

It is significant that the inverse of $[I_3 - C]$ exists, and that all of its entries are nonnegative. Because of this and the fact that the matrix D contains only nonnegative entries, the matrix X will also have only nonnegative entries. This means there is a meaningful solution to the accounting problem:

$$X = \begin{bmatrix} 1638.00 \\ 2569.00 \\ 1562.00 \end{bmatrix}$$

Thus, $x_1 = \$1638.00$, $x_2 = \$2569.00$, and $x_3 = \$1562.00$. All direct and indirect costs can now be determined by substituting these values in Table 3, as shown in Table 4.

Table 4

Department	Total Costs, Dollars	Direct Costs, Dollars	Indirect Costs for Services from Departments, Dollars		
			S_1	S_2	S_3
S_1	1629.15	600	409.50	385.35	234.30
S_2	2577.60	1100	573.30	513.80	390.50
S_3	1567.40	600	163.80	256.90	546.70
P_1	3222.25	2100	245.70	642.25	234.30
P_2	2672.60	1500	245.70	770.70	156.20

From Table 4, we learn that department P_1 pays \$1122.25 for the services it receives from S_1, S_2, S_3, and P_2 pays \$1172.60 for the services it receives from these departments. The procedure we have followed charges the direct costs of the service departments to the production departments, and each production department is charged according to the services it utilizes. Furthermore, the total cost for P_1 and P_2 is \$5894.85, and this figure approximates the sum of the direct costs of the three service departments and the two production departments. The results are consistent with conventional accounting procedure. Discrepancies that occur are due to rounding off.

Finally, a comment should be made about the allocation of charges for services as shown in Table 3. How is it determined that 25% of the total cost x_1 of S_1 should be charged to S_1, 35% to S_2, 10% to S_3, 15% to P_1, and 15% to P_2? The services of each department may be measured in some suitable unit, and each department may be charged according to the number of these units of service it receives. If 20% of the accounting items concern a given department, that department is charged 20% of the total cost of the accounting department. When services are not readily measurable, the allocation basis is subjectively determined. □

Exercise 2.6D 1. Consider the accounting problem described by the data in the table:

Department	Total Costs	Direct Costs, Dollars	Indirect Costs S_1	Indirect Costs S_2
S_1	x_1	2000	$\frac{1}{9}x_1$	$\frac{3}{9}x_2$
S_2	x_2	1000	$\frac{3}{9}x_1$	$\frac{4}{9}x_2$
P_1	x_3	2500	$\frac{1}{9}x_1$	$\frac{2}{9}x_2$
P_2	x_4	1500	$\frac{3}{9}x_1$	$\frac{1}{9}x_2$
P_3	x_5	3000	$\frac{1}{9}x_1$	$\frac{2}{9}x_2$
Totals			x_1	x_2

Determine whether this accounting problem has a solution. If it does, find the total costs. Prepare a table similar to Table 4. Show that the total of the service charges allocated to P_1, P_2, and P_3 is equal to the sum of the direct costs of the service departments S_1 and S_2.

2. Follow the directions of Problem 1 for the accounting problem described by the following data:

Department	Total Costs	Direct Costs, Dollars	Indirect Costs for Services from Departments S_1	Indirect Costs for Services from Departments S_2	Indirect Costs for Services from Departments S_3
S_1	x_1	500	$0.20x_1$	$0.10x_2$	$0.10x_3$
S_2	x_2	1000	$0.40x_1$	$0.15x_2$	$0.30x_3$
S_3	x_3	500	$0.10x_1$	$0.05x_2$	$0.30x_3$
P_1	x_4	2000	$0.20x_1$	$0.35x_2$	$0.20x_3$
P_2	x_5	1500	$0.10x_1$	$0.35x_2$	$0.10x_3$
Totals		5500	x_1	x_2	x_3

CHAPTER REVIEW

Important Terms

row
column
dimension of a matrix
diagonal of a matrix
square matrix
vector
zero matrix
scalar multiplication

matrix multiplication
identity matrix
inverse of a matrix
augmented matrix
row operation
reduced row-echelon form of a matrix
parameter

*Leontief model (open and closed)
*input–output matrix
transpose
symmetric

True–False Questions

(Answers on page 604)

T   F   1. Matrices of the same dimension can always be added.

T   F   2. Matrices of the same dimension can always be multiplied.

T   F   3. A square matrix will always have an inverse.

T   F   4. The reduced row-echelon form of a matrix A is unique.

Fill in the Blanks

(Answers on page 604)

1. If matrix A is of dimension 3×4 and matrix B is of dimension 4×2, then AB is of dimension _____ .

2. A system of three linear equations in three unknowns has either _____ solution, or no solutions, or _____ _____ solutions.

3. If A is a matrix of dimension 3×4, the 3 tells the number of _____ and the 4 tells the number of _____ .

4. If $AB = I$, the identity matrix, then B is called the _____ of A.

Review Exercises

Answers to Odd-Numbered Problems begin on page 604.

In Problems 1–14 compute the given expression for

$$A = \begin{bmatrix} -2 & 0 & 7 \\ 1 & 8 & 3 \\ 2 & 4 & 21 \end{bmatrix} \quad B = \begin{bmatrix} 1 & 3 & 9 \\ 2 & 7 & 5 \\ 3 & 6 & 8 \end{bmatrix} \quad C = \begin{bmatrix} 0 & 1 & 2 \\ 0 & 5 & 1 \\ 8 & 7 & 9 \end{bmatrix}$$

1. $A + B$

2. $B + A$

3. $3(A + B)$

4. $3A + 3B$

5. $3A - 3B$

6. $B - C$

7. $2(5A)$

8. $\frac{3}{4}A$

9. $2A + \frac{1}{2}B - 3C$

10. $A - 2B + 3C$

11. AB

12. BA

13. $(B - A)C$

14. $BC - AC$

---

* From optional section.

In Problems 15–22 find the inverse, if it exists, of each matrix.

15. $\begin{bmatrix} 3 & 0 \\ -2 & 1 \end{bmatrix}$

16. $\begin{bmatrix} 4 & 1 \\ 3 & 1 \end{bmatrix}$

17. $\begin{bmatrix} 1 & 2 & 3 \\ 2 & 4 & 5 \\ 3 & 5 & 6 \end{bmatrix}$

18. $\begin{bmatrix} -1 & 2 & 0 \\ 3 & 2 & -1 \\ 4 & 0 & 3 \end{bmatrix}$

19. $\begin{bmatrix} 4 & 3 & -1 \\ 0 & 2 & 2 \\ 3 & -1 & 0 \end{bmatrix}$

20. $\begin{bmatrix} -6 & 6 & 2 \\ 13 & 3 & 1 \\ 8 & -8 & 8 \end{bmatrix}$

21. $\begin{bmatrix} 1 & 2 & -3 \\ 4 & 6 & 2 \\ -3 & -6 & 9 \end{bmatrix}$

22. $\begin{bmatrix} 9 & 6 & -3 \\ 2 & -6 & 4 \\ -3 & 2 & 1 \end{bmatrix}$

In Problems 23–34 find the solution, if it exists, of each system of linear equations. If the system has infinitely many solutions, list at least three solutions.

23. $2x_1 - x_2 + x_3 = 1$
$x_1 + x_2 - x_3 = 2$
$3x_1 - x_2 + x_3 = 0$

24. $2x_1 + 3x_2 - x_3 = 5$
$x_1 - x_2 + x_3 = 1$
$3x_1 - 3x_2 + 3x_3 = 3$

25. $x_1 - 2x_2 = 6$
$3x_1 + 2x_2 - x_3 = 2$
$4x_1 + 3x_3 = -1$

26. $2x_1 - x_2 + 3x_3 = 5$
$x_1 + 2x_3 = 0$
$3x_1 + 2x_2 + x_3 = -3$

27. $x_1 - 3x_2 = 5$
$3x_2 + x_3 = 0$
$2x_1 - x_2 + 2x_3 = 2$

28. $x_1 - x_3 = 2$
$2x_1 - x_2 = 4$
$x_1 + x_2 + x_3 = 6$

29. $3x_1 + x_2 - 2x_3 = 3$
$x_1 - 2x_2 + x_3 = 4$

30. $2x_1 - x_2 - 3x_3 = 0$
$x_1 - 2x_2 + x_3 = 4$

31. $x_1 + 2x_2 - x_3 = 5$
$2x_1 - x_2 + 2x_3 = 0$

32. $x_1 - x_2 + 2x_3 = 6$
$2x_1 + 2x_2 - x_3 = -1$

33. $2x_1 - x_2 = 6$
$x_1 - 2x_2 = 0$
$3x_1 - x_2 = 6$

34. $x_1 - 2x_2 = 0$
$2x_1 + x_2 = 5$
$x_1 - 3x_2 = -3$

35. What must be true about x, y, z, w, if the matrices

$$A = \begin{bmatrix} x & y \\ z & w \end{bmatrix} \quad \text{and} \quad B = \begin{bmatrix} 1 & 1 \\ -1 & 1 \end{bmatrix}$$

are to commute? That is, $AB = BA$.

36. Let $t = [t_1 \quad t_2]$, with $t_1 + t_2 = 1$, and let $A = \begin{bmatrix} \frac{1}{4} & \frac{3}{4} \\ \frac{2}{3} & \frac{1}{3} \end{bmatrix}$. Find t such that $tA = t$.

37. Associate numbers to letters as follows:

1 2 3 4 5 6 7 8 9 10 11 12 13 14 15 16 17 18 19 20 21 22 23 24 25 26
↓ ↓
A B C D E F G H I J K L M N O P Q R S T U V W X Y Z

The matrix A used to encode a message has as its inverse the matrix

$$A^{-1} = \begin{bmatrix} 2 & -3 \\ -1 & 2 \end{bmatrix}$$

Decode the message

11 7 84 51 51 28 66 43 44 29 107 65 64 41

38. Associate numbers to letters as in Problem 23, and use the matrix

$$A = \begin{bmatrix} 1 & 0 & 0 \\ 3 & 1 & 5 \\ -2 & 0 & 1 \end{bmatrix}$$

to encode the message IT'S OVER

LINEAR PROGRAMMING PART I: GEOMETRIC APPROACH

3.1 INTRODUCTION

Whenever the analysis of a problem leads to minimizing or maximizing a linear expression in which the variable must obey a collection of linear inequalities, a solution may be obtained using linear programming techniques.

Historically, linear programming problems evolved out of the need to solve problems involving resource allocation during World War II by the United States Army. Among those who worked on such problems for the Air Force was George Dantzig, who later gave a general formulation of the linear programming problem and offered a method for solving it. His technique, called the **simplex method,** is discussed in Chapter 4.

In this chapter, we shall study ways to solve linear programming problems that involve only two variables. As a result, we can use a geometric approach to solve the problems. But first we need to discuss linear inequalities.

3.2 LINEAR INEQUALITIES

THE GRAPH OF A LINEAR INEQUALITY □ SYSTEMS OF LINEAR INEQUALITIES □ SOME TERMINOLOGY □ APPLICATION

We have already discussed linear equations (linear equalities) in two variables x and y. (Section 1.3). These are equations of the form

$$Ax + By = C \tag{1}$$

where A, B, C are real numbers and A and B are not both zero. If in Equation (1) we replace the equal sign by an inequality symbol, namely, one of the symbols $<, >, \leq, \geq$, we obtain a *linear inequality in two variables x and y.*

Linear Inequality in Two Variables

For example, the expressions

$$3x + 2y \geq 4, \qquad 2x - 3y < 0, \qquad 3x + 5y > -8$$

Nonstrict Inequality

Strict Inequality

are each linear inequalities in two variables. The first of these is called a *nonstrict inequality* since the inequality symbol $\geq$ is nonstrict; the remaining two linear inequalities are *strict*.

THE GRAPH OF A LINEAR INEQUALITY

Graph of a Linear Inequality

The *graph of a linear inequality* in two variables x and y is the set of all points (x, y) for which the inequality holds.

Let's look at an example.

GEORGE DANTZIG is one of the pioneering creators of linear programming, which is one of the most important developments in applied mathematics in the last half-century. He developed the simplex method in 1946. A historical perspective worth reading is George Dantzig, "Reminiscences about the Origins of Linear Programming," *Operations Research Letters,* **1,** 2 (April 1982).

□ **Example 1**   Graph the inequality: $2x + 3y \geq 6$

Solution   First, we graph the line

$$L: \quad 2x + 3y = 6$$

Any point on the line L obeys the inequality $2x + 3y \geq 6$, since we are seeking all points (x, y) for which $2x + 3y$ is greater than *or equal to* 6. See Figure 1(a).

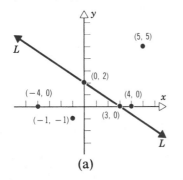

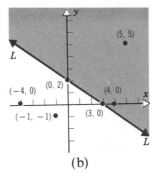

Figure 1   (a)   (b)

Now, let's test a few points, such as $(-1, -1)$, $(5, 5)$, $(4, 0)$, $(-4, 0)$, to see if they obey the inequality. We do this by substituting the coordinates of each point into the left member of the inequality and determining whether the result is ≥ 6 or < 6.

	$2x \quad + 3y$	*Conclusion*
$(-1, -1)$:	$2(-1) + 3(-1) = -2 - 3 = -5 < 6$	Not part of graph
$(5, 5)$:	$2(5) \quad + 3(5) \quad = 25 > 6$	Part of graph
$(4, 0)$:	$2(4) \quad + 3(0) \quad = 8 > 6$	Part of graph
$(-4, 0)$:	$2(-4) + 3(0) \quad = -8 < 6$	Not part of graph

Notice that the two points $(4, 0)$ and $(5, 5)$ that are part of the graph both lie on one side of L, while the points $(-4, 0)$ and $(-1, -1)$ (not part of the graph) lie on the other side of L. This is not an accident. The graph of the inequality is the shaded region of Figure 1(b).   □

Let's outline the procedure for graphing a linear inequality:

Graphing a
Linear Inequality

Step 1: Graph the corresponding linear equation, a line L.

Step 2: Select a point P not on the line L.

Step 3: If the coordinates of this point P satisfy the linear inequality, then all points on the same side of L as the point P satisfy the inequality. If the coordinates of the point P do not obey the linear inequality, then all points on the opposite side of L from P satisfy the inequality.

Points on the line L itself may or may not obey the inequality. Here is an example of a case when the points on L do not satisfy the inequality.

□ **Example 2**   Graph the linear inequality: $2x - y < -4$

Solution   The corresponding linear equation is the line

$$L: \quad 2x - y = -4$$

For its graph, see Figure 2(a).

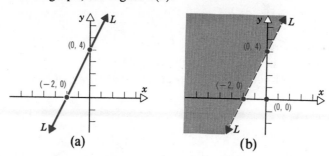

Figure 2   (a)   (b)

We select a point on either side of L to be tested, for example $(0, 0)$:

$$2(0) - 0 = 0 > -4$$

Since $(0, 0)$ does not obey the inequality, all points on the opposite side of L from $(0, 0)$ are on the graph.

Since no point on L can be on the graph (why?), the graph is the shaded region of Figure 2(b) and the line L is dashed to indicate that it is not part of the graph. □

Half-Plane   The set of points belonging to the graph of a linear inequality (for example, the shaded region in Figure 2(b)) is sometimes called a *half-plane.*

SYSTEMS OF LINEAR INEQUALITIES

System of   A *system of linear inequalities* is a collection of two or more linear inequalities. To
Linear Inequalities   **graph** a system of two inequalities we locate all points that obey each linear inequality of the system.

Let's look at a system of two linear inequalities in two unknowns. There are several possible graphs that can result. For example, suppose L and M are the lines corresponding to two linear inequalities, and suppose L and M intersect. See Figure 3. Then the two lines L and M divide the plane into four regions a, b, c, and d. One of these regions is the solution of the system.

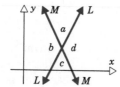

Figure 3

□ **Example 3**   Graph the system:

$$2x - y \le -4$$
$$x + y \ge -1$$

Solution   The lines corresponding to these linear inequalities are

$$L: \quad 2x - y = -4$$
$$M: \quad x + y = -1$$

The graphs of L and M are shown in Figure 4.

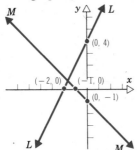

Figure 4

If we graph each linear inequality as a separate problem and then find the region common to the two resulting half-planes, we will have the solution of the system. The heavily shaded region in Figure 5 is the solution.   □

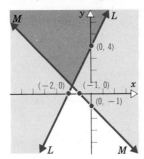

Figure 5

If the lines L and M are parallel, the system of linear inequalities may or may not have a solution. Examples of such situations are given below.

□ **Example 4**   Graph the system:

$$2x - y \le -4$$
$$2x - y \le -2$$

Solution   The lines corresponding to these linear inequalities are

$$L: \quad 2x - y = -4$$
$$M: \quad 2x - y = -2$$

These lines are parallel. Their graphs are shown in Figure 6.

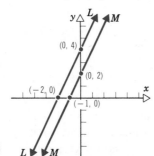

Figure 6

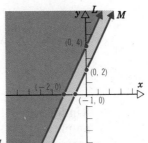

Figure 7

The graphs of the two linear inequalities are shown in Figure 7, and the solution is the heavily shaded region.   □

Notice that the solution of this system is the same as that of the single linear inequality $2x - y \le -4$.

□ **Example 5**   The solution of the system

$$2x - y \ge -4$$
$$2x - y \le -2$$

is the heavily shaded region in Figure 8.   □

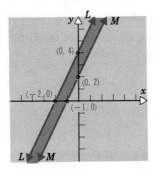

Figure 8

□ **Example 6**   The system

$$2x - y \le -4$$
$$2x - y \ge -2$$

has no solution, as Figure 9 indicates, because the two half-planes have no points in common.   □

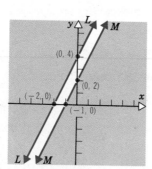

Figure 9

Until now, we have considered systems of only two linear inequalities. The next example is of a system of four linear inequalities. As we shall see, the technique for graphing such systems is the same as that used for graphing systems of two linear inequalities in two unknowns.

□ **Example 7**   Graph the system:

$$x + y \geq 2$$
$$2x + y \geq 3$$
$$x \geq 0$$
$$y \geq 0$$

Solution   Again, we first graph the four lines:

$$L_1: \quad x + y = 2$$
$$L_2: \quad 2x + y = 3$$
$$L_3: \qquad x = 0$$
$$L_4: \qquad y = 0$$

The graph of the system is the intersection of the four regions determined by each of the four inequalities. See Figure 10.   □

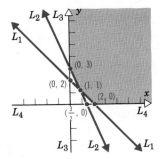

Figure 10

□ **Example 8**   Graph the system:

$$x + y \leq 2$$
$$2x + y \leq 3$$
$$x \geq 0$$
$$y \geq 0$$

Solution   Since the lines associated with these linear inequalities are the same as those of the previous example, we proceed directly to the graph. See Figure 11.   □

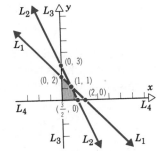

Figure 11

SOME TERMINOLOGY

Unbounded
Bounded

Compare the graphs of the systems of linear inequalities given in Examples 7 and 8. The graph in Figure 10 is said to be *unbounded* in the sense that it extends infinitely far in some direction; the graph in Figure 11 is *bounded* in the sense that it can be enclosed by some circle of sufficiently large radius.

The boundary of each of the graphs in Figures 10 and 11 consists of line segments. In fact, the graph of any system of linear inequalities will have line segments as boundaries. The point of intersection of two line segments that form the boundary is called a *vertex* of the graph. For example, the graph of the system given in Example 7 has the vertices $(0, 3)$, $(1, 1)$, and $(2, 0)$. See Figure 10. The graph of the system given in Example 8 has the vertices $(0, 2)$, $(0, 0)$, $(\frac{3}{2}, 0)$, $(1, 1)$. See Figure 11.

We shall soon see that the vertices of the graph of a system of linear inequalities play a major role in the procedure for solving linear programming problems.

APPLICATION

□ **Example 9**   Nutt's Nuts has 75 pounds of cashews and 120 pounds of peanuts. These are to be mixed in 1 pound packages as follows: A low-grade mixture that contains 4 ounces of cashews and 12 ounces of peanuts and a high-grade mixture that contains 8 ounces of cashews and 8 ounces of peanuts.

(a)   Using x to denote the number of the packages of low-grade mixture and using y to denote the number of packages of the high-grade mixture, write down a system of linear inequalities that describes the possible number of each kind of package.

(b)   Graph the system and list its vertices.

Solution   (a)   We begin by naming the variables

$$x = \text{number of packages of low-grade mixture}$$
$$y = \text{number of packages of high-grade mixture}$$

First, we note that the only meaningful values for x and y are nonnegative values. Thus we must restrict x and y so that

$$x \geq 0 \qquad y \geq 0$$

Next, we note that there is a limit to the number of pounds of cashews and peanuts available. First, the total number of pounds of cashews cannot exceed 75 pounds (1200 ounces), and the number of pounds of peanuts cannot exceed 120 pounds (1920 ounces). This means that

$$\begin{pmatrix} \text{Ounces of} \\ \text{cashews} \\ \text{required} \\ \text{for low-grade} \\ \text{mixture} \end{pmatrix} \begin{pmatrix} \text{Number of} \\ \text{packages of} \\ \text{low-grade} \\ \text{mixture} \end{pmatrix} + \begin{pmatrix} \text{Ounces of} \\ \text{cashews} \\ \text{required} \\ \text{for high-} \\ \text{grade} \\ \text{mixture} \end{pmatrix} \begin{pmatrix} \text{Number of} \\ \text{packages} \\ \text{of high-} \\ \text{grade} \\ \text{mixture} \end{pmatrix} \begin{matrix} \text{cannot} \\ \text{exceed} \end{matrix} \; 1200$$

$$\begin{pmatrix} \text{Ounces of} \\ \text{peanuts} \\ \text{required} \\ \text{for low-grade} \\ \text{mixture} \end{pmatrix} \begin{pmatrix} \text{Number of} \\ \text{packages of} \\ \text{low-grade} \\ \text{mixture} \end{pmatrix} + \begin{pmatrix} \text{Ounces of} \\ \text{peanuts} \\ \text{for high-} \\ \text{grade} \\ \text{mixture} \end{pmatrix} \begin{pmatrix} \text{Number of} \\ \text{packages of} \\ \text{high-grade} \\ \text{mixture} \end{pmatrix} \begin{matrix} \text{cannot} \\ \text{exceed} \end{matrix} \; 1920$$

In terms of the data given and the variables introduced, we can write these statements compactly as

$$4x + 8y \le 1200$$
$$12x + 8y \le 1920$$

The system of linear inequalities that gives the possible values x and y can take on, is

$$x \ge 0$$
$$y \ge 0$$
$$4x + 8y \le 1200$$
$$12x + 8y \le 1920$$

(b) The system of linear inequalities given above can be simplified to the equivalent form

$$x \ge 0 \qquad \text{①}$$
$$y \ge 0 \qquad \text{②}$$
$$x + 2y \le 300 \qquad \text{③}$$
$$3x + 2y \le 480 \qquad \text{④}$$

in which, for convenience, we have numbered each linear inequality. The graph of the system is given in Figure 12. The vertices of the graph are the points of intersection of the lines ① and ②, ① and ③, ② and ④, and ③ and ④. The first three are easy to identify by inspection; the last one requires that we solve the system of equations

$$x + 2y = 300$$
$$3x + 2y = 480$$

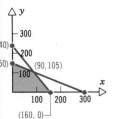

Figure 12 The vertices are

$$(0, 0),\ (0, 150),\ (160, 0),\ (90, 105) \qquad \square$$

Exercise 3.2   *Answers to Odd-Numbered Problems begin on page* 605.

In Problems 1–10 graph each inequality.

1. $x \geq 0$

2. $y \geq 0$

3. $x \geq 0, \quad y \geq 0$

4. $x \leq 0, \quad y \leq 0$

5. $2x - 3y \leq -6$

6. $3x + 2y \geq 6$

7. $5x + y \leq -10$

8. $x - 2y > -4$

9. $x \geq 5$

10. $y \leq -2$

In Problems 11–20 graph each system of linear inequalities. Tell whether the graph is bounded or unbounded and list each vertex of the graph.

11.
$$x \geq 0$$
$$y \geq 0$$
$$x + y \leq 2$$

12.
$$x \geq 0$$
$$y \geq 0$$
$$2x + 3y \leq 6$$

13.
$$x \geq 0$$
$$y \geq 0$$
$$x + y \geq 2$$
$$2x + 3y \leq 6$$

14.
$$x \geq 0$$
$$y \geq 0$$
$$x + y \geq 2$$
$$2x + 3y \leq 12$$
$$3x + 2y \leq 12$$

15.
$$x \geq 0$$
$$y \geq 0$$
$$2 \leq x + y$$
$$x + y \leq 8$$
$$2x + y \leq 10$$

16.
$$x \geq 0$$
$$y \geq 0$$
$$2 \leq x + y$$
$$x + y \leq 8$$
$$1 \leq x + 2y$$

17.
$$x \geq 0$$
$$y \geq 0$$
$$x + y \geq 2$$
$$2x + 3y \leq 12$$
$$3x + y \leq 12$$

18.
$$x \geq 0$$
$$y \geq 0$$
$$2 \leq x + y$$
$$x + y \leq 10$$
$$2x + y \leq 3$$

19.
$$x \geq 0$$
$$y \geq 0$$
$$1 \leq x + 2y$$
$$x + 2y \leq 10$$

20.
$$x \geq 0$$
$$y \geq 0$$
$$1 \leq x + 2y$$
$$x + 2y \leq 10$$
$$2 \leq x + y$$
$$x + y \leq 8$$

Applications

21. Rework Example 9 if 120 pounds of cashews and 80 pounds of peanuts are available.

22. Rework Example 9 if the high-grade mixture contains 10 ounces of cashews and 6 ounces of peanuts.

23. Mike's Famous Toy Trucks company manufactures two kinds of a toy truck — a dumpster and a tanker. In the manufacturing process, each dumpster requires 3 hours of grinding and 4 hours of finishing, while each tanker requires 2 hours of grinding and 3

hours of finishing. The Company has 2 grinders and 3 finishers, each of whom work 40 hours per week.

(a) Using x to denote the number of dumpsters and y to denote the number of tankers, write down a system of linear inequalities that describes the possible numbers of each truck that can be manufactured.

(b) Graph the system and list its vertices.

24. Repeat Problem 23 if 1 grinder and 2 finishers, each of whom work 40 hours per week are available.

3.3 A GEOMETRIC APPROACH TO LINEAR PROGRAMMING PROBLEMS

We begin by restating a portion of Example 9 given in the previous section: Nutt's Nuts has 75 pounds of cashews and 120 pounds of peanuts. These are to be mixed in 1 pound packages as follows: a low-grade mixture that contains 4 ounces of cashews and 12 ounces of peanuts and a high-grade mixture that contains 8 ounces of cashews and 8 ounces of peanuts.

Suppose that in addition to the information given above, we also know what the profit will be on each type of mixture. For example, suppose the profit is $0.25 on each package of the low-grade mixtures and is $0.45 on each package of the high-grade mixture. The question of importance to the manager is "How many packages of each type of mixture should be prepared to maximize the profit?"

If P symbolizes the profit, x is the number of packages of low-grade mixture, and y is the number of high-grade packages, then the question can be restated as "What are the values of x and y so that the expression

$$P = \$0.25x + \$0.45y$$

is a maximum?

The problem above is typical of a *linear programming problem.* It requires that a certain linear expression, the profit, be maximized. This linear expression is called Objective the **objective function.** Furthermore, the problem requires that the maximum profit Function be achieved under certain restrictions or **constraints,** each of which are linear inequal-Constraints ities involving the variables. The linear programming problem may be restated as
Maximize

$$P = \$0.25x + \$0.45y \qquad \text{Objective function}$$

subject to the conditions that

$$x \geq 0 \qquad \text{Nonnegativity constraint}$$
$$y \geq 0 \qquad \text{Nonnegativity constraint}$$
$$x + 2y \leq 300 \qquad \text{Cashew constraint}$$
$$3x + 2y \leq 480 \qquad \text{Peanut constraint}$$

In general, every linear programming problem has two components:

1. A linear objective function to be maximized or minimized.
2. A collection of linear inequalities that must be satisfied simultaneously.

Linear Programming Problem *A linear programming problem* in two variables, *x* and *y*, consists of *maximizing* or *minimizing* an *objective function*

$$z = Ax + By$$

where *A* and *B* are given real numbers, subject to certain conditions or *constraints* expressible as linear inequalities in *x* and *y*.

Let's look at this more closely. To maximize (or minimize) the quantity $z = Ax + By$ means to locate the points (x, y) that make the expression for z the largest (or smallest). But not all points (x, y) are eligible. Only the points that obey *all* the constraints are potential solutions. Hence, we refer to such points as *feasible solutions*.

Feasible Solution

In a linear programming problem, we want to find the feasible solution that maximizes (or minimizes) the objective function.

Solution of a
Linear
Programming
Problem

By a *solution* to a linear programming problem we mean a point (x, y) in the set of feasible solutions together with the value of the objective function at that point, that maximizes (or minimizes) the objective function.

If none of the feasible solutions maximize (or minimize) the objective function, or if there are no feasible solutions, then the linear programming problem has no solution.

☐ **Example 1**   Minimize the quantity

$$z = x + 2y$$

subject to the constraints

$$x + y \geq 1 \qquad x \geq 0 \qquad y \geq 0$$

Solution   The objective function to be minimized is $z = x + 2y$. The constraints are the linear inequalities

$$x + y \geq 1 \qquad x \geq 0 \qquad y \geq 0$$

The shaded portion of Figure 13 illustrates the set of feasible solutions.

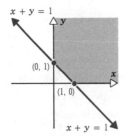

Figure 13

To see if there is a smallest z, we graph $z = x + 2y$ for some choice of z, say, $z = 3$. See Figure 14. By moving the line $x + 2y = 3$ parallel to itself, we can observe what happens for different values of z. Since we want a minimum value for z, we try to move $z = x + 2y$ down as far as possible while keeping some part of the line within the set of feasible solutions. The "best" solution is obtained when the line just touches one corner, or *vertex,* of the set of feasible solutions. If you refer to Figure 14, you will see that the best solution is $x = 1$, $y = 0$, which yields $z = 1$. There is no other feasible solution for which z is smaller.   □

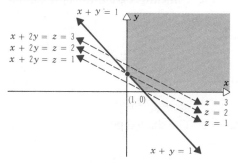

Figure 14

In Example 1, we can see that the feasible solution that minimizes z occurs at a vertex. This is not an unusual situation. If there is a feasible solution minimizing (or maximizing) the objective function, it is *usually* located at a vertex of the set of feasible solutions.

However, it is possible for a feasible solution that is not a vertex to minimize (or maximize) the objective function. This occurs when the slope of the objective function is the same as the slope of one side of the set of feasible solutions. The following example illustrates this possibility.

□ **Example 2**   Minimize the quantity

$$z = x + 2y$$

subject to the constraints

$$x + y \geq 1 \qquad 2x + 4y \geq 3 \qquad x \geq 0 \qquad y \geq 0$$

Solution   Again, we first graph the constraints. The shaded portion of Figure 15 illustrates the set of feasible solutions.

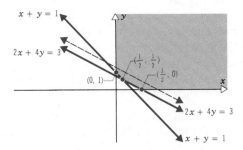

Figure 15

If we graph the objective equation $z = x + 2y$ for some choice of z and move it down, we see that a minimum is reached when $z = \frac{3}{2}$. In fact, any point on the line $2x + 4y = 3$ between $(\frac{1}{2}, \frac{1}{2})$ and $(\frac{3}{2}, 0)$ will minimize the objective function. Of course, the reason any feasible point on $2x + 4y = 3$ minimizes the objective equation $z = x + 2y$ is that these two lines are parallel (both have slope $-\frac{1}{2}$). Thus, this linear programming problem has infinitely many solutions. □

The next example illustrates a linear programming problem that has no solution.

□ **Example 3**   Maximize the quantity

$$z = x + 2y$$

subject to the constraints

$$x + y \geq 1 \qquad x \geq 0 \qquad y \geq 0$$

Solution   First, we graph the constraints. The shaded portion of Figure 16 illustrates the set of feasible solutions.

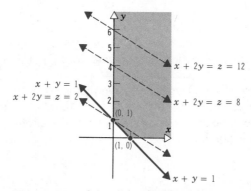

Figure 16

The graphs of the objective function $z = x + 2y$ for $z = 2$, $z = 8$, and $z = 12$ are also shown in Figure 16. Observe that we continue to get larger values for z by moving the graph of the objective function upward. But there is no feasible point that will make z *largest*. No matter how large a value is assigned to z, there is a feasible point that will give a larger value. Since there is no feasible point that makes z largest, we conclude that this linear programming problem has no solution. □

For any linear programming problem that has a solution, the following general result is true:

If a linear programming problem has a solution, it is located at a vertex of the set of feasible solutions; if a linear programming problem has multiple solutions, at least one of them is located at a vertex of the set of feasible solutions. In either case, the corresponding value of the objective function is unique.

The result stated above requires knowing in advance whether the linear programming problem has a solution. If the set of feasible solutions is bounded—that is, if it can be enclosed within some circle—the linear programming problem will have a solution.

If the set of feasible solutions is not bounded (see Example 3), then the graphs of the objective function for several values of z should be used to determine whether a solution exists or does not exist.

Based on these comments, we can outline a procedure for solving a linear programming problem provided that it has a solution.

Solving
a Linear
Programming
Problem

> **Step 1:** Write an expression for the quantity that is to be maximized or mini-mized (the objective function).
>
> **Step 2:** Determine all the constraints and graph them.
>
> **Step 3:** List the vertices of the set of feasible solutions.
>
> **Step 4:** Determine the value of the objective function at each vertex.
>
> **Step 5:** Select the optimal solution, that is, the maximum or minimum value of the objective function.

Let's look at some examples.

□ **Example 4** Maximize and minimize the objective function

$$z = x + 5y$$

subject to the constraints

① $x + 4y \le 12$ ② $x \le 8$ ③ $x + y \ge 2$ ④ $x \ge 0$ ⑤ $y \ge 0$

Solution   The objective function and the constraints (numbered for convenience) are given (this will not be the case when we do word problems), so we can proceed to graph the constraints. The shaded portion of Figure 17 illustrates the set of feasible solutions. Since this set is bounded, we know a solution exists.

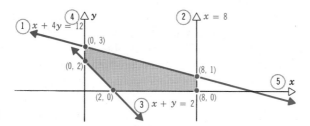

Figure 17

Now we locate the vertices of the set of feasible solutions at the points of intersection of lines ① and ④, ① and ②, ② and ⑤, ③ and ⑤, and ③ and ④. Using methods discussed earlier, we find that the vertices are

$$(0, 3), \quad (8, 1), \quad (8, 0), \quad (2, 0), \quad (0, 2)$$

To find the maximum and minimum value of $z = x + 5y$, we set up a table:

Vertex (x, y)	Value of Objective Function $z = x + 5y$
(0, 3)	$z = 0 + 5(3) = 15$
(8, 1)	$z = 8 + 5(1) = 13$
(8, 0)	$z = 8 + 5(0) = 8$
(2, 0)	$z = 2 + 5(0) = 2$
(0, 2)	$z = 0 + 5(2) = 10$

The maximum value of z is 15, and it occurs at the point (0, 3). The minimum value of z is 2, and it occurs at the point (2, 0).   □

Now, let's solve the problem of the cashews and peanuts.

□ **Example 5**   Maximize

$$P = 0.25x + 0.45y$$

subject to the constraints

① $x \geq 0$ ② $y \geq 0$ ③ $x + 2y \leq 300$ ④ $3x + 2y \leq 480$

Solution   Before applying the method of this chapter to solve this problem, let's discuss a solution that might be suggested by intuition. Namely, since the profit is higher for the high-grade mixture, you might think that Nutt's Nuts should prepare as many packages of the high-grade mixture as possible. If this were done, then there would be a total of 150 packages (8 ounces divides into 75 pounds of cashews exactly 150 times) and the total profit would be

$$150(0.45) = \$67.50$$

As we shall see, this is not the best solution to the problem. This is because there would be several pounds of peanuts left over ($120 - 75 = 45$, to be exact) that would be neither packaged nor sold.

To use more of the peanuts and thus make a higher profit, Nutt's Nuts has to make both high-grade *and* low-grade packages. We are still asking ourselves how many packages of each mixture should be made to obtain the maximum profit, but now we will use linear programming to solve the problem. The graph of the set of feasible solutions is given in Figure 18.

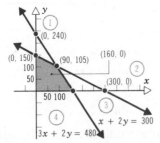

Figure 18

Since this set is bounded, we proceed to locate its vertices. The vertices of the set of feasible solutions are the points of intersection of lines ① and ②, ① and ③, ② and ④, and ③ and ④:

$$(0, 0), \quad (0, 150), \quad (160, 0), \quad (90, 105)$$

(Notice that the points of intersection of lines ① and ④ and lines ② and ③ are not feasible solutions.) It remains only to evaluate the objective equation at each vertex:

Vertex (x, y)	Value of Objective Function $P = (\$0.25)x + (\$0.45)y$
$(0, 0)$	$P = (0.25)(0) + (0.45)(0) = 0$
$(0, 150)$	$P = (0.25)(0) + (0.45)(150) = \$67.50$
$(160, 0)$	$P = (0.25)(160) + (0.45)(0) = \$40.00$
$(90, 105)$	$P = (0.25)(90) + (0.45)(105) = \$69.75$

Thus, a maximum profit is obtained if 90 packages of low-grade mixture and 105 packages of high-grade mixture are made. The maximum profit obtainable under the conditions described is $69.75.   □

□ **Example 6**   Mike's Famous Toy Trucks manufactures two kinds of toy trucks—a standard model and a deluxe model. In the manufacturing process, each standard model requires 2 hours of grinding and 2 hours of finishing, and each deluxe model needs 2 hours of grinding and 4 hours of finishing. The company has 2 grinders and 3 finishers, each of whom work 40 hours per week. Each standard model toy truck brings a profit of $3 and each deluxe model a profit of $4. Assuming that every truck made will be sold, how many of each should be made to maximize profits?

Solution   First, we name the variables:

$$x = \text{Number of standard models made}$$
$$y = \text{Number of deluxe models made}$$

The quantity to be maximized is the profit, which we denote by P:

$$P = \$3x + \$4y$$

This is the objective function. To manufacture one standard model requires 2 grinding hours and to make one deluxe model requires 2 grinding hours. Thus, the number of grinding hours of x standard and y deluxe models is

$$2x + 2y$$

But the total amount of grinding time available is 80 hours per week. This means we have the constraint

$$2x + 2y \leq 80 \qquad \text{Grinding time constraint}$$

Similarly, for the finishing time we have the constraint

$$2x + 4y \leq 120 \qquad \text{Finishing time constraint}$$

Simplifying each of these constraints and adding the nonnegativity constraints $x \geq 0$ and $y \geq 0$, we may list all the constraints for this problem.

$$x + y \leq 40 \qquad x + 2y \leq 60 \qquad x \geq 0 \qquad y \geq 0$$

Figure 19 illustrates the set of feasible solutions, which is bounded.

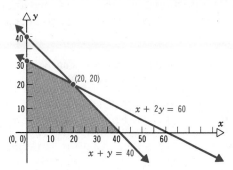

Figure 19

The vertices of the set of feasible solutions are

$$(0, 0), \quad (0, 30), \quad (40, 0), \quad (20, 20)$$

The table lists the corresponding values of the objective equation:

Vertex (x, y)	Value of Objective Function $P = \$3x + \$4y$
(0, 0)	$P = 0$
(0, 30)	$P = \$120$
(40, 0)	$P = \$120$
(20, 20)	$P = 3(20) + 4(20) = \$140$

Thus, a maximum profit is obtained if 20 standard trucks and 20 deluxe trucks are manufactured. The maximum profit is $140. □

□ **Example 7**
Investment Strategy

A retired couple have up to $30,000 they wish to invest in fixed-income securities. Their broker recommends investing in two bonds: one a AAA bond yielding 12%; the other a B+ bond paying 15%. After some consideration, the couple decide to invest at most $12,000 in the B+-rated bond and at least $6000 in the AAA bond. They also want the amount invested in the AAA bond to exceed or equal the amount invested in the B+ bond. What should the broker recommend if the couple (quite naturally) want to maximize their return on investment?

Solution   First, we name the variables:

$$x = \text{Amount invested in AAA bond}$$
$$y = \text{Amount invested in B}^+ \text{ bond}$$

The quantity to be maximized — return on investment — which we denote by P, is

$$P = 0.12x + 0.15y$$

This is the objective function. The conditions specified by the problem are:

Up to $30,000 available to invest	$x + y \le 30,000$
Invest at most $12,000 in B$^+$ bond	$y \le 12,000$
Invest at least $6000 in AAA bond	$x \ge 6,000$
Amount in AAA bond must exceed or equal amount in B$^+$ bond	$x \ge y$

In addition, we must have the conditions $x \ge 0$ and $y \ge 0$. The total list of constraints is

$\textcircled{1}$ $x + y \le 30,000$ $\textcircled{2}$ $y \le 12,000$ $\textcircled{3}$ $x \ge 6000$

$\textcircled{4}$ $x \ge y$ $\textcircled{5}$ $x \ge 0$ $\textcircled{6}$ $y \ge 0$

Figure 20 illustrates the set of feasible solutions, which is bounded. The vertices of the set of feasible solutions are

(6000, 0),   (6000, 6000),   (12,000 12,000),   (18,000, 12,000),   (30,000, 0)

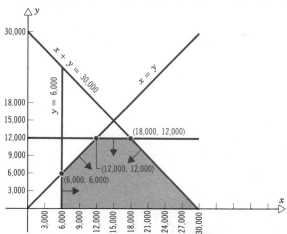

Figure 20

The corresponding return on investment at each vertex is:

$$P = 0.12(6000) + 0.15(0) = \$720$$
$$P = 0.12(6000) + 0.15(6000) = 720 + 900 = \$1620$$
$$P = 0.12(12,000) + 0.15(12,000) = 1440 + 1800 = \$3240$$
$$P = 0.12(18,000) + 0.15(12,000) = 2160 + 1800 = \$3960$$
$$P = 0.12(30,000) + 0.15(0) = \$3600$$

Thus, the maximum return on investment is $3960, obtained by placing $18,000 in the AAA bond and $12,000 in the B$^+$ bond.   □

□ **Example 8**

Urban Economics
Model*

This example concerns reclaimed land and its allocation into two major uses—agricultural and urban (or nonagricultural). The reclamation of land for urban purposes cost $400 per acre and for agricultural uses, $300. The primal problem is that the reclamation agency wishes to minimize the total cost C of reclaiming the land:

$$C = \$400x + \$300y$$

where x = the number of acres of urban land and y = the number of acres of agricultural land. Although this equation can be minimized by setting both x and y at zero, that is, reclaiming nothing, the problem derives from a number of constraints due to three different groups.

The first is an urban group, which insists that at least 4000 acres of land be reclaimed for urban purposes. The second group is concerned with agriculture and says that at least 5000 acres of land must be reclaimed for agricultural uses. Finally, the third group is concerned only with reclamation and is quite uninterested in the use to which the land will be put. The third group, however, says that at least 10,000 acres of land must be reclaimed. The primal problem and the constraints can, therefore, be written in full as follows:

Minimize

$$C = \$400x + \$300y$$

subject to the constraints

$$x \geq 4000$$
$$y \geq 5000$$
$$x + y \geq 10,000$$
$$x \geq 0$$
$$y \geq 0$$

Figure 21 illustrates the set of feasible solutions, which is not bounded. However, it is apparent that this problem has a solution since lowering the graph of the objective function (dashed black line) will eventually lead to a smallest value for C.

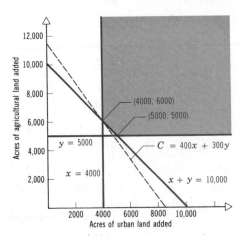

Figure 21

* This example is adapted from Maurice Yeates, *An Introduction to Quantitative Analysis in Economic Geography*, McGraw-Hill, New York, 1968.

The combination of urban and agricultural land at the vertex (4000, 6000) reveals that if 4000 acres are devoted to urban purposes and 6000 acres to agricultural purposes, the cost is a minimum and is

$$C = (\$400)(4000) + (\$300)(6000) = \$3,400,000 \qquad \square$$

MODEL: POLLUTION CONTROL

The following model is taken from a paper by Robert E. Kohn.* In this paper, a linear programming model is proposed that can be useful in determining what air pollution controls should be adopted in an airshed. The methodology is based on the premise that air quality goals should be achieved at the least possible cost. Advantages of the model are its simplicity, its emphasis on economic efficiency, and its appropriateness for the kind of data that are already available.

To illustrate the model, consider a hypothetical airshed with a single industry, cement manufacturing. Annual production is 2,500,000 barrels of cement. Although the kilns are equipped with mechanical collectors for air pollution control, they are still emitting 2 pounds of dust for every barrel of cement produced. The industry can be required to replace the mechanical collectors with four-field electrostatic precipitators, which would reduce emissions to 0.5 pound of dust per barrel of cement or with five-field electrostatic precipitators, which would reduce emissions to 0.2 pound per barrel. If the capital and operating costs of the four-field precipitator are $0.14 per barrel of cement produced and of the five-field precipitator are $0.18 per barrel, what control methods should be required of this industry? Assume that, for this hypothetical airshed, it has been determined that particulate emissions (which now total 5,000,000 pounds per year) should be reduced by 4,200,000 pounds.

If C represents the cost of control, x is the number of barrels of annual cement production subject to the four-field electrostatic precipitator (cost is $0.14 a barrel of cement produced and pollutant reduction is $2 - 0.5 = 1.5$ pounds of particulates per barrel of cement produced), and y is the number of barrels of annual cement production subject to the five-field electrostatic precipitator (cost is $0.18 a barrel and pollutant reduction is $2 - 0.2 = 1.8$ pounds per barrel of cement produced), then the problem can be stated as follows:

Minimize

$$C = \$0.14x + \$0.18y$$

subject to

$$x + y \le 2,500,000$$
$$1.5x + 1.8y \ge 4,200,000$$
$$x \ge 0$$
$$y \ge 0$$

* R. E. Kohn, "A Mathematical Programming Model for Air Pollution Control," *School Science and Mathematics* (June 1969), pp. 487–499.

The first equation states that our objective is to minimize air pollution control costs; the second that barrels of cement production subject to the two control methods cannot exceed the annual production; the third that the particulate reduction from the two methods must be greater than or equal to the particulate reduction target; and the last two expressions mean that we cannot have negative quantities of cement. Figure 22 illustrates a graphic solution to the problem.

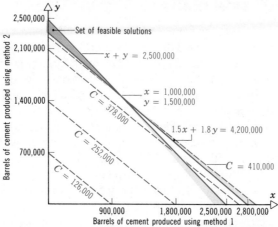

Figure 22

The least costly solution would be to install the four-field precipitator on kilns producing 1,000,000 ($x = 1,000,000$) and the five-field precipitator on kilns producing 1,500,000 ($y = 1,500,000$) barrels of cement at a cost of $C = \$410,000$.

A further analysis of this type of problem is found in Chapter 4.

Exercise 3.3 *Answers to Odd-Numbered Problems begin on page 606.*

In Problems 1–6 the figure below illustrates the graph of the set of feasible solutions of a linear programming problem. Find the maximum and minimum values of each objective function.

1. $z = 2x + 3y$ 2. $z = 3x + 27y$ 3. $z = x + 8y$
4. $z = 3x + y$ 5. $z = x + 6y$ 6. $z = x + 5y$

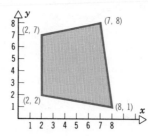

In Problems 7–14 maximize (if possible) the quantity $z = 5x + 7y$ subject to the given constraints.

7. $x \geq 0$
$y \geq 0$
$x + y \leq 2$

8. $x \geq 0$
$y \geq 0$
$2x + 3y \leq 6$

9.

$$x \geq 0$$
$$y \geq 0$$
$$x + y \geq 2$$
$$2x + 3y \leq 6$$

10.

$$x \geq 0$$
$$y \geq 0$$
$$x + y \geq 2$$
$$2x + 3y \leq 12$$
$$3x + 2y \leq 12$$

11.

$$x \geq 0$$
$$y \geq 0$$
$$2 \leq x + y$$
$$x + y \leq 8$$
$$2x + y \leq 10$$

12.

$$x \geq 0$$
$$y \geq 0$$
$$2 \leq x + y$$
$$x + y \leq 8$$
$$1 \leq x + 2y$$
$$x + 2y \leq 10$$

13.

$$x \geq 0$$
$$y \geq 0$$
$$x + 3y \geq 6$$

14.

$$x \geq 0$$
$$y \geq 0$$
$$2x + 3y \geq 12$$

In Problems 15–20 minimize (if possible) the quantity $z = 2x + 3y$ subject to the given constraints.

15.

$$x \geq 0$$
$$y \geq 0$$
$$x + y \geq 2$$

16.

$$x \geq 0$$
$$y \geq 0$$
$$2x + y \geq 2$$

17.

$$x \geq 0$$
$$y \geq 0$$
$$x + y \geq 2$$
$$2x + 3y \leq 12$$
$$3x + y \leq 12$$

18.

$$x \geq 0$$
$$y \geq 0$$
$$2 \leq x + y$$
$$x + y \leq 10$$
$$2x + 3y \leq 6$$

19.

$$x \geq 0$$
$$y \geq 0$$
$$1 \leq x + 2y$$
$$x + 2y \leq 10$$

20.

$$x \geq 0$$
$$y \geq 0$$
$$1 \leq x + 2y$$
$$x + 2y \leq 10$$
$$2 \leq x + y$$
$$x + y \leq 8$$

In Problems 21–26 find the maximum and minimum values (if possible) of the given objective function subject to the constraints

$$x \geq 0 \quad y \geq 0 \quad x + y \leq 10 \quad 2x + y \geq 10 \quad x + 2y \geq 10$$

21. $z = x + y$

22. $z = 2x + 3y$

23. $z = 5x + 2y$

24. $z = x + 2y$

25. $z = 3x + 4y$

26. $z = 3x + 6y$

Applications

27. In Example 5 (page 130), if the profit on the low-grade mixture is $0.30 per package and the profit on the high-grade mixture is $0.40 per package, how many packages of each mixture should be made for a maximum profit?

28. Using the information supplied in Example 6 (page 131), suppose the profit on each standard model is $4 and the profit on each deluxe model is $4. How many of each should be manufactured in order to maximize profit?

29. Using the information supplied in Example 6 (page 131), suppose the profit on each standard model is $4 and the profit on each deluxe model is $3. How many of each should be manufactured in order to maximize profit?

30. *Investment Strategy.* An investment broker wants to invest up to $20,000. She can purchase a type A bond yielding a 10% return on the amount invested and she can purchase a type B bond yielding a 15% return on the amount invested. She also wants to invest at least as much in the type A bond as in the type B bond. She will also invest at least $5000 in the type A bond and no more than $8000 in the type B bond. How much should she invest in each type of bond to maximize her return?

31. A factory manufactures two products, each requiring the use of three machines. The first machine can be used at most 70 hours; the second machine at most 40 hours; and the third machine at most 90 hours. The first product requires 2 hours on Machine 1, 1 hour on Machine 2, and 1 hour on Machine 3; the second product requires 1 hour each on Machines 1 and 2 and 3 hours on Machine 3. If the profit is $40 per unit for the first product and $60 per unit for the second product, how many units of each product should be manufactured to maximize profit?

32. *Diet Problem.* A diet is to contain at least 400 units of vitamins, 500 units of minerals, and 1400 calories. Two foods are available: F_1, which costs $0.05 per unit, and F_2, which costs $0.03 per unit. A unit of food F_1 contains 2 units of vitamins, 1 unit of minerals, and 4 calories; a unit of food F_2 contains 1 unit of vitamins, 2 units of minerals, and 4 calories. Find the minimum cost for a diet that consists of a mixture of these two foods and also meets the minimal nutrition requirements.

33. *Diet Problem.* Danny's Chicken Farm is a producer of frying chickens. In order to produce the best fryers possible, the regular chicken feed is supplemented by four vitamins. The minimum amount of each vitamin required per 100 ounces of feed is: Vitamin 1, 50 units; Vitamin 2, 100 units; Vitamin 3, 60 units; Vitamin 4, 180 units. Two supplements are available: Supplement I costs $0.03 per ounce and contains 5 units of Vitamin 1 per ounce, 25 units of Vitamin 2 per ounce, 10 units of Vitamin 3 per ounce, and 35 units of Vitamin 4 per ounce. Supplement II costs $0.04 per ounce and contains 25 units of Vitamin 1 per ounce, 10 units of Vitamin 2 per ounce, 10 units of Vitamin 3 per ounce, and 20 units of Vitamin 4 per ounce. How much of each supplement should Danny buy to add to each 100 ounces of feed in order to minimize his cost, but still have the desired vitamin amounts present?

34. *Optimal Use of Land.* A farmer has 70 acres of land available on which to grow some soybeans and some corn. The cost of cultivation per acre, the workdays needed per acre, and the profit per acre are indicated in the table:

	Soybeans	Corn	Total Available
Cultivation cost per acre	$60	$30	$1800
Days of work per acre	3 days	4 days	120 days
Profit per acre	$300	$150	

As indicated in the last column, the acreage to be cultivated is limited by the amount of money available for cultivation costs and by the number of working days that can be put into this part of the business. Find the number of acres of each crop that should be planted in order to maximize the profit.

35. The manager of a supermarket meat department finds that there are 160 pounds of round steak, 600 pounds of chuck steak, and 300 pounds of pork in stock on Saturday morning. From experience, the manager knows that half these quantities can be sold as straight cuts. The remaining meat will have to be ground into hamburger patties and picnic patties for which there is a large weekend demand. Each pound of hamburger patties contains 20% ground round and 60% ground chuck. Each pound of picnic patties contains 30% ground pork and 50% ground chuck. The remainder of each product consists of an inexpensive nonmeat filler which the store has in unlimited quantities. How many pounds of each product should be made if the objective is to maximize the amount of meat used to make the patties?

36. J. B. Rug Manufacturers has available 1200 square yards of wool and 1000 square yards of nylon for the manufacture of two grades of carpeting: high-grade, which sells for $500 per roll, and low-grade, which sells for $300 per roll. Twenty square yards of wool and 40 square yards of nylon are used in a roll of high-grade carpet, and 40 square yards of nylon are used in a roll of low-grade carpet. Forty work-hours are required to manufacture each roll of the high-grade carpet, and 20 work-hours are required for each roll of the low-grade carpet, at an average cost of $6.00 per work-hour. A maximum of 800 work-hours are available. The cost of wool is $5.00 per square yard and the cost of nylon is $2.00 per square yard. How many rolls of each type of carpet should be manufactured to maximize income? [*Hint:* Income = Revenue from sale − (Production cost for material + labor)]

37. The rug manufacturer in Problem 36 finds that maximum income occurs when no high-grade carpet is produced. If the price of the low-grade carpet is kept at $300 per roll, in what price range should the high-grade carpet be sold so that income is maximized by selling some rolls of each type carpet? Assume all other data remain the same.

38. Maximize
$$P = 2x + y + 3z$$

subject to
$$x + 2y + z \leq 25$$
$$3x + 2y + 3z \leq 30$$
$$x \geq 0 \quad y \geq 0 \quad z \geq 0$$

[*Hint:* Solve the constraints three at a time, find the points that are in the set of feasible solutions, and test each of them in the objective function. Assume a solution exists.]

CHAPTER REVIEW

Important	linear inequality in two	systems of linear inequalities	constraints
Terms	variables	unbounded graph	feasible solution
	nonstrict linear inequality	bounded graph	solution of a linear
	strict linear inequality	vertex of the graph	programming problem
	graph of a linear inequality	linear programming problem	
	half-plane	objective function	

True–False Questions

(Answers on page 607 *)*

T   F   1. The graph of a system of linear inequalities may be bounded or unbounded.

T   F   2. The graph of the set of constraints of a linear programming problem, under certain conditions, could have a circle for a boundary.

T   F   3. The objective function of a linear programming problem is always a linear equation involving the variables.

T   F   4. In a linear programming problem, there may be more than one point that maximizes or minimizes the objective function.

T   F   5. Some linear programming problems will have no solution.

T   F   6. If a linear programming problem has a solution, it is located at the center of the set of feasible solutions.

Fill in the Blanks

(Answers on page 607 *)*

1. The graph of a linear inequality in two variables is called a _____ .

2. In a linear programming problem, the quantity to be maximized or minimized is referred to as the _____ function.

3. The points that obey the collection of constraints of a linear programming problem are called _____ solutions.

4. A linear programming problem will always have a solution if the set of feasible solutions is _____ .

5. If a linear programming problem has a solution, it is located at a _____ of the set of feasible solutions.

Review Exercises

Answers to Odd-Numbered Problems begin on page 607.

In Problems 1–4, graph each linear inequality.

1. $x - 3y < 0$ **2.** $4x + y \geq 8$

3. $5x + y \geq 10$ **4.** $2x + 3y > 6$

In Problems 5–10, graph each system of linear inequalities. Locate the vertices and tell whether the graph is bounded or unbounded.

5. $x \geq 0,\ y \geq 0,\ 3x + 2y \leq 12,\ x + y \geq 1$.

6. $x \geq 0,\ y \geq 0,\ x + y \leq 8,\ 2x + y \geq 2$.

7. $x \geq 0,\ y \geq 0,\ x + 2y \geq 4,\ 3x + y \geq 6$.

8. $x \geq 0,\ y \geq 0,\ 2x + y \geq 4,\ 3x + 2y \geq 6$.

9. $x \geq 0,\ y \geq 0,\ 3x + 2y \geq 6,\ 3x + 2y \leq 12,\ x + 2y \leq 8$.

10. $x \geq 0,\ y \geq 0,\ x + 2y \geq 2,\ x + 2y \leq 10,\ 2x + y \leq 10$.

In Problems 11–18 use the constraints below to solve each linear programming problem.

$$x \geq 0$$
$$y \geq 0$$
$$x + 2y \leq 40$$
$$2x + y \leq 40$$
$$x + y \geq 10$$

11. Maximize $z = x + y$

12. Maximize $z = 2x + 3y$

13. Minimize $z = 5x + 2y$

14. Minimize $z = 3x + 2y$

15. Maximize $z = 2x + y$

16. Maximize $z = x + 2y$

17. Minimize $z = 2x + 5y$

18. Minimize $z = x + y$

In Problems 19–22 maximize and minimize (if possible) the quantity $z = 15x + 20y$ subject to the given constraints

19.
$$x \geq 0$$
$$y \geq 0$$
$$x \leq 5$$
$$y \leq 8$$
$$3x + 4y \geq 12$$

20.
$$x \geq 0$$
$$y \geq 0$$
$$x \leq 6$$
$$y \leq 6$$
$$3x + 2y \geq 6$$

21.
$$x \geq 0$$
$$y \geq 0$$
$$2x + 3y \leq 22$$
$$x \leq 5$$
$$y \leq 6$$

22.
$$x \geq 0$$
$$y \geq 0$$
$$x + 2y \leq 20$$
$$x + 10y \geq 36$$
$$5x + 2y \geq 36$$

23. *Diet Problem.* Katy needs at least 60 units of carbohydrates, 45 units of protein, and 30 units of fat each month. From each pound of Food A, she receives 5 units of carbohydrates, 3 of protein, and 4 of fat. Food B contains 2 units of carbohydrates, 2 units of protein, and 1 unit of fat per pound. If Food A costs $1.30 per pound and Food B costs $0.80 per pound, how many pounds of each food should Katy buy each month to keep costs at a minimum?

24. The ACE Meat Market makes up a combination package of ground beef and ground pork for meat loaf. The ground beef is 75% lean (75% beef, 25% fat) and costs the market 70¢ per pound. The ground pork is 60% lean (60% pork, 40% fat) and costs the market 50¢ per pound. If the meat loaf is to be at least 70% lean, how much ground beef and ground pork should be mixed to keep cost at a minimum?

25. A ski manufacturer makes two types of skiis: downhill and cross-country. Using the information given in the table below, how many of each type of ski should be made for a maximum profit to be achieved? What is the maximum profit?

	Downhill	Cross-Country	Maximum Time Available
Manufacturing time per ski	2 hours	1 hour	40 hours
Finishing time per ski	1 hour	1 hour	32 hours
Profit per ski	$70	$50	

26. Rework Problem 25 if the manufacturing unit has a maximum of 48 hours available.

Mathematical Questions

From CPA and CMA Exams (Answers on page 141 *)*

Use the following information to answer Problems 1–3:

CPA Exam—May 1975

The Random Company manufactures two products, Zeta and Beta. Each product must pass through two processing operations. All materials are introduced at the start of Process No. 1. There are no work-in-process inventories. Random may produce either one product exclusively or various combinations of both products subject to the following constraints:

	Process No. 1	Process No. 2	Contribution Margin per Unit
Hours required to produce one unit of:			
Zeta	1 hour	1 hour	$4.00
Beta	2 hours	3 hours	5.25
Total capacity in hours per day	1000 hours	1275 hours	

A shortage of technical labor has limited Beta production to 400 units per day. There are no constraints on the production of Zeta other than the hour constraints in the above schedule. Assume that all relationships between capacity and production are linear, and that all of the above data and relationships are deterministic rather than probabilistic.

1. Given the objective to maximize total contribution margin, what is the production constraint for Process No. 1?
   (a) Zeta + Beta ≤ 1000   (b) Zeta + 2Beta ≤ 1000
   (c) Zeta + Beta ≥ 1000   (d) Zeta + 2Beta ≥ 1000

2. Given the objective to maximize total contribution margin, what is the labor constraint for production of Beta?
   (a) Beta ≤ 400   (b) Beta ≥ 400
   (c) Beta ≤ 425   (d) Beta ≥ 425

3. What is the objective function of the data presented?
   (a) Zeta + 2Beta = $9.25
   (b) ($4.00)Zeta + 3($5.25)Beta = Total contribution margin
   (c) ($4.00)Zeta + ($5.25)Beta = Total contribution margin
   (d) 2($4.00)Zeta + 3($5.25)Beta = Total contribution margin

4. *CPA Exam—November 1976*
   Williamson Manufacturing intends to produce two products, X and Y. Product X requires 6 hours of time on Machine 1 and 12 hours of time on Machine 2. Product Y requires 4 hours of time on Machine 1 and no time on Machine 2. Both machines are available for 24 hours. Assuming that the objective function of the total contribution margin is $2X + $1Y, what product mix will produce the maximum profit?
   (a) No units of Product X and 6 units of Product Y
   (b) 1 unit of Product X and 4 units of Product Y
   (c) 2 units of Product X and 3 units of Product Y
   (d) 4 units of Product X and no units of Product Y

5. *CPA Exam—May 1975*
   Quepea Company manufactures two products, Q and P, in a small building with limited

capacity. The selling price, cost data, and production time are given below:

	Product Q	Product P
Selling price per unit	$20	$17
Variable costs of producing and selling a unit	$12	$13
Hours to produce a unit	3	1

Based on this information, the profit maximization objective function for a linear programming solution may be stated as:

(a) Maximize $20Q + $17P.
(b) Maximize $12Q + $13P.
(c) Maximize $3Q + $1P.
(d) Maximize $8Q + $4P.

6. *CPA Exam—November 1975*
Patsy, Inc., manufactures two products, X and Y. Each product must be processed in each of three departments: machining, assembling, and finishing. The hours needed to produce one unit of product per department and the maximum possible hours per department follow:

Department	Production Hours per Unit X	Y	Maximum Capacity in Hours
Machining	2	1	420
Assembling	2	2	500
Finishing	2	3	600

Other restrictions follow:

$$X \geq 50 \qquad Y \geq 50$$

The objective function is to maximize profits where profit $= $4X + $2Y$. Given the objective and constraints, what is the most profitable number of units of X and Y, respectively, to manufacture?

(a) 150 and 100
(b) 165 and 90
(c) 170 and 80
(d) 200 and 50

7. *CPA Exam—November 1979*
Milford Company manufactures two models, medium and large. The contribution margin expected is $12 for the medium model and $20 for the large model. The medium model is processed 2 hours in the machining department and 4 hours in the polishing department. The large model is processed 3 hours in the machining department and 6 hours in the polishing department. How would the formula for determining the maximization of total contribution margin be expressed?

(a) $5X + 10Y$
(b) $6X + 9Y$
(c) $12X + 20Y$
(d) $12X(2 + 4) + 20Y(3 + 6)$

8. *CMA Exam—December 1979*
The Elon Company manufactures two industrial products—X-10, which sells for $90 a unit, and Y-12, which sells for $85 a unit. Each product is processed through both of the

company's manufacturing departments. The limited availability of labor, material, and equipment capacity has restricted the ability of the firm to meet the demand for its products. The production department believes that linear programming can be used to routinize the production schedule for the two products.

The following data are available to the production department:

	Amount Required per Unit	
	X-10	Y-12
Direct Material: Weekly supply is limited to 1800 pounds at $12.00 per pound	4 lb	2 lb
Direct Labor:		
Department 1 — Weekly supply limited to 10 people at 40 hours each at an hourly cost of $6.00	$\frac{2}{3}$ hour	1 hour
Department 2 — Weekly supply limited to 15 people at 40 hours each at an hourly rate of $8.00	$1\frac{1}{4}$ hours	1 hour
Machine Time:		
Department 1 — Weekly capacity limited to 250 hours	$\frac{1}{2}$ hour	$\frac{1}{2}$ hour
Department 2 — Weekly capacity limited to 300 hours	0 hours	1 hour

The overhead costs for Elon are accumulated on a plantwide basis. The overhead is assigned to products on the basis of the number of direct labor hours required to manufacture the product. This base is appropriate for overhead assignment because most of the variable overhead costs vary as a function of labor time. The estimated overhead cost per direct labor hour is:

Variable overhead cost	$ 6.00
Fixed overhead cost	6.00
Total overhead cost per direct labor hour	$12.00

The production department formulated the following equations for the linear programming statement of the problem:

$$A = \text{Number of units of X-10 to be produced}$$
$$B = \text{Number of units of Y-12 to be produced}$$

Objective function to minimize costs:

$$\text{Minimize} \quad Z = 85A + 62B$$

Constraints:

Material	$4A + 2B \leq 1800$ lb
Department 1 labor	$\frac{2}{3}A + 1B \leq 400$ hours
Department 2 labor	$1\frac{1}{4}A + 1B \leq 600$ hours
Nonnegativity	$A \geq 0 \qquad B \geq 0$

(a)   The formulation of the linear programming equations as prepared by Elon Company's production department is incorrect. Explain what errors have been made in the formulation prepared by the production department.

(b)   Formulate and label the proper equations for the linear programming statement of Elon Company's production problem.

(c)   Explain how linear programming could help Elon Company determine how large a change in the price of direct materials would have to be to change the optimum production mix of X-10 and Y-12.

9. *CPA Exam — November 1977*

Hale Company manufactures products A and B, each of which requires two processes, polishing and grinding. The contribution margin is $3 for Product A and $4 for Product B. The illustration shows the maximum number of units of each product that may be processed in the two departments.

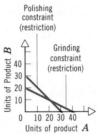

Considering the constraints (restrictions) on processing, which combination of products A and B maximizes the total contribution margin?

(a)   0 units of A and 20 units of B

(b)   20 units of A and 10 units of B

(c)   30 units of A and 0 units of B

(d)   40 units of A and 0 units of B

10. *CPA Exam — November 1980*

Johnson, Inc., manufactures product X and product Y, which are processed as follows:

	Type A Machine	Type B Machine
Product X	6 hours	4 hours
Product Y	9 hours	5 hours

The contribution margin is $12 for product X and $7 for product Y. The available time daily for processing the two products is 120 hours for machine Type A and 80 hours for machine Type B. How would the restriction (constraint) for machine Type B be expressed?

(a) $4X + 5Y$

(b) $4X + 5Y \leq 80$

(c) $6X + 9Y \leq 120$

(d) $12X + 7Y$

11. *CMA Exam—June 1983*

    A small company makes only two products, with the following two production constraints representing two machines and their maximum availability:

    $$2X + 3Y \leq 18$$
    $$2X + Y \leq 10$$

    where $X =$ the units of the first product
    $Y =$ the units of the second product

    If the profit equation is $Z = \$4X + \$2Y$, the maximum possible profit is

    (a) $20
    (b) $21
    (c) $18
    (d) $24
    (e)   Some profit other than those given above

CMA Exam—December 1983

Questions 12 through 14 are based on the Jarten Company, which manufactures and sells two products. Demand for the two products has grown to such a level that Jarten can no longer meet the demand with its facilities. The company can work a total of 600,000 direct labor hours annually using three shifts. A total of 200,000 hours of machine time is available annually. The company plans to use linear programming to determine a production schedule that will maximize its net return.

   The company spends $2,000,000 in advertising and promotion and incurs $1,000,000 for general and administrative costs. The unit sale price for Model A is $27.50; Model B sells for $75.00 each. The unit manufacturing requirement and unit cost data are as shown below. Overhead is assigned on a machine hour (MH) basis.

	Model A		**Model B**	
Raw material		$ 3		$ 7
Direct labor	1 DLH @ $8	8	1.5 DLH @ $8	12
Variable overhead	.5 MH @ $12	6	2.0 MH @ $12	24
Fixed overhead	.5 MH @ $4	2	2.0 MH @ $4	8
		$19		$51

12. The objective function that would maximize Jarten's net income is

   (a) $10.50A + 32.00B$
   (b) $8.50A + 24.00B$
   (c) $27.50A + 75.00B$
   (d) $19.00A + 51.00B$
   (e) $17.00A + 43.00B$

13. The constraint function for the direct labor is

   (a) $1A + 1.5B \leq 200,000$
   (b) $8A + 12B \leq 600,000$
   (c) $8A + 12B \leq 200,000$
   (d) $1A + 1.5B \leq 4,800,000$
   (e) $1A + 1.5B \leq 600,000$

14. The constraint function for the machine capacity is

(a) $6A + 24B \le 200{,}000$

(b) $1/.5A + 1.5/2.0B \le 800{,}000$

(c) $.5A + 2B \le 200{,}000$

(d) $(.5 + .5)A + (2 + 2)B \le 200{,}000$

(e) $(0.5 \times 1) + (1.5 \times 2.00) \le (200{,}000 \times 600{,}000)$

15. *CPA Exam—November 1984*

Boaz Company manufactures two models, medium (X) and large (Y). The contribution margin expected is \$24 for the medium model and \$40 for the large model. The medium model is processed two hours in the machining department and four hours in the polishing department. The large model is processed three hours in the machining department and six hours in the polishing department. If total contribution margin is to be maximized, using linear programming, how would the objective function be expressed?

(a) $24X(2 + 4) + 40Y(3 + 6)$

(b) $24X + 40Y$

(c) $6X + 9Y$

(d) $5X + 10Y$

4

LINEAR PROGRAMMING PART II: THE SIMPLEX METHOD

4.1 THE SIMPLEX TABLEAU; PIVOTING

INTRODUCTION □ STANDARD FORM OF A MAXIMUM PROBLEM
□ SLACK VARIABLES AND THE SIMPLEX TABLEAU □ THE PIVOT OPERATION

INTRODUCTION

In Chapter 3 we described a geometrical method (using graphs) for solving linear programming problems. Unfortunately, this method is useful only when there are no more than two variables and the number of constraints is small.

If we have a large number of either variables or constraints, it is still true that the optimal solution will be found at a vertex of the set of feasible solutions. In fact, we could find these vertices by writing all the equations corresponding to the inequalities of the problem and then proceeding to solve all possible combinations of these equations. We would of course, have to discard any solutions that are not feasible (because they do not satisfy one or more of the constraints). Then we could evaluate the objective function at the remaining feasible solutions. After all this, we might discover that the problem has no optimal solution after all.

Just how difficult is this procedure? Well, if there were just 4 variables and 7 constraints, we would have to solve all possible combinations of 4 equations chosen from a set of 7 equations—that would be 35 solutions in all. Each of these solutions would then have to be tested for feasibility. So, even for this relatively small number of variables and constraints, the work would be quite tedious. In the real world of applications, it is fairly common to encounter problems with *hundreds,* even *thousands,* of variables and constraints. Of course, such problems must be solved by computer. Even so, choosing a more efficient problem-solving strategy than the geometrical method might reduce the computer's running time from hours to seconds, or, for very large problems, from years to hours.

A more systematic approach would involve choosing a solution at one vertex of the feasible set, then moving from there to another vertex at which the objective function has a better value, and continuing in this way until the best possible value is found. One very efficient and popular way of doing this is the subject of the present chapter: the *simplex method.*

STANDARD FORM OF A MAXIMUM PROBLEM

Maximum Linear Programming Problem Standard Form

A linear programming problem in which the objective function is to be maximized is referred to as a *maximum linear programming problem.* Such problems are said to be in *standard form* provided two conditions are met:

Condition 1. All the variables are nonnegative.

Condition 2. All other constraints are written as a linear expression that is less than or equal to a positive constant.

□ **Example 1**   Determine which of the following maximum linear programming problems are in standard form.

(a)   Maximize

$$z = 5x_1 + 4x_2$$

subject to the constraints

$$3x_1 + 4x_2 \leq 120 \qquad x_1 \geq 0$$
$$4x_1 + 3x_2 \leq 20 \qquad x_2 \geq 0$$

(b) Maximize

$$z = 8x_1 + 2x_2 + 3x_3$$

subject to the constraints

$$4x_1 + 8x_2 \leq 120 \qquad x_1 \geq 0$$
$$3x_2 + 4x_3 \leq 120 \qquad x_2 \geq 0$$

(c) Maximize

$$z = 6x_1 - 8x_2 + x_3$$

subject to the constraints

$$3x_1 + x_2 \leq 10 \qquad x_1 \geq 0$$
$$4x_1 - x_2 \leq 5 \qquad x_2 \geq 0$$
$$x_1 + x_2 + x_3 \geq -3 \qquad x_3 \geq 0$$

(d) Maximize

$$z = 8x_1 + x_2$$

subject to the constraints

$$3x_1 + 4x_2 \geq 2 \qquad x_1 \geq 0$$
$$x_1 + x_2 \leq 6 \qquad x_2 \geq 0$$

Solution   (a) This is a maximum problem containing two variables x_1 and x_2. Since both variables are nonnegative and since the other constraints

$$3x_1 + 4x_2 \leq 120$$
$$4x_1 + x_2 \leq 20$$

Linear	Less	Positive
expressions	than or	
	equal	

are each written as linear expressions less than or equal to a positive constant, we conclude the maximum problem is in standard form.

(b) This is a maximum problem containing three variables x_1, x_2, and x_3. Since the variable x_3 is not given as nonnegative, the maximum problem is not in standard form.

(c) This is a maximum problem containing three variables x_1, x_2, and x_3. Each variable is nonnegative. The other constraints

$$3x_1 + x_2 \leq 10$$
$$4x_1 - x_2 \leq 5$$
$$x_1 + x_2 + x_3 \geq -3$$

contains $x_1 + x_2 + x_3 \geq -3$, which is not a linear expression that is $\leq$ a positive constant. Thus, the maximum problem is not in standard form. Notice, however, that by multiplying this constraint by -1, we get

$$-x_1 - x_2 - x_3 \leq 3$$

which is in the desired form. Thus, although the maximum problem as stated is not in standard form, it can easily be modified to conform to the requirements of the standard form.

(d) The maximum problem contains two variables x_1 and x_2 each of which is nonnegative. Of the other constraints, the first one, $3x_1 + 4x_2 \geq 2$ does not conform. Thus, the maximum problem is not in standard form. Notice that we cannot modify this problem to place it in standard form. Even though multiplying by -1 will change the $\geq$ to $\leq$, in so doing the 2 will change to -2. □

SLACK VARIABLES AND THE SIMPLEX TABLEAU

In order to apply the simplex method to a maximum problem, we need to first

1. Introduce *slack variables.*

2. Construct the *initial simplex tableau.*

We will show how these steps are done by working with a specific maximum problem in standard form. (This problem is Example 6 of Chapter 3, page 131.) Maximize

$$P = 3x_1 + 4x_2$$

subject to the constraints

$$2x_1 + 4x_2 \leq 120 \qquad x_1 \geq 0$$
$$2x_1 + 2x_2 \leq 80 \qquad x_2 \geq 0$$

This problem is in standard form for a maximum linear programming problem. When we say that $2x_1 + 4x_2 \leq 120$, we mean that there is a number greater than or equal to 0, which we might as well call s_1, such that

$$2x_1 + 4x_2 + s_1 = 120$$

This number s_1 is a variable. It must be nonnegative since it is the difference between 120 and a number that is less than or equal to 120. We call it a *slack variable* since it "takes up the slack" between the left and right sides of the inequality.

Similarly, when we say that $2x_1 + 2x_2 \leq 80$, we are saying that there is a slack variable s_2 such that

$$2x_1 + 2x_2 + s_2 = 80$$

Furthermore, the objective function $P = 3x_1 + 4x_2$ can be rewritten as

$$-3x_1 - 4x_2 + P = 0$$

In effect, we have now replaced our original system of constraints and the objective function by a system of three equations in five unknowns:

$$2x_1 + 4x_2 + s_1 = 120$$
$$2x_1 + 2x_2 + s_2 = 80$$
$$-3x_1 - 4x_2 + P = 0$$

Here, it is understood that each of the five variables is required to be nonnegative. To solve the maximum problem is to find the particular solution (x_1, x_2, s_1, s_2, P) that gives the largest possible value for P. The augmented matrix for this system is

$$
\begin{array}{ccccc}
x_1 & x_2 & s_1 & s_2 & P \\
\end{array}
$$
$$
\left[
\begin{array}{ccccc|c}
2 & 4 & 1 & 0 & 0 & 120 \\
2 & 2 & 0 & 1 & 0 & 80 \\
-3 & -4 & 0 & 0 & 1 & 0 \\
\end{array}
\right]
$$

This augmented matrix is called the *initial simplex tableau* for the problem. Notice that we have written the name of each variable above the column in which its coefficients appear.

So far, we have seen this much of the simplex method:

> For a maximum problem in standard form
>
> 1. The constraints are changed from inequalities to equations by the introduction of extra variables — one for each constraint and all nonnegative — called *slack variables.*
>
> 2. These equations, together with one that describes the objective function, are placed in an augmented matrix called the *initial simplex tableau.*

Slack Variables

Initial Simplex Tableau

□ **Example 2** The following maximum problems are in standard form. For each one introduce slack variables and set up the initial simplex tableau.

(a) Maximize

$$P = 3x_1 + 2x_2 + x_3$$

subject to the constraints

$$3x_1 + x_2 + x_3 \le 30 \qquad x_1 \ge 0$$
$$5x_1 + 2x_2 + x_3 \le 24 \qquad x_2 \ge 0$$
$$x_1 + x_2 + 4x_3 \le 20 \qquad x_3 \ge 0$$

(b) Maximize

$$P = x_1 + 4x_2 + 3x_3 + x_4$$

subject to the constraints

$$2x_1 + x_2 \le 10 \qquad x_1 \ge 0 \qquad x_2 \ge 0$$
$$3x_1 + x_2 + x_3 + 2x_4 \le 18 \qquad x_3 \ge 0 \qquad x_4 \ge 0$$
$$x_1 + x_2 + x_3 + x_4 \le 14$$

Solution (a) For each constraint we introduce a nonnegative slack variable to obtain the following equations:

$$3x_1 + x_2 + x_3 + s_1 = 30 \qquad x_1 \ge 0 \qquad s_1 \ge 0$$
$$5x_1 + 2x_2 + x_3 + s_2 = 24 \qquad x_2 \ge 0 \qquad s_2 \ge 0$$
$$x_1 + x_2 + 4x_3 + s_3 = 20 \qquad x_3 \ge 0 \qquad s_3 \ge 0$$

These equations, together with the objective function P, give the initial simplex tableau:

$$
\begin{array}{ccccccc}
x_1 & x_2 & x_3 & s_1 & s_2 & s_3 & P \\
\left[\begin{array}{ccccccc|c}
3 & 1 & 1 & 1 & 0 & 0 & 0 & 30 \\
5 & 2 & 1 & 0 & 1 & 0 & 0 & 24 \\
1 & 1 & 4 & 0 & 0 & 1 & 0 & 20 \\
-3 & -2 & -1 & 0 & 0 & 0 & 1 & 0
\end{array}\right]
\end{array}
$$

(b) For each constraint, we introduce a nonnegative slack variable to obtain the equations

$$2x_1 + x_2 + s_1 = 10 \qquad x_1 \ge 0, x_2 \ge 0, x_3 \ge 0, x_4 \ge 0$$
$$3x_1 + x_2 + x_3 + 2x_4 + s_2 = 18 \qquad s_1 \ge 0, s_2 \ge 0, s_3 \ge 0$$
$$x_1 + x_2 + x_3 + x_4 + s_3 = 14$$

These equations, together with the objective function P, give the initial simplex tableaux:

$$
\begin{array}{cccccccc}
x_1 & x_2 & x_3 & x_4 & s_1 & s_2 & s_3 & P \\
\left[\begin{array}{cccccccc|c}
2 & 1 & 0 & 0 & 1 & 0 & 0 & 0 & 10 \\
3 & 1 & 1 & 2 & 0 & 1 & 0 & 0 & 18 \\
1 & 1 & 1 & 1 & 0 & 0 & 1 & 0 & 14 \\
-1 & -4 & -3 & -1 & 0 & 0 & 0 & 1 & 0
\end{array}\right]
\end{array} \qquad \square
$$

Notice that in each initial simplex tableaux an identity matrix appears under the column headed by the slack variables and the objective function. Notice too that the right-hand column will always contain nonnegative constants.

THE PIVOT OPERATION

Before going any further in our discussion of the simplex method, we need to discuss the matrix operation known as *pivoting*. The first thing one does in a pivot operation is to choose a *pivot element*. However, for now the pivot element will be specified in advance; the method of selecting pivot elements in the simplex tableau will be shown in the next section.

Pivoting To *pivot* a matrix about a given element—called the *pivot element*—is to apply row operations so that the pivot element is replaced by a 1 and all other entries in the same column—called the *pivot column*—become 0's.

Steps for Pivoting

> The correct sequence of steps is:
>
> **Step 1:** In the *pivot row* (where the pivot element appears), divide each entry by the *pivot element* (we assume it is not 0).
>
> **Step 2:** Obtain 0's elsewhere in the *pivot column* by performing row operations.

The following example illustrates a pivot operation.

□ **Example 3**   Perform a pivot operation on the matrix given below, where the pivot element is circled, and the pivot row and pivot column are marked by arrows:

$$\rightarrow \begin{bmatrix} x_1 & x_2 & s_1 & s_2 & P & \\ 2 & ④ & 1 & 0 & 0 & 120 \\ 2 & 2 & 0 & 1 & 0 & 80 \\ -3 & -4 & 0 & 0 & 1 & 0 \end{bmatrix} \qquad (1)$$
$$\uparrow$$

Solution   In this matrix, the pivot column is column 2 and the pivot row is row 1. Step 1 of the pivoting procedure tells us to divide row 1 by 4:

$$\begin{bmatrix} x_1 & x_2 & s_1 & s_2 & P & \\ \frac{1}{2} & ① & \frac{1}{4} & 0 & 0 & 30 \\ 2 & 2 & 0 & 1 & 0 & 80 \\ -3 & -4 & 0 & 0 & 1 & 0 \end{bmatrix}$$

Now, to accomplish Step 2, we multiply row 1 by -2 and add it to row 2; in addition, we multiply row 1 by 4 and add it to row 3. The row operations specified are

$$R_2 = -2r_1 + r_2 \qquad R_3 = 4r_1 + r_3$$

The new matrix looks like this:

$$\begin{bmatrix} x_1 & x_2 & s_1 & s_2 & P & \\ \frac{1}{2} & ① & \frac{1}{4} & 0 & 0 & 30 \\ 1 & 0 & -\frac{1}{2} & 1 & 0 & 20 \\ -1 & 0 & 1 & 0 & 1 & 120 \end{bmatrix} \begin{matrix} x_2 \\ s_2 \\ P \end{matrix} \qquad (2)$$

This completes the pivot operation, since the pivot column has been replaced by

$$\begin{matrix} 1 \\ 0 \\ 0 \end{matrix}$$

□

Just what has the pivot operation done? To see, we look again at the original matrix (1). Observe that the entries in columns s_1, s_2, and P form an identity matrix (I_3, to be exact). This makes it easy to solve for s_1, s_2, and P, using the other variables as parameters:

$$2x_1 + 4x_2 + s_1 = 120 \qquad \text{or} \qquad s_1 = 120 - 2x_1 - 4x_2$$
$$2x_1 + 2x_2 + s_2 = 80 \qquad \text{or} \qquad s_2 = 80 - 2x_1 - 2x_2$$
$$-3x_1 - 4x_2 + P = 0 \qquad \text{or} \qquad P = 3x_1 + 4x_2$$

For additional emphasis, we write s_1, s_2, and P to the right of the corresponding rows of the tableau as follows:

$$\rightarrow
\begin{bmatrix}
x_1 & x_2 & s_1 & s_2 & P & \\
2 & ④ & 1 & 0 & 0 & 120 \\
2 & 2 & 0 & 1 & 0 & 80 \\
-3 & -4 & 0 & 0 & 1 & 0
\end{bmatrix}
\begin{matrix}
\\ s_1 \\ s_2 \\ P
\end{matrix}$$

After pivoting, we obtain the matrix (2).

Notice that the identity matrix I_3 now appears in columns 2, 4, and 5, which helps us solve for x_2, s_2, and P in terms of x_1 and s_1:

$$x_2 = 30 - \tfrac{1}{2}x_1 - \tfrac{1}{4}s_1$$
$$s_1 = 20 - x_1 + \tfrac{1}{2}s_1$$
$$P = 120 + x_1 - s_1$$

This is why we wrote x_2, s_2, and P to the right of the matrix (2).

□ **Example 4** Perform another pivot operation on

$$\rightarrow
\begin{bmatrix}
x_1 & x_2 & s_1 & s_2 & P & \\
\tfrac{1}{2} & 1 & \tfrac{1}{4} & 0 & 0 & 30 \\
① & 0 & -\tfrac{1}{2} & 1 & 0 & 20 \\
-1 & 0 & 1 & 0 & 1 & 120
\end{bmatrix}
\begin{matrix}
\\ x_2 \\ s_2 \\ P
\end{matrix}$$

where the new pivot element has been circled.

Solution Since the pivot element happens to be a 1 in this case, we skip Step 1. For Step 2, we perform the row operations

$$R_1 = -\frac{1}{2}r_2 + r_1 \qquad R_3 = r_2 + r_3$$

The result is

$$\begin{bmatrix}
x_1 & x_2 & s_1 & s_2 & P & \\
0 & 1 & \tfrac{1}{2} & -\tfrac{1}{2} & 0 & 20 \\
1 & 0 & -\tfrac{1}{2} & 1 & 0 & 20 \\
0 & 0 & \tfrac{1}{2} & 1 & 1 & 140
\end{bmatrix}
\begin{matrix}
\\ x_2 \\ x_1 \\ P
\end{matrix}$$

□

Notice that in Example 4 the identity matrix I_3 now appears in columns 1, 2, and 5 — with shifted columns, as

$$\begin{matrix} 0 & 1 & 0 \\ 1 & 0 & 0 \\ 0 & 0 & 1 \end{matrix}$$

We may now solve for x_2, x_1, and P in terms of s_1 and s_2, as indicated on the right of the matrix.

Exercise 4.1 *Answers to Odd-Numbered Exercises Begin on Page* 608 .

In Problems 1–10 determine which maximum linear programming problems are in standard form. Do not attempt to solve them!

1. Maximize

$$P = 2x_1 + x_2$$

subject to the constraints

$$x_1 + x_2 \le 5 \qquad x_1 \ge 0$$
$$2x_1 + 3x_2 \le 2 \qquad x_2 \ge 0$$

2. Maximize

$$P = 3x_1 + 4x_2$$

subject to the constraints

$$3x_1 + x_2 \le 6 \qquad x_1 \ge 0$$
$$x_1 + 4x_2 \le 4 \qquad x_2 \ge 0$$

3. Maximize

$$P = 3x_1 + x_2 + x_3$$

subject to the constraints

$$x_1 + x_2 + x_3 \le 6 \qquad x_1 \ge 0$$
$$2x_1 + 3x_2 + 4x_3 \le 10$$

4. Maximize

$$P = 2x_1 + x_2 + 4x_3$$

subject to the constraints

$$2x_1 + x_2 + x_3 \le 10 \qquad x_2 \ge 0$$

5. Maximize

$$P = 3x_1 + x_2 + x_3$$

subject to the constraints

$$x_1 + x_2 + x_3 \le 8 \qquad x_1 \ge 0$$
$$2x_1 + x_2 + 4x_3 \ge 6 \qquad x_2 \ge 0$$

6. Maximize

$$P = 2x_1 + x_2 + 4x_3$$

subject to the constraints

$$2x_1 + x_2 + x_3 \leq -1, \qquad x_1 \geq 0$$
$$x_2 \geq 0$$

7. Maximize

$$P = 2x_1 + x_2$$

subject to the constraints

$$x_1 + x_2 \geq -6 \qquad x_1 \geq 0$$
$$2x_1 + x_2 \leq 4 \qquad x_2 \geq 0$$

8. Maximize

$$P = 3x_1 + x_2$$

subject to the constraints

$$x_1 + 3x_2 \leq 4 \qquad x_1 \geq 0$$
$$2x_1 - x_2 \geq 1 \qquad x_2 \geq 0$$

9. Maximize

$$P = 2x_1 + x_2 + 3x_3$$

subject to the constraints

$$x_1 + x_2 - x_3 \leq 10 \qquad x_1 \geq 0, \quad x_2 \geq 0$$
$$x_2 + x_3 \leq 4 \qquad x_3 \geq 0$$

10. Maximize

$$P = 2x_1 + 2x_2 + 3x_3$$

subject to the constraints

$$x_1 - x_2 + x_3 \leq 6 \qquad x_1 \geq 0, \quad x_2 \geq 0$$
$$x_1 \leq 4 \qquad x_3 \geq 0$$

In Problems 11–16, each maximum problem is not in standard form. Determine if the problem can be modified so as to be in standard form. If it can, write the modified version.

11. Maximize

$$P = x_1 + x_2$$

subject to the constraints

$$3x_1 - 4x_2 \leq -6, \qquad x_1 \geq 0$$
$$x_1 + x_2 \leq 4 \qquad x_2 \geq 0$$

12. Maximize

$$P = 2x_1 + 3x_2$$

subject to the constraints

$$-4x_1 + 2x_2 \geq -8, \quad x_1 \geq 0$$
$$x_1 - x_2 \leq 6 \quad x_2 \geq 0$$

13. Maximize

$$P = x_1 + x_2 + x_3$$

subject to the constraints

$$x_1 + x_2 + x_3 \leq 6, \quad x_1 \geq 0, \quad x_2 \geq 0$$
$$4x_1 + 3x_2 \geq 12, \quad x_3 \geq 0$$

14. Maximize

$$P = 2x_1 + x_2 + 3x_3$$

subject to the constraints

$$x_1 + x_2 + x_3 \geq -8 \quad x_1 \geq 0, \quad x_2 \geq 0$$
$$x_1 - x_2 \leq -6 \quad x_3 \geq 0$$

15. Maximize

$$P = 2x_1 + x_2 + 3x_3$$

subject to the constraints

$$-x_1 + x_2 + x_3 \geq -6 \quad x_1 \geq 0, \quad x_2 \geq 0$$
$$2x_1 - 3x_2 \geq -12 \quad x_3 \geq 0$$

16. Maximize

$$P = x_1 + x_2 + x_2$$

subject to the constraints

$$2x_1 - x_2 + 3x_3 \leq 8 \quad x_1 \geq 0, \quad x_2 \geq 0$$
$$x_1 - x_2 \geq 6 \quad x_3 \geq 0$$

In Problems 17–24, each maximum problem is in standard form. For each one introduce slack variables and set up the initial simplex tableaux.

17. Maximize

$$P = 2x_1 + x_2 + 3x_3$$

subject to the constraints

$$5x_1 + 2x_2 + x_3 \leq 20$$
$$6x_1 + x_2 + 4x_3 \leq 24$$
$$x_1 + x_2 + 4x_3 \leq 16$$
$$x_1 \geq 0, \quad x_2 \geq 0, \quad x_3 \geq 0$$

18. Maximize

$$P = 3x_1 + 2x_2 + x_3$$

subject to the constraints

$$3x_1 + 2x_2 - x_3 \leq 10$$
$$x_1 - x_2 + 3x_3 \leq 12$$
$$2x_1 + x_2 + x_3 \leq 6$$
$$x_1 \geq 0, \quad x_2 \geq 0, \quad x_3 \geq 0$$

19. Maximize

$$P = 3x_1 + 5x_2$$

subject to the constraints

$2.2x_1 - 1.8x_2 \le 5$

$0.8x_1 + 1.2x_2 \le 2.5$

$x_1 + x_2 \le 0.1$

$x_1 \ge 0, \quad x_2 \ge 0$

20. Maximize

$$P = 2x_1 + 3x_2$$

subject to the constraints

$1.2x_1 - 2.1x_2 \le 0.5$

$0.3x_1 + 0.4x_2 \le 1.5$

$x_1 + x_2 \le 0.7$

$x_1 \ge 0, \quad x_2 \ge 0$

21. Maximize

$$P = 2x_1 + 3x_2 + x_3$$

subject to the constraints

$x_1 + x_2 + x_3 \le 50$

$3x_1 + 2x_2 + x_3 \le 10$

$x_1 \ge 0, \quad x_2 \ge 0, \quad x_3 \ge 0$

22. Maximize

$$P = x_1 + 4x_2 + 2x_3$$

subject to the constraints

$3x_1 + x_2 + x_3 \le 10$

$x_1 + x_2 + 3x_3 \le 5$

$x_1 \ge 0, \quad x_2 \ge 0, \quad x_3 \ge 0$

23. Maximize

$$P = 3x_1 + 4x_2 + 2x_3$$

subject to the constraints

$3x_1 + x_2 + 4x_3 \le 5$

$x_1 + x_2 \le 5$

$2x_1 - x_2 + x_3 \le 6$

$x_1 \ge 0, \quad x_2 \ge 0, \quad x_3 \ge 0$

24. Maximize

$$P = 2x_1 + x_2 + 3x_3$$

subject to the constraints

$2x_1 + x_2 + x_3 \le 2$

$x_1 - x_2 \le 4$

$2x_1 + x_2 - x_3 \le 5$

$x_1 \ge 0, \quad x_2 \ge 0, \quad x_3 \ge 0$

In Problems 25–29 perform a pivot operation on each augmented matrix. Write the original system of equations and the final system of equations. The pivot element is circled.

25.

x_1	x_2	s_1	s_2	P		
1	②	1	0	0	300	s_1
3	2	0	1	0	480	s_2
−1	−2	0	0	1	0	P

26.

x_1	x_2	s_1	s_2	P		
1	4	1	0	0	100	s_1
2	⑤	0	1	0	50	s_2
−2	−1	0	0	1	0	P

27.

x_1	x_2	x_3	s_1	s_2	s_3	P		
1	2	4	1	0	0	0	24	s_1
2	−1	1	0	1	0	0	32	s_2
3	②	4	0	0	1	0	18	s_3
−1	−2	−3	0	0	0	1	0	P

28.

$$\begin{array}{ccccccc} x_1 & x_2 & x_3 & s_1 & s_2 & s_3 & P \end{array}$$

$$\begin{bmatrix} 1 & ② & 1 & 1 & 0 & 0 & 0 & | & 6 \\ 2 & 3 & 1 & 0 & 1 & 0 & 0 & | & 12 \\ 1 & -2 & 3 & 0 & 0 & 1 & 0 & | & 0 \\ -1 & -2 & -3 & 0 & 0 & 0 & 1 & | & 0 \end{bmatrix} \begin{array}{c} s_1 \\ s_2 \\ s_3 \\ P \end{array}$$

29.

$$\begin{array}{ccccccccc} x_1 & x_2 & x_3 & x_4 & s_1 & s_2 & s_3 & s_4 & P \end{array}$$

$$\begin{bmatrix} -3 & 0 & 1 & 0 & 1 & 0 & 0 & 0 & 0 & | & 20 \\ ② & 0 & 0 & 1 & 0 & 1 & 0 & 0 & 0 & | & 24 \\ 0 & -3 & 1 & 0 & 0 & 0 & 1 & 0 & 0 & | & 28 \\ 0 & -3 & 0 & 1 & 0 & 0 & 0 & 1 & 0 & | & 24 \\ -1 & -2 & -3 & -4 & 0 & 0 & 0 & 0 & 1 & | & 0 \end{bmatrix} \begin{array}{c} s_1 \\ s_2 \\ s_3 \\ s_4 \\ P \end{array}$$

4.2 THE SIMPLEX METHOD: THE MAXIMUM PROBLEM

THE PIVOTING PROCESS □ GEOMETRY OF THE SIMPLEX METHOD □ THE UNBOUNDED CASE
□ SUMMARY OF THE SIMPLEX METHOD □ RECENT ADVANCES IN LINEAR PROGRAMMING

We are finally ready to state the details of the simplex method for solving a maximum linear programming problem. This method requires that the problem be in standard form and that the problem be placed in an initial simplex tableau with slack variables. We begin by looking at a maximum problem in standard form.
Maximize

$$P = 3x_1 + 4x_2$$

subject to the constraints

$$2x_1 + 4x_2 \le 120 \qquad x_1 \ge 0$$
$$2x_1 + 2x_2 \le 80 \qquad x_2 \ge 0$$

After introducing slack variables s_1 and s_2, we set up the initial simplex tableau.

$$2x_1 + 4x_2 + s_1 = 120 \qquad x_1 \ge 0 \qquad s_1 \ge 0$$
$$2x_1 + 2x_2 + s_2 = 80 \qquad x_2 \ge 0 \qquad s_2 \ge 0$$

The initial simplex tableau is

$$\begin{array}{ccccc} x_1 & x_2 & s_1 & s_2 & P \end{array}$$

$$\begin{bmatrix} 2 & 4 & 1 & 0 & 0 & | & 120 \\ 2 & 2 & 0 & 1 & 0 & | & 80 \\ \hdashline -3 & -4 & 0 & 0 & 1 & | & 0 \end{bmatrix} \begin{array}{c} s_1 \\ s_2 \\ P \end{array}$$

Notice that the bottom row contains the negatives of the coefficients in the objective function and that we have set this row off from the rest of the matrix by a dashed line.

Objective Row   We refer to this row as the *objective row*. From this point on, the simplex method consists of pivoting from one tableau to another until the optimal solution is found.

Two questions remain to be answered:
1. How is the pivot element selected?
2. When does the process end?

Pivot Element The *pivot element* for the simplex method is found using two rules:

Pivot Column

Rule 1: The *pivot column* is selected by locating the most negative entry in the objective row. If all the entries in this column are negative, the problem is unbounded and there is no solution.

Pivot Row

Rule 2: Divide each entry in the last column by the corresponding entry (from the same row) in the pivot column. (Ignore any rows in which the pivot column entry is less than or equal to 0.) The row in which the smallest positive ratio is obtained is the *pivot row*.

The *pivot element* **is the entry at the intersection of the pivot row and the pivot column.**

Note that the pivot element is never in the objective row.

In the example we have been using, we select 4 as the pivot element because -4 is the most negative entry in the last row and $120 \div 4 = 30$ is the smallest positive ratio obtainable by dividing an entry in the last column by the corresponding entry in column 2.

$$
\rightarrow \begin{bmatrix} x_1 & x_2 & s_1 & s_2 & P & \\ 2 & \textcircled{4} & 1 & 0 & 0 & 120 \\ 2 & 2 & 0 & 1 & 0 & 80 \\ \hdashline -3 & -4 & 0 & 0 & 1 & 0 \end{bmatrix} \begin{array}{l} 120 \div 4 = 30 \\ 80 \div 2 = 40 \\ \\ \end{array}
$$
$$\uparrow$$

After pivoting, we see that the smallest (in fact, only) negative entry in the objective row is the -1 in column 1. We check the row ratios in the last column:

$$
\rightarrow \begin{bmatrix} x_1 & x_2 & s_1 & s_2 & P & \\ \frac{1}{2} & 1 & \frac{1}{4} & 0 & 0 & 30 \\ \textcircled{1} & 0 & -\frac{1}{2} & 1 & 0 & 20 \\ \hdashline -1 & 0 & 1 & 0 & 1 & 120 \end{bmatrix} \begin{array}{l} 30 \div \frac{1}{2} = 60 \\ 20 \div 1 = 20 \\ \\ \end{array}
$$
$$\uparrow$$

Rule 2 tells us to select the pivot element in row 2. After pivoting (as in Example 2, Section 4.2), we have

$$
\begin{bmatrix} x_1 & x_2 & s_1 & s_2 & P & \\ 0 & 1 & \frac{1}{2} & -\frac{1}{2} & 0 & 20 \\ 1 & 0 & -\frac{1}{2} & 1 & 0 & 20 \\ \hdashline 0 & 0 & \frac{1}{2} & 1 & 1 & 140 \end{bmatrix} \begin{array}{l} x_2 \\ x_1 \\ \\ P \end{array}
$$

Now there are no negative entries in the objective row. Thus, the rules imply that no further pivots can be performed. But this is not surprising because the problem is now solved. To see why, we write the equation from the objective row, namely,

$$P = 140 - \frac{1}{2} s_1 - s_2$$

Since $s_1 \geq 0$ and $s_2 \geq 0$, any positive value of s_1 or s_2 would make the value of P less than 140. By choosing $s_1 = 0$ and $s_2 = 0$, we obtain the largest possible value for P, namely, 140. If we write the equations from the first and second rows, substituting 0 for s_1 and s_2, we have

$$x_2 = 20 - \frac{1}{2} s_1 + \frac{1}{2} s_2 = 20$$

$$x_1 = 20 + \frac{1}{2} s_1 - s_2 = 20$$

In other words, we have found the optimal solution,

$$P = 140 \quad \text{Maximum}$$

which occurs at

$$x_1 = 20 \qquad x_2 = 20$$

This same solution was found earlier in Chapter 3 (page 131) by the geometrical method.

Now, the reason we choose the most negative entry in the objective row is that it is the negative of the *largest* coefficient in the objective function:

$$P = 3x_1 + 4x_2$$

If we were to set $x_1 = x_2 = 0$, we would obtain $P = 0$ as a first approximation for the profit P. Of course, this is not a very good approximation; it can easily be improved by increasing either x_1 or x_2. But the profit per unit of x_2 is \$4, while the profit per unit of x_1 is only \$3. Thus, it is more effective to increase x_2 than x_1. But what is the largest amount by which x_2 can be increased?

We can answer this question by performing the pivot operation, as we already have in Example 1, Section 2. The matrix becomes

$$
\begin{array}{ccccc}
x_1 & x_2 & s_1 & s_2 & P \\
\end{array}
$$
$$
\left[
\begin{array}{ccccc|c}
\frac{1}{2} & \textcircled{1} & \frac{1}{4} & 0 & 0 & 30 \\
1 & 0 & -\frac{1}{2} & 1 & 0 & 20 \\
\hline
-1 & 0 & 1 & 0 & 1 & 120 \\
\end{array}
\right]
\begin{array}{c}
x_2 \\
s_2 \\
P \\
\end{array}
$$

and the corresponding equations are

$$x_2 = 30 - \frac{1}{2} x_1 - \frac{1}{4} s_1$$

$$s_2 = 20 - x_1 + \frac{1}{2} s_1$$

$$P = 120 + x_1 - s_1$$

This suggests that x_2 can be as large as 30, if we take both x_1 and s_1 to be 0, in which case P will be 120.

So we chose column 2 because we wanted to increase x_2. But why did we choose row 1, rather than row 2, as the pivot row? Let's see what would have happened if we had chosen row 2 as the pivot row. The result would have been

$$
\begin{array}{ccccc}
x_1 & x_2 & s_1 & s_2 & P \\
\end{array}
$$

$$
\left[
\begin{array}{ccccc|c}
-2 & 0 & 1 & -2 & 0 & -40 \\
1 & 1 & 0 & \frac{1}{2} & 0 & 40 \\
\hline
1 & 0 & 0 & 2 & 1 & 160 \\
\end{array}
\right]
\begin{array}{c}
s_1 \\
x_2 \\
P \\
\end{array}
$$

But this is not acceptable because of the negative number in the last column. (In effect, this matrix tells us that we could get P to be as large as 160, by setting $x_1 = 0$, $x_2 = 40$, and $s_1 = -40$; but this is not a feasible solution because s_1 is supposed to be greater than or equal to 0.)

The reason we get a feasible solution if we choose row 1 to pivot, and an apparent but false solution if we choose row 2, is because the row ratio ($120 \div 4$) for row 1 is smaller (hence, better) than the row ratio ($80 \div 2$) for row 2.

So, the reasoning behind the simplex method is fairly complicated, but the process of "moving to a better solution" is made quite easy simply by following the rules. Briefly, the pivoting strategy works like this:

> Rule 1 forces us to pivot the variable that will most effectively improve the value of the objective function.
>
> Rule 2 prevents us from making this variable *too large* to be feasible.

In general, the reasoning used in the above problem shows that

> If there are no negative entries in the objective row, the optimal solution has been found.

Final Tableau   We thus have a stopping or termination criterion for the simplex method. The tableau reached when the optimal solution is found is called a *final tableau.*

Let's work another one.

□ **Example 1**   Maximize

$$P = 6x_1 + 8x_2 + x_3$$

subject to

$$
\begin{array}{ll}
3x_1 + 5x_2 + 3x_3 \le 20 & x_1 \ge 0 \\
x_1 + 3x_2 + 2x_3 \le 9 & x_2 \ge 0 \\
6x_1 + 2x_2 + 5x_3 \le 30 & x_3 \ge 0 \\
\end{array}
$$

Solution   Note that the problem is in standard form. Introducing slack variables s_1, s_2, and s_3, the system becomes

$$
\begin{aligned}
3x_1 + 5x_2 + 3x_3 + s_1 &= 20 \quad & x_1 \geq 0 \quad & s_1 \geq 0 \\
x_1 + 3x_2 + 2x_3 + s_2 &= 9 \quad & x_2 \geq 0 \quad & s_2 \geq 0 \\
6x_1 + 2x_2 + 5x_3 + s_3 &= 30 \quad & x_3 \geq 0 \quad & s_3 \geq 0 \\
-6x_1 - 8x_2 - x_3 + P &= 0
\end{aligned}
\tag{1}
$$

The initial simplex tableau is

$$
\begin{array}{c}
\quad x_1 \quad x_2 \quad x_3 \quad s_1 \quad s_2 \quad s_3 \quad P \\
\left[
\begin{array}{ccccccc|c}
3 & 5 & 3 & 1 & 0 & 0 & 0 & 20 \\
1 & ③ & 2 & 0 & 1 & 0 & 0 & 9 \\
6 & 2 & 5 & 0 & 0 & 1 & 0 & 30 \\
\hline
-6 & -8 & -1 & 0 & 0 & 0 & 1 & 0
\end{array}
\right]
\begin{array}{l}
20 \div 5 = 4 \\
9 \div 3 = 3 \\
30 \div 2 = 15 \\
\\
\end{array}
\end{array}
$$

The pivot column is found by locating the column containing the smallest entry in the objective row (-8 in column 2).

The pivot row is obtained by dividing each entry in the last column by the corresponding entry in the pivot column and selecting the smallest nonnegative ratio. Thus, the second row is the pivot row and the pivot element in that row is the circled element 3. Notice that the column under P in any tableau is the same as in the initial tableau. This is why from now on, we will omit the column for P. After pivoting, the new tableau is

$$
\begin{array}{c}
\quad x_1 \quad\; x_2 \;\; x_3 \;\; s_1 \;\; s_2 \;\; s_3 \\
\left[
\begin{array}{cccccc|c}
④/₃ & 0 & -\frac{1}{3} & 1 & -\frac{5}{3} & 0 & 5 \\
\frac{1}{3} & 1 & \frac{2}{3} & 0 & \frac{1}{3} & 0 & 3 \\
\frac{16}{3} & 0 & \frac{11}{3} & 0 & -\frac{2}{3} & 1 & 24 \\
\hline
-\frac{10}{3} & 0 & \frac{13}{3} & 0 & \frac{8}{3} & 0 & 24
\end{array}
\right]
\begin{array}{l}
5 \div \frac{4}{3} = 3.75 \\
3 \div \frac{1}{3} = 9 \\
24 \div \frac{16}{3} = 4.5 \\
\\
\end{array}
\end{array}
$$

By the same procedure as before, we determine the next pivot element to be $\frac{4}{3}$, in the upper left corner. After pivoting, we get

$$
\begin{array}{c}
\quad x_1 \;\; x_2 \;\; x_3 \;\; s_1 \;\; s_2 \;\; s_3 \\
\left[
\begin{array}{cccccc|c}
1 & 0 & -\frac{1}{4} & \frac{3}{4} & -\frac{5}{4} & 0 & \frac{15}{4} \\
0 & 1 & \frac{3}{4} & -\frac{1}{4} & \frac{3}{4} & 0 & \frac{7}{4} \\
0 & 0 & 5 & -4 & ⑥ & 1 & 4 \\
\hline
0 & 0 & \frac{7}{2} & \frac{5}{2} & -\frac{3}{2} & 0 & \frac{73}{2}
\end{array}
\right]
\end{array}
$$

Since we still observe a negative entry in the objective row, we pivot again. (Remember, in finding the pivot element, we ignore rows in which the pivot column contains a negative number—in this case, $-\frac{3}{4}$.) The new tableau is

$$
\begin{array}{cccccc}
x_1 & x_2 & x_3 & s_1 & s_2 & s_3 \\
\end{array}
$$

$$
\left[
\begin{array}{cccccc|c}
1 & 0 & \frac{19}{24} & -\frac{1}{12} & 0 & \frac{5}{24} & \frac{55}{12} \\
0 & 1 & \frac{1}{8} & \frac{1}{4} & 0 & -\frac{1}{8} & \frac{5}{4} \\
0 & 0 & \frac{5}{6} & -\frac{2}{3} & 1 & \frac{1}{6} & \frac{2}{3} \\
\hdashline
0 & 0 & \frac{19}{4} & \frac{3}{2} & 0 & \frac{1}{4} & \frac{75}{2}
\end{array}
\right]
\begin{array}{c}
x_1 \\ x_2 \\ s_2 \\ \\ P
\end{array}
$$

This is a final tableau; the last column says that

$$ P = \tfrac{75}{2} \qquad x_1 = \tfrac{55}{12} \qquad x_2 = \tfrac{5}{4} \qquad x_3 = 0 $$

We see that $x_3 = 0$, because its column contains a number greater than 0 in the last row. We also see that $s_1 = 0$, $s_2 = \frac{2}{3}$, and $s_3 = 0$. These values can be used to check that these are, in fact, solutions of the system of equations (1). □

□ **Example 2**   Mike's Famous Toy Trucks specializes in making four kinds of toy trucks: a delivery truck, a dump truck, a garbage truck, and a gasoline truck. Three machines—a metal casting machine, a paint spray machine, and a packaging machine—are used in the production of these trucks. The time, in hours, each machine works to make each type of truck and the profit for each truck are given in Table 1. The maximum time available per week for each machine is: metal casting 4000 hours, paint spray 1800 hours, and packaging 1000 hours. How many of each type truck should be produced to maximize profit? Assume that every truck made is sold.

Table 1

	Metal Casting	Paint Spray	Packaging	Profit
Delivery Truck	2 hours	1 hour	0.5 hour	$0.50
Dump Truck	2.5 hours	1.5 hours	0.5 hour	$1.00
Garbage Truck	2 hours	1 hour	1 hour	$1.50
Gasoline Truck	2 hours	2 hours	1 hour	$2.00

Solution   Let x_1, x_2, x_3, and x_4 denote the number of delivery trucks, dump trucks, garbage trucks, and gasoline trucks, respectively, to be made. If P denotes the profit to be maximized, we have the problem:

Maximize

$$ P = 0.5x_1 + x_2 + 1.5x_3 + 2x_4 $$

subject to the conditions

$$
\begin{aligned}
2x_1 + 2.5x_2 + 2x_3 + 2x_4 &\le 4000 \qquad x_1 \ge 0 \qquad x_3 \ge 0 \\
x_1 + 1.5x_2 + x_3 + 2x_4 &\le 1800 \qquad x_2 \ge 0 \qquad x_4 \ge 0 \\
0.5x_1 + 0.5x_2 + x_3 + x_4 &\le 1000
\end{aligned}
$$

Since this problem is in standard form, we introduce slack variables s_1, s_2, and s_3, write the initial simplex tableau, and solve:

$$
\begin{array}{ccccccc}
x_1 & x_2 & x_3 & x_4 & s_1 & s_2 & s_3 \\
\end{array}
$$

$$
\left[
\begin{array}{ccccccc|c}
2 & 2.5 & 2 & 2 & 1 & 0 & 0 & 4000 \\
1 & 1.5 & 1 & ② & 0 & 1 & 0 & 1800 \\
0.5 & 0.5 & 1 & 1 & 0 & 0 & 1 & 1000 \\
\hline
-0.5 & -1 & -1.5 & -2 & 0 & 0 & 0 & 0
\end{array}
\right]
\begin{array}{c}
s_1 \\ s_2 \\ s_3 \\ \\
\end{array}
$$

$$
\begin{array}{ccccccc}
x_1 & x_2 & x_3 & x_4 & s_1 & s_2 & s_3 \\
\end{array}
$$

$$
\left[
\begin{array}{ccccccc|c}
1 & 1 & 1 & 0 & 1 & -1 & 0 & 2200 \\
0.5 & 0.75 & 0.5 & 1 & 0 & 0.5 & 0 & 900 \\
0 & -0.25 & ⑤ & 0 & 0 & -0.5 & 1 & 100 \\
\hline
0.5 & 0.5 & -0.5 & 0 & 0 & 1 & 0 & 1800
\end{array}
\right]
\begin{array}{c}
s_1 \\ x_4 \\ s_3 \\ \\
\end{array}
$$

$$
\begin{array}{ccccccc}
x_1 & x_2 & x_3 & x_4 & s_1 & s_2 & s_3 \\
\end{array}
$$

$$
\left[
\begin{array}{ccccccc|c}
1 & 1.5 & 0 & 0 & 1 & 0 & -2 & 2000 \\
0.5 & 1 & 0 & 1 & 0 & 1 & -1 & 800 \\
0 & -0.5 & 1 & 0 & 0 & -1 & 2 & 200 \\
\hline
0.5 & 0.25 & 0 & 0 & 0 & 0.5 & 1 & 1900
\end{array}
\right]
\begin{array}{c}
s_1 \\ x_4 \\ x_3 \\ \\
\end{array}
$$

This is a final tableau. The maximum profit is $P = \$1900$, and it is attained for

$$x_1 = 0 \qquad x_2 = 0 \qquad x_3 = 200 \qquad x_4 = 800 \qquad \square$$

The practical considerations of the situation described in Example 2 are that delivery trucks and dump trucks are too costly to produce or too little profit is being gained from their sale. Since the slack variable s_1 has a value of 2000 for maximum P and since s_1 represents the number of hours the metal casting machine is printing no truck (that is, the time the machine is idle), it may be possible to release this machine for other duties.

GEOMETRY OF THE SIMPLEX METHOD

The maximum value (provided it exists) of the objective function will occur at one of the vertices of the feasible region. The simplex method is designed to move from vertex to vertex of the feasible region, at each stage improving the value of the objective function until an optimal solution is found. More precisely, the geometry behind the simplex method is this:

1. A given tableau corresponds to a vertex of the feasible region.
2. The operation of pivoting moves us to an adjacent vertex, where the objective function has a value at least as large as it did at the previous vertex.
3. The process continues until the final tableau is reached—which produces a vertex that maximizes the objective function.

Though drawings of this can be rendered in only 2 or 3 dimensions (that is, when the objective function has 2 or 3 variables in it), the same interpretation can be shown to hold regardless of the number of variables involved. Let's look at an example.

☐ **Example 3** Maximize

$$P = 3x_1 + 5x_2$$

subject to the constraints

$$x_1 + x_2 \le 60 \qquad x_1 \ge 0$$
$$x_1 + 2x_2 \le 80 \qquad x_2 \ge 0$$

The feasible region is shown in Figure 1.

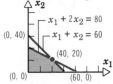

Figure 1

Below, on the left we apply the simplex method, indicating on the right the vertex corresponding to each tableau and the value of the objective function there. The reader is urged to supply the details.

	Tableau		Vertex	Value of $P = 3x_1 + 5x_2$ at the Vertex

$$
\begin{array}{ccccc}
x_1 & x_2 & s_1 & s_2 & P \\
\end{array}
$$

$$
\left[
\begin{array}{ccccc|c}
1 & 1 & 1 & 0 & 0 & 60 \\
1 & 2 & 0 & 1 & 0 & 80 \\
\hline
-3 & -5 & 0 & 0 & 1 & 0 \\
\end{array}
\right]
\begin{array}{l} s_1 \\ s_2 \end{array} \quad (0, 0) \qquad 0
$$

↓

$$
\left[
\begin{array}{ccccc|c}
\frac{1}{2} & 0 & 1 & -\frac{1}{2} & 0 & 20 \\
\frac{1}{2} & 1 & 0 & \frac{1}{2} & 0 & 40 \\
\hline
-\frac{1}{2} & 0 & 0 & \frac{5}{2} & 1 & 200 \\
\end{array}
\right]
\begin{array}{l} s_1 \\ x_2 \end{array} \quad (0, 40) \qquad 200
$$

↓

$$
\left[
\begin{array}{ccccc|c}
1 & 0 & 2 & -1 & 0 & 40 \\
0 & 1 & -1 & 1 & 0 & 20 \\
\hline
0 & 0 & 1 & 2 & 1 & 220 \\
\end{array}
\right]
\begin{array}{l} x_1 \\ x_2 \end{array} \quad \begin{array}{l} (40, 20) \qquad 220 \\ \text{(maximum value)} \end{array}
$$

(final tableau)

THE UNBOUNDED CASE

So far in our discussion, it has always been possible to continue to choose pivot elements until the problem has been solved. But it may turn out that all the entries in a column of a tableau are 0 or negative at some stage. If this happens, it means that the problem is *unbounded* and a maximum solution does not exist.

For example, consider the tableau

$$
\begin{array}{cccc}
x_1 & x_2 & s_1 & s_2 \\
\end{array}
$$

$$
\left[
\begin{array}{cccc|c}
-1 & 1 & 1 & 0 & 2 \\
1 & -1 & 0 & 1 & 2 \\
\hline
-1 & -1 & 0 & 0 & 0 \\
\end{array}
\right]
\begin{array}{l} s_1 \\ s_2 \end{array}
$$

When there are two equal smallest negative entries in the last row, you may choose either column as the pivot column. Suppose we arbitrarily choose column 1 to pivot, and the tableau becomes

$$\begin{array}{c} \begin{array}{cccc} x_1 & x_2 & s_1 & s_2 \end{array} \\ \left[\begin{array}{cccc|c} 0 & 0 & 1 & 1 & 4 \\ 1 & -1 & 0 & 1 & 2 \\ \hline 0 & -2 & 0 & 1 & 2 \end{array} \right] \begin{array}{l} s_1 \\ x_1 \\ \\ \end{array} \end{array}$$

Now the only negative entry in the last row is in column 2, and it is impossible to choose a pivot element in that column. This implies that the objective function is unbounded. Indeed, it is easy to see that if the only constraints are $-x_1 + x_2 \leq 2$, $x_1 - x_2 \leq 2$, $x_1 \geq 0$, and $x_2 \geq 0$, then $P = x_1 + x_2$ has no maximum. The feasible region is shown in Figure 2.

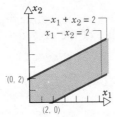

Figure 2

SUMMARY OF THE SIMPLEX METHOD

The general procedure for solving a maximum linear programming using the simplex method can be outlined as follows.

1. The maximum problem is stated in standard form as:
   Maximize

$$P = c_1 x_1 + c_2 x_2 + \cdots + c_n x_n$$

   subject to the constraints

$$\begin{aligned} a_{11} x_1 + a_{12} x_2 + \cdots + a_{1n} x_n &\leq b_1 \\ a_{21} x_1 + a_{22} x_2 + \cdots + a_{2n} x_n &\leq b_2 \\ &\vdots \\ a_{m1} x_1 + a_{n2} x_2 + \cdots + a_{mn} x_n &\leq b_m \end{aligned} \qquad x_1 \geq 0, x_2 \geq 0, \ldots, x_n \geq 0$$

   in which $b_1 > 0, b_2 > 0, \cdots b_m > 0$.

2. Introduce slack variables $s_1, s_2, \ldots s_m$ so that the constraints take the form of equations

$$\begin{aligned} a_{11} x_1 + a_{12} x_2 + \cdots + a_{1n} x_n + s_1 &= b_1 \\ a_{21} x_1 + a_{22} x_2 + \cdots + a_{2n} x_n + s_2 &= b_2 \\ &\vdots \\ a_{m1} x_1 + a_{m2} x_2 + \cdots + a_{mn} x_n + s_m &= b_m \end{aligned} \qquad \begin{aligned} x_1 &\geq 0, x_2 \geq 0, \ldots, x_n \geq 0 \\ s_1 &\geq 0, s_2 \geq 0, \ldots, s_m \geq 0 \end{aligned}$$

3. Set up the initial simplex tableau

$$
\begin{array}{c}
\begin{array}{cccccccc}
x_1 & x_2 & \cdots & x_n & s_1 & s_2 & \cdots & s_m & P
\end{array}\\
\left[\begin{array}{cccccccc|c}
a_{11} & a_{12} & \cdots & a_{1n} & 1 & 0 & \cdots & 0 & 0 & b_1 \\
a_{21} & a_{22} & & a_{2n} & 0 & 1 & \cdots & 0 & 0 & b_2 \\
\cdot & & & & & & & & & \\
\cdot & & & & & & & & & \\
\cdot & & & & & & & & & \\
a_{m1} & a_{m2} & & a_{mn} & 0 & 0 & \cdots & 1 & 0 & b_m \\
\hline
-c_1 & -c_2 & & -c_n & 0 & 0 & & 0 & 1 & 0
\end{array}\right]
\begin{array}{c}
s_1 \\ s_2 \\ \\ \\ \\ s_m \\ P
\end{array}
\end{array}
$$

4. Pivot until
   (a)   All the entries in the objective row are nonnegative. This is a final tableau from which a solution can be read.

   or
   (b)   The selection of the pivot column is a column whose entries are negative or zero. In this case the problem is unbounded and there is no solution.

The flowchart in Figure 3 illustrates the steps to be used in solving maximum linear programming problems.

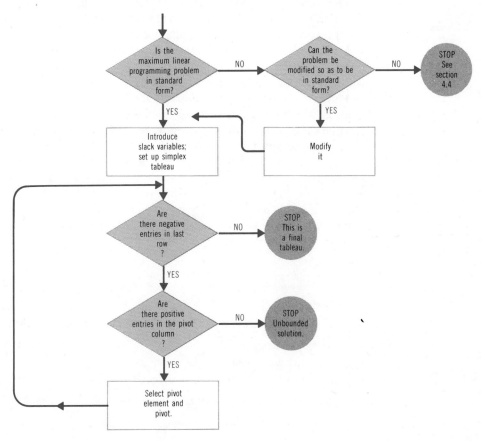

Figure 3

RECENT ADVANCES IN LINEAR PROGRAMMING

Since its introduction in the 1940s linear programming has gained ever wider acceptance and application. The 1975 Nobel Prize in Economics was shared by the recently deceased (1986) Soviet economist Leonid Kantorovich who made essential use of linear programming in his work. Today, airlines, brokerage houses and oil companies routinely construct large scale linear programming problems involving thousands, even tens of thousands, of variables and constraints. To date the method of choice for solving these problems has been the simplex algorithm developed some forty years ago by George Dantzig.

Computer implementation of the simplex algorithm has been relatively successful, yet practitioners in the field have always asked if perhaps some algorithm other than the simplex method might not be more appropriate. The reason was twofold: there were already scattered instances of problems that required too much computer time to solve with the simplex method and, also, the demands of industry could easily envision problems involving hundreds of thousands of variables for which a quicker algorithm would be more cost efficient and even necessary.

In 1979 a young Soviet mathematician named Leonid Khachian proposed an algorithm, called the *ellipsoid method,* that proceeded to find the optimal solution by successively surrounding the feasible region by ellipsoids. Though this algorithm did better on some problems, its practical significance was diminished by the fact that it performed no better on the average than the simplex method.

More recently, in 1984, Narendra Karmarkar, a researcher at A.T.&T. Bell Laboratories, announced a linear programming technique that he and his colleagues claim will substantially speed up the handling of current problems and will allow the tackling of problems that would otherwise be out of reach. Unlike the simplex method, which moves along the edges of the feasible region from vertex to vertex, the Karmarkar algorithm deals with points in the interior of the feasible region in its search for the optimum. Tests conducted in 1986 at the University of California, Berkeley, showed that the Karmarkar algorithm solved certain selected problems about three to four times faster than the simplex algorithm. Prospects for it look encouraging, though as of this writing it was too early to tell whether the Karmarkar algorithm would live up to all of its predictions. But were it to significantly better the performance of the simplex method on a broad range of problems, the cost savings to industry users would be substantial.

Exercise 4.2   *Answers to Odd-Numbered Problems begin on page* 609 .

In Problems 1–6 determine which of the following statements is true about each tableau:

(a)   It is the final tableau.
(b)   It requires additional pivoting.
(c)   It indicates no solution to the problem.

   If the answer is (a), write down the solution; if the answer is (b), indicate the pivot element.

1.
$$\begin{array}{cccc} x_1 & x_2 & s_1 & s_2 \\ \end{array}$$
$$\left[\begin{array}{cccc|c} 1 & 0 & 1 & -\frac{1}{2} & 20 \\ \frac{1}{2} & 1 & 0 & \frac{1}{4} & 30 \\ \hline -1 & 0 & 0 & 1 & 120 \end{array}\right]\begin{array}{l} s_1 \\ x_2 \\ \\ \end{array}$$

2.
$$\begin{array}{cccc} x_1 & x_2 & s_1 & s_2 \\ \end{array}$$
$$\left[\begin{array}{cccc|c} 1 & 0 & 1 & -\frac{1}{2} & 20 \\ 0 & 1 & -\frac{1}{2} & \frac{1}{2} & 20 \\ \hline 0 & 0 & 1 & \frac{1}{2} & 140 \end{array}\right]\begin{array}{l} x_1 \\ x_2 \\ \\ \end{array}$$

3.
$$\begin{array}{cccc} x_1 & x_2 & s_1 & s_2 \\ \end{array}$$
$$\left[\begin{array}{cccc|c} 0 & \frac{1}{14} & 1 & -\frac{1}{7} & \frac{186}{21} \\ 1 & \frac{12}{7} & 0 & \frac{4}{7} & \frac{32}{7} \\ \hline 0 & \frac{12}{7} & 0 & \frac{32}{7} & \frac{256}{7} \end{array}\right]\begin{array}{l} s_1 \\ x_1 \\ \\ \end{array}$$

4.
$$\begin{array}{cccc} x_1 & x_2 & s_1 & s_2 \\ \end{array}$$
$$\left[\begin{array}{cccc|c} \frac{1}{4} & \frac{1}{2} & 1 & 0 & 10 \\ \frac{7}{4} & 3 & 0 & 1 & 8 \\ \hline -8 & -12 & 0 & 0 & 0 \end{array}\right]\begin{array}{l} s_1 \\ s_2 \\ \\ \end{array}$$

5.
$$\begin{array}{cccc} x_1 & x_2 & s_1 & s_2 \\ \end{array}$$
$$\left[\begin{array}{cccc|c} 1 & -2 & 0 & 4 & 24 \\ 0 & -2 & 1 & 4 & 36 \\ \hline 5 & -10 & 12 & 4 & 20 \end{array}\right]\begin{array}{l} x_1 \\ s_1 \\ \\ \end{array}$$

6.
$$\begin{array}{cccc} x_1 & x_2 & s_1 & s_2 \\ \end{array}$$
$$\left[\begin{array}{cccc|c} 1 & 3 & 1 & 0 & 30 \\ 2 & 1 & 0 & 1 & 12 \\ \hline -2 & -5 & 0 & 0 & 0 \end{array}\right]\begin{array}{l} s_1 \\ s_2 \\ \\ \end{array}$$

In Problems 7–22 use the simplex method to solve each maximum linear programming problem.

7. Maximize

$$P = 5x_1 + 7x_2$$

subject to

$$2x_1 + 3x_2 \le 12 \qquad x_1 \ge 0$$
$$3x_1 + x_2 \le 12 \qquad x_2 \ge 0$$

8. Maximize

$$P = x_1 + 5x_2$$

subject to

$$2x_1 + x_2 \le 10 \qquad x_1 \ge 0$$
$$x_1 + 2x_2 \le 10 \qquad x_2 \ge 0$$

9. Maximize

$$P = 5x_1 + 7x_2$$

subject to

$$x_1 + 2x_2 \le 2 \qquad x_1 \ge 0$$
$$2x_1 + x_2 \le 2 \qquad x_2 \ge 0$$

10. Maximize

$$P = 5x_1 + 4x_2$$

subject to

$$x_1 + x_2 \le 2 \qquad x_1 \ge 0$$
$$2x_1 + 3x_2 \le 6 \qquad x_2 \ge 0$$

11. Maximize

$$P = 3x_1 + x_2$$

subject to

$$x_1 + x_2 \le \;\; 2 \qquad x_1 \ge 0$$
$$2x_1 + 3x_2 \le 12 \qquad x_2 \ge 0$$
$$3x_1 + x_2 \le 12$$

12. Maximize

$$P = 3x_1 + 5x_2$$

subject to

$$2x_1 + x_2 \le 4 \qquad x_1 \ge 0$$
$$x_1 + 2x_2 \le 6 \qquad x_2 \ge 0$$

13. Maximize

$$P = 2x_1 + x_2 + x_3$$

subject to

$$-2x_1 + x_2 - 2x_3 \le 4 \qquad x_1 \ge 0$$
$$x_1 - 2x_2 + x_3 \le 2 \qquad x_2 \ge 0$$
$$x_3 \ge 0$$

14. Maximize

$$P = 4x_1 + 2x_2 + 5x_3$$

subject to

$$x_1 + 3x_2 + 2x_3 \le 30 \qquad x_1 \ge 0$$
$$2x_1 + x_2 + 3x_3 \le 12 \qquad x_2 \ge 0$$
$$x_3 \ge 0$$

15. Maximize

$$P = 2x_1 + x_2 + 3x_3$$

subject to

$$x_1 + 2x_2 + x_3 \le 25 \qquad x_1 \ge 0$$
$$3x_1 + 2x_2 + 3x_3 \le 30 \qquad x_2 \ge 0$$
$$x_3 \ge 0$$

16. Maximize
$$P = 6x_1 + 3x_2 + 2x_3$$
subject to
$$2x_1 + 2x_2 + 3x_3 \leq 30 \qquad x_1 \geq 0$$
$$2x_1 + 2x_2 + x_3 \leq 12 \qquad x_2 \geq 0$$
$$x_3 \geq 0$$

17. Maximize
$$P = 2x_1 + 4x_2 + x_3 + x_4$$
subject to
$$2x_1 + x_2 + 2x_3 + 3x_4 \leq 12 \qquad x_1 \geq 0$$
$$2x_2 + x_3 + 2x_4 \leq 20 \qquad x_2 \geq 0$$
$$2x_1 + x_2 + 4x_3 \leq 16 \qquad x_3 \geq 0$$
$$x_4 \geq 0$$

18. Maximize
$$P = 2x_1 + 4x_2 + x_3$$
subject to
$$-x_1 + 2x_2 + 3x_3 \leq 6 \qquad x_1 \geq 0$$
$$-x_1 + 4x_2 + 5x_3 \leq 5 \qquad x_2 \geq 0$$
$$-x_1 + 5x_2 + 7x_3 \leq 7 \qquad x_3 \geq 0$$

19. Maximize
$$P = 2x_1 + x_2 + x_3$$
subject to
$$x_1 + 2x_2 + 4x_3 \leq 20 \qquad x_1 \geq 0$$
$$2x_1 + 4x_2 + 4x_3 \leq 60 \qquad x_2 \geq 0$$
$$3x_1 + 4x_2 + x_3 \leq 90 \qquad x_3 \geq 0$$

20. Maximize
$$P = x_1 + 2x_2 + 4x_3$$
subject to
$$8x_1 + 5x_2 - 4x_3 \leq 30 \qquad x_1 \geq 0$$
$$-2x_1 + 6x_2 + x_3 \leq 5 \qquad x_2 \geq 0$$
$$-2x_1 + 2x_2 + x_3 \leq 15 \qquad x_3 \geq 0$$

21. Maximize
$$P = x_1 + 2x_2 + 4x_3 - x_4$$
subject to
$$5x_1 + 4x_3 + 6x_4 \leq 20 \qquad x_1 \geq 0 \qquad x_3 \geq 0$$
$$4x_1 + 2x_2 + 2x_3 + 8x_4 \leq 40 \qquad x_2 \geq 0 \qquad x_4 \geq 0$$

22. Maximize

$$P = x_1 + 2x_2 - x_3 + 3x_4$$

subject to

$$2x_1 + 4x_2 + 5x_3 + 6x_4 \leq 24 \qquad x_1 \geq 0 \qquad x_3 \geq 0$$
$$4x_1 + 4x_2 + 2x_3 + 2x_4 \leq 4 \qquad x_2 \geq 0 \qquad x_4 \geq 0$$

23. *Mixture Problem.* Nutt's Nut Company has 500 pounds of peanuts, 100 pounds of pecans, and 50 pounds of cashews on hand. They package three types of 5-pound cans of nuts: Can I contains 3 pounds peanuts, 1 pound pecans, and 1 pound cashews; Can II contains 4 pounds peanuts, $\frac{1}{2}$ pound pecans, and $\frac{1}{2}$ pound cashews; and Can III contains 5 pounds peanuts. The selling price for each can is $8 for Can I, $7 for Can II, and $5 for Can III. How many cans of each kind should be made to maximize revenue?

24. One of the methods used by the Alexander Company to separate copper, lead, and zinc from ores is the flotation separation process. This process consists of three steps: oiling, mixing, and separation. These steps must be applied for 2, 2, and 1 hour, respectively, to produce 1 unit of copper; 2, 3, and 1 hour, respectively, to produce 1 unit of lead; and 1, 1, and 3 hours, respectively, to produce 1 unit of zinc. The oiling and separation phases of the process can be in operation for a maximum of 10 hours a day, while the mixing phase can be in operation for a maximum of 11 hours a day. The Alexander Company makes a profit of $45 per unit of copper, $30 per unit lead, and $35 per unit zinc. The demand for these metals is unlimited. How many units of each metal should be produced daily by use of the flotation process to achieve the highest profit?

25. A wood cabinet manufacturer produces cabinets for television consoles, stereo systems, and radios, each of which must be assembled, decorated, and crated. Each television console requires 3 hours to assemble, 5 hours to decorate, and 0.1 hour to crate and returns a profit of $10. Each stereo system requires 10 hours to assemble, 8 hours to decorate, and 0.6 hour to crate and returns a profit of $25. Each radio requires 1 hour to assemble, 1 hour to decorate and 0.1 hour to crate and returns a profit of $3. The manufacturer has 30,000, 40,000, and 120 hours available weekly for assembling, decorating, and crating, respectively. How many units of each product should be manufactured to maximize profit?

26. The finishing process in the manufacture of cocktail tables and end tables requires sanding, staining, and varnishing. The time in minutes, required for each finishing process is given in the table below:

	Sanding	Staining	Varnishing
End table	8	10	4
Cocktail table	4	4	8

The equipment required for each process is used on one table at a time and is available for 6 hours each day. If the profit on each cocktail table is $20 and on each end table is $15, how many of each should be manufactured each day in order to maximize profit?

27. A large TV manufacturer has warehouse facilities for storing its 25″ color TVs in Chicago, New York, and Denver. Each month the city of Atlanta is shipped at most 400 25″ TVs. The cost of transporting each TV to Atlanta from Chicago, New York, and Denver averages $20, $20, and $40, respectively, while the cost of labor required for packing averages $6, $8, and $4, respectively. Suppose $10,000 is allocated each month for

transportation costs and $3000 is allocated for labor costs. If the profit on each TV made in Chicago is $50, in New York is $80, and Denver is $40, how should monthly shipping arrangements be scheduled to maximize profit?

4.3 THE SIMPLEX METHOD: THE MINIMUM PROBLEM

STANDARD FORM OF A MINIMUM PROBLEM □ DUAL OF A MINIMUM PROBLEM

So far in this chapter, we have discussed only maximum linear programming problems, in which the optimal solution yields the largest possible value for the objective function. In this section we discuss *minimum* problems, where the smallest possible value is desired. Among a number of techniques for solving such problems is one developed by John Von Neumann and others, in which the solution (if it exists) of a minimum problem is found by solving a related maximum problem called the *dual problem.*

Before constructing the dual problem, the minimum problem must be placed in *standard form.*

STANDARD FORM OF A MINIMUM PROBLEM

A minimum problem is said to be in standard form provided the following conditions are met

Standard Form for a Minimum Problem

Condition 1. All the variables must be nonnegative.

Condition 2. All the other constraints must be written with ≥ signs. (This is just the opposite of the standard form requirement for a maximum problem.)

Condition 3. The objective function to be minimized must be written with nonnegative coefficients.

□ **Example 1** Determine which of the following minimum problems are in standard form.

(a) Minimize

$$C = 2x_1 + 3x_2$$

subject to the constraints

$$x_1 + 3x_2 \geq 24 \qquad x_1 \geq 0, \quad x_2 \geq 0$$
$$2x_1 + x_2 \geq 18$$

(b) Minimize

$$C = 3x_1 - x_2 + 4x_3$$

subject to the constraints

$$3x_1 + x_2 + x_3 \geq 12 \qquad x_1 \geq 0, \quad x_2 \geq 0$$
$$x_1 + x_2 + x_3 \geq 8 \qquad x_3 \geq 0$$

(c) Minimize
$$C = 2x_1 + x_2 + x_3$$

subject to the constraints

$$x_1 - 3x_2 + x_3 \le 12 \qquad x_1 \ge 0, \quad x_2 \ge 0$$
$$x_1 + x_2 + x_3 \ge 1 \qquad x_3 \ge 0$$

(d) Minimize
$$C = 2x_1 + x_2 + 3x_3$$

subject to the constraints

$$-x_1 + 2x_2 + x_3 \ge -2 \qquad x_1 \ge 0, \quad x_2 \ge 0$$
$$x_1 + x_2 + x_3 \ge \quad 6 \qquad x_3 \ge 0$$

Solution (a) Since all three conditions are met, this minimum problem is in standard form.

(b) Conditions 1 and 2 are met but condition 3 is not, since the coefficient of x_2 in the objective function is negative. Thus, this minimum problem is not in standard form.

(c) Conditions 1 and 3 are met but condition 2 is not, since the first constraint $x_1 - 3x_2 + x_3 \le 12$ is not written with a $\ge$ sign. Thus, the minimum problem, as stated, is not in standard form. Notice however, that by multiplying by -1, we can write this constraint as $-x_1 + 3x_2 - x_3 \ge -12$. Written in this way, the minimum problem is in standard form.

(d) Conditions 1, 2, and 3 are each met, so this minimum problem is in standard form.   □

THE DUAL OF A MINIMUM PROBLEM

We illustrate by example how to obtain the dual problem.

□ **Example 2**   Obtain the dual problem of the minimum problem:
Minimize

$$C = 300x_1 + 480x_2$$

subject to the conditions

$$x_1 + 3x_2 \ge 0.25 \qquad x_1 \ge 0$$
$$2x_1 + 2x_2 \ge 0.45 \qquad x_2 \ge 0$$

Solution Observe that the minimum problem is in standard form. We begin by constructing a special matrix for the coefficients of the constraints of this problem without introducing slack variables. As in a simplex tableau, we place the objective function in the last row. The result is

$$\begin{array}{cc} x_1 & x_2 \end{array}$$
$$\begin{bmatrix} 1 & 3 & | & 0.25 \\ 2 & 2 & | & 0.45 \\ 300 & 480 & | & 0 \end{bmatrix}$$

Similarly, the special matrix for the maximum problem in Example 5 of Chapter 3 (page 130) would be

$$\begin{bmatrix} 1 & 2 & 300 \\ 3 & 2 & 480 \\ 0.25 & 0.45 & 0 \end{bmatrix}$$

Observe that this matrix is the transpose of the previous one; that is, the rows of the first matrix (for the minimum problem) are the columns of the second matrix (for the maximum problem). When a maximum and a minimum problem have this rela-

Dual Problems   tionship, they are called *dual problems* of each other.

Thus, the dual problem of the given minimum problem is:
Maximize

$$P = 0.25y_1 + 0.45y_2$$

subject to the conditions

$$y_1 + 2y_2 \leq 300 \qquad y_1 \geq 0$$
$$3y_1 + 2y_2 \leq 480 \qquad y_2 \geq 0 \qquad \qquad \square$$

This duality relationship is significant because of the following principle:

> **Von Neumann Duality Principle** The optimal solution of a minimum linear programming problem, if the solution exists, has the same value as the optimal solution of the maximum problem that is its dual.

In other words, one way to solve a minimum problem in linear programming is to solve the dual problem. To obtain this dual problem, proceed as follows:

Obtaining the Dual Problem

> **Step 1:** Write the minimum problem in standard form.
>
> **Step 2:** Construct the special matrix from the constraints and the objective function.
>
> **Step 3:** Interchange the rows and columns to form the special matrix of the dual problem.
>
> **Step 4:** Translate this matrix into a maximum problem in standard form.

Dualization   This process is known as *dualization.* It is illustrated in the next example.

JOHN von NEUMANN (1903–1957) was born in Budapest, Hungary, but spent most of his life at Princeton University and the Institute for Advanced Study. He developed the theory of games at the age of 25 and is largely responsible for inventing the digital computer. Von Neumann, probably the greatest mathematical genius of this century, had a fantastic capacity for doing mental calculations and possessed a photographic memory. He contributed to quantum mechanics, economics, and computer science, and developed a technique that accelerated the production of the first atomic bomb.

☐ **Example 3**   Find the dual of the minimum problem:
Minimize

$$C = 2x_1 + 3x_2$$

subject to

$$2x_1 + x_2 \geq 6 \qquad x_1 \geq 0$$
$$x_1 + 2x_2 \geq 4 \qquad x_2 \geq 0$$
$$x_1 + x_2 \geq 5$$

Solution   Observe that the minimum problem is in standard form. The special matrix is

$$\begin{bmatrix} 2 & 1 & | & 6 \\ 1 & 2 & | & 4 \\ 1 & 1 & | & 5 \\ 2 & 3 & | & 0 \end{bmatrix}$$

Interchanging rows and columns, we obtain the matrix

$$\begin{bmatrix} 2 & 1 & 1 & | & 2 \\ 1 & 2 & 1 & | & 3 \\ 6 & 4 & 5 & | & 0 \end{bmatrix}$$

This is the special matrix form of the following maximum problem:
Maximize

$$P = 6y_1 + 4y_2 + 5y_3$$

subject to

$$2y_1 + y_2 + y_3 \leq 2 \qquad y_1 \geq 0$$
$$y_1 + 2y_2 + y_3 \leq 3 \qquad y_2 \geq 0$$
$$y_3 \geq 0$$

This maximum problem is in standard form and is the dual of the original problem.   ☐

Some observations about this example:

1. The variables (x_1, x_2) of the minimum problem have different names from the variables of its dual problem (y_1, y_2, y_3).
2. The minimum problem has three constraints and two variables, while the dual problem has two constraints and three variables. (In general, if a problem has m constraints and n variables, its dual will have n constraints and m variables.)
3. The inequalities defining the constraints are $\geq$ for the minimum problem and $\leq$ for the maximum problem.
4. Since the coefficients in the minimal objective function are positive, the dual problem has nonnegative numbers to the right of the $\leq$ signs.
5. We follow the custom of denoting an objective function by C (for *Cost*) if it is to be minimized, and P (for *Profit*) if it is to be maximized.

□ **Example 4**   Solve the maximum problem of Example 3 by the simplex method and thereby obtain the solution for the minimum problem.

Solution   We introduce slack variables s_1 and s_2 to get

$$2y_1 + y_2 + y_3 + s_1 = 2$$
$$y_1 + 2y_2 + y_3 + s_2 = 3$$

The initial simplex tableau is

$$
\begin{array}{ccccc}
y_1 & y_2 & y_3 & s_1 & s_2 \\
\end{array}
\left[
\begin{array}{ccc|cc|c}
② & 1 & 1 & 1 & 0 & 2 \\
1 & 2 & 1 & 0 & 1 & 3 \\
\hline
-6 & -4 & -5 & 0 & 0 & 0
\end{array}
\right]
\begin{array}{c}
s_1 \\
s_2 \\
\\
\end{array}
$$

omitting the column for P. We have drawn an extra vertical line in the tableau to set off the columns of s_1 and s_2. (As you will see, the slack variable columns play a special role in the solution of a dual problem.) Now, using the 2 circled above as a pivot element, we pivot and get

$$
\begin{array}{ccccc}
y_1 & y_2 & y_3 & s_1 & s_2 \\
\end{array}
\left[
\begin{array}{ccc|cc|c}
1 & \frac{1}{2} & ⟨\frac{1}{2}⟩ & \frac{1}{2} & 0 & 1 \\
0 & \frac{3}{2} & \frac{1}{2} & -\frac{1}{2} & 1 & 2 \\
\hline
0 & -1 & -2 & 3 & 0 & 6
\end{array}
\right]
\begin{array}{c}
y_1 \\
s_2 \\
\\
\end{array}
$$

This time, the entry in row 1, column 3 is the pivot. When we pivot, we obtain

$$
\begin{array}{ccccc}
y_1 & y_2 & y_3 & s_1 & s_2 \\
\end{array}
\left[
\begin{array}{ccc|cc|c}
2 & 1 & 1 & 1 & 0 & 2 \\
-1 & 1 & 0 & -1 & 1 & 1 \\
\hline
4 & 1 & 0 & 5 & 0 & 10
\end{array}
\right]
\begin{array}{c}
y_3 \\
s_2 \\
\\
\end{array}
$$

Now all the entries in the objective row are greater than or equal to 0, so this is a final tableau and an optimal solution has been reached. We read from it that the solution to the maximum problem is

$$P = 10 \qquad y_1 = 0 \qquad y_2 = 0 \qquad y_3 = 2$$

The duality principle states that the minimum value of the objective function in the original problem is the same as the maximum value in the dual; that is,

$$C = 10$$

But which values of x_1 and x_2 will yield this minimum value? There are some details of the duality principle and its application that we have omitted here; these concern the relationships between the variables of the original problem and the slack variables used in the solution of the dual problem. As a consequence of these relationships, the entire minimal solution can be read from the right end of the objective row of the final tableau:

$$x_1 = 5 \qquad x_2 = 0 \qquad C = 10 \qquad\qquad □$$

Notice in the solution to Example 4 that the value of x_1 is found at the bottom of the column corresponding to s_1 and x_2 is similarly found in the column corresponding to s_2. In general, the values of the slack variables are not the same as those of the original variables. Observe that here

$$x_1 = 5 \qquad x_2 = 0$$

while

$$s_1 = 0 \qquad s_2 = 1$$

We summarize how to solve a minimum linear programming problem below:

Solving a
Minimum Problem

> **Step 1:** Write the dual (maximum) problem.
>
> **Step 2:** Solve this maximum problem by the simplex method.
>
> **Step 3:** Read the optimal solution for the original problem from the objective row of the final simplex tableau. The variables will appear as the last entries in the columns corresponding to the slack variables.
>
> **Step 4:** The minimum value of the objective function (C) will appear in the lower right corner of the final tableau; it is equal to the maximum value of the dual objective function (P).

□ **Example 5**   Minimize

$$C = 6x_1 + 8x_2 + x_3$$

subject to

$$
\begin{aligned}
3x_1 + 5x_2 + 3x_3 &\geq 20 & x_1 &\geq 0 \\
x_1 + 3x_2 + 2x_3 &\geq 9 & x_2 &\geq 0 \\
6x_1 + 2x_2 + 5x_3 &\geq 30 & x_3 &\geq 0
\end{aligned}
$$

Solution   This minimum problem is in standard form. The special matrix of this problem is

$$
\left[\begin{array}{ccc|c}
3 & 5 & 3 & 20 \\
1 & 3 & 2 & 9 \\
6 & 2 & 5 & 30 \\
6 & 8 & 1 & 0
\end{array}\right]
$$

We interchange rows and columns to get

$$
\left[\begin{array}{ccc|c}
3 & 1 & 6 & 6 \\
5 & 3 & 2 & 8 \\
3 & 2 & 5 & 1 \\
20 & 9 & 30 & 0
\end{array}\right]
$$

The dual problem is:
Maximize

$$P = 20y_1 + 9y_2 + 30y_3$$

subject to

$$3y_1 + y_2 + 6y_3 \le 6 \qquad y_1 \ge 0$$
$$5y_1 + 3y_2 + 2y_3 \le 8 \qquad y_2 \ge 0$$
$$3y_1 + 2y_2 + 5y_3 \le 1 \qquad y_3 \ge 0$$

We introduce slack variables s_1, s_2, and s_3. The initial tableau for this problem is

$$
\begin{array}{cccccc}
y_1 & y_2 & y_3 & s_1 & s_2 & s_3 \\
\end{array}
$$

$$
\left[
\begin{array}{ccc|ccc|c}
3 & 1 & 6 & 1 & 0 & 0 & 6 \\
5 & 3 & 2 & 0 & 1 & 0 & 8 \\
3 & 2 & 5 & 0 & 0 & 1 & 1 \\
\hline
-20 & -9 & -30 & 0 & 0 & 0 & 0 \\
\end{array}
\right]
$$

The final tableau (as you may verify) is

$$
\begin{array}{cccccc}
y_1 & y_2 & y_3 & s_1 & s_2 & s_3 \\
\end{array}
$$

$$
\left[
\begin{array}{ccc|ccc|c}
0 & -1 & 1 & 1 & 0 & -1 & 5 \\
0 & -\frac{1}{3} & -\frac{19}{3} & 0 & 1 & -\frac{5}{3} & \frac{19}{3} \\
1 & \frac{2}{3} & \frac{5}{3} & 0 & 0 & \frac{1}{3} & \frac{1}{3} \\
\hline
0 & \frac{13}{3} & \frac{10}{3} & 0 & 0 & \frac{20}{3} & \frac{20}{3} \\
\end{array}
\right]
\begin{array}{l}
s_1 \\
s_2 \\
y_1 \\
\\
\end{array}
$$

The solution to the maximum problem is

$$P = \frac{20}{3} \qquad y_1 = \frac{1}{3} \qquad y_2 = 0 \qquad y_3 = 0$$

For the minimum problem, the values of x_1, x_2, and x_3 are read as the last entries in the columns under s_1, s_2, and s_3, respectively. Hence, the optimal solution to the minimum problem is

$$x_1 = 0 \qquad x_2 = 0 \qquad x_3 = \frac{20}{3}$$

and the minimum value is $C = \frac{20}{3}$.   □

□ **Example 6**
Transportation
Problem

The Red Tomato Company operates two plants for canning its tomatoes and has two warehouses for storing the finished products until they are purchased by retailers. The company wants to arrange its shipments from the plants to the warehouses so that the requirements of the warehouses are met and shipping costs are kept at a minimum. The schedule shown in the table represents the per case shipping costs from plant to warehouse.

		Warehouse	
		A	B
Plant	I	$0.25	$0.18
	II	$0.25	$0.14

Each week, Plant I can produce at most 450 cases and Plant II can produce no more than 350 cases of tomatoes. Also, each week, Warehouse A requires at least 300 cases and Warehouse B requires at least 500 cases. If we represent the number of cases shipped from Plant I to Warehouse A by x_1, from Plant I to Warehouse B by x_2, and so on, the above data can be represented by the following table:

		Warehouse		Maximum Available
		A	B	
Plant	I	x_1	x_2	450
	II	x_3	x_4	350
Minimum demand		300	500	

The linear programming problem is stated as follows:
Minimize the cost equation

$$C = 0.25x_1 + 0.18x_2 + 0.25x_3 + 0.14x_4$$

subject to

$$x_1 + x_2 \leq 450 \qquad x_1 \geq 0$$
$$x_3 + x_4 \leq 350 \qquad x_2 \geq 0$$
$$x_1 + x_3 \geq 300 \qquad x_3 \geq 0$$
$$x_2 + x_4 \geq 500 \qquad x_4 \geq 0$$

To get the problem in standard form, we multiply both sides of the first two inequalities by -1:

$$-x_1 - x_2 \geq -450$$
$$-x_3 - x_4 \geq -350$$
$$x_1 + x_3 \geq 300$$
$$x_2 + x_4 \geq 500$$

The special matrix for the minimum problem is

$$\begin{bmatrix} -1 & -1 & 0 & 0 & -450 \\ 0 & 0 & -1 & -1 & -350 \\ 1 & 0 & 1 & 0 & 300 \\ 0 & 1 & 0 & 1 & 500 \\ 0.25 & 0.18 & 0.25 & 0.14 & 0 \end{bmatrix}$$

The dual matrix is

$$\begin{bmatrix} -1 & 0 & 1 & 0 & 0.25 \\ -1 & 0 & 0 & 1 & 0.18 \\ 0 & -1 & 1 & 0 & 0.25 \\ 0 & -1 & 0 & 1 & 0.14 \\ -450 & -350 & 300 & 500 & 0 \end{bmatrix}$$

and the dual (maximum) problem is:
Maximize

$$P = -450y_1 - 350y_2 + 300y_3 + 500y_4$$

subject to

$$-y_1 + y_3 \le 0.25 \qquad y_1 \ge 0$$
$$-y_1 + y_4 \le 0.18 \qquad y_2 \ge 0$$
$$-y_2 + y_3 \le 0.25 \qquad y_3 \ge 0$$
$$-y_2 + y_4 \le 0.14 \qquad y_4 \ge 0$$

Introducing the slack variables s_1, s_2, s_3, and s_4, we construct the initial simplex tableau and proceed to solve the dual problem:

$$
\rightarrow
\begin{array}{cccccccc|cc}
y_1 & y_2 & y_3 & y_4 & s_1 & s_2 & s_3 & s_4 & & \\
\hline
-1 & 0 & 1 & 0 & 1 & 0 & 0 & 0 & 0.25 & s_1 \\
-1 & 0 & 0 & 1 & 0 & 1 & 0 & 0 & 0.18 & s_2 \\
0 & -1 & 1 & 0 & 0 & 0 & 1 & 0 & 0.25 & s_3 \\
0 & -1 & 0 & ① & 0 & 0 & 0 & 1 & 0.14 & s_4 \\
\hline
450 & 350 & -300 & -500 & 0 & 0 & 0 & 0 & 0 &
\end{array}
$$
$$\uparrow$$

$$
\rightarrow
\begin{array}{cccccccc|c}
y_1 & y_2 & y_3 & y_4 & s_1 & s_2 & s_3 & s_4 & \\
\hline
-1 & 0 & ① & 0 & 1 & 0 & 0 & 0 & 0.25 \\
-1 & 1 & 0 & 0 & 0 & 1 & 0 & -1 & 0.04 \\
0 & -1 & 1 & 0 & 0 & 0 & 1 & 0 & 0.25 \\
0 & -1 & 0 & 1 & 0 & 0 & 0 & 1 & 0.14 \\
\hline
450 & -150 & -300 & 0 & 0 & 0 & 0 & 500 & 70
\end{array}
$$
$$\uparrow$$

$$
\rightarrow
\begin{array}{cccccccc|c}
y_1 & y_2 & y_3 & y_4 & s_1 & s_2 & s_3 & s_4 & \\
\hline
-1 & 0 & 1 & 0 & 1 & 0 & 0 & 0 & 0.25 \\
-1 & ① & 0 & 0 & 0 & 1 & 0 & -1 & 0.04 \\
1 & -1 & 0 & 0 & -1 & 0 & 1 & 0 & 0 \\
0 & -1 & 0 & 1 & 0 & 0 & 0 & 1 & 0.14 \\
\hline
150 & -150 & 0 & 0 & 300 & 0 & 0 & 500 & 145
\end{array}
$$
$$\uparrow$$

$$
\begin{array}{cccccccc|cc}
y_1 & y_2 & y_3 & y_4 & s_1 & s_2 & s_3 & s_4 & & \\
\hline
-1 & 0 & 1 & 0 & 1 & 0 & 0 & 0 & 0.25 & y_3 \\
-1 & 1 & 0 & 0 & 0 & 1 & 0 & 1 & 0.04 & y_2 \\
0 & 0 & 0 & 0 & -1 & 1 & 1 & -1 & 0.04 & s_3 \\
-1 & 0 & 0 & 1 & 0 & 1 & 0 & 0 & 0.18 & y_4 \\
\hline
0 & 0 & 0 & 0 & 300 & 150 & 0 & 350 & 151 &
\end{array}
$$

$$\underbrace{\qquad}_{} $$

$$x_1 \qquad x_2 \qquad x_3 \qquad x_4 \qquad C$$

The final tableau yields the solution to the original minimum problem:

$$C = \$151 \qquad x_1 = 300 \qquad x_2 = 150 \qquad x_3 = 0 \qquad x_4 = 350$$

This means Plant I should deliver 300 cases to Warehouse A and 150 cases to Warehouse B; and Plant II should deliver 350 cases to Warehouse B to keep costs at the minimum ($151).

□

A final note for this section: If you find that the dual of a minimum problem has an unbounded solution, then the minimum problem has no feasible solution; the solution set of its constraints is empty.

Exercise 4.3 *Answers to Odd-Numbered Problems begin on page* 609.

In Problems 1–6 determine which of the given minimum problems are in standard form.

1. Minimize

$$C = 2x_1 + 3x_2$$

subject to the constraints

$$4x_1 - x_2 \geq 2 \qquad x_1 \geq 0$$
$$x_1 + x_2 \geq 1 \qquad x_2 \geq 0$$

2. Minimize

$$C = 3x_1 + 5x_2$$

subject to the constraints

$$3x_1 - x_2 \geq 4 \qquad x_1 \geq 0$$
$$x_1 - 2x_2 \geq 3 \qquad x_2 \geq 0$$

3. Minimize

$$C = 2x_1 - x_2$$

subject to the constraints

$$2x_1 - x_2 \geq 1 \qquad x_1 \geq 0$$
$$-2x_1 \geq -3 \qquad x_2 \geq 0$$

4. Minimize

$$C = 2x_1 + 3x_2$$

subject to the constraints

$$x_1 - x_2 \leq 3 \qquad x_1 \geq 0$$
$$2x_1 + 3x_2 \geq 4 \qquad x_2 \geq 0$$

5. Minimize

$$C = 3x_1 + 7x_2 + x_3$$

subject to the constraints

$$x_1 + x_3 \leq 6 \qquad x_1 \geq 0, \ x_2 \geq 0$$
$$2x_1 + x_2 \geq 4 \qquad x_3 \geq 0$$

6. Minimize

$$C = x_1 - x_2 + x_3$$

subject to the constraints

$$x_1 + x_2 \geq 6 \qquad x_1 \geq 0, \quad x_2 \geq 0$$
$$2x_1 - x_3 \geq 4 \qquad x_3 \geq 0$$

In Problems 7–10 write the dual problem for each minimum linear programming problem.

7. Minimize

$$C = 2x_1 + 3x_2$$

subject to

$$x_1 + x_2 \geq 2 \qquad x_1 \geq 0$$
$$2x_1 + 3x_2 \geq 6 \qquad x_2 \geq 0$$

8. Minimize

$$C = 3x_1 + 4x_2$$

subject to

$$2x_1 + x_2 \geq 2 \qquad x_1 \geq 0$$
$$2x_1 + x_2 \geq 6 \qquad x_2 \geq 0$$

9. Minimize

$$C = 3x_1 + x_2 + x_3$$

subject to

$$x_1 + x_2 + x_3 \geq 5 \qquad x_1 \geq 0$$
$$2x_1 + x_2 \geq 4 \qquad x_2 \geq 0$$
$$x_3 \geq 0$$

10. Minimize

$$C = 2x_1 + x_2 + x_3$$

subject to

$$2x_1 + x_2 + x_3 \geq 4 \qquad x_1 \geq 0$$
$$x_1 + 2x_2 + x_3 \geq 6 \qquad x_2 \geq 0$$
$$x_3 \geq 0$$

In Problems 11–16 solve each minimum linear programming problem by using the simplex method.

11. Minimize

$$C = 6x_1 + 3x_2$$

subject to

$$x_1 + x_2 \geq 2 \qquad x_1 \geq 0$$
$$2x_1 + 6x_2 \geq 6 \qquad x_2 \geq 0$$

12. Minimize

$$C = 3x_1 + 4x_2$$

subject to

$$x_1 + x_2 \geq 3 \qquad x_1 \geq 0$$
$$2x_1 + x_2 \geq 4 \qquad x_2 \geq 0$$

13. Minimize

$$C = 6x_1 + 3x_2$$

subject to

$$x_1 + x_2 \geq 4 \qquad x_1 \geq 0$$
$$3x_1 + 4x_2 \geq 12 \qquad x_2 \geq 0$$

14. Minimize

$$C = 2x_1 + 3x_2 + 4x_3$$

subject to

$$x_1 - 2x_2 - 3x_3 \geq -2 \qquad x_1 \geq 0$$
$$x_1 + x_2 + x_3 \geq 2 \qquad x_2 \geq 0$$
$$2x_1 + x_3 \geq 3 \qquad x_3 \geq 0$$

15. Minimize

$$C = x_1 + 2x_2 + x_3$$

subject to

$$x_1 - 3x_2 + 4x_3 \geq 12 \qquad x_1 \geq 0$$
$$3x_1 + x_2 + 2x_3 \geq 10 \qquad x_2 \geq 0$$
$$x_1 - x_2 - x_3 \geq -8 \qquad x_3 \geq 0$$

16. Minimize

$$C = x_1 + 2x_2 + 4x_3$$

subject to

$$x_1 - x_2 + 3x_3 \geq 4 \qquad x_1 \geq 0$$
$$2x_1 + 2x_2 - 3x_3 \geq 6 \qquad x_2 \geq 0$$
$$-x_1 + 2x_2 + 3x_3 \geq 2 \qquad x_3 \geq 0$$

17. *Mixture Problem.* Minimize the cost of preparing the following mixture, which is made up of three foods, I, II, III. Food I costs $2 per unit, Food II costs $1 per unit, and Food III costs $3 per unit. Each unit of Food I contains 2 ounces of protein and 4 ounces of carbohydrate; each unit of Food II has 3 ounces of protein and 2 ounces of carbohydrate; and each unit of Food III has 4 ounces of protein and 2 ounces of carbohydrate. The mixture must contain at least 20 ounces of protein and 15 ounces of carbohydrate.

18. *Advertising.* A local appliance store has decided on an advertising campaign utilizing newspaper and radio. Each dollar spent on newspaper advertising is expected to reach 50 people in the "Under $25,000" and 40 in the "Over $25,000" bracket. Each dollar spent on radio advertising is expected to reach 70 people in the "Under $25,000" and 20 people in the "Over $25,000". If the store wants to reach at least 100,000 people in the "Under $25,000" and at least 120,000 in the "Over $25,000" bracket, how should it proceed so that the cost of advertising is minimized?

4.4 THE SIMPLEX METHOD WITH MIXED CONSTRAINTS; PHASE I/PHASE II

MIXED CONSTRAINTS □ THE SIMPLEX METHOD WITH MIXED CONSTRAINTS
□ THE MINIMUM PROBLEM □ EQUALITY CONSTRAINTS □ MODEL: POLLUTION CONTROL
□ MODEL: ECOLOGY

Thus far we have only developed the simplex method for solving maximum and minimum problems in standard form. In this section, we develop the simplex method for linear programming problems that cannot be written in standard form.

MIXED CONSTRAINTS

Recall that for a maximum problem in standard form each constraint must be of the form

$$a_1 x_1 + a_2 x_2 + \cdots + a_n x_n \leq b_1, \qquad b_1 > 0$$

Mixed Constraints

That is, each is a linear expression *less than or equal to a positive constant.* When the constraints are of any other form—greater than or equal to or equal to—we have what are called *mixed constraints.* The following example will illustrate the simplex method for solving these problems with mixed constraints.

THE SIMPLEX METHOD WITH MIXED CONSTRAINTS

□ **Example 1**   Maximize

$$P = 20x_1 + 15x_2$$

subject to the constraints

$$x_1 + x_2 \geq 7 \qquad x_1 \geq 0$$
$$9x_1 + 5x_2 \leq 45 \qquad x_2 \geq 0$$
$$2x_1 + x_2 \geq 8$$

Solution   We first observe this is a maximum problem that is not in standard form. Second, it cannot be modified so as to be in standard form.

> **Step 1:** Write each constraint except the nonnegative constraints as an inequality with the variables on the left side of a $\leq$ sign.

To do this, we merely multiply the first and third inequality by -1. The result is that the constraints become

$$-x_1 - x_2 \leq -7$$
$$9x_1 + 5x_2 \leq 45$$
$$-2x_1 - x_2 \leq -8$$

> **Step 2:** Introduce nonnegative variables on the left side of each inequality to form an equality.

To do this, we will use the variables, s_1, s_2, s_3 to obtain

$$-x_1 - x_2 + s_1 = -7 \qquad s_1 \geq 0$$
$$9x_1 + 5x_2 + s_2 = 45 \qquad s_2 \geq 0$$
$$-2x_1 - x_2 + s_3 = -8 \qquad s_3 \geq 0$$

Step 3: Set up the initial simplex tableau.

$$
\begin{array}{ccccc}
x_1 & x_2 & s_1 & s_2 & s_3 \\
\end{array}
$$
$$
\left[
\begin{array}{ccccc|c}
-1 & -1 & 1 & 0 & 0 & -7 \\
9 & 5 & 0 & 1 & 0 & 45 \\
-2 & -1 & 0 & 0 & 1 & -8 \\
\hline
-20 & -15 & 0 & 0 & 0 & 0 \\
\end{array}
\right]
$$

This initial tableau represents the solution $x_1 = 0$, $x_2 = 0$, $s_1 = -7$, $s_2 = 45$, $s_3 = -8$. This is not a feasible solution. The reason for this lies in the existence of the two negative constraints in the right-hand column. That is, this tableau represents a solution that causes two of the variables to be negative, in violation of the nonnegativity requirement. Whenever this occurs, the simplex algorithm consists of two phases.

Phase I/Phase II

Step 4: Determine whether Phase I or Phase II applies. Phase I is used whenever negative entries appear in the right-hand column; Phase II is used whenever all the entries in the right-hand column are nonnegative. In determining whether Phase I or Phase II applies, the objective row is ignored.

Step 5: Select the pivot element.
Phase I: The pivot row is the row with the most negative value in the right column. If all entries in the pivot row are nonnegative, there are no feasible solutions and the problem has no solution.
For each column with a negative entry in the pivot row, form the ratio using the right-hand column entry as denominator. The largest of these is the pivot column.
Phase II. Follow the pivoting strategy given on page 161 of Section 4.2.

For our example, we use Phase I. The pivot row is row 3 (due to the -8). To find the pivot column we form the ratios $-2/-8 = 1/4$ and $-1/-8 = 1/8$, the largest being 1/4. Thus, the pivot column is column 1.

Step 6: Go back to Step 4 unless a final tableau has been reached.

For our example, after pivoting on the entry in row 3, column 1, we get the tableau

$$
\begin{array}{ccccc}
x_1 & x_2 & s_1 & s_2 & s_3 \\
\end{array}
$$

$$
\left[
\begin{array}{ccccc|c}
0 & -\frac{1}{2} & 1 & 0 & -\frac{1}{2} & -3 \\
0 & \frac{1}{2} & 0 & 1 & \frac{9}{2} & 9 \\
1 & \frac{1}{2} & 0 & 0 & -\frac{1}{2} & 4 \\
\hline
0 & -5 & 0 & 0 & -10 & 80
\end{array}
\right]
$$

Step 4: Phase I applies.

Step 5: The pivot row is row 1; the pivot column is column 2 (or column 5). After pivoting, we get the tableau

$$
\begin{array}{ccccc}
x_1 & x_2 & s_1 & s_2 & s_3 \\
\end{array}
$$

$$
\left[
\begin{array}{ccccc|c}
0 & 1 & -2 & 0 & 1 & 6 \\
0 & 0 & 1 & 1 & 4 & 6 \\
1 & 0 & 1 & 0 & -1 & 1 \\
\hline
0 & 0 & -10 & 0 & -5 & 110
\end{array}
\right]
$$

Step 4: Phase II applies.

Step 5: The pivot column is column 3; the pivot row is row 3. After pivoting, we get the tableau

$$
\begin{array}{ccccc}
x_1 & x_2 & s_1 & s_2 & s_3 \\
\end{array}
$$

$$
\left[
\begin{array}{ccccc|c}
2 & 1 & 0 & 0 & -1 & 8 \\
-1 & 0 & 0 & 1 & 5 & 5 \\
1 & 0 & 1 & 0 & -1 & 1 \\
\hline
10 & 0 & 0 & 0 & -15 & 120
\end{array}
\right]
$$

Step 4: Phase II applies.

Step 5: The pivot column is column 5; the pivot row is row 2. After pivoting, we get the tableau

$$
\begin{array}{ccccc}
x_1 & x_2 & s_1 & s_2 & s_3 \\
\end{array}
$$

$$
\left[
\begin{array}{ccccc|c}
\frac{9}{5} & 1 & 0 & \frac{1}{5} & 0 & 9 \\
-\frac{1}{5} & 0 & 0 & \frac{1}{5} & 1 & 1 \\
\frac{4}{5} & 0 & 1 & \frac{1}{5} & 0 & 2 \\
\hline
7 & 0 & 0 & 3 & 0 & 135
\end{array}
\right]
\begin{array}{c}
x_2 \\
s_3 \\
s_1 \\
\\
\end{array}
$$

This is a final tableau. The maximum value of P is 135 and it is achieved when $x_1 = 0$, $x_2 = 9$, $s_1 = 2$, $s_2 = 0$, $s_3 = 1$. ☐

THE MINIMUM PROBLEM

Earlier we presented a method of solving the minimum problem if it was in standard form. In general, a minimum problem can be changed to a maximum problem by realizing that in order to minimize C we must maximize $-C$. The following example will illustrate this method.

□ **Example 2** Minimize

$$C = 5x_1 + 6x_2$$

subject to the constraints

$$x_1 \geq 0, \qquad x_2 \geq 0$$
$$x_1 + x_2 \leq 10$$
$$x_1 + 2x_2 \geq 12$$
$$2x_1 + x_2 \geq 12$$
$$x_1 \geq 3$$

Solution We change our problem from minimizing $C = 5x_1 + 6x_2$ to maximizing $z = -C = -5x_1 - 6x_2$.

Step 1: Write each constraint with $\leq$.

$$x_1 + x_2 \leq 10$$
$$-x_1 - 2x_2 \leq -12$$
$$-2x_1 - x_2 \leq -12$$
$$-x_1 \leq -3$$

Step 2: Introduce nonnegative variables to form equalities:

$$s_1 \geq 0, \qquad s_2 \geq 0, \qquad s_3 \geq 0, \qquad s_4 \geq 0$$
$$x_1 + x_2 + s_1 = 10$$
$$-x_1 - 2x_2 + s_2 = -12$$
$$-2x_1 - x_2 + s_3 = -12$$
$$-x_1 + s_4 = -3$$

Step 3: Set up initial simplex tableau:

$$
\begin{array}{cccccc}
x_1 & x_2 & s_1 & s_2 & s_3 & s_4 \\
\end{array}
$$

$$
\left[
\begin{array}{cccccc|c}
1 & 1 & 1 & 0 & 0 & 0 & 10 \\
-1 & -2 & 0 & 1 & 0 & 0 & -12 \\
-2 & -1 & 0 & 0 & 1 & 0 & -12 \\
-1 & 0 & 0 & 0 & 0 & 1 & -3 \\
\hdashline
5 & 6 & 0 & 0 & 0 & 0 & 0 \\
\end{array}
\right]
$$

Step 4: Phase I applies.

Step 5: The pivot row is row 2 (or 3) and for this row the pivot column is column 2. After pivoting we get the tableau:

$$
\begin{array}{cccccc}
x_1 & x_2 & s_1 & s_2 & s_3 & s_4 \\
\end{array}
$$

$$
\left[
\begin{array}{cccccc|c}
\frac{1}{2} & 0 & 1 & \frac{1}{2} & 0 & 0 & 4 \\
\frac{1}{2} & 1 & 0 & -\frac{1}{2} & 0 & 0 & 6 \\
-\frac{3}{2} & 0 & 0 & -\frac{1}{2} & 1 & 0 & -6 \\
-1 & 0 & 0 & 0 & 0 & 1 & -3 \\
\hdashline
2 & 0 & 0 & 3 & 0 & 0 & -36 \\
\end{array}
\right]
$$

Step 4: Phase I applies.

Step 5: The pivot row is row 3, the pivot column is column 1. After pivoting we get the tableau:

$$
\begin{array}{cccccc}
x_1 & x_2 & s_1 & s_2 & s_3 & s_4 \\
\end{array}
$$

$$
\left[
\begin{array}{cccccc|c}
0 & 0 & 1 & \frac{1}{3} & \frac{1}{3} & 0 & 2 \\
0 & 1 & 0 & -\frac{2}{3} & \frac{1}{3} & 0 & 4 \\
1 & 0 & 0 & \frac{1}{3} & -\frac{2}{3} & 0 & 4 \\
0 & 0 & 0 & \frac{1}{3} & -\frac{2}{3} & 1 & 1 \\
\hline
0 & 0 & 0 & \frac{7}{3} & \frac{4}{3} & 0 & -44
\end{array}
\right]
\begin{array}{c}
s_1 \\ x_2 \\ x_1 \\ s_4 \\ \\
\end{array}
$$

This is a final tableau. Since the maximum value of $z = -44$, the minimum value of $C = 44$. This occurs when $x_1 = 4$, $x_2 = 4$, $s_1 = 2$, $s_2 = 0$, $s_3 = 0$, $s_4 = 1$ □

EQUALITY CONSTRAINTS

So far all our constraints used $\leq$ or $\geq$. What can be done if one of the constraints is an equality? One way is to replace the $=$ constraint with two constraints $\leq$ and $\geq$. The next example illustrates this way.

□ **Example 3**   Minimize

$$
C = 7x_1 + 5x_2 + 6x_3
$$

subject to the constraints

$$
x_1 \geq 0, \qquad x_2 \geq 0, \qquad x_3 \geq 0
$$
$$
x_1 + x_2 + x_3 = 10
$$
$$
x_1 + 2x_2 + 3x_3 \leq 19
$$
$$
2x_1 + 3x_3 \geq 21
$$

Solution   We wish to maximize $z = -C = -7x_1 - 5x_2 - 6x_3$ subject to the constraints

$$
x_1 \geq 0, \qquad x_2 \geq 0, \qquad x_3 \geq 0
$$
$$
x_1 + x_2 + x_3 \leq 10
$$
$$
x_1 + x_2 + x_3 \geq 10
$$
$$
x_1 + 2x_2 + 3x_3 \leq 19
$$
$$
2x_1 + 3x_3 \geq 21
$$

Step 1: Rewrite the constraints with $\leq$:

$$
x_1 + x_2 + x_3 \leq 10
$$
$$
-x_1 - x_2 - x_3 \leq -10
$$
$$
x_1 + 2x_2 + 3x_3 \leq 19
$$
$$
-2x_1 - 3x_3 \leq -21
$$

Step 2: Introduce nonnegative variables:

$$s_1 \geq 0, \qquad s_2 \geq 0, \qquad s_3 \geq 0, \qquad s_4 \geq 0$$
$$x_1 + x_2 + x_3 + s_1 = 10$$
$$-x_1 - x_2 - x_3 + s_2 = -10$$
$$x_1 + 2x_2 + 3x_3 + s_3 = 19$$
$$-2x_1 - 3x_2 + s_4 = -21$$

Step 3: Set up the initial simplex tableau:

x_1	x_2	x_3	s_1	s_2	s_3	s_4	
1	1	1	1	0	0	0	10
-1	-1	-1	0	1	0	0	-10
1	2	3	0	0	1	0	19
-2	-3	0	0	0	0	1	-21
7	5	6	0	0	0	0	0

Step 4: Phase I applies.

Step 5: The pivot row is row 4, the pivot column is column 2. Pivoting we get the tableau:

x_1	x_2	x_3	s_1	s_2	s_3	s_4	
$\frac{1}{3}$	0	1	1	0	0	$\frac{1}{3}$	3
$-\frac{1}{3}$	0	-1	0	1	0	$-\frac{1}{3}$	-3
$-\frac{1}{3}$	0	3	0	0	1	$\frac{2}{3}$	5
$\frac{2}{3}$	1	0	0	0	0	$-\frac{1}{3}$	7
$\frac{11}{3}$	0	6	0	0	0	$\frac{5}{3}$	-35

Step 4: Phase I applies.

Step 5: The pivot row is row 2; the pivot column is column 3. Pivoting we get the tableau

x_1	x_2	x_3	s_1	s_2	s_3	s_4	
0	0	0	1	1	0	0	0
$\frac{1}{3}$	0	1	0	-1	0	$\frac{1}{3}$	3
$-\frac{4}{3}$	0	0	0	3	1	$-\frac{1}{3}$	-4
$\frac{2}{3}$	1	0	0	0	0	$-\frac{1}{3}$	7
$\frac{5}{3}$	0	0	0	6	0	$-\frac{1}{3}$	-53

Step 4: Phase I applies.

Step 5: The pivot row is row 3, the pivot column is column 1. Pivoting we get the tableau

x_1	x_2	x_3	s_1	s_2	s_3	s_4	
0	0	0	1	1	0	0	0
0	0	1	0	$-\frac{1}{4}$	$\frac{1}{4}$	$\frac{1}{4}$	2
1	0	0	0	$-\frac{9}{4}$	$-\frac{3}{4}$	$\frac{1}{4}$	3
0	1	0	0	$\frac{3}{2}$	$\frac{1}{2}$	$-\frac{1}{2}$	5
0	0	0	0	$\frac{39}{4}$	$\frac{5}{4}$	$-\frac{3}{4}$	-58

Step 4: Phase II applies.

Step 5: The pivot column is column 7, the pivot row is row 2. Pivoting we get the tableau:

$$
\begin{array}{ccccccc}
x_1 & x_2 & x_3 & s_1 & s_2 & s_3 & s_4 \\
\end{array}
$$

$$
\left[
\begin{array}{ccccccc|c}
0 & 0 & 0 & 1 & 1 & 0 & 0 & 0 \\
0 & 0 & 4 & 0 & -1 & 1 & 1 & 8 \\
1 & 0 & -1 & 0 & -2 & -1 & 0 & 1 \\
0 & 1 & 2 & 0 & 1 & 1 & 0 & 9 \\
\hline
0 & 0 & 3 & 0 & 9 & 2 & 0 & -52 \\
\end{array}
\right]
$$

This is a final tableau. Since the maximum value of z is -52, the minimum value of c is 52. This occurs when $x_1 = 1$, $x_2 = 9$, $x_3 = 0$, $s_1 = 0$, $s_2 = 0$, $s_3 = 0$, $s_4 = 8$. ☐

MODEL: POLLUTION CONTROL

In the pollution control model we presented in Chapter 3, we considered an extremely simplified application. A more realistic version is given in the following model.* In this example we merely indicate the complicated nature of attempting to solve a real-world problem. As a result, the linear programming problem is set up, but no solution is actually given.

There are many pollution sources and five (not one) major pollutants in this larger model. The required pollutant reductions in the St. Louis airshed for the year 1970 are given as folows:

Sulfur dioxide	485,000,000 pounds
Carbon monoxide	1,300,000,000 pounds
Hydrocarbons	280,000,000 pounds
Nitrogen oxides	75,000,000 pounds
Particulate matter	180,000,000 pounds

The model includes a wide variety of possible control methods. Among them are the installation of exhaust and crankcase devices on used as well as new automobiles; the substitution of natural gas for coal; the installation of catalytic oxidation systems to convert sulfur dioxide in the stacks of power plants to salable sulfuric acid; and even the municipal collection of leaves as an alternative to burning.

The most contested control method in the St. Louis airshed has been a restriction on the sulfur content of coal. Consider a particular category of traveling grate stokers that burns 3.1% sulfur coal. Let control method 3 be the substitution of 1.8% sulfur coal for the high-sulfur coal in these stokers. The variable X_3 represents the number of tons of 3.1% sulfur coal replaced with low-sulfur coal.

Total cost of this control method is

$$C = (\$2.50)X_3$$

---

* Robert E. Kohn, "Application of Linear Programming to a Controversy on Air Pollution Control," *Management Science,* **17,** 10 (June 1971), pp. B609–B621.

where \$2.50 is an estimate of the incremental cost of the low-sulfur coal.

Just as the number of barrels of cement controlled by any process was constrained in our simple example (see Chapter 3), so

$$X_3 \leq 200,000$$

where 200,000 tons is the estimate of the quantity of coal that will be burned in this category of traveling grate stokers in 1970.

For every ton of 3.1% sulfur coal replaced by 1.8% sulfur coal, sulfur dioxide emissions are reduced by

$$\left[\left(\begin{array}{c} 0.031 \\ \text{sulfur} \\ \text{content} \end{array} \right) \left(\begin{array}{c} 2000 \text{ lb} \\ \text{per ton} \\ \text{of coal} \end{array} \right) \left(\begin{array}{c} 0.95 \\ \text{complete} \\ \text{burning} \end{array} \right)(2) \right]$$

$$- \left[(0.944) \left(\begin{array}{c} 0.018 \\ \text{sulfur} \\ \text{content} \end{array} \right)(2000 \text{ lb})(0.95)(2) \right] = 53.2 \text{ lb}$$

where the factor (2) doubles the weight of sulfur burned to get the weight of sulfur dioxide; where the factor (0.944) accounts for the higher BTU content of the low-sulfur coal, which permits 0.944 ton of it to replace 1 ton of the high-sulfur coal; and where (0.95) incorporates an assumption of 95% complete burning. The two expressions within brackets represent emission of sulfur dioxide from 3.1% and 1.8% sulfur coal, respectively. Thus, we have

$$(53.2)X_3 = \text{Pounds of sulfur dioxide reduced}$$

The remaining pollutant reductions are

$$(0.2)X_3 = \text{Pounds of carbon monoxide reduced}$$

$$(0.1)X_3 = \text{Pounds of hydrocarbons reduced}$$

$$(1.1)X_3 = \text{Pounds of nitrogen oxides reduced}$$

$$(12.2)X_3 = \text{Pounds of particulates reduced}$$

The relatively high reduction in particulates reflects not only the fact that 0.944 ton of the 1.8% sulfur coal is burned in place of 1 ton, but also the lower ash content of the substituted coal. (Reduction coefficients are not always positive; low-sulfur coal in a pulverized coal boiler that is equipped with a high-efficiency electrostatic precipitator can cause an increase in particulate emissions. The presence of less sulfur dioxide in the flue gas reduces the chargeability of the particles so that the benefits of the lower ash and higher BTU content may be offset by the reduced efficiency of the electrostatic precipitator.)

The mathematical programming model for 1970 is shown below. Notice that control methods X_1 and X_2 for the cement industry are included (see Chapter 3), as well as control method X_3. The dots represent the remaining 200–300 control methods.

Minimize $C = \$0.14X_1 + \$0.18X_2 + \$2.50X_3 + \cdots$

subject to

$$X_1 + X_2 \leq 2{,}500{,}000$$
$$X_3 + \cdots \leq 200{,}000$$
$$\vdots \qquad \vdots$$
$$53.2X_3 + \cdots \geq 485{,}000{,}000 \text{ lb of sulfur dioxide}$$
$$0.2X_3 + \cdots \geq 1{,}300{,}000{,}000 \text{ lb of carbon monoxide}$$
$$0.1X_3 + \cdots \geq 280{,}000{,}000 \text{ lb of hydrocarbons}$$
$$1.1X_3 + \cdots \geq 75{,}000{,}000 \text{ lb of nitrogen oxides}$$
$$1.5X_1 + 1.8X_2 + \cdots \geq 180{,}000{,}000 \text{ lb of particulates}$$
$$X_1, X_2, X_3, \cdots \geq 0$$

The pollution reduction requirements mentioned above appear in the model. In summing the pollutant reductions contributed by the various control methods, we are assuming that all pounds of any pollutant are homogeneous, regardless of where or when they are emitted. This is a limitation of the model because it is dependent on a close correspondence between a pollutant reduction and a specific concentration measured in parts per million or micrograms per cubic meter of that pollutant in the ambient air.

However, where necessary, meteorological sophistication can be incorporated in the model by selective weighting of those sources that seem to have a greater or lesser proportional effect on air quality than others.

MODEL: ECOLOGY

The next model is quoted from an article in *Some Mathematical Models in Biology*.* This model is an interesting application of linear programming to a bioeconomic situation; it is a good illustration of how the given information must be analyzed, sifted, and interpreted in order to formulate a useful mathematical model.

In the Edwards Plateau country of west Texas the vegetation is easily modified by grazing animals from a mixed vegetation to a dominance of grasses, or forbs, or browse, or various combinations of these. It is common to see in pastures in this area herds of cattle, bands of sheep, and flocks of mohair goats. Whitetail deer and wild turkey are common if there is sufficient browse and mixed vegetation. Catfish will thrive in ponds if there is suitable vegetation cover to prevent siltation. Ranchers sell beef, wool, mutton, mohair and lease deer and turkey hunting and catfishing rights. The relative monetary income values per animal are: cattle, 10.; goats, 1.; sheep, 1. (wool and mutton combined); deer, 0.5; turkey, 0.05; and fish, 0.001. A rancher owns

* G. M. Van Dyne and Kenneth R. Rebman, "Maintaining a Profitable Ecological Balance," in Robert M. Thrall, ed., *Some Mathematical Models in Biology,* University of Michigan, 1967.

10 sections of such land which has a maximum carrying capacity of 10 animal units per section per year. The animal unit equivalents for the various species per animal are: cattle, 1.; sheep, 0.2; goats, 0.25; deer, 0.3; and essentially zero for turkeys and fish. To properly organize his operation for livestock production, he has to have at least 20 cattle and at least 20 goats on his ranch. The rancher wants at least some sheep and some deer on his ranch. He can maintain the desired vegetation cover for turkey and fish if he has (a) cattle, sheep, goats, and deer, (b) cattle, sheep, and goats, or (c) cattle, goats, and deer, but no more than 75% of the grazing load (measured in animal units) may be due to cattle and goats combined. Of course, he wants his total stocking rate of all organisms combined to be equal to or less than the carrying capacity of the range. Furthermore, he can put in no more than one pond per section each of which will support no more than 500 fish each, and can harvest no more than 25% of the catfish per pond per year. The requirements and habits of the wild turkey are such that he cannot maintain more than 2 flocks of 10 birds per flock per section and he cannot harvest more than 20% of the population per year. He keeps only castrated male goats for mohair and shears them once each year. His cattle, sheep, and deer harvests which will maintain a given population are respectively about 25, 35, and 15% of the population per year. For simplification, the 35% for sheep includes both wool and mutton.

The first step is to isolate the salient points from this description. They are:

(1)   The relative monetary income values per animal are:

Cattle	10
Goats	1
Sheep	1
Deer	0.5
Turkey	0.05
Fish	0.001

(2)   There are 10 sections of land, each with a maximum carrying capacity of 10 animal units per year.

(3)   Animal unit equivalents for the species are:

Cattle	1
Goats	0.25
Sheep	0.2
Deer	0.3
Turkey	0
Fish	0

(4)   The ranch must have at least 20 cattle and 20 goats.

(5)   There must be some sheep and some deer.

(6)   If there are to be any turkey and fish, there must be
　　　(a)   cattle, sheep, and goats
　　or
　　　(b)   cattle, goats, and deer

(7) Cattle and goats can comprise no more than 75% of the animal units.
(8) Total animal units cannot exceed the carrying capacity.
(9) A maximum of 500 fish per section, with a 25% annual harvest.
(10) A maximum of 20 birds per section, with a 20% annual harvest.
(11) Harvest percentages:

Cattle	25%
Goats	100%
Sheep	35%
Deer	15%

(12) How many individuals of each species should the rancher have in order to maximize annual profit?

The next step is to quantify these conditions.

In the first place the rancher is hoping for an answer that is something like: have 30 cattle, 22 sheep, etc. He will be understandably upset if he is told that to realize a maximum profit, he requires 33.25 cattle and 21.7 sheep. The rancher is certainly anticipating the answer to be in integers. However, any programming problem that imposes integer constraints on the variables is apt to be extremely difficult to solve. Thus, the first simplification is to treat the problem as a continuous programming problem. It may even turn out that all or some of the optimal values of the variables of this problem *are* actually integers. If not, the solution can be rounded to the nearest integer solution. It is important to realize that this rounded solution may *not* be the best integer solution. However, if

p_0 is the maximum profit for the continuous problem

p_1 is the profit obtained by rounding the optimal solution

p_2 is the maximum profit to the integer problem

then clearly $p_1 \leq p_2 \leq p_0$. If $p_0 - p_1$ is very small, the rancher will not care anyway.

The next step is to determine the variables. Since he has 10 parcels of land, each being able to support 6 different species, the first inclination is to use 60 variables x_{ij}, $i = 1 \ldots 6, j = 1 \ldots 10$. Then x_{ij} will represent the number of species i to be placed on parcel j. However, since the conditions for survival are the same in any parcel, it is much simpler to consider the entire 10 parcels as a single unit. Then only 6 variables $x_i, i = 1 \ldots 6$ are needed, where x_i represents the total number of species i. In the final solution, $\frac{1}{10}$ of x_i can be placed in each parcel. (Or other adjustments can be made, at the rancher's preference.) (Note that we cannot just maximize profit over a single parcel. The constraints would require *some* deer on *every* parcel, which is not required in the given problem.)

Thus we define the following 6 variables:

x_1: Number of cattle

x_2: Number of goats

x_3: Number of sheep

x_4: Number of deer

x_5: Number of turkey

x_6: Number of fish

The conditions then give the following constraints: Condition (2) says the maximum carrying capacity available is 100 units. Condition (3) gives the animal units for each species. Condition (7) gives the constraint:

$$1x_1 + 0.25x_2 \leq 75$$

Condition (8) becomes:

$$1x_1 + 0.25x_2 + 0.2x_3 + 0.3x_4 \leq 100$$

Condition (4) is:

$$x_1 \geq 20$$
$$x_2 \geq 20$$

Condition (5) is:

$$x_3 \geq \text{``Some''}$$
$$x_4 \geq \text{``Some''}$$

where "Some" is the minimum number of sheep and deer the rancher wants. Since the rancher is vague about this, let us assume that "Some" = 1. So lower bound constraints are:

$$x_1 \geq 20$$
$$x_2 \geq 20$$
$$x_3 \geq 1$$
$$x_4 \geq 1$$

Now we see that condition (6) is irrelevant. The lower bound constraints guarantee that (6)(a) and (b) will *always* be satisfied. Hence, it will always be possible to have turkey ($x_5 > 0$) and fish ($x_6 > 0$). Conditions (9) and (10) give

$$x_6 \leq 5000$$
$$x_5 \leq 200$$

Finally, it is only needed to calculate the profit. Condition (1) gives profit per animal. Not all animals can be harvested, however. Harvest percentages are given in (9), (10), and (11). The annual profit from each species is:

Cattle	$(10)(0.25x_1)$
Goat	$(1)(x_2)$
Sheep	$(1)(0.35x_3)$
Deer	$(0.5)(0.15x_4)$
Turkey	$(0.05)(0.20x_5)$
Fish	$(0.001)(0.25x_6)$

Thus the rancher's problem is:
Subject to the constraints

$$x_1 + 0.25x_2 \leq 75$$
$$x_1 + 0.25x_2 + 0.2x_3 + 0.3x_4 \leq 100$$
$$x_1 \geq 20$$
$$x_2 \geq 20$$
$$x_3 \geq 1$$
$$x_4 \geq 1$$
$$0 < x_5 \leq 200$$
$$0 < x_6 \leq 5000$$

maximize the objective function

$$z = 2.5x_1 + x_2 + 0.35x_3 + 0.075x_4 + 0.01x_5 + 0.00025x_6$$

For maximum annual profit, the rancher's selection should be:

70	Cattle for a profit of	175.
20	Goats for a profit of	20.
123.5	Sheep for a profit of	43.225
1	Deer for a profit of	0.075
200	Turkeys for a profit of	2.
5000	Fish for a profit of	1.25

giving a profit of 241.55 units.

Of course, the rancher will have to have only 123 sheep, reducing his profit by 0.175. He will not be able to realize any profit on his single deer, which he insisted on having. So his profit is further reduced by 0.075.

Thus, his total profit, with an integer number of species, is 241.30.

Since the *best* integer solution can give no more than 241.55 profit, it is probably not worth finding it. (In fact this is very likely it.)

If the rancher now decides that one deer does not constitute "some," then the problem can be redone, giving a larger lower bound for x_4.

It only remains to distribute the species over the 10 parcels. If each parcel must have an integer number of species to itself, each parcel will have

7	Cattle
2	Goats
2	Flocks of 10 birds each
1	Pond with 500 fish

Putting an integer number of sheep on each parcel means that only 12 sheep can be on any parcel. This further reduces the profit by 1.05, since only 120 sheep are present. (Now, the total profit is only 240.25, but the *best* integer solution can give a profit no greater than 241.55.)

Note that the 7 cattle, 2 goats, and 12 sheep on each parcel use a total of 9.9 land units. Thus, no single parcel can support the deer. However, the deer can presumably roam over all 10 parcels, in which case there are enough land units to support 3 deer, which are still not enough for a deer "harvest."

Exercise 4.4   *Answers to Odd-Numbered Problems begin on page* 610

1. Maximize $P = 3x_1 + 4x_2$ subject to the constraints

$$x_1 \geq 0, \qquad x_2 \geq 0$$
$$x_1 + x_2 \leq 12$$
$$5x_1 + 2x_2 \geq 36$$
$$7x_1 + 4x_2 \geq 14$$

2. Maximize $P = 5x_1 + 2x_2$ subject to the constraints

$$x_1 \geq 0, \qquad x_2 \geq 0$$
$$x_1 + x_2 \geq 11$$
$$2x_1 + 3x_2 \geq 24$$
$$x_1 + 3x_2 \leq 18$$

3. Maximize $P = 3x_1 + 2x_2 - x_3$ subject to the constraints

$$x_1 \geq 0, \qquad x_2 \geq 0, \qquad x_3 \geq 0$$
$$x_1 + 3x_2 + x_3 \leq 9$$
$$2x_1 + 3x_2 - x_3 \geq 2$$
$$3x_1 - 2x_2 + x_3 \geq 5$$

4. Maximize $P = 3x_1 + 2x_2 - x_3$ subject to the constraints

$$x_1 \geq 0, \qquad x_2 \geq 0, \qquad x_3 \geq 0$$
$$2x_1 - x_2 - x_3 \leq 2$$
$$x_1 + 2x_2 + x_3 \geq 2$$
$$x_1 - 3x_2 - 2x_3 \leq -5$$

5. Minimize $C = 6x_1 + 8x_2 + x_3$ subject to the constraints

$$x_1 \geq 0, \qquad x_2 \geq 0, \qquad x_3 \geq 0$$
$$3x_1 + 5x_2 + 3x_3 \geq 20$$
$$x_1 + 3x_2 + 2x_3 \geq 9$$
$$6x_1 + 2x_2 + 5x_3 \geq 30$$
$$x_1 + x_2 + x_3 \leq 10$$

6. Minimize $C = 2x_1 + x_2 + x_3$ subject to the constraints

$$x_1 \geq 0, \qquad x_2 \geq 0, \qquad x_3 \geq 0$$
$$3x_1 - x_2 - 4x_3 \leq -12$$
$$x_1 + 3x_2 + 2x_3 \geq 10$$
$$x_1 - x_2 + x_3 \leq 8$$

7. Maximize $P = 3x_1 + 2x_2$ subject to the constraints
$$x_1 \geq 0, \qquad x_2 \geq 0$$
$$2x_1 + x_2 \leq 4$$
$$x_1 + x_2 = 3$$

8. Maximize $P = 45x_1 + 27x_2 + 18x_3 + 36x_4$ subject to the constraints
$$x_1 \geq 0, \qquad x_2 \geq 0, \qquad x_3 \geq 0, \qquad x_4 \geq 0$$
$$5x_1 + x_2 + x_3 + 8x_4 = 30$$
$$2x_1 + 4x_2 + 3x_3 + 2x_4 = 30$$

9. Private Motors, Inc., has 2 plants, M1 and M2, which manufactures engines; the company also has 2 assembly plants, A1 and A2, which assemble the cars. M1 can produce at most 600 engines per week. M2 can product at most 400 engines per week. A1 needs at least 500 engines per week and A2 needs at least 300 engines per week. The following is a table of charges to ship engines to assembly plants.

	A1	A2
M1	$400	$100
M2	$200	$300

How many engines should be shipped each week to each assembly plant from M1? M2? [*Hint:* Consider four variables: x_1 = number of units shipped from M1 to A1, x_2 = number of units shipped from M1 to A2, x_3 = number of units shipped from M2 to A1, and x_4 = number of units shipped from M2 to A2.]

10. Quality Oak Tables, Inc., has an individual who does all its finishing work and it wishes to use him in this capacity at least 6 hours each day. The assembly area can be used at most 8 hours each day. The company has three models of oak tables T1, T2, T3. T1 requires 1 hour for assembly, 2 hours for finishing, and 9 board feet of oak. T2 requires 1 hour for assembly, 1 hour for finishing, and 9 board feet of oak. T3 requires 2 hours for assembly, 1 hour for finishing, and 3 board feet of oak. If we wish to minimize the board feet of oak used, how many of each model should be made?

CHAPTER REVIEW

Important Terms		
maximum linear programming problem	pivot element	dual problem
standard form	pivot row	duality principle
slack variables	pivot column	mixed constraints
initial simplex tableau	final tableau	Phase I/Phase II
objective row	simplex method	
pivot operation	standard form of a minimum problem	

True–False Questions *(Answers on page 610)*

T F 1. In a maximum problem written in standard form each of the constraints, with the exception of the nonnegativity constraints, are written with a $\leq$ symbol.

T F 2. In a maximum problem written in standard form the slack variables are sometimes negative.

T F 3. Once the pivot element is identified in a tableau, the pivot operation causes the pivot element to become a 1 and causes the remaining entries in the pivot column to become 0's.

T F 4. The pivot element is sometimes in the objective row.

T F 5. One way to solve a minimum problem is to first solve its dual, which is a maximum problem.

Fill in the Blanks *(Answers on page 610)*

1. The constraints of a maximum problem in standard form are changed from an inequality to an equation by introducing _____ _____ .

2. The pivot _____ is located by selecting the most negative entry in the objective row.

3. For a minimum problem to be in standard form all the constraints must be written with _____ signs.

4. When the rows of the special matrix of a minimum problem are the columns of the special matrix of a maximum problem, we say the problems are _____ .

5. The _____ _____ _____ principle states that the optimal solution of a minimum linear programming problem, if it exists, has the same value as the optimal solution of the maximum problem, which is its dual.

Review Exercises *Answers to Odd-Numbered Problems begin on page 610.*

1. Maximize

$$P = 100x + 200y + 50z$$

subject to the constraints

$$5x + 5y + 10z \leq 1000$$
$$10x + 8y + 5z \leq 2000$$
$$10x + 5y \leq 500$$
$$x \geq 0$$
$$y \geq 0$$
$$z \geq 0$$

2. Maximize

$$P = x + 2y + z$$

subject to the constraints

$$3x + y + z \leq 3$$
$$x - 10y - 4z \leq 20$$
$$x \geq 0$$
$$y \geq 0$$

3. Maximize

$$P = 40x_1 + 60x_2 + 50x_3$$

subject to the constraints

$$2x_1 + 2x_2 + x_3 \leq 8$$
$$x_1 - 4x_2 + 3x_3 \leq 12$$
$$x_1 \geq 0, \qquad x_2 \geq 0, \qquad x_3 \geq 0$$

4. Maximize

$$P = 2x_1 + 8x_2 + 10x_3 + x_4$$

subject to the constraints

$$x_1 + 2x_2 + x_3 + x_4 \leq 50$$
$$3x_1 + x_2 + 2x_3 + x_4 \leq 100$$
$$x_1 \geq 0, \qquad x_2 \geq 0, \qquad x_3 \geq 0, \qquad x_4 \geq 0$$

5. Minimize

$$C = 2x_1 + x_2$$

subject to

$$2x_1 + 2x_2 \leq 8$$
$$x_1 - x_2 \leq 2$$
$$x_1 \geq 0$$
$$x_2 \geq 0$$

6. Minimize

$$C = 4x_1 + 2x_2$$

subject to

$$x_1 + 2x_2 \leq 4$$
$$x + 4x_2 \leq 6$$
$$x_1 \geq 0$$
$$x_2 \geq 0$$

7. Minimize

$$C = 5x_1 + 4x_2 + 3x_3$$

subject to the constraints

$$x_1 + x_2 + x_3 \geq 100$$
$$2x_1 + x_2 \geq 50$$
$$x_1 \geq 0, \qquad x_2 \geq 0, \qquad x_3 \geq 0$$

8. Minimize

$$c = 2x_1 + x_2 + 3x_3 + x_4$$

subject to

$$x_1 + x_2 + x_3 + x_4 \geq 50$$
$$3x_1 + x_2 + 2x_3 + x_4 \geq 100$$
$$x_1 \geq 0, \qquad x_2 \geq 0, \qquad x_3 \geq 0, \qquad x_4 \geq 0$$

9. *Optimal Land Use.* A farmer has 1000 acres of land on which corn, wheat, or soybeans can be grown. Each acre of corn costs $100 for preparation, requires 7 days of labor, and yields a profit of $30. An acre of wheat costs $120 to prepare, requires 10 days of labor, and yields $40 profit. An acre of soybeans costs $70 to prepare, requires 8 days of labor, and yields $40 profit. If the farmer has $10,000 for preparation, and can count on enough workers to supply 8000 days of labor, how many acres should be devoted to each crop to maximize profits?

Mathematical Questions

From CPA Exams (Answers on page 610)

Use the following information to answer Problems 1-4:

CPA Exam—May 1973

The Ball Company manufactures three types of lamps which are labeled A, B, and C. Each lamp is processed in two departments—I and II. Total available man-hours per day for departments I and II are 400 and 600, respectively. No additional labor is available. Time requirements and profit per unit for each lamp type are as follows:

	A	B	C
Man-hours required in Department I	2	3	1
Man-hours required in Department II	4	2	3
Profit per unit (Sales price less all variable costs)	$5	$4	$3

The company has assigned you, as the accounting member of its profit planning committee, to determine the number of types of A, B, and C lamps that it should produce in order to maximize its total profit from the sale of lamps. The following questions relate to a linear programming model that your group has developed.

1. The coefficients of the objective function would be

   (a) 4, 2, 3   (b) 2, 3, 1
   (c) 5, 4, 3   (d) 400, 600

2. The constraints in the model would be

   (a) 2, 3, 1   (b) 5, 4, 3
   (c) 4, 2, 3   (d) 400, 600

3. The constraint imposed by the available man-hours in Department I could be expressed as

(a) $4X_1 + 2X_2 + 3X_3 \leq 400$ (b) $4X_1 + 2X_2 + 3X_3 \geq 400$
(c) $2X_1 + 3X_2 + 1X_3 \leq 400$ (d) $2X_1 + 3X_2 + 1X_2 \geq 400$

4. The most types of lamps that would be included in the optimal solution would be

(a) 2   (b) 1
(c) 3   (d) 0

5. CPA Exam—May 1972; January 1979
In a system of equations for a linear programming model, what can be done to equalize an inequality such as $3X + 2Y \leq 15$?

(a) Nothing.   (b) Add a slack variable.
(c) Add a tableau.   (d) Multiply each element by -1.

Use the following information to answer Problems 6 and 7:

CPA Exam—November 1974
The Golden Hawk Manufacturing Company wants to maximize the profits on products A, B, and C. The contribution margin for each product follows:

Product	Contribution Margin
A	$2
B	$5
C	$4

The production requirements and departmental capacities, by departments, are as follows:

Department	Production Requirements by Product (Hours)		
	A	B	C
Assembling	2	3	2
Painting	1	2	2
Finishing	2	3	1

Department	Departmental Capacity (Total Hours)
Assembling	30,000
Painting	38,000
Finishing	28,000

6. What is the profit maximization formula for the Golden Hawk Company?

(a) $\$2A + \$5B + \$4C = X$ (where $X = $ Profit)
(b) $5A + 8B + 5C \leq 96{,}000$
(c) $\$2A + \$5B + \$4C \leq X$ (where $X = $ Profit)
(d) $\$2A + \$5B + \$4C = 96{,}000$

7. What is the constraint for the Painting Department of the Golden Hawk Company?

(a) $1A + 2B + 2C \geq 38{,}000$ (c) $1A + 2B + 2C \leq 38{,}000$
(b) $\$2A + \$5B + \$4C \geq 38{,}000$ (d) $2A + 3B + 2C \leq 30{,}000$

8. *CPA Exam—May 1976*

Watch Corporation manufactures products *A*, *B*, and *C*. The daily production requirements are shown below.

Product	Profit per Unit	Hours Required per Unit per Department		
		Machining	Plating	Polishing
A	$10	1	1	1
B	$20	3	1	2
C	$30	2	3	2
Total Hours per Day per Department		16	12	6

What is Watch's objective function in determining daily production of each unit?

(a) $A + B + C \leq \$60$
(b) $\$3A + \$6B + \$7C = \$60$
(c) $A + B + C \leq$ Profit
(d) $\$10A + \$20B + \$30C =$ Profit

CIA Exam—May 1980

Questions 9–11 are based on a company, that uses a linear programming model to schedule the production of three products. The per-unit selling prices, variable costs, and labor time required to produce these products are presented below. Total labor time available is 200 hours.

Product	Selling Price	Variable Cost	Labor Hours
A	$4.00	$1.00	2
B	$2.00	$ .50	2
C	$3.50	$1.50	3

9. The objective function to maximize the company's gross profit (Z) is

(a) $4A + 2B + 3.5C = Z$
(b) $2A + 2B + 3C = Z$
(c) $5A + 2.5B + 5C = Z$
(d) $3A + 1.5B + 2C = Z$
(e) $A + B + C = Z$

10. The constraint of labor time available is represented by

(a) $2A + 2B + 3C \leq 200$
(b) $2A + 2B + 3C \geq 200$
(c) $A + B + C \geq 200$
(d) $4A + 2B + 3.5C = 200$
(e) $A/2 + B/2 + C/3 = 200$

11. A linear programming model produces an optimal solution by

(a)   Ignoring resource constraints
(b)   Minimizing production costs
(c)   Minimizing both variable production costs and labor costs
(d)   Maximizing the objective function subject to resource constraints
(e)   Finding the point at which various resource constraints intersect

FINANCE

5.1 SIMPLE INTEREST AND SIMPLE DISCOUNT

SIMPLE INTEREST □ SIMPLE DISCOUNT

Interest

Very simply, *interest* is money paid for the use of money. The total amount of money borrowed, whether by an individual from a bank in the form of a loan or by a bank from an individual in the form of a savings account, is called the *principal*.

Principal

Rate of Interest

The *rate of interest* is the amount charged for the use of the principal for a given length of time, usually on a yearly, or *per annum,* basis. Rates of interest are usually expressed as percentages: 10% per annum; 14% per annum; and so on. However, when using rates of interest in calculations, we use the decimal equivalent: 0.10 for 10%; 0.14 for 14% and so on.

SIMPLE INTEREST

The easiest type of interest to deal with is called *simple interest.*

Simple Interest   **Simple interest is interest computed on the principal for the entire period it is borrowed.**

If a *principal P* is borrowed at a simple interest rate of *r* per annum (where *r* is a decimal) for a period of *t* years, the interest charge *I* is

$$I = Prt$$

□ **Example 1**

A loan of $250 is made for 9 months at a simple interest rate of 10% per annum. What is the interest charge?

Solution

The actual period the money is borrowed for is 9 months, which is $\frac{3}{4}$ of a year. The interest charge is the product of the amount borrowed, $250, the annual rate of interest, 0.10, and the length of time in years, $\frac{3}{4}$. Thus,

$$\text{Interest charge} = (\$250)(0.10)\left(\frac{3}{4}\right) = \$18.75$$

□

The *amount A* owed at the end of *t* years is the sum of the principal borrowed and the interest charge:

$$A = P + I = P + Prt = P(1 + rt)$$

□ **Example 2**

A person borrows $1000 for a period of 6 months. What simple interest rate is being charged if the amount *A* that must be repaid after 6 months is $1045?

Solution The principal P is $1000 and the period is $\frac{1}{2}$ year (6 months), the amount A owed after 6 months is $1045. We seek r in the equation:

$$A = P + Prt$$

$$1045 = 1000 + 1000r \left(\frac{1}{2}\right)$$

$$45 = 500r$$

$$r = \frac{45}{500} = 0.09$$

The per annum rate of interest is 9%. □

☐ **Example 3** A bank borrows $1,000,000 for 1 month at a simple interest rate of 9% per annum. How much must the bank pay back at the end of 1 month?

Solution The principal P is $1,000,000, the period t is $\frac{1}{12}$ year and the rate r is 0.09.

$$A = P(1 + rt)$$

$$A = 1,000,000 \left[1 + 0.09 \left(\frac{1}{12}\right)\right]$$

$$= 1,000,000(1.0075)$$

$$= \$1,007,500$$ □

SIMPLE DISCOUNT

If a lender deducts the interest at the time the loan is made, the loan is said to be

Simple Discount *discounted.* The interest discounted from a loan is referred to as the *simple discount.*
Proceeds The amount the borrower receives is called the *proceeds,* and the amount to be repaid
Maturity Value is called the *maturity value.*

☐ **Example 4** A borrower signs a note and agrees to pay $1000 in 9 months at 10% simple discount. How much does this borrower receive?

Solution Here $A = 1000$, $r = .10$, and $t = \frac{9}{12}$. The discount d is given by

$$d = Art = \$1000(0.10) \left(\frac{9}{12}\right) = \$75$$

This amount is deducted from the maturity value of $1000, that is, the proceeds is

$$P = A - Art \qquad 1000 - 75 = \$925$$ □

☐ **Example 5** What simple interest rate is the borrower in Example 4 paying on the $925 that was borrowed for 9 months?

Solution   The principal P is $925, t is $\frac{3}{4}$ of a year, and the amount A is $1000.

$$A = P + Prt$$

$$1000 = 925 + 925r\left(\frac{3}{4}\right)$$

$$75 = 693.75r$$

$$r = \frac{75}{693.75} = 0.108108$$

The per annum rate of interest is 10.81%.   □

If r is the simple discount rate, t the time in years, and A the amount repaid on maturity value then P, the proceeds, is given by

$$P = A - Art = A(1 - rt)$$

□ **Example 6**   You wish to borrow $10,000 for 3 months. If the person you are borrowing from offers an 8% simple discount, how much must you repay at the end of 3 months?

Solution   The amount P you borrow is $10,000, the discount rate r is 0.08, and the time t is $\frac{1}{4}$ year.

$$P = A(1 - rt)$$

$$10,000 = A\left[1 - 0.08\left(\frac{1}{4}\right)\right]$$

$$10,000 = 0.98A$$

$$A = \frac{10,000}{0.98}$$

$$= \$10,204.08$$ □

Exercise 5.1   *Answers to Odd-Numbered Problems begin on page* 610.

In Problems 1–6 find the interest due on each loan.

1. $1000 is borrowed for 3 months at 10% simple interest.
2. $100 is borrowed for 6 months at 8% simple interest.
3. $500 is borrowed for 9 months at 12% simple interest.
4. $800 is borrowed for 8 months at 12% simple interest.
5. $1000 is borrowed for 18 months at 10% simple interest.
6. $100 is borrowed for 24 months at 12% simple interest.

In Problems 7–12 find the simple interest rate for each loan.

7. $1000 is borrowed; the amount owed after 6 months is $1050.
8. $500 is borrowed; the amount owed after 8 months is $600.
9. $300 is borrowed; the amount owed after 12 months is $400.

10. $600 is borrowed; the amount owed after 9 months is $660.

11. $900 is borrowed; the amount owed after 10 months is $1000.

12. $800 is borrowed; the amount owed after 3 months is $900.

In Problems 13–16 find the proceeds for the given amount repaid, time, and simple discount rate.

13. $1200 repaid in 6 months with a simple discount rate of 10%.

14. $500 repaid in 8 months with a simple discount rate of 9%.

15. $2000 repaid in 24 months with a simple discount rate of 8%.

16. $1500 repaid in 18 months with a simple discount rate of 10%.

In Problems 17–20 find the amount you must repay.

17. You borrow $1200 for 6 months at a simple discount rate of 10%.

18. You borrow $500 for 8 months at a simple discount rate of 9%.

19. You borrow $2000 for 24 months at a simple discount rate of 8%.

20. You borrow $1500 for 18 months at a simple discount rate of 10%.

In Problems 21–22 determine at which rate the borrower pays the least interest.

21. A loan for 6 months using a simple discount rate of 9% or using a simple interest rate of 10%.

22. A loan for 9 months using a simple discount rate of 8% or using a simple interest rate of $8\frac{1}{2}$%.

5.2 COMPOUND INTEREST

COMPOUND INTEREST □ PRESENT VALUE

COMPOUND INTEREST

Compound
Interest
Effective Rate of
Interest

If the interest due at the end of a unit payment period is added to the principal, so that the interest computed for the next unit payment period is based on this new principal amount (old principal plus interest), then the interest is said to have been *compounded*. That is, *compound interest* is interest paid on previously earned interest.

Quite often, the term *effective rate of interest* is used. This is the equivalent annual rate of interest due to compounding. When interest is compounded annually, there is no difference between the per annum rate and the effective rate; however, when interest is compounded more than once a year, the effective rate always exceeds the per annum rate. The following example illustrates this distinction.

□ **Example 1** A bank pays 6% per annum compounded quarterly. If $200 is placed in a savings account and the quarterly interest is left in the account, how much money is in the account after 1 year? What is the effective rate of interest?

Solution   At the first quarter (3 months), the interest earned is

$$I = (\$200)\left(\frac{1}{4}\right)(0.06) = \$3.00$$

The new principal is $P + I = \$203$. The interest on this principal at the second quarter is

$$I = (\$203)\left(\frac{1}{4}\right)(0.06) = \$3.05$$

The interest at the third quarter on the principal of $206.05 ($203 + $3.05) is

$$I = (\$206.05)\left(\frac{1}{4}\right)(0.06) = \$3.09$$

The interest for the fourth quarter is

$$I = (\$209.14)\left(\frac{1}{4}\right)(0.06) = \$3.14$$

Thus, after 1 year, the total in the savings account is $212.28.

To find out what the effective rate of interest rate is, we use the formula $I = Prt$. The total interest paid for the 1 year period is $12.28 on a principal of $200. Thus,

$$\$12.28 = (\$200)(r)(1)$$

Solving for r, we obtain

$$r = 0.0614$$

The effective rate of interest is thus 6.14%.   □

Let's develop a formula for computing the amount when interest is compounded. Suppose the principal is P, the rate of interest per payment period is i (in decimal form), n is the number of payment periods, and A_n is the amount accrued after n payment periods. Then at the end of the first payment period,

$$A_1 = P + Pi = P(1 + i)$$

At the end of the second payment period, and subsequent ones,

$$A_2 = A_1 + A_1 i = A_1(1 + i) = P(1 + i)(1 + i) = P(1 + i)^2$$
$$A_3 = A_2 + A_2 i = A_2(1 + i) = P(1 + i)^3$$

$$\cdot$$
$$\cdot$$
$$\cdot$$

$$A_n = A_{n-1} + A_{n-1} i = A_{n-1}(1 + i) = P(1 + i)^n$$

Compound
Interest Formula

> The amount A_n accrued on a principal P after n payment periods at i interest (i in decimal form) per payment period is
>
> $$A_n = P(1 + i)^n$$

This formula is usually referred to as the *compound interest formula.* When using the compound interest formula, remember that

$$i = \frac{r}{n} \quad \frac{\text{annual rate of interest}}{\text{Number of payment periods per year}}$$

For example, if the annual rate of interest is 10% and the compounding is monthly, then there are 12 payment periods per year and

$$i = \frac{0.10}{12} = 0.00833$$

If 18% is the annual rate compounded daily (365 payment periods), then

$$i = \frac{0.18}{365} = 0.0004932$$

Using a calculator with a y^x key, we generate the following tables.

The Per Annum Interest Rate Is	Annual Compounding (One Payment Period Per Year)		
	8% $i = 0.08$	**10%** $i = 0.10$	**12%** $i = 0.12$
No. of Payment Periods (Years) n	$(1 + i)^n$	$(1 + i)^n$	$(1 + i)^n$
1	1.08	1.1	1.12
5	1.46933	1.61051	1.76234
10	2.15892	2.59374	3.10585
20	4.66096	6.7275	9.6463
30	10.0627	17.4494	29.9599
40	21.7245	45.2593	93.05097

The Per Annum Interest Rate Is	Monthly Compounding (12 Payment Periods per Year)		
	8% $i = 0.00667$	**10%** $i = 0.00833$	**12%** $i = 0.01$
No. of Payment Periods (months) n	$(1 + i)^n$	$(1 + i)^n$	$(1 + i)^n$
1	1.00667	1.00833	1.01
12	1.0829995	1.104713	1.126825
24	1.172888	1.22039	1.26973
36	1.27024	1.34818	1.43077
60	1.48985	1.64531	1.816697
120	2.21964	2.70704	3.30039

	Daily Compounding (365 Payment Periods per Year)		
The Per Annum Interest Rate Is	8% $i = 0.0002192$	10% $i = 0.00027397$	12% $i = 0.0003288$
No. of Payment Periods (Days) n	$(1 + i)^n$	$(1 + i)^n$	$(1 + i)^n$
365	1.083278	1.105156	1.127475
730	1.17349	1.22137	1.271199
1825	1.49176	1.64861	1.82194
3650	2.22535	2.71791	3.31946
7300	4.95216	7.38703	11.01883

From these tables we can compare the effective rates of interest for 8%, 10%, 12% compounded monthly and compounded daily.

	Effective Rate	
Per Annum Rate	Compounded Monthly	Compounded Daily
8%	8.30%	8.33%
10%	10.47%	10.52%
12%	12.68%	12.75%

□ **Example 2** If $1000 is invested at an annual rate of interest of 10%, what is the amount after 5 years if the compounding takes place:
(a) Annually? (b) Monthly? (c) Daily?

Solution The principal is $P = \$1000$.

(a) We look at the annual compounding table where $n = 5$. The amount A is

$$A = P(1 + i)^n = (\$1000)(1.61051) = \$1610.51$$

(b) For monthly compounding, $n = 60$. The amount A is

$$A = P(1 + i)^n = (\$1000)(1.64531) = \$1645.31$$

(c) For daily compounding, $n = 1825$. The amount A is

$$A = P(1 + i)^n = (\$1000)(1.64861) = \$1648.61 \qquad \square$$

PRESENT VALUE

If we solve for P in the compound interest formula, we obtain

$$P = A_n(1 + i)^{-n}$$

Present Value   In this formula, P is called the *present value* of the amount A_n due at the end of n interest periods at a rate i per interest period. In other words, P is the amount that must be invested for n interest periods at a rate i per interest period in order to accumulate the amount A_n.

Values for $(1 + i)^{-n}$ can be found using a hand-held calculator with a y^x key.

The compound interest formula and the present value formula can be used to solve many different kinds of problems. The examples below illustrate some of these applications.

□ **Example 3**   How much money should be invested at 8% per annum so that after 2 years the amount will be $10,000 when the interest is compounded:

(a) Annually?   (b) Monthly?   (c) Daily?

Solution   In this problem, we want to find the principal P when we know that the amount A after 2 years is going to be $10,000. That is, we want to find the present value of $10,000. Using a calculator

(a) Since compounding is once per year for 2 years, $n = 2$. We find

$$P = A(1 + i)^{-n}$$
$$= 10,000(1 + 0.08)^{-2}$$
$$= 10,000(0.8573388)$$
$$= \$8573.39$$

(b) Since compounding is 12 times per year for 2 years, $n = 24$. We find

$$P = A(1 + i)^{-n}$$
$$= 10,000 \left(1 + \frac{0.08}{12}\right)^{-24}$$
$$= 10,000(0.852596)$$
$$= \$8525.96$$

(c) Since compounding is 365 times per year for 2 years, $n = 730$. We find

$$P = A(1 + i)^{-n}$$
$$= 10,000 \left(1 + \frac{0.08}{365}\right)^{-730}$$
$$= 10,000(0.8521587)$$
$$= \$8521.59 \qquad \qquad □$$

□ **Example 4**   What annual rate of interest compounded annually should you seek if you want to double your investment in 5 years?

Solution
If P is the principal and we want P to double, the amount A will be $2P$. We use the compound interest formula with $n = 5$ to find i:

$$2P = P(1 + i)^5$$
$$2 = (1 + i)^5$$
$$1 + i = \sqrt[5]{2}$$
$$i = \sqrt[5]{2} - 1 = 1.148698 - 1 = 0.148698$$

↑
Use your calculator

The annual rate of interest needed to double the principal in 5 years is 14.87%. □

Exercise 5.2 *Answers to Odd-Numbered Problems begin on page* 610.

In Problems 1–6 find the amount owed.

1. $1000 is borrowed at 10% compounded monthly for 36 months.
2. $100 is borrowed at 14% compounded monthly for 36 months.
3. $500 is borrowed at 9% compounded annually for 1 year.
4. $200 is borrowed at 10% compounded annually for 10 years.
5. $800 is borrowed at 12% compounded daily for 200 days.
6. $400 is borrowed at 10% compounded daily for 180 days.

In Problems 7–10 find the principal needed now to get each amount.

7. To get $100 in 6 months at 10% compounded monthly
8. To get $500 in 1 year at 12% compounded annually
9. To get $500 in 1 year at 9% compounded daily
10. To get $800 in 2 years at 10% compounded monthly
11. What annual rate of interest is required to double an investment in 3 years?
12. What annual rate of interest is required to double an investment in 10 years?
13. Approximately how long will it take to triple an investment at 10% compounded annually?
14. Approximately how long will it take to triple an investment at 9% compounded annually?
15. Mr. Nielsen wants to borrow $1000 for 2 years. He is given the choice of (a) a simple interest loan of 12% or (b) a loan at 10% compounded monthly. Which loan results in less interest due?
16. Rework Problem 15 if the simple interest loan is 15% and the other loan is at 14% compounded daily.
17. What principal is needed now to get $1000 one year from today and $1000 two years from today at 9% compounded annually?
18. Repeat Problem 17 using 9% compounded daily.
19. Find the effective rate of interest for $5\frac{1}{4}$% compounded quarterly.
20. Repeat Problem 19 using 6% compounded quarterly.

21. What interest rate compounded quarterly will give an effective interest rate of 7%.

22. Repeat Problem 21 using 10%.

In Problems 23–26 which of the two rates would yield the larger amount in one year: [*Hint:* Start with a principal $10,000 in each instance.].

23. 6% compounded quarterly or $6\frac{1}{4}$% compounded annually?

24. 9% compounded quarterly or $9\frac{1}{4}$% compounded annually?

25. 9% compounded monthly or 8.8% compounded daily?

26. 8% compounded semiannually or 7.9% compounded daily?

27. If the price of homes rises an average of 5% per year for the next four years, what will be the selling price of a home that is selling for $90,000 today four years from today?

5.3 ANNUITY: SINKING FUND

ANNUITY □ SINKING FUND

ANNUITY

In the previous sections we saw how to compute the future value of an investment when a fixed amount of money is deposited in an account that pays interest compounded periodically. Often, however, people and financial institutions do not deposit money and then sit back and watch it grow. Rather, money is invested in small amounts at periodic intervals. Examples of such investments are annual life insurance premiums, monthly deposits in a bank, installment loan payments, and so on.

An *annuity* is a sequence of equal periodic payments. When the payments are made at the same time the interest is credited, the annuity is termed *ordinary*. We shall only concern ourselves with *ordinary annuities* in this book.

Ordinary Annuity

The *payment period* can be annual, semiannual, quarterly, monthly or any fixed length of time.

Amount of an Annuity The *amount of an annuity* is the sum of all payments made plus all interest accumulated.

□ **Example 1** Find the amount of an annuity after 5 payments if each payment is equal to $100 and is made on an annual basis at an interest rate of 10% per annum compounded annually.

Solution After 5 payments, the first $100 payment will have accumulated interest compounded annually at 10% for 4 years. Its value A_1 after 4 years is

$$A_1 = \$100(1 + 0.10)^4 = \$100(1.4641) = \$146.41$$

↑
Use your calculator

The second payment of $100, made 1 year after the first payment, will accumulate interest compounded at 10% for 3 years. Its value A_2 at the end of the fifth payment is

$$A_2 = \$100(1 + 0.10)^3 = \$100(1.331) = \$133.10$$

Similarly, the third, fourth, and fifth payments will have the values

$$A_3 = \$100(1 + 0.10)^2 = \$100(1.21) = \$121.00$$
$$A_4 = \$100(1 + 0.10)^1 = \$100(1.10) = \$110.00$$
$$A_5 = \$100$$

The amount of the annuity after 5 payments is

$$A_1 + A_2 + A_3 + A_4 + A_5 = \$146.41 + \$133.10 + \$121.00 + \$110.00 + \$100.00$$
$$= \$610.51 \qquad \square$$

To develop a formula for the amount of an annuity, suppose $1 is the payment for an annuity at an interest rate of i percent per payment period (in decimal form) and with a term of n payment periods. Since payments are made at the end of each period, the first payment will accumulate the value A_1 compounded over $n - 1$ periods at i percent per payment period. The second payment will accumulate the value A_2 compounded over $n - 2$ periods at i percent per payment period, and so on. Then

$$A_1 = \$1(1 + i)^{n-1}, \qquad A_2 = \$1(1 + i)^{n-2}, \qquad \ldots, \qquad A_n = \$1(1 + i)^0 = \$1$$

The total amount of the annuity after n payment periods, denoted by $A(n, i)$, is

$$A(n, i) = A_1 + \cdots + A_n = (1 + i)^{n-1} + (1 + i)^{n-2} + \cdots + (1 + i) + 1$$
$$= [1 + (1 + i) + \cdots + (1 + i)^{n-1}]$$
$$= \frac{[1 + (1 + i) + \cdots + (1 + i)^{n-1}][1 - (1 + i)]}{1 - (1 + i)}$$
$$= \frac{[1 - (1 + i)^n]}{-i} = \frac{[(1 + i)^n - 1]}{i}$$

If P represents the payment in dollars made at each payment period for an annuity at i percent interest per payment period, the amount A of the annuity after n payment periods is

$$A = P \cdot A(n, i)$$

where

$$A(n, i) = \frac{(1 + i)^n - 1}{i}$$

Table 1, page 220, lists values for $A(n, i)$ per annum rates of 8%, 10%, and 12% compounded annually and monthly over a variety of time periods. A calculator may also be used to find $A(n, i)$.

☐ **Example 2** Find the amount of an annuity if a payment of $100 per year is made for 5 years at 10% compounded annually.

Solution For $P = \$100$, $n = 5$, and $i = 0.10$, we find from Table 1(a) that

$$A = P \cdot A(n, i) = \$100(6.105100) = \$610.51 \qquad \square$$

☐ **Example 3** Mary decides to put aside $100 every month in a money market fund that pays 8% compounded monthly. After making 12 deposits, how much money does Mary have?

Solution This is an annuity problem in which $P = \$100$. To find the amount after 12 payments, we look in Table 1(b) under monthly compounding at 8%. The amount A after 12 deposits is

$$A = P \cdot A(n, i) = \$100(12.44993) = \$1244.99 \qquad \square$$

☐ **Example 4** To save for his son's college education, Mr. Graff decides to put $50 aside every month in a credit union account paying 10% interest compounded monthly. If he begins this savings program when his son is 3 years old, how much will he have saved by the time his son is 18 years old?

Solution When his son is 18 years old, Mr. Graff will have made his 180th payment, so he will have

$$A = P \cdot A(n, i) = \$50(414.4703) = \$20,723.52 \qquad \square$$

☐ **Example 5** Joe, at age 35, decides to invest in an IRA. He will put aside $2000 per year for the next 30 years. How much will he have at age 65 if his rate of return is assumed to be 10% per annum?

Solution This is an annuity problem in which $P = \$2000$. We use Table 1(a), annual compounding at 10%, with $n = 30$. The amount A in Joe's IRA after 30 years is

$$A = P \cdot A(n, i) = \$2000(164.494023) = \$328,988.05 \qquad \square$$

☐ **Example 6** If Joe had begun his IRA at age 25, instead of 35, his IRA at age 65 would amount to

$$A = \$2000(442.592556) = \$885,185.11 \qquad \square$$

SINKING FUND

Quite often, a person with a debt decides to accumulate sufficient funds to pay off the debt by agreeing to set aside enough money each month (or quarter, or year) so that when the debt becomes payable, the money set aside each month plus the interest earned will equal the debt. The fund created by such a plan is called a *sinking fund*. Companies use sinking funds to accumulate capital for the purpose of purchasing new equipment.

Sinking Fund

We shall limit our discussion of sinking funds to those in which equal payments are made at equal time intervals. Usually, the debtor agrees to pay interest on the debt as a separate item, so that the amount needed in a sinking fund is only the amount originally borrowed.

□ **Example 7**   A woman borrows $3000 and agrees to pay interest monthly at an annual rate of 12%. At the same time, she sets up a sinking fund in order to repay the loan at the end of 5 years. If the sinking fund earns interest at the rate of 8% compounded annually, find the size of each annual sinking fund deposit. Construct a table showing the growth of the sinking fund.

Solution   The monthly interest payments due on the debt are

$$\$3000(0.01) = \$30$$

The size of the sinking fund deposit is calculated by using the formula

$$A = P \cdot A(n, i)$$

in which A represents the amount to be saved, P is the payment, $n = 5$, and the rate is 8%. The required payment is

$$P = \$3000 \; \frac{1}{A(n, i) \; \uparrow} = (\$3000)(0.17045645) = \$511.37$$

$$\text{Table 1(a)}$$

Thus, annual sinking fund payments of $511.37 are needed.
The growth of the sinking fund is shown in Table 1.

Table 1

Payment	Interest	Sinking Fund Deposit	Total
0	—	—	—
1	0	511.37	511.37
2	40.91	511.37	1063.65
3	85.09	511.37	1660.11
4	132.81	511.37	2304.29
5	184.34	511.37	3000.00

Note: Because of round-off error, the final total will sometimes be slightly off.   □

□ **Example 8**
Depletion Investment   A gold mine is expected to yield an annual net return of $200,000 for the next 10 years, after which it will be worthless. An investor wants an annual return on his investment of 18%. If he can establish a sinking fund earning 10% annually, how much should he be willing to pay for the mine?

Solution   Let p denote the purchase price. Then $0.18p$ represents an 18% return on investment. The annual sinking fund contribution needed to obtain the amount p in 10 years is $p[1/A(n, i)]$, where $n = 10$ and the rate is 10%. The investor should be willing to pay an amount p so that

Return on investment + Sinking fund requirement = Annual return

$$0.18p + p\,\frac{1}{A(n,\,i)} = \$200{,}000$$
$$0.18p + (0.06274539)p = \$200{,}000$$
$$0.24274539p = \$200{,}000$$
$$p = \$823{,}909 \qquad \square$$

Exercies 5.3   *Answers to Odd-Numbered Problems begin on page* 610 .

In Problems 1–6 find the amount of each annuity.

1. The payment is $100 annually for 10 years at 10% compounded annually.
2. The payment is $200 monthly for 1 year at 8% compounded monthly.
3. The payment is $400 monthly for 1 year at 12% compounded monthly.
4. The payment is $1000 annually for 5 years at 10% compounded annually.
5. The payment is $200 monthly for 3 years at 10% compounded monthly.
6. The payment is $2000 annually for 20 years at 10% compounded annually.
7. A company establishes a sinking fund to provide for the payment of a $100,000 debt, maturing in 4 years. Contributions to the fund are to be made at the end of every year. Find the amount of each annual deposit if interest is 8% per annum.
8. A state has $5,000,000 worth of bonds that are due in 20 years. A sinking fund is established to pay off the debt. If the state can earn 10% annually on its money, what is the annual sinking fund deposit needed?
9. *Depletion Investment.* An investor wants to know the amount she should pay for an oil well expected to yield an annual return of $30,000 for the next 30 years, after which the well will be dry. Find the amount she should pay to yield a 14% annual return if a sinking fund earns 10% annually.
10. If you deposit $10,000 every year in an account paying 8% compounded annually, how long will it take to accumulate $1,000,000?

5.4 PRESENT VALUE OF AN ANNUITY; AMORTIZATION

Present Value of an Annuity   The *present value* of an annuity is the sum of the present values of the payments.

In other words, the present value of an annuity is the amount of money needed now so that if it is invested at i percent, n equal payments can be withdrawn without any money left over.

□ **Example 1**   Compute the amount of money required to pay out $100 per year for 5 years at 10% compounded annually.

Solution For the first payment, the present value V_1 is

$$V_1 = \$100(1 + 0.10)^{-1} = \$100(0.909091) = \$90.91$$

For the second payment, the present value V_2 is

$$V_2 = \$100(1 + 0.10)^{-2} = \$100(0.826446) = \$82.64$$

Similarly,

$$V_3 = \$100(1 + 0.10)^{-3} = \$100(0.751315) = \$75.13$$
$$V_4 = \$100(1 + 0.10)^{-4} = \$100(0.683014) = \$68.30$$
$$V_5 = \$100(1 + 0.10)^{-5} = \$100(0.620921) = \$62.09$$

The present value V for 5 payments is

$$V = V_1 + V_2 + V_3 + V_4 + V_5 = \$90.91 + \$82.64 + \$75.13 + \$68.30 + \$62.09$$
$$= \$379.07$$

Thus, a person would need $379.07 now invested at 10% per annum in order to withdraw $100 per year for the next 5 years.

Table 2(a) summarizes these results. Table 2(b) lists the amount at the beginning of each subsequent year.

Table 2(a)

Payment	Present Value
1st	$100(1.10)^{-1} = \$\ 90.91$
2nd	$100(1.10)^{-2} = \$\ 82.64$
3rd	$100(1.10)^{-3} = \$\ 75.13$
4th	$100(1.10)^{-4} = \$\ 68.30$
5th	$100(1.10)^{-5} = \$\ 62.09$
Total	$379.07

Table 2(b)

Year	Amount at the Beginning of the Year	Interest
1	379.07	37.91
2	316.98	31.70
3	248.68	24.87
4	173.55	17.36
5	90.91	9.09
6	0	—

To develop a formula for present value, suppose $1 is the payment for an annuity at an interest rate of i percent per payment period (in decimal form) and with a term of n payment periods. Then the present value V_1 of the first payment is

$$V_1 = (1 + i)^{-1}$$

The present value V_2 for the second payment is

$$V_2 = (1 + i)^{-2}$$

The present value V_n for the nth payment is

$$V_n = (1 + i)^{-n}$$

The total present value $P(n, i)$ of the annuity is

$$P(n, i) = V_1 + \cdots + V_n = (1 + i)^{-1} + \cdots + (1 + i)^{-n}$$
$$= (1 + i)^{-n}[1 + (1 + i) + \cdots + (1 + i)^{n-1}]$$
$$= \frac{1 - (1 + i)^n}{1 - (1 + i)}(1 + i)^{-n} = \frac{(1 + i)^n - 1}{i(1 + i)^n} = \frac{1 - (1 + i)^{-n}}{i}$$

If P represents the payment made in dollars, the present value V of the annuity at a rate i per payment period for n payment periods is

$$V = P \cdot P(n, i)$$

where

$$P(n, i) = \frac{1 - (1 + i)^{-n}}{i}$$

Some values for $P(n, i)$ are given in Table 2, page 222 .

□ Example 2 A man agrees to pay $300 per month for 48 months to pay off a car loan. If interest of 12% per annum is charged monthly, how much did the car originally cost? How much interest was paid?

Solution This is the same as asking for the present value V of an annuity of $300 per month at 12% for 48 months. Using Table 2(b) page 222, we find that the original cost of the car is

$$V = P \cdot P(n, i) = \$300(37.9739595) = \$11,392.19$$

The total payment is ($300)(48) = $14,400. Thus, the interest paid is

$$\$14,400 - \$11,392.19 = \$3007.81 \qquad \square$$

AMORTIZATION

A loan with a fixed rate of interest is said to be *amortized* if both principal and interest are paid by a sequence of equal payments made over equal periods of time.

When a loan of V dollars is amortized at a particular rate r of interest per payment period over n payment periods, the question is, "What is the payment P?" In other words, in amortization problems, we want to find the amount of payment P which, after n payment periods at i percent interest per payment period, gives us a present value equal to the amount of the loan. Thus, we need to find P in the formula

$$V = P \cdot P(n, i)$$

Since we are interested in P, we solve for P, obtaining

$$P = V \frac{1}{P(n, i)}$$

Table 2, page 222, lists typical values for $1/P(n, i)$.

□ **Example 3**   What monthly payment is necessary to pay off a loan of $800 at 10% per annum:
(a)   In 2 years?   (b)   In 3 years?

Solution   (a)   For the 2 year loan, $V = \$800$ and $n = 24$. Consulting the monthly compounding schedule in Table 2(b) at 10%, we find that the monthly payment is

$$P = V \frac{1}{P(n,\ i)} = \$800(0.04614493) = \$36.92$$

(b)   For the 3 year loan, $V = \$800$ and $n = 36$. The monthly payment P is

$$P = V \frac{1}{P(n,\ i)} = \$800(0.03226719) = \$25.81$$

□

For the 2 year loan in Example 3, the total amount paid out is $(\$36.92)(24) = \$886.08$; for the 3 year loan, the total amount paid out is $(\$25.81)(36) = \$929.16$. It should be clear that the longer the term of a debt, the more it costs the borrower to pay off the loan.

For amortization problems involving long-term mortgages with monthly payments, it is convenient to use a table of mortgages such as Table 3, in which appropriate values of $P(n,\ i)$ and $1/P(n,\ i)$ are listed.

Table 3
Mortgage Table

Monthly Payments n	8% per Annum $P(n,\ i)$	9% per Annum $P(n,\ i)$	10% per Annum $P(n,\ i)$	8% per Annum $1/P(n,\ i)$	9% per Annum $1/P(n,\ i)$	10% per Annum $1/P(n,\ i)$
60	49.3184	48.17337	47.0654	0.020276	0.020758	0.021247
120	82.42148	78.94169	75.6712	0.012133	0.012668	0.0132151
180	104.64059	98.5934	93.0574	0.009557	0.010143	0.0107461
240	119.55429	111.14495	103.625	0.008364	0.008997	0.0096502
300	129.5645	119.1616	110.047	0.007718	0.008392	0.00908701

□ **Example 4**   Mr. and Mrs. Corey have just purchased a $70,000 house and have made a down
House Mortgage   payment of $15,000. They can amortize the balance ($55,000) at 9% for 25 years.
(a)   What are the monthly payments?
(b)   What is their total interest payment?
(c)   After 20 years, what equity do they have in their house?

Solution (a) The monthly payment P needed to pay off the loan of $55,000 at 9% for 25 years (300 months) is

$$P = \$55,000 \left[\frac{1}{P(n,\ i)} \right]$$
$$= \$55,000(0.008392) = \$461.56$$

(b) The total paid out for the loan is

$$(\$461.56)(300) = \$138,468.00$$

Thus, the interest on this loan amounts to

$$\$138,468 - \$55,000 = \$83,468.00$$

(c) After 20 years (240 months) there remains 5 years (or 60 months) of payments. The present value of the loan is the present value of a monthly payment of $461.56 for 60 months at 9%, namely,

$$(\$461.56)P(n,\ i) = (\$461.56)(48.17337) = \$22,234.90$$

Thus, the equity after 20 years is

downpayment + amount paid on loan $= \$15,000 + [\$55,000 - \$22,234.90]$
$$= \$47,765.10 \qquad \square$$

Usually, the monthly payment is rounded up to the next dollar to insure liquidation in the alloted term. The final payment is then not the same as the rest of the payments.

Table 4 gives a partial schedule of payments for the loan in Example 4. The Amount Paid on Loan column was obtained by the method of Example 4 using Table 4. However, the data in the Principal and Interest columns were obtained through a computer program. It is interesting to observe how slowly the amount paid on the loan increases early in the payment schedule, with very little of the payment used to reduce principal, and how quickly the amount paid on the loan increases during the last 5 years.

Table 4

Payment Number	Monthly Payment	Principal	Interest	Amount Paid on Loan
1	$461.56	$49.06	$412.50	$49.06
60	$461.56	$75.94	$385.62	$3,699.94
120	$461.56	$119.27	$342.29	$9,493.23
180	$461.56	$186.85	$274.71	$18,563.67
240	$461.56	$292.56	$169.00	$32,765.10
300	$461.56	$458.16	$3.40	$55,000.00

☐ Example 5 When Mr. Nicholson died, he left an inheritance of $15,000 for his family to be paid to them over a 10 year period in equal amounts at the end of each year. If the $15,000 is invested at 10%, what is the annual payout to the family?

Solution This example asks what annual payment is needed at 10% for 10 years to give a total of $15,000. That is, we can think of the $15,000 as a loan amortized at 10% for 10 years. The payment needed to pay off the loan is the yearly amount Mr. Nicholson's family will receive. Thus, the yearly payout P is

$$P = \$15,000 \left[\frac{1}{P(n, i)} \right] = \$15,000(0.16274539) = \$2441.18$$

↑
Use Table 2a   ☐

☐ Example 6 Kathy is 20 years away from retiring and starts saving $100 a month in an account paying 6% compounded monthly. When she retires she wishes to withdraw a fixed amount each month for 25 years. What will this fixed amount be?

Solution After 20 years, the amount accumulated in her account

$$A = P \cdot A(n, i) = 100 \cdot A(240, 0.005) = 100 \cdot (462.0408951) = \$46,204.09$$

To find the amount she can withdraw for 300 payments (25 years) at 0.005% per payment (6% compounded monthly)

$$V = P \cdot P(n, i)$$
$$46,204.09 = P \cdot P(300, 0.005)$$
$$P = \frac{46,204.09}{P(300, 0.005)} = \frac{46,204.09}{155.206864} = \$297.69 \qquad ☐$$

Exercise 5.4 *Answers to Odd-Numbered Problems begin on page* 611 .

In Problems 1–6 find the present value of each annuity.

1. The payment is to be $500 per month for 36 months at 10% compounded monthly.
2. The payment is to be $1000 per year for 3 years at 8% compounded annually.
3. The payment is to be $100 per month for 9 months at 12% compounded monthly.
4. The payment is to be $400 per month for 18 months at 10% compounded monthly.
5. The payment is to be $10,000 per year for 20 years at 10% compounded annually.
6. The payment is to be $2000 per month for 3 years at 12% compounded monthly.
7. A husband and wife contribute $4000 per year to an IRA paying 10% compounded annually for 20 years. What is the value of their IRA?
8. Rework Problem 7 if the interest rate is 8%.
9. What annual payment is needed to pay off a loan of $10,000 amortized at 12% compounded monthly for 2 years?
10. What monthly payment is needed to pay off a loan of $500 amortized at 12% per month for 2 years?

11. In Example 4, if Mr. and Mrs. Corey amortize the $55,000 loan at 10% for 20 years, what is their monthly payment?

12. In Example 4, if Mr. and Mrs. Corey amortize their $55,000 loan at 12% for 15 years, what is their monthly payment?

13. In Example 5, if Mr. Nicholson left $15,000 to be paid over 20 years in equal yearly payments and if this amount were invested at 12%, what would the annual payout be?

14. Joan has a sum of $30,000 that she invests at 10% compounded monthly. What equal monthly payments can she receive over a 10 year period? Over a 20 year period?

15. Mr. Doody, at age 65, can expect to live for 20 years. If he can invest at 10% per annum compounded monthly, how much does he need now to guarantee himself $250 every month for the next 20 years?

16. Ms. Joy, at age 65, can expect to live for 25 years. If she can invest at 10% per annum compounded monthly, how much does she need now to guarantee herself $300 every month for the next 25 years?

17. *House Mortgage.* A couple wishes to purchase a house for $120,000 with a down payment of $25,000. They can amortize the balance either at 8% for 20 years or at 9% for 25 years. Which monthly payment is greater? For which loan is the total interest paid greater? After 10 years, which loan provides the greater equity?

18. *House Mortgage.* A couple have decided to purchase a $100,000 house using a down payment of $20,000. If they can amortize the balance at 8% for 25 years, what is their monthly payment? What is the total interest paid? What is their equity after 5 years? What is the equity after 20 years?

19. John is 45 years old and wants to retire at 65. He wishes to make monthly deposits in an account paying 9% compounded monthly and when he retires withdraw $300 a month for 30 years. How much should John deposit each month?

20. The grand prize in the Illinois Lottery was $6,000,000 paid out in 20 equal yearly payments of $300,000 each. How much should they deposit in an account paying 8% compounded annually to achieve this goal?

5.5 LEASING; CAPITAL EXPENDITURE; BONDS

LEASING □ CAPITAL EXPENDITURE □ BONDS

LEASING

□ **Example 1**
Leasing Problem

A corporation may obtain a particular machine either by leasing it for 4 years (the useful life) at an annual rent of $1000 or by purchasing the machine for $3000.

(a) Which alternative is preferable if the corporation can invest money at 10% per annum?

(b) What if it can invest at 14% per annum?

Solution (a) Suppose the corporation may invest money at 10% per annum. The present value of an annuity of $1000 for 4 years at 10% equals $3169.87, which exceeds the purchase price. Therefore, purchase is preferable.

(b) Suppose the corporation may invest at 14% per annum. The present value of an annuity of $1000 for 4 years at 14% equals $2913.71, which is less than the purchase price. Hence, leasing is preferable. □

CAPITAL EXPENDITURE

□ **Example 2**
Capital Expenditure

A corporation is faced with a choice between two machines, both of which are designed to improve operations by saving on labor costs. Machine A costs $8000 and will generate an annual labor savings of $2000. Machine B costs $6000 and will save $1800 annually. However, Machine A has a useful life of 7 years while Machine B has a useful life of only 5 years. Assuming that the time value of money (investment opportunity rate) of the corporation is 10% per annum, which machine is preferable? (Assume annual compounding and that the savings is realized at the end of each year).

Solution

Machine A costs $8000 and has a life of 7 years. Since an annuity of $1 for 7 years at 10% interest has a present value of $4.87, the cost of Machine A may be considered the present value of an annuity:

$$\frac{\$8000}{4.87} = \$1642.71$$

The $1642.71 may be termed the *equivalent annual cost* of Machine A. Similarly, the equivalent annual cost of Machine B may be calculated by reference to the present value of an annuity of 5 years, namely,

$$\frac{\$6000}{3.79} = \$1583.11$$

Thus, the net annual savings of each machine is as follows:

	A	B
Labor savings	$2000.00	$1800.00
Equivalent annual cost	1642.71	1583.11
Net savings	$ 357.29	$ 216.80

Therefore, Machine A is preferable. □

BONDS

We begin our third application with some definitions of terms concerning corporate bonds. A calculator will be needed for the example that follows.

Face Amount (Face Value or Par Value) **The denomination of the bond.**

This is normally $1000. Generally, the face amount is the amount paid to the bondholder at maturity.

Nominal Interest (Coupon Interest) The contractual periodic interest payments on the bond.

This is normally quoted as an annual percentage of the face amount. Nominal interest payments are conventionally made semiannually, and semiannual periods are used for compound interest calculations. The nominal interest rate does not purport to be a true or effective interest rate, but merely fixes the amount of the semiannual cash payments to bondholders. These semiannual payments are calculated by multiplying half the annual nominal interest rate by the face amount.

Bond Price The amount paid by the bondholder to the corporation at the time of the bond's original issuance, or the price at which the bond is traded between investors in bond markets after issuance.

Bond prices are stated as a percentage of face amount. Thus, a price of 101 is equal to 101% of the face amount. When the bond price is higher than the face amount, the excess is referred to as a *bond premium.* If the price is lower than face amount, the difference is called a *bond discount.*

Effective Interest Rate   *True,* or *effective, interest rates* are determined in the marketplace, influenced by such factors as the supply and demand of money, the open-market activities of the Federal Reserve Board, credit standing, etc. Accordingly, effective interest rates vary from time to time. Inasmuch as the nominal interest rates are fixed for the entire life of the bond, effective interest rates are adjusted by varying the price of a bond.

A bond may be thought of as consisting of a combination of an annuity of semiannual interest payments plus a single future amount payable at maturity. The price of a bond is therefore the sum of the present value of the annuity of semiannual interest payments plus the present value of the single future payment at maturity. This present value is calculated by discounting at the effective interest rate and assuming semiannual discounting periods.

□ **Example 3**
Corporate Bonds   A bond has a face amount of $1000 and matures in 10 years. The nominal interest rate is 8.5%. What is the price of the bond to yield an effective interest rate of 8%?

Solution   **Step 1:** Calculate the amount of each semiannual interest payment, half the nominal rate times the face amount:

$$\left(\frac{1}{2}\right)(0.085)(\$1000) = \$42.50$$

Step 2: Calculate the present value of the annuity of semiannual payments:

Amount of each payment from Step 1	$ 42.50
Number of payments (2 × 10 years): 20	
Effective interest rate per period (half of stated effective rate): 4%	
Factor from formula for $P(n, i)$ (use a calculator)	13.5903
Present value of interest payments	$ 577.59

Step 3: Calculate the present value of the amount payable at maturity:

Amount payable at maturity	$ 1000
Number of semiannual compounding periods before maturity: 20	
Effective interest rate per period: 4%	
Factor from formula for $(1 + i)^{-n}$ (use a calculator)	.45639
Present value of maturity value	$ 456.39

Step 4: Determine the price of the bond:

Present value of interest payments	$ 577.59
Present value of maturity payment	456.39
Price of bond	$1033.98

□

Exercise 5.5   *Answers to Odd-Numbered Problems begin on page* 611.

1. *Leasing Problem.* A corporation may obtain a machine either by leasing it for 5 years (the useful life) at an annual rent of $2000 or by purchasing the machine for $8100. If the corporation can borrow money at 10% per annum, which alternative is preferable?

2. If the corporation in Problem 1 can borrow money at 14% per annum, which alternative is preferable?

3. *Capital Expenditure Analysis.* Machine A costs $10,000 and has a useful life of 8 years, and Machine B costs $8000 and has a useful life of 6 years. Suppose Machine A generates an annual labor savings of $2000 while Machine B generates an annual labor savings of $1800. Assuming the time value of money (investment opportunity rate) is 10% per annum, which machine is preferable?

4. In Problem 3, if the time value of money is 14% per annum, which machine is preferable?

5. *Corporate Bonds.* A bond has face amount of $1000 and matures in 15 years. The nominal interest rate is 9%. What is the price of the bond that will yield an effective interest rate of 8%?

6. For the bond in Problem 5, what is the price of the bond to yield an effective interest rate of 10%?

CHAPTER REVIEW

Important Terms		
interest	compound interest	present value of annuity
principal	effective rate of interest	amortization
rate of interest	compound interest formula	leasing
per annum	present value	capital expenditure analysis
simple interest	annuity	bond
amount	ordinary annuity	face amount
simple discount	payment period	par value

proceeds   amount of annuity   nominal interest
maturity value   sinking fund   coupon interest

Review   *Answers to Odd-Numbered Problems begin on page* 611.
Exercises

1. Find the interest (I) and amount (A) if $400 is borrowed for 9 months at 12% simple interest.

2. Dan borrows $500 at 9% per annum simple interest for 1 year and 2 months. What is the interest charged and what is the amount of the loan?

3. Find the amount of an investment of $100 after *2* years and 3 months at 10% compounded monthly.

4. Mike places $200 in a savings account that pays 10% per annum compounded monthly. How much is in his account after 9 months?

5. A car dealer offers Mike the choice of two loans:
   (a) $3000 for 3 years at 12% per annum simple interest
   (b) $3000 for 3 years at 10% per annum compounded monthly
   Which loan costs Mike the least?

6. A money market fund pays 9% per annum compounded monthly. How much should I invest now so that 2 years from now I will have $100.00 in the account?

7. Katy wants to buy a bicycle that costs $75 and will purchase it in 6 months. How much should she put in her savings account for this if she can get 10% per annum compounded monthly?

8. Mike decides he needs $500.00 1 year from now to buy a used car. If he can invest at 8% compounded monthly, how much should he save each month to buy the car?

9. Mr. and Mrs. Corey are newlyweds and want to purchase a home, but they need a down payment of $10,000. If they want to buy their home in 2 years, how much should they save each month in their savings account that pays 10% per annum compounded monthly?

10. Mike has just purchased a used car on time and will make equal payments of $50 per month for 18 months at 12% per annum charged monthly. How much did the car actually cost?

11. *House Mortgage.* Mr. and Mrs. Ostedt have just purchased an $80,000 home and made a 25% down payment. The balance can be amortized at 10% for 25 years. What are the monthly payments? How much interest will be paid? What is their equity after 5 years?

12. An inheritance of $25,000 is to be paid in equal amounts over a 5 year period at the end of each year. If the $25,000 can be invested at 10% per annum, what is the annual payment?

13. *House Mortgage.* A mortgage of $125,000 is to be amortized at 9% per annum for 25 years. What are the monthly payments? What is the equity after 10 years?

14. A state has $8,000,000 worth of construction bonds that are due in 25 years. What annual sinking fund deposit is needed if the state can earn 10% per annum on its money?

15. *Depletion Problem.* How much should Mr. Graff pay for a gold mine expected to yield an annual return of $20,000 and to have a life expectancy of 20 years, if he wants to have a 15% annual return on his investment and he can set up a sinking fund that earns 10% a year?

16. Mr. Doody, at age 70, is expected to live for 15 years. If he can invest at 12% per annum compounded monthly, how much does he need now to guarantee himself $300 every month for the next 15 years?

17. *Depletion Problem.* An oil well is expected to yield an annual net return of $25,000 for the next 15 years, after which it will run dry. An investor wants a return on his investment of 20%. He can establish a sinking fund earning 10% annually. How much should he pay for the oil well?

18. Hal deposited $100 a month in an account paying 9% per annum compounded monthly for 25 years. What is the largest amount he may withdraw monthly for 35 years?

Mathematical Questions

From CPA Exams (Answers on page 611 *)*

1. *CPA Exam—May 1973*
Which of the following tables should be used to calculate the amount of the equal periodic payments which could be equivalent to an outlay of $3000 at the time of the last payment?
- (a) Amount of 1
- (b) Amount of an annuity of 1
- (c) Present value of an annuity of 1
- (d) Present value of 1

2. *CPA Exam—November 1976*
A businessman wants to withdraw $3000 (including principal) from an investment fund at the end of each year for 5 years. How should he compute his required initial investment at the beginning of the first year if the fund earns 6% compounded annually?
- (a) $3000 times the amount of an annuity of $1 at 6% at the end of each year for 5 years
- (b) $3000 divided by the amount of an annuity of $1 at 6% at the end of each year for 5 years
- (c) $3000 times the present value of an annuity of $1 at 6% at the end of each year for 5 years
- (d) $3000 divided by the present value of an annuity of $1 at 6% at the end of each year for 5 years

3. *CPA Exam—November 1976*
A businessman wants to invest a certain sum of money at the end of each year for 5 years. The investment will earn 6% compounded annually. At the end of 5 years, he will need a total of $30,000 accumulated. How should he compute his required annual investment?
- (a) $30,000 times the amount of an annuity of $1 at 6% at the end of each year for 5 years
- (b) $30,000 divided by the amount of an annuity of $1 at 6% at the end of each year for 5 years
- (c) $30,000 times the present value of an annuity of $1 at 6% at the end of each year for 5 years
- (d) $30,000 divided by the present value of an annuity of $1 at 6% at the end of each year for 5 years

4. *CPA Exam—November 1974*
Shaid Corporation issued $2,000,000 of 6%, 10 year convertible bonds on June 1, 1973, at 98 plus accrued interest. The bonds were dated April 1, 1973, with interest payable April 1 and October 1. Bond discount is amortized semiannually on a straight-line basis.
   On April 1, 1974, $500,000 of these bonds were converted into 500 *shares of* – 20 par value common stock. Accrued interest was paid in cash at the time of conversion.

What was the effective interest rate on the bonds when they were issued?

(a) 6%
(b) Above 6%
(c) Below 6%
(d) Cannot be determined from the information given.

CPA Exam—November 1974

Items 5 through 7 apply to the appropriate use of present-value tables. Given below are the present-value factors for $1.00 discounted at 8% for one to five periods. Each of the following items is based on 8% interest compounded annually from day of deposit to day of withdrawal.

Periods	Present Value of $1 Discounted at 8% per Period
1	0.926
2	0.857
3	0.794
4	0.735
5	0.681

5. What amounts should be deposited in a bank today to grow to $1000 three years from today?

(a) $\dfrac{\$1000}{0.794}$

(b) $\$1000 \times 0.926 \times 3$

(c) $(\$1000 \times 0.926) + (\$1000 \times 0.857) + (\$1000 \times 0.794)$

(d) $\$1000 \times 0.794$

6. What amount should an individual have in his bank account today before withdrawal if he needs $2000 each year for 4 years with the first withdrawal to be made today and each subsequent withdrawal at 1 year intervals? (He is to have exactly a zero balance in his bank account after the fourth withdrawal.)

(a) $\$2000 + (\$2000 \times 0.926) + (\$2000 \times 0.857) + (\$2000 \times 0.794)$

(b) $\dfrac{\$2000}{0.735} \times 4$

(c) $(\$2000 \times 0.926) + (\$2000 \times 0.857) + (\$2000 \times 0.794) + (\$2000 \times 0.735)$

(d) $\dfrac{\$2000}{0.926} \times 4$

7. If an individual put $3000 in a savings account today, what amount of cash would be available 2 years from today?

(a) $\$3000 \times 0.857$

(b) $\$3000 \times 0.857 \times 2$

(c) $\dfrac{\$3000}{0.857}$

(d) $\dfrac{\$3000}{0.926} \times 2$

PART TWO

PROBABILITY

SETS; COUNTING TECHNIQUES

6.1 SETS

SET PROPERTIES AND SET NOTATION □ OPERATION ON SETS
□ THE NUMBER OF ELEMENTS IN A SET □ APPLICATIONS

SET PROPERTIES AND SET NOTATION

Recall from Chapter 1 that a *set* is a collection of objects considered as a whole. The objects of a set S are called *elements* of S, or *members* of S. A set that has no elements, called the *empty set* or *null set,* is denoted by the symbol $\varnothing$.

The elements of a set are not repeated. Thus, we never write {3, 2, 2} but rather write {3, 2}. Also, the order in which the elements of a set are listed does not make any difference. Thus, the three sets

$$\{3, 2, 4\} \qquad \{2, 3, 4\} \qquad \{4, 3, 2\}$$

are different listings of the same set. The *elements* of a set distinguish the set — not the order in which the elements are written.

Some other examples of sets are the following:

(a) Let

$$E = \{\text{All possible outcomes resulting from tossing a coin three times}\}$$

If we let H denote "heads" and T denote "tails," then the set E can also be written as

$$E = \{TTT, HTT, THT, TTH, HHT, HTH, THH, HHH\}$$

where, for instance, THT means the first toss resulted in tails, the second toss in heads, and the third toss in tails.

(b) Let

$$F = \{\text{Possible arrangements of the digits}\}$$

Some typical elements of F are:

$$1478906532, \qquad 4875326019, \qquad 3214569870$$

The number of elements in F is very large, so listing all of them is impractical. Later on in this chapter we will study a technique to compute the number of elements in F.

Equality of Sets **Let A and B be two sets. We say that A *is equal to B*, written as**

$$A = B$$

GEORG F. L. P. CANTOR (1845–1918) was born in St. Petersburg, Russia. His father was a Danish merchant and his mother was a talented artist. The family, which was of Jewish descent converted to Christianity, moved to Frankfurt, Germany in 1856. Cantor was educated at Zurich and the University of Berlin. At Berlin his instructors were the famous mathematicians Kummer, Weierstrauss, and Kronecker. After receiving his Ph.D. degree in 1867, Cantor had an active professional career, but spent it at a mediocre university. At the age of 29 he published his revolutionary paper on the theory of infinite sets, a work that provided a common language for most of mathematics.

if and only if A and B have the same elements. If two sets A and B are not equal, we write

$$A \neq B$$

Subset   Let A and B be two sets. We say that A *is a subset of* B or that A *is contained in B*, written as

$$A \subseteq B$$

if and only if every element of A is also an element of B. If a set A *is not a subset* of a set B, we write

$$A \not\subseteq B$$

When we say that A is a subset of B, we can also say "there are no elements in set A that are not also elements in set B." Of course, $A \subseteq B$ if and only if whenever $x \in A$, then $x \in B$ for all x. This latter way of interpreting the meaning of $A \subseteq B$ is useful for obtaining various laws that sets obey.

Proper Subset   Let A and B be two sets. We say that A *is a proper subset of* B or that A *is properly contained in B*, written as

$$A \subset B$$

if and only if every element of the set A is also an element of set B, but there is at least one element in set B that is *not* in set A.

Notice that "A is a proper subset of B" means that there are *no* elements of A that are not also elements of B, but there is at least one element of B that is not in A.

If a set A is *not* a proper subset of a set B, we write

$$A \not\subset B$$

The following example illustrates some uses of the three relationships, $=$, $\subseteq$, and $\subset$, just defined.

□ **Example 1**   Consider three sets A, B, and C given by

$$A = \{1, 2, 3\} \qquad B = \{1, 2, 3, 4, 5\} \qquad C = \{1, 2, 3\}$$

Some of the relationships between pairs of these sets are:
(a) $A = C$ (b) $A \subseteq B$ (c) $A \subseteq C$ (d) $A \subset B$ (e) $C \subseteq A$ □

In comparing the two definitions of *subset* and *proper subset,* you should notice that if a set A is a subset of a set B, then either A is a proper subset of B or else A equals B. That is,

$$A \subseteq B \text{ if and only if either } A \subset B \text{ or } A = B$$

Also, if A is a proper subset of B, we can infer that A is a subset of B, but A does not equal B. That is,

$$A \subset B \text{ if and only if } A \subseteq B \text{ and } A \neq B$$

The distinction that is made between *subset* and *proper subset* is rather subtle, but quite important.

We can think of the relationship $\subset$ as a refinement of $\subseteq$. On the other hand, the relationship $\subseteq$ is an extension of $\subset$, in the sense that $\subseteq$ may include equality whereas with $\subset$, equality cannot be included.

Because of the way the relationship $\subseteq$ (is a subset of) has been defined, it is easy to see that for any set A, we have

$$\varnothing \subseteq A$$

Since the empty set $\varnothing$ has no elements, there is no element of the set $\varnothing$ that is not also in A.

Also, if A is any nonempty set, that is, any set having at least one element, then

$$\varnothing \subset A$$

In applications, the elements that may be considered are usually limited to some specific all-encompassing set. For example, in discussing students eligible to graduate from Midwestern University, the discussion would be limited to students enrolled at the university.

Universal Set The *universal set U* **is defined as the set consisting of all elements under consideration.**

Thus, if A is any set and if U is the universal set, then every element in A must be in U (since U consists of all elements under consideration). Hence, we may write

$$A \subseteq U$$

for *any* set A.

It is convenient to represent a set as the interior of a circle. Pairs of sets are usually depicted as interlocking circles enclosed in a rectangle, which represents the universal set. Such diagrams of sets are called *Venn diagrams*. See Figure 1.

Venn Diagram

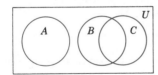

Figure 1

OPERATIONS ON SETS

Next, we introduce operations that may be performed on sets.

Union of Sets Let A and B be any two sets. The *union of A with B,* written as

$$A \cup B$$

is defined to be the set consisting of those elements either in A **or in** B **or in both** A **and** B**. That is,**

$$A \cup B = \{x \,|\, x \in A \text{ or } x \in B\}$$

In the Venn diagram in Figure 2 the shaded area corresponds to $A \cup B$.

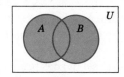

Figure 2

Intersection of Sets Let A and B be any two sets. The *intersection of A with B*, written as

$$A \cap B$$

is defined as the set consisting of those elements that are both in A and in B. That is,

$$A \cap B = \{x \mid x \in A \text{ and } x \in B\}$$

In other words, to find the intersection of two sets A and B means to find the elements *common* to A and B. In the Venn diagram in Figure 3 the shaded region is $A \cap B$.

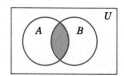

Figure 3

□ **Example 2** For the sets

$$A = \{1, 3, 5\} \qquad B = \{3, 4, 5, 6\} \qquad C = \{6, 7\}$$

find: (a) $A \cup B$ (b) $A \cap B$ (c) $A \cap C$

Solution (a) $A \cup B = \{1, 3, 5\} \cup \{3, 4, 5, 6\} = \{1, 3, 4, 5, 6\}$
(b) $A \cap B = \{1, 3, 5\} \cap \{3, 4, 5, 6\} = \{3, 5\}$
(c) $A \cap C = \{1, 3, 5\} \cap \{6, 7\} = \varnothing$ □

□ **Example 3** Let T be the set of all taxpayers and let S be the set of all people over 65 years of age. Describe $T \cap S$.

Solution $T \cap S$ is the set of all taxpayers who are also over 65 years of age.   □

Disjoint Sets If two sets A and B have no elements in common, that is, if

$$A \cap B = \varnothing$$

then A and B are called *disjoint sets.*

JOHN VENN (1834–1923), the son of a minister, graduated from Gonville and Caius College in Cambridge, England in 1853, after which he pursued theological interests as a curate in the parishes of London. In addition to his work in logic, he made important contributions to the mathematics of probability. He was an accomplished linguist, a botanist, and a noted mountaineer.

Two disjoint sets A and B are illustrated in the Venn diagram in Figure 4. Since the areas corresponding to A and B do not overlap anywhere, $A \cap B$ is empty.

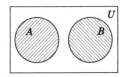

Figure 4

□ **Example 4** Suppose that a die* is tossed. Let A be the set of outcomes in which an even number turns up; let B be the set of outcomes in which an odd number shows. Find $A \cap B$.

Solution
$$A = \{2, 4, 6\} \qquad B = \{1, 3, 5\}$$

We note that A and B have no elements in common, since an even number and an odd number cannot occur simultaneously on a single toss of a die. Therefore, $A \cap B = \varnothing$ and the sets A and B are disjoint sets. □

Suppose we consider all the employees of some company as our universal set U. Let A be the subset of employees who smoke. Then all the nonsmokers will make up some subset of U that is called the *complement* of the set of smokers.

Complement Let A be any set. The *complement of A,* written as

$$\overline{A} \quad (\text{or } A', \quad \text{or } -A)$$

is defined as the set consisting of elements in the universe U that are not in A. Thus,

$$\overline{A} = \{x \mid x \notin A\}$$

The shaded region in Figure 5 illustrates the complement, $\overline{A}$.

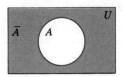

Figure 5

□ **Example 5** Let

$$U = \{a, b, c, d, e, f\} \qquad A = \{a, b, c\} \qquad B = \{a, c, f\}$$

List the elements of the following sets:
(a) $\overline{A}$ (b) $\overline{B}$ (c) $\overline{A \cup B}$
(d) $\overline{A} \cap \overline{B}$ (e) $\overline{A \cap B}$ (f) $\overline{A} \cup \overline{B}$

* A *die* (plural *dice*) is a cube with the numbers 1, 2, 3, 4, 5, 6 showing on the six faces.

Solution   (a) $\bar{A}$ consists of all the elements in U that are not in A, namely, $\bar{A} = \{d, e, f\}$.

(b)   Similarly, $\bar{B} = \{b, d, e\}$.

(c)   To determine $\overline{A \cup B}$, we first determine the elements in $A \cup B$:

$$A \cup B = \{a, b, c, f\}$$

The complement of the set $A \cup B$ is then

$$\overline{A \cup B} = \{d, e\}$$

(d)   From parts (a) and (b) we find that

$$\bar{A} \cap \bar{B} = \{d, e\}$$

(e)   As in part (c), we first determine the elements in $A \cap B$:

$$A \cap B = \{a, c\}$$

Then,

$$\overline{A \cap B} = \{b, d, e, f\}$$

(f) From parts (a) and (b) we find that

$$\bar{A} \cup \bar{B} = \{b, d, e, f\}$$ □

The answers to parts (c) and (d) in Example 5 are the same, and so are the results from parts (e) and (f). This is no coincidence. There are two fundamental formulas involving intersections and unions of complements of sets. They are known as *De Morgan's laws*.

De Morgan's Laws   Let A and B be any two sets.

   (a) $\overline{A \cup B} = \bar{A} \cap \bar{B}$ (b) $\overline{A \cap B} = \bar{A} \cup \bar{B}$

De Morgan's laws state that all we need to do to form the complement of a union (or intersection) of sets is to form the complements of the individual sets and then change the union symbol to an intersection (or the intersection to a union). We shall employ Venn diagrams to verify De Morgan's laws.

(a)   First, we draw two diagrams, as shown in Figure 6.

Figure 6

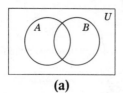
(a)

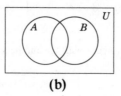
(b)

We will use the diagram on the left for $\overline{A} \cap \overline{B}$ and the one on the right for $\overline{A \cup B}$. Figure 7 illustrates the completed Venn diagrams of these sets.

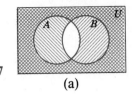 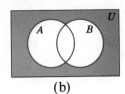

Figure 7

(a)   (b)

Thus, in Figure 7(a) $\overline{A} \cap \overline{B}$ is represented by the cross-hatched region and in Figure 7(b) $\overline{A \cup B}$ is represented by the shaded region. Since these regions correspond, this illustrates that the two sets $\overline{A} \cap \overline{B}$ and $\overline{A \cup B}$ are equal.

(b)   This verification is left to you. See Problem 28, part (c).

□ **Example 6**   Use a Venn diagram to illustrate

$$A \cup B = (A \cap \overline{B}) \cup (A \cap B) \cup (\overline{A} \cap B)$$

Solution   First, we construct Figure 8.

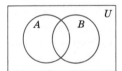

Figure 8

Now, shade the regions $A \cap \overline{B}$, $A \cap B$, and $\overline{A} \cap B$, as shown in Figure 9.

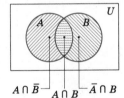

Figure 9 $A \cap \overline{B}$ $A \cap B$ $\overline{A} \cap B$

The three regions together represent the set $A \cup B$.   □

□ **Example 7**   Use a Venn diagram to illustrate

$$(A \cup B) \cap C$$

Solution First we construct Figure 10(a). Then we shade $A \cup B$ and C as in Figure 10(b). The cross-hatched region of Figure 10(b) is the set $(A \cup B) \cap C$.

□

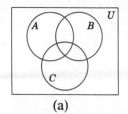
(a)

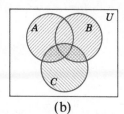
(b)

Figure 10

We list without any further discussion several results we will be using in later chapters:

(a) $A \cup \varnothing = A$ (b) $A \cap \varnothing = \varnothing$ (c) $A \cup \overline{A} = U$

(d) $A \cap \overline{A} = \varnothing$ (e) $\overline{U} = \varnothing$ (f) $\overline{\varnothing} = U$

(g) $\overline{(\overline{A})} = A$

THE NUMBER OF ELEMENTS IN A SET

When you count objects, what you are actually doing is taking each object to be counted and matching each of these objects exactly once to the counting numbers 1, 2, 3, and so on, until *no* objects remain. Even before numbers had names and symbols assigned to them, this method of counting was used. Early cavemen determined how many of their herd of cattle did not return from pasture by using rocks. As each cow left, a rock was placed aside. As each cow returned, a rock was removed from the pile. If rocks remained after all the cows returned, it was then known that some cows were missing. It is important to realize that cavemen were able to do this without developing a language or symbolism for numbers.

We will need some new notation. If A is any set, we will denote by $c(A)$ the number of elements in A. Thus, for example, for the set L of letters in the alphabet,

$$L = \{a, b, c, d, e, f, \ldots, x, y, z\}$$

we write $c(L) = 26$ and say "the number of elements in L is 26."

Also, for the set

$$N = \{1, 2, 3, 4, 5\}$$

we write $c(N) = 5$.

The empty set $\varnothing$ has no elements, and we write

$$c(\varnothing) = 0$$

Finite If the number of elements in a set is zero or a positive integer, we say that the set is Mathematics *finite.* Otherwise, the set is said to be *infinite.* The area of mathematics that deals with the study of finite sets is called *finite mathematics.*

□ **Example 8**   A survey of a group of people indicated there were 25 with brown eyes and 15 with black hair. If 10 people had both brown eyes and black hair and 23 people had neither, how many people were interviewed?

Solution   Let A denote the set of people with brown eyes and B the set of people with black hair. Then the data given tell us

$$c(A) = 25 \qquad c(B) = 15 \qquad c(A \cap B) = 10$$

Now, the number of people with either brown eyes or black hair cannot be $c(A) + c(B)$, since those with both would be counted twice. The correct procedure then would be to subtract those with both. That is,

$$c(A \cup B) = c(A) + c(B) - c(A \cap B) = 25 + 15 - 10 = 30$$

The sum of people found either in A or in B and those found neither in A nor in B is the total interviewed. Thus, the number of people interviewed is

$$30 + 23 = 53$$

See Figure 11.

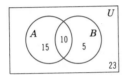

Figure 11

In Example 8 we discovered the following important relationship:

Let A and B be two finite sets. Then
$$c(A \cup B) = c(A) + c(B) - c(A \cap B)$$

□

APPLICATIONS

□ **Example 9**   In a survey of 75 consumers, 12 indicated they were going to buy a new car, 18 said
Consumer Survey   they were going to buy a new refrigerator, and 24 said they were going to buy a new stove. Of these, 6 were going to buy both a car and a refrigerator, 4 were going to buy a car and a stove, and 10 were going to buy a stove and refrigerator. One person indicated he was going to buy all three items.

(a)   How many were going to buy none of these items?
(b)   How many were going to buy only a car?
(c)   How many were going to buy only a stove?
(d)   How many were going to buy only a refrigerator?

Solution   Denote the sets of people buying cars, refrigerators, and stoves by C, R, and S, respectively. Then we know from the data given that

$$c(C) = 12 \qquad c(R) = 18 \qquad c(S) = 24$$
$$c(C \cap R) = 6 \qquad c(C \cap S) = 4 \qquad c(S \cap R) = 10$$
$$c(C \cap R \cap S) = 1$$

We use the information given above in the reverse order and put it into a Venn diagram. Thus, beginning with the fact that $c(C \cap R \cap S) = 1$, we place a 1 in that set, as shown in Figure 12(a). Now, $c(C \cap R) = 6$, $c(C \cap S) = 4$, and $c(S \cap R) = 10$.

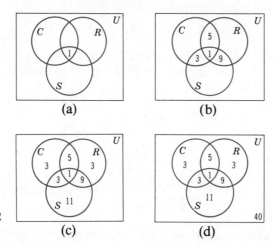

Figure 12

(a)   (b)

(c)   (d)

Thus, we place $6 - 1 = 5$ in the proper region (giving a total of 6 in the set $C \cap R$). Similarly, we place 3 and 9 in the proper regions for the sets $C \cap S$ and $S \cap R$. See Figure 12(b). Now, $c(C) = 12$ and 9 of these 12 are already accounted for. Also, $c(R) = 18$ with 15 accounted for and $c(S) = 24$ with 13 accounted for. See Figure 12(c). Finally, the number in $\overline{C \cup R \cup S}$ is the total of 75 less those accounted for in C, R, and S, namely $3 + 5 + 1 + 3 + 3 + 9 + 11 = 35$. Thus,

$$c(\overline{C \cup R \cup S}) = 75 - 35 = 40$$

See Figure 12(d). From this figure, we can see that: (a) 40 were going to buy none of the items, (b) 3 were going to buy only a car, (c) 11 were going to buy only a stove, and (d) 3 were going to buy only a refrigerator.

□ **Example 10**   In a survey of 10,281 people restricted to those who were either black or male or over
Demographic Survey   18 years of age, the following data were obtained:

Black: 3490

Male: 5822

Over 18:   4722

Black males: 1745

Over 18 and male: 859

Over 18 and black: 1341

Black male over 18: 239

The data are inconsistent. Why?

Solution We denote the set of people who were black by B, male by M, and over 18 by H. Then we know that

$$c(B) = 3490 \qquad c(M) = 5822 \qquad c(H) = 4722$$
$$c(B \cap M) = 1745 \qquad c(H \cap M) = 859$$
$$c(H \cap B) = 1341 \qquad c(H \cap M \cap B) = 239$$

Since $H \cap M \cap B \neq \varnothing$, we use the Venn diagram shown in Figure 13. This means that

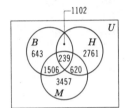

Figure 13

$$239 + 1102 + 620 + 1506 + 3457 + 643 + 2761 = 10{,}328$$

people were interviewed. However, it is given that only 10,281 were interviewed. This means the data are inconsistent. ☐

Exercise 6.1 *Answers to Odd-Numbered Problems begin on page* 611.

In Problems 1–10 replace the asterisk by the symbol(s) =, ⊂, and/or ⊆ to give a true statement. If none of these relationships hold, write "None of these."

1. $\{1, 3, 7\} * \{1, 3\}$
2. $\{4, 9\} * \{9, 10, 4\}$
3. $\{5, 7\} * \{5, 8\}$
4. $\{0, 1, 4\} * \{0, 5, 8, 9\}$
5. $\varnothing * \{1, 3\}$
6. $\{0\} * \{1, 3\}$
7. $\{1, 3\} * \{1, 3, 5, 8\}$
8. $\{5, 8, 9, 15\} * \{9\}$
9. $\{2, 3\} * \{2, 3, 6, 8, 0\}$
10. $\{2, 3\} * \{2, 3\}$

11. If $A \subseteq B$ and $B \subseteq C$, what do you conclude? Why?

12. Write down all possible subsets of the set $\{a, b, c\}$.

13. Write down all possible subsets of the set $\{a, b, c, d\}$.

14. If the universal set is the set of people, let A denote the subset of fat people, let B denote the subset of bald people, and let C denote the subset of bald and fat people. Write down several correct relationships involving A, B, and C.

In Problems 15–22, use $A = \{1, 2, 3\}$, $B = \{3, 4, 5, 6\}$, $C = \{3, 5, 7\}$ to evaluate each set.

15. $A \cap B$ **16.** $A \cap C$

17. $A \cup C$ **18.** $B \cup C$

19. $(A \cup B) \cap C$ **20.** $(A \cap B) \cap C$

21. $A \cup (B \cup C)$ **22.** $(A \cap B) \cup C$

23. If $U =$ Universal set $= \{0, 1, 2, 3, 4, 5, 6, 7, 8, 9\}$ and if $A = \{0, 1, 5, 7\}$, $B = \{2, 3, 5, 8\}$, $C = \{5, 6, 9\}$, find:

(a) $A \cup B$ (b) $B \cap C$

(c) $A \cap B$ (d) $\overline{A \cap B}$

(e) $\overline{A} \cap \overline{B}$ (f) $A \cup (B \cap A)$

(g) $(C \cap A) \cap (\overline{A})$ (h) $(A \cap B) \cup (B \cap C)$

24. If $U =$ Universal set $= \{1, 2, 3, 4, 5\}$ and if $A = \{3, 5\}$, $B = \{1, 2, 3\}$, $C = \{2, 3, 4\}$, find:

(a) $\overline{A} \cap \overline{C}$ (b) $(A \cup B) \cap C$

(c) $A \cup (B \cap C)$ (d) $(A \cup B) \cap (A \cup C)$

(e) $\overline{A \cap C}$ (f) $\overline{A \cup B}$

(g) $\overline{A} \cap \overline{B}$ (h) $(A \cap B) \cup C$

25. Let

$U = \{$All letters of the alphabet$\}$

$A = \{b, c, d\}$ $B = \{c, e, f, g\}$

List the elements of the sets:

(a) $A \cup B$ (b) $A \cap B$ (c) $\overline{A} \cap \overline{B}$ (d) $\overline{A} \cup \overline{B}$

26. Let

$$U = \{a, b, c, d, e, f\} \quad A = \{b, c\} \quad B = \{c, d, e\}$$

List the elements of the sets:

(a) $A \cup B$ (b) $A \cap B$ (c) $\overline{A}$

(d) $\overline{B}$ (e) $\overline{A \cap B}$ (f) $\overline{A \cup B}$

27. Use Venn diagrams to illustrate the following sets:

(a) $\overline{A} \cap B$ (b) $(\overline{A} \cap \overline{B}) \cup C$

(c) $A \cap (A \cup B)$ (d) $A \cup (A \cap B)$

(e) $(A \cup B) \cap (A \cup C)$ (f) $A \cup (B \cap C)$

(g) $A = (A \cap B) \cup (A \cap \overline{B})$ (h) $B = (A \cap B) \cup (\overline{A} \cap B)$

28. Use Venn diagrams to illustrate the following laws:

(a) $A \cap (B \cup C) = (A \cap B) \cup (A \cap C)$ (Distributive law)

(b) $A \cap (A \cup B) = A$ (Absorption law)

(c) $\overline{A \cap B} = \overline{A} \cup \overline{B}$ (De Morgan's law)

(d) $(A \cup B) \cup C = A \cup (B \cup C)$ (Associative law)

In Problems 29–32 use

$$A = \{x|x \text{ is a customer of IBM}\}$$
$$B = \{x|x \text{ is a secretary employed by IBM}\}$$
$$C = \{x|x \text{ is a computer operator at IBM}\}$$
$$D = \{x|x \text{ is a stockholder of IBM}\}$$
$$E = \{x|x \text{ is a member of the Board of Directors of IBM}\}$$

to describe each set.

29. $A \cap E$

30. $B \cap D$

31. $A \cup D$

32. $C \cap E$

In Problems 33–36 use

$$U = \{\text{All college students}\}$$
$$M = \{\text{All male students}\}$$
$$S = \{\text{All students who smoke}\}$$

to describe each set.

33. $M \cap S$ **34.** $\overline{M}$ **35.** $\overline{M} \cap \overline{S}$ **36.** $M \cup S$

In Problems 37–40 find the number of elements in each set.

37. $\{1, 3, 5, 7\}$

38. $\{0, 1, 2\}$

39. $\{0, 1, 2, 3, 4, 5, 6, 7, 8, 9\}$

40. $\{2, 4\}$

In Problems 41–46 use the sets $A = \{1, 2, 3, 5\}$ and $B = \{4, 6, 8\}$ to find the number of elements in each set.

41. A

42. B

43. $A \cap B$

44. $A \cup B$

45. $(A \cap B) \cup A$

46. $(B \cap A) \cup B$

In Problems 47–50 use the sets $A = \{1, 3, 6, 8\}$, $B = \{8\}$, and $C = \{8, 10\}$ to find the number of elements in each set.

47. $A \cup (B \cap C)$

48. $A \cup (B \cup C)$

49. $A \cap (B \cap C)$

50. $(A \cap B) \cup C$

51. Find $c(A \cup B)$, given that $c(A) = 4$, $c(B) = 3$, and $c(A \cap B) = 2$.

52. Find $c(A \cup B)$, given that $c(A) = 14$, $c(B) = 11$, and $c(A \cap B) = 6$.

53. Find $c(A \cap B)$, given that $c(A) = 5$, $c(B) = 4$, and $c(A \cup B) = 7$.

54. Find $c(A \cap B)$, given that $c(A) = 8$, $c(B) = 9$, and $c(A \cup B) = 16$.

55. Find $c(A)$, given that $c(B) = 8$, $c(A \cap B) = 4$, and $c(A \cup B) = 14$.

56. Find $c(B)$, given that $c(A) = 10$, $c(A \cap B) = 5$, and $c(A \cup B) = 29$.

57. Motors, Inc., manufactured 325 cars with automatic transmissions, 216 with power steering, and 89 with both these options. How many cars were manufactured if every car has at least one option?

58. Suppose that out of 1500 first-year students at a certain college, 350 are taking history, 300 are taking mathematics, and 270 are taking both history and mathematics. How many first-year students are taking history or mathematics?

In Problems 59–67 use the data in the figure below to answer each question.

59. How many are in set A?
60. How many are in set B?
61. How many are in A or B?
62. How many are in B or C?
63. How many are in A but not B?
64. How many are in B but not C?
65. How many are in all three?
66. How many are in none?
67. How many are in A and B and C?

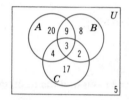

Applications   68. *Voting Patterns.* In 1948, according to a study made by Berelsa, Lazarfeld, and McPhee, the influence of religion and age on voting in Elmira, New York, was given by the following table:

	Age		
	Below 35	**35–54**	**Over 54**
Protestant Voting Republican	82	152	111
Protestant Voting Democratic	42	33	15
Catholic Voting Republican	27	33	7
Catholic Voting Democratic	44	47	33

Find:

(a) The number of voters who are Catholic or Republican or both.
(b) The number of voters who are Catholic or over 54 or both.
(c) The number of Democratic voters below 35 or over 54.

69. The Venn diagram on page 251 illustrates the number of seniors (S), female students (F), and students on the dean's list (D) at a small western college. Describe each number.

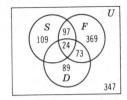

70. At a small midwestern college:

31	female seniors were on the dean's list
62	females were on the dean's list who were not seniors
45	male seniors were on the dean's list
87	female seniors were not on the dean's list
96	male seniors were not on the dean's list
275	females were not seniors and were not on the dean's list
89	men were on the dean's list who were not seniors
227	men were not seniors and were not on the dean's list

(a) How many were seniors?

(b) How many were females?

(c) How many were on the dean's list?

(d) How many were seniors on the dean's list?

(e) How many were female seniors?

(f) How many were females on the dean's list?

(g) How many were students at the college?

71. In a survey of 75 college students, it was found that of the three weekly news magazines *Time, Newsweek,* and *U.S. News and World Report:*

23	read *Time*
18	read *Newsweek*
14	read *U.S. News and World Report*
10	read *Time* and *Newsweek*
9	read *Time* and *U.S. News and World Report*
8	read *Newsweek* and *U.S. News and World Report*
5	read all three

(a) How many read none of these three magazines?

(b) How many read *Time* alone?

(c) How many read *Newsweek* alone?

(d) How many read *U.S. News and World Report* alone?

(e) How many read neither *Time* nor *Newsweek?*

(f) How many read *Time* or *Newsweek* or both?

72. Of the cars sold during the month of July, 90 had air conditioning, 100 had automatic transmissions, and 75 had power steering. Five cars had all three of these extras. Twenty cars had none of these extras. Twenty cars had only air conditioning; 60 cars had only automatic transmissions; and 30 cars had only power steering. Ten cars had both automatic transmission and power steering.

(a)   How many cars had both power steering and air conditioning?

(b)   How many had both automatic transmission and air conditioning?

(c)   How many had neither power steering nor automatic transmission?

(d)   How many cars were sold in July?

(e)   How many had automatic transmission or air conditioning or both?

73.   A staff member at a large engineering school was presenting data to show that the students there received a liberal education as well as a scientific one. "Look at our record," she said. "Out of one senior class of 500 students, 281 are taking English, 196 are taking English and History, 87 are taking History and a foreign language, 143 are taking a foreign language and English, and 36 are taking all of these." She was fired. Why?

74.   *Blood Classification.*   Blood is classified as being either Rh-positive or Rh-negative and according to type. If blood contains an A antigen, it is type A; if it has a B antigen, it is type B; if it has both A and B antigens, it is type AB; and if it has neither antigen, it is type O. Use a Venn diagram to illustrate these possibilities. How many different possibilities are there?

75.   A survey of 52 families from a suburb of Chicago indicated that there was a total of 241 children below the age of 18. Of these, 109 were male; 132 were below the age of 11; 143 had played Little League; and 69 males were below the age of 11. If 45 females under 11 had played Little League and 30 males under 11 had played Little League, how many children over 11 and under 18 had played Little League?

6.2 THE MULTIPLICATION PRINCIPLE

In this section we introduce a general principle of counting, the *Multiplication Principle*. We begin with two examples.

□ **Example 1**   In traveling from New York to Los Angeles, Mr. Doody wishes to stop over in Chicago. If he has 5 different routes to choose from in driving from New York to Chicago and has 3 routes to choose from in driving from Chicago to Los Angeles, in how many ways can Mr. Doody travel from New York to Los Angeles?

Solution   The task of traveling from New York to Los Angeles is composed of two consecutive operations:

| Choose a route from New York to Chicago Task 1 | Choose a route from Chicago to Los Angeles Task 2 |

In Figure 14, we see that following each of the 5 routes from New York to Chicago there are 3 routes from Chicago to Los Angeles. Thus, in all, there are $5 \cdot 3 = 15$ different routes.

Figure 14

These 15 different routes can be enumerated as

$$1A, 1B, 1C \qquad 2A, 2B, 2C \qquad 3A, 3B, 3C \qquad 4A, 4B, 4C \qquad 5A, 5B, 5C$$

Notice that the total number of ways the trip can be taken is simply the product of the number of ways of doing task 1 with the number of ways of doing task 2.

Tree Diagram The different routes in Example 1 can also be depicted in a *tree diagram*. See Figure 15.

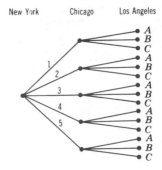

Figure 15

☐ **Example 2** In a city election, there are 4 candidates for mayor, 3 candidates for vice-mayor, 6 candidates for treasurer, and 2 for secretary. In how many ways can these four offices be filled?

Solution The task of filling an office can be divided into four consecutive operations:

| Select a mayor | Select a vice-mayor | Select a treasurer | Select a secretary |

Corresponding to each of the 4 possible mayors, there are 3 vice-mayors. These two offices can be filled in $4 \cdot 3 = 12$ different ways. Also, corresponding to each of these 12 possibilities, we have 6 different choices for treasurer—giving $12 \cdot 6 = 72$ different possibilities. Finally, to each of these 72 possibilities there can correspond 2 choices for secretary. Thus, all told, these offices can be filled in $4 \cdot 3 \cdot 6 \cdot 2 = 144$ different ways. A partial illustration is given by the tree diagram in Figure 16. ☐

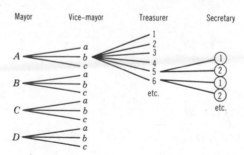

Figure 16

The examples just solved demonstrate a general type of counting problem, which can be solved by the Multiplication Principle.

> **Multiplication Principle** If we can perform a first task in p different ways, a second task in q different ways, a third task in r different ways, . . . , then the total act of performing the first task, followed by performing the second task, and so on, can be done in $p \cdot q \cdot r \cdot \ldots$ different ways

☐ **Example 3** (a) How many possible batting orders can the manager of a baseball team construct
Batting Orders   from nine available players?

(b) If the manager adheres to the rule that the pitcher always bats last and the star homerun hitter is always fourth (cleanup), then how many batting orders are possible from nine given players?

Solution (a) In the first slot, any of the 9 players can be chosen. In the second slot, any one of the remaining 8 can be chosen; and so on, so that there are

$$9 \cdot 8 \cdot 7 \cdot 6 \cdot 5 \cdot 4 \cdot 3 \cdot 2 \cdot 1 = 362{,}880$$

possible batting orders.

(b) The first position can be filled in any one of 7 ways, the second in any of 6 ways, the third in any of 5 ways, the fourth has been designated, the fifth in any of 4 ways, . . . , so that here there are

$$7 \cdot 6 \cdot 5 \cdot 4 \cdot 3 \cdot 2 \cdot 1 = 5040$$

different batting orders of 9 players after 2 have been designated. ☐

☐ **Example 4** License plates in the state of Maryland consist of 3 letters of the alphabet followed by 3 digits.

(a) The Maryland system will allow how many possible license plates?

(b) Of these, how many will have all their digits distinct?

Solution (a) There are 6 positions on the plate to be filled, the first 3 by letters and the last 3 by digits.

Positions 1, 2, and 3 can be filled in any one of 26 ways, while the remaining positions can each be filled in any of 10 ways. The total number of plates, by the Multiplication Principle, is then

$$26 \cdot 26 \cdot 26 \cdot 10 \cdot 10 \cdot 10 = 17,576,000$$

(b) Here, the tasks involved in filling the digit positions are slightly different. The first digit can be any one of 10, but the second digit can be only any one of 9 (we cannot duplicate the first digit); there are the 8 choices for the third digit (we cannot duplicate either the first or the second). Thus there are

$$26 \cdot 26 \cdot 26 \cdot 10 \cdot 9 \cdot 8 = 12,654,720$$

plates with no repeated digit. ☐

Exercise 6.2 *Answers to Odd-Numbered Problems begin on page* 613.

1. There are two roads between towns A and B. There are 4 roads between towns B and C. How many different routes may one travel between towns A and C?

2. A woman has 4 blouses and 5 skirts. How many different outfits can she wear?

3. XYZ Company wants to build a complex consisting of a factory, office building, and warehouse. If the building contractor has 3 different kinds of factories, 2 different office buildings, and 4 different warehouses, how many models must be built to show all possibilities to XYZ Company?

4. Cars, Inc., has 3 different car models and 6 color schemes. If you are one of the dealers, how many cars must you display to show each possibility?

5. A man has 3 pairs of shoes, 8 pairs of socks, 4 pairs of slacks, and 9 sweaters. How many outfits can he wear?

6. There are 14 teachers in a Math Department. A student is asked to indicate her favorite and her least favorite. In how many ways is this possible?

7. A house has 3 doors and 12 windows. In how many ways can a burglar rob the house by entering through a window and exiting through a door?

8. A man has 4 pairs of gloves. In how many ways can he select a right-hand glove and a left-hand glove that do not match?

9. A corporation has a board of directors consisting of 12 members. The board must select from its members a chairman, vice chairman, and a secretary. In how many ways can this be done?

10. How many license plates consisting of 2 letters followed by 2 digits are possible?

11. A restaurant offers 6 different salads, 5 different main courses, 10 different desserts, and 4 different drinks. How many different lunches—each consisting of a salad, a main course, a dessert and a drink are possible?

12. Five different mathematics books, 3 different physics books, and 2 different computer science books are to be arranged on a student's desk. The student wants the books to be grouped by subject matter. How many arrangements are possible?

13. How many ways can 6 people be seated in a row of 6 seats? 8 people be seated in a row of 8 seats?

14. How many different words can be formed using the 5 letters of the word "CLIPS"?

15. How many four-letter code words are possible from the first of 6 letters of the alphabet with no letters repeated? Allowing letters to repeat?

16. How many outcomes are there for the experiment of flipping 2 coins?

17. How many outcomes are there for the experiment of flipping 4 coins?

18. Refer to Problem 17. In how many of the outcomes are the first and the last toss identical?

19. How many ways are there to rank 7 candidates who apply for a job?

20. (a) How many different ways are there to arrange 7 letters in the word "PROBLEM"? (b) If we insist that the letter P comes first, now how many ways are there? (c) If we insist that the letter P come first and the letter M be last, now how many ways are there?

21. On a math test there are 10 multiple-choice questions with 4 possible answers and 15 true-false questions. In how many possible ways can the 25 questions be answered?

22. Using the digits 1, 2, 3, and 4, how many different 4 digit numbers can be formed?

23. How many different license plate numbers can be made using 2 letters followed by 4 digits selected from the digits 0 through 9, if

    (a) Letters and digits may be repeated?
    (b) Letters may be repeated, but digits are not repeated?
    (c) Neither letters nor digits may be repeated?

24. *Security.* A system has seven switches, each of which may be either open or closed. The state of the system is described by indicating for each switch whether it is open or closed. How many different states of the system are there?

25. *Psychology Testing.* In an ESP experiment a person is asked to select and arrange 3 cards from a set of 6 cards labeled *A, B, C, D, E,* and *F.* Without seeing the card a second person is asked to give the arrangement he thinks he perceives. Determine the number of possible responses by the second person if he simply guesses.

26. Find the number of 7-digit telephone numbers

    (a) With no repeated digits (lead 0 is allowed).
    (b) With no repeated digits (lead 0 not allowed).
    (c) With repeated digits allowed including a lead 0.

27. *Product Choice.* An automobile manufacturer produces 3 different models. Models *A* and *B* can come in any of 3 body styles; Model *C* can come in only 2 body styles. Each car also comes in either black or green. How many distinguishable car types are there?

6.3 PERMUTATIONS

FACTORIAL ☐ PERMUTATIONS

In the next two sections we use the Multiplication Principle to discuss two general types of counting problems, called *permutations* and *combinations*. These concepts arise often in applications, especially in probability.

FACTORIAL

Before discussing the nature of permutations, we shall introduce a useful shorthand notation — the *factorial symbol.*

Factorial The symbol *n!*, read as *"n factorial,"* means

$$0! = 1 \qquad 1! = 1 \qquad n! = n(n-1)(n-2) \cdots (3)(2)(1), \quad n \geq 1 \qquad \text{is an integer}$$

Thus, to compute *n!*, we find the product of all consecutive integers from 1 to *n* inclusive.

A formula we shall find useful is

$$(n+1)! = (n+1) \cdot n!$$

☐ **Example 1** (a) $4! = (4)(3)(2)(1) = 24$

(b) $\dfrac{5!}{4!} = \dfrac{5 \cdot 4!}{4!} = 5$

(c) $\dfrac{52!}{5!47!} = \dfrac{52 \cdot 51 \cdot 50 \cdot 49 \cdot 48 \cdot 47!}{5 \cdot 4 \cdot 3 \cdot 2 \cdot 47!} = 2{,}598{,}960$

(d) $\dfrac{7!}{(7-5)!5!} = \dfrac{7!}{2!5!} = \dfrac{7 \cdot 6 \cdot 5!}{2!5!} = \dfrac{7 \cdot 6}{2} = 21$ ☐

PERMUTATIONS

We start with an example.

☐ **Example 2** Suppose we are setting up a code of 3 letter words and have 6 different letters, *a, b, c, d, e,* and *f,* from which to choose. If the code must not repeat any letter and if such words as *abc* and *bac* are considered different, how many different words can be formed?

Solution   We solve the problem by using the Multiplication Principle. In selecting a first letter, we have 6 choices. Since whatever letter is chosen cannot be repeated, we have 5 choices available for the second letter and 4 for the last letter. In all, then, there are $6 \cdot 5 \cdot 4 = 120$ words of 3 letters than can be formed. See Figure 17 for a partial tree diagram of this solution.   □

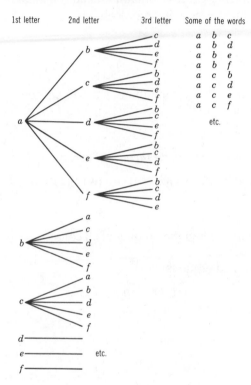

Figure 17

A way of rephrasing the question posed in the above example would be to ask: How many ordered arrangements using 3 distinct letters can be formed from the 6 letters a through f?

In general, we could ask: Given n distinct objects, how many ordered arrangements can be formed using r of the objects?

Permutation   Ordered arrangements of objects are called *permutations*. **An r permutation of a set of n objects is an ordered arrangement using r of the n objects. $P(n, r)$ is defined to be the *number* of r permutations of a set of n distinct objects.**

$P(n, r)$ is also referred to as the number of *permutations of n different objects taken r at a time.*

Thus, $P(n, r)$ is the number of ordered arrangements that can be formed using r objects chosen from a set of n distinct objects. To help you feel more comfortable, here is a list of short problems with their solutions given in $P(n, r)$ notation.

Find the Number of	Solution
Ways of choosing 5 people from a group of 10 and arranging them in a line.	$P(10, 5)$
Six-letter "words" that can be formed with no letter repeated.	$P(26, 6)$
Seven-digit telephone numbers, with no repeated digit (allow 0 for a first digit).	$P(10, 7)$
Ways of arranging 8 people in a line.	$P(8, 8)$

Note that in all of the above examples, *order is important.*

We now proceed to find a formula for $P(n, r)$.

In computing $P(n, r)$, we want to find the number of possible different arrangements of r quantities that are chosen from n different quantities in which no item is repeated and order is important. The first entry can be filled by any one of the n possibilities, the second by any one of the remaining $(n - 1)$, the third by any one of the now remaining $(n - 2)$, and so on. Since there are r positions to be filled, the number of possibilities is

$$P(n, r) = \underbrace{n(n - 1)(n - 2) \cdots (n - r + 1)}_{r \text{ factors}}$$

For example, if $n = 6$ and $r = 2$,

$$P(6, 2) = \underbrace{6 \cdot 5}_{2 \text{ factors}} = 30$$

Other examples are

$$P(7, 3) = \underbrace{7 \cdot 6 \cdot 5}_{3 \text{ factors}} = 210 \qquad P(5, 5) = \underbrace{5 \cdot 4 \cdot 3 \cdot 2 \cdot 1}_{5 \text{ factors}} = 5! = 120$$

To obtain the last factor in the expression for $P(n, r)$, we observe the following pattern:

First factor is n

Second factor is $n - 1$

Third factor is $n - 2$

.

.

.

rth factor is $n - (r - 1) = n - r + 1$

The number of different arrangements using r objects chosen from n objects in which

1. The n objects are all different
2. No object is repeated more than once in an arrangement
3. Order is important

is given by the formula

$$P(n, r) = n(n-1) \cdots (n-r+1)$$

Multiplying the right side by 1 in the form of $(n-r)!/(n-r)!$, we obtain

$$P(n, r) = n(n-1)(n-2) \cdots \cdots (n-r+1) \frac{(n-r)!}{(n-r)!}$$

Thus, since $n(n-1)(n-2) \cdots \cdots (n-r+1)(n-r)! = n!$, we get the following useful formula for $P(n, r)$:

$$P(n, r) = \frac{n!}{(n-r)!}$$

□ **Example 3**   There are 8 different mathematics books and 6 different computer science books. How many ways can a shelf arrangement using 5 of the mathematics books be formed?

Solution   We are seeking the number of arrangements using 5 of the 8 mathematics books. The answer is given by

$$P(8, 5) = \frac{8!}{(8-5)!} = \frac{8!}{3!}$$
$$= 8 \cdot 7 \cdot 6 \cdot 5 \cdot 4 = 6720 \qquad \qquad \square$$

□ **Example 4**   A student has 6 questions on an examination and is allowed to answer the questions in any order. In how many different orders could the student answer these questions?

Solution   The student wants the number of ordered arrangements of the 6 questions using all 6 of them. The number is given by

$$P(6, 6) = \frac{6!}{(6-6)!} = \frac{6!}{0!} = \frac{6!}{1} = 720 \qquad \qquad \square$$

In general the number of permutations (arrangements) of n different objects using all n of them is given by

$$P(n, n) = n!$$

So, in a class of n students, there are $n!$ ways of coercing all the students into a straight line.

□ **Example 5**   From the 8 mathematics books and the 6 computer science books of Example 3, seven positions on a shelf are to be filled. If the first 4 positions are to be occupied by math books and the last 3 by computer science books, in how many ways can this be done?

Solution   We think of the problem as consisting of 2 tasks. Task 1 is to fill the first 4 positions with 4 of the 8 mathematics books. This can be done in $P(8, 4)$ ways. Task 2 is to fill the remaining three positions with 3 of 6 computer books. This can be done in $P(6, 3)$ ways. By the Multiplication Principle, the seven positions can be filled as specified in

$$P(8, 4) \cdot P(6, 3) = \frac{8!}{4!} \cdot \frac{6!}{3!} = 8 \cdot 7 \cdot 6 \cdot 5 \cdot 6 \cdot 5 \cdot 4 = 201{,}600 \text{ ways}$$ □

Exercise 6.3   *Answers to Odd-Numbered Problems begin on page* 613.

In Problems 1–20 evaluate each expression.

1. $\dfrac{5!}{2!}$ 2. $\dfrac{8!}{2!}$ 3. $\dfrac{6!}{3!}$ 4. $\dfrac{9!}{3!}$

5. $\dfrac{10!}{8!}$ 6. $\dfrac{11!}{9!}$ 7. $\dfrac{9!}{8!}$ 8. $\dfrac{10!}{9!}$

9. $\dfrac{8!}{2!6!}$ 10. $\dfrac{9!}{3!6!}$ 11. $P(7, 2)$ 12. $P(5, 1)$

13. $P(8, 1)$ 14. $P(6, 6)$ 15. $P(5, 0)$ 16. $P(6, 4)$

17. $\dfrac{8!}{(8-3)!3!}$ 18. $\dfrac{9!}{(9-5)!5!}$ 19. $\dfrac{6!}{(6-6)!6!}$ 20. $\dfrac{7!}{(0-0)!7!}$

21. (a)   How many different ways are there to arrange the 6 letters in the word SUNDAY?
    (b)   If we insist that the letter S come first, now how many ways are there?
    (c)   If we insist that the letter S come first and the letter Y be last, now how many ways are there?

22. How many ways are there to rank 8 candidates who apply for a job?

23. From a pool of 10 job applicants, a list ranking the top 4 must be made. How many such lists are possible?

24. How many different 5 letter 'words" (sequences of letters) can be formed from the standard alphabet if repeated letters are not allowed? If repeated letters are allowed?

25. A station wagon has 9 seats. In how many different ways can 5 people be seated in it?

26. There are 5 different French books and 5 different Spanish books. How many ways are there to arrange them on a shelf if
    (a)   Books of the same language must be grouped together?
    (b)   French and Spanish books must alternate in the grouping?

27. In how many ways can 8 different books be distributed to 12 children if no child gets more than one book?

28. A computer must assign each of 4 outputs to one of 8 different printers. In how many ways can it do this provided no printer gets more than one output?

29. *Lottery Tickets.* From the 1500 lottery tickets that are sold, 3 tickets are to be selected for first, second, and third prizes. How many possible outcomes are there?

30. *Personnel Assignment.* A salesperson is needed in each of 7 different sales territories. If 10 equally qualified persons apply for the jobs, in how many ways can the job be filled?

31. *Slate Assignment.* A club has 15 members. In how many ways can they choose a slate of four officers consisting of a president, vice president, secretary and treasurer?

32. *Name Assignment.* A newborn child is to be given a first name and a middle name from a selection of 15 names. How many different possibilities are there?

33. How many basketball games are played in the Big Ten, if every team plays every other team twice?

6.4 COMBINATIONS

COMBINATIONS □ PASCAL TRIANGLE

Permutations focus on the order in which objects are arranged. However, in many cases, order is not important. For example, in a draw poker hand, the order in which you receive the cards is not relevant — all that matters is what cards are received. That is, with poker hands, we are concerned only with what *combination* of cards we have — not the particular order of the cards.

COMBINATIONS

To further emphasize the distinction between ordered and unordered selections, suppose we have 4 letters a, b, c, d, and wish to choose 2 of them without repeating any letter. If order is important, then we have $P(4, 2) = 4 \cdot 3 = 12$ possible arrangements, namely

$$ab, ac, ad \quad bc, bd, cd \quad ba, ca, da \quad cb, db, dc$$

If order is not a consideration, we have only 6 selections, namely,

$$ab, ac, ad, bc, bd, cd$$

Notice that in this example there are twice as many permutations (ordered selections) as unordered selections. The reason is that any selection can occur in one of two orderings — for example, the arrangements ab and ba both correspond to the unordered selection ab. Unordered selections are called *combinations*.

Combinations $C(n, r)$ **is defined to be the *number* of ways of choosing *r* distinct objects from a set of *n* distinct objects, without regard to the order of the selection.**

$C(n, r)$ is also referred to as the number of *combinations of n objects taken r at a time*.

The following table lists problems whose solutions are given in $C(n, r)$ notation.

Find the Number of	Solution
Ways of selecting 4 people from a group of six	$C(6, 4)$
Five card unordered poker hands	$C(52, 5)$
Committees of 6 that can be formed from the U. S. Senate (100 members)	$C(100, 6)$
Ways of selecting 5 courses from a catalog containing 200	$C(200, 5)$

In order to obtain a formula for $C(n, r)$, we observe that each unordered selection of r objects from a set of n can be arranged or permuted in $r!$ different ways.

For example, the unordered selection a, b, c gives rise to the orderings listed below.

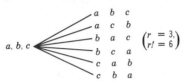

Thus, since each unordered selection yields $r!$ orderings or permutations, the number of permutations of r objects chosen from a set of n is $r!$ times as big as the number of unordered selections of r objects from a set of n.

That is,

$$r!C(n, r) = P(n, r)$$

and if we use our previously developed formula for $P(n, r)$,

$$C(n, r) = \frac{P(n, r)}{r!} = \frac{n!}{r!(n-r)!}$$

The number of different selections of r objects chosen from n objects in which

1. The n objects are all different
2. No object is repeated
3. Order is not important

is given by the formula

$$C(n, r) = \frac{n!}{r!(n-r)!}$$

□ **Example 1** Compute the following numbers:

(a) $C(50, 2)$ (b) $C(7, 5)$ (c) $C(7, 7)$ (d) $C(7, 0)$

Solution (a) $C(50, 2) = \dfrac{50!}{2!(50-2)!} = \dfrac{50!}{2!48!} = 1225$

(b) $C(7, 5) = \dfrac{7!}{5!(7-5)!} = \dfrac{7!}{5!2!} = 21$

(c) $C(7, 7) = \dfrac{7!}{7!(7-7)!} = \dfrac{7!}{7!0!} = 1$

(d) $C(7, 0) = \dfrac{7!}{0!(7-0)!} = \dfrac{7!}{0!7!} = 1$ □

□ **Example 2** From a deck of 52 cards, a hand of 5 cards is dealt. How many different hands are possible?

Solution   Such a hand is an unordered selection of 5 cards from a deck of 52. So, the number of different hands is

$$C(52, 5) = \frac{52!}{5!47!} = \frac{52 \cdot 51 \cdot 50 \cdot 49 \cdot 48}{5 \cdot 4 \cdot 3 \cdot 2 \cdot 1}$$
$$= 2,598,960 \qquad \square$$

☐ **Example 3**
Computer Science

A bit is a 0 or a 1. A 6 bit string is a sequence of length 6 consisting of 0's and 1's. How many 6 bit strings contain

(a)   Exactly one 1
(b)   Exactly two 1's?

Solution   (a)   To form a 6 bit string having one 1, we need but specify where the single 1 is located (the other positions are 0's). The location for the 1 can be chosen in

$$C(6, 1) = 6 \text{ ways}$$

(b)   Here, we must choose two of the 6 positions to contain 1's. Hence there are

$$C(6, 2) = 15 \text{ such strings} \qquad \square$$

☐ **Example 4**
Sampling

A sociologist needs a sample of 12 welfare recipients located in a large metropolitan area. He divides the city into 4 areas—northwest, northeast, southwest, southeast. Each section contains 25 welfare recipients. The sociologist may select the 12 recipients in any way he wants—all from the same area, 2 from the southwest area and 10 from the northwest area, and so on. How many different groups of 12 recipients are there?

Solution   Since order of selection is not important and since the selection is of 12 things from a possible $4 \cdot 25 = 100$ things, there are $C(100, 12)$ different groups. That is,

$$C(100, 12) = \frac{100!}{12!88!} \qquad \square$$

☐ **Example 5**

From 5 faculty members and 4 students, a committee of 4 is to be chosen that includes 2 students and 2 faculty members. In how many ways can this be done?

Solution   The faculty members can be chosen in $C(5, 2)$ ways. The students can be chosen in $C(4, 2)$ ways. By the Multiplication Principle, there are then

$$C(5, 2) \cdot C(4, 2) = \frac{5!}{2!3!} \cdot \frac{4!}{2!2!} = 10 \cdot 6 = 60 \text{ different ways} \qquad \square$$

PASCAL'S TRIANGLE

Binomial Coefficient

Sometimes the notation $\binom{n}{r}$, read as "*n* choose *r*," is used in place of $C(n, r)$. $\binom{n}{r}$ is called a *binomial coefficient* because of its connection with the Binomial Theorem (discussed in Section 8.2). A triangular display of $\binom{n}{r}$ for $n = 0$ to $n = 6$ is given in Figure 18. This triangular display is called *Pascal's triangle*.

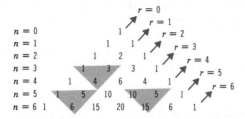

Figure 18

For example, $\binom{5}{2} = 10$, is found in the row marked $n = 5$ and on the diagonal marked $r = 2$.

In the Pascal triangle, successive entries can be obtained by adding the two nearest entries in the row above it. The shaded triangles in Figure 18 illustrate this. For example, $10 + 5 = 15$, etc.

The Pascal triangle, as the figure indicates, is symmetric. That is, when n is even, the largest entry occurs in the middle, and corresponding entries on either side are equal. When n is odd, there are two equal middle entries with corresponding equal entries on either side.

The reasons behind these properties of Pascal's triangle as well as other properties of binomial coefficients are discussed in Chapter 8.

Exercise 6.4   *Answers to Odd-Numbered Problems begin on page* 613 .

In Problems 1–8 find the value of each expression.

1. $C(6, 4)$ **2.** $C(5, 4)$ **3.** $C(7, 2)$ **4.** $C(8, 7)$

5. $\binom{5}{1}$ **6.** $\binom{8}{1}$ **7.** $\binom{8}{6}$ **8.** $\binom{8}{4}$

9. In how many ways can a committee of 3 senators be selected from a group of 8 senators?

10. In how many ways can a committee of 4 representatives be selected from a group of 9 representatives?

11. A Math Department is allowed to tenure 4 of 17 eligible teachers. In how many ways can the selection for tenure be made?

12. How many different hands are possible in a bridge game? (A bridge hand consists of 13 cards dealt from a deck of 52 cards.)

13. There are 25 students in the Math Club. How many ways can 3 officers be selected?

14. How many different relay teams of 4 persons can be chosen from a group of 10 runners?

15. A basketball team has 6 players who play at guard (2 of 5 starting positions). How many different teams are possible, assuming the remaining 3 positions are filled and it is not possible to distinguish a left guard from a right guard?

16. On a basketball team of 12 players, 2 play only at center, 3 play only at guard, and the rest play at forward (5 men on a team: 2 forwards, 2 guards, and 1 center). How many

BLAISE PASCAL (1623–1662) is most well-known for his creation of a theory of probability. He constructed the first computer, and later in life became interested in theology, contributing several literary masterpieces in this area. The computer language PASCAL is named for him.

different teams are possible, assuming it is not possible to distinguish left and right guards and left and right forwards?

17. The Student Affairs Committee has 3 faculty, 2 administration members, and 5 students on it. In how many ways can a subcommittee of 1 faculty, 1 administration member, and 2 students be formed?

18. Of 1352 stocks traded in 1 day on the New York Stock Exchange, 641 advanced, 234 declined, and the remainder were unchanged. In how many ways can this happen?

19. How many different ways can an offensive football team be formed from a squad that consists of 20 linemen, 3 quarterbacks, 8 halfbacks, and 4 fullbacks? This football team must have 1 quarterback, 2 halfbacks, 1 fullback, and 7 linemen.

20. How many different ways can a baseball team be made up from a squad of 15 players, if 3 players are used only as pitchers and the remaining players can be placed at any position except pitcher (9 players on a team)?

21. A little girl has 1 penny, 1 nickel, 1 dime, 1 quarter, and 1 half dollar in her purse. If she pulls out 3 coins, how many different sums are possible?

22. How many 8 bit strings contain

    (a)   Exactly two 1's?
    (b)   Exactly three 1's?

23. A state of Maryland million dollar lottery ticket consists of 6 distinct numbers chosen from the range 00 through 99. The order in which the numbers appear on the ticket is irrelevant. How many distinct lottery tickets can be issued?

24. How many poker hands contain all spades?

25. How many committees of 5 can be formed from members of the U. S. Senate?

26. A test has 3 parts. In part 1 a student must do 3 of 5 questions, in part 2 a student must choose 2 of 4 questions, and in part 3 a student must pick 3 of 6 questions. In how many different ways can a student complete the test?

27. In how many ways can a committee of 4 be selected from 6 men and 8 women if the committee must contain at least 2 women?

28. A man wants to invite 1 or more of his 4 friends to dinner. In how many ways can he do this?

29. How many 8 bit strings contain an even number of 1's? An odd number of 1's?

In Problems 30–38, use the Multiplication Principle, permutations or combinations, as appropriate.

30. *Location of Office Secretaries.* An office manager must locate 12 secretaries into three offices that hold respectively 6, 4, and 2 secretaries. In how many ways can the three groups be chosen to occupy the three offices?

31. *Test Panel Selection.* A sample of 8 persons is selected for a test from a group containing 40 smokers and 15 nonsmokers. In how many ways can the 8 persons be selected?

32. *Resource Allocation.* A trucking company has 8 trucks and 6 drivers available when requests for 4 trucks are received. How many different ways are there of selecting the trucks and the drivers to meet these requests.

33. *Group Selection.* From a group of 5 people, we are required to select a different person to participate in each of 3 different tests. In how many ways can the selections be made?

34. *Congressional Committees.* In the U. S. Congress, a conference committee is to be composed of 5 senators and 4 representatives. In how many ways can this be done? (There are 435 representatives and 100 senators.)

35. *Quality Control.* A box contains 24 light bulbs. The quality control engineer will pick a sample of 4 light bulbs for inspection. How many different samples are there?

36. *Mating.* A horse stable has 12 mares and 4 stallions. How many different ways can they be mated.

37. *Rating.* A sportswriter makes a preseason guess of the top 15 university basketball teams (in order) from among 50 major university teams. How many different possibilities are there?

38. *Packaging.* A manufacturer produces 8 different items. He packages assortments of equal parts of 3 different items. How many different assortments can be packaged?

CHAPTER REVIEW

Important Terms	set	union ($\cup$)	factorial
	empty set	intersection ($\cap$)	tree diagram
	subset ($\subseteq$)	disjoint sets	multiplication principle
	proper subset ($\subset$)	complement	permutation
	universal set	De Morgan's laws	combination
	Venn diagram	finite sets	Pascal triangle

True–False Questions

(Answers on page 613)

T F 1. If $A \cup B = A \cap B$, then $A = B$.

T F 2. If A and B are disjoint sets, then $c(A \cup B) = c(A) + c(B)$.

T F 3. The number of permutations of 4 different objects taken 4 at a time is 12.

T F 4. $C(5, 3) = 20$

Fill in the Blanks

(Answers on page 613)

1. Two sets that have no elements in common are called _____.

2. The number of different arrangements of r objects from n objects in which (a) the n objects are different, (b) no object is repeated more than once in an arrangement, and (c) order is important is called a _____.

3. If in Problem 2 above, condition (c) is replaced by "order is not important," we have a _____.

4. A triangular display of combinations is called the _____ triangle.

5. The combinations $\binom{n}{r}$ are sometimes called _____ _____.

Review Exercises

Answers to Odd-Numbered Problems begin on page 613 .

In Problems 1–16 replace the asterisk by the symbol(s) $\in$, $\subset$, $\subseteq$, and/or $=$ to give a true statement. If none of these relationships hold, write "None of these."

1. $0 * \varnothing$

2. $\{0\} * \{1, 0, 3\}$

3. $\{5, 6\} \cap \{2, 6\} * \{8\}$

4. $\{2, 3\} \cup \{3, 4\} * \{3\}$

5. $\{8, 9\} * \{9, 10, 11\}$

6. $1 * \{1, 3, 5\} \cup \{3, 4\}$

7. $5 * \{0, 5\}$

8. $\varnothing * \{1, 2, 3\}$

9. $\varnothing * \{1, 2\} \cap \{3, 4, 5\}$

10. $\{2, 3\} * \{3, 4\}$

11. $\{1, 2\} * \{1\} \cup \{3\}$

12. $5 * \{1\} \cup \{2, 3\}$

13. $\{4, 5\} \cap \{5, 6\} * \{4, 5\}$

14. $\{6, 8\} * \{8, 9, 10\}$

15. $\{6, 7, 8\} \cap \{8\} * \{6\}$

16. $4 * \{6, 8\} \cap \{4, 8\}$

17. For the sets

$$A = \{1, 3, 5, 6, 8\} \qquad B = \{2, 3, 6, 7\} \qquad C = \{6, 8, 9\}$$

find:

(a) $(A \cap B) \cup C$

(b) $(A \cap B) \cap C$

(c) $(A \cup B) \cap B$

18. For the sets U = Universal set = $\{1, 2, 3, 4, 5, 6, 7\}$ and

$$A = \{1, 3, 5, 6\} \qquad B = \{2, 3, 6, 7\} \qquad C = \{4, 6, 7\}$$

find:

(a) $\overline{A \cap B}$

(b) $(B \cap C) \cap A$

(c) $\overline{B} \cup \overline{A}$

19. If A and B are sets and if $c(A) = 24$, $c(A \cup B) = 33$, $c(B) = 12$, find $c(A \cap B)$.

20. During June, Colleen's Motors sold 75 cars with air conditioning, 95 with power steering, and 100 with automatic transmission. Twenty cars had all three options, 10 cars had none of these options, and 10 cars were sold that had only air conditioning. In addition, 50 cars had both automatic transmission and power steering, and 60 cars had both automatic transmission and air conditioning.

(a) How many cars were sold in June?

(b) How many cars had only power steering?

21. In a survey of 125 college students, it was found that of three newspapers, the *Wall Street Journal, New York Times,* and *Chicago Tribune:*

60	read the *Chicago Tribune*
40	read the *New York Times*
15	read the *Wall Street Journal*
25	read the *Chicago Tribune* and *New York Times*
8	read the *New York Times* and *Wall Street Journal*
3	read the *Chicago Tribune* and *Wall Street Journal*
1	read all three

(a) How many read none of these papers?

(b) How many read only the *Chicago Tribune?*

(c) How many read neither the *Chicago Tribune* nor the *New York Times?*

22. If $U =$ Universal set $= \{1, 2, 3, 4, 5\}$ and $B = \{1, 4, 5\}$, find all sets A for which $A \cap B = \{1\}$.

23. Compute $P(6, 3)$.

24. Compute $C(6, 2)$.

25. In how many different ways can a committee of 3 people be formed from a group of 5 people?

26. In how many different ways can 4 people line up?

27. In how many different ways can 3 books be placed on a shelf?

28. In how many different ways can 3 people be seated in 4 chairs?

29. How many house styles are possible if a contractor offers 3 choices of roof designs, 4 choices of window designs, and 6 choices of brick?

30. How many different answers are possible in a true–false test consisting of 10 questions?

31. You are to set up a code of 2 digit words using the digits 1, 2, 3, 4 without using any digit more than once. What is the maximum number of words in such a language? If the words 12 and 21, for example, designate the same word, how many words are possible?

32. You are to set up a code of 3 digit words using the digits 1, 2, 3, 4, 5, 6 without using any digit more than once in the same word. What is the maximum number of words in such a language? If the words 124, 142, etc., designate the same word, how many different words are possible?

33. A small town consists of a north side and a south side. The north side has 16 houses and the south side has 10 houses. A pollster is asked to visit 4 houses on the north side and 3 on the south side. In how many ways can this be done?

34. *Program Selection.* A ceremony is to include 7 speeches and 6 musical selections.

    (a) How many programs are possible?

    (b) How many programs are possible if speeches and musical selections are to be alternated?

35. There are 7 boys and 6 girls willing to serve on a committee. How many 7 member committees are possible if a committee is to contain:

    (a) 3 boys and 4 girls?

    (b) At least one member of each sex?

36. Colleen's Ice Cream Parlor offers 31 different flavors to choose from, and specializes in double dip cones.

    (a) How many different cones are there to choose from if you may select the same flavor for each dip?

    (b) How many different cones are there to choose from if you cannot repeat any flavor? Assume that a cone with vanilla on top of chocolate is different from a cone with chocolate on to of vanilla.

    (c) How many different cones are there if you consider any cone having chocolate on top and vanilla on the bottom the same as having vanilla on top and chocolate on the bottom?

37. A person has 4 History, 5 English, and 6 Mathematics books. How many ways can they be arranged on a shelf if books on the same subject must be together?

38. Five people are to line up for a group photograph. If 2 of them refuse to stand next to each other, in how many ways can the photograph be taken?

39. The figure below indicates the locations of two houses, *A* and *B*, in a city, where the lines represent streets. A person at *A* wishes to reach *B* and can only travel in two directions, to the right and up. How many different paths are there from *A* to *B*?

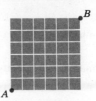

40. *Selecting a Route.* A cab driver picks up a passenger at point *A* (see the figure below) whose destination is point *B*. After completing the trip, the driver is to proceed to the garage at point *C*. If the cab must travel to the right or up, how many different routes are there from *A* to *C*?

41. In how many ways can we choose three words, one each from five 3 letter words, six 4 letter words, and eight 5 letter words?

42. A newborn child can be given 1, 2, or 3 names. In how many ways can a child be named if we can choose from 100 names?

43. In how many ways can 5 girls and 3 boys be divided into 2 teams of 4 if each team is to include at least 1 boy?

44. A meeting is to be addressed by 5 speakers, *A, B, C, D, E*. In how many ways can the speakers be ordered if *B* must not precede *A*?

45. What is the answer to Problem 44 if *B* is to speak immediately after *A*?

46. *License Plate Numbers.* An automobile license number contains 1 or 2 letters followed by a 4 digit number. Compute the maximum number of different licenses.

7

INTRODUCTION TO PROBABILITY

7.1 INTRODUCTION

Random Event

Probability theory is a part of mathematics that is useful for discovering and investigating the *regular* features of *random events*. Although it is not really possible to give a precise and simple definition of what is meant by the words *random* and *regular*, we hope that the explanation and the examples given below will help you understand these concepts.

Certain phenomena in the real world may be considered *chance phenomena*. These phenomena do not always produce the same observed outcome, and the outcome of any given observation of the phenomena may not be predictable. But they have a long-range behavior known as *statistical regularity*.

In some cases, we are familiar enough with the phenomenon under investigation to feel justified in making *exact* predictions with respect to the result of each individual observation. For example, if you want to know the time and place of a solar eclipse, you may not hesitate to predict an exact time, based on astronomical data.

However, in many cases our knowledge is not precise enough to allow exact predictions in particular situations. Some examples of such cases, called *random events,* are:

(a) Tossing a fair coin gives a result that is either a head or a tail. For any one throw, we cannot predict the result, although it is obvious that it is determined by definite causes (such as the initial velocity of the coin, the initial angle of throw, and the surface on which the coin rests). Even though some of these causes can be controlled, we cannot predetermine the result of any particular toss. Thus, the result of tossing a coin is a *random event*.

(b) In a series of throws with an ordinary die, each throw yields as its result one of the numbers 1, 2, 3, 4, 5, or 6. Thus, the result of throwing a die is a *random event*.

(c) The sex of a newborn baby is either male or female. However, the sex of a newborn baby cannot be predicted in any particular case. This, too, is an example of a *random event*.

The above examples demonstrate that in studying a sequence of random experiments, it is not possible to forecast individual results. These are subject to irregular, random fluctuations that cannot be exactly predicted. However, if the number of observations is large, that is, if we deal with a *mass phenomenon*, some regularity appears.

In Example (a), we cannot predict the result of any particular toss of the coin. However, if we perform a long sequence of tosses, we notice that the number of times heads occurs is approximately equal to the number of times tails appears. That is, it seems *reasonable* to say that in any toss of this fair coin, a head or a tail is *equally likely* to occur. As a result, we might *assign a probability* of $\frac{1}{2}$ for obtaining a head (or tail) on a particular toss.

For Example (b), the appearance of any particular face of the die is a random event. However, if we perform a long series of tosses, any face is as *equally likely* to occur as any other, provided the die is fair. Here we might *assign a probability* of $\frac{1}{6}$ for obtaining a particular face.

For Example (c), our intuition tells us that a boy baby and a girl baby are *equally likely* to occur. If we follow this reasoning, we might *assign a probability* of $\frac{1}{2}$ to having a girl baby. However, if we consult the data found in Table 1,† we see that it might be more accurate to *assign a probability* of .487 to having a girl baby.

Table 1

Year of Birth	Number of Births		Total Number of Births $b + g$	Ratio of Births	
	Boys b	Girls g		$\dfrac{b}{b+g}$	$\dfrac{g}{b+g}$
1970	1,915,378	1,816,008	3,731,386	.513	.487
1971	1,822,910	1,733,060	3,555,970	.513	.487
1972	1,669,927	1,588,484	3,258,411	.512	.488
1973	1,608,326	1,528,639	3,136,965	.513	.487
1974	1,622,114	1,537,844	3,159,958	.513	.487
1975	1,613,135	1,531,063	3,144,198	.513	.487
1976	1,624,436	1,543,352	3,167,788	.513	.487
1977	1,705,916	1,620,716	3,326,632	.513	.487
1978	1,709,394	1,623,885	3,333,279	.513	.487
1979	1,791,267	1,703,131	3,494,398	.513	.487
Total	17,082,803	16,226,182	33,308,985	.513	.487

The examples below illustrate some of the kinds of problems we shall encounter and solve in this and the next chapter.

□ **Example 1**   A fair die is thrown. With what probability will the face 5 occur?   □

□ **Example 2**   A fair coin is tossed. If it comes up heads (H), a fair die is rolled and the experiment is finished. If the coin comes up tails (T), the coin is tossed again and the experiment is finished. With what probability will the situation heads first, 5 second, occur?   □

□ **Example 3**   A room contains 50 people. With what probability will at least 2 of them have the same birthday?   □

□ **Example 4**   A factory produces light bulbs of which 80% are not defective. A sample of 6 bulbs is taken. With what probability will 3 or more of them be defective?   □

□ **Example 5**   Two dice are rolled. If they are fair, with what probability will the total be 11? If one is "loaded" in a certain way, what is the probability of an 11?   □

□ **Example 6**   A group of 1200 people includes 50 who qualify for an executive position and 500 females. Furthermore, suppose 35 females qualify. With what probability will a person chosen at random be both qualified and female?   □

† U.S. Census, 1970–1979.

Other questions that can be answered by using probability theory are given below. They are listed here merely as illustrations of the power of probability theory.

□ **Example 7**   Consider a telephone exchange with a finite number of lines. Suppose that the exchange is constructed in such a way that an incoming call that finds all the lines busy does not wait, but is lost. This is called an *exchange without waiting lines.* The most important problem to be solved *before* the exchange is constructed is to determine for any time t, the probability of finding all the lines busy at time t.   □

□ **Example 8**   People arrive at random times at a ticket counter to be served by an attendant, lining up in a queue if others are waiting. Given information about the rate of arrival and the length of time an attendant requires to serve each customer, how much of the time is the attendant idle? How much of the time is the line more than 15 persons long? What would be the effect of adding another attendant? If the people are not allowed to wait in line but must go elsewhere, what percentage of arrivals go unanswered? The same questions can be asked about gas stations, toll booths on roads, hospital beds, and so on.   □

□ **Example 9**   The following problem occurs quite often in physics and biology and was formulated by Galton in 1874 in his study of the disappearance of family lines: Given that a man of a known family has a probability of $p_0, p_1, p_2, \ldots$ of producing 0, 1, 2 male offspring, what is the probability that the family will eventually die out?   □

□ **Example 10**   Suppose that an infectious disease is spread by contact, that a susceptible person has a chance of catching it with each contact with an infected person, but that one becomes immune after having had the disease and can no longer transmit it. Some of the questions we would like answered are: How many susceptibles will be left when the number of infected is 0? How long will the epidemic last? For a given community, what is the probability that the disease will die out?   □

Exercise 7.1
1. Consult the United States census from 1970–1979. What probability would you assign to the birth of a boy baby based on these data?

2. Pick a page at random in your telephone directory and list the last digit of every number. Are all digits used equally often?

3. Toss a die six times and record the face shown. Denote this number by x (x can take the values 1, 2, 3, 4, 5, 6). Repeat the experiment 20 more times and tabulate the results. Do you observe any regularity?

4. *Buffon Needle Problem.* Suppose a needle is dropped at random onto a floor that is marked with parallel lines 6 inches apart. Suppose the needle is 4 inches long. With what probability does the needle fall between the two lines? Perform the experiment 20 times and record the number of times the needle rests completely within the two lines. An

illustration is provided below and a solution may be found in *Mathematics in the Modern World.**

5. *Gambler's Ruin Problem.* Conduct the following experiment with a classmate. Assume that you have $90 and your classmate has $10. Flip a fair coin. If you lose, you give your classmate $1, and if you win, your classmate gives you $1. The game ends when one of you loses all your money. Can you guess how long the game will last? Can you guess who has the better chance of winning?

6. *Birthday Problem.* Conduct the following experiment in your class. Find out how many students would bet that no 2 students have the same birthday. List the birthdays of all the students and determine whether any 2 have the same birthday. Would you have won or lost the bet? (See page 298 for a table that provides a rationale for betting one way or the other.)

7. *Chevalier de Mere's Problem.*† Which of the following random events do you think is more likely to occur?
   (a) To obtain a 1 on at least one die in a simultaneous throw of four fair dice.
   (b) To obtain at least one pair of 1's in a series of 24 throws of a pair of fair dice.
   (See Problem 23, page 316.)

8. Pick an editorial from your daily newspaper that contains at least 1000 words. List the number of times each letter of the alphabet is used. Based on this, what probability might you assign to the occurrence of a letter in an editorial?

7.2 SAMPLE SPACES AND ASSIGNMENT OF PROBABILITIES

SAMPLE SPACES □ EVENTS AND SIMPLE EVENTS □ PROBABILITY OF AN EVENT

In studying probability we are concerned with experiments, real or conceptual, and their outcomes. In this study we try to formulate in a precise manner a mathematical theory that closely resembles the experiment in question. The first stage of development of a mathematical theory is the building of what is termed a *mathematical model*. This model is then used as a predictor of outcomes of the experiment. The purpose of this section is to learn how a *probabilistic model* can be constructed.

---

* *Mathematics in the Modern World,* Readings from *Scientific American,* W. H. Freeman, San Francisco, 1968, pp. 169ff.
† CHEVALIER DE MERE (1607–1684), a philosopher and a man of letters, was a prominent figure at the court of Louis XIV. A French knight, de Mere was an ardent dice gambler and tried to become rich by this game. He was constantly thinking of various complicated rules that he hoped would help him reach his goal. He knew and corresponded with almost all leading mathematicians of his time, including Pascal, seeking their assistance.

SAMPLE SPACES

We begin by writing down the associated *sample space* of an experiment; that is, we write down all outcomes that can occur as a result of the experiment.

For example, if the experiment consists of flipping a coin, we would ordinarily agree that the only possible outcomes are heads, H, and tails, T. Therefore, a sample space for the experiment is the set $\{H, T\}$.

☐ **Example 1**   Consider an experiment in which, for the sake of simplicity, one die is green and the other is red. When the 2 dice are rolled, the set of outcomes consists of all the different ways that the dice may come to rest. This is referred to as a set of all *logical possibilities*. This experiment can be displayed in two different ways. One way is to use a tree diagram, as shown in Figure 1.

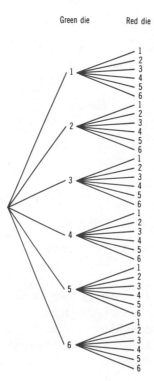

Green die   Red die

Figure 1

Another way is to let g and r denote, respectively, the number that comes up on the green die and the red die. Then an *outcome* can be represented by an ordered pair (g, r), where both g and r can assume any of the values 1, 2, 3, 4, 5, 6. Thus, a sample space S for this experiment is the set

Outcome

$$S = \{(g, r) | 1 \leq g \leq 6, \quad 1 \leq r \leq 6\}$$

Also, notice that the Multiplication Principle shows that the number of elements in S is 36, since there are 6 choices for g, 6 choices for r, and $6 \cdot 6 = 36$.

Figure 2 gives a graphical representation of the elements of S. ☐

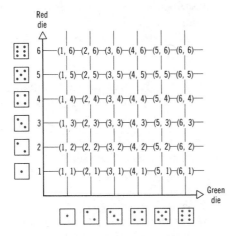

Figure 2

Sample Space A *sample space S,* associated with a real or conceptual experiment, is the set of all logical possibilities that can occur as a result of the experiment. Each element of a sample space S is called an *outcome.*

In the table below we list some experiments and their sample spaces.

	Experiment	Sample Space
(a)	Tossing two coins, a penny and a nickel, and noting the upturned faces when they come to rest.	$S = \{HH, HT, TH, TT\}$
(b)	An experiment consists of selecting three manufactured parts from the production process and observing whether they are acceptable (A) or defective (D).	$S = \{AAA, AAD, ADA,$ $ADD, DAA, DAD,$ $DDA, DDD\}$
(c)	Polling customers at a supermarket whether they *like* (L) a certain product or *dislike* (D) it and recording their response.	$S = \{L, D\}$
(d)	A spinner is marked from 1 to 8. An experiment consists of spinning the dial once.	$S = \{1, 2, 3, 4, 5, 6, 7, 8\}$
(e)	Surveying whether a customer entering a fast food restaurant orders a hamburger (H), french fries (F), both (B), or neither (N).	$S = \{H, F, B, N\}$

The theory of probability begins as soon as a sample space has been specified. The sample space of an experiment plays the same role as the universal set in set theory for all questions concerning the experiment.

In this chapter, we confine our attention to those cases for which the sample space is finite, that is, to those situations in which it is possible to have only a finite number of outcomes.

Notice that in our definition we say *a* sample space, rather than *the* sample space, since an experiment can be described in many different ways. In general, it is a safe guide to include as much detail as possible in the description of the outcomes of the experiment in order to answer all pertinent questions concerning the result of the experiment.

□ Example 2 Consider the set of all different types of families with 3 children. Describe the sample space for the experiment of drawing one family from the set of all possible 3 child families.

Solution One way of describing the sample space is by denoting the number of girls in the family. The only possibilities are members of the set

$$\{0, 1, 2, 3\}$$

That is, a 3 child family can have 0, 1, 2, or 3 girls.

This sample space has four outcomes. A disadvantage of describing the experiment using this sample space is that a question such as "Was the second child a girl?" cannot be answered. Thus, this method of classifying the outcomes may be too coarse, since it may not provide enough wanted information.

Another way of describing the sample space is by first defining B and G as "Boy" and "Girl," respectively. Then the sample space might be given as

$$\{BBB, BBG, BGB, BGG, GBB, GBG, GGB, GGG\}$$

where *BBB* means first child is a boy, second child is a boy, third child is a boy; and so on. This experiment can be depicted by the tree diagram in Figure 3. Notice that the experiment has 8 possible outcomes. □

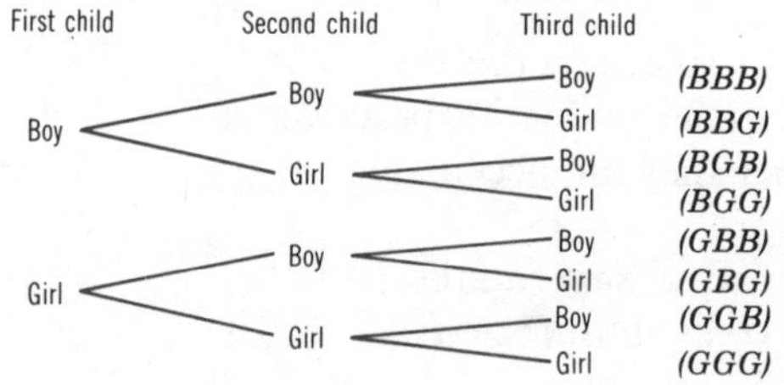

Figure 3

The advantage of the second type of classification of the sample space in Example 2 is that each outcome of the experiment corresponds to exactly one element in the sample space.

EVENTS AND SIMPLE EVENTS

Event; Simple Event An *event* is a subset of the sample space. If an event has exactly one element, that is, consists of only one outcome, it is called a *simple event*.

Every event can be written as the union of simple events. For example, consider the sample space of Example 2. The event E that the family consists of exactly 2 boys is

$$E = \{BBG, BGB, GBB\}$$

The event E is the union of the three simple events $\{BBG\}$, $\{BGB\}$, $\{GBB\}$. That is,

$$E = \{BBG\} \cup \{BGB\} \cup \{GBB\}$$

Since a sample space S is also an event, we can express a sample space as the union of simple events. Thus, if the sample space S consists of n outcomes,

$$S = \{e_1, e_2, \ldots, e_n\}$$

then

$$S = \{e_1\} \cup \{e_2\} \cup \ldots \cup \{e_n\}$$

□ **Example 3**   In the experiment of Example 1, involving a green die and a red die, let A be the event that the green die comes up less than or equal to 3 and the red die is 5. Let B be the event that the green die is 2 and the red die is 5 or 6. Describe the event A *or* B.

Solution

$$A = \{(g, r) \mid g \le 3, \quad r = 5\} \qquad B = \{(g, r) \mid g = 2, \quad r = 5, 6\}$$
$$= \{(1, 5), (2, 5), (3, 5)\} \qquad\qquad = \{(2, 5), (2, 6)\}$$

Note that A has three members and B has two members. Now the event A *or* B is merely the union of A with B. Thus,

$$A \cup B = \{(1, 5), (2, 5), (3, 5), (2, 6)\}$$

We conclude the event A *or* B has four members. [The event A *and* B, $A \cap B$, has one member, namely, (2, 5).]   □

PROBABILITY OF AN EVENT

We are now in a position to formulate a definition for the probability of a simple event of a sample space.

Probability of a Simple Event   Let S denote a sample space. To each simple event $\{e\}$ of S, we assign a real number, $P(e)$, called the *probability of the simple event* $\{e\}$, which has the two properties:

(I) $P(e) \ge 0$ for all simple events $\{e\}$ in S
(II)   The sum of the probabilities of all the simple events of S equals 1   (1)

If the sample space S is given by

$$S = \{e_1, e_2, \ldots, e_n\}$$

then

(I) $P(e_1) \ge 0, \quad P(e_2) \ge 0, \quad \ldots, \quad P(e_n) \ge 0$
(II) $P(e_1) + P(e_2) + \cdots + P(e_n) = 1$

The real number assigned to the simple event {e} is *completely arbitrary* within the framework of the above restrictions. For example, let a die be thrown. A sample space S is then

$$S = \{1, 2, 3, 4, 5, 6\}$$

There are six simple events in S: {1}, {2}, {3}, {4}, {5}, {6}. Either of the following two assignments of probabilities is acceptable.

(a)
$$P(1) = \frac{1}{6} \quad P(2) = \frac{1}{6} \quad P(3) = \frac{1}{6}$$

$$P(4) = \frac{1}{6} \quad P(5) = \frac{1}{6} \quad P(6) = \frac{1}{6}$$

This choice is in agreement with the definition, since the probability of each simple event is nonnegative and their sum is 1. This is an example of a "fair" die in which each simple event is equally likely to occur.

(b)
$$P(1) = 0 \quad P(2) = 0 \quad P(3) = \frac{1}{3}$$

$$P(4) = \frac{2}{3} \quad P(5) = 0 \quad P(6) = 0$$

This choice is also acceptable, even though it is unnatural. It implies that the die is "loaded," since only a 3 or a 4 appears and a 4 is twice as likely to occur as a 3.

☐ **Example 4**   A coin is weighted so that heads {H} is 5 times more likely to occur than tails {T}. What probability should we assign to heads? To tails?

Solution   Let x denote the probability that tails occurs. Then,

$$P(T) = x \quad \text{and} \quad P(H) = 5x$$

Since the sum of the probabilities of all the simple events equals 1, we must have

$$P(H) + P(T) = 5x + x = 1$$

$$6x = 1$$

$$x = \frac{1}{6}$$

Thus, we assign the probabilities

$$P(H) = \frac{5}{6} \quad P(T) = \frac{1}{6}$$

☐

Suppose probabilities have been assigned to each simple event of S. We now raise the question, "What is the probability of an event?" Let S be a sample space and let E be any event of S. It is clear that either $E = \varnothing$ or E is a simple event or E is the union of two or more simple events.

Probability of an Event If $E = \varnothing$, we define the *probability of* $\varnothing$ to be   **(2)**

$$P(\varnothing) = 0$$

In this case, the event $E = \varnothing$ is said to be *impossible*.

If E is simple, (1) is applicable.

If E is the union of r simple events $\{e_{i_1}\}, \{e_{i_2}\}, \ldots , \{e_{i_r}\}$, we define the *probability of E* to be

$$P(E) = P(e_{i_1}) + P(e_{i_2}) + \cdots + P(e_{i_r})$$

In particular, if the sample space S is given by

$$S = \{e_1, e_2, \ldots , e_n\}$$

we must have

$$P(S) = P(e_1) + \cdots + P(e_n) = 1$$

Thus, the probability of S, the sample space, is 1.

□ **Example 5**   Let 2 coins be tossed. A sample space S is

$$S = \{HH, TH, HT, TT\}$$

Let E be the event that they are both heads or both tails.

This can be depicted in two ways. See Figure 4.

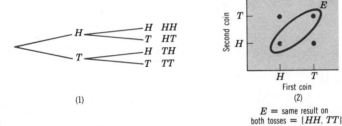

(1)

Figure 4

E = same result on both tosses = $\{HH, TT\}$

(2)

Compute the probability for event E with the following two assignments of probabilities:

(a) $P(HH) = P(TH) = P(HT) = P(TT) = \frac{1}{4}$

(b) $P(HH) = \frac{1}{9}, \quad P(TH) = \frac{2}{9}, \quad P(HT) = \frac{2}{9}, \quad P(TT) = \frac{4}{9}$

Solution   The event E is $\{HH, TT\}$.

(a) $P(E) = P(HH) + P(TT) = \frac{1}{4} + \frac{1}{4} = \frac{1}{2}$

(b) $P(E) = P(HH) + P(TT) = \frac{1}{9} + \frac{4}{9} = \frac{5}{9}$ □

The fact that we obtained different probabilities for the same event in Example 5 is not unexpected, since it results from our original assignment of probabilities to the simple events of the experiment. Any assignment that conforms to the restrictions given in (1) is mathematically correct.   The question of which assignment make is not a mathematical question, but is one that depends on the real-world situation to which the theory is applied. In this example the coins were fair in case (a) and were loaded in case (b).

Now that we have introduced the concepts of sample space, event, and probability of events, we introduce the idea of a *probabilistic model*.

Constructing a
Probabilistic Model

To construct a *probabilistic model* we need to do the following:

Step 1: List all possible outcomes of the experiment under investigation; that is, give a sample space or, if this is not easy to do, determine the number of simple events in the sample space.

Step 2: Assign to each simple event a probability $P(e)$ such that (1) is satisfied.

□ **Example 6**   A fair coin is tossed. If it comes up heads, H, a fair die is rolled and the experiment is finished. It comes up tails, T, the coin is tossed once more. Describe a probabilistic model for this experiment.

Solution   All the possible outcomes of this experiment are

$$S = \{H1, H2, H3, H4, H5, H6, TT, TH\}$$

where $H1$ indicates heads for the coin and then 1 for the die, and so on. See Figure 5 for the tree diagram.

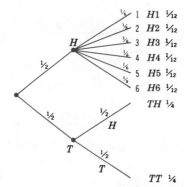

Figure 5

To these eight possible outcomes we assign the following probabilities:

$$P(H1) = P(H2) = P(H3) = P(H4) = P(H5) = P(H6) = \frac{1}{12}$$

$$P(TH) = P(TT) = \frac{1}{4}$$

The above discussion constitutes a model, called a *probabilistic* or *stochastic model,* for the experiment.   □

□ **Example 7**   For the model described in Example 6, let E be the event

$$E = \{H2, H4, TH\}$$

The probability of the event E is

$$P(E) = P(H2) + P(H4) + P(TH)$$

$$= \frac{1}{12} + \frac{1}{12} + \frac{1}{4} = \frac{5}{12}$$

□

Exercise 7.2 *Answers to Odd-Numbered Problems begin on page* 613 − 614.

1. A nickel and a dime are tossed. List the elements of the sample space:

   (a) If we are interested in whether the dime falls heads (H) or tails (T).
   (b) If we are interested only in the number of heads that appear on a single toss of the two coins.
   (c) If we are interested in whether the coins match (M) or do not match (D).

2. A card is selected from a standard deck of playing cards and its color — red (R) or black (B) is recorded. Describe an appropriate sample space for this experiment.

In Problems 3–6 describe the sample space associated with each random experiment. List the elements in each sample space.

3. Tossing a coin 3 times
4. Tossing 3 coins once
5. Tossing a coin 2 times and then a die
6. Tossing a coin and then a die

In Problems 7–14 use the spinners pictured below to list the elements in the sample space associated with each experiment described.

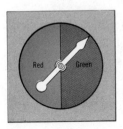
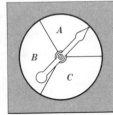
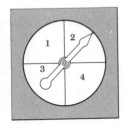

7. First Spinner 1 is spun and then Spinner 2 is spun.
8. First Spinner 3 is spun and then Spinner 1 is spun.
9. Spinner 1 is spun twice.
10. Spinner 3 is spun twice.
11. Spinner 2 is spun twice and then Spinner 3 is spun.
12. Spinner 3 is spun once and then Spinner 2 is spun twice.
13. Spinners 1, 2, 3 are each spun once in this order.
14. Spinners 3, 2, 1 are each spun once in this order.

In Problems 15–20 count the elements in the sample space associated with each random experiment.

15. Tossing a coin 4 times

16. Tossing a coin 5 times

17. Tossing 3 dice

18. Tossing 2 dice and then a coin

19. Selecting 2 cards (without replacement) from an ordinary deck of 52 cards*

20. Selecting 3 cards (without replacement) from an ordinary deck of 52 cards*

In Problems 21–24 consider the experiment of tossing a coin twice. The table lists six possible assignments of probabilities for this experiment:

Simple Event		Sample Space			
		HH	HT	TH	TT
Assignments	1	$\frac{1}{4}$	$\frac{1}{4}$	$\frac{1}{4}$	$\frac{1}{4}$
	2	0	0	0	1
	3	$\frac{3}{16}$	$\frac{5}{16}$	$\frac{5}{16}$	$\frac{3}{16}$
	4	$\frac{1}{2}$	$\frac{1}{2}$	$-\frac{1}{2}$	$\frac{1}{2}$
	5	$\frac{1}{8}$	$\frac{1}{4}$	$\frac{1}{4}$	$\frac{1}{8}$
	6	$\frac{1}{9}$	$\frac{2}{9}$	$\frac{2}{9}$	$\frac{4}{9}$

Using this table, answer the following questions.

21. Which of the assignments of probabilities satisfy the restrictions in (1)?

22. Which of the assignments should be used if the coin is known to be fair?

23. Which of the assignments of probabilities should be used if the coin is known to always come up tails?

24. What assignment of probabilities should be used if tails is twice as likely as heads to occur?

In Problems 25–28 assign valid probabilities to the simple events of each random experiment.

25. Tossing a fair coin twice

26. Tossing a fair coin three times

27. Tossing a fair die and then a fair coin

28. Tossing a fair die and then 2 fair coins

* An ordinary *deck of cards* has 52 cards. There are four suits of 13 cards each. The suits are called *clubs* (black), *diamonds* (red), *hearts* (red), and *spades* (black). In each suit the 13 cards are labeled A (ace), 2, 3, 4, 5, 6, 7, 8, 9, 10, J (jack), Q (queen), and K (king).

In Problems 29–34 the random experiment consists of tossing a fair coin four times.

29. List the elements of the sample space and assign probabilities to each simple event.

30. Write the elements of the event, "The first two tosses are heads."

31. Write the elements of the event, "The last three tosses are tails."

32. Write the elements of the event, "Exactly three tosses come up tails."

33. Write the elements of the event, "The number of heads exceeds 1 but is fewer than 4."

34. Write the elements of the event, "The first two tosses are heads and the second two are tails."

In Problems 35–40 the random experiment consists of tossing 2 fair dice. Construct a probabilistic model for this experiment and find the probability of each given event.

35. $A = \{(1, 2), (2, 1)\}$

36. $B = \{(1, 5), (2, 4), (3, 3), (4, 2), (5, 1)\}$

37. $C = \{(1, 4), (2, 4), (3, 4), (4, 4)\}$

38. $D = \{(1, 2), (2, 1), (2, 4), (4, 2), (3, 6), (6, 3)\}$

39. $E = \{(1, 1), (2, 2), (3, 3), (4, 4), (5, 5), (6, 6)\}$

40. $F = \{(6, 6)\}$

In Problems 41–46 the random experiment consists of tossing a fair die and then a fair coin. Construct a probabilistic model for this experiment and find the probability of each given event.

41. A: The coin comes up heads

42. B: The die comes up 1

43. C: The die does *not* come up 1

44. D: The die comes up 5 or 6

45. E: The die comes up 3, 4, or 5

46. F: The coin comes up heads and the die comes up a number less than 4

47. In Example 5, if the events E, F, G are defined as

E: At least 1 head F: Exactly 1 tail G: Tails on both tosses

find $P(E)$, $P(F)$, $P(G)$ for the two given assignments of probabilities.

48. If the events E and F are defined as

E: Common stocks are a good buy F: Corporate bonds are a good buy

state in words the meaning of:

(a) $P(E \cup F)$ (b) $P(\overline{E})$ (c) $P(\overline{E} \cap \overline{F})$

(d) $P(E \cup \overline{F})$ (e) $P(\overline{E} \cup F)$ (f) $P(\overline{E} \cap F)$

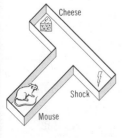

49. *T-maze.* In a T-maze a mouse may turn to the right (R) and receive a mild shock, or to the left (L) and get a piece of cheese. Its behavior in making such "choices" is studied by psychologists. Suppose a mouse runs a T-maze three times. List the set of all possible outcomes and assign valid probabilities to each simple event. Find the probability of each of the following events:

(a) E: Run to the right two consecutive times

(b) F: Never run to the right

(c) G: Run to the left on the first trial

(d) H: Run to the right on the second trial

50. A marketing study reveals two major rival companies, G and H, and four minor firms, a, b, c, d, who always ally themselves with one of the two major companies on prices. Free competition results if a major company is backed by two smaller ones. Construct a sample space and list the events that maintain free competition.

51. A red die and a green die are tossed. If r denotes the result on the red die and g the result on the green die, give verbal descriptions of the following algebraically described events:

(a) $r = 3g$ (b) $r - g = 1$ (c) $r \leq g$

(d) $r + g = 8$ (e) $g = r^2$ (f) $r = g$

Graph each of these events using Figure 2 as a backdrop.

52. Let $S = \{e_1, e_2, e_3, e_4, e_5, e_6, e_7\}$ be a given sample space. Let the probabilities assigned to the simple events be given as follows:

$$P(e_1) = P(e_2) = P(e_6)$$

$$P(e_3) = 2P(e_4) = \frac{1}{2} P(e_1)$$

$$P(e_5) = \frac{1}{2} P(e_7) = \frac{1}{4} P(e_1)$$

(a) Find $P(e_1)$, $P(e_2)$, $P(e_3)$, $P(e_4)$, $P(e_5)$, $P(e_6)$, $P(e_7)$.

(b) If $A = \{e_1, e_2\}$, $B = \{e_2, e_3, e_4\}$, $C = \{e_5, e_6, e_7\}$, and $D = \{e_1, e_5, e_6\}$, find $P(A)$, $P(B)$, $P(C)$, $P(D)$, $P(A \cup B)$, $P(A \cap D)$, $P(D \cap B)$, and $P(A \cap B)$.

53. Three cars, C_1, C_2, C_3, are in a race. If the probability of C_1 winning is p, that is, $P(C_1) = p$, and $P(C_1) = \frac{1}{2}P(C_2)$ and $P(C_3) = \frac{1}{2}P(C_2)$, find $P(C_1)$, $P(C_2)$, and $P(C_3)$. Also, find $P(C_1 \cup C_2)$ and $P(C_1 \cup C_3)$.

54. Consider an experiment with a loaded die such that the probability of any of the faces appearing in a toss is equal to that face times the probability that a 1 will occur. That is, $P(6) = 6 \cdot P(1)$, and so on.

(a) Describe the sample space.

(b) Find $P(1)$, $P(2)$, $P(3)$, $P(4)$, $P(5)$, and $P(6)$.

(c) Let the events A, B, and C be described as

A: Even-numbered face

B: Odd-numbered face

C: Prime number on face (2, 3, 5 are prime)

Find $P(A)$, $P(B)$, $P(C)$, $P(A \cup B)$, and $P(A \cup \overline{C})$.

7.3 PROPERTIES OF THE PROBABILITY OF AN EVENT

MUTUALLY EXCLUSIVE EVENTS □ ADDITIVE RULE □ COMPLEMENT OF AN EVENT □ ODDS

In this section, we state and prove results involving the probability of an event after the probabilistic model has been determined. The main tool we employ is set theory.

MUTUALLY EXCLUSIVE EVENTS

Mutually Exclusive Events   Two or more events of a sample space S are said to be *mutually exclusive* if and only if they have no outcomes in common.

That is, if we treat the events as sets, they are disjoint.

The following result gives us a way of computing probabilities for mutually exclusive events.

> Let E and F be two events of a sample space S. If E and F are mutually exclusive, that is, if $E \cap F = \varnothing$, then the probability of the event E or F is the sum of their probabilities, namely,
>
> $$P(E \cup F) = P(E) + P(F) \qquad (1)$$

Since E and F can be written as a union of simple events in which no simple event of E appears in F and no simple event of F appears in E, the result follows.

□ Example 1   In the experiment of tossing 2 fair dice, what is the probability of obtaining either a sum of 7 or a sum of 11?

Solution   Let E and F be the events

$$E: \quad \text{Sum is 7} \qquad F: \quad \text{Sum is 11}$$

Since the dice are fair,

$$P(E) = \frac{6}{36} \qquad P(F) = \frac{2}{36}$$

The two events E and F are mutually exclusive. Therefore, by (1), the probability that the sum is 7 or 11 is

$$P(E \cup F) = P(E) + P(F) = \frac{6}{36} + \frac{2}{36} = \frac{8}{36} = \frac{2}{9} \qquad \qquad □$$

The probability of any simple event of a sample space S is nonnegative. Furthermore, since any event E of S is the union of simple events in S, and since $P(S) = 1$, it is easy to see that

$$0 \le P(E) \le 1$$

> To summarize, the probability of an event E of a sample space S has the following three properties:
>
> (I)   *Positiveness:* $0 \le P(E) \le 1$ for every event E of S
>
> (II)   *Certainty:* $P(S) = 1$
>
> (III) *Union:* $P(E \cup F) = P(E) + P(F)$ for any two events E and F of S for which $E \cap F = \varnothing$

ADDITIVE RULE

The following result, called the *additive rule,* provides a technique for finding the probability of the union of two events when they are not disjoint.

Additive Rule For any two events E and F of a sample space S,

$$P(E \cup F) = P(E) + P(F) - P(E \cap F)$$

Proof From Example 6 in Section 6.1 (page 243), we have

$$E \cup F = (E \cap \overline{F}) \cup (E \cap F) \cup (\overline{E} \cap F)$$

Since $E \cap \overline{F}$, $E \cap F$, and $\overline{E} \cap F$ are pairwise disjoint, we can use property (III) to write

$$P(E \cup F) = P(E \cap \overline{F}) + P(E \cap F) + P(\overline{E} \cap F) \qquad (2)$$

We may write the sets E and F in the form

$$E = (E \cap F) \cup (E \cap \overline{F})$$
$$F = (E \cap F) \cup (\overline{E} \cap F)$$

Since $E \cap F$ and $E \cap \overline{F}$ are disjoint and $E \cap F$ and $\overline{E} \cap F$ are disjoint, we have

$$P(E) = P(E \cap F) + P(E \cap \overline{F})$$
$$P(F) = P(E \cap F) + P(\overline{E} \cap F) \qquad (3)$$

Combining the results in (2) and (3), we get

$$P(E \cup F) = P(E) + P(F) - P(E \cap F)$$

□

□ **Example 2** Consider the two events

E: A shopper spends at least \$40 for food

F: A shopper spends at least \$15 for meat

Because of recent studies, we might assign

$$P(E) = .56 \qquad P(F) = .63$$

Suppose the probability that a shopper spends at least \$40 for food and \$15 for meat is .33. What is the probability that a shopper spends at least \$40 for food or at least \$15 for meat?

Solution Since we are looking for the probability of $E \cup F$, we use the additive rule and find that

$$P(E \cup F) = P(E) + P(F) - P(E \cap F)$$
$$= .56 + .63 - .33 = .86$$

□

Often a Venn diagram is helpful in solving probability problems. A Venn diagram depicting the information of Example 2 is given in Figure 6. From this figure, we conclude that the probability of the event E, but not F, is .23 and that the probability of neither E nor F is .14.

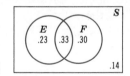

Figure 6

□ **Example 3**   In an experiment with 2 fair dice, consider the events

$$E: \quad \text{The sum of the faces is 8}$$
$$F: \quad \text{Doubles are thrown}$$

What is the probability of obtaining E or F?

Solution

$$E = \{(2, 6), (3, 5), (4, 4), (5, 3), (6, 2)\}$$
$$F = \{(1, 1), (2, 2), (3, 3), (4, 4), (5, 5), (6, 6)\}$$
$$E \cap F = \{(4, 4)\}$$

Also,

$$P(E) = \frac{5}{36} \quad P(F) = \frac{6}{36} \quad P(E \cap F) = \frac{1}{36}$$

Thus, the probability of E or F is

$$P(E \cup F) = \frac{5}{36} + \frac{6}{36} - \frac{1}{36} = \frac{10}{36} = \frac{5}{18}$$

□

COMPLEMENT OF AN EVENT

Let E be an event of a sample space S. The complement of E is the event "Not E" in S. The next result gives a relationship between their probabilities.

Let E be an event of a sample space S. Then

$$P(\overline{E}) = 1 - P(E) \tag{4}$$

where $\overline{E}$ is the complement of E.

Proof   We know that

$$S = E \cup \overline{E} \quad E \cap \overline{E} = \varnothing$$

Since E and $\overline{E}$ are mutually exclusive,

$$P(S) = P(E) + P(\overline{E})$$

Now, we apply property (II), setting $P(S) = 1$. It follows that

$$P(\overline{E}) = 1 - P(E)$$

This result gives us a tool for finding the probability that an event does not occur if we know the probability that it does occur. Thus, the probability $P(\overline{E})$ that E does not occur is obtained by subtracting from 1 the probability $P(E)$ that E does occur. □

□ **Example 4**   A study of people over 40 with an MBA degree shows that it is reasonable to assign a probability of .756 that such a person will have annual earnings in excess of $30,000. The probability that such a person will earn $30,000 or less is then

$$1 - .756 = .244$$ □

□ **Example 5**   In an experiment using 2 fair dice find:

(a)   The probability that the sum of the faces is less than or equal to 7
(b)   The probability that the sum of the faces is greater than 7

Solution   (a)   The number of simple events in the event E described is 21. The number of simple events of the sample space S is 36. Thus, because the dice are fair,

$$P(E) = \frac{21}{36} = \frac{7}{12}$$

(b)   We need to find $P(\overline{E})$. From (4)

$$P(\overline{E}) = 1 - P(E) = 1 - \frac{7}{12} = \frac{5}{12}$$

That is, the probability that the sum of the faces is greater than 7 is $\frac{5}{12}$.   □

ODDS

In many instances, the probability of an event may be expressed as *odds*—either *odds for* an event or *odds against* an event.

If E is an event:

The *odds for E* are $\dfrac{P(E)}{P(\overline{E})}$ or $P(E)$ to $P(\overline{E})$

The *odds against E* are $\dfrac{P(\overline{E})}{P(E)}$ or $P(\overline{E})$ to $P(E)$

□ **Example 6**   The probability of the event

$$E: \quad \text{It will rain}$$

is .3. The odds for rain are

$$\frac{.3}{.7} \quad \text{or} \quad 3 \text{ to } 7$$

The odds against rain are

$$\frac{.7}{.3} \quad \text{or} \quad 7 \text{ to } 3 \qquad \square$$

To obtain the probability of the event E when either the odds for E or the odds against E are known, we use the following formulas:

If the odds for E are a to b, then

$$P(E) = \frac{a}{a+b} \tag{5}$$

If the odds against E are a to b, then

$$P(E) = \frac{b}{a+b}$$

The proof of (5) is given after the following example.

□ **Example 7**   (a)   The odds for a Republican victory in the 1988 Presidential election are 7 to 5. What is the probability that a Republican victory occurs?

(b)   The odds against the Chicago Cubs winning the league pennant are 200 to 1.* What is the probability that the Cubs win the pennant?

Solution   (a)   The event E is "A Republican victory occurs." The odds for E are 7 to 5. Thus,

$$P(E) = \frac{7}{7+5} = \frac{7}{12} \approx .583$$

(b)   The event F is "The Cubs win the pennant." The odds against F are 200 to 1. Thus,

$$P(F) = \frac{1}{200+1} = \frac{1}{201} \approx .00498 \qquad \square$$

Proof of (5)   Suppose the odds for E are a to b. Then, by the definition of odds,

$$\frac{P(E)}{P(\overline{E})} = \frac{a}{b}$$

But, $P(\overline{E}) = 1 - P(E)$. So,

$$\frac{P(E)}{1 - P(E)} = \frac{a}{b}$$

* Las Vegas odds for the 1987 season.

Cross-multiplying, we get

$$bP(E) = a[1 - P(E)] = a - aP(E)$$

or

$$aP(E) + bP(E) = a$$

Solving for $P(E)$ yields

$$P(E) = \frac{a}{a + b}$$

□

Exercise 7.3   *Answers to Odd-Numbered Problems begin on page* 614.

In Problems 1–6 find the probability of the indicated event when $P(A) = .20$ and $P(B) = .30$.

1. $P(\overline{A})$

2. $P(\overline{B})$

3. $P(A \cup B)$ if A, B are mutually exclusive

4. $P(A \cap B)$ if A, B are mutually exclusive

5. $P(A \cup B)$ if $P(A \cap B) = .15$

6. $P(A \cap B)$ if $P(A \cup B) = .40$

7. In tossing 2 fair dice, are the events "Sum is 2" and "Sum is 12" mutually exclusive? What is the probability of obtaining either a 2 or a 12?

8. In tossing 2 fair dice, are the events "Sum is 6" and "Sum is 8" mutually exclusive? What is the probability of obtaining either a 6 or an 8?

9. The Chicago Bulls basketball team has a probability of winning of .65. What is their probability of losing?

10. The Chicago Black Hawks hockey team has a probability of winning of .6 and a probability of losing of .25. What is the probability of a tie?

11. Jill needs to pass both mathematics and English in order to graduate. She estimates her probability of passing mathematics at .4 and English at .6, and she estimates her probability of passing at least one of them at .8. What is her probability of passing both courses?

12. After midterm exams, the student in Problem 11 reassesses her probability of passing mathematics to .7. She feels her probability of passing at least one of these courses is still .8, but she has only a probability of .1 of passing both courses. If her probability of passing English is less than .4, she will drop English. Should she drop English? Why?

13. Let A and B be events of a sample space S and let $P(A) = .5$, $P(B) = .3$, and $P(A \cap B) = .1$. Find the probabilities for each of the following events:

    (a) A or B (b) A but not B

    (c) B but not A (d) Neither A nor B

14. If A and B represent two mutually exclusive events such that $P(A) = .35$ and $P(B) = .50$, find each of the following:

    (a) $P(A \cup B)$ (b) $P(\overline{A \cup B})$ (c) $P(\overline{B})$

    (d) $P(\overline{A})$ (e) $P(A \cap B)$

15. At the Milex, tune-up and brake repair shop, the manager has found that a car will require a tune-up with probability .6, a brake job with probability .1, and both with probability .02.

(a) What is the probability that a car requires either a tune-up or a brake job?

(b) What is the probability that a car requires a tune-up but not a brake job?

(c) What is the probability that a car requires neither type of repair?

16. A factory needs two raw materials, say E and F. The probability of not having an adequate supply of material E is .06, whereas the probability of not having an adequate supply of material F is .04. A study shows that the probability of a shortage of both E and F is .02. What is the probability of the factory being short of either material E or F?

17. In a survey of the number of TV sets in a house, the following probability table was constructed:

Number of TV sets	0	1	2	3	4 or more
Probability	.05	.24	.33	.21	.17

Find the probability of a house having:

(a) 1 or 2 TV sets   (b) 1 or more TV sets

(c) 3 or fewer TV sets   (d) 3 or more TV sets

(e) Less than 2 TV sets   (f) Less than 1 TV set

(g) 1, 2, or 3 TV sets   (h) 2 or more TV sets

18. Through observation it has been determined that the probability for a given number of people waiting in line at a particular checkout register of a supermarket is:

Number waiting in line	0	1	2	3	4 or more
Probability	.10	.15	.20	.24	.31

Find the probability of:

(a) At most 2 people in line

(b) At least 2 people in line

(c) At least 1 person in line

In Problems 19–24 determine the probability of E for the given odds.

19. 3 to 1 for E 20. 4 to 1 against E

21. 7 to 5 against E 22. 2 to 9 for E

23. 1 to 1 for E (even)   24. 50 to 1 for E

In Problems 25–28 determine the odds for and against each event for the given probability.

25. $P(E) = .7$ 26. $P(H) = \frac{1}{3}$ 27. $P(F) = \frac{4}{5}$ 28. $P(G) = .01$

29. If 2 fair dice are thrown, what are the odds of obtaining a 7? An 11? A 7 or 11?

30. If the odds for event A are 1 to 5 and the odds for event B are 1 to 3, what are the odds for the event A or B, assuming the event A and B is impossible?

31. In a track contest, the odds that A will win are 1 to 2 and the odds that B will win are 2 to 3. Find the probability and the odds that A or B wins the race, assuming a tie is impossible.

32. It has been estimated that in 70% of the fatal accidents involving two cars, at least one of the drivers is drunk. If you hear of a two-car fatal accident, what odds should you give a friend for the event that at least one of the drivers is drunk?

33. Generalize the additive rule by showing that the probability of the occurrence of at least one of the three events A, B, C is given by

$$P(A \cup B \cup C) = P(A) + P(B) + P(C)$$
$$- P(A \cap B) - P(A \cap C) - P(B \cap C)$$
$$+ P(A \cap B \cap C)$$

7.4 PROBABILITY FOR THE CASE OF EQUALLY LIKELY EVENTS

□ EXAMPLES USING COUNTING TECHNIQUES

Equally Likely Events — So far, we have seen that in some cases it is reasonable to assign the same probability to each simple event of the sample space. Such events are termed *equally likely events*.

Equally likely events occur when items are selected randomly. For example, in randomly selecting 1 person from a group of 10, the probability of selecting a particular individual is $\frac{1}{10}$. If a card is chosen randomly from a deck of 52 cards, the probability of drawing a particular card is $\frac{1}{52}$. In general, if a sample space S has n equally likely simple events, the probability assigned to each simple event is $\frac{1}{n}$.

Let a sample space S be given by

$$S = \{e_1, e_2, \ldots, e_n\}$$

Suppose each of the simple events $\{e_1\}, \ldots, \{e_n\}$ are equally likely to occur. If E is the union of m of these n simple events, then

$$P(E) = \frac{m}{n} \qquad (1)$$

Proof   Since the simple events $e_1, \ldots, e_n$ are equally likely, we know that

$$P(e_1) = \cdots = P(e_n) \qquad (2)$$

Since

$$S = \{e_1\} \cup \cdots \cup \{e_n\}$$

we have

$$P(S) = P(e_1) + \cdots + P(e_n) = 1 \qquad (3)$$

To satisfy both (2) and (3) we must have

$$P(e_1) = P(e_2) = \cdots = P(e_n) = \frac{1}{n}$$

Now, for the event E of S, in which the m events have been reordered for convenience, we have

$$E = \{e_1\} \cup \cdots \cup \{e_m\}$$

Thus,

$$P(E) = P(e_1) + \cdots + P(e_m) = \underbrace{\frac{1}{n} + \cdots + \frac{1}{n}}_{m \text{ times}} = \frac{m}{n}$$

□

The above result is sometimes stated in the following way:

If an experiment has n equally likely outcomes, among which the event E occurs m times, then the probability of event E, written as $P(E)$, is m/n. That is,

$$P(E) = \frac{\text{Number of possible ways the event } E \text{ can take place}}{\text{Number of outcomes in } S} = \frac{m}{n}$$

If the fact that the event E has occurred is termed a *success,* then

$$P(E) = \frac{\text{Number of successes}}{\text{Number of outcomes in } S} = \frac{m}{n} \tag{4}$$

Event E not occurring is referred to as a *failure.*

Thus, to compute the probability of an event E in which the outcomes are equally likely, count the number $c(E)$ of simple events in E, and divide by the total number $c(S)$ of simple events in the sample space. Then,

$$P(E) = \frac{c(E)}{c(S)}$$

Statement (1) is often used to define *probability.* Using this definition, the properties (I), (II), and (III) previously stated in Section 7.3 are still valid.

Suppose an experiment resulted in no successes at all. By (1), we have

$$P(\text{Success}) = \frac{0}{n} = 0 \tag{5}$$

If the experiment resulted in all events in the sample space being successes, then $m = n$, and

$$P(\text{Success}) = \frac{m}{n} = \frac{n}{n} = 1$$

From this result and (5), we see that

$$0 \leq P(\text{Success}) \leq 1$$

Suppose E is an event with m successes in a sample space S of n elements. Then

$$P(E) = \frac{m}{n}$$

Now $\overline{E}$ contains $n - m$ elements. Hence,

$$P(\overline{E}) = \frac{(n - m)}{n} = \frac{n}{n} - \frac{m}{n} = 1 - \frac{m}{n} = 1 - P(E)$$

□ Example 1   In an experiment with 2 dice, we present the following in terms of events:

(a)   The sum of the faces is 3.
(b)   The sum of the faces is 7.
(c)   The sum of the faces is 7 or 3.
(d)   The sum of the faces is 7 and 3.

Find the probability of these events, assuming the dice are fair.

Solution   (a)   The sum of the faces is 3 if and only if the outcome is the event $A = \{(1, 2),$ $(2, 1)\}$. Since $c(A) = 2$ and $c(S) = 36$, we have

$$P(A) = \frac{2}{36} = \frac{1}{18}$$

(b)   The sum of the faces is 7 if and only if the outcome is a member of the event $B = \{(1, 6), (2, 5), (3, 4), (4, 3), (5, 2), (6, 1)\}$. Since $c(B) = 6$, we have

$$P(B) = \frac{6}{36} = \frac{1}{6}$$

(c)   The sum of the faces is 7 or 3 if and only if the outcome is a member of $A \cup B$, as defined in parts (a) and (b).

$$A \cup B = \{(2, 1), (1, 2), (1, 6), (2, 5), (3, 4), (4, 3), (5, 2), (6, 1)\}$$

Since $c(A \cup B) = 8$,

$$P(A \cup B) = \frac{8}{36} = \frac{2}{9}$$

(d)   The sum of the faces is 3 and 7 if and only if the outcome is a member of $A \cap B$. Since $A \cap B = \varnothing$, the event is impossible. That is, $P(A \cap B) = 0$.   □

□ Example 2   What is the probability that a random 4-digit telephone extension has one or more repeated digits?

Solution   There are $10^4 = 10,000$ distinct 4-digit telephone extensions; this, therefore, is the number of simple events in the sample space.

We wish to find the probability that a random 4-digit telephone extension has one or more repeated digits. Since it is difficult to count the elements in this event, we first compute the probability of the event.

E: No repeated digits in four-digit extension

Notice that the event $\overline{E}$ is one or more repeated digits. By the Multiplication Principle, the number of 4-digit extensions that have *no* repeated digits is

$$10 \cdot 9 \cdot 8 \cdot 7 = 5040$$

Hence

$$P(E) = \frac{5040}{10,000} = .504$$

Therefore, the probability of one or more repeated digits is

$$P(\overline{E}) = 1 - .504 = .496 \qquad \Box$$

□ **Example 3**   An interesting problem in which formula (4) is used is the so-called *birthday problem.* In general, the problem is to find the probability that in a group of *r* people there are at least 2 people who have the same birthday (the same month and day of the year).

Solution   To solve the problem, let us first determine the number of simple events in the sample space. There are 365 possibilities for each person's birthday (we exclude February 29 for simplicity). Since there are *r* people in the group, there are 365^r possibilities for the birthdays. [For 1 person in the group, there are 365 days on which his or her birthday can fall; for 2 people, there are $(365)(365) = 365^2$ pairs of days; and, in general, using the multiplication principle, for *r* people there are 365^r possibilities.]

Next, we assume a person is no more likely to be born on one day than another, so that we assign the probability $1/365^r$ to each simple event.

We wish to find the probability that at least 2 people have the same birthday. It is difficult to count the elements in this set; it is much easier to count the elements of the event

$$E: \quad \text{No 2 people have the same birthday}$$

Notice that the event $\overline{E}$ is that at least 2 people have the same birthday. To find the probability of *E*, we proceed as follows: Choose 1 person at random. There are 365 possibilities for his or her birthday. Choose a second person. There are 364 possibilities for this birthday, if no 2 people are to have the same birthday. Choose a third person. There are 363 possibilities left for this birthday. Finally, we arrive at the *r*th person. There are $365 - (r - 1)$ possibilities left for this birthday. By the multiplication principle, the total number of possibilities is $365 \cdot 364 \cdot 363 \cdots \cdots (365 - r + 1)$.

Hence, the probability of event *E* is

$$P(E) = \frac{365 \cdot 364 \cdot 363 \cdots \cdots (365 - r + 1)}{365^r}$$

The probability of 2 or more people having the same birthday is then $P(\overline{E}) = 1 - P(E)$.   □

The table below gives the probabilities for 2 or more people having the same birthday for some values of *r*. Notice that the probability is better than $\frac{1}{2}$ for any group of 23 or more people.

	Number of People														
	5	10	15	20	21	22	23	24	25	30	40	50	60	70	80	90
Probability that 2 or more have same birthday	.027	.117	.253	.411	.444	.476	.507	.538	.569	.706	.891	.970	.994	.99916	.99991	.99999

EXAMPLES USING COUNTING TECHNIQUES

The next two examples utilize counting techniques developed in the previous chapter.

□ **Example 4**   A box contains 12 light bulbs of which 5 are defective. All bulbs look alike and have equal probability of being chosen. Three light bulbs are picked at random.

(a)   What is the probability that all 3 are defective?

(b)   What is the probability that at least 2 are defective?

Solution   (a)   The number of elements in the sample space S is equal to the number of combinations of 12 light bulbs taken 3 at a time, namely,

$$\binom{12}{3} = \frac{12!}{3!9!} = 220$$

Define E as the event, "3 bulbs are defective." Then E can occur in $\binom{5}{3}$ ways, that is, the number of ways in which 3 defective bulbs can be chosen from 5 defectives ones. The probability $P(E)$ is

$$P(E) = \frac{\binom{5}{3}}{\binom{12}{3}} = \frac{\frac{5!}{3!2!}}{220} = \frac{10}{220} = .04545$$

(b)   What is the probability of the event F: At least 2 are defective? The event F is equivalent to asking for the probability of selecting either 2 or 3 defective bulbs. Thus,

$$P(F) = \frac{\binom{5}{2}\binom{7}{1}}{\binom{12}{3}} + P(E) = \frac{70}{220} + \frac{10}{220} = .36364$$

□

□ **Example 5** Find the probability of obtaining (a) a straight and (b) a flush in a poker hand. (A poker hand is a set of 5 cards chosen at random from a deck of 52 cards.)

Solution (a) A straight consists of 5 consecutive cards, not all of the same suit. The sample space contains $\binom{52}{5}$ simple events, each equally likely to occur. Now, for the straight 4, 5, 6, 7, 8, the 4 can be drawn in 4 different ways, as can the 5, the 6, the 7, and the 8, for a total of 4^5 ways. There are a total of 10 different kinds of straights (A, 2, 3, 4, 5), (2, 3, 4, 5, 6), . . . , (9, 10, J, Q, K), and (10, J, Q, K, A). Thus, all together, there are $10 \cdot 4^5$ straights. However, among these are the straight flushes (36 straights all in one suit) and the four royal flushes (straight flushes consisting of 10, J, Q, K, A), which should not be included in the straight category. Thus, there are

$$10 \cdot 4^5 - 36 - 4 = 10{,}240 - 40 = 10{,}200 \text{ straights}$$

The probability of drawing a straight is therefore

$$\frac{10{,}200}{\binom{52}{5}} = .0039$$

(b) A flush consists of 5 cards in a single suit. The number of ways of obtaining a flush in a given suit is $\binom{13}{5} = 1287$, and there are four different suits, for a total of $4(1287) = 5148$ flushes. However, straight flushes (36) and the four royal flushes should not be included in the flush category. Thus, there are

$$5148 - 36 - 4 = 5108 \text{ flushes}$$

The probability of drawing a flush is therefore

$$\frac{5108}{\binom{52}{5}} = .0020$$

□

Exercise 7.4 *Answers to Odd-Numbered Problems begin on page* 614 .

In Problems 1 – 10 a card is drawn at random from a regular deck of 52 cards .   Calculate the probability of each event.

1. The ace of hearts is drawn.   2. An ace is drawn.

3. A spade is drawn.   4. A red card is drawn.

5. A picture card (J, Q, K) is drawn.

6. A number card (A, 2, 3, 4, 5, 6, 7, 8, 9, 10) is drawn.

7. A card with a number less than 6 is drawn (count A as 1).

8. A card with a value of 10 or higher is drawn.

9. A card that is not an ace is drawn.

10. A card that is either a queen or king of any suit is drawn.

In Problems 11–18 a ball is picked at random from a box containing 3 white, 5 red, 8 blue, and 7 green balls. Find the probability of each event.

11. White ball is picked.

12. Blue ball is picked.

13. Green ball is picked.

14. Red ball is picked.

15. White or red ball is picked.

16. Green or blue ball is picked.

17. Neither red nor green ball is picked.

18. Red or white or blue ball is picked.

19. In a throw of 2 fair dice, what is the probability that the number on one die is double the number on the other?

20. In a throw of 2 fair dice, what is the probability that one die gives a 5 and the other die a number less than 5?

21. From a sales force of 150 people, 1 person will be chosen to attend a special sales meeting. If 52 are single, 72 are college graduates, and, of the 52 who are single, $\frac{3}{4}$ are college graduates, what is the probability that a salesperson selected at random will be neither single nor a college graduate?

22. In an election, two amendments were proposed. The results indicate that of 850 people eligible to cast a ballot, 480 voted in favor of Amendment I, 390 voted for Amendment II, 120 voted for both, and 100 approved of neither. If an eligible voter is selected at random (that is, any one is as likely to be chosen as another), compute the following probabilities:

    (a) The voter is in favor of I, but not II.

    (b) The voter is in favor of II, but not I.

23. What is the probability that, in a group of 3 people, at least 2 were born in the same month (disregard day and year)?

24. What is the probability that, in a group of 6 people, at least 2 were born in the same month (disregard day and year)?

25. A box contains 100 slips of paper numbered from 1 to 100. If 3 slips are drawn in succession with replacement, what is the probability that at least 2 of them have the same number?

26. If, in Problem 25, 10 slips are drawn with replacement, what is the probability that at least 2 of them have the same number?

27. Use a calculator and the idea behind Example 3 to find the approximate probability that 2 or more United States Senators have the same birthday. (There are 100 Senators.)

28. Follow the directions of Problem 27 for the House of Representatives. (There are more than 365 Representatives.)

29. Through a mix-up on the production line, 6 defective refrigerators were shipped out with 44 good ones. If 5 are selected at random, what is the probability that all 5 are defective? What is the probability that at least 2 of them are defective?

30. In a shipment of 50 transformers, 10 are known to be defective. If 30 transformers are picked at random, what is the probability that all 30 are nondefective? Assume that all transformers look alike and have an equal probability of being chosen.

31. Five cards are dealt at random from a regular deck of 52 playing cards. Find the probability that:

    (a) All are hearts.
    (b) Exactly 4 are spades.
    (c) Exactly 2 are clubs.

32. *Bridge.* In a game of bridge, find the probability that a hand of 13 cards consists of 5 spades, 4 hearts, 3 diamonds, and 1 club.

33. *Poker.* Find the probability of obtaining each of the following poker hands:

    (a) Royal flush (10, J, Q, K, A in a single suit)
    (b) Straight flush (5 cards in sequence in a single suit, but not a royal flush)
    (c) Four of a kind (4 cards of the same face value)
    (d) Full house (one pair and one triple of the same face values)
    (e) Straight or better

34. *Elevator Problem.*† An elevator starts with 5 passengers and stops at 8 floors. Find the probability that no 2 passengers leave at the same floor. Assume that all arrangements of discharging the passengers have the same probability.

7.5 CONDITIONAL PROBABILITY

CONDITIONAL PROBABILITY □ PRODUCT RULE □ PROBABILITY TREE

In this section we introduce *conditional probability.* Recall that whenever we compute the probability of an event we do it relative to the entire sample space in question. Thus, when we ask for the probability $P(E)$ of the event E, this probability $P(E)$ represents an appraisal of the likelihood that a chance experiment will produce an outcome in the set E relative to a sample space S.

However, sometimes we would like to compute the probability of an event E of a sample space relative to another event F of the same sample space. That is, if we have *prior* information that the outcome must be in a set F, this information should be used to reappraise the likelihood that the outcome will also be in E. This reappraised

Conditional Probability   probability is denoted by $P(E|F)$, and is read as the *conditional probability of E given F.* It represents the answer to the question, how probable is E, given that F has occurred?

Let's discuss some examples to illustrate conditional probability and then state the definition.

□ **Example 1**   Consider the experiment of flipping 2 fair coins. As we have previously seen, the sample space S is

$$S = \{HH, HT, TH, TT\}$$

† William Feller, *An Introduction to Probability Theory and Its Applications,* 3rd ed., Wiley, New York, 1968.

Figure 7 illustrates the sample space and, for convenience, the probability of each event.

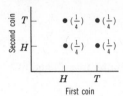

Figure 7

Suppose the experiment is performed by another person and we have no knowledge of the result, but we are informed that at least 1 tail was tossed. This information means the outcome *HH* could not have occurred. But the remaining outcomes *HT*, *TH*, *TT* are still possible. How does this alter the probabilities of the remaining outcomes?

For instance, we might be interested in calculating the probability of the event $\{TT\}$. The three simple events $\{TH\}, \{HT\}, \{TT\}$ were each assigned the probability $\frac{1}{4}$ *before* we knew the information that at least 1 tail occurred, so it is not reasonable to assign them this same probability now. Since only three outcomes are now possible, we assign to each of them the probability $\frac{1}{3}$. See Figure 8.   □

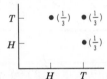

Figure 8

□ **Example 2**   Consider the experiment of drawing a single card from a deck of 52 playing cards. We are interested in the event *E* consisting of the outcome that a black ace is drawn. Since we may assume that there are 52 equally likely possible outcomes and there are 2 black aces in the deck, we have

$$P(E) = \frac{2}{52}$$

However, suppose a card is drawn and we are informed that it is a spade. How should this information be used to *reappraise* the likelihood of the event *E*?

Solution   Clearly, since the event *F* "A spade has been drawn" has occurred, the event "Not spade" is no longer possible. Hence, the sample space has changed from 52 playing cards to 13 spade cards, and the number of black aces that can be drawn has been reduced to 1. Therefore, we must compute the probability of event *E* relative to the new sample space *F*. This probability is denoted by $P(E|F)$ and has the value

$$P(E|F) = \frac{1}{13}$$ □

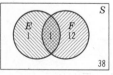

Figure 9

Let's analyze the situation in Example 2 more carefully. The event *E* is "A black ace is drawn." We have computed the probability of event *E* knowing event *F* has occurred. This means we are computing a probability relative to a *new sample space* *F*. That is, *F* is treated as the universal set. We should consider only that part of *E* that is included in *F*; that is, we consider $E \cap F$. See Figure 9.

Thus, the probability of E given F is the ratio of the number of entries in $E \cap F$ to the number of entries in F. Since $c(E \cap F) = 1$ and $c(F) = 13$, then

$$P(E|F) = \frac{c(E \cap F)}{c(F)} = \frac{1}{13}$$

Notice that

$$P(E|F) = \frac{1}{13} = \frac{\frac{1}{52}}{\frac{13}{52}} = \frac{P(E \cap F)}{P(F)}$$

In fact, for sample spaces involving equally likely events, this formula can be proved. Suppose E and F are two events for a particular experiment. Assume that the sample space S for this experiment has n possible equally likely outcomes. Suppose event F has m outcomes, while $E \cap F$ has k outcomes ($k \le m$). Since the events are equally likely we have

$$P(F) = \frac{[\text{Number of outcomes in } F]}{n} = \frac{m}{n}$$

and

$$P(E \cap F) = \frac{[\text{Number of outcomes in } E \cap F]}{n} = \frac{k}{n}$$

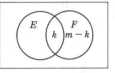

Figure 10

We wish to compute $P(E|F)$, the probability that E occurs given that F has occurred. Since we assume F has occurred, look only at the m outcomes in F. Of these m outcomes, there are k outcomes where E also occurs, since $E \cap F$ has k outcomes. See Figure 10. Thus

$$P(E|F) = \frac{k}{m}$$

Divide numerator and denominator by n to get

$$P(E|F) = \frac{\dfrac{k}{n}}{\dfrac{m}{n}} = \frac{P(E \cap F)}{P(F)}$$

With this result in mind we choose to define conditional probability as follows:

Conditional Probability Let E and F be events of a sample space S and suppose $P(F) > 0$. The *conditional probability of event E assuming the event F,* denoted by $P(E|F)$, is defined as

$$P(E|F) = \frac{P(E \cap F)}{P(F)} \tag{1}$$

Thus, if E is any subset of the sample space S, then $P(E|F)$ provides the reappraisal of the likelihood that an outcome of the experiment will be in the set E if we have prior information that it must be in the set F. Thus we call $P(E|F)$ the conditional probability of E given F.

$P(E|F)$ satisfies the three properties (I), (II), and (III) presented in Section 7.3, page 287. The student is asked to verify this in Problem 44.

□ **Example 3**   Suppose a population of 1000 people includes 70 accountants and 520 females. Let E be the event "A person is an accountant." Let F be the event "A person is female." Then

$$P(E) = \frac{70}{1000} = .07 \qquad P(F) = \frac{520}{1000} = .52$$

Instead of studying the entire population, we may want to investigate the female subpopulation and ask for the probability that a female chosen at random is also an accountant. If there are 40 females who are accountants, the ratio $\frac{40}{520}$ represents the conditional probability of the event E (accountant) assuming the event F (the person chosen is female). In symbols, we would write

$$P(E|F) = \frac{40}{520} = \frac{1}{13}$$

□

Figure 11 illustrates that in computing $P(E|F)$ in Example 3, we form the ratio of the numbers of those entries in E and in F with the numbers that are in F.

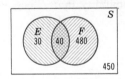

Figure 11

Alternately, using the definition of conditional probability, we see that

$$P(E \cap F) = \frac{40}{1000} \qquad P(F) = \frac{520}{1000}$$

$$P(E|F) = \frac{\frac{40}{1000}}{\frac{520}{1000}} = \frac{40}{520} = \frac{1}{13}$$

In the definition of conditional probability, if we replace F by S, the sample space, we get

$$P(E|S) = \frac{P(E \cap S)}{P(S)}$$

But $E \cap S = E$ and $P(S) = 1$. This reduces to

$$P(E|S) = P(E)$$

as expected.

The symbol $P(E|F)$ is usually read as "the probability of E given F."

□ **Example 4**   Consider a 3 child family* for which the sample space S is

$$S = \{BBB, BBG, BGB, BGG, GBB, GBG, GGB, GGG\}$$

We assume each simple event is equally likely, so that each is assigned a probability of $\frac{1}{8}$. Let E be the event, "The family has exactly 2 boys" and let F be the event "The first child is a boy." What is the probability that the family has 2 boys, given that the first child is a boy?

Solution   We want to find $P(E|F)$. The events E and F are

$$E = \{BBG, BGB, GBB\} \qquad F = \{BBB, BBG, BGB, BGG\}$$

Clearly, $E \cap F = \{BBG, BGB\}$, so we have

$$P(E \cap F) = \frac{1}{4} \qquad P(F) = \frac{1}{2}$$

$$P(E|F) = \frac{P(E \cap F)}{P(F)} = \frac{\frac{1}{4}}{\frac{1}{2}} = \frac{1}{2}$$

□

□ **Example 5**   Motors, Inc., has two plants to manufacture cars. Plant I manufactures 80% of the cars and Plant II manufactures 20%. At Plant I, 85 out of every 100 cars are rated standard quality or better. At Plant II, only 65 out of every 100 cars are rated standard quality or better. We would like to find the answers to the following questions:

(a)   What is the probability that a customer obtains a standard quality car if he buys a car from Motors, Inc.?

(b)   What is the probability that the car came from Plant I if it is known that the car is of standard quality?

Solution   Let the events A, B, C, and D be defined as follows:

> A: The car purchased is of standard quality
> B: The car is of standard quality and came from Plant I
> C: The car is of standard quality and came from Plant II
> D: The car came from Plant I

As a preliminary step, we make the following computations: The percentage of cars that are both manufactured in Plant I and of standard quality is 85% of 80%, which is equal to 68%. Similarly, the percentage of cars manufactured in Plant II and of standard quality is 65% of 20%, which is equal to 13%.

(a)   We have

$$P(B) = .68 \qquad P(C) = .13$$

Since $B \cap C = \varnothing$,

$$P(A) = P(B \cup C) = P(B) + P(C) = .68 + .13 = .81$$

Thus, a total of 81% of the cars are of standard quality.

*Refer to Example 2 in Section 7.2, (page 278).

(b)   We need to compute $P(D|A)$. Since $D \cap A = B$, we have

$$P(D|A) = \frac{P(D \cap A)}{P(A)} = \frac{P(B)}{P(A)} = \frac{.68}{.81} = .8395 \qquad \square$$

PRODUCT RULE

If in formula (1), we multiply both sides of the equation by $P(F)$, we obtain the following useful relationship, which is referred to as the *product rule:*

$$P(E \cap F) = P(F) \cdot P(E|F)$$

The next example illustrates how the product rule is used to compute the probability of an event which is itself a sequence of two events.

□ **Example 6**   Two cards are drawn at random (without replacement) from a standard deck of 52 cards. What is the probability that the first card is a diamond and the second is red?

Solution   We seek the probability of an event which is a sequence of two events, namely,

E: The first card is a diamond

F: The second card is red

Since there are 52 cards in the deck, of which 13 are diamonds, it follows that

$$P(E) = \frac{13}{52} = \frac{1}{4}$$

If E occurred, that means that there are only 51 cards left in the deck, of which 25 are red, so

$$P(F|E) = \frac{25}{51}$$

By the product rule,

$$P(F \cap E) = P(E) \cdot P(F|E) = \frac{1}{4} \cdot \frac{25}{51} = \frac{25}{204} \qquad \square$$

PROBABILITY TREE

Many experiments consists of a sequence of two or more events. A *probability tree* provides a useful device for structurally defining the relationships within such experiments and for computing probabilities associated with possible outcomes.

The probability tree for Example 6 is given in Figure 12.

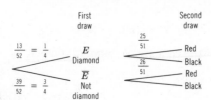

Figure 12

□ **Example 7**   From a box containing 4 white, 3 yellow and 1 green ball, two balls are drawn one at a time without replacing the first before the second is drawn. Use the probability tree to find the probability that one white and one yellow ball are drawn.

Solution   We seek the probability of an event that is a sequence of two events, namely,

$$W: \quad \text{drawing a white ball}$$
$$Y: \quad \text{drawing a yellow ball}$$

Since 4 of the eight balls are white, on the first draw we have

$$P(W) = P(W \text{ on 1st}) = \frac{4}{8} = \frac{1}{2}$$

Since one white ball has been removed leaving 7 balls in the box of which 3 are yellow, on the second draw we have

$$P(Y|W) = P(Y \text{ on 2nd}|W \text{ on 1st}) = \frac{3}{7}$$

The event drawing one white ball and one yellow ball can occur in two ways: drawing a white ball first and then a yellow ball (path 2 of the probability tree in Figure 13), or drawing a yellow ball first and then a white ball (path 4).

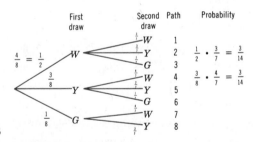

Figure 13

For Path 2, we have

$$P(W) \cdot P(Y|W) = P(W \text{ on 1st}) \cdot P(Y \text{ on 2nd}|W \text{ on 1st}) = \frac{1}{2} \cdot \frac{3}{7} = \frac{3}{14}$$

For Path 4 we have

$$P(Y) \cdot P(W|Y) = P(Y \text{ on 1st}) \cdot P(W \text{ on 2nd}|Y \text{ on 1st}) = \frac{3}{8} \cdot \frac{4}{7} = \frac{3}{14}$$

Since the two events are mutually exclusive, the final probability is the sum of these two probabilities

$$\frac{3}{14} + \frac{3}{14} = \frac{6}{14} = \frac{3}{7}$$

□

Exercise 7.5   *Answers to Odd-Numbered Problems begin on page* 614.

In Problems 1–6 find the indicated probabilities by referring to the following probability tree:

1. $P(C)$ 4. $P(D|A)$
2. $P(D)$ 5. $P(C|D)$
3. $P(C|A)$ 6. $P(D|C)$

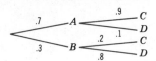

In Problems 7–14 use the table below to obtain probabilities for events in a sample space S. Read the following directly from the table:

	E	F	G	Totals
H	.10	.06	.08	.24
I	.30	.14	.32	.76
Totals	.40	.20	.40	1.00

7. $P(E)$ 8. $P(G)$ 9. $P(H)$ 10. $P(I)$
11. $P(E \cap H)$ 12. $P(E \cap I)$ 13. $P(G \cap H)$ 14. $P(G \cap I)$

In Problems 15–18 use equation (1) and the appropriate values from the above table to compute the conditional probability.

15. $P(E|H)$ 16. $P(E|I)$ 17. $P(G|H)$ 18. $P(G|I)$

19. If E and F are events with $P(E) = .4$, $P(F) = .2$, and $P(E \cap F) = .1$, find the probability of E given F. Find $P(F|E)$.

20. If E and F are events with $P(E) = .6$, $P(F) = .5$, and $P(E \cap F) = .3$, find the probability of E given F. Find $P(F|E)$.

21. If E and F are events with $P(E \cap F) = .1$ and $P(E|F) = .2$, find $P(F)$.

22. If E and F are events with $P(E \cap F) = .2$ and $P(E|F) = .5$, find $P(F)$.

23. A card is drawn at random from a regular deck of 52 cards. What is the probability that:
 (a) The card is a red ace?
 (b) The card is a red ace if it is known an ace was picked?
 (c) The card is a red ace if it is known a red card was picked?

24. A card is drawn at random from a regular deck of 52 cards. What is the probability that:
 (a) The card is a black jack?
 (b) The card is a black jack if it is known a jack was picked?
 (c) The card is a black jack if it is known a black card was picked?

25. A recent poll of residents in a certain community revealed the following information about voting preferences:

	Democrat	Republican	Independent
Male	50	40	30
Female	60	30	25

Events M, F, D, R, and I are defined as follows:

M: Resident is male

F: Resident is female

D: Resident is a Democrat

R: Resident is a Republican

I: Resident is an Independent

Find:

(a) $P(F|I)$ 　　　　(b) $P(R|F)$ 　　　　(c) $P(M|D)$

(d) $P(D|M)$ 　　　　(e) $P(M|R \cup I)$ 　　(f) $P(I|M)$

26. Let E be the event, "A person is an executive" and let F be the event "A person earns over \$25,000 per year." State in words what is expressed by each of the following probabilities:

(a) $P(E|F)$ 　　(b) $P(F|E)$ 　　(c) $P(\overline{E}|\overline{F})$ 　　(d) $P(\overline{E}|F)$

27. For a 3 child family, find the probability of exactly 2 girls, given that the first child is a girl.

28. For a 3 child family, find the probability of exactly 1 girl, given that the first child is a boy.

29. A fair coin is tossed four successive times. Find the probability of obtaining 4 heads. Does the probability change if we are told that the second throw resulted in a head?

30. A pair of fair dice is thrown and we are told that at least one of them shows a 2. If we know this, what is the probability that the total is 7?

31. In a small town, it is known that 25% of the families have no children, 25% have 1 child, 18% have 2 children, 16% have 3 children, 8% have 4 children, and 8% have 5 or more children. Find the probability that a family has more than 2 children if it is known that it has at least 1 child.

32. A sequence of 2 cards is drawn from an ordinary deck of 52 cards (without replacement). What is the probability that the first card is red and the second is black?

In Problems 33–36, use a probability tree to find the indicated probabilities.

33. Two cards are drawn at random (without replacement) from a standard deck of 52 cards. What is the probability that the first card is a heart and the second is red?

34. From a box containing 3 white, 2 green and 1 yellow ball, two balls are drawn at a time without replacing the first before the second is drawn. Find the probability that one white and one yellow ball are drawn.

35. If two cards are drawn from a 52- card deck without replacement, what is the probability that the second card is a queen?

36. *Test Screening.* "Temp Help" uses a preemployment test to screen applicants for the job of a programmer. The test is passed by 70% of the applicants. Among those who pass the test 85% complete training successfully. In an experiment, a random sample of applicants who do not pass the test is also employed. Training is successfully completed by only 40% of this group. If no preemployment test is used, what percentage of applicants would you expect to complete training successfully?

37. In a sample survey, it is found that 35% of the men and 70% of the women are under 160 pounds. Assume that 50% of the sample are men. If a person is selected at random and this person is under 160 pounds, what is the probability that this person is a woman?

38. If the probability that a married man will vote in a given election is .50, the probability that a married woman will vote in the election is .60, and the probability that a woman will vote in the election, given that her husband votes is .90, find:

   (a) The probability that a husband and wife will both vote in the elections.
   (b) The probability that a married man will vote in the election, given that at least one member of the married couple will vote.

39. Of the first-year students in a certain college, it is known that 40% attended private secondary schools and 60% attended public schools. The registrar reports that 30% of all students who attended private schools maintain an A average in their first year at college and that 24% of all first-year students had an A average. At the end of the year, one student is chosen at random from the class. If the student has an A average, what is the conditional probability that the student attended a private school? [*Hint:* Use a probability tree.]

40. In a rural area in the north, registered Republicans outnumber registered Democrats by 3 to 1. In a recent election, all Democrats voted for the Democratic candidate and enough Republicans also voted for the Democratic candidate so that the Democrat won by a ratio of 5 to 4. If a voter is selected at random, what is the probability he or she is Republican? What is the probability a voter is Republican, if it is known that he or she voted for the Democratic candidate?

41. If E and F are two events with $P(E) > 0$ and $P(F) > 0$, show that
$$P(F) \cdot P(E|F) = P(E) \cdot P(F|E)$$

42. Show that $P(E|E) = 1$ when $P(E) \neq 0$.

43. Show that $P(E|F) + P(\overline{E}|F) = 1$.

44. Show that $P(E|F)$ satisfies the three properties (I), (II), and (III) stated in Section 7.3.

7.6 INDEPENDENT EVENTS

One of the most important concepts in probability is that of independence. In this section we define what is meant by two events being *independent*. First, however, we try to develop an intuitive idea of the meaning of independent events.

□ **Example 1**   Consider a group of 36 students. Suppose that E and F are two properties that each student either has or does not have. For example, the events E and F might be

E: Student has blue eyes
F: Student is a male

With regard to these two properties, suppose it is found that the 36 students are distributed as follows:

	Blue Eyes E	Not Blue Eyes $\overline{E}$	Totals
Male, F	6	6	12
Female, $\overline{F}$	12	12	24
Totals	18	18	36

If we choose a student at random, the probabilities corresponding to the events E and F are

$$P(E) = \frac{18}{36} = \frac{1}{2}$$

$$P(F) = \frac{12}{36} = \frac{1}{3}$$

$$P(E \cap F) = \frac{6}{36} = \frac{1}{6}$$

$$P(E|F) = \frac{P(E \cap F)}{P(F)} = \frac{\frac{1}{6}}{\frac{1}{3}} = \frac{1}{2} = P(E)$$ □

In Example 1, the probability of E given F equals the probability of E. This situation can be described by saying that the information that the event F has occurred does not affect the probability of the event E. If this is the case, we say that E *is independent of F.*

Independent Events Let E and F be two events of a sample space S with $P(F) > 0$. The *event E is independent of the event F* if and only if

$$P(E|F) = P(E)$$

In Problem 41, Exercise 7.5, you were asked to show that

$$P(F) \cdot P(E|F) = P(E) \cdot P(F|E) \tag{1}$$

provided $P(E) > 0$ and $P(F) > 0$. If E is independent of F, then we know that $P(E|F) = P(E)$. Substituting this into (1), we find that

$$P(F|E) = P(F)$$

That is, the event F is independent of E.

Thus, if two events E and F have positive probabilities and if the event E is independent of F, then F is also independent of E. In this case, E and F are called *independent events.*

We also have the following result concerning independent events:

Test for Independence Two events E and F of a sample space S are independent events if and only if

$$P(E \cap F) = P(E) \cdot P(F) \qquad (2)$$

That is, the probability of E and F is equal to the product of the probability of E and the probability of F.

Proof   If E and F are independent events, then

$$P(E|F) = \frac{P(E \cap F)}{P(F)} \qquad \text{and} \qquad P(E|F) = P(E)$$

Thus,

$$\frac{P(E \cap F)}{P(F)} = P(E) \qquad \text{or} \qquad P(E \cap F) = P(E) \cdot P(F)$$

Conversely, if $P(E \cap F) = P(E) \cdot P(F)$, then

$$P(E|F) = \frac{P(E \cap F)}{P(F)} = \frac{P(E) \cdot P(F)}{P(F)} = P(E)$$

That is, E and F are independent events.

This result is used to verify whether two events are independent.   □

□ **Example 2**   Suppose a red die and a green die are thrown. Let event E be "Throw a 5 with the red die," and let event F be "Throw a 6 with the green die."

Solution   In this experiment, the events E and F are

$$E = \{(5, 1), (5, 2), (5, 3), (5, 4), (5, 5), (5, 6)\}$$
$$F = \{(1,6), (2, 6), (3, 6), (4, 6), (5, 6), (6, 6)\}$$

and

$$P(E) = \frac{1}{6} \qquad P(F) = \frac{1}{6}$$

Also, the event E and F is

$$E \cap F = \{(5, 6)\}$$

so that

$$P(E \cap F) = \frac{1}{36}$$

Since $P(E) \cdot P(F) = \frac{1}{6} \cdot \frac{1}{6} = \frac{1}{36} = P(E \cap F)$, E and F are independent events.   □

□ **Example 3**   For the data in the T-maze problem (Problem 49, Exercise 7.2), show that the events E and G are not independent, but that the events G and H are independent, where E, G, and H are defined as before:

> E: Run to the right two consecutive times
> G: Run to the left on the first trial
> H: Run to the right on the second trial

Solution   The events E and G are

$$E = \{RRL, LRR, RRR\}$$
$$G = \{LLL, LLR, LRL, LRR\}$$

The sample space S has eight elements so that

$$P(E) = \frac{3}{8} \qquad P(G) = \frac{1}{2}$$

Also, the event E and G is

$$E \cap G = \{LRR\}$$

so that

$$P(E \cap G) = \frac{1}{8}$$

Since $P(E \cap G) \neq P(E) \cdot P(G)$, the events E and G are not independent. Thus, running to the right two consecutive times and running to the left on the first trial are dependent.

Next, the event H is

$$H = \{RRL, RRR, LRL, LRR\}$$

so that

$$P(H) = \frac{1}{2}$$

The event G and H and its probability are

$$G \cap H = \{LRL, LRR\} \qquad P(G \cap H) = \frac{1}{4}$$

Since $P(G \cap H) = P(G) \cdot P(H)$, the events G and H are independent. Thus, running to the left on the first trial and running to the right on the second trial are independent events.   □

Example 3 illustrates that the question of whether two events are independent can be answered simply by determining whether formula (2) is satisfied. Although we may often suspect two events E and F of being independent, our intuition must be checked by computing $P(E)$, $P(F)$, and $P(E \cap F)$ and determining whether $P(E \cap F) = P(E) \cdot P(F)$.

Steps to Check for
Independence

The following steps summarize the procedure to use to check for events E and F being independent:

Step 1: Compute the probability of event E.

Step 2: Compute the probability of event F.

Step 3: Compute the probability of the event E and F, $P(E \cap F)$.

Step 4: If $P(E \cap F) = P(E) \cdot P(F)$, the events are independent.
If $P(E \cap F) \neq P(E) \cdot P(F)$, the events are not independent.

For some probabilistic models, an assumption of independence is made. In such instances when two events are independent, formula (2) may be used to compute the probability that both events occur. The following example illustrates such a situation.

□ **Example 4**   In a group of seeds, $\frac{1}{4}$ of which should produce white plants, the best germination that can be obtained is 75%. If one seed is planted, what is the probability that it will grow into a white plant?

Solution   Let G and W be the events

G: The plant will grow

W: The seed will produce a white plant

Assume that W does not depend on G and vice versa, so that W and G are independent events.

Then, the probability that the plant grows and is white, namely, $P(W \cap G)$ is

$$P(W \cap G) = P(W) \cdot P(G) = \frac{1}{4} \cdot \frac{3}{4} = \frac{3}{16}$$

A white plant will grow 3 out of 16 times.   □

There is a danger that mutually exclusive events and independent events may be confused. A source of this confusion is the common expression. "Events are independent if they have nothing to do with each other" This expression provides a description of independence when applied to everyday events; but when it is applied to sets, it suggests nonoverlapping. Nonoverlapping sets are mutually exclusive but in general are not independent. See Problem 17 in Exercise 7.6.

Exercise 7.6   *Answers to Odd-Numbered Problems begin on page* 615 .

1. If E and F are independent events and if $P(E) = .3$ and $P(F) = .5$, find $P(E \cap F)$.

2. If E and F are independent events and if $P(E) = .6$ and $P(E \cap F) = .3$, find $P(F)$.

3. If E and F are independent events, find $P(F)$ if $P(E) = .2$ and $P(E \cup F) = .3$.

4. If E and F are independent events, find $P(E)$ if $P(F) = .3$ and $P(E \cup F) = .6$.

5. If $P(E) = .3$, $P(F) = .2$, and $P(E \cup F) = .4$, what is $P(E|F)$? Are E and F independent?

6. If $P(E) = .4$, $P(F) = .6$, and $P(E \cup F) = .7$, what is $P(E|F)$? Are E and F independent?

7. A fair die is rolled. Let E be the event "1, 2, or 3 is rolled" and let F be the event "3, 4, or 5 is rolled." Are E and F independent?

8. A loaded die is rolled. The probabilities for this die are $P(1) = P(2) = P(4) = P(5) = \frac{1}{8}$ and $P(3) = P(6) = \frac{1}{4}$. Are the events defined in Problem 7 independent in this case?

9. For a 3 child family, let E be the event "The family has at most 1 boy" and let F be the event "The family has children of each sex." Are E and F independent events?

10. For a 2 child family, are the events E and F as defined in Problem 9 independent?

11. A first card is drawn at random from a regular deck of 52 cards and is then put back in the deck. A second card is drawn. What is the probability that:

   (a) The first card is a club?
   (b) The second card is a heart, given that the first is a club?
   (c) The first card is a club and the second is a heart?

12. For the situation described in Problem 11, what is the probability that:

   (a) The first card is an ace?
   (b) The second card is a king, given that the first card is an ace?
   (c) The first card is an ace and the second is a king?

13. In the T-maze problem (Problem 49, Exercise 7.2), are the two events E and F independent?

14. Define the events E and F to be

   E: A head turns up on the first throw of a fair coin
   F: A tail turns up on the second throw of a fair coin

   Show that E and F are independent events.

15. A die is loaded so that

$$P(1) = P(2) = P(3) = \frac{1}{4} \qquad P(4) = P(5) = P(6) = \frac{1}{12}$$

   If $A = \{1, 2\}$, $B = \{2, 3\}$, $C = \{1, 3\}$, show that any pair of these events is independent.

16. In a survey of 100 people, categorized as drinkers or nondrinkers, with or without a liver ailment, the following data were obtained:

	F Liver Ailment	$\overline{F}$ No Liver Ailment
Drinkers, E	52	18
Nondrinkers, $\overline{E}$	8	22

   (a) Are the events E and F independent?
   (b) Are the events $\overline{E}$ and $\overline{F}$ independent?
   (c) Are the events E and $\overline{F}$ independent?

17. Give an example of two events that are:

   (a) Independent, but not mutually exclusive (disjoint)

      (b)   Not independent, but mutually exclusive (disjoint)

      (c)   Not independent and not mutually exclusive (disjoint)

18. Show that whenever two events are both independent and mutually exclusive, then at least one of them is impossible.

19. Let E be any event. If F is an impossible event, show that E and F are independent.

20. Show that if E and F are independent events, so are $\overline{E}$ and F. [*Hint:* Use De Morgan's law.]

21. Show that if E and F are independent events and if $P(E) \neq 0$, $P(F) \neq 0$, then E and F are not mutually exclusive.

22. Three events E, F, and G are *independent* if any two of them are independent and

$$P(E \cap F \cap G) = P(E) \cdot P(F) \cdot P(G)$$

Use this definition to determine whether the events E, F, and G defined below for the experiment of tossing 2 fair dice are independent.

      E: The first die shows a 6

      F: The second die shows a 3

      G: The sum on the 2 dice is 7

23. *Chevalier de Mere's Problem.* Solve Problem 7 in Exercise 7.1 (page 275). [*Hint:* Part (a) $P(\text{No 1's are obtained}) = \frac{5^4}{6^4} = \frac{625}{1296} = .4823$. Part (b) The probability of not obtaining a double 1 on any given toss is $\frac{35}{36}$. Thus, $P(\text{No double 1's are obtained}) = (\frac{35}{36})^{24} = .509$.]

24. A woman has 10 keys but only 1 fits her door. She tries them successively (without replacement). Find the probability that a key fits in exactly 5 tries.†

7.7 BAYES' FORMULA

PARTITIONS AND PROBABILITIES □ BAYES' FORMULA □ *A PRIORI* AND *A POSTERIORI* PROBABILITIES

In this section we consider experiments with sample spaces that can be divided or partitioned into two (or more) mutually exclusive events. This study involves a further application of conditional probabilities and leads us to the famous formula of Thomas Bayes, first published in 1763.

---

† William Feller, *An Introduction to Probability Theory and Its Applications,* 3rd ed., Wiley, New York, 1968.

    THOMAS BAYES (1702–1761), born in London, was the son of a Presbyterian minister. Bayes, who was also ordained and began his ministry by assisting his father, was elected a Fellow of the Royal Society in 1742. He published several theological papers, but is most famous for his paper on probability, which was published after his death by a friend who found it among his effects. This work is noteworthy because it is the first discussion of inductive inference in precise quantitive form.

We begin by considering the following example.

□ **Example 1**   Given two urns, I and II, suppose Urn I contains 4 black and 7 white balls. Urn II contains 3 black, 1 white, and 4 yellow balls. We select an urn at random and then draw a ball. What is the probability that we obtain a black ball?

Solution   Let U_I and U_{II} stand for the events "Urn I is chosen" and "Urn II is chosen," respectively. Similarly, let B, W, Y stand for the event that "A black," "A white," or "A yellow ball is chosen," respectively.

A solution to Example 1 can be depicted using a probability tree, as shown in Figure 14.

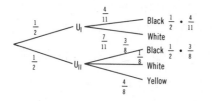
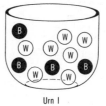
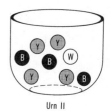

Urn I   Urn II

Figure 14

$$P(U_I) = P(U_{II}) = \frac{1}{2}$$

$$P(B|U_I) = \frac{4}{11} \qquad P(B|U_{II}) = \frac{3}{8}$$

The event B can be written as

$$B = (B \cap U_I) \cup (B \cap U_{II})$$

Since $B \cap U_I$ and $B \cap U_{II}$ are disjoint, we add their probabilities. Then

$$P(B) = P(B \cap U_I) + P(B \cap U_{II})$$

Using the definition of conditional probability, we have

$$P(B|U_I) = \frac{P(B \cap U_I)}{P(U_I)} \qquad\qquad P(B|U_{II}) = \frac{P(B \cap U_{II})}{P(U_{II})}$$

$$P(B \cap U_I) = P(U_I) \cdot P(B|U_I) \qquad P(B \cap U_{II}) = P(U_{II}) \cdot P(B|U_{II})$$

Thus,

$$P(B) = P(U_I) \cdot P(B|U_I) + P(U_{II}) \cdot P(B|U_{II})$$

$$= \frac{1}{2} \cdot \frac{4}{11} + \frac{1}{2} \cdot \frac{3}{8} = \frac{65}{176} = .369$$

□

PARTITIONS AND PROBABILITIES

Suppose A_1 and A_2 are two nonempty, mutually exclusive events of a sample space S and the union of A_1 and A_2 is S; that is,

$$A_1 \neq \emptyset \qquad A_2 \neq \emptyset \qquad A_1 \cap A_2 = \emptyset \qquad S = A_1 \cup A_2$$

Partition   In this case, we say that A_1 and A_2 form a *partition of S*. See Figure 15.

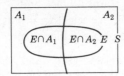

Figure 15

Now, if we let E be any event in S, we may write the set E in the form

$$E = (E \cap A_1) \cup (E \cap A_2)$$

The sets $E \cap A_1$ and $E \cap A_2$ are disjoint, since

$$(E \cap A_1) \cap (E \cap A_2) = (E \cap E) \cap (A_1 \cap A_2) = E \cap \emptyset = \emptyset$$

Using the definition for conditional probability, the probability of E is therefore

$$
\begin{aligned}
P(E) &= P(E \cap A_1) + P(E \cap A_2) \\
&= P(A_1) \cdot P(E|A_1) + P(A_2) \cdot P(E|A_2)
\end{aligned}
\tag{1}
$$

The above formula is used to find the probability of an event E of a sample space when the sample space is partitioned into two sets A_1 and A_2.

□ **Example 2**   Of the applicants to a medical school, it is felt that 80% are eligible to enter and 20% are not. To aid in the selection process, an admissions test is administered which is designed so that an eligible candidate will pass 90% of the time, while an ineligible candidate will pass only 30% of the time. What is the probability that an applicant for admission will pass the admissions test?

Solution   The sample space S consists of the applicants for admission, and S can be partitioned into the following two events:

$$A_1: \text{ Eligible applicant} \qquad A_2: \text{ Ineligible applicant}$$

These two events are disjoint, and their union is S. See Figure 16.

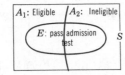

Figure 16

The event E is E: Applicant passes admissions test

Now,

$$P(A_1) = .8 \qquad P(A_2) = .2$$
$$P(E|A_1) = .9 \qquad P(E|A_2) = .3$$

Using formula (1), we have

$$P(E) = P(A_1) \cdot P(E|A_1) + P(A_2) \cdot P(E|A_2) = (.8)(.9) + (.2)(.3) = .78$$

Thus, the probability that an applicant will pass the admissions test is .78.   □

If we partition a sample space S into three sets A_1, A_2, and A_3 so that

$$S = A_1 \cup A_2 \cup A_3$$
$$A_1 \cap A_2 = \emptyset \quad A_2 \cap A_3 = \emptyset \quad A_1 \cap A_3 = \emptyset$$
$$A_1 \neq \emptyset \quad A_2 \neq \emptyset \quad A_3 \neq \emptyset$$

we may write any set E in S in the form

$$E = (E \cap A_1) \cup (E \cap A_2) \cup (E \cap A_3)$$

Since $E \cap A_1$, $E \cap A_2$, and $E \cap A_3$ are disjoint, the probability of event E is

$$P(E) = P(E \cap A_1) + P(E \cap A_2) + P(E \cap A_3)$$
$$= P(A_1) \cdot P(E|A_1) + P(A_2) \cdot P(E|A_2) + P(A_3) \cdot P(E|A_3) \tag{2}$$

See Figure 17.

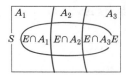

Figure 17

Formula (2) is used to find the probability of an event E of a sample space when the sample space is partitioned into three sets A_1, A_2, and A_3.

□ **Example 3**   Three machines, I, II, and III, manufacture .4, .5, and .1 of the total production in a plant, respectively. The percentage of defective items produced by I, II, and III is 2%, 4%, and 1%, respectively. For an item chosen at random, what is the probability that it is defective?

Solution   In this example, the sample space S is partitioned into three events A_1, A_2, and A_3 defined as follows:

A_1: Item produced by Machine I
A_2: Item produced by Machine II
A_3: Item produced by Machine III

Clearly, the events A_1, A_2, and A_3 are mutually exclusive, and their union is S. Define the event E in S to be

E: Item is defective

Now,

$$P(A_1) = .4 \qquad P(A_2) = .5 \qquad P(A_3) = .1$$
$$P(E|A_1) = .02 \qquad P(E|A_2) = .04 \qquad P(E|A_3) = .01$$

Thus, using formula (2), we see that

$$P(E) = (.4)(.02) + (.5)(.04) + (.1)(.01)$$
$$= .008 + .020 + .001 = .029 \qquad \square$$

Figure 18 gives a probability tree solution to Example 3.

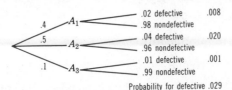

Figure 18   Probability for defective .029

To generalize formulas (1) and (2) to a sample space S partitioned into n subsets, we first introduce the following definition:

Partition A sample space S is *partitioned* into n subsets $A_1, A_2, \ldots, A_n$, provided:

(a) **The intersection of any two of the subsets is empty.**
(b) **Each subset is nonempty.**
(c) $A_1 \cup A_2 \cup \cdots \cup A_n = S$

Let S be a sample space and let $A_1, A_2, A_3, \ldots, A_n$ be n events that form a partition of the set S. If E is any event in S, then

$$E = (E \cap A_1) \cup (E \cap A_2) \cup \cdots \cup (E \cap A_n)$$

Clearly, $E \cap A_1, E \cap A_2, \ldots, E \cap A_n$ are mutually exclusive events. Hence,

$$P(E) = P(E \cap A_1) + P(E \cap A_2) + \cdots + P(E \cap A_n) \qquad (3)$$

In (3), replace $P(E \cap A_1), P(E \cap A_2), \ldots, P(E \cap A_n)$ using the definition of conditional probability. Then we obtain the formula

$$P(E) = P(A_1) \cdot P(E|A_1) + P(A_2) \cdot P(E|A_2) + \cdots + P(A_n) \cdot P(E|A_n) \qquad (4)$$

☐ **Example 4**   In Example 2, suppose an applicant passes the admissions test. What is the probability that he or she was among those eligible; that is, what is the probability $P(A_1|E)$?

Solution   By the definition of conditional probability,

$$P(A_1|E) = \frac{P(A_1 \cap E)}{P(E)} = \frac{P(A_1) \cdot P(E|A_1)}{P(E)}$$

But $P(E)$ is given by (4) when $n = 2$, or, by (1). Thus,

$$P(A_1|E) = \frac{P(A_1) \cdot P(E|A_1)}{P(A_1) \cdot P(E|A_1) + P(A_2) \cdot P(E|A_2)} \qquad (5)$$

Using the information supplied in Example 2, we find

$$P(A_1|E) = \frac{(.8)(.9)}{.78} = \frac{.72}{.78} = .923$$

The admissions test is a reasonably effective device. Less than 8% of the students passing the test are ineligible. □

BAYES' FORMULA

Equation (5) is a special case of *Bayes' formula* when the sample space is partitioned into two sets A_1 and A_2. The general formula is given next.

Bayes' Formula Let S be a sample space partitioned into n events, $A_1, \ldots, A_n$. Let E be any event of S for which $P(E) > 0$. The probability of the event A_j ($j = 1, 2, \ldots, n$), given the event E, is

$$P(A_j|E) = \frac{P(A_j) \cdot P(E|A_j)}{P(E)}$$

$$= \frac{P(A_j) \cdot P(E|A_j)}{P(A_1) \cdot P(E|A_1) + P(A_2) \cdot P(E|A_2) + \cdots + P(A_n) \cdot P(E|A_n)} \tag{6}$$

The proof is left as an exercise (see Problem 26, Exercise 7.7).

The following example illustrates a use for Bayes' formula when the sample space S is partitioned into three events.

□ **Example 5** Motors, Inc., has three plants, I, II, and III. Plant I produces 35% of the car output, Plant II produces 20%, and Plant III produces the remaining 45%. One percent of the output of Plant I is defective, as is 1.8% of the output of Plant II, and 2% of the output of Plant III. The annual total output of Motors, Inc., is 1,000,000 cars. A car is chosen at random from the annual output and it is found to be defective. What is the probability that it came from Plant I? Plant II? Plant III?

Solution To answer these questions, let's define the following events:

$$E: \quad \text{Car is defective}$$
$$A_1: \quad \text{Car produced by Plant I}$$
$$A_2: \quad \text{Car produced by Plant II}$$
$$A_3: \quad \text{Car produced by Plant III}$$

Also, $P(A_1|E)$ indicates the probability that a car is produced by Plant I, given that it was defective; $P(A_2|E)$ and $P(A_3|E)$ are similarly defined. To find these probabilities, we proceed as follows.

From the data given in the problem, we can determine the following:

$$\begin{array}{ll} P(A_1) = .35 & P(E|A_1) = .010 \\ P(A_2) = .20 & P(E|A_2) = .018 \\ P(A_3) = .45 & P(E|A_3) = .020 \end{array} \tag{7}$$

Now,

$A_1 \cap E$ is the event "Produced by Plant I and is defective"

$A_2 \cap E$ is the event "Produced by Plant II and is defective"

$A_3 \cap E$ is the event "Produced by Plant III and is defective"

From the definition of conditional probability, we find

$$P(A_1 \cap E) = P(A_1) \cdot P(E|A_1) = (.35)(.010) = .0035$$
$$P(A_2 \cap E) = P(A_2) \cdot P(E|A_2) = (.20)(.018) = .0036$$
$$P(A_3 \cap E) = P(A_3) \cdot P(E|A_3) = (.45)(.020) = .0090$$

Since $E = (A_1 \cap E) \cup (A_2 \cap E) \cup (A_3 \cap E)$, we have

$$P(E) = P(A_1 \cap E) + P(A_2 \cap E) + P(A_3 \cap E)$$
$$= .0035 + .0036 + .0090$$
$$= .0161$$

Thus, the probability that a defective car is chosen is .0161.

Given that the car chosen is defective, the probability that it came from Plant I is $P(A_1|E)$, from Plant II is $P(A_2|E)$, and from Plant III is $P(A_3|E)$. To compute these probabilities, we use Bayes' formula:

$$P(A_1|E) = \frac{P(A_1) \cdot P(E|A_1)}{P(A_1) \cdot P(E|A_1) + P(A_2) \cdot P(E|A_2) + P(A_3) \cdot P(E|A_3)}$$

$$= \frac{P(A_1) \cdot P(E|A_1)}{P(E)} = \frac{(.35)(.01)}{.0161} = .217$$

$$P(A_2|E) = \frac{P(A_2) \cdot P(E|A_2)}{P(E)} = \frac{.0036}{.0161} = .224$$

$$P(A_3|E) = \frac{P(A_3) \cdot P(E|A_3)}{P(E)} = \frac{.0090}{.0161} = .559$$

(8)

A PRIORI, A POSTERIORI PROBABILITIES

In Bayes' formula, the probabilities $P(A_j)$ are referred to as *a priori* probabilities, while the $P(A_j|E)$ are called *a posteriori* probabilities. We use Example 5 to explain the reason for this terminology. Knowing nothing else about a car, the probability that it was produced by Plant 1 is given by $P(A_1)$. Thus, $P(A_1)$ can be regarded as a "before the fact" or *a priori* probability. With the additional information that the car is defective, we reassess the likelihood of whether it came from Plant 1 and compute $P(A_1|E)$. Thus, $P(A_1|E)$ can be viewed as an "after the fact" or *a posteriori* probability.

Note that $P(A_1) = .35$, while $P(A_1|E) = .217$. So, the knowledge that a car is defective decreases the chances that it came from Plant 1.

□ **Example 6**   The residents of a community are examined for cancer. The examination results are classified as positive (+), if a malignancy is suspected, and as negative (−), if there are no indications of a malignancy. If a person has cancer, the probability of a suspected malignancy is .98; and the probability of reporting cancer where none existed is .15. If 5% of the community has cancer, what is the probability of a person not having cancer if the examination is positive?

Solution   Let us define the following events:

$$A_1: \quad \text{Person has cancer}$$
$$A_2: \quad \text{Person does not have cancer}$$
$$E: \quad \text{Examination is positive}$$

We want to know the probability of a person not having cancer if it is known that the examination is positive; that is, we wish to find $P(A_2|E)$. Now,

$$P(A_1) = .05 \qquad P(A_2) = .95$$
$$P(E|A_1) = .98 \qquad P(E|A_2) = .15$$

Using Bayes' formula, we get

$$P(A_2|E) = \frac{P(A_2) \cdot P(E|A_2)}{P(A_1) \cdot P(E|A_1) + P(A_2) \cdot P(E|A_2)}$$

$$= \frac{(.95)(.15)}{(.05)(.98) + (.95)(.15)} = .744$$

Thus, even if the examination is positive, the person examined is more likely not to have cancer than to have cancer. The reason the test is designed this way is that it is better for a healthy person to be examined more thoroughly, than for someone with cancer to go undetected. Simply stated, the test is useful because of the high probability that a person with cancer will not go undetected.   □

□ **Example 7**   The manager of a car repair shop knows from past experience that when a call is received from a person whose car will not start, the probabilities for various troubles (assuming no two can occur simultaneously) are as follows:

Event	Trouble	Probability
A_1:	Flooded	.3
A_2:	Battery cable loose	.2
A_3:	Points bad	.1
A_4:	Out of gas	.3
A_5:	Something else	.1

The manager also knows that if the person will hold the gas pedal down and try to start the car, the probability that it will start (E) is

$$P(E|A_1) = .9 \qquad P(E|A_2) = 0 \qquad P(E|A_3) = .2$$
$$P(E|A_4) = 0 \qquad P(E|A_5) = .2$$

(a)   If a person has called and is instructed to "hold the pedal down . . . ," what is the probability that the car will start?

(b) If the car does start after holding the pedal down, what is the probability that the car was flooded?

Solution (a) We need to compute $P(E)$. Using formula (4) for $n = 5$ (the sample space is partitioned into five disjoint sets), we have

$$P(E) = P(A_1) \cdot P(E|A_1) + P(A_2) \cdot P(E|A_2) + P(A_3) \cdot P(E|A_3)$$
$$+ P(A_4) \cdot P(E|A_4) + P(A_5) \cdot P(E|A_5)$$
$$= (.3)(.9) + (.2)(0) + (.1)(.2) + (.3)(0) + (.1)(.2)$$
$$= .27 + .02 + .02 = .31$$

(b) We use Bayes' formula to compute the *a posteriori* probability $P(A_1|E)$:

$$P(A_1|E) = \frac{P(A_1) \cdot P(E|A_1)}{P(E)} = \frac{(.3)(.9)}{.31} = \frac{.27}{.31} = .87$$

Thus, the probability that the car is flooded, after it is known that holding down the pedal started the car, is .87. □

When the probability of each event of the partition is equally likely,

$$P(A_1) = P(A_2) = \cdots = P(A_n)$$

we obtain a special case of Bayes' formula:

$$P(A_j|E) = \frac{P(E|A_j)}{P(E|A_1) + P(E|A_2) + \cdots + P(E|A_n)} \tag{9}$$

Let's return to Example 5 and assume that $P(A_1) = P(A_2) = P(A_3)$, so that the three plants' share of the total production is the same. In this case, it is easier to use (9) to obtain the probability that a car is produced at Plant I, given that it was defective:

$$P(A_1|E) = \frac{P(E|A_1)}{P(E|A_1) + P(E|A_2) + P(E|A_3)}$$
$$= \frac{.010}{.010 + .018 + .020} = \frac{.010}{.048} = \frac{5}{24} = .208$$

Exercise 7.7 *Answers to Odd-Numbered Problems begin on page 615.*

In Problems 1–6 find the indicated probabilities by referring to the following probability tree and using Bayes' formula:

1. $P(A|E)$		2. $P(B|\overline{E})$
3. $P(C|E)$		4. $P(A|\overline{E})$
5. $P(B|E)$		6. $P(C|\overline{E})$

7. Events A_1 and A_2 form a partition of a sample space S with $P(A_1) = .3$ and $P(A_2) = .7$. If E is an event in S with $P(E|A_1) = .01$ and $P(E|A_2) = .02$, compute $P(E)$.

8. Events A_1 and A_2 form a partition of a sample space S with $P(A_1) = .4$ and $P(A_2) = .6$. If E is an event in S with $P(E|A_1) = .03$ and $P(E|A_2) = .01$, compute $P(E)$.

9. Events A_1, A_2, and A_3 form a partition of a sample space S with $P(A_1) = .5$, $P(A_2) = .3$, and $P(A_3) = .2$. If E is an event in S with $P(E|A_1) = .01$, $P(E|A_2) = .03$, and $P(E|A_3) = .02$, compute $P(E)$.

10. Events A_1, A_2, and A_3 form a partition of a sample space S with $P(A_1) = .3$, $P(A_2) = .3$, and $P(A_3) = .4$. If E is an event in S with $P(E|A_1) = .01$, $P(E|A_2) = .02$, and $P(E|A_3) = .02$, compute $P(E)$.

11. Use the information in Problem 7 to find $P(A_1|E)$ and $P(A_2|E)$.

12. Use the information in Problem 8 to find $P(A_1|E)$ and $P(A_2|E)$.

13. Use the information in Problem 9 to find $P(A_1|E)$, $P(A_2|E)$, and $P(A_3|E)$.

14. Use the information in Problem 10 to find $P(A_1|E)$, $P(A_2|E)$, and $P(A_3|E)$.

15. In Example 3 (page 319), suppose it is known that a defective item was produced. Find the probability that it came from Machine I; from Machine II; from Machine III.

16. In Example 5 (page 321), suppose $P(A_1) = P(A_2) = P(A_3) = \frac{1}{3}$. Find $P(A_2|E)$ and $P(A_3|E)$.

17. In Example 7 (page 323), compute the *a posteriori* probabilities $P(A_2|E)$, $P(A_3|E)$, $P(A_4|E)$, and $P(A_5|E)$.

18. In Example 6 (page 322), compute $P(A_1|E)$.

19. Three urns contain colored balls as follows:

Urn	Red, R	White, W	Blue, B
I	5	6	5
II	3	4	9
III	7	5	4

One urn is chosen at random and a ball is withdrawn. The ball is red. What is the probability that it came from Urn I? From Urn II? From Urn III? [*Hint:* Define the events E: Ball selected is red, U_I: Urn I selected, U_{II}: Urn II selected, and U_{III}: Urn III selected. Determine $P(U_I|E)$, $P(U_{II}|E)$, and $P(U_{III}|E)$ by using Bayes' formula.]

20. Suppose that if a person with tuberculosis is given a TB screening, the probability that his or her condition will be detected is .90. If a person without tuberculosis is given a TB screening, the probability that he or she will be diagnosed incorrectly as having tuberculosis is .3. Suppose, further, that 11% of the adult residents of a certain city have tuberculosis. If one of these adults is diagnosed as having tuberculosis based on the screening, what is the probability that he or she actually has tuberculosis? Interpret your result.

21. Cars are being produced by two factories, I and II, but Factory I produces twice as many cars as Factory II in a given time. Factory I is known to produce 2% defectives and Factory II produces 1% defectives. A car is examined and found to be defective. What are the *a priori* and *a posteriori* probabilities that the car was produced by Factory I?

22. An absent-minded nurse is to give Mr. Brown a pill each day. The probability that the nurse forgets to administer the pill is $\frac{2}{3}$. If he receives the pill, the probability that Brown will die is $\frac{1}{3}$. If he does not get his pill, the probability that he will die is $\frac{3}{4}$. Mr. Brown died. What is the probability that the nurse forgot to give Brown the pill?

23. An oil well is to be drilled in a certain location. The soil there is either rock (probability .53), clay (probability .21), or sand. If it is rock, a geological test gives a positive result with 35% accuracy; if it is clay, this test gives a positive result with 48% accuracy; and if it is sand, the test gives a positive result with 75% accuracy. Given that the test is positive, what is the probability that the soil is rock? What is the probability that the soil is clay? What is the probability that the soil is sand?

24. A geologist is using seismographs to test for oil. It is found that if oil is present, the test gives a positive result 95% of the time, and if oil is not present, the test gives a positive result 2% of the time. Finally oil is discovered in 1% of the cases tested. If the test shows positive, what is the probability that oil is present?

25. *Political Polls.* In conducting a political poll, a pollster divides the United States into four sections: Northeast (*N*), containing 40% of the population; South (*S*), containing 10% of the population; Midwest (*M*), containing 25% of the population; and West (*W*), containing 25% of the population. From the poll, it is found that in the next election 40% of the people in the Northeast say they will vote for Republicans, in the South 56% will vote Republican, in the Midwest 48% will vote Republican, and in the West 52% will vote Republican. What is the probability that a person chosen at random will vote Republican? Assuming a person votes Republican, what is the probability that he or she is from the Northeast?

26. Prove Bayes' formula (6).

CHAPTER REVIEW

Important Terms	random event	additive rule	product rule
	probabilistic model	odds for	independent events
	outcome	odds against	probability tree
	sample space	equally likely	Bayes' formula
	event	success	partition
	simple event	failure	*a priori* probability
	mutually exclusive	conditional probability	*a posteriori* probability

True–False Questions

(Answers on page 615)

T   F   1. If the odds for an event *E* are 2 to 1, then $P(E) = \frac{2}{3}$.

T   F   2. The conditional probability of *E* given *F* is

$$P(E|F) = \frac{P(E \cap F)}{P(E)}$$

T   F   3. If two events in a sample space have no simple events in common, they are said to be *independent*.

T   F   4. Bayes' formula is useful for computing *a posteriori* probability.

Fill in the Blanks

(Answers on page 615)

1. If $P(E) = .6$, the odds _____ *E* are 3 to 2.

2. When each simple event in a sample space is assigned the same probability, the events are termed _____ _____.

3. If two events in a sample space have no simple events in common, they are said to be

_____ _____.

4. The formula

$$P(A_1|E) = \frac{P(A_1) \cdot P(E|A_1)}{P(E)}$$

is called _____ _____.

Review Exercises

Answers to Odd-Numbered Problems begin on page 616.

1. A survey of families with 2 children is made, and the sexes of the children are recorded. Describe the sample space and draw a tree diagram of this random experiment.

2. A fair coin is tossed three times.

   (a) Construct a probabilistic model corresponding to this experiment.

   (b) Find the probabilities of the following events:
   (i) The first toss is T.
   (ii) The first toss is H.
   (iii) Either the first toss is T or the third toss is H.
   (iv) At least one of the tosses is H.
   (v) There are at least two T's.
   (vi) No tosses are H.

3. An urn contains 3 white marbles, 2 yellow marbles, 4 red marbles, and 5 blue marbles. Two marbles are picked at random. What is the probability that:

   (a) Both are blue?

   (b) Exactly 1 is blue?

   (c) At least 1 is blue?

4. Let A and B be events with $P(A) = .3$, $P(B) = .5$, and $P(A \cap B) = .2$. Find the probability that:

   (a) A or B happens.

   (b) A does not happen.

   (c) Neither A nor B happens.

   (d) Either A does not happen or B does not happen.

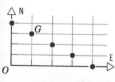

5. Jones lives at O (see the figure). He owns 5 gas stations located 4 blocks away (dots). Each afternoon he checks on one of his gas stations. He starts at O. At each intersection he flips a fair coin. If it shows heads, he will head North (N); otherwise, he will head toward the East (E). What is the probability that he will end up at gas station G before coming to one of the other stations?

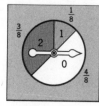

6. Consider the experiment of spinning the spinner in the figure three times. (Assume the spinner cannot fall on a line.)

   (a) Are all outcomes equally likely?

   (b) If not, which of the outcomes has the highest probability?

   (c) Let F be the event, "Each digit will occur exactly once." Find $P(F)$.

7. If E and F are events with $P(E \cup F) = \frac{5}{8}$, $P(E \cap F) = \frac{1}{3}$, and $P(E) = \frac{1}{2}$, find:

   (a) $P(\overline{E})$ (b) $P(F)$ (c) $P(\overline{F})$

8. If E and F represent mutually exclusive events, $P(E) = .30$, and $P(F) = .45$, find each of the following probabilities:

   (a) $P(\overline{E})$
   (b) $P(\overline{F})$
   (c) $P(E \cap F)$
   (d) $P(E \cup F)$
   (e) $P(\overline{E \cap F})$
   (f) $P(\overline{E \cup F})$
   (g) $P(\overline{E} \cup \overline{F})$
   (h) $P(\overline{E} \cap \overline{F})$

9. Three envelopes are addressed for three secret letters written in invisible ink. A secretary randomly places each of the letters in an envelope and mails them. What is the probability that at least one person receives the correct letter?

10. What are the odds in favor of a 5 when a fair die is thrown?

11. A better is willing to give 7 to 6 odds that the Bears will win the NFL title. What is the probability of the Bears winning?

12. A biased coin is such that the probability of heads (H) is $\frac{1}{4}$ and the probability of tails (T) is $\frac{3}{4}$. Show that in flipping this coin twice the events E and F defined below are independent.

   E: A head turns up in the first throw

   F: A tail turns up in the second throw

13. The records of Midwestern University show that in one semester, 38% of the students failed Mathematics, 27% of the students failed Physics, and 9% of the students failed Mathematics and Physics. A student is selected at random.

   (a) If a student failed Physics, what is the probability that he or she failed Mathematics?
   (b) If a student failed Mathematics, what is the probability that he or she failed Physics?
   (c) What is the probability that he or she failed Mathematics or Physics?

14. The table below indicates a survey conducted by a deodorant producer:

	Like the Deodorant	Did Not Like the Deodorant	No Opinion
Group I	180	60	20
Group II	110	85	12
Group III	55	65	7

   Let the events E, F, G, H, and K be defined as follows:

   E: Customer likes the deodorant

   F: Customer does not like the deodorant

   G: Customer is from Group I

   H: Customer is from Group II

   K: Customer is from Group III

   Find:

   (a) $P(E|G)$
   (b) $P(G|E)$
   (c) $P(H|E)$
   (d) $P(K|E)$
   (e) $P(F|G)$
   (f) $P(G|F)$
   (g) $P(H|F)$
   (h) $P(K|F)$

15. In a certain population of people, 25% are blue-eyed and 75% are brown-eyed. Also, 10% of the blue-eyed people are left-handed and 5% of the brown-eyed people are left-handed.

    (a) What is the probability that a person chosen at random is blue-eyed and left-handed?
    (b) What is the probability that a person chosen at random is left-handed?
    (c) What is the probability that a person is blue-eyed, given that the person is left-handed?

16. Three machines in a factory, A_1, A_2, A_3, produce 55%, 30% and 15% of total production, respectively. The percentage of defective output of these machines is 1%, 2% and 3%, respectively. An item is chosen at random and it is defective. What is the probability that it came from machine A_1? From A_2? From A_3?

17. A lung cancer test has been found to have the following reliability. The test can detect 85% of the people who have cancer and does not detect 15% of these people. Among the noncancerous group it detects 92% of the people not having cancer, whereas 8% of this group are detected erroneously as having lung cancer. Statistics show that about 1.8% of the population have cancer. Suppose an individual is given the test for lung cancer and it detects the disease. What is the probability that the person actually has cancer?

18. A pair of fair dice is thrown three times. What is the probability that on the first toss the sum of the 2 dice is even, on the second toss the sum is less than 6, and on the third toss the sum is 7?

Mathematical Questions

From Actuary Exams (Answers on page 616)

1. *Actuary Exam—Part I*
    If P and Q are events having positive probability in the sample space S such that $P \cap Q = \varnothing$, then all of the following pairs are independent EXCEPT:
    (a) $\varnothing$ and P (b) P and Q (c) P and S
    (d) P and $P \cap Q$ (e) $\varnothing$ and the complement of P

2. *Actuary Exam—Part I*
    A box contains 12 varieties of candy and exactly 2 pieces of each variety. If 12 pieces of candy are selected at random, what is the probability that a given variety is represented?

    (a) $\dfrac{2^{12}}{(12!)^2}$ (b) $\dfrac{2^{12}}{24!}$ (c) $\dfrac{2^{12}}{\binom{24}{12}}$ (d) $\dfrac{11}{46}$ (e) $\dfrac{35}{46}$

3. *Actuary Exam—Part II*
    What is the probability that a 3-card hand drawn at random and without replacement from an ordinary deck consists entirely of black cards?
    (a) $\frac{1}{17}$ (b) $\frac{2}{17}$ (c) $\frac{1}{8}$ (d) $\frac{3}{17}$ (e) $\frac{4}{17}$

4. *Actuary Exam—Part II*
    Events S and T are independent with $\Pr(S) < \Pr(T)$, $\Pr(S \cap T) = \frac{6}{25}$, and $\Pr(S|T) + \Pr(T|S) = 1$. What is $\Pr(S)$?
    (a) $\frac{1}{25}$ (b) $\frac{1}{5}$ (c) $\frac{6}{25}$ (d) $\frac{2}{5}$ (e) $\frac{3}{5}$

5. *Actuary Exam—Part II*
   What is the least number of independent times that an unbiased die must be thrown to make the probability that all throws do not give the same result greater than .999?
   (a) 3   (b) 4   (c) 5   (d) 6   (e) 7

6. *Actuary Exam—Part II*
   In a group of 20,000 men and 10,000 women, 6% of the men and 3% of the women have a certain affliction. What is the probability that an afflicted member of the group is a man?
   (a) $\frac{3}{5}$ (b) $\frac{2}{3}$ (c) $\frac{3}{4}$ (d) $\frac{4}{3}$ (e) $\frac{8}{9}$

7. *Actuary Exam—Part II*
   An unbiased die is thrown two independent times. Given that the first throw resulted in an even number, what is the probability that the sum obtained is 8?
   (a) $\frac{5}{36}$ (b) $\frac{1}{6}$ (c) $\frac{4}{21}$ (d) $\frac{7}{36}$ (e) $\frac{1}{3}$

8. *Actuary Exam—Part II*
   If the events S and T have equal probability and are independent with $\Pr(S \cap T) = p > 0$, then $\Pr(S) =$
   (a) $\sqrt{p}$ (b) p^2 (c) $\dfrac{p}{2}$ (d) p (e) $2p$

9. *Actuary Exam—Part II*
   The probability that both S and T occur, the probability that S occurs and T does not, and the probability that T occurs and S does not are all equal to p. What is the probability that either S or T occurs?
   (a) p (b) $2p$ (c) $3p$ (d) $3p^2$ (e) p^3

10. *Actuary Exam—Part II*
    What is the probability that a bridge hand contains 1 card of each denomination (i.e., 1 ace, 1 king, 1 queen, . . . , 1 three, 1 two)?

    (a) $\dfrac{13!}{13^{13}}$ (b) $\dfrac{4^{13}}{\binom{52}{13}}$ (c) $\dfrac{\binom{52}{4}}{\binom{52}{13}}$ (d) $\left(\dfrac{1}{13}\right)^{13}$ (e) $\dfrac{13^4}{\binom{52}{13}}$

ADDITIONAL TOPICS IN PROBABILITY

8.1 MORE COUNTING TECHNIQUES

EXAMPLES □ PERMUTATIONS WITH REPETITION
□ PROBABILITY PROBLEMS USING COUNTING TECHNIQUES

In this section we consider some counting problems that will be useful in our discussion of probability and that are also meant to sharpen your counting skills.

EXAMPLES

The first example deals with a coin-tossing experiment in which a coin is tossed a fixed number of times. There are exactly two possible outcomes on each trial or toss (heads, H, or tails, T). For instance, in tossing a coin three times, one possible outcome is HTH — heads on the first toss, tails on the second toss, and heads on the third toss.

□ **Example 1**   Suppose an experiment consists of tossing a fair coin 8 times.

(a)   How many different outcomes are possible?
(b)   How many different outcomes have exactly 3 tails?
(c)   How many outcomes have at most 2 tails?
(d)   How many outcomes have at least 3 tails?

Solution   (a)   Each outcome of the experiment consists of a sequence of eight letters H or T, where the first letter records the result of the first toss, the second letter the result of the second toss, and so forth. Thus, the process can be visualized as filling an empty box at each toss with either an H or a T. Since each box can be filled in two ways, by the Multiplication Principle, the sequence of eight boxes can be filled in

$$\underbrace{2 \cdot 2 \cdot 2 \cdot \cdots \cdot 2}_{8 \text{ factors}} = 2^8 = 256 \text{ ways}$$

Thus, there are $2^8 = 256$ different possible outcomes.

(b)   Any sequence that contains exactly $3T$'s must contain 5 H's. A particular outcome is determined as soon as we decide where to place the T's in the eight boxes. The three boxes to receive the T's can be selected from the eight boxes in $C(8, 3)$ different ways. So the number of outcomes with exactly 3 tails is

$$C(8, 3) = \frac{8!}{3!5!} = 8 \cdot 7 = 56$$

(c)   The outcomes with at most 2 tails correspond to the sequences with 0, 1, or 2 T's, and they are:

$0\ T$:   One outcome is possible, namely $HHHHHHHH$.

$1\ T$:   This outcome is determined by selecting one box out of eight in which to place the single T. This can be done in $C(8, 1) = 8$ ways.

2 *T*:   This outcome is determined by selecting two boxes out of eight in which to place the 2 *T*'s. This can be done in $C(8, 2) = 28$ ways.

Thus, the number of outcomes with at most 2 tails is just the sum of all these outcomes, which is $1 + 8 + 28 = 37$ ways.

(d) The outcomes with at least 3 tails are the results with 3, 4, 5, 6, 7, or 8 tails. The total number of such outcomes is

$$C(8, 3) + C(8, 4) + C(8, 5) + C(8, 6) + C(8, 7) + C(8, 8)$$

But there is a simpler way of obtaining the answer. If we start with the total number of outcomes obtained in part (a) and subtract the number of outcomes of at most 2 tails obtained in part (c), we get the number of outcomes with at least 3 tails:

$$256 - 37 = 219 \text{ ways}$$ □

Part (d) of the above example illustrates a counting technique that is often useful: Count the outcomes that are not favorable to you and subtract from the total number of outcomes. This "backdoor" approach can be easier at times than a direct attack. Here is another example of its use.

□ **Example 2**   Find the number of 7 digit telephone numbers that have at least 1 repeated digit. Lead 0's are allowed.

Solution   A direct application of the Multiplication Principle shows that there are 10^7 total possible 7-digit telephone numbers. The number that have *no* repeated digits is

$$P(10, 7) = \frac{10!}{3!} = 604{,}800$$

Hence, the number that have at least 1 repeated digit is

$$10^7 - \frac{10!}{3!} = 9{,}395{,}200$$ □

□ **Example 3**   An urn contains 8 white balls and 4 red balls. Four balls are selected. In how many ways can the 4 balls be drawn from the total of 12 balls:

(a) If the color is not considered?
(b) If 3 balls are white and 1 is red?
(c) If all 4 balls are white?
(d) If all 4 balls are red?

Solution   (a) Since order is not important, this experiment is simply a selection of 4 balls out of 12. There are $C(12, 4)$ possible ways to select the balls, that is,

$$C(12, 4) = \frac{12!}{4!8!} = \frac{12 \cdot 11 \cdot 10 \cdot 9}{4 \cdot 3 \cdot 2 \cdot 1} = 495 \text{ ways}$$

(b) The desired answer involves two operations: first, the selection of 3 white balls from 8; and second, the selection of 1 red ball from 4:

Select 3 white balls Operation 1	Select 1 red ball Operation 2

The first operation can be performed in $C(8, 3)$ ways; the second operation can be performed in $C(4, 1)$ ways. By the Multiplication Principle, the answer is

$$C(8, 3) \cdot C(4, 1) = \frac{8!}{3!5!} \cdot \frac{4!}{1!3!} = 224$$

(c) Since all 4 balls must be selected from the 8 that are white, the answer is

$$C(8, 4) = \frac{8!}{4!4!} = \frac{8 \cdot 7 \cdot 6 \cdot 5}{4 \cdot 3 \cdot 2 \cdot 1} = 70 \text{ ways}$$

(d) Since the 4 red balls must be selected from 4 red balls, the answer is 1 way. □

It is important in counting problems to be sure that what you are computing corresponds to the problem. The next example illustrates that sometimes more than one approach is possible.

□ **Example 4** From a group of 3 men and 2 women, how many committees of 3 can be formed that contain at least 1 woman?

Solution We use an indirect attack. The total number of committees of 3 that can be chosen is $C(5, 3)$. The number of committees that contain *no* women is $C(3, 3)$.
  Hence, there are

$$C(5, 3) - C(3, 3) = 9$$

committees that contain at least 1 woman.
  Here is another way to solve Example 4. □

Solution The required committee will have either 1 woman and 2 men, or 2 women and 1 man. The number of committees of the first type is

$$\underset{\substack{\text{Choose} \\ \text{woman}}}{C(2, 1)} \cdot \underset{\substack{\text{Choose} \\ \text{men}}}{C(3, 2)} = 2 \cdot 3 = 6$$

the number of committees of the second type is

$$\underset{\substack{\text{Choose} \\ \text{women}}}{C(2, 2)} \cdot \underset{\substack{\text{Choose} \\ \text{man}}}{C(3, 1)} = 1 \cdot 3 = 3$$

Hence, the desired answer is given by

$$C(2, 1) \cdot C(3, 2) + C(2, 2) \cdot C(3, 1) = 6 + 3 = 9$$ □

Now that we solved the example the correct way, we illustrate how an error can occur when setting up counting problems. Suppose we start the problem by using the Multiplication Principle.

Task 1: Choose a woman for the committee.

Task 2: Choose the remaining two people for the committee.

Task 1 can be done in $C(2, 1)$ ways, while task 2 can be done in $C(4, 2)$ ways since the other two people must be chosen from the 3 men and one woman remaining.

We would thus assert that there are

$$C(2, 1) \cdot C(4, 2) = 12$$

committees containing at least 1 woman.

But, the *total* number of committees of 3 that can be formed from this group is $C(5, 3) = 10$. Our answer of 12 is clearly in *error*.

The source of our difficulty lies at the start. In using the Multiplication Principle, we are asserting that every time we perform Task 1 followed by Task 2, a *different* committee will result. Here, this is not so. To see this, suppose we label the women as W_1, W_2 and the men as M_1, M_2, M_3. One way of performing Task 1 followed by Task 2 would be

Task 1   Choose W_1
Task 2   Choose W_2, M_1

A different way of performing this sequence of tasks is

Task 1   Choose W_2
Task 2   Choose W_1, M_1

Both ways have resulted in the same committee W_1, W_2, M_1; yet, in applying the Multiplication Principle, we have behaved as if these outcomes were different. This is the source of our miscount.

The message is: In applying the Multiplication Principle we must take care to ensure that different sequences of tasks correspond to different outcomes.

PERMUTATIONS WITH REPETITION

Our previous discussion of permutations required that the objects we were rearranging be distinct. We now examine what happens when repetitions are allowed. The following example shows that allowing repetition of some objects introduces modifications.

□ **Example 5**   How many 3 letter words (real or imaginary) can be formed from the letters in the word

(a)   MAD   (b)   DAD?

Solution   (a)   The three distinct letters in MAD can be rearranged in

$$P(3, 3) = 3! = 6 \text{ ways}$$

(b)   Straightforward listing shows that there are only 3 ways of rearranging the letters in the word DAD:

DAD, DDA, and ADD □

The word DAD in the above example contains 2 D's and it would seem that it is this duplication that results in fewer rearrangements for DAD than for MAD. In the next example we describe a way of dealing with the problem of duplication.

□ **Example 6**   How many distinct "words" can be formed using all the letters of the word

M A M M A L   ?

Solution   Any such word will have 6 letters formed from 3 M's, 2 A's, and 1 L. To form a word think of six blank positions that will have to be filled in by the above letters.

$$\overline{1}\ \overline{2}\ \overline{3}\ \overline{4}\ \overline{5}\ \overline{6}$$

We separate the construction of a word into 3 tasks.

Task 1: Choose 3 of the positions for the M's.

Task 2: Choose 2 of the remaining positions for the A's.

Task 3: Choose the remaining position for the L.

Doing this sequence of tasks will result in a word and, conversely, every rearrangement of MAMMAL can be interpreted as resulting from this sequence of tasks.

Task 1 can be done in $C(6, 3)$ ways. There are now 3 positions left for the 2 A's, so task 2 can be done in $C(3, 2)$ ways. Five blanks have been filled, so that the L must go in the remaining blank. That is, task 3 can be done in $C(1, 1)$ ways. The Multiplication Principle says that the number of rearrangements is

$$C(6, 3) \cdot C(3, 2) \cdot C(1, 1) = \frac{6!}{3!3!} \cdot \frac{3!}{2!1!} \cdot \frac{1!}{1!}$$

$$= \frac{6!}{3!2!1!}$$ □

The form of the answer in the above example is suggestive. Had the letters in MAMMAL been distinct, there would have been 6! rearrangements possible. The presence of 3 M's, 2 A's and 1 L yielded the denominator above. The very same reasoning used in Example 6 can be used to derive the following general result.

The number of distinct permutations of n things of which n_1 are of one kind, n_2 of a second kind, . . . , n_k of a kth kind, is

$$\frac{n!}{n_1! \cdot n_2! \cdot \cdots \cdot n_k!}$$

☐ **Example 7**   How many different vertical arrangements are possible for 10 flags, if 2 are white, 3 are red, and 5 are blue.

Solution   Here we want the different arrangements of 10 objects, which are not all different. Following the result above, we have

$$\frac{10!}{2!3!5!} = \frac{10 \cdot 9 \cdot 8 \cdot 7 \cdot \cancel{6} \cdot \cancel{5!}}{2 \cdot \cancel{3} \cdot \cancel{2} \cdot \cancel{5!}} = 2520 \text{ different arrangements}$$ ☐

☐ **Example 8**   How many different 11 letter words (real or imaginary) can be formed from the word below?

MISSISSIPPI

Solution   Here we want the number of distinct 11 letter words with 4 I's, 4 S's, 2 P's, and 1 M, so that the total number of 11 letter words is

$$\frac{11!}{2!4!4!} = \frac{39{,}916{,}800}{1152} = 34{,}650$$ ☐

The ideas above can be adapted to problems involving assignments of objects to locations.

☐ **Example 9**   A sorority house has 3 bedrooms and 10 students. One bedroom has 3 beds, the second has 2 beds, and the third has 5 beds. In how many different ways can the students be assigned rooms?

Solution   Designate the bedrooms as A, B, and C. We think of the 10 students as standing in a row and we hand each student a letter corresponding to her assigned bedroom. An assignment of rooms can then be visualized as a sequence of length 10 (the number of students) containing 3 A's, 2 B's, and 5 C's (the capacity of the rooms). For example, the sequence

A B B C . . .

would have the first student in room A, students 2 and 3 in room B, and so on. There are

$$\frac{10!}{3!2!5!} = 2520$$

such sequences and, hence, room assignments.   ☐

PROBABILITY PROBLEMS USING COUNTING TECHNIQUES

The following three examples utilize counting techniques to solve probability problems.

☐ **Example 10**   A class contains 10 male students and 12 female students. Two students are selected at random. What is the probability that they are of opposite sex?

Solution   Since there are 22 students in the class, there are $\binom{22}{2}$ ways of selecting two of them. If they are to be of opposite sex, we must obviously choose one male and one female. The first task can be accomplished in $\binom{10}{1}$ ways, while the second can be done in $\binom{12}{1}$

ways. The Multiplication Principle yields $\binom{10}{1} \cdot \binom{12}{1}$ ways of picking a male and a female. Consider the event

$$E: \text{"Students are of opposite sex"}$$

The desired probability is then

$$P(E) = \frac{\binom{10}{1} \cdot \binom{12}{1}}{\binom{22}{2}} = .519$$

An alternate way of attacking the problem would be to consider the event

$$\overline{E}: \text{"Students chosen are of the same sex"}$$

There are $\binom{10}{2}$ ways of picking two males and $\binom{12}{2}$ ways of selecting two females. So the probability that both are of the same sex is

$$P(\overline{E}) = \frac{\binom{10}{2} + \binom{12}{2}}{\binom{22}{2}} = .481$$

Since $1 - .481 = .519$, the same answer results.

□ **Example 11** A fair coin is tossed 10 times.

(a) What is the probability of obtaining exactly 5 heads and 5 tails?
(b) What is the probability of obtaining between 4 and 6 heads?

Solution (a) The number of tosses containing exactly 5 heads (and 5 tails) is $\binom{10}{5}$. Hence, the probability of an equal number of heads and tails is

$$\frac{\binom{10}{5}}{2^{10}} = .2461$$

(b) The sample space consists of all possible outcomes resulting from tossing a coin 10 times and has 2^{10} elements (two possibilities, H or T, on each of 10 tosses). We are interested in how many outcomes result in 4, 5, or 6 heads. There are $\binom{10}{4}$ tosses with exactly 4 heads since counting them is the same as choosing which 4 of the 10 tosses should contain H's. Likewise, there are $\binom{10}{5}$ and $\binom{10}{6}$ tosses, respectively, with exactly 5 heads and 6 heads. Hence, the probability of obtaining between 4 and 6 heads is given by

$$\frac{\binom{10}{4} + \binom{10}{5} + \binom{10}{6}}{2^{10}} = .6563$$

□ **Example 12**   If the letters in the word MISTER are randomly scrambled, what is the probability that the resulting rearrangement has the I preceding the E?

Solution   The total number of ways of rearranging the letters in MISTER is 6!, which forms the denominator of our desired probability. The numerator counts the number of arrangements having the I before the E. To compute this, we imagine any rearrangement as resulting from some placement of the letters in the following six positions

— — — — — —

We consider the formation of an arrangement having I preceding E as consisting of two tasks. Task 1 is to choose two of the six positions for the I and E—the I would then of necessity have to occupy the leftmost position of the two chosen.

Task 1 can be done in $\binom{6}{2}$ ways.

Task 2 would be to arrange the letters MSTR in the remaining 4 positions. This can be done in 4! ways. Hence, by the Multiplication Principle, the number of arrangements with the I preceding the E is

$$\binom{6}{2} \cdot 4!$$

So, the desired probability is

$$\frac{\binom{6}{2} \cdot 4!}{6!} = \frac{\frac{6!}{2!4!} \cdot 4!}{6!} = \frac{1}{2!} = .5$$

□

The answer should be intuitively plausible—we would expect one-half of the arrangements to have I before E and the other half to have E before I.

Exercise 8.1   *Answers to Odd-Numbered Problems begin on page* 616.

1. An experiment consists of tossing a coin 10 times.

    (a)   How many different outcomes are possible?
    (b)   How many different outcomes have exactly 4 heads?
    (c)   How many different outcomes have at most 2 heads?
    (d)   How many different outcomes have at least 3 heads?

2. An experiment consists of tossing a coin six times.

    (a)   How many different outcomes are possible?
    (b)   How many different outcomes have exactly 3 heads?
    (c)   How many different outcomes have at least 2 heads?
    (d)   How many different outcomes have 4 heads or 5 heads?

3. An urn contains 7 white balls and 3 red balls. Three balls are selected. In how many ways can the 3 balls be drawn from the total of 10 balls:

    (a)   If the color is not considered?   (c)   If all 3 balls are white?
    (b)   If 2 balls are white and 1 is red?   (d)   If all 3 balls are red?

4. An urn contains 15 red balls and 10 white balls. Five balls are selected. In how many ways can the 5 balls be drawn from the total of 25 balls:

    (a) If the color is not considered?   (c) If 3 balls are red and 2 are white?
    (b) If all balls are red?   (d) If at least 4 are red balls?

5. In the World Series the American League team (A) and the National League team (N) play until one team wins four games. If the sequence of winners is designated by letters (for example, $NAAAA$ means the National League team won the first game and the American League team won the next four), how many different sequences are possible?

6. How many different ways can 3 red, 4 yellow, and 5 blue bulbs be arranged in a string of Christmas tree lights with 12 sockets?

7. In how many ways can 3 apple trees, 4 peach trees, and 2 plum trees be arranged along a fence line if one does not distinguish between trees of the same kind?

8. How many different 9 letter words (real or imaginary) can be formed from the letters in the word ECONOMICS?

9. How many different 11 letter words (real or imaginary) can be formed from the letters in the word MATHEMATICS?

10. The United States Senate has 100 members. Suppose it is desired to place each senator on exactly 1 of 7 possible committees. The first committee has 22 members, the second has 13, the third has 10, the fourth has 5, the fifth has 16, and the sixth and seventh have 17 apiece. In how many ways can these committees be formed?

11. In how many ways can 10 children be placed on 3 distinct teams of 3, 3, and 4 members?

12. A group of 9 people is going to be split into committees of 4, 3, and 2 people. How many committees can be formed if:

    (a) A person can serve on any number of committees?
    (b) No person can serve on more than one committee?

13. A group consists of 5 men and 8 women. A committee of 4 is to be formed from this group, and policy dictates that at least 1 woman be on this committee.

    (a) How many committees can be formed that contain exactly 1 man?
    (b) How many committees can be formed that contain exactly 2 women?
    (c) How many committees can be formed that contain at least 1 man?

14. How many distinct 7-digit telephone numbers can be formed if (a) using the digits 1, 1, 2, 2, 5, 5, 5? (b) If it is required that the first digit be a 5?

15. In how many ways can 30 diplomats be assigned to 5 countries, with each country receiving an equal number of diplomats?

16. How many rearrangements of the letters in the word SUCCESS have the U before the E?

17. An experiment consists of tossing a coin 8 times. How many outcomes have more heads then tails?

18. Eight couples (husband and wife) are present at a meeting where a committee of 3 is to be chosen. How many ways can this be done so that the committee

    (a) Contains a couple?
    (b) Contains no couple?

19. A fair coin is tossed 10 times. Find the probability that 6 heads and 4 tails result.

20. A fair coin is tossed 8 times. Find the probability that

    (a) Four heads and 4 tails occur.
    (b) Between 3 and 5 heads occur.
    (c) More heads than tails occur.

21. Five distinct letters are randomly picked from the alphabet. What is the probability that at least one of them is a vowel (a, e, i, o, u)?

22. What is the probability that a 5-digit telephone extension has

    (a) No repeated digits?
    (b) One or more repeated digits?
    (c) Contains the number 2?

23. A room contains 10 married couples. Two people are chosen randomly from the room. What is the probability that they are husband and wife?

24. A room contains 5 males and 8 females. If two people are chosen at random, what is the probability that they are of opposite sex?

25. If the letters in EQUAL are randomly rearranged, what is the probability that the result has them in alphabetical order?

26. In a random rearrangement of the letters in the word CARPET, what is the probability that the R precedes the P?

27. If the letters in RANDOM are scrambled, what is the probability that the result has the M preceding the O?

28. A fair coin is tossed 10 times. What is the probability of obtaining an odd number of tails?

8.2 THE BINOMIAL THEOREM

INTRODUCTION □ BINOMIAL IDENTITIES

INTRODUCTION

The *binomial theorem* deals with the problem of expanding an expression of the form $(x + y)^n$, where n is a positive integer.

Expressions such as $(x + y)^2$ and $(x + y)^3$ are not too difficult to expand. For example.

$$(x + y)^2 = x^2 + 2xy + y^2 \qquad (x + y)^3 = x^3 + 3x^2y + 3xy^2 + y^3$$

However, expanding expressions such as $(x + y)^6$ or $(x + y)^8$ by the normal process of multiplication would be tedious and time-consuming. It is here that the binomial theorem is especially useful.

Recall that

$$C(n, r) = \binom{n}{r} = \frac{n!}{r!(n - r)!}$$

Then, for example, the expression

$$(x + y)^2 = x^2 + 2xy + y^2$$

can be written as

$$(x + y)^2 = \binom{2}{0} x^2 + \binom{2}{1} xy + \binom{2}{2} y^2$$

The expansion of $(x + y)^3$ can be written as

$$(x + y)^3 = x^3 + 3x^2y + 3xy^2 + y^3 = \binom{3}{0} x^3 + \binom{3}{1} x^2y + \binom{3}{2} xy^2 + \binom{3}{3} y^3$$

The binomial theorem generalizes this pattern.

Binomial Theorem   If n is a positive integer,

$$(x + y)^n = \binom{n}{0} x^n + \binom{n}{1} x^{n-1}y + \binom{n}{2} x^{n-2}y^2$$

$$+ \cdots + \binom{n}{k} x^{n-k}y^k + \cdots + \binom{n}{n} y^n \qquad (1)$$

Observe that the powers of x begin at n and decrease by 1, while the powers of y begin with 0 and increase by 1. Also, the coefficient of the term involving y^k is always $\binom{n}{k}$.

Let's get some practice in using the binomial theorem.

□ **Example 1**   Expand $(x + y)^6$ using the binomial theorem.

Solution

$$(x + y)^6 = \binom{6}{0} x^6 + \binom{6}{1} x^5y + \binom{6}{2} x^4y^2 + \binom{6}{3} x^3y^3$$

$$+ \binom{6}{4} x^2y^4 + \binom{6}{5} xy^5 + \binom{6}{6} y^6$$

$$= x^6 + 6x^5y + 15x^4y^2 + 20x^3y^3 + 15x^2y^4 + 6xy^5 + y^6 \qquad □$$

Note that the coefficients in the expansion of $(x + y)^6$ are the entries in the Pascal triangle for $n = 6$. (See Figure 18, page 265.)

□ **Example 2**   Find the coefficient of x^3y^4 in the expansion of $(x + y)^7$.

Solution   The coefficient of x^3y^4 is

$$\binom{7}{4} = \frac{7 \cdot 6 \cdot 5}{3 \cdot 2 \cdot 1} = 35 \qquad □$$

□ **Example 3**   Expand $(x + 2y)^4$ using the binomial theorem.

Solution   Here, we let "$2y$" play the role of "y" in the binomial theorem. We then get

$$(x + 2y)^4 = \binom{4}{0} x^4 + \binom{4}{1} x^3(2y) + \binom{4}{2} x^2(2y)^2$$
$$+ \binom{4}{3} x(2y)^3 + \binom{4}{4} (2y)^4$$
$$= x^4 + 8x^3y + 24x^2y^2 + 32xy^3 + 16y^4 \qquad \square$$

To explain why the binomial theorem is true, we take a close look at what happens when we compute $(x + y)^3$. Think of $(x + y)^3$ as the product of 3 factors, namely,

$$(x + y)^3 = (x + y)(x + y)(x + y)$$

Were we to multiply these three factors together without any attempt at simplification or collecting of terms we would get

$$\underset{\substack{\text{Factor} \\ 1}}{(x + y)} \, \underset{\substack{\text{Factor} \\ 2}}{(x + y)} \, \underset{\substack{\text{Factor} \\ 3}}{(x + y)} = xxx + xyx + yxx + yyx + xxy + xyy + yxy + yyy$$

Notice that the terms on the right yield all possible products that can be formed by picking either an x or y from each of the three factors on the left. Thus, for example.

$\qquad xyx \qquad$ results from choosing an x from factor 1,
$\qquad\qquad\qquad$ a y from factor 2, and an x from factor 3

Now, the number of terms on the right that will simplify to, say, xy^2, will be those terms that resulted from choosing y's from 2 of the factors and an x from the remaining factor. How many such terms are there? There are as many as there are ways of choosing 2 of the 3 factors to contribute y's—that is, there are $C(3, 2) = \binom{3}{2}$ such terms. This is why the coefficient of xy^2 in the expansion of $(x + y)^3$ is $\binom{3}{2}$.

In general, if we think of $(x + y)^n$ as the product of n factors,

$$(x + y)^n = \underbrace{(x + y) \cdot (x + y) \, \cdots \, (x + y)}_{n \text{ factors}}$$

Then upon multiplying out and simplifying there will be as many terms of the form $x^{n-k} y^k$ as there are ways of choosing k of the n factors to contribute y's (and the remaining $n - k$ to contribute x's). There are $C(n, k)$ ways of making this choice. So, the coefficient of $x^{n-k} y^k$ is thus $\binom{n}{k}$, and this is the assertion of the binomial theorem.

BINOMIAL IDENTITIES

Binomial coefficients are involved in many relations that can be useful when applying them. We discuss some of these in the examples below.

□ **Example 4**   Show that

$$\binom{n}{k} = \binom{n}{n - k}$$

Solution   By definition,

$$\binom{n}{k} = \frac{n!}{k!(n-k)!}$$

while

$$\binom{n}{n-k} = \frac{n!}{(n-k)![n-(n-k)]!}$$

Since $n - (n - k) = k$, a comparison of the expressions shows that they are equal.

□

Another way of explaining the equality would be to imagine that we wanted to pick a team of k players from n people. Then choosing those k who will play is the same as choosing those $n - k$ who will not. So the number of ways of choosing the players equals the number of ways of choosing the nonplayers. The players can be chosen in $C(n, k) = \binom{n}{k}$ ways, while those to be left out can be chosen in $\binom{n}{n-k}$ ways and the equality follows.

Thus,

$$\binom{5}{3} = \binom{5}{2}, \qquad \binom{10}{2} = \binom{10}{8}$$

and so on. This identity accounts for the symmetry in the rows of Pascal's triangle.

□ **Example 5**   Show that

$$\binom{n}{k} = \binom{n-1}{k} + \binom{n-1}{k-1}$$

Solution   We could expand both sides of the above identity using the definition of binomial coefficients and, after some algebra, demonstrate the equality. But we choose the route of posing a problem that we solve two different ways. Equating the two solutions will prove the identity.

A committee of k is to be chosen from n people. The total number of ways this can be done is $C(n, k) = \binom{n}{k}$.

We now count the total number of committees a different way. Assume that one of the n people is Mr. Martin. We compute

(1)   those not containing Mr. Martin

and

(2)   those containing Mr. Martin

The number of committees of type (1) is $\binom{n-1}{k}$ since the k people must be chosen from the $n - 1$ people who are not Mr. Martin. The number of committees of type (2) will correspond to the number of ways we can choose the $k - 1$ people other than Mr. Martin to be on the committee. So, the number of committees of type (2) is given by $\binom{n-1}{k-1}$. Since the number of committees of type (1) plus the number of committees of type (2) equals the total number of committees, our identity follows.

□

For example, $\binom{8}{5} = \binom{7}{5} + \binom{7}{4}$. It is precisely this identity that explains the reason why an entry in Pascal's triangle can be obtained by adding the nearest two entries in the row above it. Due to a recursive character, the identity in Example 5 is sometimes used in computer programs that evaluate binomial coefficients.

☐ **Example 6**   Explain why

$$\binom{6}{3} = \binom{2}{2} + \binom{3}{2} + \binom{4}{2} + \binom{5}{2}$$

Solution   We make repeated use of the identity in Example 5.

$$\text{So, } \binom{6}{3} = \binom{5}{3} + \binom{5}{2}$$

$$= \binom{4}{3} + \binom{4}{2} + \binom{5}{2} \quad \left[\text{applying the identity to } \binom{5}{3}\right]$$

$$= \binom{3}{3} + \binom{3}{2} + \binom{4}{2} + \binom{5}{2} \quad \left[\text{applying the identity to } \binom{4}{3}\right]$$

$$= \binom{2}{2} + \binom{3}{2} + \binom{4}{2} + \binom{5}{2}. \quad \left[\text{Since } \binom{2}{2} = \binom{3}{3} = 1\right]$$ ☐

☐ **Example 7**   Show that

$$\binom{n}{0} + \binom{n}{1} + \binom{n}{2} + \cdots + \binom{n}{n} = 2^n$$

Solution   We make use of the binomial theorem. Since the binomial theorem is valid for all x and y, we may set $x = y = 1$ in (1). This gives

$$2^n = (1 + 1)^n = \binom{n}{0} + \binom{n}{1} + \binom{n}{2} + \cdots + \binom{n}{n}$$ ☐

This shows, for example, that the sum of the elements in the row marked $n = 6$ of Pascal's triangle is $2^6 = 64$. The result in Example 7 has an interpretation in terms of the number of subsets of a set with n elements. $\binom{n}{0}$ gives the number of subsets with 0 elements; $\binom{n}{1}$ the number of subsets with 1 element; $\binom{n}{2}$ the number of subsets with 2 elements; and so on. The sum $\binom{n}{0} + \binom{n}{1} + \cdots + \binom{n}{n}$ is thus the total number of subsets of a set with n elements. The result in Example 7 can then be rephrased as:

> A set with n elements has 2^n subsets.

Thus, a set with 5 elements has $2^5 = 32$ subsets.

☐ **Example 8**   Show that

$$\binom{n}{0} - \binom{n}{1} + \binom{n}{2} - \cdots + (-1)^n \binom{n}{n} = 0$$

(The last term will be preceded by a plus or minus sign depending on whether n is even or odd.)

Solution   We again make use of the binomial theorem. This time we let $x = 1$ and $y = -1$ in (1). This produces

$$0 = (1-1)^n = \binom{n}{0} + \binom{n}{1}(-1) + \binom{n}{2}(-1)^2 + \binom{n}{3}(-1)^3 + \cdots + \binom{n}{n}(-1)^n$$

$$= \binom{n}{0} - \binom{n}{1} + \binom{n}{2} - \cdots + (-1)^n \binom{n}{n}$$ ☐

We mention an interpretation of this identity by examining the instance where $n = 5$. The identity gives

$$\binom{5}{0} - \binom{5}{1} + \binom{5}{2} - \binom{5}{3} + \binom{5}{4} - \binom{5}{5} = 0$$

Transposing this equality yields

$$\binom{5}{0} + \binom{5}{2} + \binom{5}{4} = \binom{5}{1} + \binom{5}{3} + \binom{5}{5}$$

This says that a set with 5 elements has as many subsets containing an even number of elements as it has subsets containing an odd number of elements.

Exercise 8.2   *Answers to Odd-Numbered Problems begin on page* 616.

In Problems 1–6 use the binomial theorem to expand each expression.

1. $(x+y)^5$
2. $(x+y)^4$
3. $(x+3y)^3$
4. $(2x+y)^3$
5. $(2x-y)^4$
6. $(x-y)^4$
7. What is the coefficient of x^2y^3 in the expansion of $(x+y)^5$?
8. What is the coefficient of x^2y^6 in the expansion of $(x+y)^8$?
9. What is the coefficient of x^8 in the expansion of $(x+3)^{10}$?
10. What is the coefficient of x^3 in the expansion of $(x+2)^5$?
11. How many different subsets can be chosen from a set with 5 elements?
12. How many different subsets can be chosen from a set of 50 elements?
13. How many nonempty subsets does a set with 10 elements have?
14. How many subsets with an even number of elements does a set with 10 elements have?
15. How many subsets with an odd number of elements does a set with 10 elements have?
16. Explain why

$$\binom{8}{5} = \binom{4}{4} + \binom{5}{4} + \binom{6}{4} + \binom{7}{4}$$

17. Explain why

$$\binom{10}{7} = \binom{6}{6} + \binom{7}{6} + \binom{8}{6} + \binom{9}{6}$$

18. Show that

$$\binom{7}{1} + \binom{7}{3} + \binom{7}{5} + \binom{7}{7} = 2^6$$

19. Replace $\binom{11}{6} + \binom{11}{5}$ by a single binomnial coefficient.

20. Replace $\binom{8}{8} + \binom{9}{8} + \binom{10}{8}$ by a single binomial coefficient.

8.3 THE BINOMIAL PROBABILITY MODEL

BERNOULLI TRIALS □ BINOMIAL PROBABILITIES □ MODEL: TESTING A SERUM OR VACCINE □ MODEL: ERROR CORRECTION IN ELECTRONIC TRANSMISSION OF DATA

BERNOULLI TRIALS

In this section we study practical situations that can be interpreted by using a simple probabilistic model, called the *binomial probability model*. The model was first studied by J. Bernoulli about 1700 and, for this reason, the model is sometimes referred to as a *Bernoulli trial*.

The binomial probability model is a sequence of trials, each of which consists of repetition of a single experiment. We assume the outcome of one experiment does not affect the outcome of any other one; that is, we assume the trials to be independent. Furthermore, we assume that there are only two possible outcomes for each trial and label them *S*, for *Success*, and *F*, for *Failure*. The probability of success, $p = P(S)$, remains the same from trial to trial. In addition, since there are only two outcomes in each trial, the probability of failure must be $1 - p$, and we write

$$q = 1 - p = P(F)$$

Thus, $p + q = 1$.

Any random experiment for which the binomial probability model is appropriate is called a *Bernoulli trial*.

Bernoulli Trial **Random experiments are called *Bernoulli trials* if:**

(a) **The same experiment is repeated several times.**

(b) **There are only two possible outcomes, success and failure.**

(c) **The repeated trials are independent.**

(d) **The probability of each outcome remains the same for each trial.**

Many real-world situations have the characteristics of the binomial probability model. For example, in repeatedly running a subject through a T-maze, we may label

---

* JAMES (JACQUES) BERNOULLI (1654–1705) was a member of a family of famous Swiss mathematicians. At the insistence of his father, he studied theology. Later, he refused a church appointment and began lecturing on experimental physics at the University of Basel. Thanks to Bernoulli's contributions, probability theory was raised to the status of a science. In 1713, his book *Ars Conjectardi* was published in Latin by his nephew Nicholas Bernoulli, who also was a mathematician.

a turn to the left by S and a turn to the right by F. The assumption of independence of each trial is equivalent to presuming the subject has no memory.

In opinion polls, one person's response is independent of any other person's response, and we may designate the answer "Yes" by an S and any other answer ("No" or "Don't know") by an F.

In testing TV's, we have a sequence of independent trials (each test of a particular TV is a trial) and we label a nondefective TV with an S and a defective one with an F.

In determining whether 9 out of 12 persons will recover from a tropical disease, we assume that each of the 12 persons has the same chance of recovery from the disease and that their recoveries are independent (say they are not treated by the same doctor or in the same hospital). We may designate "recovery" by S and "nonrecovery" by F.

Next we consider an experiment that will lead us to formulate a general expression for the probability of obtaining k successes in a sequence of n Bernoulli trials ($k \leq n$).

The experiment is to test a drug to be administered to a group of people infected by a tropical disease. In such a case, we can define a success to be when a person is recovered and a failure to occur if he or she does not recover. Then p is the probability of recovery and q is the probability of not recovering.

The probability tree in Figure 1 lists all the possible outcomes and their respective probabilities for a group of three persons.

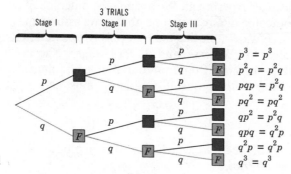

Figure 1

The set of outcomes is

$$SSS, \ SSF, \ SFS, \ SFF, \ FSS, \ FSF, \ FFS, \ FFF$$

Here for example, SSF means that the first two people recover (successes) and the third does not (failure).

The outcome SSS, in which all three recover, has a probability $ppp = p^3$, since each Bernoulli trial has a probability p of resulting in success.

If we wish to calculate the probability that exactly two people will recover, we consider only the outcomes

$$SSF, \ SFS, \ FSS$$

The outcome SSF has probability $ppq = p^2q$ since the two successes each have probability p and the failure has probability q. In the same way, the other two outcomes SFS and FSS, in which there are two successes and one failure, also have probabilities p^2q. Therefore the probability that exactly two people recover and one does not is equal to the sum of the probabilities of the three outcomes and, hence, is given by $3p^2q$.

In a similar way we compute the following probabilities:

$$P \text{ (exactly one person recovering and two not recovering)} = 3pq^2$$
$$P \text{ (all three recovered)} = p^3$$
$$P \text{ (all three not recovering)} = q^3$$

BINOMIAL PROBABILITIES

When considering a group larger than three it would be extremely tedious, to say the least, to solve problems of this type using a probability tree. This is why we want a general expression.

Suppose the probability of a success in a Bernoulli trial is p, and suppose we wish to find the probability of exactly k successes in n repeated trials. One possible outcome is

$$\underbrace{SSS---S}_{k \text{ successes}} \underbrace{FF---F}_{n-k \text{ failures}} \tag{1}$$

where k successes come first, followed by $n - k$ failures. The probability of this outcome is

$$= \underbrace{ppp---p}_{k \text{ factors}} \underbrace{qq---q}_{n-k \text{ factors}}$$

$$= p^k q^{n-k}$$

The k successes could also be obtained by rearranging the letters in (1) above. The number of such sequences must be equal to the number of ways of choosing k of the n trials to contain successes—namely, $\binom{n}{k}$. If we multiply this number by the probability of obtaining any one such sequence, we arrive at the following result:

In a Bernoulli trial the probability of exactly k successes in n trials is given by

$$b(n, k; p) = \binom{n}{k} p^k \cdot q^{n-k} = \frac{n!}{k!(n-k)!} p^k \cdot q^{n-k} \tag{2}$$

where $q = 1 - p$.

Binomial Probability   The symbol $b(n, k; p)$, which represents the probability of exactly k successes in n trials, is called a *binomial probability*.

□ **Example 1**   A common example of a Bernoulli trial is a coin-flipping experiment:

1. There are exactly two possible mutually exclusive outcomes on each trial or toss (heads or tails).
2. The probability of a particular outcome (say, H) remains constant from trial to trial (toss to toss).
3. The outcome on any trial (toss) is independent of the outcome on any other trial (toss).

We would like to compute the probability of obtaining exactly 1 tail in 6 tosses of a fair coin.

Solution   Let S denote the simple event "Tail shows" and let F denote the simple event "Head shows." Using Formula (2) in which $k = 1$, $n = 6$, and $p = \frac{1}{2} = P(S)$, we obtain

$$P(\text{Exactly one success}) = b\left(6, 1; \frac{1}{2}\right) = \binom{6}{1}\left(\frac{1}{2}\right)^1\left(\frac{1}{2}\right)^{6-1}$$

$$= \frac{6}{64} \approx .0938 \qquad \square$$

☐ **Example 2**   A typist makes at least one error on the average in every fifth typed page. If nine pages
Typist Error   are typed in one day, what is the probability that

(a)   Exactly three of them have errors.

(b)   None of them has an error.

(c)   No more than 7 pages have errors.

Solution   In this example, $P(\text{success}) = P(\text{making an error}) = \frac{1}{5} = .2$. The number of trials n is the number of typed pages and k is the number of pages containing errors.

(a) $n = 9$, $k = 3$, and $q = 1 - .2 = .8$.

$$P(\text{exactly } 3) = b(9, 3; .2) = \binom{9}{3}(.2)^3(.8)^6 = .1762$$

(b)   If none of the 9 pages had any errors, $k = 0$.

$$P(\text{exactly } 0) = b(9, 0; .2) = \binom{9}{0}(.2)^0(.8)^9 = .1342$$

For part (c), as in many other applications, it is necessary to compute the probability not of exactly k successes, but of *at least* or *at most* k successes. To obtain such probabilities we have to compute all the individual probabilities and add them.

(c)   "No more than 7 pages have errors" means 0, 1, 2, 3, 4, 5, 6, or 7 pages with errors. We could add $b(9, 0; .2)$, $b(9, 1; .2)$, and so on, but it is easier to use the formula $P(E) = 1 - P(\overline{E})$. The complement of "no more than 7" is "8 or more."

$$P(\text{no more than } 7) = 1 - P(8 \text{ or more})$$

$$= 1 - [b(9, 8; .2) + b(9, 9; .2)] = .9999 \qquad \square$$

☐ **Example 3**   A machine produces light bulbs to meet certain specifications, and 80% of the bulbs
Quality Control   produced meet these specifications. A sample of 6 bulbs is taken from the machine's production. What is the probability that 3 or more of them fail to meet the specifications?

Solution   In this example we are looking for the probability of the event

$$E: \text{At least 3 fail to meet specifications}$$

But this event is just the union of the mutually exclusive events "Exactly 3 failures,"

"Exactly 4 failures," "Exactly 5 failures," and "Exactly 6 failures." Hence, we use formula (2) for $n = 6$ and $k = 3, 4, 5$, and 6. Since the probability of failure is .20, we have

$$P(\text{Exactly 3 failures}) = b(6, 3; .20) = .0819$$
$$P(\text{Exactly 4 failures}) = b(6, 4; .20) = .0154$$
$$P(\text{Exactly 5 failures}) = b(6, 5; .20) = .0015$$
$$P(\text{Exactly 6 failures}) = b(6, 6; .20) = .0001$$

Therefore,

$$P(\text{At least 3 failures}) = P(E) = .0819 + .0154 + .0015 + .0001 = .0989 \quad \square$$

Another way of getting this answer is to compute the probability of the complementary event

$$\overline{E}: \text{Less than 3 failures}$$

Then,

$$P(\overline{E}) = P(\text{Exactly 2 failures}) + P(\text{Exactly 1 failure}) + P(\text{Exactly 0 failures})$$
$$= b(6, 2; .20) + b(6, 1; .20) + b(6, 0; .20)$$
$$= .2458 + .3932 + .2621 = .9011$$

As a result,

$$P(\text{At least 3 failures}) = 1 - P(E) = 1 - .9011 = .0989$$

□ Example 4
Product Promotion

A man claims to be able to distinguish between two kinds of wine with 90% accuracy and presents his claim to an agency interested in promoting the consumption of one of the two kinds of wine. The following experiment is conducted to check his claim. The man is to taste the two types of wine and distinguish between them. This is to be done 9 times with a 3 minute break after each taste. It is agreed that if the man is correct at least 6 out of the 9 times, he will be hired.

The main questions to be asked are, on the one hand, whether the above procedure gives sufficient protection to the hiring agency against a person guessing and, on the other hand, whether the man is given sufficient chance to be hired if he is really a wine connoisseur.

Solution

To answer the first question, let's assume that the man is guessing. Then in each trial he has probability $\frac{1}{2}$ of identifying the wine correctly. Let k be the number of correct identifications. Let's compute the binomial probability for $k = 6, 7, 8, 9$, to find the likelihood of the man being hired while guessing:

$$b\left(9, 6; \frac{1}{2}\right) + b\left(9, 7; \frac{1}{2}\right) + b\left(9, 8; \frac{1}{2}\right) + b\left(9, 9; \frac{1}{2}\right)$$
$$= .1641 + .0703 + .0176 + .0020 = .2540$$

Thus, there is a likelihood of .254 that he will pass if he is just guessing.

To answer the second question in the case where the claim is true, we need to find the sum of the probabilities $b(9, k; .90)$ for $k = 6, 7, 8, 9$:

$b(9, 6; .90) + b(9, 7; .90) + b(9, 8; .90) + b(9, 9; .90)$

$$= .0446 + .1722 + .3874 + .3874 = .9916 \quad \square$$

Notice that the test in Example 4 is fair to the man, since it practically assures him the position if his claim is true. However, the company may not like the test because 25% of the time a person who guesses will pass the test.

MODEL: TESTING A SERUM OR VACCINE*

Suppose that the normal rate of infection of a certain disease in cattle is 25%. To test a newly discovered serum, healthy animals are injected with it. How can we evaluate the result of the experiment?

For an absolutely worthless serum, the probability that exactly k of n test animals remain free from infection may be equated to $b(n, k; .75)$. For $k = n = 10$, this probability is about $b(10, 10; .75) = .056$. Thus, if out of 10 test animals none catches infection, this may be taken as an indication that the serum has had an effect, although it is not conclusive proof. Notice that, without serum, the probability that out of 17 animals at most 1 catches infection is $b(17, 0; .25) + b(17, 1; .25) = .0501$. Therefore, there is *stronger evidence* in favor of the serum if out of 17 test animals at most 1 gets infected than if out of 10 all remain healthy. For $n = 23$ the probability of at most 2 animals catching infection is about .0492 and, thus, at most 2 failures out of 23 is again better evidence for the serum than at most 1 out of 17 or 0 out of 10.

MODEL: ERROR CORRECTION IN ELECTRONIC TRANSMISSION OF DATA

Electronically transmitted data, be it from computer to computer or from a satellite to a ground station, is normally in the form of strings of 0's and 1's—that is, in binary form. Bursts of noise or faults in relays, for example, may at times garble the transmission and produce errors so that the message received is not the same as the one originally sent. For example,

001	$\longmapsto\!\!\rightsquigarrow\!\!\longrightarrow$	101	
Message	Noisy	Message	(3)
sent	channel	received	

is a transmission where the message received is in error since the initial 0 has been changed to a 1.

A naive way of trying to protect against such error would be to repeat the message twice. So, instead of transmitting 001, we would send 001001. Then, were the exact same error to creep in as did in (3), the received message would be

$$101001$$

The receiver would certainly know an error has occurred since the last half of the message is not a duplicate of the first half. But, he would have no way of recovering the original message, since he would not know where the error happened. For example, he would not be able to distinguish between the two messages

$$001001 \text{ and } 101101$$

There are more sophisticated ways of coding binary data with redundancy that allow not only the detection of errors, but simultaneously permit their location and correction so that the original message can be recovered. These are referred to as *error-correcting codes* and are commonly used today in computer-implemented transmissions. One such is the (7, 4) Hamming code named after Richard Hamming, a former researcher at A.T. & T. Laboratories. It is a code of length 7, meaning that an individual message is a string consisting of 7 items, each of which is either a 0 or 1. (The 4 refers to the fact that the first 4 elements in the string can be freely chosen by the sender, while the remaining 3 are determined by a fixed rule and constitute the redundancy that gives the code its error correction capability.) The (7, 4) Hamming code is capable of locating and correcting a single error. That is, if during transmission a 1 has been changed to a 0 or vice versa in one of the 7 locations, the Hamming code is capable of detecting and correcting this. While we will not explain how or why the Hamming code works, we will analyze the benefit obtained by its use.

By an error we mean that an individual 1 has been changed to a 0 or that a 0 has been changed to a 1. We assume that the probability of an error happening remains constant during transmission and we designate this probability by q. Thus, $p = 1 - q$ is the probability that an individual symbol remains unchanged. This is summarized in the diagram.

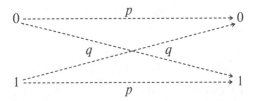

(In practice, values of q are normally small and values of p close to 1, since we would normally be using a relatively reliable channel.)

We also assume that errors occur randomly and independently. In short, we can think of the transmission of a binary string of length 7 as a Bernoulli trial, with failure corresponding to a symbol being received in error.

For a message of length 7, if *no* coding were used, the probability that the receiver would get the correct message would be

$$b(7, 7; p) = p^7$$

since none of the 7 symbols could have been altered. For $p = .98$, this gives $(.98)^7 = .8681$.

Using the Hamming code, the receiver will get the correct message even if one error has occurred. Hence, the corresponding probability of correct reception would be

$$\underbrace{b(7, 7; p)}_{\text{No errors}} + \underbrace{b(7, 6; p)}_{\text{One error}} = p^7 + 7p^6 q$$

For $p = .98$ this now gives $.8681 + .1240 = .9921$, which shows a considerable improvement.

There are codes in use that correct more than a single error. One such code, known by the initials of its originators as a BCH code, is a code of length 15 (messages are binary strings of length 15) that corrects up to 2 errors. Sending a message of length 15 with no attempt at coding would result in a probability of $b(15, 15; p) = p^{15}$ of the correct message being received. For $p = .98$ this gives $b(15, 15; .98) = .7386$. Using the BCH code that can correct 2 or fewer errors, the probability that a message will be correctly received becomes

$$\underbrace{b(15, 15; p)}_{\text{No errors}} + \underbrace{b(15, 14; p)}_{\text{One error}} + \underbrace{b(15, 13; p)}_{\text{Two errors}}$$

Evaluating this for $p = .98$ we get

$$.7386 + .2261 + .0323 = .9970$$

Codes that can correct a high number of errors are clearly very desirable. Yet a basic result in the theory of codes states that; as the error-correcting capability of a code increases, so, of necessity, must its length. But lengthier codes require more time for transmission and are clumsier to use. Thus, here, speed and correctness are at odds.

Exercise 8.3   *Answers to Odd-Numbered Problems begin on page* 616 .

In Problems 1–14 use formula (2), page 349, and a calculator to compute each binomial probability.

1. $b(7, 5; .30)$ **2.** $b(8, 6; .40)$

3. $b(15, 8; .70)$ **4.** $b(8, 5; .60)$

5. $b(15, 10; \frac{1}{2})$ **6.** $b(12, 6; .90)$

7. $b(15, 3; .3) + b(15, 2; .3) + b(15, 1; .3) + b(15, 0; .3)$

8. $b(8, 6; .4) + b(8, 7; .4) + b(8, 8; .4)$

9. $n = 3$, $k = 2$, $p = \frac{1}{3}$ 10. $n = 3$, $k = 1$, $p = \frac{1}{3}$

11. $n = 3$, $k = 0$, $p = \frac{1}{6}$ 12. $n = 3$, $k = 3$, $p = \frac{1}{6}$

13. $n = 5$, $k = 3$, $p = \frac{2}{3}$ 14. $n = 5$, $k = 0$, $p = \frac{2}{3}$

15. Find the probability of obtaining exactly 6 successes in 10 trials when the probability of success is .3.

16. Find the probability of obtaining exactly 5 successes in 9 trials when the probability of success is .2.

17. Find the probability of obtaining exactly 9 successes in 12 trials when the probability of success is .8.

18. Find the probability of obtaining exactly 8 successes in 15 trials when the probability of success is .75.

19. Find the probability of obtaining at least 5 successes in 8 trials when the probability of success is .25.

20. Find the probability of obtaining at most 3 successes in 7 trials when the probability of success is .15.

In Problems 21–25 a fair coin is tossed eight times.

21. What is the probability of obtaining exactly 1 head?

22. What is the probability of obtaining exactly 2 heads?

23. What is the probability of obtaining at least 5 tails?

24. What is the probability of obtaining at most 2 tails?

25. What is the probability of obtaining exactly 2 heads if it is known that at least 1 head appeared?

26. To screen prospective employees, a company gives a 10 question multiple choice test. Each question has 4 possible answers, of which one is correct. The chance of answering the questions correctly by just guessing is $\frac{1}{4}$ or 25%. Find the probability of answering, by chance:

    (a) Exactly 3 questions correctly   (b) No questions correctly

    (c) At least 8 correctly   (d) No more than 7 questions correctly

27. *Opinion Poll.* Mr. Austin and Mr. Moran are running for public office. A survey conducted just before the day of election indicates that 60% of the voters prefer Mr. Austin and 40% prefer Mr. Moran. If 8 people are chosen at random and asked their preference, find the probability that all 8 people will express a preference for Mr. Moran.

28. *Working Habits.* If 40% of the workers at a large factory bring their lunch each day, what is the probability that in a randomly selected sample of eight workers

    (a) Exactly two bring their lunch each day?

    (b) At least two bring their lunch each day?

    (c) No one brings lunch?

    (d) No more than three bring lunch each day?

29. What is the probability of obtaining 7's exactly two times in 5 rolls of 2 fair dice?

30. What is the probability of obtaining 11's exactly three times in 7 rolls of 2 fair dice?

31. *Quality Control.* Suppose that 5% of the items produced by a factory are defective. If 8 items are chosen at random, what is the probability that:

    (a) Exactly 1 is defective?   (b) Exactly 2 are defective?
    (c) At least 1 is defective?   (d) Less than 3 are defective?

32. *Opinion Polls.* Suppose that 60% of the voters intend to vote for a conservative candidate. What is the probability that a survey polling 8 people reveals that 3 or fewer intend to vote for a conservative candidate?

33. Assuming all sex distributions to be equally probable, what is the probability that a family with exactly 6 children will have 3 boys and 3 girls?

34. *Family Structure.* What is the probability that in a family of 7 children:

    (a) 4 will be girls?
    (b) At least 2 are girls?
    (c) At least 2 and not more than 4 are girls?

35. An experiment is performed four times, with 2 possible outcomes F (Failure) and S (Success) with probabilities $\frac{1}{4}$ and $\frac{3}{4}$, respectively.

    (a) Draw the tree diagram describing the experiment.
    (b) Calculate the probability of exactly 2 successes and 2 failures by using the tree diagram from part (a).
    (c) Verify your answer to part (b) by using formula (2).

36. *Batting Averages.* For a baseball player with a .250 batting average, what is the probability that the player will have at least 2 hits in four times at bat? What is the probability of at least 1 hit in four times at bat?

37. If the probability of hitting a target is $\frac{1}{5}$ and 10 shots are fired independently, what is the probability of the target being hit at least twice?

38. *Quality Control.* A television manufacturer tests a random sample of 15 picture tubes to determine whether any are defective. The probability that a picture tube is defective has been found from past experience to be .05.

    (a) What is the probability that there are no defective tubes in the sample?
    (b) What is the probability that more than 2 of the tubes are defective?

39. *True and False Tests.* In a 15 item true–false examination, what is the probability that a student who guesses on each question will get at least 10 correct answers? If another student has .8 probability of correctly answering each question, what is the probability that this student will answer at least 12 questions correctly?

40. What is the probability of obtaining exactly 3 tails if it is known that at least 1 tail appeared?

41. *Product Testing.* A supposed coffee connoisseur claims she can distinguish between a cup of instant coffee and a cup of percolator coffee 75% of the time. You give her 6 cups of coffee and tell her that you will grant her claim if she correctly identifies at least 5 of the 6 cups.

    (a) What are her chances of having her claim granted if she is in fact only guessing?
    (b) What are her chances of having her claim rejected when in fact she really does have the ability she claims?

42. *Opinion Polls.* Opinion polls based on small samples often yield misleading results. Suppose 65% of the people in a city are opposed to a bond issue and the others favor it. If 7 people are asked for their opinion, what is the probability that a majority of them will favor the bond issue?

43. There is a Hamming code of length 15 that corrects a single error. Assuming $p = .98$, find the probability that a message transmitted using this code will be correctly received.

44. There is a binary code of length 23 (called the Golay code) that can correct up to 3 errors. With $p = .98$, find the probability that a message transmitted using the Golay code will be correctly received.

45. What is the probability that the birthdays of 6 people fall in 2 calendar months, leaving exactly 10 months free? (Assume independent and equal probabilities for all months.)

46. A book of 500 pages contains 500 misprints. Estimate the chance that a given page contains at least 3 misprints.

47. In a Bernoulli trial with $p = \frac{1}{3}$, for what least value of n does the probability of exactly 2 successes have its only maximum value?

48. How many times should a fair coin be flipped in order to have the probability of at least 1 head appear to be greater than .98?

49. Prove the identity

$$b(n, k; p) = b(n, n - k; 1 - p)$$

[Hint: Refer to Example 4, page 343].

8.4 EXPECTATION

EXPECTED VALUE □ EXPECTED VALUE OF BERNOULLI TRIALS □ DERIVATION OF $E = np$

EXPECTED VALUE

An important concept, which has its origin in gambling and which uses probability, is *expected value.* For instance, gamblers are quite concerned with the *expectation,* or *expected value,* of a game. Suppose, for example, that 1000 tickets are printed and raffled off. Out of all these tickets one ticket has a cash value of $300, two are worth $100, and 100 are worth $1, while the remaining are worth $0. The *expected* (average) *value* of a ticket is then

$$E = \frac{\$300 + \$100 + \$100 + \$1 + \$1 + \cdots + \$1 + \$0 + \$0 + \cdots + \$0}{1000}$$

$$= \$300 \cdot \frac{1}{1000} + \$100 \cdot \frac{2}{1000} + \$1 \cdot \frac{100}{1000} + \$0 \cdot \frac{897}{1000}$$

$$= \frac{\$600}{\$1000} = \$0.60$$

Thus, if the raffle is to be nonprofit to all, the charge for each ticket should be $0.60. The result can also be viewed as saying that if we entered such a raffle many times, $\frac{1}{1000}$ of the time we would win $300, $\frac{2}{1000}$ of the time we would win $100, and so on, with our winnings in the long run averaging $0.60 per ticket.

As another example of expectation, suppose that you are to receive $3.00 each time you obtain 2 heads on a single toss of 2 coins and $0 otherwise. Then the *expected value* is

$$E = \$3.00 \cdot \frac{1}{4} + \$0 \cdot \frac{3}{4} = \$0.75$$

This means that you should be willing to pay $0.75 each time you toss the coins if the game is to be a fair one. We arrive at the expected value E by multiplying the amount earned for a given result of the toss times the probability for that toss to occur, and adding all the products.

Another example is a game consisting of flipping a single coin. If a head shows, the player loses $1; but if a tail shows, the player wins $2. Thus, half the time the player loses $1 and the other half the player wins $2. The expected value E of the game is

$$E = \$2 \cdot \frac{1}{2} + (-\$1) \cdot \frac{1}{2} = \frac{1}{2} = \$0.50$$

The player is expected to win an average of $0.50 on each play.

In each of the above examples, we have dealt with experiments involving payoffs (numerical values) and their corresponding probabilities. In the expression for the expected value in the raffle problem, the term $\$300 \cdot \frac{1}{1000}$ is the pairing of the value $300 with its corresponding probability $\frac{1}{1000}$, namely the probability of picking a $300 ticket. Likewise, the probability of getting a $1 ticket is $\frac{100}{1000}$ and this produces the term $\$1 \cdot \frac{100}{1000}$ in the expression for the expected value, E. So the expression for E is obtained by multiplying each ticket value by the probability of its occurrence and adding the results.

In the second example in the expressions for the expected value, the term $\$3.00 \cdot \frac{1}{4}$ is the pairing of the value $3.00 with its corresponding probability $\frac{1}{4}$, namely the probability of obtaining HH. Likewise the probability of getting HT, TH, and TT is $\frac{3}{4}$ with payoff 0, and this produces $\$0 \cdot \frac{3}{4}$ in the expression for the expected value.

Finally in the last example, in the expression for the expected value, the term $\$2 \cdot \frac{1}{2}$ is the pairing of the value $2.00 with its corresponding probability $\frac{1}{2}$, namely the probability of obtaining T. Likewise the probability of getting H is $\frac{1}{2}$ with payoff $-\$1$.

This leads to the following definition.

Expected Value* If an experiment has n outcomes that are assigned the payoffs $m_1, m_2, \ldots, m_n$ occurring with probabilities $p_1, p_2, \ldots, p_n$, respectively, then the expected value is given by

$$E = m_1 \cdot p_1 + m_2 \cdot p_2 + \cdots + m_n \cdot p_n$$

The term *expected value* should not be interpreted as a value that actually occurs in the experiment. For example, there was no raffle ticket paying $.60. Rather, it

---

* In more rigorous treatments, the assignment of numerical values to outcomes of an experiment is called a *random variable* and E is called the expected value or mean of the random variable.

represents the average value per experiment were we to repeat the experiment many times.

In gambling, for instance, E is interpreted as the average winnings expected for the player in the long run. If E is positive, we say that the game is *favorable* to the player; if $E = 0$, we say the game is *fair*; and if E is negative, we say the game is *unfavorable* to the player.

When the payoff assigned to an outcome of an experiment is positive, it can be interpreted as a profit, winnings, or gain. When it is negative, it represents losses, penalties, or deficits.

The following steps outline the general procedure involved in determining the expected value.

Steps to Compute Expectation

Step 1: Determine the sample space S, which describes the possible outcomes when the experiment is performed and assign an appropriate probability to each simple event in S.

Step 2: Determine the payoff values $m_1, m_2, \ldots, m_n$.

Step 3: Determine $p_1, p_2, \ldots, p_n$ for each payoff $m_1, m_2, \ldots, m_n$.

Step 4: Calculate $E = m_1 \cdot p_1 + m_2 \cdot p_2 + \cdots + m_n \cdot p_n$.

☐ **Example 1** What is the expected number of heads in tossing a fair coin three times?

Solution **Step 1:** The sample space is
$$S = \{HHH, HHT, HTH, HTT, THH, THT, TTH, TTT\}.$$

Step 2: A coin tossed three times can have 0, 1, 2 or 3 heads. We treat these values as payoffs.

Step 3: The probabilities corresponding to 0, 1, 2 or 3 heads in Step 2 are $\frac{1}{8}, \frac{3}{8}, \frac{3}{8}$, and $\frac{1}{8}$, respectively.

Step 4: The expected number of heads can now be found by multiplying each payoff by its corresponding probability and finding the sum of these values.

$$\text{Expected number of heads} = E = 0 \cdot \frac{1}{8} + 1 \cdot \frac{3}{8} + 2 \cdot \frac{3}{8} + 3 \cdot \frac{1}{8} = \frac{3}{2} = 1.5$$

Thus, on the average, tossing a coin three times will result in 1.5 heads. ☐

☐ **Example 2** Consider the experiment of rolling a fair die. The player recovers an amount of dollars equal to the number of dots on the face that turns up, except when face 5 or 6 turns up, in which case the player will lose $5 or $6, respectively. What is the expected value of the game?

Solution Since all faces are equally likely to occur, we assign a probability of $\frac{1}{6}$ to each of them.

The payoffs for the outcomes 1, 2, 3, 4, 5, 6 are, respectively, $1, $2, $3, $4, −$5, −$6. Steps 1, 2, and 3 are summarized in the following table.

Outcome	1	2	3	4	5	6
Probability	$\frac{1}{6}$	$\frac{1}{6}$	$\frac{1}{6}$	$\frac{1}{6}$	$\frac{1}{6}$	$\frac{1}{6}$
Payoff	$1	$2	$3	$4	−$5	−$6

Step 4: The expected value of the game is:

$$E = \$1 \cdot \frac{1}{6} + \$2 \cdot \frac{1}{6} + \$3 \cdot \frac{1}{6} + \$4 \cdot \frac{1}{6} + (-\$5) \cdot \frac{1}{6} + (-\$6) \cdot \frac{1}{6}$$

$$= -\$\frac{1}{6} = -16.7¢$$

The player would expect to lose an average of 16.7¢ on each throw. □

□ **Example 3** An oil company may bid for only one of two contracts for oil drilling in two different areas, I and II. It is estimated that a profit of $300,000 would be realized from the first field and $400,000 from the second field. Legal and other costs of bidding for the first oil field are $2500 and for the second are $5000. The probability of discovering oil in the first field is .60 and in the second is .70. The question is which oil field should the company bid for; that is, for which oil field is the expectation larger?

Solution In the first field, the company expects to discover oil .6 of the time at a gain of $300,000. Thus, it would not discover oil .4 of the time at a loss of $2500. The expectation E_{I} is therefore

$$E_{\mathrm{I}} = (\$300,000)(.6) + (-\$2500)(.4) = \$179,000$$

Similarly, for the second field, the expectation E_{II} is

$$E_{\mathrm{II}} = (\$400,000)(.7) + (-\$5000)(.3) = \$278,500$$

Since the expected value for the second field exceeds that for the first, the oil company should bid on the second field. □

□ **Example 4** A laboratory contains 10 electron microscopes, of which 2 are defective. If all microscopes are equally likely to be chosen and if 4 are chosen, what is the expected number of defective microscopes?

Solution The sample of 4 microscopes can contain 0, 1, or 2 defective microscopes. The probability p_0 that none in the sample is defective is

$$p_0 = \frac{\binom{2}{0}\binom{8}{4}}{\binom{10}{4}} = \frac{1}{3}$$

Similarly, the probabilities p_1 and p_2 for 1 and 2 defective microscopes are

$$p_1 = \frac{\binom{2}{1}\binom{8}{3}}{\binom{10}{4}} = \frac{8}{15} \quad \text{and} \quad p_2 = \frac{\binom{2}{2}\binom{8}{2}}{\binom{10}{4}} = \frac{2}{15}$$

Since we are interested in determining the expected number of defective microscopes, we assign a payoff of 0 to the outcome "0 defectives are selected," a payoff of 1 to the outcome "1 defective is chosen," and a payoff of 2 to the outcome "2 defectives are chosen." The expected value E is

$$E = 0 \cdot p_0 + 1 \cdot p_1 + 2 \cdot p_2 = \frac{8}{15} + \frac{4}{15} = \frac{4}{5}$$

Of course, we cannot have $\frac{4}{5}$ of a defective microscope. However, we can interpret this to mean that in the long run such a sample will average just under one defective microscope. □

We point out that $\frac{4}{5}$ is a reasonable answer for the expected number of defective microscopes since $\frac{1}{5}$ of the microscopes in the laboratory are defective and we are selecting a random sample consisting of four of these microscopes.

EXPECTED VALUE OF BERNOULLI TRIALS

In 100 tosses of a coin, what is the expected number of heads? If a student guesses at random on a true–false exam with 50 questions, what is her expected grade? These are specific instances of the following more general question:

In n trials of a Bernoulli process, what is the expected number of successes?

We now compute this expected value. As before, p denotes the probability of success on any individual trial.

If $n = 1$ (there is but one trial), then the expected number of successes is

$$E = 1 \cdot p + 0 \cdot (1 - p) = p$$

If $n = 2$ (two trials), then either 0, 1, or 2 successes can occur. Computing the probability of each, we get

$$E = 2 \cdot p^2 + 1 \cdot 2p(1 - p) + 0 \cdot (1 - p)^2 = 2p$$

This would seem to suggest that with n trials the expected value E would be given by $E = np$. This is indeed the case and we have the following result:

> In a Bernoulli process with n trials, the expected number of successes is
> $$E = np$$
> where p is the probability of success on any single trial.

A derivation of this result is included at the end of this section. The intuitive idea behind the result is fairly simple. Thinking of probabilities as percentages, if success results p percent of the time then out of n attempts p percent of them, namely np, should be successful.

□ **Example 5**   In flipping a fair coin five times, there are 6 possible outcomes: 0 tails, 1 tail, 2 tails, 3 tails, 4 tails, or 5 tails, each with the respective probabilities

$$\binom{5}{0}\left(\frac{1}{2}\right)^5, \binom{5}{1}\left(\frac{1}{2}\right)^5, \binom{5}{2}\left(\frac{1}{2}\right)^5, \binom{5}{3}\left(\frac{1}{2}\right)^5, \binom{5}{4}\left(\frac{1}{2}\right)^5, \binom{5}{5}\left(\frac{1}{2}\right)^5$$

The expected number of tails is

$$E = 0 \cdot \binom{5}{0}\left(\frac{1}{2}\right)^5 + 1 \cdot \binom{5}{1}\left(\frac{1}{2}\right)^5 + 2 \cdot \binom{5}{2}\left(\frac{1}{2}\right)^5$$

$$+ 3 \cdot \binom{5}{3}\left(\frac{1}{2}\right)^5 + 4 \cdot \binom{5}{4}\left(\frac{1}{2}\right)^5 + 5 \cdot \binom{5}{5}\left(\frac{1}{2}\right)^5 = \frac{5}{2}$$

Clearly, using the result $E = np$ is much easier, since for $n = 5$ and $p = \frac{1}{2}$, we obtain $E = (5)(\frac{1}{2}) = \frac{5}{2}$.   □

□ **Example 6**   In a true-false test with 100 questions, what is the expected number of correct answers if a person guesses on each question?

Solution   This is an example of a Bernoulli trial. The probability for success (a correct answer) when guessing is $p = \frac{1}{2}$. Since there are $n = 100$ questions, the expected number of correct answers is

$$E = np = (100)(\tfrac{1}{2}) = 50$$ □

DERIVATION OF $E = np$

The derivation is an exercise in handling binomial coefficients and using the Binomial Theorem. We will make use of the following identity:

$$k\binom{n}{k} = n\binom{n-1}{k-1} \tag{1}$$

This can be established by expanding both sides using the definition of a binomial coefficient. (See Problem 30, Exercise 8.4, page 366.)

Recall that the probability of obtaining exactly k successes in n trials is given by $b(n, k; p) = \binom{n}{k}p^k q^{n-k}$. Thus the expected number of successes is

$$E = 0 \cdot \binom{n}{0} p^0 q^n + 1 \cdot \binom{n}{1} p^1 q^{n-1} + 2 \cdot \binom{n}{2} p^2 q^{n-2} +$$

$$\cdots + k \underbrace{\binom{n}{k}}_{\substack{\text{No. of} \\ \text{successes}}} \underbrace{p^k q^{n-k}}_{\substack{\text{Corresponding} \\ \text{probability}}} + \cdots + n \binom{n}{n} p^n$$

Using (1) above,

$$E = n\binom{n-1}{0}pq^{n-1} + n\binom{n-1}{1}p^2q^{n-2} + \cdots$$

$$+ n\binom{n-1}{k-1}p^kq^{n-k} + \cdots + n\binom{n-1}{n-1}p^n$$

Now, factor out an n and a p from each of the terms on the right to get

$$E = np\left[\binom{n-1}{0}q^{n-1} + \binom{n-1}{1}pq^{n-2} + \cdots\right.$$

$$\left. + \binom{n-1}{k-1}p^{k-1}q^{(n-1)-(k-1)} + \cdots + \binom{n-1}{n-1}p^{n-1}\right]$$

The expression in brackets is $(p+q)^{n-1}$. To see why, use the binomial theorem. Thus,

$$E = np(p+q)^{n-1}$$

Since $p + q = 1$, the result $E = np$ follows.

Exercise 8.4   *Answers to Odd-Numbered Problems begin on page* 617.

1. For the data given below, compute the expected value.

Outcome	e_1	e_2	e_3	e_4
Probability	.4	.2	.1	.3
Payoff	2	3	-2	0

2. For the data below, compute the expected value.

Outcome	e_1	e_2	e_3	e_4
Probability	$\frac{1}{3}$	$\frac{1}{6}$	$\frac{1}{4}$	$\frac{1}{4}$
Payoff	1	0	4	-2

3. Attendance at a football game in a certain city results in the following pattern. If it is extremely cold, the attendance will be 35,000; if it is cold, it will be 40,000; if it is moderate, 48,000; and if it is warm, 60,000. If the probabilities for extremely cold, cold, moderate, and warm are .08, .42, .42, and .08, respectively, how many fans are expected to attend the game?

4. A player rolls a fair die and receives a number of dollars equal to the number of dots appearing on the face of the die. What is the least the player should expect to pay in order to play the game?

5. Mary will win $8 if she draws an ace from a set of 10 different cards from ace to 10. How much should she pay for one draw?

6. Thirteen playing cards, ace through king, are placed randomly with faces down on a table. The prize for guessing correctly the value of any given card is $1. What would be a fair price to pay for a guess?

7. David gets $10 if he throws a double on a single throw of a pair of dice. How much should he pay for a throw?

8. You pay a $1 to toss 2 coins. If you toss 2 heads, you get $2 (including your $1); if you toss only 1 head, you get back your $1; and if you toss no heads, you lose your $1. Is this a fair game to play?

9. *Raffles.* In a raffle, 1000 tickets are being sold at 60¢ each. The first prize is $100, and there are three second prizes of $50 each. By how much does the price of a ticket exceed its expected value?

10. *Raffles.* In a raffle, 1000 tickets are being sold at 60¢ each. The first prize is $100. There are two second prizes of $50 each, and five third prizes of $10 each (there are eight prizes in all). Laura buys one ticket. How much more than the expected value of the ticket does she pay?

11. A fair coin is tossed three times, and a player wins $3 if 3 tails occur, wins $2 if 2 tails occur, and loses $3 if no tails occur. If 1 tail occurs, no one wins.

    (a) What is the expected value of the game?

    (b) Is the game fair?

    (c) If the answer to part (b) is "No," how much should the player win or lose for a toss of exactly 1 tail to make the game fair?

12. Colleen bets $1 on a 2 digit number. She wins $75 if she draws her number from the set of all 2 digit numbers, {00, 01, 02, . . . , 99}; otherwise, she loses her $1.

    (a) Is this game fair to the player?

    (b) How much is Colleen expected to lose in a game?

13. Two teams, A and B, have played each other 14 times. Team A won 9 games, and team B won 5 games. They will play again next week. Bob offers to bet $6 on team A while you bet $4 on team B. The winner gets the $10. Is the bet fair to you in view of the past records of the two teams? Explain your answer.

14. A department store wants to sell 11 purses that cost them $41 each and 32 purses that cost them $9 each. If all purses are wrapped in 43 identical boxes and if each customer picks a box randomly, find:

    (a) Each customer's expectation.

    (b) The department store's expected profit if it charges $13 for each box.

15. Caryl draws a card from a deck of 52 cards. She receives 40¢ for a heart, 50¢ for an ace, and 90¢ for the ace of hearts. If the cost of a draw is 15¢, should she play the game? Explain.

16. *Family Size.* The following data give information about family size in the United States for a household in which the wife resides and the male head of household is in the 30–34 age bracket:

Number of Children	0	1	2	3
Proportion of Families	10.2%	15.9%	31.8%	42.1%

A family is chosen at random. Find the expected number of children in the family.

17. Assume that the odds for a certain race horse to win are 7 to 5. If a better receives $5 when the horse wins, how much should he bet when the horse loses to make the game fair?

18. In roulette, there are 38 equally likely possibilities: the numbers 1–36, 0, and 00 (double zero). See the figure. What is the expected value for a gambler who bets $1 on number 15 if she wins $35 each time the number 15 turns up and loses $1 if any other number turns up? If the gambler plays the number 15 for 200 consecutive times, what is the total expected gain?

19. *Site Selection.* A company operating a chain of supermarkets plans to open a new store in one of two locations. They conducted a survey of the two locations and estimated that the first location will show an annual profit of $15,000 if it is successful and a $3000 loss otherwise. For the second location, the estimated annual profit is $20,000 if successful and a $6000 loss results otherwise. The probability of success at each location is $\frac{1}{2}$. What location should the management decide on in order to maximize its expected profit?

20. For Problem 19 assume the probability of success at the first location is $\frac{2}{3}$ and at the second location is $\frac{1}{2}$. What location should be chosen?

21. Find the number of times the face 5 is expected to occur in a sequence of 2000 throws of a fair die.

22. What is the expected number of tails that will turn up if a fair coin is tossed 582 times?

23. A certain kind of light bulb has been found to have .02 probability of being defective. A shop owner receives 500 light bulbs of this kind. How many of these bulbs are expected to be defective?

24. A student enrolled in a Math course has .9 probability of passing the course. In a class of 20 students, how many would you expect to fail the Math course?

25. *Drug Reaction.* A doctor has found that the probability that a patient who is given a certain drug will have unfavorable reactions to the drug is .002. If a group of 500 patients is going to be given the drug, how many of them does the doctor expect to have unfavorable reactions?

26. A true–false test consisting of 30 questions is scored by subtracting the number of wrong answers from the number of right ones. Find the expected number of correct answers of a student who just guesses on each question. What will the test score be?

27. A coin is weighted so that $P(H) = \frac{1}{4}$ and $P(T) = \frac{3}{4}$. Find the expected number of tosses of the coin required in order to obtain either a head or 4 tails.

28. A box contains 3 defective bulbs and 9 good bulbs. If 5 bulbs are drawn from the box without replacement, what is the expected number of defective bulbs?

29. Prove that if the numerical values assigned to the outcomes of an experiment that has expected value E are all multiplied by the constant k, then the expected value of the new experiment is $k \cdot E$. Similarly, if to all the numerical values we add the same constant k, prove that the expected value of the new game is $E + k$.

30. Verify that $k\binom{n}{k} = n\binom{n-1}{k-1}$.

8.5 APPLICATIONS

OPERATIONS RESEARCH □ MODEL: SELECTING A MORTGAGE

OPERATIONS RESEARCH

The field of *operations research,* the science of making optimal or best decisions, has experienced remarkable growth and development since the 1940s. The purpose of this section is to introduce you to some examples from operations research that utilize the concept of expectation.

□ **Example 1**

Market Assessment

A national car rental agency rents cars for $16 per day (gasoline and mileage are additional expenses to the customer). The daily cost per car (for example, lease costs and overhead) is $6 per day. The daily profit to the company is $10 per car if the car is rented, and the company incurs a daily loss of $6 per car if the car is not rented. The daily profit depends on two factors: the demand for cars and the number of cars the company has available to rent. Previous rental records show that the daily demand is:

Number of customers	8	9	10	11	12
Probability	.10	.10	.30	.30	.20

Find the expected number of customers and determine the optimal number of cars the company should have available for rental. (This is the number that yields the largest expected profit.)

Solution

The expected number of customers is

$$8(.1) + 9(.1) + 10(.3) + 11(.3) + 12(.2) = 10.4$$

If 10.4 customers are expected, how many cars should be on hand? Surely, the number should not exceed 11, since fewer than 11 customers are expected. However, the number may not be the integer closest to 10.4, since costs play a major role in the determination of profit. We need to compute the expected profit for each possible number of cars. The largest expected profit will tell us how many cars to have on hand.

For example, if there are 10 cars available, the expected profit for 8, 9, or 10 customers is

$$68(.1) + 84(.1) + 100(.8) = \$95.20$$

We obtain the entry 68(.1) by noting that the 10 cars cost the company $60, and 8 cars rented with probability .10 bring in $128, for a profit of $68. Similarly, we obtain the entry 84(.1) by noting that the 10 cars cost the company $60, and 9 cars rented with probability .10 bring in $144, for a profit of $84. The entry 100(.8) is obtained since for 10 or more customers (probability $.3 + .3 + .2 = .8$) the profit is $10 \times \$16 - \$60 = \$100$.

The table lists the expected profit for 8 to 12 cars. Clearly, the optimal stock size is 11 cars, since this number of cars maximizes expected profit.

Number of cars	8	9	10	11	12
Expected profit	$80.00	$88.40	$95.20	$97.20	$94.40

□

□ **Example 2**
Quality Control

A factory produces electronic components, and each component must be tested. If the component is good, it will allow the passage of current; if the component is defective, it will block the passage of current. Let p denote the probability that a component is good. See Figure 2.

Figure 2

With this system of testing, a large number of components requires an equal number of tests. This increases the production cost of the electronic components since it requires one test per component. To reduce the number of tests, a quality control engineer proposes, instead, a new testing procedure: Connect the components pairwise in series, as shown in Figure 3.

Figure 3

If the current passes two components in series, then both components are good and only one test is required. The probability that two components are good is p^2. If the current does not pass, they must be sent individually to the quality control department, where each component is tested separately. In this case, three tests are required. The probability that three tests are needed is $1 - p^2$ (1 minus probability of success p^2). The expected number of tests for a pair of components is

$$E = 1 \cdot p^2 + 3 \cdot (1 - p^2) = p^2 + 3 - 3p^2 = 3 - 2p^2$$

The number of tests saved for a pair is

$$2 - (3 - 2p^2) = 2p^2 - 1$$

The number of tests saved per component is

$$\frac{2p^2 - 1}{2} = p^2 - \frac{1}{2} \text{ tests}$$

The greater the probability p that the component is good, the greater the saving. For example, if p is almost 1, we have a saving of almost $1 - \frac{1}{2}$ or $\frac{1}{2}$, which is 50% of the original number of tests needed. Of course, if p is small, say less than .7, we do not save anything since $(.7)^2 - \frac{1}{2}$ is less than 0, and we are wasting tests. □

If the reliability of the components manufactured in Example 2 is very high, it might even be advisable to make larger groups. Suppose three components are connected in series. See Figure 4.

Figure 4

For individual testing, we need three tests. For group testing, we have

1   test needed with probability p^3

4   tests needed with probability $1 - p^3$

The expected number of tests is

$$E = 1 \cdot p^3 + 4 \cdot (1 - p^3) = 4 - 3p^3 \text{ tests}$$

The number of tests saved per component is

$$\frac{3p^3 - 1}{3} = p^3 - \frac{1}{3} \text{ tests}$$

In a similar way we can show that if the components are arranged in groups of four connected in series, then the number of tests saved per component is

$$p^4 - \frac{1}{4} \text{ tests}$$

In general, for groups of n, the number of tests saved per component is

$$p^n - \frac{1}{n} \text{ tests}$$

Notice from the above formula that as n, the group size, gets very large, the number of tests saved per component gets very, very small.

To determine the optimal group size for $p = .9$, we refer to Table 1. From the table, we can see that the optimal group size is 4, resulting in a substantial saving of approximately 41%.

We also note that larger group sizes do not increase savings.

Table 1

Group Size	Expected Tests Saved per Component $p = .9$	Percent Saving
2	$p^2 - \frac{1}{2} = .81 - .50 = .31$	31
3	$p^3 - \frac{1}{3} = .729 - .333 = .396$	39.6
4	$p^4 - \frac{1}{4} = .6561 - .25 = .4061$	40.61
5	$p^5 - \frac{1}{5} = .59049 - .2 = .39049$	39.05
6	$p^6 - \frac{1}{6} = .531 - .167 = .364$	36.4
7	$p^7 - \frac{1}{7} = .478 - .143 = .335$	33.5
8	$p^8 - \frac{1}{8} = .430 - .125 = .305$	30.5

☐ **Example 3**   A $75,000 oil detector is lowered under the sea to detect oil fields, and it becomes detached from the ship. If the instrument is not found within 24 hours, it will crack under the pressure of the sea. It is assumed that a skin diver will find it with probability .85, but it costs $500 to hire him. How many skin divers should be hired?

Solution   Let's assume that x skin divers are hired. The probability that they will fail to discover the instrument is $.15^x$. Thus, the instrument will be found with probability $1 - .15^x$.

The expected gain from hiring the skin divers is

$$\$75,000(1 - .15^x) = \$75,000 - \$75,000(.15^x)$$

while the cost for hiring them is

$$\$500 \cdot x$$

Thus, the expected net gain, denoted by $E(x)$, is

$$E(x) = \$75,000 - \$75,000(.15^x) - \$500x$$

The problem is then to choose x so that $E(x)$ is maximum.

We begin by evaluating $E(x)$ for various values of x:

$$E(1) = \$75,000 - \$75,000(.15^1) - \$500(1) = \$63,250.00$$
$$E(2) = \$75,000 - \$75,000(.15^2) - \$500(2) = \$72,312.50$$
$$E(3) = \$75,000 - \$75,000(.15^3) - \$500(3) = \$73,246.88$$
$$E(4) = \$75,000 - \$75,000(.15^4) - \$500(4) = \$72,962.03$$
$$E(5) = \$75,000 - \$75,000(.15^5) - \$500(5) = \$72,494.30$$
$$E(6) = \$75,000 - \$75,000(.15^6) - \$500(6) = \$71,999.15$$

Thus, the expected net gain is optimal when 3 divers are hired. Notice that hiring additional skin divers does not necessarily increase expected net gain. In fact, the expected net gain declines if more than 3 divers are hired.   □

MODEL: SELECTING A MORTGAGE*

A couple plans to buy a condominium for investment purposes and has several types of mortgages to choose from, obviously aiming to pick one that is least costly to them. Their choices are:

1. A 3 year adjustable rate mortgage (ARM), where payments are fixed over the first three years of the mortgage and then the interest rate is adjusted triennially based on the Federal Reserve's three-year treasury (T) bill rates. We assume this is currently available to them at $12\frac{3}{4}\%$.
2. A 5 year ARM where an interest adjustment is made every fifth year based on the Federal Reserve's five-year T-bill rate. This is currently available for $13\frac{1}{8}\%$.
3. A conventional fixed rate mortgage at $14\frac{1}{8}\%$.

If interest rates on T-bills could be predicted with some certainty, then the couple's decision would be straightforward. Sadly, such is not the case, and it is precisely the variability of interest rates that must be built into any analysis of these mortgage choices.

The situation described above was considered by Luna and Reid in the article referenced below. They studied the variation in T-bill interest rates over a 30 year period and built a statistical model to estimate the probabilities of future interest rate

* Adapted from Robert E. Luna and Richard A. Reid, "Mortgage Selection Using a Decision Tree Approach," *Interfaces* **16**:3 (May–June 1986), pp. 73–81.

changes. Interest rate changes were divided into three types — a change to a low rate, a mean rate, or a high rate. They used their model to estimate what each of these changes would be, along with the probabilities of each happening. Based on their estimates, for example, a 3 year ARM currently at $12\frac{3}{4}\%$ would face the following probable readjustments at the end of the first three year period.

Current	Readjustment	Probability
	$18\frac{7}{8}$	.27
$12\frac{3}{4}$	$15\frac{3}{4}$	.46
	12	.27

The effect of these predictions on invested dollars was computed and a summary of this data is contained in Figure 5. The probability tree represents the cost per $1000

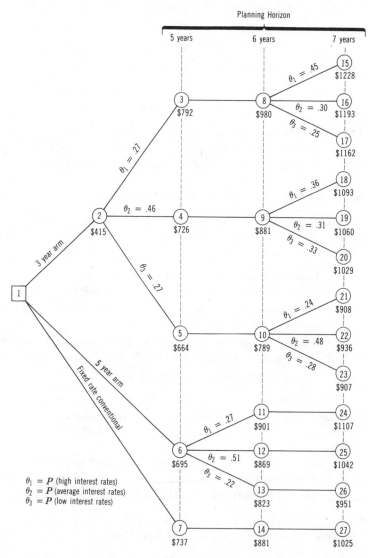

Figure 5

of a mortgage under various options over a period of seven years. The branches labeled θ_1, θ_2, θ_2 represent probabilities attached to readjustments to high, mean or low rates, respectively. The nodes represent accumulated mortgage costs at various times. For example, node 3 represents an incurred cost of $792 at the end of 5 years under a 3 year ARM that was readjusted using a high interest rate (and the assumed probability of that high rate is .27).

Which of the three mortgage options is best for the couple? One way to assess this would be to compute and compare the *expected costs* of each option. We do this for the 5 year ARM and compute expected cost at the end of 5, 6, and 7 years. Our information is drawn directly from Figure 5.

At the end of 5 years, the expected cost is $695.

At the end of 6 years, the expected cost is

$$.27 (\$901) + .51 (\$869) + .22 (\$823) = \$876.52$$

At the end of 7 years, the expected cost is

$$.27 (\$1107) + .51 (\$1042) + .22 (\$951) = \$1039.53$$

The same expected cost computations can be done for the other two types of mortgages. (Clearly, the fixed rate mortgage is by its nature very predictable.) The results, rounded to the nearest dollar, are recorded in the following table.

Type of Mortgage	5 years	6 years	7 years
3 year ARM	$727	$883	$1061
5 year ARM	695	868	1040
Conventional	737	881	1025

Thus, if the condominium is held for 5 or 6 years the 5 year ARM produces the lowest expected cost, though in the seventh year the conventional mortgage becomes more favorable.

It should be noted that this analysis is dependent heavily on assumptions regarding probabilities of interest rate fluctuations. Also, the averaging involved in expected value computations is perhaps more appropriate to a situation where a large number of similar mortgage choices have to be made rather than for one single choice. There are alternate criteria that could be used to distinguish options. One such choice, for example, would be to assume that in all instances the highest possible interest rates prevail and then to pick the mortgage type that with those assumptions produces the lowest cost. This "best of the worst" approach is called a *minimax* criterion.

Exercise 8.5 *Answers to Odd-Numbered Problems begin on page* 617.

1. *Market Assessment.* A car agency has fixed costs of $8 per car per day and the revenue for each car rented is $14 per day. The daily demand is given in the table:

Number of customers	7	8	9	10	11
Probability	.10	.20	.40	.20	.10

Find the expected number of customers. Determine the optimal number of cars the company should have on hand each day. What is the expected profit in this case?

2. In Example 2 in this section, suppose $p = .8$. Show that the optimal group size is 3.

3. In Example 2 in this section, suppose $p = .95$. Show that the optimal group size is 5.

4. In Example 2 in this section, suppose $p = .99$. Compute savings for group sizes 10, 11, and 12, and thus show that 11 is the optimal group size. Determine the percent saving.

5. In Example 3 in this section, suppose the probability of the skin divers discovering the instrument is .95. Find:

   (a) An equation expressing the net expected gain.

   (b) The number x of skin divers that maximizes the net gain.

6. An airline must decide which of two aircraft it will use on a flight from New York to Los Angeles. Aircraft A has a seating capacity of 200, while aircraft B has a capacity of 300. Previous experience has allowed the airline to estimate the number of passengers on the flight as follows:

No. of passengers	150	180	200	250	300
Probability	.2	.3	.2	.2	.1

Regardless of aircraft used, the cost of a ticket is $300, but there are different operating costs attached to each aircraft. There is a fixed cost (fuel, crew, etc.) of $6000 attached to using aircraft A, while aircraft B has a fixed cost of $8000. There is also a per passenger cost (meals, luggage, added fuel) of $120 for aircraft A and $130 for aircraft B.

Which aircraft should the airline schedule so that it maximizes its profit on the flight?

7. In the mortgage model, verify the computations for the expected cost of the 3 year ARM at the end of 5, 6, and 7 years.

8. In the mortgage model, make the assumption that, whenever an interest rate change is due, the highest rate will always go into effect. Under this assumption, compute the cost of

   (a) The 3 year ARM

   (b) The 5 year ARM

   at the end of 5, 6, and 7 years. Which is the better choice?

CHAPTER REVIEW

Important Terms	binomial theorem	Bernoulli trial	expected value
	binomial probability	expectation	

True-False Questions *(Answers are on page 618)*

T F 1. $2^n = \binom{n}{0} + \binom{n}{1} + \binom{n}{2} + \cdots + \binom{n}{n}$

T F 2. In the binomial expansion of $(x + 1)^7$, the coefficient of x^4 is 4.

T F 3. $b(n, k; p)$ gives the probability of exactly n trials in k successes.

T F 4. In flipping a fair coin 10 times, the expected number of trials is 5.

Fill in the Blanks

1. To expand an expression such as $(x + y)^n$ where n is a positive integer, we use the _____ _____.

2. Random experiments are called Bernoulli trials if:
   (a) The same experiment is repeated several times.
   (b) There are only two possible outcomes, success and failure.
   (c) The repeated trials are _____.
   (d) The probability of each outcome remains the _____ for each trial.

3. If an experiment has n outcomes that are assigned the payoffs $m_1, m_2, \ldots, m_n$, occurring with probabilities $p_1, p_2, \ldots, p_n$, then $E = m_1 p_1 + m_2 p_2 + \cdots + m_n p_n$ is the _____ _____.

Review Exercises

Answers to Odd-Numbered Problems begin on page 618 .

1. There are 5 rotten plums in a crate of 25 plums. How many samples of 4 of the 25 plums contain
   (a) Only good plums?
   (b) Three good plums and 1 rotten plum?
   (c) One or more rotten plum?

2. An admissions test given by a university contains 10 true–false questions. Eight or more of the questions must be answered correctly in order to be admitted.
   (a) How many different ways can the answer sheet be filled out?
   (b) How many different ways can the answer sheet be filled out so that 8 or more questions are answered correctly?

3. Management believes that 1 out of 5 people watching a television advertisement about their new product will purchase the product. Five people who watched the advertisement are picked at random. What is the probability that 0, 1, 2, 3, 4, or 5 of these people will purchase the product?

4. Suppose that the probability of a player hitting a home run is $\frac{1}{20}$. In five tries, what is the probability that the player hits at least 1 home run?

5. In a 12 item true–false examination:
   (a) What is the probability that a student will obtain all correct answers by chance if he or she is guessing?
   (b) If 7 correct answers constitute a passing grade, what is the probability that he or she will pass?
   (c) What are the odds in favor of passing?

6. In a 20 item true–false examination:
   (a) What is the probability that a student will obtain all correct answers by chance if he or she is guessing?
   (b) If 12 correct answers constitute a passing grade, what is the probability that he or she will pass?
   (c) What are the odds in favor of passing?

7. In a certain game, a player has the probability $\frac{1}{7}$ of winning a prize worth $89.99 and the probability $\frac{1}{3}$ of winning another prize worth $49.99. What is the expected cost of the game for the player?

8. Frank pays 70¢ to play a certain game. He draws 2 balls (together) from a bag containing 2 red balls and 4 green balls. He receives $1 for each red ball that he draws. If he draws no red balls, he loses his 70¢. Has he paid too much? By how much?

9. In a lottery, 1000 tickets are sold at 25¢ each. There are three cash prizes: $100, $50, and $30. Alice buys five tickets.

   (a) What would have been a fair price for a ticket?
   (b) How much extra did Alice pay?

10. The figure below shows a spinning game for which a person pays $0.30 to purchase an opportunity to spin the dial. The numbers in the figure indicate the amount of payoff and its corresponding probability. Find the expected value of this game. Is the game fair?

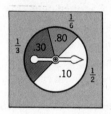

11. Consider the three boxes in the figure below. The game is played in two stages. The first stage is to choose a ball from Box A. If the result is a ball marked I, then we go to Box I, and select a ball from there. If the ball is marked II, then we select a ball from Box II. The number drawn on the second stage is the gain. Find the expected value of this game.

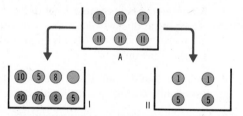

12. What is the expected number of heads that will turn up if a biased coin, $P(H) = \frac{1}{4}$, is tossed 200 times?

13. *European Roulette.* A European roulette wheel has only 37 compartments, 18 red, 18 black, and 1 green. A player will be paid $2 (including his $1 bet) if he picks correctly the color of the compartment in which the ball finally rests. Otherwise, he loses $1. Is the game fair to the player? Compare this answer to the answer obtained in Problem 18, Exercise 8.4.

14. *The Blood Testing Problem.** A group of 1000 people are subjected to a blood test that can be administered in two ways: (1) each person can be tested separately (in this case 1000 tests are required) or (2) the blood samples of 30 people can be pooled and analyzed together. If we use the second way and the test is negative, then one test suffices for 30

---

* William Feller, *An Introduction to Probability Theory and Its Applications,* 3rd ed., Wiley, New York, 1968, pp. 239–240.

people. If the test is positive, each of the 30 people can then be tested separately, and, in all, $30 + 1$ tests are required for the 30 people. Assume the probability p that the test is positive is the same for all people and that the people to be tested are independent.

(a) What is the probability that the test for a pooled sample of 30 people will be positive?

(b) What is the expected number of tests necessary under plan (2)?

15. What is the expected number of girls in families having exactly three children?

16. Find the probability of throwing an 11 at least three times in five throws of a pair of fair dice.

Mathematical Questions

From CPA and Actuary Exams (Answers on page 618 .)

1. *CPA Exam—May 1975*
The Stat Company wants more information on the demand for its products. The following data are relevant:

Units Demanded	Probability of Unit Demand	Total Cost of Units Demanded
0	.10	$0
1	.15	1.00
2	.20	2.00
3	.40	3.00
4	.10	4.00
5	.05	5.00

What is the total expected value or payoff with perfect information?

(a) $2.40   (b) $7.40   (c) $9.00   (d) $9.15

2. *CPA Exam—May 1976*
Your client wants your advice on which of two alternatives he should choose. One alternative is to sell an investment now for $10,000. Another alternative is to hold the investment 3 days after which he can sell it for a certain selling price based on the following probabilities:

Selling Price	Probability
$5,000	.4
$8,000	.2
$12,000	.3
$30,000	.1

Using probability theory, which of the following is the most reasonable statement?

(a) Hold the investment 3 days because the expected value of holding exceeds the current selling price.

(b) Hold the investment 3 days because of the chance of getting $30,000 for it.

(c) Sell the investment now because the current selling price exceeds the expected value of holding.

(d) Sell the investment now because there is a 60% chance that the selling price will fall in 3 days.

3. *CPA Exam—May 1979*

The Polly Company wishes to determine the amount of safety stock that it should maintain for Product D that will result in the lowest cost.

The following information is available:

Stockout cost	$80 per occurrence
Carrying cost of safety stock	$2 per unit
Number of purchase orders	5 per year

The available options open to Polly are as follows:

Units of Safety Stock	10	20	30	40	50	55
Probability	50%	40%	30%	20%	10%	5%

The number of units of safety stock that will result in the lowest cost are:

(a) 20   (b) 40   (c) 50   (d) 55

4. *CPA Exam—December 1977*

The ARC Radio Company is trying to decide whether to introduce as a new product a wrist "radiowatch" designed for shortwave reception of exact time as broadcast by the National Bureau of Standards. The "radiowatch" would be priced at $60, which is exactly twice the variable cost per unit to manufacture and sell it. The incremental fixed costs necessitated by introducing this new product would amount to $240,000 per year. Subjective estimates of the probable demand for the product are shown in the following probability distribution:

Annual Demand	6,000	8,000	10,000	12,000	14,000	16,000
Probability	.2	.2	.2	.2	.1	.1

The expected value of demand for new product is

(a) 11,000 units
(b) 10,200 units
(c) 9,000 units
(d) 10,600 units
(e) 9,800 units

5. *CPA Exam—May 1982*

In planning its budget for the coming year, King Company prepared the following payoff probability distribution describing the relative likelihood of monthly sales volume levels and related contribution margins for product A:

Monthly Sales Volume	Contribution Margin	Probability
4,000	$ 80,000	.20
6,000	120,000	.25
8,000	160,000	.30
10,000	200,000	.15
12,000	240,000	.10

What is the expected value of the monthly contribution margin for product A?

(a) $140,000
(b) $148,000
(c) $160,000
(d) $180,000

6. *CPA Exam — December 1983*

A decision tree has been formulated for the possible outcomes of introducing a new product line.

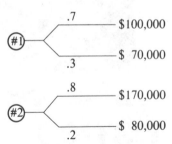

Branches related to Alternative 1 reflect the possible payoffs from introducing the product without an advertising campaign. The branches for Alternative 2 reflect the possible payoffs with an advertising campaign costing $40,000. The expected values of Alternatives 1 and 2, respectively, are

(a) #1: $(.7 \times \$100,000) + (.3 \times \$70,000)$
    #2: $(.8 \times \$170,000) + (.2 \times \$80,000)$

(b) #1: $(.7 \times \$100,000) + (.3 \times \$70,000)$
    #2: $(.8 \times \$130,000) + (.2 \times \$40,000)$

(c) #1: $(.7 \times \$100,000) + (.3 \times \$70,000)$
    #2: $(.8 \times \$170,000) + (.2 \times \$80,000) - \$40,000$

(d) #1: $(.7 \times \$100,000) + (.3 \times \$70,000) - \$40,000$
    #2: $(.8 \times \$170,000) + (.2 \times \$80,000) - \$40,000$

7. *CPA Exam — December 1983*

A battery manufacturer warrants its automobile batteries to perform satisfactorily for as long as the owner keeps the car. Auto industry data show that only 20% of car buyers retain their cars for three years or more. Historical data suggest

Number of Years Owned	Probability of Battery Failure	Battery Exchange Costs	Percentage of Failed Batteries Returned
Less than 3 years	0.4	$50	75%
3 years or more	0.6	$20	50%

If 50,000 batteries were sold this year, what is the estimated warranty cost?

(a) $375,000   (b) $435,000
(c) $500,000   (d) $660,000

8. *Actuary Exam — Part II*

What is the probability that 10 independent tosses of an unbiased coin result in no fewer than 1 head and no more than 9 heads?

(a) $(\frac{1}{2})^9$ (b) $1 - 11(\frac{1}{2})^9$ (c) $1 - 11(\frac{1}{2})^{10}$ (d) $1 - (\frac{1}{2})^9$
(e) $1 - (\frac{1}{2})^{10}$

STATISTICS

9.1 INTRODUCTORY REMARKS

*S*tatistics is the science of collecting, organizing, analyzing, and interpreting numerical facts. By making observations, statisticians obtain *data* in the form of measurements or counts. The *organization of data* involves the presentation of the collected measurements or counts in a form suitable for determining logical conclusions. Usually, tables or graphs are used to represent the collected data. The *analysis of data* is the process of extracting, from given measurements or counts, related and relevant information from which a brief numerical description can be formulated. In this process we use concepts known as the *mean, median, range, variance,* and *standard deviation.* By *interpretation of data* we mean the art of drawing conclusions from the analysis of the data. This involves the formulation of predictions concerning a large collection of objects based on the information available from a small collection of similar objects.

In collecting data concerning varied characteristics, it is often impossible or impractical to observe an entire group. Instead of examining an entire group, called the *population,* a small segment, called the *sample,* is chosen. It would be difficult, for example, to question all cigarette smokers in order to study the effects of smoking. Therefore, appropriate samples of smokers are usually selected for questioning.

The method of selecting the sample is extremely important if we want the results to be reliable. All members of the population under investigation should have an equal probability of being selected; otherwise, a *biased sample* could result. For example, if we want to study the relationship between smoking cigarettes and lung cancer, we cannot choose a sample of smokers who all live in the same location. The individuals chosen might have dozens of characteristics peculiar to their area, which would give a false impression with regard to all smokers.

As an example, suppose we want to study the effects of drugs on youths. If we decide to choose a sample from a group of students at a specific university or from a group of youths in a ghetto, we will get a biased sample, since university students and ghetto youths may be heavy users of drugs. It would be more appropriate to arrange the sample so that all members of the population under investigation have an equal probability of being selected.

Samples collected in such a way that each selection is equally likely to be chosen are called *random samples.* Of course, there are many random samples that can be chosen from a population. By combining the results of more than one random sample of a population, it is possible to obtain a more accurate representation of the population.

If a sample is representative of a population, important conclusions about the population can often be inferred from analysis of the sample. The phase of statistics dealing with conditions under which such inference is valid is called *inductive statistics* or *statistical inference.* Since such inference cannot be absolutely certain, the language of probability is often used in stating conclusions. Thus, when a meteorologist makes a forecast, weather data collected over a large region are studied, and based on this study, the weather forecast is given in terms of chances. A typical forecast might be "There is a 20% possibility for rain tomorrow."

Margin notes:
Organization of Data
Analysis of Data
Population
Sample
Random Sample
Inductive Statistics

To summarize, in statistics we are interested in four principles: gathering data or information, organizing it, analyzing it, and interpreting it.

In gathering data or in choosing a random sample it is important to:

1. Describe the method for choosing the sample clearly and carefully.
2. Choose the sample so that it is random, that is, so that it is dependable and not subject to personal choice or bias.

□ **Example 1**   Suppose television tubes on an assembly line pass an inspection, and suppose it is desired to test on the average one out of four tubes. If the test is to be performed in a random fashion, how should the inspection proceed?

Solution   To remove any personal choice on the part of the inspector, 2 fair coins can be flipped. Then, whenever 2 tails appear (probability $\frac{1}{4}$), the inspector can select a tube for testing.

□

Exercise 9.1   *Answers to Odd-Numbered Problems begin on page* 618 .

In Problems 1–6 list some possible ways to choose random samples for each study.

1. A study to determine opinion about a certain television program.
2. A study to detect defective radio resistors.
3. A study of the opinions of people toward Medicare.
4. A study to determine opinions about an election of a United States president.
5. A study of the number of savings accounts per family in the United States.
6. A national study of the monthly budget for a family of 4.
7. The following is an example of a biased sample: In a study of political party preferences, poorly dressed interviewers obtained a significantly greater proportion of answers favoring Democratic party candidates in their samples than did their well-dressed and wealthier-looking counterparts. Give two more examples of biased samples.
8. In a study of the number of savings accounts per family, a sample of accounts totaling less than $10,000 was taken, and, from the owners of these accounts, information about the total number of accounts owned by all family members was obtained. Criticize this sample.
9. It is customary for newsreporters to sample the opinions of a few people to find out how the population at large feels about the events of the day. A reporter questions people on a downtown street corner. Is there anything wrong with such an approach?
10. In 1936 the Literary Digest conducted a poll to predict the presidential election. Based on its poll it predicted the election of Landon over Roosevelt. In the actual election, Roosevelt won. The sample was taken by drawing the mailing list from telephone directories and lists of car owners. What was wrong with the sample?

9.2 ORGANIZATION OF DATA

FREQUENCY TABLE ☐ HISTOGRAM ☐ FREQUENCY POLYGON
☐ CUMULATIVE FREQUENCY DISTRIBUTION

Quite often a study results in a collection of large masses of data. If the data are to be understood and, at the same time, effective, they must be summarized in some manner. Two methods of presenting data are in common use. One method involves a summarized presentation of the numbers themselves according to order in a tabular form; the other involves presenting the quantitative data in pictorial form, such as by using graphs or diagrams.

☐ **Example 1** Suppose a random sample of 71 children from a group of 10,000 indicate their weight measurements, as shown in Table 1:

Table 1
Weight Measurements of 71 Students, in Pounds

69	71	71	55	52	55	58	58	58	62	67	94
82	94	95	89	89	104	93	93	58	62	67	62
94	85	92	75	75	79	75	82	94	105	115	104
105	109	94	92	89	85	85	89	95	92	105	71
72	72	79	79	85	72	79	119	89	72	72	69
79	79	69	93	85	93	79	85	85	69	79	

Certain information available from the sample becomes more evident once the data are ordered according to some scheme. If the 71 measurements are written in order of magnitude, we obtain Table 2:

Table 2

52	55	55	58	58	58	58	62	62	62	67	67
69	69	69	69	71	71	71	72	72	72	72	72
75	75	75	79	79	79	79	79	79	79	79	82
82	85	85	85	85	85	85	85	89	89	89	89
89	92	92	92	93	93	93	93	94	94	94	94
94	95	95	104	104	105	105	105	109	115	119	

☐

FREQUENCY TABLE

The data in Table 2 can be presented in a so-called *frequency table*. This is done as follows: Tally marks are used to record the occurrence of the respective scores. Then the *frequency f* with which each score occurs can be determined. In doing this, further information may become evident. See Table 3.

Table 3

Score	Tally	Frequency, f	Score	Tally	Frequency, f
119	/	1	82	//	2
115	/	1	79	ʇʜʇ ///	8
109	/	1	75	///	3
105	///	3	72	ʇʜʇ	5
104	//	2	71	///	3
95	//	2	69	////	4
94	ʇʜʇ	5	67	//	2
93	////	4	62	///	3
92	///	3	58	////	4
89	ʇʜʇ	5	55	//	2
85	ʇʜʇ //	7	52	/	1

Line Chart   A graph representation of the same data may be presented in a *line chart,* which is obtained in the following way: If we let the vertical axis denote the frequency f and the horizontal axis denote the score data, we obtain the graph shown in Figure 1.

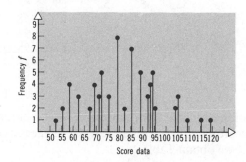

Figure 1

In studying data, a distinction should be made as to whether the data are *discrete* or *continuous.*

Variable; Continuous Variable; Discrete Variable   A measurable characteristic is called a *variable.* If a variable can assume any real value between certain limits, it is called a *continuous variable.* It is called a *discrete variable* if it can assume only a finite set of values or as many values as there are whole numbers.

Examples of continuous variables are weight, height, length, time, etc. Examples of discrete variables are the number of votes a candidate gets, number of cars sold, etc.

□ **Example 2**   A random sample of 71 children from a group of 10,000 indicate their weight measurements, as shown in Table 4 (these are the data from Table 2, but measured more accurately).

Table 4

52.30	55.61	55.71	58.01	58.41	58.51	58.91	62.33	62.50	62.71
67.13	67.23	69.51	69.67	69.80	69.82	71.34	71.65	71.83	72.15
72.22	72.41	72.59	72.67	75.11	75.71	75.82	79.03	79.06	79.09
79.15	79.28	79.32	79.51	79.62	82.32	82.61	85.09	85.13	85.25
85.31	85.41	85.51	85.58	89.21	89.32	89.49	89.61	89.78	92.41
92.63	92.89	93.05	93.19	93.28	93.91	94.17	94.28	94.31	94.52
94.71	95.32	95.51	104.31	104.71	105.21	105.37	105.71	109.34	115.71
119.38									

The data in Table 4 illustrate an example of a continuous variable, whereas the data given in Table 1 are discrete. The difference is in the accuracy of the measuring device.   □

Raw Data   The data in Table 4 are ordered, but are still considered to be *raw data* because they have not yet been subjected to any kind of statistical treatment. To begin to classify the raw data, two decisions must be made:

1. We have to decide on the *number of classes* into which the data are to be grouped.
2. We must decide on the *range of values* each class is to cover.

In grouping any data, experience indicates that we should seldom use fewer than six classes or more than twenty classes. This is, of course, not a firm rule and there are exceptions to it.

The size of each class depends to a large extent on the nature of the data, and above all, on the actual number of items within each class. For the data in Table 4, the smallest value is 52.30 and the largest value is 119.38. In order to use all the data, we have to cover the interval from 52.30 to 119.38.

Range The *range* of a set of numbers is the difference between the largest and the smallest value in the data under consideration. Thus,

$$\text{Range} = (\text{Largest value}) - (\text{Smallest value})$$

For the weight measurements of Example 2, the range is

$$119.38 - 52.30 = 67.08$$

HISTOGRAM

Class Interval
Class Limit

Now, we would like to present the data in Table 4 in the form of a graph called a *histogram*. To do this, we must first determine the *class intervals* and the *class limits*. The class intervals for our data will be obtained by dividing the range into equal intervals. Tables 5 and 6 show the use of two different class intervals — one of size 5 and the other of size 10. In choosing intervals of size 5 and 10, we will be able to cover all the scores.

Lower Class Limit
Upper Class Limit

The intervals given in column 2 of Tables 5 and 6 are called *class intervals.* Numbers such as 49.995–59.995 are called *class limits:* 49.995 is the *lower class limit* and 59.995 is the *upper class limit* for the class interval. To avoid confusion, we will always use one decimal place more for class limits than appears in the raw data. Thus, for our data, we choose the class intervals 114.995–119.995, 109.995–114.995, and so on, so that each score could be assigned to one and only one class interval. In performing arithmetic computations with the class limits, we will use the nearest integer value instead of the actual value.

Notice that once raw data are converted to grouped data, it is impossible to retrieve or recover the original data from the frequency table. The best we can do is to choose the midpoint of each class interval as a representative for each class. In Table 5, for example, the actual scores of 105.21, 105.37, 105.71, and 109.34 are viewed as being represented by the midpoint of the class interval 104.995–109.995, namely, $(105 + 110)/2 = 107.500$.

Table 5

Class	Class Interval	Tally	Frequency
14	114.995–119.995	//	2
13	109.995–114.995		0
12	104.995–109.995	////	4
11	99.995–104.995	//	2
10	94.995– 99.995	//	2
9	89.995– 94.995	7HL 7HL //	12
8	84.995– 89.995	7HL 7HL //	12
7	79.995– 84.995	//	2
6	74.995– 79.995	7HL 7HL /	11
5	69.995– 74.995	7HL ///	8
4	64.995– 69.995	7HL /	6
3	59.995– 64.995	///	3
2	54.995– 59.995	7HL /	6
1	49.995– 54.995	/	1

Table 6

Class	Class Interval	Tally	Frequency
7	109.995–119.995	//	2
6	99.995–109.995	7HL /	6
5	89.995– 99.995	7HL 7HL ////	14
4	79.995– 89.995	7HL 7HL ////	14
3	69.995– 79.995	7HL 7HL 7HL ////	19
2	59.995– 69.995	7HL ////	9
1	49.995– 59.995	7HL //	7

To build a histogram for the data in Table 6, we construct a set of rectangles having as a base the size of the class interval and as height the frequency of occurrence of data in that particular interval. The center of the base is the mid-point of each class interval. See Figure 2.

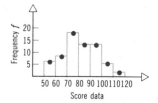

Figure 2

FREQUENCY POLYGON

If we connect all the midpoints of the tops of the rectangles in Figure 2, we obtain a line graph called a *frequency polygon*. (In order not to leave the graph hanging, we always connect it to the horizontal axis on both sides.) See Figure 3.

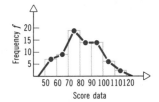

Figure 3

Sometimes it is useful to learn how many cases fall below (or above) a certain value. For the data of Table 6, we may want to know how many students had weights less than 99.995 or less than 69.995 (or how many had weights more than 59.995 or more than 99.995). If this is the case, we can convert the data as follows: Start at the lowest class interval (49.995–59.995) and note how many scores are below the upper limit of this interval. The number is 7. So we write 7 in the column labeled cf of Table 7 in the row for 49.995–59.995. Next, we ask how many scores fall below the upper

Table 7

Class Interval	Tally	f	cf
109.995–119.995	//	2	71
99.995–109.995	//// /	6	69
89.995– 99.995	//// //// ////	14	63
79.995– 89.995	//// //// ////	14	49
69.995– 79.995	//// //// //// ////	19	35
59.995– 69.995	//// ////	9	16
49.995– 59.995	//// //	7	7

limit of the next class interval (59.995–69.995); that is, how many scores are below 69.995? The answer is $7 + 9 = 16$. The process is continued upward. The top entry of the last column should agree with the total number of scores in the sample. The numbers in this column are called the *cumulative (less than) frequencies*.

Cumulative
Frequency

CUMULATIVE FREQUENCY DISTRIBUTION

The graph in which the horizontal axis represents class intervals and the vertical axis represents cumulative frequencies is called the *cumulative (less than) frequency distribution.* See Figure 4 for the cumulative frequency distribution for the data from Table 7. Notice that the points obtained are connected by lines in order to aid interpretation of the graph.

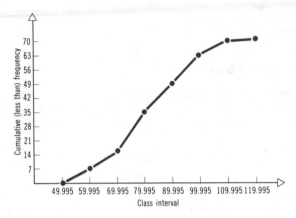

Figure 4

In a similar manner, the *cumulative (more than) frequency distribution* can be obtained.

Exercise 9.2 *Answers to Odd-Numbered Problems begin on page* 619.

1. Consider the data given in the table.

Votes Cast	Number of Precincts
600–649	1
550–599	9
500–549	26
450–499	48
400–449	67
350–399	104
300–349	150
250–299	190
200–249	120
150–199	33
100–149	4
50–99	1
	Total: 753

Distribution of Cleveland Voting Precincts according to total vote cast for governor.

SOURCE: *Ohio Election Statistics,* 1932, pp. 218–242.

With reference to this table, determine the following:

(a)   The lower limit of the fifth class
(b)   The upper limit of the fourth class
(c)   The midpoint of the fifth class
(d)   The size of the fifth interval
(e)   The frequency of the third class
(f)   The class interval having the largest frequency
(g)   The number of precincts with less than 600 votes
(h)   Construct the histogram
(i)   Construct the frequency polygon

2. The following scores were made on a 53-item test:

25	30	34	37	41	42	46	49	53
26	31	34	37	41	42	46	50	53
28	31	35	37	41	43	47	51	54
29	32	36	38	41	44	48	52	54
30	33	36	39	41	44	48	52	55
30	33	37	40	42	45	48	52	

(a) Set up a frequency table for the above data. What is the range?

(b) Draw a line chart for the data.

(c) Draw a histogram for the data using a class interval of size 2.

(d) Draw the frequency polygon for this histogram.

(e) Find the cumulative (less than) frequencies.

(f) Draw the cumulative (less than) frequency distribution.

(g) Find the cumulative (more than) frequencies.

(h) Draw the cumulative (more than) frequency distribution.

3. For Table 5 in the text:

(a) Draw a line chart.

(b) Draw a histogram.

(c) Draw the frequency polygon.

(d) Find the cumulative (less than) frequencies.

(e) Draw the cumulative (less than) frequency distribution.

4. *Commercial Bank Earnings.* According to the *Fortune Directory* (June 15, 1967), the following are the earnings of the 50 largest commercial banks in the United States (as percentage of capital funds for the year 1966):

12.2	9.9	11.2	12.5	9.8
11.5	11.8	11.1	12.3	10.1
11.4	9.2	12.8	9.8	12.6
9.9	10.2	12.6	14.4	10.9
10.2	10.3	11.6	10.2	13.1
10.4	10.9	8.4	14.6	13.4
12.3	11.4	9.2	12.8	11.0
11.2	10.9	10.1	10.9	12.9
11.2	13.2	10.2	16.0	13.6
10.9	11.4	11.6	11.7	13.0

Answer the same questions as in Problem 2, using a class interval of 0.5 beginning with 8.05.

5. *Number of Physicians.* The following are the number of physicians per 100,000 population in 110 selected large American cities in 1962 (*Statistical Abstract of the United States,* 1967):

131	245	145	129	155	232	256	204	296	222
185	166	198	127	153	230	175	161	240	169
169	158	116	171	111	152	126	140	218	142
141	116	176	127	156	185	207	218	153	128

176	162	100	138	129	211	178	198	132	289
165	129	137	78	146	148	145	146	161	119
119	116	245	137	95	169	131	156	136	122
194	113	184	132	172	91	110	188	185	144
105	166	154	108	144	202	212	190	165	128
131	157	115	153	127	224	171	154	149	112
134	190	130	192	123	224	131	190	136	123

Answer the same questions as in Problem 2, using a class interval of 10 beginning with 70.5.

9.3 MEASURES OF CENTRAL TENDENCY

MEAN □ MEDIAN □ MODE

Average
The idea of taking an *average* is familiar to practically everyone. Quite often we hear people talk about average salary, average height, average grade, average family, and so on. However, the idea of averages is so commonly used that it should not surprise you to learn that several kinds of averages have been introduced in statistics.

MEAN

Averages are called *measures of central tendency.* The three most common measures of central tendency are the *arithmetic mean, median,* and *mode.*

Mean The *arithmetic mean,* or *mean,* of a set of real numbers $x_1, x_2, \ldots, x_n$ is denoted by $\overline{X}$ and is defined as

$$\overline{X} = \frac{x_1 + x_2 + \cdots + x_n}{n} \tag{1}$$

□ **Example 1**
The grades of a student on eight examinations were 70, 65, 69, 85, 94, 62, 79, and 100. Find the mean.

Solution
In this example, $n = 8$. The mean of this set of grades is

$$\overline{X} = \frac{70 + 65 + 69 + 85 + 94 + 62 + 79 + 100}{8} = 78$$

□

An interesting fact about the mean is that the sum of deviations of each item from the mean is zero. In Example 1, the deviation of each score from the mean $\overline{X} = 78$ is $(100 - 78)$, $(94 - 78)$, $(85 - 78)$, $(79 - 78)$, $(70 - 78)$, $(69 - 78)$, $(65 - 78)$, and

$(62 - 78)$. Table 8 lists each score, the mean, and the deviation from the mean. If we add up the deviations from the mean, we obtain a sum of zero.

Table 8

Score	Mean	Deviation from Mean
100	78	22
94	78	16
85	78	7
79	78	1
70	78	-8
69	78	-9
65	78	-13
62	78	-16
		Sum of Deviations: 0

For any group of data, the following result is true:

The sum of the deviations from the mean is zero.

As a matter of fact, we could have defined the mean as that real number for which the sum of the deviations is zero.

Another interesting fact about the mean is that if Y is any guessed or assumed mean (which may be any real number) and if we let d_j denote the deviation of each item of the data from the assumed mean, $(d_j = x_j - Y)$, then the actual mean is

$$\overline{X} = Y + \frac{d_1 + d_2 + \cdots d_n}{n} \tag{2}$$

Consider Example 1. We know that the actual mean is 78. Suppose we had guessed the mean to be 52. Then, using formula (2), we obtain

$$\overline{X} = 52 + \frac{\begin{array}{c}(100 - 52) + (94 - 52) + (85 - 52) + (79 - 52)\\ + (70 - 52) + (69 - 52) + (65 - 52) + (62 - 52)\end{array}}{8}$$

$$= 52 + 26 = 78$$

which agrees with what we have already found.

The purpose of introducing equation (2) to find the mean is that, if the numbers to be added in finding the mean are large, (2) can simplify the computation.

A method for computing the mean for grouped data given in a frequency table is illustrated here by the use of an example.

□ **Example 2**   Find the mean for the grouped data given in Table 6.

Solution
1. Take the midpoint (m_i) of each of the intervals as a reference point and enter the result in column 3 of Table 9. For example, the midpoint of the interval 79.995–89.995 is 85.
2. Next, multiply the entry in column 3 by the frequency f_i for that class interval and enter the product in column 4, which is labeled $f_i m_i$.
3. Add the entries in column 4.

The mean is then computed by dividing the sum by the number of entries. That is,

$$\overline{X} = \frac{\Sigma f_i m_i}{n} \qquad (3)$$

where

Σ means to add up the entries

$f_i = $ Number of entries in the ith class interval

$m_i = $ Midpoint of ith class interval

$n = $ Number of items

Table 9 displays the information needed to complete the example.

Table 9

Class Interval	f_i	m_i	$f_i m_i$
109.995–119.995	2	115	230
99.995–109.995	6	105	630
89.995– 99.995	14	95	1330
79.995– 89.995	14	85	1190
69.995– 79.995	19	75	1425
59.995– 69.995	9	65	585
49.995– 59.995	7	55	385
$n = 71$			$5775 = $ Sum of $f_i m_i$

Now we can use the data in Table 9 and equation (3) to find the mean:

$$\overline{X} = \frac{5775}{71} = 81.34$$

□

MEDIAN

When data is grouped, the original data are lost due to grouping. As a result, the number obtained by using equation (3) is only an approximation to the actual mean. The reason for this is that using (3) amounts to computing the weighted average midpoint of a class interval (weighted by the frequency of scores in that interval) and therefore cannot be a computation for $\overline{X}$ exactly.

Median The *median* of a set of real numbers arranged in order of magnitude is the **middle value if the number of items is odd, and it is the mean of the two middle values if the number of items is even.**

□ **Example 3**   (a)   The group of data 2, 2, 3, 4, 5, 7, 7, 7, 11 has median 5.

(b)   The group of data 2, 2, 3, 3, 4, 5, 7, 7, 7, 11 has median 4.5, since

$$\frac{4+5}{2} = 4.5$$

□

To find the median for the grouped data in Table 6, page 384, we proceed as follows: The median is that point in the data that will have 50% of the cases above it and 50% below it. Now, 50% of 71 cases is 35.5 cases, so we are interested in finding the point in the distribution with 35 cases above it and 35 below it.

We start by counting up from the bottom until we come as close to 35 cases as possible, but not exceeding it. This brings us through the interval 69.995–79.995. Thus, the median must lie in the interval 79.995–89.995. Now, the median will equal

Interpolation Factor   the lower limit of the interval 79.995–89.995, namely 79.995, plus an *interpolation factor*. The interpolation factor is determined as follows:

1. Count the number p of entries or fractional entries needed to reach the median (in our example, the number is 0.5).

2. If the frequency for the interval is q, divide the interval into q parts.

3. The interpolation factor I is

$$I = \frac{p}{q} \cdot i$$

where

$$p = \text{Number of entries needed to reach the median}$$
$$q = \text{Number of entries in the interval}$$
$$i = \text{Size of the interval}$$

The median M is then given by

$$M = (\text{Lower limit of interval}) + (\text{Interpolation factor})$$

For the data of Table 6, the median M is

$$M = 79.995 + \frac{0.5}{14} \cdot 10 = 80.352$$

Again, keep in mind that this median is an approximation to the actual median, since it is obtained from grouped data. If we go back to the original data listed in Table 4, we obtain $M = 82.32$.

Centile Point   The median is sometimes called the *centile point* and is denoted by C_{50} to indicate that 50% of the data are below it and 50% are above it. Similarly, we can find C_{25}, or the first quartile, and C_{75}, or the third quartile.

For the data in Table 9, C_{25} is formed by first finding the class interval containing the tally equal to 25% of all the tallies. Thus, the tally corresponding to C_{25} is found in the class interval 69.995–79.995, since

$$25\% \text{ of } 71 = 17.75$$

and 16 tallies lie in the first two class intervals. Using the interpolation factor, we find that

$$C_{25} = 69.995 + (1.75)\frac{1}{19}(10) = 69.995 + 0.921 = 70.916$$

MODE

Mode The *mode* of a set of real numbers is the value that occurs with the greatest frequency exceeding a frequency of 1.

The mode does not necessarily exist, and if it does, it is not always unique. For the data in Table 3, page 382, the mode is 79 (8 is the highest frequency).

□ Example 4   The group of data 2, 3, 4, 5, 7, 15 has no mode.   □

□ Example 5   The group of data 2, 2, 2, 3, 3, 7, 7, 7, 11, 15 has two modes 2 and 7, and is called
Bimodal   *bimodal.*   □

When data have been listed in a frequency table, the mode is defined as the midpoint of the interval consisting of the largest number of cases. For example, the mode for the data in Table 6, page 384, is 75 (the midpoint of the interval 69.995–79.995).

Of the three measures of central tendency considered so far, the mean is the most important, the most reliable, and the one most frequently used. The reason for this is that it is easy to understand, easy to compute, and uses all the data in the collection. If two samples are chosen from the same population, the two means corresponding to the two samples will not generally differ by as much as the two medians of these samples.

The second most reliable measure is the median. It, too, is easy to understand and most of the time easy to compute. One advantage of the median over the mean is that it is independent of extreme values.

Exercise 9.3   *Answers to Odd-Numbered Problems begin on page 622.*

In Problems 1–6 compute the mean, median, and mode of the given raw data.

1. 21, 25, 43, 36
2. 16, 18, 24, 30
3. 55, 55, 80, 92, 70
4. 65, 82, 82, 95, 70
5. 62, 71, 83, 90, 75
6. 48, 65, 80, 92, 80

In Problems 7–8 use the given histograms to determine the mean and median.

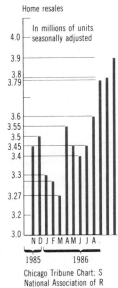

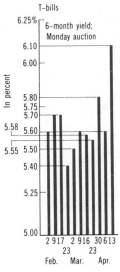

9. If an investor purchased 50 shares of IBM stock at $155 per share, 90 shares at $190 per share, 120 shares at $210 per share, and another 75 shares at $255 per share, what is the average cost per share?

10. If a farmer sells 120 bushels of corn at $2 per bushel, 80 bushels at $2.10 per bushel, 150 bushels at $1.90 per bushel, and 120 bushels at $2.20 per bushel, what is the average income per bushel?

11. The annual salaries of five faculty members in the Mathematics Department at a large university are $24,000, $25,000, $26,000, $26,500, and $45,000. Compute the mean and median. Which measure describes the situation more realistically? If you were among the four lowest-paid members, which measure would you use to describe the situation? What if you were the one making $45,000?

12. For the grouped data in Table 5, page 384, compute the mean, median, and mode.

13. The distribution of the monthly earnings of 1155 secretaries in May 1987 in the Chicago metropolitan area is summarized in the table. Find the mean salary and the median salary.

Monthly Earnings	Number of Secretaries
Under $1000	25
$1000–$1250	55
$1250–$1500	325
$1500–$1750	410
$1750–$2000	215
$2000–$2250	75
Over $2250	50

14. For the data given in Problems 2, 4, and 5 in Exercise 9.2 (page 387), find the mean, median, and mode.

15. Find C_{75} and C_{40} for the grouped data in Tables 5 and 6.

16. In a labor–management wage negotiation in which the laborers are the lowest paid of the workers in the company, which measure of central tendency would labor tend to use as an argument for more pay? Which would management use? Why?

17. For the data given in Problem 1 in Exercise 9.2 (page 386), find the mean, using an assumed mean.

18. In a frequency table, the score x_1 appears f_1 times, the score x_2 appears f_2 times, . . . , and the score x_n appears f_n times. Show that the mean $\overline{X}$ is given by the formula

$$\overline{X} = \frac{x_1 \cdot f_1 + x_2 \cdot f_2 + \cdots + x_n \cdot f_n}{f_1 + f_2 + \cdots + f_n}$$

9.4 MEASURES OF DISPERSION

RANGE □ STANDARD DEVIATION □ STANDARD DEVIATION FOR GROUPED DATA □ CHEBYCHEV'S THEOREM

We begin with an example.

□ **Example 1** Consider the following sets of scores:

$$S_1: \quad 4, 6, 8, 10, 12, 14, 16$$
$$S_2: \quad 4, 7, 9, 10, 11, 13, 16$$

Notice that the mean of S_1 and S_2 is 10, and the median of S_1 and S_2 is 10. The scores in each set are different, but those in S_2 seem to be more closely clustered around 10 than those in S_1. □

We need a statistical measure to indicate the extent to which the scores in Example 1 are spread out. Such measures are called *measures of dispersion.*

RANGE

Range   The simplest measure of dispersion is the *range,* which we have already defined as the difference between the largest value and the smallest value. For S_1 and S_2 the range is $16 - 4 = 12$. We can see that the range is a poor measure of dispersion since it depends on only two measures and tells us nothing about the rest of the scores.

Deviation from   Another measure of dispersion is the *deviation from the mean.* Recall that this
the Mean   measure is characterized by the fact that if the deviations from the mean of each score are all added up, the result is zero. Because of this, it is not widely used as a measure of dispersion.

We need a measure that will give us an idea of how much deviation is involved without having these deviations add up to zero. By squaring each deviation from the mean, adding them, and dividing by the number of scores, we obtain an average

Variance squared deviation, which is called the *variance* of the set of scores. The formula for the variance, which is denoted by σ^2, is*

$$\sigma^2 = \frac{(x_1 - \overline{X})^2 + (x_2 - \overline{X})^2 + \cdots + (x_n - \overline{X})^2}{n}$$

where $\overline{X}$ is the mean of the scores $x_1, x_2, \ldots, x_n$ and n is the number of scores.

STANDARD DEVIATION

Standard
Deviation
In order to apply this measure in practical situations (for instance, if our data represent dollars, we cannot talk about "squared dollars"), we use the square root of the variance. This is called the *standard deviation* of a set of scores. The standard deviation is denoted by σ and is given by the formula

$$\sigma = \sqrt{\frac{(x_1 - \overline{X})^2 + (x_2 - \overline{X})^2 + \cdots + (x_n - \overline{X})^2}{n}}$$

where $\overline{X}$ and the x_i's are defined the same way as for the variance.

For the data in Example 1, the standard deviation for S_1 is

$$\sigma = \sqrt{\frac{36 + 16 + 4 + 0 + 4 + 16 + 36}{7}} = \sqrt{\frac{112}{7}} = \sqrt{16} = 4$$

and the standard deviation for S_2 is

$$\sigma = \sqrt{\frac{36 + 9 + 1 + 0 + 1 + 9 + 36}{7}} = \sqrt{\frac{92}{7}} = \sqrt{13.14} = 3.625$$

The fact that the standard deviation of the set S_2 is less than that for the set S_1 is an indication that the scores of S_2 are more clustered around the mean than those of S_1.

□ **Example 2** Find the standard deviation for the data

100, 90, 90, 85, 80, 75, 75, 75, 70, 70, 65, 65, 60, 40, 40, 40

Solution The mean is

$$\overline{X} = \frac{100 + 2 \cdot 90 + 85 + 80 + 3 \cdot 75 + 2 \cdot 70 + 2 \cdot 65 + 60 + 3 \cdot 40}{16} = 70$$

The deviations from the mean and their squares are given in Table 10 on page 396. The standard deviation is

$$\sigma = \sqrt{\frac{4950}{16}} = \frac{70.4}{4} = 17.6$$

* The Greek letter sigma.

□ **Example 3**   Find the standard deviation for the data

$$80, 80, 80, 80, 75, 75, 75, 75, 75, 70, 70, 65, 65, 60, 60, 55, 55$$

Solution   Here the mean is $\overline{X} = 70$ for the 16 scores. Table 11 gives the deviations from the mean and their squares. The standard deviation is

$$\sigma = \sqrt{\frac{1200}{16}} = \sqrt{75} = 8.7$$

□

Table 10

Scores x	Deviation from the Mean $x - \overline{X}$	Deviation Squared $(x - \overline{X})^2$
100	30	900
90	20	400
90	20	400
85	15	225
80	10	100
75	5	25
75	5	25
75	5	25
70	0	0
70	0	0
65	−5	25
65	−5	25
60	−10	100
40	−30	900
40	−30	900
40	−30	900
Mean = 70 $n = 16$	Sum = 0	Sum = 4950

Table 11

Scores x	Deviation from the Mean $x - \overline{X}$	Deviation Squared $(x - \overline{X})^2$
80	10	100
80	10	100
80	10	100
80	10	100
75	5	25
75	5	25
75	5	25
75	5	25
70	0	0
70	0	0
65	−5	25
65	−5	25
60	−10	100
60	−10	100
55	−15	225
55	−15	225
Mean = 70 $n = 16$	Sum = 0	Sum = 1200

These two examples show that although the samples have the same mean, 70, and the same sample size, 16, the scores in the first set deviate further from the mean than do the scores in the second set.

> In general, a relatively small standard deviation indicates that the measures tend to cluster close to the mean, and a relatively high standard deviation shows that the measures are widely scattered from the mean.

CHEBYCHEV'S THEOREM

Suppose we are observing an experiment with numerical outcomes and that the experiment has mean $\overline{X}$ and standard deviation σ. We wish to estimate the fractions of outcomes that lie within k units of the mean.

> **Chebychev's Theorem*** For any distribution of numbers with mean $\overline{X}$ and standard deviation σ the probability that a randomly chosen outcome lies between $\overline{X} - k$ and $\overline{X} + k$ is at least $1 - \dfrac{\sigma^2}{k^2}$.

☐ **Example 4** Suppose that an experiment with numerical outcomes has mean 4 and standard deviation 1. Use Chebychev's theorem to estimate the probability that an outcome lies between 2 and 6.

Solution Here $\overline{X} = 4$, $\sigma = 1$. Since we wish to estimate the probability that an outcome lies between 2 and 6, the value of k is $k = 6 - \overline{x} = 6 - 4 = 2$ (or $k = \overline{x} - 2 = 4 - 2 = 2$). Then by Chebychev's theorem the desired probability is at least

$$1 - \frac{\sigma^2}{k^2} = 1 - \frac{1}{2^2} = 1 - \frac{1}{4} = .75$$

That is, we expect at least 75% of the outcomes of this experiment will lie between 2 and 6. ☐

☐ **Example 5** An office supply company sells boxes containing 100 paper clips. Because of the packaging procedure not every box contains exactly 100 clips. From previous data it is known that the average number of clips in a box is indeed 100 and the standard deviation is 3. If the company ships 10,000 boxes, estimate the number of boxes having between 94 and 106 clips inclusive.

Solution Our experiment involves counting the number of clips in the box. For this experiment we have $\overline{X} = 100$, and $\sigma = 3$. Therefore by Chebychev's theorem the fraction of boxes having between $100 - 6$ and $100 + 6$ clips ($k = 6$) should be at least

$$1 - \frac{3^2}{6^2} = 1 - \frac{9}{36} = \frac{27}{36} = .75$$

That is, we expect at least 75% of 10,000 boxes, or 7500 boxes to have between 94 and 106 clips. ☐

The importance of Chebychev's theorem stems from the fact that it applies to *any* data — only the mean and standard deviation must be known. However the estimate is a crude one. Other results (such as the *normal distribution* given later) produce more accurate estimates about the probability of falling within k units of the mean.

---

* Named after the nineteenth-century Russian mathematician P. L. Chebychev.

STANDARD DEVIATION FOR GROUPED DATA

To find the standard deviation for grouped data we use the formula

$$\sigma = \sqrt{\frac{(x_1 - \overline{X})^2 \cdot f_1 + (x_2 - \overline{X})^2 \cdot f_2 + \cdots + (x_n - \overline{X})^2 \cdot f_n}{n}}$$

where $x_1, x_2, \ldots, x_n$ are the class midpoints; $f_1, f_2, \ldots, f_n$ are the respective frequencies; n is the sum of the frequencies, that is, $n = f_1 + f_2 + \cdots + f_n$; and $\overline{X}$ is the mean.

□ **Example 6**   Find the standard deviation for the grouped data given in Table 9, page 390.

Solution   We have already found that the mean for the grouped data is

$$\overline{X} = 81.3$$

The class midpoints are 55, 65, 75, 85, 95, 105, and 115. The deviations of the mean from the class midpoints, their squares, and the products of the squares by the respective frequencies are listed in Table 12. The standard deviation is

$$\sigma = \sqrt{\frac{16{,}447.99}{71}} = \sqrt{231.66} = 15.22$$

□

Table 12

Class Midpoint	f_i	$x_i - \overline{X}$	$(x_i - \overline{X})^2$	$(x_i - \overline{X})^2 \cdot f_i$
115	2	33.7	1,135.69	2,271.38
105	6	23.7	561.69	3,370.14
95	14	13.7	187.69	2,627.66
85	14	3.7	13.69	191.66
75	19	−6.3	39.69	754.11
65	9	−16.3	265.69	2,391.21
55	7	−26.3	691.69	4,841.83
Sum	71			16,447.99

A little computation shows that the sum of the deviations of the approximate mean from the class midpoints is not exactly zero. This is because we are using only an approximation to the mean, since we cannot compute the exact mean for grouped data.

Exercise 9.4 *Answers to Odd-Numbered Problems begin on page* 623 .

1. Use histograms (*a*) and (*b*) to determine by inspection which distribution has the largest variance.

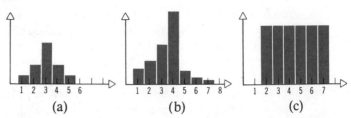
(a)   (b)   (c)

2. Use histograms (*b*) and (*c*) to determine by inspection which distribution has the largest variance.

In Problems 3–8 compute the standard deviation for the given raw data.

3. 4, 5, 9, 9, 10, 14, 25   4. 6, 8, 10, 10, 11, 12, 18

5. 62, 58, 70, 70   6. 55, 65, 80, 80, 90

7. 85, 75, 62, 78, 100   8. 92, 82, 75, 75, 82

9. The lifetimes of six light bulbs are 968, 893, 769, 845, 922, and 815 hours. Calculate the mean lifetime and the standard deviation.

10. A group of 25 applicants for admission to Midwestern University made the following scores on the quantitative part of an aptitude test:

591	570	425	472	555
490	415	479	517	570
606	614	542	607	441
502	506	603	488	460
550	551	420	590	482

Find the mean and standard deviation of these scores.

11. Find the standard deviation for the data given in Problem 1, Exercise 9.2 (page 386).

12. Find the standard deviation for the grouped data given in Table 5 (page 384).

13. Suppose that an experiment with numerical outcomes has mean 25 and standard deviation 3. Use Chebychev's theorem to tell what percent of outcomes lie

(a) between 19 and 31   (b) between 20 and 30
(c) between 16 and 34   (d) less than 19 or more than 31
(e) less than 16 or more than 34

14. A watch company determines that the number of defective watches in each box averages 6 with standard deviation 2. Suppose that 1000 boxes are produced. Extimate the number of boxes having between 0 and 12 defective watches.

9.5 NORMAL DISTRIBUTION

NORMAL CURVE □ STANDARD NORMAL CURVE
□ THE NORMAL CURVE AS AN APPROXIMATION TO THE BINOMIAL DISTRIBUTION

Frequency polygons or frequency distributions can assume almost any shape or form, depending on the data. However, the data obtained from many experiments often follow a common pattern. For example, heights of people, weights of people, test scores, and coin tossing all lead to data which have the same kind of frequency distribution. This distribution is referred to as the *normal distribution* or the *Gaussian distribution.* Because it occurs so often in practical situations, it is generally regarded as the most important distribution, and much statistical theory is based on it. The graph of the normal distribution, called the *normal curve,* is the bell-shaped curve shown in Figure 5.

Normal
Distribution

Normal Curve

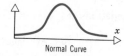

Figure 5   Normal Curve

NORMAL CURVE

Some properties of the normal curve are listed below.

1. Normal curves are bell-shaped and are symmetrical with respect to a vertical line. See Figure 6.

2. The mean is at the center. See Figure 6.

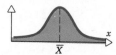

Figure 6 $\overline{X}$

3. Irrespective of the shape, the area enclosed by the curve and the *x*-axis is always equal to 1. See the shaded region in Figure 6.

4. The probability that an outcome of a normally distributed experiment is between *a* and *b* equals the area under the associated normal curve from $x = a$ to $x = b$. See the shaded region in Figure 7.

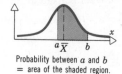

Figure 7   Probability between *a* and *b*
= area of the shaded region.

CARL FRIEDRICH GAUSS (1777–1855), sometimes called the "prince of mathematicians," made profound contributions to number theory, the theory of functions, probability and statistics. He discovered a way to calculate the orbits of asteroids, made basic discoveries in electromagnetic theory, and invented a telegraph.

5. The standard deviation of a normal distribution plays a major role in describing the area under the normal curve. As shown in Figure 8, the standard deviation is related to the area under the normal curve as follows:

(a) Within 1 standard deviation (from $\overline{X} - \sigma$ to $\overline{X} + \sigma$) is about 95.45% of the total area under the curve

(b) Within 2 standard deviations (from $\overline{X} - 2\sigma$ to $\overline{X} + 2\sigma$) is about 95.45% of the total area under the curve.

(c) Within 3 standard deviations (from $\overline{X} - 3\sigma$ to $\overline{X} + 3\sigma$) is about 99.73% of the total area under the curve

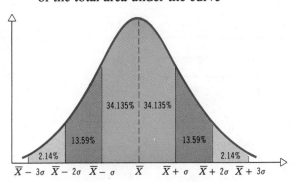

Figure 8

It is also important to recognize that, in theory, the normal curve will never touch the x-axis, but will extend to infinity in either direction. In addition, every normal distribution has its mean, median, and mode at the same point.

☐ **Example 1**   At Jefferson High School, the average IQ score of the 1200 students is 100, with a standard deviation of 15. The IQ scores have a normal distribution.

(a) How many students will have an IQ between 85 and 115?

(b) How many students will have an IQ between 70 and 130?

(c) How many students will have an IQ between 55 and 145?

(d) How many students will have an IQ under 55 or over 145?

(e) How many students will have an IQ over 145?

Solution   (a)   Since we are assuming that the IQ scores have a normal distribution, we know that the mean is 100. Since the standard deviation σ is 15, then 1σ either side of the mean is from 85 to 115. By property 5(a) we know that 68.27% of 1200, or

$$(0.6827)(1200) = 819 \text{ students}$$

have IQ's between 85 and 115.

(b)   The scores from 70 to 130 extend $2\sigma\, (= 30)$ either side of the mean. By property 5(b) we know that 95.45% of 1200, or

$$(0.9545)(1200) = 1145 \text{ students}$$

have IQ's between 70 and 130.

(c)   The scores from 55 to 145 extend $3\sigma (= 45)$ either side of the mean. By property 5(c) we know that 99.73% of 1200, or

$$(0.9973)(1200) = 1197 \text{ students}$$

have IQ's between 55 and 145.

(d)   There are about 3 students $(1200 - 1197)$ who have scores that are not between 55 and 145.

(e)   About 1 or 2 of them are above 145.

See Figure 9.   ☐

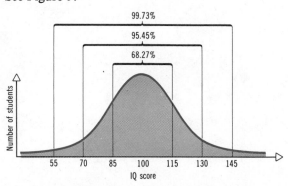

Figure 9

A normal distribution curve is completely determined by $\overline{X}$ and σ. Hence, different normal distributions of data with different means and standard deviations give rise to different shapes of the normal curve. Figure 10 indicates how the normal curve changes when the standard deviation changes. For the sake of clarity, we assume all data have mean 0.

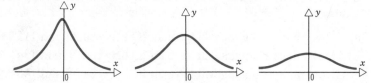

Figure 10

As the standard deviation increases, the normal curve flattens out. A flatter curve indicates a greater likelihood for the outcomes to be spread out. A sharper curve indicates that the outcomes are more likely to be close to the mean.

STANDARD NORMAL CURVE

It would be a hopeless task to attempt to set up separate tables of normal curve areas for every conceivable value of $\overline{X}$ and σ. Fortunately, we are able to transform all the observations to one table — the table corresponding to the so-called *standard normal curve,* which is the normal curve for which $\overline{X} = 0$ and $\sigma = 1$. This can be achieved by introducing new score data, called *Z-scores,* defined as

Z-Score

$$Z = \frac{\text{Distance between } x \text{ and } \overline{X}}{\text{Standard deviation}} = \frac{x - \overline{X}}{\sigma} \qquad (1)$$

where

$$x = \text{Old score data}$$
$$\overline{X} = \text{Mean of the old data}$$
$$\sigma = \text{Standard deviation of the old data}$$

Standard Score   The new score data defined by (1) will always have a *zero mean* and a *unit standard deviation*. Such data are said to be expressed in *standard units* or *standard scores*. By expressing data in terms of standard units, it becomes possible to make a comparison of distributions. Furthermore, as for all normal curves, the total area under a standard normal curve is equal to 1.

□ **Example 2**   On a test, 80 is the mean and 7 is the standard deviation. What is the Z-score of a score of:

(a)   88?   (b)   62?

Interpret your results.

Solution   (a)   Here, 88 is the regular score. Using (1) with $x = 88$, $\overline{X} = 80$, $\sigma = 7$, we get

$$Z = \frac{x - \overline{X}}{\sigma} = \frac{88 - 80}{7} = \frac{8}{7} = 1.1429$$

(b)   Here, 62 is the regular score. Using (1) with $x = 62$, $\overline{X} = 80$, and $\sigma = 7$, we get

$$Z = \frac{62 - 80}{7} = \frac{-18}{7} = -2.5714$$

The Z-score of 1.1429 tells us that the original score of 88 is 1.1429 standard deviations *above* the mean. See Figure 11. The Z-score of −2.5714 tells us that the original score of 62 is 2.5714 standard deviations *below* the mean. A negative Z-score always means that the score is below the mean. See Figure 11. □

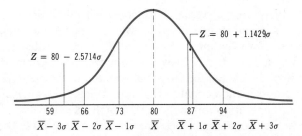

Figure 11

The curve in Figure 10 with mean $\overline{X} = 0$ and standard deviation $\sigma = 1$ is the standard normal curve. For this curve, the areas between $Z = -1$ and 1, $Z = -2$ and 2, $Z = -3$ and 3 are equal, respectively, to 68.27%, 95.45%, and 99.73% of the total area under the curve, which is 1. To find the areas cut off between other points, we proceed as in the following example.

□ **Example 3**   Suppose, to begin with, we consider the standard normal curve illustrated in Figure 12. We wish to find the proportion of the area, or the proportion of cases, included between the two points 0.6 and 1.86 units from the mean.

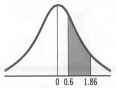

Figure 12

Solution

Normal Curve Table

This problem is worked by using a *normal curve table,* Table 3 on page 382. We begin by checking the table to find the area of the curve cut off between the mean and a point equivalent to a standard score of 0.6 from the mean. This value appears in the second column of the table next to 0.6 and is found to be 0.2257. Next, we continue down the table in the left-hand column until we come to a standard score of 1.8. By looking across the row to the column below 0.06 (column 8), we find that 0.4686 of the area is included between the mean and this point. Then the area of the curve between these two points is the difference between the two areas, 0.4686 − 0.2257, which is 0.2429. We can then state that approximately 24.29% of the cases fall between 0.6 and 1.86, or that *the probability of a score falling between these two points is about .2429.*   □

In the next example, we take two points that are on different sides of the mean.

□ **Example 4**   We want to determine what proportion of the area of the normal curve falls between a standard score of −0.39 and one of 1.86 for the standard normal curve given in Figure 13.

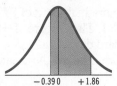

Figure 13

Solution

There are no values for negative standard scores in Table 3. Because of the symmetry of normal curves, equal standard scores, whether positive or negative, give equal areas when taken from the mean. From Table 3, we find that a standard score of −0.39 cuts off an area of 0.1517 between it and the mean. A standard score of 1.86 includes 0.4686 of the area of the curve between it and the mean. The area included between both points is then equal to the sum of these two areas, 0.1517 + 0.4686, which is 0.6203. Thus, approximately 62.03% of the area is between −0.39 and 1.86. In other words, the probability of a score falling between these two points is about 0.6203.   □

□ **Example 5**   A student receives a grade of 82 on a final examination in Biology for which the mean is 73 and the standard deviation is 9. In his final examination in Sociology for which the mean grade is 81 and the standard deviation is 15, he receives an 89. In which examination is his relative standing higher?

Solution In their present form, these distributions are not comparable, since they have different means and, more important, different standard deviations. In order to compare the data, we transform the data to standard scores. For the Biology test data, the new score data for the student's examination score are

$$Z = \frac{82 - 73}{9} = \frac{9}{9} = 1$$

For the Sociology test data, the new score data for the student's examination score are

$$Z = \frac{89 - 81}{15} = \frac{8}{15} = 0.533$$

This means the student's score in the Biology exam is 1 standard unit above the mean, while his score in the Sociology exam is 0.533 standard unit above the mean. Hence, his *relative standing* is higher in Biology. □

THE NORMAL CURVE AS AN APPROXIMATION TO THE BINOMIAL DISTRIBUTION

We start with an example.

□ **Example 6** Consider an experiment in which a fair coin is tossed 10 times. Find the frequency distribution for the probability of tossing a head.

Solution The probability for obtaining exactly k heads is given by a binomial distribution $b(10, k; \frac{1}{2})$. Thus, we obtain the distribution given in Table 13. If we graph this frequency distribution, we obtain the line chart shown in Figure 14. When we connect the tops of the lines of the line chart, we obtain a *normal curve,* as shown.

Table 13

No. of Heads	Probability $b(10, k; \frac{1}{2})$
0	.0010
1	.0098
2	.0439
3	.1172
4	.2051
5	.2461
6	.2051
7	.1172
8	.0439
9	.0098
10	.0010

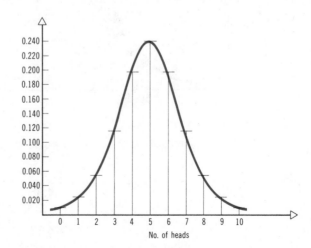

Figure 14

No. of heads

□

This particular distribution for $n = 10$ and $p = \frac{1}{2}$ is not a result of the choice of n or p. As a matter of fact, the line chart for any binomial probability $b(n, k; p)$ will give an approximation to a normal curve. You should verify this for the cases in which $n = 15$, $p = .3$, and $n = 8$, $p = \frac{3}{4}$.

Probabilities associated with binomial experiments are readily obtainable from the formula $b(n, k; p)$ when n is small. If n is large, we can compute the binomial probabilities by an approximating procedure using a normal curve. It turns out that the normal distribution provides a very good approximation to the binomial distribution when n is large or p is close to $\frac{1}{2}$.

In Chapter 8, Section 4, we have shown that the mean $\overline{X}$ for the binomial distribution is given by $\overline{X} = np$. Moreover, it can be shown that the standard deviation is $\sigma = \sqrt{npq}$.

☐ **Example 7**   A company manufactures 60,000 pencils each day. Quality control studies have shown that, on the average, 4% of the pencils are defective. A random sample of 500 pencils is selected from each day's production and tested. What is the probability that in the sample there are:

(a)   At least 12 and no more than 24 defective pencils?

(b)   32 or more defective pencils?

Solution   (a)   Since $n = 500$ is very large, it is appropriate to use a normal curve approximation for the binomial distribution. Thus, with $n = 500$ and $p = .04$,

$$\overline{X} = np = 500(.04) = 20 \qquad \sigma = \sqrt{npq} = \sqrt{500(.04)(.96)} \approx 4.38$$

To find the approximate probability of the number of defective pencils in a sample being at least 12 and no more than 24, we find the area under a normal curve from $x = 12$ to $x = 24$. See Figure 15.

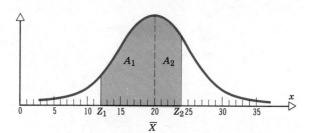

Figure 15

Areas A_1 and A_2 are found as follows:

$$Z_1 = \frac{x - \overline{X}}{\sigma} = \frac{12 - 20}{4.38} = -1.83 \qquad A_1 = 0.4664$$

$$Z_2 = \frac{x - \overline{X}}{\sigma} = \frac{24 - 20}{4.38} = 0.91 \qquad A_2 = 0.3186$$

Total area $= A_1 + A_2 = 0.4664 + 0.3186 = 0.785$

Thus, the approximate probability of the number of defective pencils in the sample being at least 12 and not more than 24 is 0.785.

(b)   We want to find the area A_2 indicated in Figure 16. We know that the area to the

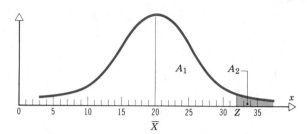

Figure 16

right of the mean is 0.5, and if we subtract the area A_1 from 0.5, we will obtain A_2. Therefore, we find the area A_1:

$$Z = \frac{x - \overline{X}}{\sigma} = \frac{32 - 20}{4.38} = 2.74 \qquad A_1 = 0.4969$$

Then,

$$A_2 = 0.5 - A_1 = 0.5 - 0.4969 = 0.0031$$

Thus, the approximate probability of finding 32 or more defective pencils in the sample is .0031.   ◻

Exercise 9.5   *Answers to Odd-Numbered Problems begin on page* 623.

In Problems 1–4 determine $\overline{X}$ and σ by inspection.

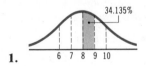

1.

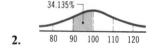

2.

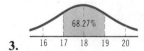

3.

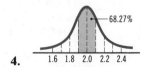

4.

5.   Given a normal distribution with a mean of 13.1 and a standard deviation of 9.3, find the Z-score equivalent of the following scores in the distribution:

$$7, 9, 13, 15, 29, 37, 41$$

6.   Given a normal distribution with a mean of 15.2 and a standard deviation of 5.1, find the Z-score equivalent of the following scores in the distribution:

$$8, 9, 15, 16, 22, 23, 25$$

In Problems 7–10 use Table 3, page 382, to find each area of the shaded region under the standard normal curve.

7.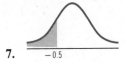
-0.5

8.
$1\quad 2$

9.
1.5

10.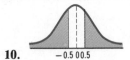
$-0.5\ 0\ 0.5$

11. Given the following Z-scores on a standard normal distribution, find the area from the mean to each score.

   (a) 0.89   (b) 1.10   (c) 2.50   (d) 3.00

   (e) -0.75 (f) -2.31 (g) 0.80   (h) 3.03

12. An instructor assigns grades in an examination according to the following procedure:

        A   if score exceeds $\overline{X} + 1.6\sigma$

        B   if score is between $\overline{X} + 0.6\sigma$ and $\overline{X} + 1.6\sigma$

        C   if score is between $\overline{X} - 0.3\sigma$ and $\overline{X} + 0.6\sigma$

        D   if score is between $\overline{X} - 1.4\sigma$ and $\overline{X} - 0.3\sigma$

        F   if score is below $\overline{X} - 1.4\sigma$

   What percentage of each grade does this instructor give, assuming that the scores are normally distributed?

13. The average height of 2000 women in a random sample is 64 inches. The standard deviation is 2 inches. The heights have a normal distribution.

   (a) How many women are between 62 and 66 inches tall?

   (b) How many women are between 60 and 68 inches tall?

   (c) How many women are between 58 and 70 inches tall?

14. Corn flakes come in a box that says it holds a mean weight of 16 ounces of cereal. The standard deviation is 0.1 ounce. Suppose that the manufacturer packages 600,000 boxes with weights that have a normal distribution.

   (a) How many boxes weigh between 15.9 and 16.1 ounces?

   (b) How many boxes weigh between 15.8 and 16.2 ounces?

   (c) How many boxes weigh between 15.7 and 16.3 ounces?

   (d) How many boxes weigh under 15.7 or over 16.3 ounces?

   (e) How many boxes weigh under 15.7 ounces?

15. The weight of 100 college students closely follows a normal distribution with a mean of 130 pounds and a standard deviation of 5.2 pounds.

   (a) How many of these students would you expect to weigh at least 142 pounds?

(b) What range of weights would you expect to include the middle 70% of the students in this group?

16. *Life Expectancy of Clothing.* If the average life of a certain make of clothing is 40 months with standard deviation of 7 months, what percentage of these clothes can be expected to last from 28 months to 42 months? Assume that clothing lifetime follows a normal distribution.

17. *Life Expectancy of Shoes.* Records show that the average life expectancy of a pair of shoes is 2.2 years with a standard deviation of 1.7 years. A manufacturer guarantees that shoes lasting less than a year are replaced free. For every 1000 shoes sold, how many shoes should the manufacturer expect to replace free?

18. The attendance over a weekly period of time at a movie theater is normally distributed with a mean of 10,000 and a standard deviation of 1000 persons. Find:

   (a) The number in the lowest 70% of the attendance figures
   (b) The percentage of attendance figures that falls between 8500 and 11,000 persons
   (c) The percentage of attendance figures that differs from the mean by 1500 persons or more

19. Caryl, Mary, and Kathleen are vying for a position as secretary. Caryl, who is tested with Group I, gets a score of 76 on her test; Mary, who is tested with Group II, gets a score of 89; and Kathleen, who is tested with Group III, gets a score of 21. If the average score for Group I is 82, for Group II is 93, and for Group III is 24, and if the standard deviation for each group is 7, 2, and 9, respectively, which person has the highest relative standing?

20. In Mathematics 135, the average final grade is 75.0 and the standard deviation is 10.0. The professor's grade distribution shows that 15 students with grades from 68.0 to 82.0 received C's. Assuming the grades follow a normal distribution, how many students are in Mathematics 135?

21. Draw the line chart and frequency curve for the probability of a head in an experiment in which a biased coin is tossed 15 times and the probability that a head occurs is .3. [*Hint:* Find $b(15, k; .30)$ for $k = 0, 1, \ldots, 15$.]

22. Follow the same directions as in Problem 21 for an experiment in which a biased coin is tossed 8 times and the probability that heads appears is $\frac{3}{4}$.

In Problems 23–28 suppose a binomial experiment consists of 750 trials and the probability of success for each trial is .4. Then

$$\overline{X} = np = 300 \qquad \text{and} \qquad \sigma = \sqrt{npq} = \sqrt{(750)(.4)(.6)} \approx 13$$

Approximate the probability of obtaining the number of successes indicated by using a normal curve.

23. 285–315

24. 280–320

25. 300 or more

26. 300 or less

27. 325 or more

28. 275 or less

CHAPTER REVIEW

Important Terms			
population	frequency polygon	measure of dispersion
sample	cumulative (less than) frequency	range
biased sample		variance
random sample	cumulative (more than) frequency	standard deviation
inductive statistics		Chebychev's theorem
frequency table	measure of central tendency	normal distribution
line chart	mean	normal curve, bell-shaped curve
continuous variable	median	
discrete variable	mode	standard normal curve
histogram	deviation from the mean	Z-score
class interval	interpolation factor	standard score
upper class limit	centile point	normal curve table
lower class limit	bimodal	

True–False Questions

T F 1. The range of a set of numbers is the difference between the standard deviation and the mean.

T F 2. Two sets of scores can have the same mean and median yet be different.

T F 3. A relatively small standard deviation indicates that measures are widely scattered from the mean.

T F 4. The sum of the deviations from the mean is zero.

T F 5. For the normal distribution 68.27% of the total area under the curve is within 2 standard deviations of the mean.

Fill in the Blanks

1. The three most common measures of central tendency are (a) _____ (b) _____ (c) _____ .

2. The square root of the variance is called _____ .

3. The graph of the normal distribution has a _____ shape.

4. The formula $\dfrac{x - \overline{X}}{\sigma}$ is called the _____ .

5. The formula $1 - \dfrac{\sigma^2}{k^2}$ measures the probability that a randomly chosen variable lies between _____ and _____ .

Review Exercises

Answers to Odd-Numbered Problems begin on page 624 .

1. The following scores were made on a math exam:

80	99	82	21	100	55	80	26	78	52
12	73	20	44	72	63	19	85	33	66
78	42	87	90	30	10	48	75	83	77
63	85	69	80	14	87	66	52	17	60
74	70	73	95	89	14	92	8	100	72

(a) Set up a frequency table for the above data. What is the range?

(b) Draw a line chart for the data.

(c) Draw a histogram for the data using a class interval of size 5 beginning with 4.5.

(d) Draw the frequency polygon for the histogram.

(e) Find the cumulative (more than) frequencies.

(f) Find the cumulative (less than) frequencies.

2. Find the mean, the median, and the mode for each of the following sets of measurements:

   (a) 12, 10, 8, 2, 0, 4, 10, 5, 4, 4, 8, 0

   (b) 195, 5, 2, 2, 2, 2, 1, 0

   (c) 2, 5, 5, 7, 7, 7, 9, 9, 11

3. In which of the sets of data in Problem 2 is the mean a poor measure of central tendency? Why?

4. Give an example of data in which the preferred measure of central tendency would be the:

   (a) Mean   (b) Mode   (c) Median

5. Give an example of two sets of scores for which the mean is the same and the standard deviation is different.

6. Give one advantage of the standard deviation over the variance. Give an example.

7. In seven different rounds of golf, Joe scores 74, 72, 76, 81, 77, 76, and 73. What is the standard deviation of his scores?

8. A normal distribution has a mean of 25 and a standard deviation of 5.

   (a) What proportion of the scores fall between 20 and 30?

   (b) What proportion of the scores will lie above 35?

9. A set of 600 scores is normally distributed. How many scores would you expect to find:

   (a) Between $\pm 1\sigma$ above the mean?

   (b) Between 1σ and 3σ above the mean?

   (c) Between $\pm\frac{2}{3}\sigma$ of the mean?

10. *Average Life of a Dog.* The average life expectancy of a dog is 14 years, with a standard deviation of about 1.25 years. Assuming that the life spans of dogs are normally distributed, approximately how many dogs will die before reaching the age of 10 years, 4 months?

11. Use Table 3, page 382, to calculate the area under the normal curve between:

    (a) $Z = -1.35$ and $Z = -2.75$

    (b) $Z = 1.2$ and $Z = 1.75$

12. Bob got an 89 on the final exam in Mathematics and a 79 on the Sociology exam. In the Mathematics class the average grade was 79 with a standard deviation of 5, and in the Sociology class the average grade was 72 with a standard deviation of 3.5. Assuming that the grades in both subjects were normally distributed, in which class did Bob rank higher?

13. Suppose it is known that the number of items produced in a factory has a mean of 40. If the variance of a week's production is known to equal 25, then what can be said about the probability that this week's production will be between 30 and 50?

14. From past experience a teacher knows that the test scores of students taking an examination have a mean of 75 and a variance of 25.

    (a) What can be said about the probability that a student will score between 65 and 85?

(b) How many students would have to take the examination so as to ensure, with probability of at least .9, that the class average would be within 5 of 75?

Mathematical Questions

From Actuary Exams (Answers on page 625 *.)*

1. *Actuary Exam—Part II*
    Under the hypothesis that a pair of dice are fair, the probability is approximately 0.95 that the number of 7's appearing in 180 throws of the dice will lie within $30 \pm K$. What is the value of K?
    (a) 2   (b) 4   (c) 6   (d) 8   (e) 10

2. *Actuary Exam—Part II*
    If X is normally distributed with mean μ and variance μ^2 and if $\Pr(-4 < X < 8) = 0.9974$, then $\mu =$
    (a) 1   (b) 2   (c) 4   (d) 6   (e) 8

3. *Actuary Exam—Part II*
    A manufacturer makes golf balls whose weights average 1.62 ounces, with a standard deviation of 0.05 ounce. What is the probability that the weight of a group of 100 balls will lie in the interval 162 ± 0.5 ounces?
    (a) 0.18   (b) 0.34   (c) 0.68   (d) 0.84   (e) 0.96

10

APPLICATIONS TO GAMES OF STRATEGY

10.1 INTRODUCTION

Game theory, as a branch of mathematics, is a relatively new field. It is concerned with the analysis of human behavior in conflicts of interest. In other words, game theory gives mathematical expression to the strategies of opposing players and offers techniques for choosing the best possible strategy. In most parlor games, it is relatively easy to define winning and losing and, on this basis, to quantify the best strategy for each player. However, game theory is not merely a tool for the gambler so that he or she can take advantage of the odds; nor is it merely a method for winning games like tic-tac-toe, matching pennies, or the Italian game called *Morra* (described in Section 10.3).

Gottfried Wilhelm von Leibniz is generally recognized as being the first to see the relationship between games of strategy and the theory of social behavior. For example, when union and management sit down at the bargaining table to discuss contracts, each has definite strategies open to him. Each will bluff, persuade, and try to discover the other's strategy, while at the same time trying to prevent the discovery of his own. If enough information is known, results from the theory of games can determine what is the best possible rational behavior or the best possible strategy for each player. Another application of game theory can be made to politics. If two people are vying for the same political office, each has open to him various campaign strategies. If it is possible to determine the impact of alternate strategies on the voters, the theory of games can be used to find the best strategy (usually the one that gains the most votes, while losing the least votes). Thus, game theory can be used in certain situations of conflict to indicate how people should behave to achieve certain goals. Of course, game theory does not tell us how people actually behave. Game theory is the study, then, of rational behavior in conflict situations.

Two-Person Game Any conflict or competition between two people is called a *two-person game.*

Let's consider some examples of two-person games.

□ **Example 1** In a game similar to matching pennies, Player I picks heads or tails and Player II attempts to guess the choice. Player I will pay Player II $3 if both choose heads; Player I will pay Player II $2 if both choose tails. If Player II guesses incorrectly, he will pay Player I $5. □

We use Example 1 to illustrate some terminology. First, since two players are involved, this is a two-person game. Next, notice that no matter what outcome occurs (HH, HT, TH, TT), whatever is lost (or gained) by Player I is gained (or lost) by player

Zero-Sum Games II. Such games are called *two-person zero-sum games.*

GOTTFRIED WILHELM von LEIBNIZ (1646–1716), along with Newton is credited with the development of differential and integral calculus. He was a philosopher, lawyer, theologian, and historian and wrote in several languages. His later years were clouded by a controversy over who first discovered calculus, Leibniz or Newton. In fact, both men should be credited since each discovered calculus by different means.

If we denote the gains of Player I by positive entries and his losses by negative entries, we can display this game in a 2×2 matrix as

$$\begin{array}{c} & \begin{array}{cc} H & T \end{array} \\ \begin{array}{c} H \\ T \end{array} & \begin{bmatrix} -3 & 5 \\ 5 & -2 \end{bmatrix} \end{array}$$

Payoff
Game Matrix
Each entry a_{ij} of a matrix game is termed a *payoff* and the matrix is called the *game* or *payoff matrix.*

Conversely, any $m \times n$ matrix $A = [a_{ij}]$ can be regarded as the game matrix for a two-person zero-sum game in which Player I chooses any one of the m rows of A and simultaneously Player II chooses any one of the n columns of A. The entry in the row and column chosen is the payoff.

We will assume that the game is played repeatedly, and that the problem facing each player is what choice he should make so that he gains the most benefit. Thus, Player I wishes to maximize his winnings and Player II wishes to minimize his losses. By a strategy of Player I for a given matrix game A, we mean the decision by Player I to select rows of A in some manner.

□ **Example 2**   Consider a two-person zero-sum game given by the matrix

$$\begin{bmatrix} 3 & 6 \\ -2 & -3 \end{bmatrix}$$

in which the entries denote the winnings of Player I. The game consists of Player I choosing a row and Player II simultaneously choosing a column, with the intersection of row and column giving the payoff for this play in the game. For example, if Player I chooses row 1 and Player II chooses column 2, then Player I wins $6; if Player I chooses row 2 and Player II chooses column 1, then Player I loses $2.

It is immediately evident from the matrix that this particular game is biased in favor of Player I, who will always choose row 1 since he cannot lose by doing so. Similarly, Player II, recognizing that Player I will choose row 1 will always choose column 1, since his losses are then minimized.

Best Strategy
Thus, the *best strategy* for Player I is row 1 and the *best strategy* for Player II is column 1. When both players employ their best strategy, the result is that Player I wins $3. This amount is called the *value* of the game. Notice that the payoff $3 is the minimum of the entries in its row and is the maximum of the entries in its column.

□

Strictly Determined Game A game defined by a matrix is said to be *strictly determined* if and only if there is an entry of the matrix that is the smallest element in its row and is also the largest element in its column. This entry is then called a *saddle point* and is the *value* of the game.

Fair Game
If a game has a positive value, the game favors Player I. If a game has a negative value, the game favors Player II. Any game with a value of 0 is termed a *fair game.*

If a matrix game has a saddle point, it can be shown that the row containing the saddle point is the best strategy for Player I and the column containing the saddle

Pure Strategy

point is the best strategy for Player II. This is why such games are called *strictly determined games.* Such games are also called games of *pure strategy.*

Of course, a matrix may have more than one saddle point, in which case each player has more than one best strategy available. However, the value of the game is always the same no matter how many saddle points the matrix may have. See Problem 12 in Exercise 10.1.

□ **Example 3**   Determine whether the game defined by the matrix below is strictly determined.

$$\begin{bmatrix} 3 & 0 & -2 & -1 \\ 2 & -3 & 0 & -1 \\ 4 & 2 & 1 & 0 \end{bmatrix}$$

Solution   First, we look at each row and find the smallest entry in each row:

Row 1: -2 Row 2: -3 Row 3: 0

Next, we check to see if any of the above elements are also the largest in their column. The element -2 in row 1 is not the largest entry in column 3; the element -3 in row 2 is not the largest entry in column 2; however, the element 0 in row 3 is the largest entry in column 4. Thus, this game is strictly determined. Its value is 0, so the game is fair.

□

The game of Example 3 is represented by a 3×4 matrix. This means that Player I has 3 strategies open to him, while Player II can choose from 4 strategies.

□ **Example 4**   Two franchising firms, Alpha Products and Omega Industries, are each planning to add an outlet in a certain city. It is possible for the site to be located either in the center of the city or in a large suburb of the city. If both firms decide to build in the center of the city, Alpha Products will show an annual profit of $1000 more than the profit of Omega Industries. If both firms decide to locate their outlet in the suburb, then it is determined that Alpha Products' profit will be $2000 less than the profit of Omega Industries. If Alpha locates in the suburb and Omega in the city, then Alpha will show a profit of $4000 more than Omega. Finally, if Alpha locates in the city and Omega in the suburb, then Alpha will have a profit of $3000 less than Omega's. Is there a best site for each firm to locate its franchise? In this case, by *best site* we mean the one that produces the most competition against the other firm — not the site that produces the highest gross sales. Of course, someone else may well have a different interpretation of what constitutes the best site.

Solution   If we assign rows as Alpha strategies and columns as Omega strategies and if we use positive entries to denote the gain of Alpha over Omega and negative entries for the gain of Omega over Alpha, then the matrix game for this situation is

Omega

City   Suburb

Alpha   City $\begin{bmatrix} 1 & -3 \\ 4 & -2 \end{bmatrix}$
         Suburb

where the entries are in thousands of dollars.

This game is strictly determined and the saddle point is -2, which is the value of the game. Thus, if both firms locate in the suburb, this results in the best competition. This is so since Omega will always choose to locate in the suburb, guaranteeing a larger profit than Alpha. This being the case, Alpha, in order to minimize this larger profit of Omega, must always choose the suburb. Of course, the game is not fair since it is favorable to Omega.   □

Exercise 10.1   *Answers to Odd-Numbered Problems begin on page* 626 .

In Problems 1 – 4 write the matrix game that corresponds to each two-person conflict situation.

1. Tami and Laura simultaneously each show one or two fingers. If they show the same number of fingers, Tami pays Laura one dime. If they show a different number of fingers, Laura pays Tami one dime.

2. Tami and Laura simultaneously each show one or two fingers. If the total number of fingers shown is even, Tami pays Laura that number of dimes. If the total number of fingers shown is odd, Laura pays Tami that number of dimes.

3. Tami and Laura, simultaneously and independently, each write down one of the numbers 1, 4, or 7. If the sum of the numbers is even, Tami pays Laura that number of dimes. If the sum of the numbers is odd, Laura pays Tami that number of dimes.

4. Tami and Laura, simultaneously and independently, each write down one of the numbers 3, 6, or 8. If the sum of the numbers is even, Tami pays Laura that number of dimes. If the sum of the numbers is odd, Laura pays Tami that number of dimes.

In Problems 5 – 14 determine which of the two-person, zero-sum games are strictly determined. For those that are, find the value of the game. All entries are the winnings of Player I, who plays rows.

5. $\begin{bmatrix} -1 & 2 \\ -3 & 6 \end{bmatrix}$

6. $\begin{bmatrix} 4 & 0 \\ 0 & -1 \end{bmatrix}$

7. $\begin{bmatrix} 4 & 2 \\ 3 & 1 \end{bmatrix}$

8. $\begin{bmatrix} -6 & -1 \\ 0 & 0 \end{bmatrix}$

9. $\begin{bmatrix} 2 & 0 & -1 \\ 3 & 6 & 0 \\ 1 & 3 & 7 \end{bmatrix}$

10. $\begin{bmatrix} 2 & 3 & -2 \\ -2 & 0 & 4 \\ 0 & -3 & -2 \end{bmatrix}$

11. $\begin{bmatrix} 1 & 0 & 3 \\ -1 & 2 & 1 \\ 2 & 2 & 3 \end{bmatrix}$

12. $\begin{bmatrix} 1 & -3 & -2 \\ 2 & 5 & 4 \\ 2 & 3 & 2 \end{bmatrix}$

13. $\begin{bmatrix} 6 & 4 & -2 & 0 \\ -1 & 7 & 5 & 2 \\ 1 & 0 & 4 & 4 \end{bmatrix}$

14. $\begin{bmatrix} 8 & 6 & 4 & 0 \\ -1 & 6 & 5 & -2 \\ 0 & 1 & 3 & 3 \end{bmatrix}$

15. For what values of a is the matrix below strictly determined?

$$\begin{bmatrix} a & 8 & 3 \\ 0 & a & -9 \\ -5 & 5 & a \end{bmatrix}$$

16. Show that the matrix below is strictly determined for any choice of a, b, or c.

$$\begin{bmatrix} a & a \\ b & c \end{bmatrix}$$

17. Find necessary and sufficient conditions for the matrix below to be strictly determined.

$$\begin{bmatrix} a & 0 \\ 0 & b \end{bmatrix}$$

10.2 MIXED STRATEGIES

□ **Example 1**   Consider a two-person zero-sum game given by the matrix

$$\begin{bmatrix} 6 & 0 \\ -2 & 3 \end{bmatrix}$$

in which the entries denote the winnings of Player I. Is this game strictly determined? If so, find its value.

Solution   We find that the smallest entry in each row is

Row 1:   0   Row 2:   −2

The entry 0 in row 1 is not the largest element in its column; similarly, the entry −2 in row 2 is not the largest element in its column. Thus, this game is not strictly determined.   □

At this stage, we would like to stress the point that a matrix game is not usually played just once. With this in mind, Player I in Example 1 might decide always to play row 1 since he may win $6 at best and win $0 at worst. Does this mean he should always employ this strategy? If he does, Player II would catch on and begin to choose column 2 since this strategy limits his losses to $0. However, after awhile, Player I would probably start choosing row 2 to obtain a payoff of $3. Thus, in a non-strictly determined game, it would be advisable for the players to *mix* their strategies rather than to use the same one all the time. That is, a random selection is desirable. Indeed, to make certain that the other player does not discover the pattern of moves, it may be best not to have any pattern at all. For instance, Player I may elect to play row 1 in 40% of the plays (that is, with probability .4), while Player II elects to play column 2 in 80% of the plays (that is, with probability .8). This idea of mixing strategies is important and useful in game theory. Games in which each player's strategies are

Mixed-Strategy
Games
mixed are termed *mixed-strategy games.*

Suppose we know the probability for each player to choose a certain strategy. What meaning can be given to the term *payoff of a game* if mixed strategies are used? Since the payoff has been defined for a pair of pure strategies and in a mixed-strategy situation we do not know which strategy is being used, it is not possible to define a payoff for a single game. However, in the long run, we do know how often each strategy is being used, and we can use this information to compute the *expected payoff* of the game.

In Example 1, if Player I chooses row 1 in 50% of the plays and row 2 in 50% of the plays, and if Player II chooses column 1 in 30% of the plays and column 2 in 70% of the plays, the expected payoff of the game can be computed. For example, the strategy of row 1, column 1, is chosen $(.5)(.3) = .15$ of the time. This strategy has a payoff of $6, so that the expected payoff will be $(\$6)(.15) = \$0.90$. Table 1 summarizes the entire process. Thus, the expected payoff E of this game, when the given strategies are employed, is $1.65, which makes the game favorable to Player I.

Table 1

Strategy	Payoff	Probability	Expected Payoff
Row 1—Column 1	6	.15	$0.90
Row 2—Column 1	−2	.15	−0.30
Row 1—Column 2	0	.35	0.00
Row 2—Column 2	3	.35	1.05
	Totals	1.00	$1.65

If we look very carefully at the above derivation, we get a clue as to how the expected payoff of a game that is not strictly determined should be defined.

Let's consider a game defined by the 2×2 matrix

$$A = \begin{bmatrix} a_{11} & a_{12} \\ a_{21} & a_{22} \end{bmatrix}$$

Let the strategy for Player I, who plays rows, be denoted by the row vector

$$P = \begin{bmatrix} p_1 & p_2 \end{bmatrix}$$

and the strategy for Player II, who plays columns, be denoted by the column vector

$$Q = \begin{bmatrix} q_1 \\ q_2 \end{bmatrix}$$

The probability that Player I wins the amount a_{11} is $p_1 q_1$. Similarly, the probabilities that he wins the amounts a_{12}, a_{21}, and a_{22} are $p_1 q_2, p_2 q_1$, and $p_2 q_2$, respectively. If we denote by $E(P, Q)$ the expectation of Player I, that is, the expected value of the amount he wins when he uses strategy P and Player II uses strategy Q, then

$$E(P, Q) = p_1 a_{11} q_1 + p_1 a_{12} q_2 + p_2 a_{21} q_1 + p_2 a_{22} q_2$$

Using matrix notation, the above can be expressed as

$$E(P, Q) = PAQ$$

In general, if A is an $m \times n$ matrix game, we are led to the following definition:

Expected Payoff   The *expected payoff E* of a two-person zero-sum game, defined by the matrix *A*, in which the row vector *P* and column vector *Q* define the respective strategy probabilities of Player I and Player II is

$$E = PAQ$$

If a matrix game $A = [a_{ij}]$ of dimension $m \times n$ is strictly determined, then one of the entries is a saddle point. This saddle point can always be placed in the first row and first column by simply rearranging and renumbering the rows and columns of A. The value of the game is then a_{11}, and P and Q are vectors of the form

$$P = [1 \quad 0 \quad 0 \quad 0 \quad 0 \quad \cdots \quad 0] \qquad Q = \begin{bmatrix} 1 \\ 0 \\ \cdot \\ \cdot \\ \cdot \\ 0 \end{bmatrix}$$

where P is of dimension $1 \times m$ and Q is of dimension $n \times 1$.

□ **Example 2**   Find the expected payoff of the matrix game

$$A = \begin{bmatrix} 3 & -1 \\ -2 & 1 \\ 1 & 0 \end{bmatrix}$$

if Player I and Player II decide on the strategies

$$P = [\tfrac{1}{3} \quad \tfrac{1}{3} \quad \tfrac{1}{3}] \qquad Q = \begin{bmatrix} \tfrac{1}{3} \\ \tfrac{2}{3} \end{bmatrix}$$

Solution   The expected payoff E of this game is

$$E = PAQ = [\tfrac{1}{3} \quad \tfrac{1}{3} \quad \tfrac{1}{3}] \begin{bmatrix} 3 & -1 \\ -2 & 1 \\ 1 & 0 \end{bmatrix} \begin{bmatrix} \tfrac{1}{3} \\ \tfrac{2}{3} \end{bmatrix}$$

$$= [\tfrac{2}{3} \quad 0] \begin{bmatrix} \tfrac{1}{3} \\ \tfrac{2}{3} \end{bmatrix} = \frac{2}{9}$$

Thus, the game is biased in favor of Player I and has an expected payoff of $\tfrac{2}{9}$.   □

Most games are not strictly determined. That is, most games do not give rise to best pure strategies for each player. Examples of games that are not strictly determined are matching pennies (see Example 1, Section 10.1), bridge, poker, and so on. In the next two sections, we discuss techniques for finding optimal strategies for games that are not strictly determined.

Exercise 10.2   *Answers to Odd-Numbered Problems begin on page* 626.

1. For the game of Example 1, find the expected payoff E if Player I chooses row 1 in 30% of the plays and Player II chooses column 1 in 40% of the plays.

2. For the game of Example 2, find the expected payoff E if Player I chooses row 1 with probability .3 and row 2 with probability .4, while Player II chooses column 1 half the time.

In Problems 3–6 find the expected payoff of the game $\begin{bmatrix} 4 & 0 \\ 2 & 3 \end{bmatrix}$ for the given strategies.

3. $P = \begin{bmatrix} \frac{1}{2} & \frac{1}{2} \end{bmatrix}; \quad Q = \begin{bmatrix} \frac{1}{2} \\ \frac{1}{2} \end{bmatrix}$

4. $P = \begin{bmatrix} \frac{1}{2} & \frac{1}{2} \end{bmatrix}; \quad Q = \begin{bmatrix} \frac{3}{4} \\ \frac{1}{4} \end{bmatrix}$

5. $P = \begin{bmatrix} \frac{1}{4} & \frac{3}{4} \end{bmatrix}; \quad Q = \begin{bmatrix} \frac{1}{2} \\ \frac{1}{2} \end{bmatrix}$

6. $P = \begin{bmatrix} 0 & 1 \end{bmatrix}; \quad Q = \begin{bmatrix} 0 \\ 1 \end{bmatrix}$

In Problems 7–10 find the expected payoff of each game.

7. $\begin{bmatrix} 4 & 0 \\ -3 & 6 \end{bmatrix}; \quad P = \begin{bmatrix} \frac{2}{3} & \frac{1}{3} \end{bmatrix}; \quad Q = \begin{bmatrix} \frac{1}{3} \\ \frac{2}{3} \end{bmatrix}$

8. $\begin{bmatrix} 1 & -1 \\ -2 & 3 \end{bmatrix}; \quad P = \begin{bmatrix} \frac{1}{4} & \frac{3}{4} \end{bmatrix}; \quad Q = \begin{bmatrix} \frac{1}{3} \\ \frac{2}{3} \end{bmatrix}$

9. $\begin{bmatrix} 1 & 0 & 0 \\ 0 & 1 & 0 \\ 0 & 0 & 1 \end{bmatrix}; \quad P = \begin{bmatrix} \frac{1}{3} & \frac{1}{3} & \frac{1}{3} \end{bmatrix}; \quad Q = \begin{bmatrix} \frac{1}{3} \\ \frac{1}{3} \\ \frac{1}{3} \end{bmatrix}$

10. $\begin{bmatrix} 4 & -1 & 0 \\ 2 & 3 & 1 \end{bmatrix}; \quad P = \begin{bmatrix} \frac{1}{3} & \frac{2}{3} \end{bmatrix}; \quad Q = \begin{bmatrix} \frac{2}{3} \\ \frac{1}{6} \\ \frac{1}{6} \end{bmatrix}$

11. Show that in a 2 × 2 game

$$\begin{bmatrix} a_{11} & a_{12} \\ a_{21} & a_{22} \end{bmatrix}$$

the only games that are not strictly determined are those for which either

(a) $a_{11} > a_{12}, \quad a_{11} > a_{21}, \quad a_{21} < a_{22}, \quad a_{12} < a_{22}$

or

(b) $a_{11} < a_{12}, \quad a_{11} < a_{21}, \quad a_{21} > a_{22}, \quad a_{12} > a_{22}$

Also show that all others are strictly determined.

10.3 OPTIMAL STRATEGY IN TWO-PERSON ZERO-SUM GAMES WITH 2 × 2 MATRICES

VALUE OF A GAME □ APPLICATIONS

We have already seen that the best strategy for two-person zero-sum games that are strictly determined is found in the row and column containing the saddle point. Suppose the game is not strictly determined so that the conditions given in Problem 11, Exercise 10.2, are satisfied.

In 1927, John von Neumann, along with E. Borel, initiated research in the theory of games and proved that, even in non-strictly determined games, there is a single

EMIL BOREL (1871–1956) was a prominent French mathematician. In his book, *Le Hasard,* he described the penetration of probabilistic methods into physics, biology, and other branches of science as well as the relationship between probability theory and other branches of mathematics. His pioneering work helped launch the field of measure theory on which the modern notions of length, area, and probability rest. He was a member of the Chamber of Deputies and served as the Minister of the Navy.

course of action that represents the best strategy. In practice, this means that in order to avoid always using a single strategy, a player in a game may instead choose plays randomly according to a fixed probability. This has the effect of making it impossible for the opponent to know what the player will do, since even the player will not know until the final moment. That is, by selecting a strategy randomly according to the laws of probability, the actual strategy chosen at any one time cannot be known even to the one choosing it.

For example, in the Italian game of *Morra* each player shows 1, 2, or 3 fingers and simultaneously calls out his guess as to what the sum of his and his opponent's fingers is. It can be shown that if he guesses 4 fingers each time and varies his own moves so that every twleve times he shows 1 finger five times, 2 fingers four times, and 3 fingers three times, he will, at worst, break even (in the long run).

□ **Example 1**   Consider the non-strictly determined game

$$A = \begin{bmatrix} 1 & -1 \\ -2 & 3 \end{bmatrix}$$

in which Player I plays rows and Player II plays columns. Determine the optimal strategy for each player.

Solution   If Player I chooses row 1 with probability p, then he must choose row 2 with probability $1 - p$. If Player II chooses column 1, Player I then expects to earn

$$E_I = p + (-2)(1 - p) = 3p - 2 \tag{1}$$

Similarly, if Player II chooses column 2, Player I expects to earn

$$E_I = (-1)p + 3(1 - p) = -4p + 3 \tag{2}$$

We graph these using E_I as the vertical axis and p as the horizontal axis. See Figure 1*(a)*.

Figure 1

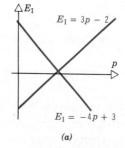

(a)

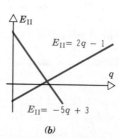

(b)

Player I wants to maximize his expected earning so he should maximize the minimum expected gain. This occurs when the two lines intersect, since for any other choice of p one or the other of the two expected earnings is less. Thus, solving equations (1) and (2) simultaneously, we obtain

$$3p - 2 = -4p + 3$$
$$7p = 5$$
$$p = \frac{5}{7}$$

The optimal strategy for Player I is therefore

$$P = [\tfrac{5}{7} \quad \tfrac{2}{7}]$$

Similarly, suppose Player II chooses column 1 with probability q (and therefore column 2 with probability $1 - q$. If Player I chooses row 1, Player II's expected earnings are

$$E_{\text{II}} = q + (-1)(1 - q) = 2q - 1$$

If Player I chooses row 2, Player II's expected earnings are

$$E_{\text{II}} = (-2)(q) + 3(1 - q) = -5q + 3$$

The optimal strategy for Player II occurs when

$$2q - 1 = -5q + 3$$
$$7q = 4$$
$$q = \frac{4}{7}$$

See Figure 1*(b)*. The optimal strategy for Player II is

$$Q = \begin{bmatrix} \tfrac{4}{7} \\ \tfrac{3}{7} \end{bmatrix}$$

The expected payoff E corresponding to these optimal strategies is

$$E = PAQ = [\tfrac{5}{7} \quad \tfrac{2}{7}] \begin{bmatrix} 1 & -1 \\ -2 & 3 \end{bmatrix} \begin{bmatrix} \tfrac{4}{7} \\ \tfrac{3}{7} \end{bmatrix} = \frac{1}{7} \qquad \square$$

VALUE OF A GAME

Now, consider a two-person zero-sum game given by the 2×2 matrix

$$A = \begin{bmatrix} a_{11} & a_{12} \\ a_{21} & a_{22} \end{bmatrix}$$

in which Player I chooses row strategies and Player II chooses column strategies.

Using the method illustrated above, it can be shown that the optimal strategy for Player I is given by $P = [p_1 \quad p_2]$, where

$$p_1 = \frac{a_{22} - a_{21}}{a_{11} + a_{22} - a_{12} - a_{21}} \qquad p_2 = \frac{a_{11} - a_{12}}{a_{11} + a_{22} - a_{12} - a_{21}} \qquad (3)$$

with $a_{11} + a_{22} - a_{12} - a_{21} \neq 0$. Notice that $p_1 + p_2 = 1$, as expected. Similarly, the optimal strategy for Player II is given by $Q = [\begin{smallmatrix} q_1 \\ q_2 \end{smallmatrix}]$, where

$$q_1 = \frac{a_{22} - a_{12}}{a_{11} + a_{22} - a_{12} - a_{21}} \qquad q_2 = \frac{a_{11} - a_{21}}{a_{11} + a_{22} - a_{12} - a_{21}} \qquad (4)$$

with $a_{11} + a_{22} - a_{12} - a_{21} \neq 0$, and $q_1 + q_2 = 1$. The expected payoff E of the game corresponding to these optimal strategies is

$$E = PAQ = \frac{a_{11} \cdot a_{22} - a_{12} \cdot a_{21}}{a_{11} + a_{22} - a_{12} - a_{21}}$$

When optimal strategies are used, the expected payoff E of the game is called the *value V of the game.*

Value of a Game

□ **Example 2**   For the game matrix

$$\begin{bmatrix} 1 & -1 \\ -2 & 3 \end{bmatrix}$$

determine the optimal strategies for Player I and Player II, and find the value of the game.

Solution   Using formula (3), we have

$$p_1 = \frac{3 - (-2)}{1 + 3 - (-1) - (-2)} = \frac{5}{7}$$

$$p_2 = \frac{1 - (-1)}{1 + 3 - (-1) - (-2)} = \frac{2}{7}$$

Thus, Player I's optimal strategy is to select row 1 with probability $\frac{5}{7}$ and row 2 with probability $\frac{2}{7}$. Also, by (4), Player II's optimal strategy is

$$q_1 = \frac{3 - (-1)}{1 + 3 - (-1) - (-2)} = \frac{4}{7}$$

$$q_2 = \frac{1 - (-2)}{1 + 3 - (-1) - (-2)} = \frac{3}{7}$$

Player II's optimal strategy is to select column 1 with probability $\frac{4}{7}$ and column 2 with probability $\frac{3}{7}$. The value V of the game is

$$V = \frac{1 \cdot 3 - (-1)(-2)}{1 + 3 - (-1) - (-2)} = \frac{1}{7}$$

Thus, in the long run, the game is favorable to Player I.   □

The results obtained in Example 2 are in agreement with those obtained earlier using the graphical technique.

□ **Example 3**   Find the optimal strategy for each player, and determine the value of the game given by the matrix

$$\begin{bmatrix} 6 & 0 \\ -2 & 3 \end{bmatrix}$$

Solution   Using the graphical technique or formulas (3) and (4), we find Player I's optimal strategy to be

$$p_1 = \frac{5}{11} \qquad p_2 = \frac{6}{11}$$

Player II's optimal strategy is

$$q_1 = \frac{3}{11} \qquad q_2 = \frac{8}{11}$$

The value V of the game is

$$V = \frac{18}{11} = 1.64$$

Thus, the game favors Player I, whose optimal strategy is $\begin{bmatrix} \frac{5}{11} & \frac{6}{11} \end{bmatrix}$.   □

APPLICATIONS

□ **Example 4**   In a presidential campaign, there are two candidates, a Democrat (D) and a Republican (R), and two types of issues, domestic issues and foreign issues. The units assigned to each candidate's strategy are given in the table. We assume that positive entries indicate a strength for the democratic candidate, while negative entries indicate a weakness. We also assume that a strength of one candidate equals a weakness of the other so that the game is zero-sum. The question is, what is the best strategy for each candidate? What is the value of the game?

		Republican	
		Domestic	**Foreign**
Democrat	Domestic	4	−2
	Foreign	−1	3

Solution   Notice first that this game is not strictly determined. If D chooses to always play foreign issues, then R will counter with domestic issues, in which case D would also talk about domestic issues, in which case, etc., etc. There is no *single* strategy either can use. We compute that the optimal strategy for the Democrat is

$$p_1 = \frac{3 - (-1)}{4 + 3 - (-2) - (-1)} = \frac{4}{10} = .4 \qquad p_2 = \frac{4 - (-2)}{10} = .6$$

The optimal strategy for the Republican is

$$q_1 = \frac{3 - (-2)}{10} = .5 \qquad q_2 = \frac{4 - (-1)}{10} = .5$$

Thus, the best strategy for the Democrat is to spend 40% of his time on domestic issues and 60% on foreign issues, while the Republician should divide his time evenly between the two issues.

The value of the game is

$$V = \frac{3 \cdot 4 - (-1)(-2)}{10} = \frac{10}{10} = 1.0$$

Thus, no matter what the Republican does, the Democrat gains at least 1.0 unit by employing his best strategy.   □

□ **Example 5**

War Game

In a naval battle, attacking bomber planes are trying to sink ships in a fleet protected by an aircraft carrier with fighter planes. The bombers can attack either high or low, with a low attack giving more accurate results. Similarly, the aircraft carrier can send its fighters at high altitudes or low altitudes to search for the bombers. If the bombers avoid the fighters, credit the bombers with 8 points; if the bombers and fighters meet, credit the bombers with −2 points. Also, credit the bombers with 3 additional points for flying low (since this results in more accurate bombing). Find optimal strategies for the bombers and the fighters. What is the value of the game?

Solution

First, we set up the game matrix. Designate the bombers as playing rows and the fighters as playing columns. Also, each entry of the matrix will denote winnings of the bombers. Then the game matrix is

$$
\begin{array}{cc}
 & \text{Fighters} \\
 & \begin{array}{cc} \text{Low} & \text{High} \end{array} \\
\text{Bombers} \begin{array}{c} \text{Low} \\ \text{High} \end{array} & \begin{bmatrix} 1 & 11 \\ 8 & -2 \end{bmatrix}
\end{array}
$$

The reason for a 1 in row 1, column 1, is that −2 points are credited for the planes meeting, but 3 additional points are credited to the bombers for a low flight.

Next, using formulas (3) and (4), the optimal strategies for the bombers $[p_1 \quad p_2]$ and for the fighters $\begin{bmatrix} q_1 \\ q_2 \end{bmatrix}$ are

$$
p_1 = \frac{-10}{-20} = \frac{1}{2} \qquad p_2 = \frac{-10}{-20} = \frac{1}{2}
$$

$$
q_1 = \frac{-13}{-20} = \frac{13}{20} \qquad q_2 = \frac{-7}{-20} = \frac{7}{20}
$$

The value V of the game is

$$
V = \frac{-2 - 88}{-20} = \frac{-90}{-20} = 4.5
$$

Thus, the game is favorable to the bombers, if both players employ their optimal strategies.

The bombers can decide whether to fly high or low by flipping a fair coin and flying high whenever heads appear. The fighters can decide whether to fly high or low by using an urn with 13 black balls and 7 white balls. Each day, a ball should be selected at random and then replaced. If the ball is black, they will go low; if it is white, they will go high.   □

Exercise 10.3 *Answers to Odd-Numbered Problems begin on page* 626.

In Problems 1–6 find the optimal strategy for each player and determine the value of each 2×2 game by using graphical techniques. Check your answers by using formulas (3) and (4).

1. $\begin{bmatrix} 1 & 2 \\ 4 & 1 \end{bmatrix}$

2. $\begin{bmatrix} 2 & 4 \\ 3 & -2 \end{bmatrix}$

3. $\begin{bmatrix} -3 & 2 \\ 1 & 0 \end{bmatrix}$

4. $\begin{bmatrix} 3 & -2 \\ -1 & 2 \end{bmatrix}$

5. $\begin{bmatrix} 2 & -1 \\ -1 & 4 \end{bmatrix}$

6. $\begin{bmatrix} 5 & 4 \\ -3 & 7 \end{bmatrix}$

7. In Example 4, suppose the candidates are assigned the following weights for each issue:

		Republican	
		Domestic	**Foreign**
Democrat	Domestic	4	−1
	Foreign	0	3

What is each candidate's best strategy? What is the value of the game and whom does it favor?

8. *War Game.* For the situation described in Example 5, credit the bomber with 4 points for avoiding the fighters and with −6 points for meeting the fighters. Also, grant the bombers 2 additional points for flying low. What are the optimal strategies and the value of the game? Give instructions to the fighters and bombers as to how they should decide whether to fly high or low.

9. A spy can leave an airport through two exits, one a relatively deserted exit and the other an exit heavily used by the public. His opponent, having been notified of the spy's presence in the airport, must guess which exit he will use. If the spy and opponent meet at the deserted exit, the spy will be killed; if the two meet at the heavily used exit, the spy will be arrested. Assign a payoff of 30 points to the spy if he avoids his opponent by using the deserted exit and of 10 points to the spy if he avoids his opponent by using the busy exit. Assign a payoff of −100 points to the spy if he is killed and −2 points if he is arrested. What are the optimal strategies and the value of the game?

10. Prove formulas (3) and (4).

11. In the matrix game

$$\begin{bmatrix} a_{11} & a_{12} \\ a_{21} & a_{22} \end{bmatrix}$$

what can be said if $a_{11} + a_{22} - a_{12} - a_{21} = 0$?

10.4 OPTIMAL STRATEGY IN OTHER TWO-PERSON ZERO-SUM GAMES USING GEOMETRIC METHODS

DOMINANT/RECESSIVE ROWS AND COLUMNS □ 2 × m OR m × 2 MATRIX GAMES □ MODEL: CULTURAL ANTHROPOLOGY

DOMINANT/RECESSIVE ROWS AND COLUMNS

So far we have discussed how to find optimal strategies for two-person zero-sum games that can be represented only by 2 × 2 matrices. In this section, we shall give techniques for finding optimal strategies when the matrix is not 2 × 2.

We begin with the following definition.

Dominant Row; Recessive Row If a matrix A contains a row r^* with entries that are all less than or equal to the corresponding entries in some other row r, then row r is said to *dominate* row r^* and r^* is said to be *recessive*.

□ **Example 1** In the matrix

$$A = \begin{bmatrix} -6 & -3 & 2 & 2 \\ -2 & 0 & 3 & 2 \\ 5 & -2 & 4 & 0 \end{bmatrix}$$

row 1 is dominated by row 2, since each entry in row 1 is less than or equal to its corresponding entry in row 2; that is,

$$-6 < -2 \quad -3 < 0 \quad 2 < 3 \quad 2 = 2$$ □

If the matrix A of Example 1 were a game in which the entries represent winnings for Player I and if Player I chooses rows, it is clear that Player I would always choose row 2 over row 1, since the values in row 2 always give greater benefit to him than those in row 1. Thus, as far as the matrix representation of this game is concerned, we could represent it by the *reduced matrix*

Reduced Matrix

$$\begin{bmatrix} -2 & 0 & 3 & 2 \\ 5 & -2 & 4 & 0 \end{bmatrix}$$

in which row 1 of matrix A is eliminated since it would never be chosen.

Dominant Column; Recessive Column If a matrix A contains a column c^* with entries that are all greater than or equal to the corresponding entries in some other column c, then column c is said to *dominate* column c^* and c^* is said to be *recessive*.

□ **Example 2** In the matrix

$$A = \begin{bmatrix} -6 & 2 & 4 \\ 4 & 4 & 2 \\ 1 & 3 & -1 \end{bmatrix}$$

column 1 dominates column 2, since each entry in column 2 is greater than or equal to its corresponding entry in column 1; that is,

$$2 > -6 \quad 4 = 4 \quad 3 > 1$$ □

If the matrix A in Example 2 were a game in which the entries denote winnings for Player I and if Player II chooses columns, it is clear that Player II would always prefer column 1 over column 2, since the smaller entries indicate lower losses. For this reason, column 2 can be eliminated from matrix A, and instead the reduced matrix below may be used:

$$\begin{bmatrix} -6 & 4 \\ 4 & 2 \\ 1 & -1 \end{bmatrix}$$

□ **Example 3**   By eliminating recessive rows and columns, find the reduced form of the matrix

$$A = \begin{bmatrix} -6 & -4 & 2 \\ 2 & -1 & 2 \\ -3 & 4 & 4 \end{bmatrix}$$

Solution   First we look at the rows of the matrix A. Notice that each entry in row 3 (and row 2) is greater than or equal to the corresponding entry in row 1. Thus, row 1 is recessive and can be eliminated. The reduced matrix is

$$\begin{bmatrix} 2 & -1 & 2 \\ -3 & 4 & 4 \end{bmatrix}$$

Neither row 1 nor row 2 in the new matrix is recessive, so we now consider the columns. Notice that each entry in column 3 is greater than or equal to the corresponding entry in column 1 (or column 2). Thus, column 3 is recessive. The reduced matrix is

$$\begin{bmatrix} 2 & -1 \\ -3 & 4 \end{bmatrix}$$

□

The above example shows how a 3×3 matrix game can sometimes be reduced to a 2×2 matrix by eliminating recessive rows and recessive columns.

□ **Example 4**   Find the optimal strategy for each player, and find the value of the two-person, zero-sum game

$$\begin{bmatrix} -6 & -4 & 2 \\ 2 & -1 & 2 \\ -3 & 4 & 4 \end{bmatrix}$$

in which the entries denote the winnings of Player I, who chooses rows, and in which each player has three possible strategies.

Solution   By eliminating recessive rows and columns, this matrix reduces to

$$\begin{bmatrix} 2 & -1 \\ -3 & 4 \end{bmatrix}$$

Using formulas (3) and (4) on page 423, we find that the optimal strategy for Player I is

$$p_1 = \frac{7}{10} \qquad p_2 = \frac{3}{10}$$

and the optimal strategy for Player II is

$$q_1 = \frac{5}{10} \qquad q_2 = \frac{5}{10}$$

The value of the game is

$$V = \frac{5}{10}$$

Thus, the game given in this example is favorable to Player I, and his best strategy is to choose row 2 in 70% of the plays and row 3 in 30% of the plays (row 1 is recessive).

□

2 × *m* OR *m* × 2 MATRIX GAMES

Suppose we now consider two-person zero-sum games with matrix representations that are $2 \times m$ or $m \times 2$ $(m > 2)$ matrices, that are not strictly determined, and that contain no recessive rows or columns. For a $2 \times m$ matrix game, Player I has two strategies and Player II has m strategies; for an $m \times 2$ matrix game, Player I has m strategies and Player II has 2 strategies.

We begin with the following example to illustrate how to find optimal strategies.

□ **Example 5**   Find the optimal strategy for each player in the 2×3 game

$$\begin{bmatrix} 4 & -1 & 0 \\ -1 & 4 & 2 \end{bmatrix}$$

in which entries denote winnings for Player I. What is the value of this game?

Solution   In the above game, Player I has two strategies and Player II has three strategies. Suppose p is the probability that Player I plays row 1. Then $1 - p$ is the probability that row 2 is played. Now let's compute the expected earnings of Player I in terms of p.

If Player II elects to play column 1, then the expected earnings E_I of Player I are equal to $4p - 1 \cdot (1 - p)$, or

$$\text{①} \; E_I = 5p - 1$$

Similarly, if Player II selects column 2 or column 3, the expected earnings for Player I are, respectively,

$$\text{②} \; E_I = 4 - 5p \qquad \text{③} \; E_I = 2 - 2p$$

Next, we graph each of these three straight lines measuring E_I along the y-axis and p along the x-axis, and we look at the situation from Player II's point of view. Player II wants to make Player I's earnings as small as possible, since then he maximizes his own earnings. Thus, Player II will always choose the lowest strategy (line), since the height of each line measures winnings of Player I. In other words, Player II's best strategy lies along the darkened line segments in Figure 2.

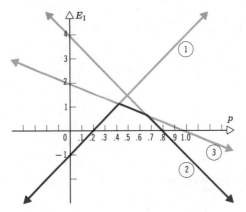

Figure 2

Player I, realizing this, will choose the value of p that yields the most earnings for him. This value occurs at the intersection of the lines

$$① \; E_1 = 5p - 1 \qquad ③ \; E_I = 2 - 2p$$

Their intersection is where

$$p = \frac{3}{7} \qquad E_I = \frac{8}{7}$$

Thus, the optimal strategy for Player I is to choose row 1 in $\frac{3}{7}$ of the plays and row 2 in $\frac{4}{7}$ of the plays. The value of the game in this case is $\frac{8}{7}$.

To find the optimal strategy for Player II, notice that Player I's optimal strategy comes from earnings calculated by using columns 1 and 3 of the matrix game. The matrix that results by eliminating column 2 from the matrix is

$$\begin{bmatrix} 4 & 0 \\ -1 & 2 \end{bmatrix}$$

The optimal strategy for Player II can now be found by formula (4), page 423. It is

$$q_1 = \frac{2}{7} \qquad q_2 = 0 \qquad q_3 = \frac{5}{7}$$

Thus, Player II's strategy is to play column 1 in $\frac{2}{7}$ of the plays and column 3 in $\frac{5}{7}$ of the plays. Since column 2 is eliminated, it is never played. □

□ **Example 6**   Find the optimal strategy for each player in the 5×2 matrix game

$$\begin{bmatrix} -2 & 2 \\ -1 & 1 \\ 2 & 0 \\ 3 & -1 \\ 4 & -2 \end{bmatrix}$$

in which the entries denote winnings for Player I. What is the value of this game?

Solution   Here, Player II has two strategies. Let q be the probability that he chooses column 1, so that $1 - q$ is the probability that he chooses column 2. Player I's earnings E_I are then

① $E_\mathrm{I} = -2q + 2(1 - q)$ ② $E_\mathrm{I} = -q + (1 - q)$
$\quad = -4q + 2$ $\quad = -2q + 1$

③ $E_\mathrm{I} = 2q$ ④ $E_\mathrm{I} = 3q - (1 - q)$
$\quad = 4q - 1$

⑤ $E_\mathrm{I} = 4q - 2(1 - q)$
$\quad = 6q - 2$

for rows 1–5, respectively. We graph these five linear equations in Figure 3.

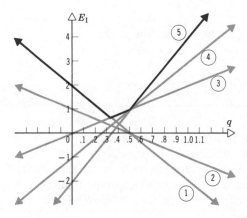

Figure 3

Player I may select any of the five strategies represented by the lines in Figure 3. Since the height of each line represents his earnings, he will employ strategies that carry him along the darkened line segments in Figure 3.

But Player II wants the earnings of Player I to be as small as possible. This occurs at the intersection of ① and ③, where $q = \frac{1}{3}$, $E_\mathrm{I} = \frac{2}{3}$. Thus, the optimal strategy for Player II is to choose column 1 in $\frac{1}{3}$ of the plays and column 2 in $\frac{2}{3}$ of the plays. The value of the game is $\frac{2}{3}$, and it is favorable to Player I.

Now, to find Player I's optimal strategy, we notice that Player II's optimal strategy comes from lines ① and ③. If we eliminate rows 2, 4, and 5 from the matrix above, we obtain the matrix

$$\begin{bmatrix} -2 & 2 \\ 2 & 0 \end{bmatrix}$$

Applying formula (3), page 423, Player I's optimal strategy is

$$p_1 = \frac{-2}{-6} = \frac{1}{3} \qquad p_3 = \frac{-4}{-6} = \frac{2}{3}$$

□

The following is an example from a paper by J. D. Williams.*

□ **Example 7**
Investment Strategy

An investor plans to invest $10,000 during a period of international uncertainty as to whether there will be peace, a continuation of the cold war, or an actual war. Her investment can be made in government bonds, armament stocks, or industrial stocks. The game is a struggle between the investor and nature. The matrix below gives the rate of interest for each player's strategy.

$$
\begin{array}{c}
\\
\\
\text{Investor}
\end{array}
\begin{array}{c}
\\
\text{Government bonds} \\
\text{Armament stocks} \\
\text{Industrial stocks}
\end{array}
\begin{array}{ccc}
\text{Hot war} & \text{Cold war} & \text{Peace} \\
\begin{bmatrix} 2 & 3 & 3.2 \\ 18 & 6 & -2 \\ 2 & 7 & 12 \end{bmatrix}
\end{array}
$$

Calculate the investor's optimal strategy.

Solution

First we look at the matrix to see if there is any row dominance or column dominance. Notice that row 3 dominates row 1 so that the reduced matrix for this game is

$$
\begin{array}{c}
\text{Armament stocks} \\
\text{Industrial stocks}
\end{array}
\begin{array}{ccc}
\text{Hot war} & \text{Cold war} & \text{Peace} \\
\begin{bmatrix} 18 & 6 & -2 \\ 2 & 7 & 12 \end{bmatrix}
\end{array}
$$

This is a 2×3 matrix that can be solved by the graphing method. The optimal strategy for the investor is

$$ p_1 = 0 \qquad p_2 = \frac{5}{17} \qquad p_3 = \frac{12}{17} $$

The value of the game is $V = 6.7$.

Thus, the investor is assured of a return of at least 6.7% when she invests $\frac{5}{17} = 29\%$ in armament stocks and $\frac{12}{17} = 71\%$ in industrial stocks. In the event of a hot war, the return is

$$ 18\left(\frac{5}{17}\right) + 2\left(\frac{12}{17}\right) = 6.7\% $$

In the event of a cold war, the return is

$$ 6\left(\frac{5}{17}\right) + 7\left(\frac{12}{17}\right) = 6.7\% $$

In the event of peace, the return is

$$ (-2)\left(\frac{5}{17}\right) + 12\left(\frac{12}{17}\right) = 7.9\% $$

□

□ **Example 8**
War Game

General White's army and the enemy are each trying to occupy three hills. General White has three regiments and the enemy has two regiments. A hill is occupied when one force has more regiments present than the other force; if both try to occupy a hill with the same number of regiments, a draw results. How should the troops be deployed to gain maximum advantage?

* J. D. Williams, *La Strategie dans les Actions Humaines,* Dunod, Paris, 1956.

Solution We denote the three strategies available to General White as follows:

3: All three regiments used together to attack one hill.

2,1: Two regiments used together and one used by itself to attack two hills.

1,1,1: All three regiments used separately to attack three hills.

White's opponent has two strategies available, namely:

2: The two regiments used together to defend one hill.

1,1: The two regiments used separately to defend two of the hills.

White will play rows, and the entries in the game matrix will denote White's expected winnings based on the rule that when White takes a hill, he earns 1 point; when a draw results, he earns 0 points; and when he is defeated, he loses 1 point. Also, for each division that is overpowered, 1 point is earned. Table 2 shows the points won (or lost) by General White for all possible deployments of his regiments. Notice that the order of deployment is quite important.

Table 2

	2,0,0	0,2,0	0,0,2	1,1,0	1,0,1	0,1,1
3,0,0	3	0	0	1	1	−1
0,3,0	0	3	0	1	−1	1
0,0,3	0	0	3	−1	1	1
2,1,0	1	−1	1	2	2	0
2,0,1	1	1	−1	2	2	0
1,2,0	−1	1	1	2	0	2
0,2,1	1	1	−1	2	0	2
1,0,2	−1	1	1	0	2	2
0,1,2	1	−1	1	0	2	2
1,1,1	0	0	0	1	1	1

For example, if White deploys his regiments as 3,0,0 and his opponent uses the deployment 2,0,0, then White captures Hill I, winning 1 point, and overpowers two regiments, winning 2 points, for a total score of 3 points. If White uses 0,2,1 and his opponent uses 0,1,1, then Hill I is a standoff, White wins Hill II and overpowers one regiment, and Hill III is a draw. Here, White has a total score of 2 points.

To determine the game matrix, we proceed as follows: If White uses a 3 deployment and his enemy uses a 2 deployment, then White expects to score 3 points $\frac{1}{3}$ of the time and score 0 points $\frac{2}{3}$ of the time. We assign an expected payoff to White of $3 \cdot \frac{1}{3} + 0 \cdot \frac{2}{3} = 1$ point in this case. If White uses a 2,1 deployment and his enemy uses a 1,1 deployment, then White expects to gain 2 points $\frac{2}{3}$ of the time and 0 points $\frac{1}{3}$ of the time for an expected payoff of $\frac{4}{3}$ points. The game matrix can be written as

$$
\begin{array}{cc}
 & \text{Enemy} \\
 & \begin{array}{cc} 2 & 1,1 \end{array} \\
\text{White} \begin{array}{c} 3 \\ 2,1 \\ 1,1,1 \end{array} & \begin{bmatrix} 1 & \frac{1}{3} \\ \frac{1}{3} & \frac{4}{3} \\ 0 & 1 \end{bmatrix}
\end{array}
$$

Notice that this matrix can be reduced, since row 2 dominates row 3. The reduced matrix is

$$
\begin{array}{cc}
 & \text{Enemy} \\
 & \begin{array}{cc} 2 & 1,1 \end{array} \\
\text{White} \begin{array}{c} 3 \\ 2,1 \end{array} & \begin{bmatrix} 1 & \frac{1}{3} \\ \frac{1}{3} & \frac{4}{3} \end{bmatrix}
\end{array}
$$

This matrix is not strictly determined. The optimal (mixed) strategy for General White is

$$ p_1 = \frac{1}{\frac{7}{3} - \frac{2}{3}} = .6 \qquad p_2 = \frac{\frac{2}{3}}{\frac{5}{3}} = .4 \qquad p_3 = 0 $$

The optimal strategy for the enemy is

$$ q_1 = \frac{1}{\frac{5}{3}} = .6 \qquad q_2 = \frac{\frac{2}{3}}{\frac{5}{3}} = .4 $$

The value of the game is

$$ V = \frac{\frac{4}{3} - \frac{1}{9}}{\frac{5}{3}} = \frac{\frac{11}{9}}{\frac{5}{3}} = \frac{11}{15} $$

The game is favorable to General White, who should deploy his troops in a 3 strategy 60% of the time and in a 2,1 strategy 40% of the time. Since no one hill is more likely to be chosen for attack than any other, it follows that each hill should be attacked by all three regiments 20% of the time. Furthermore, for the 2,1 deployment, each possible selection of the hills to receive 0,1, or 2 regiments (6 in all) will be used $\frac{.40}{6} = 6.67\%$ of the time.   □

MODEL: CULTURAL ANTHROPOLOGY

In 1960, Davenport* published an analysis of the behavior of Jamaican fishermen. Each fishing crew is confronted with a three-choice decision of fishing in the inside banks, the outside banks, or a combination of inside–outside banks. Fairly reliable estimates can be made of the quantity and quality of fish caught in these three areas under the two conditions that current is present, or not present.

* E. Davenport, "Jamaican Fishing: A Game Theory Analysis in Papers on Caribbean Anthropology," Yale University Publication in Anthropology, Nos. 57–64, 1960.

If we take the village as a whole as one player and the environment as another player, we have the components for a two-person zero-sum game, in which the village has three strategies (inside, inside–outside, outside) and the environment has two strategies (current, no current). Davenport computed an estimate of income claimed by the fishermen using each of the alternatives. This estimate is given in matrix form by

$$
\begin{array}{cc}
 & \text{Environment} \\
\end{array}
$$

$$
\text{Village} \quad
\begin{array}{l}
\text{Inside} \\
\text{Inside–Outside} \\
\text{Outside}
\end{array}
\begin{array}{cc}
\text{Current} & \text{No current} \\
\end{array}
\begin{bmatrix}
17.3 & 11.5 \\
5.2 & 17.0 \\
-4.4 & 20.6
\end{bmatrix} \qquad (1)
$$

Here the environment has two strategies. Let q be the probability of current, so that $1 - q$ is the probability of no current. If E_I represents the villagers' expected earnings, then

① $E_I = 17.3q + 11.5(1 - q)$ ② $E_I = 5.2q + 17(1 - q)$
$\quad = 5.8q + 11.5$ $\quad = -11.8q + 17$

③ $E_I = -4.4q + 20.6(1 - q)$
$\quad = -25q + 20.6$

Figure 4 shows that the optimal strategy of the environment comes from the intersection of lines ① and ②.

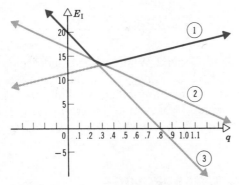

Figure 4

Computing this intersection, we obtain

$$q = .31 \quad \text{and} \quad 1 - q = .69$$

To obtain the optimal strategy of the village, we note that the optimal strategy of the environment comes from lines ① and ②. If we eliminate row 3 from the matrix in (1), we find

$$
\begin{bmatrix}
17.3 & 11.5 \\
5.2 & 17.0
\end{bmatrix}
$$

Applying formula (3), page 423, the village's optimal strategy is

$$p_1 = \frac{17.0 - 5.2}{34.3 - 16.7} = \frac{11.8}{17.6} = .67 \qquad p_2 = \frac{5.8}{17.6} = .33$$

Table 3 compares the observed frequency of strategy usage as compared with the optimal usage as predicted by the game.

Table 3

	Observed	Predicted
Outside	0	0
Inside	.69	.67
Inside–Outside	.31	.33
Current	.25	.31
No Current	.75	.69

Exercise 10.4 *Answers to Odd-Numbered Problems begin on page* 627.

In Problems 1–12, find the optimal strategy for each player, where Player I plays rows and entries denote winnings of Player I. What is the value of each game?

1.
$$\begin{bmatrix} 8 & 3 & 8 \\ 6 & 5 & 4 \\ -2 & 4 & 1 \end{bmatrix}$$

2.
$$\begin{bmatrix} 3 & -1 & 0 \\ -2 & 1 & -1 \end{bmatrix}$$

3.
$$\begin{bmatrix} 2 & 1 & 0 & 6 \\ 3 & -2 & 1 & 2 \end{bmatrix}$$

4.
$$\begin{bmatrix} -1 & 1 \\ 5 & -3 \\ 1 & -2 \\ -2 & 5 \end{bmatrix}$$

5.
$$\begin{bmatrix} 6 & -4 & 2 & -3 \\ -4 & 6 & -5 & 7 \end{bmatrix}$$

6.
$$\begin{bmatrix} 3 & -2 & 2 \\ -1 & 1 & 0 \end{bmatrix}$$

7.
$$\begin{bmatrix} 4 & -5 & 5 \\ -6 & 3 & 3 \\ 2 & -6 & 3 \end{bmatrix}$$

8.
$$\begin{bmatrix} -5 & -4 & -3 & 2 & 3 \\ 3 & 2 & 1 & -2 & -4 \end{bmatrix}$$

9.
$$\begin{bmatrix} 1 & 3 & 0 \\ 0 & -3 & 1 \\ 0 & 4 & 1 \\ -2 & 1 & 1 \end{bmatrix}$$

10.
$$\begin{bmatrix} 6 & -4 \\ 4 & -3 \\ 1 & 0 \\ -3 & 2 \\ -5 & 4 \end{bmatrix}$$

11.
$$\begin{bmatrix} 4 & 3 & -1 \\ 1 & 1 & 4 \\ 1 & 0 & 2 \end{bmatrix}$$

12.
$$\begin{bmatrix} 3 & 2 & 0 \\ 1 & 5 & -2 \\ 0 & 1 & 1 \end{bmatrix}$$

13. In a department store, one area (A) is usually very crowded and the other area (B) is usually relatively empty. The store employs two detectives and has closed-circuit television (T) to control pilferage. The television covers A and B and the detectives can be in either area A or area B or watching the television (T). The matrix below gives an estimate of the probability of the detectives finding and arresting a thief:

$$
\text{Detectives}
\begin{array}{c}
\\
TT \\
AA \\
BB \\
TA \\
TB \\
AB
\end{array}
\overset{\displaystyle \text{Thief}}{\overset{\displaystyle \begin{array}{cc} A & B \end{array}}{
\begin{bmatrix}
.51 & .75 \\
.64 & .36 \\
.19 & .91 \\
.58 & .60 \\
.37 & .85 \\
.56 & .76
\end{bmatrix}}}
$$

Here, TT means both detectives are at the television, TA means the first detective is at the television and the second is in area A, and so on. Find the optimal strategy for the thief and the detectives. What is the value of the game?

14. *Effectiveness of Antibiotics.* This problem is adapted from J. D. Williams.* Three antibiotics, A_1, A_2, and A_3, and five types of bacilli, M_1, M_1, M_3, M_4, and M_5, are involved in a study of the effectiveness of antibiotics on bacilli, with A_1 having a probability .3 of destroying M_1, and so on, as given below. Without knowing the proportion in which these germs are distributed during an epidemic, in what ratio should the antibiotics be mixed to have the greatest probability of being effective?

$$
\text{Antibiotics}
\begin{array}{c}
\\
A_1 \\
A_2 \\
A_3
\end{array}
\overset{\displaystyle \text{Bacilli}}{\overset{\displaystyle \begin{array}{ccccc} M_1 & M_2 & M_3 & M_4 & M_5 \end{array}}{
\begin{bmatrix}
.3 & .4 & .5 & 1 & 0 \\
.2 & .3 & .6 & 0 & 1 \\
.1 & .5 & .3 & .1 & 0
\end{bmatrix}}}
$$

10.5 TWO-PERSON NONZERO-SUM GAMES

So far we have been concerned only with two-person games in which the winnings of Player I are equal to the losses of Player II, and vice versa; that is, we have considered only zero-sum games. In this section we shall discuss the situation in which the play can result in a gain for both players, or a loss for both players, or a gain for one not equal to the loss of the other. Such games between two players are called *two-person nonzero-sum games.*

Cooperative Games

Noncooperative Games

We divide the class of two-person nonzero-sum games into two categories, *(1) cooperative games* in which preplay communication between the players can occur or preplay binding contracts are used, and *(2) noncooperative games* in which no sharing of information and no communication between the players takes place.

* J. D. Williams, *La Strategie dans les Actions Humaines,* Dunod, Paris, 1956.

For two-person nonzero-sum games, we use two matrices A and B to describe the payoff for a given strategy. Here, the matrix A represents the gains of player I and matrix B represents the gains of Player II. If Player I chooses to play row i and Player II plays column j, then the element a_{ij} in the matrix A gives the payoff to Player I and the entry b_{ij} in the matrix B gives the payoff to Player II.

□ **Example 1**   In a two-person nonzero-sum game, the matrices A and B below give the payoffs of Player I and Player II, respectively:

$$
\overset{\text{Player I}}{A = \begin{bmatrix} 2 & -1 & 3 \\ 1 & 4 & -3 \end{bmatrix}} \qquad \overset{\text{Player II}}{B = \begin{bmatrix} 1 & 0 & 5 \\ -2 & 6 & -3 \end{bmatrix}}
$$

Player I has two strategies and Player II has three strategies. If Player I plays row 1 and Player II plays column 3, then Player I wins 3 and Player II wins 5.   □

□ **Example 2**

Prisoners' Dilemma

Two prisoners who have committed a crime together are separated for questioning by the District Attorney, who claims to have enough evidence to convict them. Each has the choice of squealing or not squealing on the other. If only one of them confesses, he will receive a suspended sentence, while the other will be sentenced to 10 years in jail. However, if both confess, they will each get 6 years in jail. If neither confesses, each will receive a sentence of 2 years. We assume the prisoners cannot communicate with each other. Describe payoff matrices A and B for these prisoners.

Solution   Before writing the matrices, let's assign a value to each decision. If one confesses and the other does not, then the one who confessed has done quite well for himself while the one who did not confess has done very poorly. We assign a high value of 10 for confessing and a low value of 0 for not confessing. If both confess, the jail terms are not as severe as when one confesses and the other does not. We assign a value of 3 to this situation. Finally, if neither confesses, the jail terms are quite lenient for each, so we assign a value of 7 for this occurrence.

Based on this assignment of values for the possible situations, the payoff matrices A and B are

$$
A = \begin{array}{c} \\ \text{Confess} \\ \text{Not confess} \end{array} \overset{\text{Confess} \quad \text{Not confess}}{\begin{bmatrix} 3 & 10 \\ 0 & 7 \end{bmatrix}}
$$

$$
B = \begin{array}{c} \\ \text{Confess} \\ \text{Not confess} \end{array} \overset{\text{Confess} \quad \text{Not confess}}{\begin{bmatrix} 3 & 0 \\ 10 & 7 \end{bmatrix}}
$$

in which the entries of A are those of Prisoner I, who plays rows, and the entries of B are those of Prisoner II, who plays columns.   □

At this point, we confine our discussion to noncooperative games. In a manner quite similar to that of Section 10.1, we can define a *saddle point* for nonzero-sum games.

In a nonzero-sum game, let A and B denote payoff matrices in which A is the payoff matrix for Player I, who plays rows, and B is the payoff matrix for Player II, who plays columns. If each entry in the ith row of matrix A is greater than or equal to corresponding entries in the other rows of A and if each entry in the jth column of matrix B is greater than or equal to the corresponding entries in the other columns of B, then the *saddle pair* for this game is a_{ij} and b_{ij}.

Saddle Pair

For example, in the prisoner's dilemma of Example 2, each entry in row 1 of matrix A exceeds the corresponding entry of row 2. Thus, Player I would always choose to play row 1. Also, each entry in column 1 of matrix B exceeds the corresponding entry in column 2, so that Player II would always choose column 1. (Remember that the entries in matrix B denotes payoffs for Player II, so that he wishes to maximize these values if he can.) Thus, row 1 and column 1 give a saddle pair for this game.

Notice that this saddle pair (both prisoners confess) is not the *best* choice each prisoner could have made. Clearly, if neither one confesses, they (as a team) do much better. However, without cooperation and communication, the choice of confessing is the best strategy *to their knowledge*.

Just as in two-person zero-sum games, it turns out that two-person nonzero-sum games do not always possess a saddle pair. When a saddle pair exists, then a pure strategy also exists. When we try to determine an optimal strategy for two-person, nonzero-sum games, we encounter one of the more important complications of such games. For zero-sum games, we considered the notion of an expected payoff and then, in some sense, each player is found to have an optimal strategy that maximizes his expected payoff. However, this approach will not hold in general for nonzero-sum games. In fact, it is difficult to establish that any kind of optimal strategy is really optimal in a mathematical sense.

Let's now turn our attention to two-person, nonzero-sum games in which cooperation takes place.

In the prisoner's dilemma example we saw that without cooperation each prisoner finds it to his advantage to confess. In doing so, each prisoner maximizes his own position while at the same time minimizing the other prisoner's position. The dilemma occurs since each prisoner thinks it is to his personal disadvantage to choose the strategy that is most advantageous from a cooperative point of view. The only way for the prisoners to reach the attractive strategy of both not confessing, which is not maximal individual strategy, is through cooperation in the form of prior communication and agreement, which can somehow be enforced through means not described in the game matrix.

As a final note, we do not want to give you the impression that our discussion of nonzero-sum games is complete. As a matter of fact, nonzero-sum games are much too complicated to be discussed in any detail here. There are many unsolved problems in this area involving both the nature of play and possible applications.

CHAPTER REVIEW

Important Terms		
two-person game	saddle point	reduced matrix
zero-sum game	fair game	dominant column
payoff	pure strategy	recessive column
game matrix	mixed strategy	two-person nonzero-sum games
strategy	expected payoff	
best strategy	optimal strategy	cooperative games
value	dominant row	noncooperative games
strictly determined	recessive row	saddle pair

True-False Questions

T   F   1. The value of a strictly-determined game is unique.

T   F   2. In a two-person, zero-sum game, whatever is gained (lost) by Player I is lost (gained) by Player II.

T   F   3. A reduced matrix can be formed by removing dominant rows.

T   F   4. In mixed strategy games, the value of the game depends on the strategy each players uses.

Fill in the Blanks

1. Each entry of a matrix game is called a _____ .

2. In a non-strictly determined game, when optimal strategies are used, the expected payoff is called the _____ of the game.

3. Two-person nonzero-sum games are either _____ or _____ .

4. If a matrix A contains a column c* whose entries are greater than or equal to the corresponding entries of another column c, then c is said to _____ c*.

Review Exercises

Answers to Odd-Numbered Problems begin on page 626 .

1. Determine which of the following two-person zero-sum games are strictly determined. For those that are, find the value of the game.

(a) $\begin{bmatrix} 5 & 3 \\ 2 & 4 \end{bmatrix}$

(b) $\begin{bmatrix} 29 & 15 \\ 79 & 3 \end{bmatrix}$

(c) $\begin{bmatrix} 50 & 75 \\ 30 & 15 \end{bmatrix}$

(d) $\begin{bmatrix} 7 & 14 \\ 9 & 13 \end{bmatrix}$

(e) $\begin{bmatrix} 0 & 2 & 4 \\ 4 & 6 & 10 \\ 16 & 14 & 12 \end{bmatrix}$

2. Find the expected payoff of the game below for the given strategies:

$$\begin{bmatrix} -1 & 1 \\ 1 & -1 \end{bmatrix}$$

(a) $P = [\frac{1}{3} \ \frac{2}{3}]$; $Q = \begin{bmatrix} 1 \\ 0 \end{bmatrix}$

(b) $P = [0 \ 1]$; $Q = \begin{bmatrix} \frac{1}{2} \\ \frac{1}{2} \end{bmatrix}$

(c) $P = [\frac{1}{2} \ \frac{1}{2}]$; $Q = \begin{bmatrix} \frac{1}{2} \\ \frac{1}{2} \end{bmatrix}$

3. Show that if a 2×2 or 2×3 matrix game has a saddle point, then either one row dominates the other or one column dominates another column.

4. Give an example to show that the result of Problem 3 is not true for 3×3 matrix games.

5. Find the optimal strategy for each player in the following games. Assume Player I plays rows and entries denote winnings of Player I. What is the value of each game?

(a) $\begin{bmatrix} 4 & 6 & 3 \\ 1 & 2 & 5 \end{bmatrix}$ 　　　　　(b) $\begin{bmatrix} 1 & 6 \\ 5 & 2 \\ 7 & 4 \end{bmatrix}$

(c) $\begin{bmatrix} 2 & 1 \\ 4 & 0 \\ 3 & 4 \end{bmatrix}$ 　　　　　(d) $\begin{bmatrix} 0 & 3 & 2 \\ 4 & 2 & 3 \end{bmatrix}$

6. *Retail Discounting.* Consider a neighborhood in which there are only two competitive stores handling two different, but similar, brands of spark plugs. In ordinary circumstances each retailer pays $0.60 for each plug and sells it for $1.00. However, from time to time, the manufacturers have incentive plans in which they sell the plugs to the retailers for $0.40, provided that the retailer will sell them for $0.70. Each month the retailers must decide, independently of one another, what the selling price for the spark plugs should be. From previous sales patterns, each retailer observers the following pattern: At the usual price, each sells 1000 plugs per month; if one retailer discounts the price and the other does not, the discount store will sell 2000 plugs each month and the other will sell only 300 plugs; if both stores discount the price, they will each sell 1300 plugs per month. Set up the game matrix for this problem. In your opinion, how should each store manager proceed?

11

MARKOV CHAINS

* This section may be omitted without loss of continuity.

11.1 AN INTRODUCTION TO MARKOV CHAINS

MARKOV CHAINS AND TRANSITION MATRICES □ COMPUTING STATE DISTRIBUTIONS

In Chapter 8 we introduced Bernoulli trials. In discussing Bernoulli trials, we made the assumption that the outcome of each experiment is *independent* of the outcome of any previous experiment.

Here we will discuss another type of probabilistic model, called a *Markov chain,* where there is some connection between one trial and the next. Markov chains have been shown to have applications in many areas, among them business, psychology, sociology and biology.

Loosely speaking, a Markov chain or process is one in which what happens next is governed by what happened immediately before. At any stage a Markov experiment is in one of a finite number of states, with the next stage of the experiment consisting of movement to a possibly different state. The probability of moving to a certain state depends only on the state previously occupied and does not vary with time. Here are some situations that may be thought of as Markov chains:

1. There are yearly population shifts between a city and its surrounding suburbs. At any time, a person is either in the city or in the suburbs. So there are two states here with movement between them. As we track the population over time we can ask: What percentage is where?

2. Several detergents compete in the market. Each year there is some shift of customer loyalty from one brand to another. At any point in time the state of a customer would correspond to the brand of detergent he or she uses.

3. A psychology experiment consists of placing a mouse in a maze composed of rooms. The mouse moves from room to room, and we think of this movement as moving from state to state.

Let us elaborate on situation 3 with the idea of introducing some basic notions.

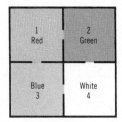

Figure 1

MARKOV CHAINS AND TRANSITION MATRICES

Consider the maze consisting of four connecting rooms shown in Figure 1. The rooms are numbered 1, 2, 3, 4 for convenience and each room contains pulsating lights of a different color. The experiment consists of releasing a mouse in a particular room and observing its behavior.

We assume an observation is made whenever a movement occurs or after a fixed time interval, whichever comes first. Since the movement of the mouse is random in nature we will use probabilistic terms to describe it.

We will refer to the rooms as states. For example, the probability p_{12} that the mouse moves from state 1 to state 2 might be $p_{12} = \frac{1}{2}$, while the probability of moving from state 1 to state 3 might be $p_{13} = \frac{1}{4}$. We are using p_{ij} to represent the probability of moving from state i to state j. So, p_{11} would represent the probability that the mouse remains in room 1 for one observation interval. Here we must have $p_{14} = 0$, since there is no direct passage between rooms 1 and 4.

A convenient way of displaying the probabilities p_{ij} would be to store them in a matrix. The resulting matrix

$$P = \begin{bmatrix} p_{11} & p_{12} & p_{13} & p_{14} \\ p_{21} & p_{22} & p_{23} & p_{24} \\ p_{31} & p_{32} & p_{33} & p_{34} \\ p_{41} & p_{42} & p_{43} & p_{44} \end{bmatrix}$$

Transition Matrix   is called the *transition matrix* of the experiment.

In our example, since there are four states, P is a 4×4 matrix. Were we to assign values to the remaining probabilities, a possible choice for the transition matrix P might be

$$P = \begin{array}{c} \\ 1 \\ 2 \\ 3 \\ 4 \end{array} \begin{array}{cccc} 1 & 2 & 3 & 4 \\ \begin{bmatrix} \frac{1}{4} & \frac{1}{2} & \frac{1}{4} & 0 \\ \frac{1}{6} & \frac{2}{3} & 0 & \frac{1}{6} \\ \frac{1}{3} & 0 & \frac{1}{3} & \frac{1}{3} \\ 0 & \frac{1}{4} & \frac{1}{2} & \frac{1}{4} \end{bmatrix} \end{array}$$

where the rows and columns are indexed by the four states (rooms). Thus P records the probabilities of where the mouse will go next given that we know where it is now. This essential idea of movement from state to state with attached probabilities can be generalized.

Markov Chain A Markov chain is a sequence of experiments each of which result in one of a finite number of states that we label 1, 2, . . . , *m*. The probability that a given state is entered depends only on the state previously occupied.

As before, we let

$$p_{ij} = \text{probability of moving from state } i \text{ to state } j$$

In a Markov chain with *m* states, the *transition matrix* $P = [p_{ij}]$ is an $m \times m$ matrix:

$$P = \begin{bmatrix} p_{11} & p_{12} & \cdots & p_{1m} \\ \vdots & & & \vdots \\ \vdots & & & \vdots \\ p_{m1} & p_{m2} & \cdots & p_{mm} \end{bmatrix}$$

Notice that P is a square matrix with entries that are always nonnegative since they represent probabilities. Also, the sum of the entries in every row is 1 since, as in the mouse and maze example, once the mouse is in a given room, it either stays there or moves to one of the other rooms with probability 1.

COMPUTING STATE DISTRIBUTIONS

The transition matrix contains the information necessary to predict what happens next, given that we know what happened before. It remains to specify what the state of affairs was at the start of the experiment. For example, what room was the mouse placed in at the start? We introduce a special row vector for this purpose.

Initial Probability Distribution

In a Markov chain with m states, the *initial probability distribution* is a $1 \times m$ row vector $v^{(0)}$ whose ith entry is the probability the experiment was in state i at the start.

For example, if the mouse was equally likely to be placed in any one of the rooms at the start, then we would have $v^{(0)} = [\frac{1}{4} \quad \frac{1}{4} \quad \frac{1}{4} \quad \frac{1}{4}]$. Whereas, if it was decided to always place the mouse initially in room 1, then we would write $v^{(0)} = [1 \quad 0 \quad 0 \quad 0]$.

Probability Vector

A *probability vector* is a vector whose entries are nonnegative and sum up to 1.

We conclude that the initial probability distribution $v^{(0)}$ of a Markov chain is a probability row vector.

□ **Example 1**

Look at the maze in Figure 1. Suppose we assign the following transition probabilities:

$$\text{From room 1 to } \begin{Bmatrix} 1 & 2 & 3 & 4 \\ \frac{1}{3} & \frac{1}{3} & \frac{1}{3} & 0 \end{Bmatrix}$$

Here, the mouse starts in room 1, and $\frac{1}{3}$ of the time it remains there during the time interval of observation, $\frac{1}{3}$ of the time it enters room 2, and $\frac{1}{3}$ of the time it enters room 3. Since it cannot go to room 4 directly from room 1, the probability assignment is 0. Similarly, the transition probabilities in moving from room 2, room 3, and room 4 may be given as follows:

$$\text{From room 2 to } \begin{Bmatrix} 1 & 2 & 3 & 4 \\ \frac{1}{3} & \frac{1}{3} & 0 & \frac{1}{3} \end{Bmatrix} \quad \text{From room 3 to } \begin{Bmatrix} 1 & 2 & 3 & 4 \\ \frac{1}{3} & 0 & \frac{1}{3} & \frac{1}{3} \end{Bmatrix}$$

$$\text{From room 4 to } \begin{Bmatrix} 1 & 2 & 3 & 4 \\ 0 & \frac{1}{3} & \frac{1}{3} & \frac{1}{3} \end{Bmatrix}$$

Find the transition matrix P. If the initial placement of the mouse is in room 4, find the initial probability distribution. What are the probabilities of being in each room after two observations?

Solution

The transition matrix P is

$$P = [p_{ij}] = \begin{matrix} & \begin{matrix} 1 & 2 & 3 & 4 \end{matrix} \\ \begin{matrix} 1 \\ 2 \\ 3 \\ 4 \end{matrix} & \begin{bmatrix} \frac{1}{3} & \frac{1}{3} & \frac{1}{3} & 0 \\ \frac{1}{3} & \frac{1}{3} & 0 & \frac{1}{3} \\ \frac{1}{3} & 0 & \frac{1}{3} & \frac{1}{3} \\ 0 & \frac{1}{3} & \frac{1}{3} & \frac{1}{3} \end{bmatrix} \end{matrix}$$

Next, since the initial placement of the mouse is in room 4, the initial probability distribution is

$$v^{(0)} = [p_1^{(0)} \quad p_2^{(0)} \quad p_3^{(0)} \quad p_4^{(0)}] = [0 \quad 0 \quad 0 \quad 1]$$

To answer the last question, we use a probability tree. See Figure 2. The numbers

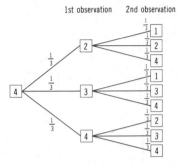

1st observation   2nd observation

Figure 2

in each square refer to the room occupied. From this tree diagram we deduce, for example, that the mouse will be in state 1 after two observations with probability

$$p_{41}^{(2)} = \frac{1}{3} \cdot \frac{1}{3} + \frac{1}{3} \cdot \frac{1}{3} = \frac{2}{9}$$

Similarly,

$$p_{42}^{(2)} = \frac{1}{3} \cdot \frac{1}{3} + \frac{1}{3} \cdot \frac{1}{3} = \frac{2}{9}$$

$$p_{43}^{(2)} = \frac{1}{3} \cdot \frac{1}{3} + \frac{1}{3} \cdot \frac{1}{3} = \frac{2}{9}$$

$$p_{44}^{(2)} = \frac{1}{3} \cdot \frac{1}{3} + \frac{1}{3} \cdot \frac{1}{3} + \frac{1}{3} \cdot \frac{1}{3} = \frac{1}{3} \tag{1}$$

□

We could record the results of Example 1 by writing $v^{(2)} = [\frac{2}{9} \quad \frac{2}{9} \quad \frac{2}{9} \quad \frac{1}{3}]$. Using this notation, the row vector $v^{(k)}$ would be used to record the probabilities of being in the various states after k trials. The ith entry of $v^{(k)}$ is the probability of being in state i at stage k. For example, $v^{(4)} = [\frac{1}{8} \quad \frac{1}{8} \quad 0 \quad \frac{3}{4}]$ would say that the probability of being in state 2 at stage 4 of the experiment is $\frac{1}{8}$.

Instead of following the procedure of the above example, it is possible to compute $v^{(k)}$ directly from the transition matrix P and the initial probability distribution $v^{(0)}$.

In a Markov chain the probability distribution $v^{(k)}$ after k observations satisfies

$$v^{(k)} = v^{(k-1)}P \tag{2}$$

where P is the transition matrix. For example, this says

$$v^{(1)} = v^{(0)}P$$

$$v^{(2)} = v^{(1)}P$$

$$v^{(3)} = v^{(2)}P, \text{ and so on}$$

Thus the succeeding distribution can always be derived from the previous one by multiplying by the transition matrix.

☐ **Example 2** Using the information from Example 1, find the probability distribution after two observations.

Solution We had $v^{(0)} = [0 \quad 0 \quad 0 \quad 1]$, so by (2)

$$v^{(1)} = v^{(0)}P = [0 \quad 0 \quad 0 \quad 1] \begin{bmatrix} \frac{1}{3} & \frac{1}{3} & \frac{1}{3} & 0 \\ \frac{1}{3} & \frac{1}{3} & 0 & \frac{1}{3} \\ \frac{1}{3} & 0 & \frac{1}{3} & \frac{1}{3} \\ 0 & \frac{1}{3} & \frac{1}{3} & \frac{1}{3} \end{bmatrix} = [0 \quad \frac{1}{3} \quad \frac{1}{3} \quad \frac{1}{3}]$$

Using (2) again,

$$v^{(2)} = v^{(1)}P = [0 \quad \frac{1}{3} \quad \frac{1}{3} \quad \frac{1}{3}] \begin{bmatrix} \frac{1}{3} & \frac{1}{3} & \frac{1}{3} & 0 \\ \frac{1}{3} & \frac{1}{3} & 0 & \frac{1}{3} \\ \frac{1}{3} & 0 & \frac{1}{3} & \frac{1}{3} \\ 0 & \frac{1}{3} & \frac{1}{3} & \frac{1}{3} \end{bmatrix} = [\frac{2}{9} \quad \frac{2}{9} \quad \frac{2}{9} \quad \frac{1}{3}]$$

This way of obtaining $v^{(2)}$ agrees with the results found in (1). ☐

A few computations using (2) lead to another result.

$$v^{(1)} = v^{(0)}P$$
$$v^{(2)} = v^{(1)}P = [v^{(0)}P]P = v^{(0)}P^2$$
$$v^{(3)} = v^{(2)}P = [v^{(0)}P^2]P = v^{(0)}P^3$$
$$v^{(4)} = v^{(3)}P = [v^{(0)}P^3]P = v^{(0)}P^4$$

In each line above we have substituted the result of the preceding line. These calculations can clearly be continued to produce the following observation.

$$v^{(k)} = v^{(0)}P^k \tag{3}$$

where P^k is the kth power of the transition matrix. Thus, the conclusion of Example 2 could also have been arrived at by squaring the transition matrix and computing

$$v^{(2)} = v^{(0)}P^2 = [0 \quad 0 \quad 0 \quad 1] \begin{bmatrix} \frac{1}{3} & \frac{2}{9} & \frac{2}{9} & \frac{2}{9} \\ \frac{2}{9} & \frac{1}{3} & \frac{2}{9} & \frac{2}{9} \\ \frac{2}{9} & \frac{2}{9} & \frac{1}{3} & \frac{2}{9} \\ \frac{2}{9} & \frac{2}{9} & \frac{2}{9} & \frac{1}{3} \end{bmatrix} = [\frac{2}{9} \quad \frac{2}{9} \quad \frac{2}{9} \quad \frac{1}{3}]$$

Equations (2) and (3) are two formulas for finding $v^{(k)}$. Equation (2) has the advantage that it lends itself better to a computer program.

☐ **Example 3**
Population
Movement

Suppose that the city of Glenwood is experiencing a movement of its population to the suburbs. At present, 85% of the total population lives in the city and 15% lives in the suburbs. But each year 7% of the city people move to the suburbs, while only 1% of the suburb people move back to the city. Assuming that the total population (city and suburbs together) remains constant, what percent of the total will remain in the city after 5 years?

Solution This problem can be expressed as a sequence of experiments in which each experiment measures the proportion of people in the city and the proportion of people in the suburbs.

In the $(n + 1)$st year, these proportions will depend for their value only on the proportions in the nth year and not on the proportions found in earlier years. Thus, we have an experiment that can be represented as a Markov chain.

The initial probability distribution for this system is

$$\begin{array}{cc} \text{City} & \text{Suburbs} \\ v^{(0)} = [.85 & .15] \end{array}$$

That is, initially, 85% of the people reside in the city and 15% in the suburbs.

The transition matrix P is

$$P = \begin{array}{c} \\ \text{City} \\ \text{Suburbs} \end{array} \begin{array}{cc} \text{City} & \text{Suburbs} \\ \begin{bmatrix} .93 & .07 \\ .01 & .99 \end{bmatrix} \end{array}$$

That is, each year 7% of the city people move to the suburbs (so that 93% remain in the city) and 1% of the suburb people move to the city (so that 99% remain in the suburbs).

To find the probability distribution after 5 years, we need to compute $v^{(5)}$:

$$v^{(1)} = v^{(0)}P = [.85 \quad .15] \begin{bmatrix} .93 & .07 \\ .01 & .99 \end{bmatrix} = [.792 \quad .208]$$

$$v^{(2)} = v^{(1)}P = [.792 \quad .208] \begin{bmatrix} .93 & .07 \\ .01 & .99 \end{bmatrix} = [.73864 \quad .26136]$$

$$v^{(3)} = v^{(2)}P = [.73864 \quad .26136] \begin{bmatrix} .93 & .07 \\ .01 & .99 \end{bmatrix} = [.68955 \quad .31045]$$

$$v^{(4)} = v^{(3)}P = [.68955 \quad .31045] \begin{bmatrix} .93 & .07 \\ .01 & .99 \end{bmatrix} = [.64439 \quad .35561]$$

$$v^{(5)} = v^{(4)}P = [.64439 \quad .35561] \begin{bmatrix} .93 & .07 \\ .01 & .99 \end{bmatrix} = [.60284 \quad .39716]$$

Thus, by the properties (2) and (3), the probability distribution after 5 years is

$$v^{(5)} = v^{(0)}P^5 = v^{(4)}P = [.60284 \quad .39716]$$

Thus, after 5 years, 60.28% of the residents live in the city and 39.72% live in the suburbs. □

This example leads us to inquire whether the situation in Glenwood ever stabilizes. That is, after a certain number of years is an equilibrium reached? Also, does the equilibrium, if attained, depend on what the initial distribution of the population was or is it independent of the initial state? We deal with these questions in the next section.

Exercise 11.1   *Answers to Odd-Numbered Problems begin on page* 630.

1. Explain why the matrix below cannot be the transition matrix for a Markov chain.

$$\begin{bmatrix} 0 & 1 & 0 \\ \frac{1}{3} & \frac{1}{3} & \frac{1}{3} \\ \frac{1}{2} & -\frac{1}{2} & \frac{1}{2} \end{bmatrix}$$

2. Explain why the matrix below cannot be the transition matrix for a Markov chain.

$$\begin{bmatrix} 1 & \frac{1}{2} & \frac{1}{3} & \frac{1}{4} \\ 0 & 1 & 0 & 0 \\ 0 & \frac{1}{2} & \frac{1}{2} & 0 \\ 1 & 0 & 0 & 0 \end{bmatrix}$$

3. Consider a Markov chain with transition matrix

$$\begin{array}{cc} & \begin{array}{cc} \text{State 1} & \text{State 2} \end{array} \\ \begin{array}{c} \text{State 1} \\ \text{State 2} \end{array} & \begin{bmatrix} \frac{1}{3} & \frac{2}{3} \\ \frac{1}{4} & \frac{3}{4} \end{bmatrix} \end{array}$$

   (a) What does the entry $\frac{2}{3}$ in this matrix represent?
   (b) Assuming that the system is initially in state 1, find the probability distribution one observation later.
   (c) Assuming that the system is initially in state 2, find the probability distribution one observation later.
   (d) Draw a probability tree to find the probability distribution two observations later.

4. Consider a Markov chain with transition matrix

$$\begin{array}{cc} & \begin{array}{cc} \text{State 1} & \text{State 2} \end{array} \\ \begin{array}{c} \text{State 1} \\ \text{State 2} \end{array} & \begin{bmatrix} .3 & .7 \\ .4 & .6 \end{bmatrix} \end{array}$$

   (a) What does the entry .4 in the matrix represent?
   (b) Assuming that the system is initially in state 1, find the probability distribution two observations later.
   (c) Assuming that the system is initially in state 2, find the probability distribution two observations later.

5. Consider the transition matrix of Problem 4. If the initial probability distribution is [.25 .75], what is the probability distribution after two observations?

6. Consider a Markov chain with transition matrix

$$P = \begin{bmatrix} .7 & .2 & .1 \\ .6 & .2 & .2 \\ .4 & .1 & .5 \end{bmatrix}$$

   If the initial distribution is [.25 .25 .5], what is the probability distribution in the next observation?

7. Find the values of a, b, and c that will make the following matrix a transition matrix for a Markov chain:

$$\begin{bmatrix} .2 & a & .4 \\ b & .6 & .2 \\ 0 & c & 0 \end{bmatrix}$$

8. In the maze of Figure 1, if the initial probability distribution is $v^{(0)} = [\frac{1}{2} \quad 0 \quad \frac{1}{2} \quad 0]$, find the probability distribution after two observations.

9. In Example 3, if the initial probability distribution for Glenwood is $v^{(0)} = [.7 \quad .3]$, what is the population distribution after 5 years?

10. A new rapid transit system has just been installed. It is anticipated that each week 90% of the commuters who used the rapid transit will continue to do so. Of those who traveled by car, 20% will begin to use the rapid transit instead.

    (a) Explain why the above is a Markov chain.

    (b) Set up the 2×2 matrix P with columns and rows labeled R (rapid transit) and C (car) to display these transitions.

    (c) Compute P^2 and P^3.

11. The voting pattern for a certain group of cities is such that 60% of the Democratic (D) mayors were succeeded by Democrats and 40% by Republicans (R). Also, 30% of the Republican mayors were succeeded by Democrats and 70% by Republicans.

    (a) Explain why the above is a Markov chain.

    (b) Set up the 2×2 matrix P with columns and rows labeled D and R to display these transitions.

    (c) Compute P^2 and P^3.

12. Consider the maze with nine rooms shown in the figure. The system consists of the maze and a mouse. We assume that the following learning pattern exists: If the mouse is in room 1, 2, 3, 4, or 5, it moves with equal probability to any room that the maze permits; if it is in room 8, it moves directly to room 9; if it is in room 6, 7, or 9, it remains in that room.

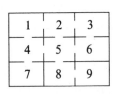

    (a) Explain why the above experiment is a Markov chain.

    (b) Construct the transition matrix P.

13. *Market Penetration.* A company is promoting a certain product, say Brand X wine. The result of this is that 75% of the people drinking Brand X wine over any given period of 1 month, continue to drink it the next month; of those people drinking other brands of wine in the period of 1 month, 35% change over to the promoted wine the next month. We would like to know what fraction of wine drinkers will drink Brand X after 2 months if 50% drink Brand X wine now.

14. A professor either walks or drives to a university. He never drives 2 days in a row, but if he walks 1 day, he is just as likely to walk the next day as to drive his car. Show that this forms a Markov chain and give the transition matrix.

15. Suppose that, during the year 1987, 45% of the drivers in a certain metropolitan area had Travelers automobile insurance, 30% had General American insurance, and 25% were insured by some other companies. Suppose also that a year later: *(1)* of those who had been insured by Travelers in 1987, 92% continued to be insured by Travelers, but 8% had switched their insurance to General American; *(2)* of those who had been insured by General American in 1987, 90% continued to be insured by General American, but 4% had switched to Travelers and 6% had switched to some other companies; *(3)* of those who had been insured by some other companies in 1987, 82% continued but 10% had switched to Travelers, and 8% had switched to General American. Using these data, answer the following questions:

    (a) What percentage of drivers in the metropolitan area were insured by Travelers and General American in 1988?

(b) If these trends continued for one more year, what percentage of the drivers were insured by Travelers and General American in 1989?

16. If A is a transition matrix, what about A^2? A^3? What do you conjecture about A^n?

17. Let

$$A = \begin{bmatrix} a_{11} & a_{12} \\ a_{21} & a_{22} \end{bmatrix}$$

be a transition matrix and

$$u = [u_1 \quad u_2]$$

be a probability row vector. Prove that uA is a probability vector.

18. Let

$$P = \begin{bmatrix} p_{11} & p_{12} \\ p_{21} & p_{22} \end{bmatrix}$$

be a transition matrix. Prove that $v^{(k)} = v^{(k-1)}P$.

11.2 REGULAR MARKOV CHAINS

POWERS OF THE TRANSITION MATRIX □ REGULAR CHAINS
□ FIXED PROBABILITY VECTOR AND EQUILIBRIUM

A fundamental question about Markov chains is: What happens in the long run? Is it the case that the distribution into states tends to stabilize over time? In this section, we investigate the conditions under which a Markov chain produces an *equilibrium,* or *steady-state,* situation. We will also give techniques for finding this equilibrium distribution, when it exists.

POWERS OF THE TRANSITION MATRIX

We begin by examining *powers* of the transition matrix P. Recall that the (i, j)th entry p_{ij} of P is the probability of moving from state i to state j in any one step. Are there corresponding interpretations for the entries in any *power* P^2, P^3, P^4, . . . of the transition matrix?

To motivate the answer we use the data of Problem 13 in Exercise 11.1. There the transition matrix is

$$P = \begin{array}{c} \\ \text{Brand } X, \quad E_1 \\ \text{Other brands, } E_2 \end{array} \begin{array}{c} \overset{\text{Brand } X}{\overset{E_1}{}} \quad \overset{\text{Other brands}}{\overset{E_2}{}} \\ \begin{bmatrix} .75 & .25 \\ .35 & .65 \end{bmatrix} \end{array}$$

A probability tree depicting 3 stages of this experiment is given in Figure 3.

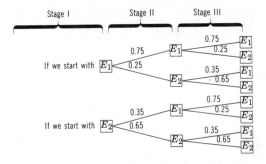

Figure 3

The probability $p_{11}^{(2)}$ of proceeding from E_1 to E_1 in two stages is

$$p_{11}^{(2)} = (.75)(.75) + (.25)(.35) = .65$$

The probability $p_{12}^{(2)}$ from E_1 to E_2 in two stages is

$$p_{12}^{(2)} = (.75)(.25) + (.25)(.65) = .35$$

The probability $p_{21}^{(2)}$ from E_2 to E_1 in two stages is

$$p_{21}^{(2)} = (.35)(.75) + (.65)(.35) = .49$$

The probability $p_{22}^{(2)}$ from E_2 to E_2 in two stages is

$$p_{22}^{(2)} = (.35)(.25) + (.65)(.65) = .51$$

If we square the matrix P, we obtain

$$P^2 = \begin{bmatrix} (.75)(.75) + (.25)(.35) & (.75)(.25) + (.25)(.65) \\ (.35)(.75) + (.65)(.35) & (.35)(.25) + (.65)(.65) \end{bmatrix}$$

$$= \begin{bmatrix} .65 & .35 \\ .49 & .51 \end{bmatrix}$$

and we notice that

$$P^2 = \begin{bmatrix} p_{11}^{(2)} & p_{12}^{(2)} \\ p_{21}^{(2)} & p_{22}^{(2)} \end{bmatrix}$$

Thus, in this example, the *square* of the transition matrix gives the probabilities for moving from one state to another state in *two* stages.

This is true in general, and higher powers of the transition matrix carry similar interpretations. More precisely,

---

If P is the transition matrix of a Markov chain, then the (i, j)th entry of P^n (nth power of P) gives the probability of passing from state i to state j in n stages.

REGULAR CHAINS

We now turn to the question involving the long-term behavior of a Markov chain and begin by observing the results of an example we have used before.

☐ **Example 1**   Take the transition matrix P of Problem 13 of Exercise 11.1 and compute some of its powers.

Solution   Some of the powers of the transition matrix P are given below.

$$P = \begin{bmatrix} .7500 & .2500 \\ .3500 & .6500 \end{bmatrix} \qquad P^7 = \begin{bmatrix} .5840 & .4159 \\ .5823 & .4176 \end{bmatrix}$$

$$P^2 = \begin{bmatrix} .6500 & .3500 \\ .4900 & .5100 \end{bmatrix} \qquad P^8 = \begin{bmatrix} .5836 & .4163 \\ .5829 & .4170 \end{bmatrix}$$

$$P^3 = \begin{bmatrix} .6100 & .3900 \\ .5460 & .4540 \end{bmatrix} \qquad P^9 = \begin{bmatrix} .5834 & .4165 \\ .5831 & .4168 \end{bmatrix}$$

$$P^4 = \begin{bmatrix} .5940 & .4060 \\ .5683 & .4316 \end{bmatrix} \qquad P^{10} = \begin{bmatrix} .5833 & .4166 \\ .5832 & .4167 \end{bmatrix}$$

$$P^5 = \begin{bmatrix} .5876 & .4124 \\ .5773 & .4226 \end{bmatrix} \qquad P^{11} = \begin{bmatrix} .5833 & .4166 \\ .5833 & .4166 \end{bmatrix} \leftarrow$$

$$P^6 = \begin{bmatrix} .5850 & .4149 \\ .5809 & .4190 \end{bmatrix} \qquad P^{12} = \begin{bmatrix} .5833 & .4166 \\ .5833 & .4166 \end{bmatrix} \leftarrow$$

No change, so we stop here ☐

We notice the interesting fact that the powers P^n seem to be converging and stabilizing around a fixed matrix. Furthermore, all rows of that matrix are identical. Also, if we let

$$\mathbf{t} = [.5833 \quad .4166]$$

and compute $\mathbf{t}P$ we find that

$$\mathbf{t}P = [.5833 \quad .4166] \begin{bmatrix} .75 & .25 \\ .35 & .65 \end{bmatrix} = [.5833 \quad .4166]$$

That is, $\mathbf{t}P = \mathbf{t}$. So, the row vector $\mathbf{t}$ is fixed by P.

Will this always happen? And what interpretation can be placed on the vector $\mathbf{t}$? Before giving the answers, we need a definition.

Regular Markov Chain   A Markov chain is said to be *regular* if for some power of its transition matrix P, all of the entries are positive.

☐ **Example 2**   The transition matrix

$$P = \begin{bmatrix} \frac{1}{2} & \frac{1}{2} \\ 1 & 0 \end{bmatrix}$$

is regular since the square of P, namely,

$$P^2 = \begin{bmatrix} \frac{3}{4} & \frac{3}{4} \\ \frac{1}{2} & \frac{1}{2} \end{bmatrix}$$

has only positive entries. ☐

☐ **Example 3** The matrix

$$P = \begin{bmatrix} 1 & 0 \\ \frac{3}{4} & \frac{1}{4} \end{bmatrix}$$

is not regular since every power of P will always have $p_{12} = 0$. The matrix

$$\begin{bmatrix} 0 & 1 \\ 1 & 0 \end{bmatrix}$$

is another example of a transition matrix that is not regular. ☐

We now turn to the question involving the long-term behavior of a Markov chain and begin by observing the results of an example we have used before.

Let P be the transition matrix of a regular Markov chain. Then,

(a) The matrices P^n approach a fixed matrix T, as n gets large. We write $P^n \rightarrow T$ (as n gets large).

(b) The rows of T are all identical and equal to a probability row vector **t**.

(c) **t** is the unique probability vector that satisfies $\mathbf{t}P = \mathbf{t}$.

FIXED PROBABILITY VECTOR AND EQUILIBRIUM

Because of (c), **t** is called the *fixed probability* vector of the transition matrix P. And, what is the significance of this vector? The answer is that it tells us what the long run distribution into states will be. More precisely, for a regular Markov chain

---

(d) If $v^{(0)}$ is any initial distribution, then $v^{(n)} \rightarrow \mathbf{t}$ as n gets large.

Thus, **t** can be thought of as representing an equilibrium state, since the state distributions $v^{(n)}$ will approach **t** as time goes on.

For example, the computations in Example 1 show that in the long run 58.33% of wine drinkers will be drinking Brand X wine.

An important point to note is that it is not necessary to compute higher and higher power P^n of the transition matrix to find T and, in the process, **t**. Result (c) allows us to find **t** by solving a system of equations.

□ **Example 4**   Find the fixed probability vector for Example 3 in Section 1.

Solution   Let $\mathbf{t} = [t_1 \quad t_2]$ be the desired fixed probability vector. Then $t_1 + t_2 = 1$ and

$$[t_1 \quad t_2] \begin{bmatrix} .93 & .07 \\ .01 & .99 \end{bmatrix} = [t_1 \quad t_2]$$

Or,

$$[.93t_1 + .01t_2 \quad .07t_1 + .99t_2] = [t_1 \quad t_2]$$

Equating corresponding entries yields the following system of two equations in two unknowns

$$.93t_1 + .01t_2 = t_1$$
$$.07t_1 + .99t_2 = t_2$$

Or,

$$-.07t_1 + .01t_2 = 0$$
$$.07t_1 - .01t_2 = 0$$

As it stands this system has infinitely many solutions. However, when we include the equation

$$t_1 + t_2 = 1$$

the resulting system is

$$-.07t_1 + .01t_2 = 0$$
$$.07t_1 - .01t_2 = 0$$
$$t_1 + t_2 = 1$$

which will have a unique solution, namely,

$$t_1 = \frac{1}{8} \qquad t_2 = \frac{7}{8}$$

In obtaining the fixed probability vector $[\frac{1}{8} \quad \frac{7}{8}]$, we learn that in the long run, $\frac{1}{8}$ of the population will live in the city while $\frac{7}{8}$ will be suburbanites.   □

□ **Example 5**   Find the fixed probability vector $\mathbf{t}$ of the transition matrix

$$P = \begin{bmatrix} \frac{1}{2} & 0 & \frac{1}{2} \\ \frac{1}{2} & \frac{1}{2} & 0 \\ \frac{1}{3} & \frac{1}{3} & \frac{1}{3} \end{bmatrix}$$

Solution   Let $\mathbf{t} = [t_1 \quad t_2 \quad t_3]$ be the fixed vector. Then $t_1 + t_2 + t_3 = 1$ and

$$[t_1 \quad t_2 \quad t_3] \begin{bmatrix} \frac{1}{2} & 0 & \frac{1}{2} \\ \frac{1}{2} & \frac{1}{2} & 0 \\ \frac{1}{3} & \frac{1}{3} & \frac{1}{3} \end{bmatrix} = [t_1 \quad t_2 \quad t_3]$$

So,

$$\tfrac{1}{2}t_1 + \tfrac{1}{2}t_2 + \tfrac{1}{3}t_3 = t_1$$
$$\tfrac{1}{2}t_2 + \tfrac{1}{3}t_3 = t_2$$
$$\tfrac{1}{2}t_1 + \tfrac{1}{3}t_3 = t_3$$

or

$$-\tfrac{1}{2}t_1 + \tfrac{1}{2}t_2 + \tfrac{1}{3}t_3 = 0$$
$$-\tfrac{1}{2}t_2 + \tfrac{1}{3}t_3 = 0$$
$$\tfrac{1}{2}t_1 - \tfrac{2}{3}t_3 = 0$$

If we add the condition that $t_1 + t_2 + t_3 = 1$, we obtain

$$-3t_1 + 3t_2 + 2t_3 = 0$$
$$-3t_2 + 2t_3 = 0$$
$$3t_1 - 4t_3 = 0$$
$$t_1 + t_2 + t_3 = 1$$

The solution of this system is the fixed vector $\quad \mathbf{t} = [\tfrac{4}{9} \quad \tfrac{2}{9} \quad \tfrac{1}{3}],$

$\square$

A nice feature is that the long run distribution $\mathbf{t}$ can be found simply by solving a system of equations. A more remarkable feature is that the same equilibrium is reached no matter what the initial distribution was. We sketch the reason for this in the 2×2 case.

Suppose $v^{(0)} = [a \quad b]$ is *any* initial distribution. Let $\mathbf{t} = [t_1 \quad t_2]$. Then, as we indicated,

$$P^n \to T = \begin{bmatrix} t_1 & t_2 \\ t_1 & t_2 \end{bmatrix}$$

Now $v^{(n)} = v^{(0)}P^n$. So, as n gets large,

$$v^{(n)} = v^{(0)}P^n \to v^{(0)}T$$

But

$$v^{(0)}T = [a \quad b]\begin{bmatrix} t_1 & t_2 \\ t_1 & t_2 \end{bmatrix} = [(a + b)t_1 \quad (a + b)t_2]$$

Since $v^{(0)}$ is a probability vector, it follows that $a + b = 1$.

Thus

$$v^{(n)} \to v^{(0)}T = [t_1 \quad t_2] = \mathbf{t}$$

That is, the same $\mathbf{t}$ is reached regardless of the entries used in $v^{(0)}$.

□ **Example 6**

Consumer Loyalty

Consider a certain community in a well-defined area with three grocery stores, I, II, and III. Within this community (we assume that the population is fixed) there always exists a shift of customers from one grocery store to another. A study was made on January 1, and it was found that $\frac{1}{4}$ of the population shopped at Store I, $\frac{1}{3}$ at Store II, and $\frac{5}{12}$ at Store III. Each month Store I retains 90% of its customers and loses 10% of them to Store II. Store II retains 5% of its customers and loses 85% of them to Store I and 10% of them to Store III. Store III retains 40% of its customers and loses 50% of them to Store I and 10% to Store II. The transition matrix P is

$$P = \begin{array}{c} \\ \text{I} \\ \text{II} \\ \text{III} \end{array} \begin{array}{ccc} \text{I} & \text{II} & \text{III} \\ \left[\begin{array}{ccc} .90 & .10 & 0 \\ .85 & .05 & .10 \\ .50 & .10 & .40 \end{array} \right] \end{array}$$

We would like to answer the following questions:

(a) What proportion of customers will each store retain by February 1?

(b) By March 1?

(c) Assuming the same pattern continues, what will be the long-run distribution of customers among the three stores?

Solution

(a) To answer the first question, we note that the initial probability distribution is $v^{(0)} = [\frac{1}{4} \quad \frac{1}{3} \quad \frac{5}{12}]$. By February 1, the probability distribution is

$$v^{(1)} = v^{(0)}P = [\frac{1}{4} \quad \frac{1}{3} \quad \frac{5}{12}] \begin{bmatrix} .90 & .10 & .00 \\ .85 & .05 & .10 \\ .50 & .10 & .40 \end{bmatrix} = [.7167 \quad .0833 \quad .2000]$$

(b) To find the probability distribution after 2 months (March 1), we compute $v^{(2)}$:

$$v^{(2)} = v^{(0)}P^2 = [\frac{1}{4} \quad \frac{1}{3} \quad \frac{5}{12}] \begin{bmatrix} .895 & .095 & .010 \\ .857 & .098 & .045 \\ .735 & .095 & .170 \end{bmatrix} = [.8155 \quad .0956 \quad .0882]$$

(c) To find the long run distribution we determine the fixed probability vector **t** of the regular transition matrix P. Let $\mathbf{t} = [t_1 \quad t_2 \quad t_3]$, where $t_1 + t_2 + t_3 = 1$. Then

$$[t_1 \quad t_2 \quad t_3] \begin{bmatrix} .90 & .10 & .00 \\ .85 & .05 & .10 \\ .50 & .10 & .40 \end{bmatrix} = [t_1 \quad t_2 \quad t_3]$$

$$[t_1 \quad t_2 \quad t_3] = [.8889 \quad .0952 \quad .0159]$$

Thus, in the long run Store I will have about 88.9% of all customers, Store II will have 9.5%, and Store III will have 1.6%.   □

□ **Example 7**

Spread of Rumor

A United States Senator has determined whether to vote Yes or No on an important bill pending in Congress and conveys this decision to an aide. The aide then passes this news on to another individual, who passes it on to a friend, and so on, each time to a new individual. Assume p is the probability that any one person passes on the information opposite to the way he heard it. Then $1 - p$ is the probability a person passes on the information the same way he heard it. With what probability will the nth person receive the information as a Yes vote?

Solution   This can be viewed as a Markov chain model. Although it is not intuitively obvious, we shall find that the answer is essentially independent of p.

To obtain the transition matrix, we observe that two states are possible: A Yes is heard or a No is heard. The transition from a Yes to a No or from a No to a Yes occurs with probability p. The transition from Yes to Yes or from No to No occurs with probability $1 - p$. Thus, the transition matrix P is

$$
\begin{array}{c c}
 & \begin{array}{c c} \text{Yes} & \text{No} \end{array} \\
\begin{array}{c} \text{Yes} \\ \text{No} \end{array} & \begin{bmatrix} 1 - p & p \\ p & 1 - p \end{bmatrix}
\end{array}
$$

The probability that the nth person will receive the information in one state or the other is given by successive powers of the matrix P, that is, by the matrices P^n. In fact, the answer in this case rapidly approaches $t_1 = \frac{1}{2}$, $t_2 = \frac{1}{2}$, after any considerable number of people are involved. This can easily be shown by verifying that the fixed probability vector is $[\frac{1}{2} \quad \frac{1}{2}]$. Hence, no matter what the Senator's initial decision is, eventually (after enough information exchange), half the people hear that the Senator is going to vote Yes and half hear that the Senator is going to vote No.   □

An interesting interpretation of this result applies to successive roll calls in Congress on the same issue. We let p represent the probability that a member changes his or her mind on an issue from one roll call to the next. Then the above example shows that if enough roll calls are forced, the Congress will eventually be near evenly split on the issue. This could perhaps serve as a model for explaining the parliamentary device of delaying actions by minority.

MODEL: SOCIAL MOBILITY*

This model is based on an article by S. J. Prais, Department of Applied Economics, Cambridge University, who analyzed the movement among social classes in late 1940s England.

In the example, the following assumptions are made.

1. Class is treated as if it related only to the male side of the family line. This is largely because in these studies social class is measured by the occupation of the father.
2. The influence of one's ancestors in determining one's class is transmitted entirely through one's father so that, if the influence of one's father has been taken into account, then the total influence of one's ancestors is accounted for.

A social transition matrix representing England in 1949 is given in Table 1.

---

* S. J. Prais, "Measuring Social Mobility," *Journal of the Royal Statistical Society,* **118** (1955), pp. 55–66.

Table 1
The Social Transition Matrix for England, 1949

	1	2	3	4	5	6	7
1. Professional and high administrative	.388	.146	.202	.062	.140	.047	.015
2. Managerial and executive	.107	.267	.227	.120	.206	.053	.020
3. High grade supervisory and nonmanual	.035	.101	.188	.191	.357	.067	.061
4. Lower grade supervisory and non-manual	.021	.039	.112	.212	.430	.124	.062
5. Skilled manual and routine nonmanual	.009	.024	.075	.123	.473	.171	.125
6. Semi-skilled manual	.000	.013	.041	.088	.391	.312	.155
7. Unskilled manual	.000	.008	.036	.083	.364	.235	.274

The element in the ith row and jth column of this matrix, denoted by p_{ij}, gives the proportion of fathers in the ith social class whose sons move into the jth social class. Furthermore, it is supposed that if there is uncertainty in the tracing of a family line through time, then p_{ij} represents the probability of transition by a family from class i into class j in the interval of one generation. For example, p_{42} indicates that .039 of the sons of fathers in class 4 (lower grade supervisory and nonmanual) move into class 2 (managerial and executive). The equilibrium probability vector for the matrix in Table 1 was found by Prais to be

$$[.023 \quad .042 \quad .088 \quad .127 \quad .409 \quad .182 \quad .129]$$

Prais compared the above result with the actual data and obtained the figures listed in Table 2.

Table 2
Actual and Equilibrium Distributions of the Social Classes in England

Class	Actual Distribution		Equilibrium Distribution (3)
	Fathers (1)	Sons (2)	
1. Professional	.037	.029	.023
2. Managerial	.043	.046	.042
3. Higher grade nonmanual	.098	.094	.088
4. Lower grade nonmanual	.148	.131	.127
5. Skilled manual	.432	.409	.409
6. Semi-skilled manual	.131	.170	.182
7. Unskilled manual	.111	.121	.129

The equilibrium distribution depends only on the structural propensities of the society and not on the distribution of the population among the classes found at any instant. The equilibrium distribution is also independent of the unit of time in which the elements of P are measured. Suppose, for example, that observations were taken showing the relationship between the social status of grandson and grandfather. Every element of the transition matrix would then be different, since it would refer to a transition during a period of two generations instead of one generation. However, the equilibrium distribution corresponding to such a matrix would be unchanged. For, if the matrix relating the status of sons to fathers is P, that relating those of grandsons to grandfathers will be P^2 (provided, of course, that nothing has happened to change the characteristics of the society in the period considered), and when these matrices are raised to the nth power, they obviously tend to the same value as n gets very large.

It can be shown that the average number of generations spent by a family in social class j is $1/(1 - p_{jj})$, where p_{jj} is the jth diagonal element of the social transition matrix. So, Prais' model would predict that a family of unskilled manual laborers would occupy that profession for aproximately $1/(1 - .274) = 1.38$ generations.

Exercise 11.2   *Answers to Odd-Numbered Problems begin on page* 630.

In Problems 1–6 determine which of the given matrices are regular. For those that are, find the fixed probability vector.

1. $\begin{bmatrix} \frac{1}{2} & \frac{1}{2} \\ 1 & 0 \end{bmatrix}$ 2. $\begin{bmatrix} \frac{1}{2} & \frac{1}{2} \\ 0 & 1 \end{bmatrix}$ 3. $\begin{bmatrix} 0 & 1 \\ \frac{1}{4} & \frac{3}{4} \end{bmatrix}$

4. $\begin{bmatrix} \frac{1}{3} & \frac{2}{3} \\ 1 & 0 \end{bmatrix}$ 5. $\begin{bmatrix} 1 & 0 & 0 \\ \frac{1}{4} & \frac{1}{2} & \frac{1}{4} \\ 0 & 1 & 0 \end{bmatrix}$ 6. $\begin{bmatrix} \frac{1}{4} & \frac{3}{4} & 0 \\ \frac{1}{2} & 0 & \frac{1}{2} \\ 0 & 1 & 0 \end{bmatrix}$

7. Show that the transition matrix P of Example 7 has a fixed probability vector $[\frac{1}{2} \quad \frac{1}{2}]$.

8. Verify the result we obtained in Example 6, part (c).

9. *Consumer Loyalty.* A grocer stocks his store with three types of detergents, A, B, C. When Brand A is sold out, the probability is .7 that he stocks up with Brand A again. When he sells out Brand B, the probability is .8 that he will stock up again with Brand B. Finally, when he sells out Brand C, the probability is .6 that he will stock up with Brand C again. When he switches to another detergent, he does so with equal probability for the remaining two brands. Find the transition matrix. In the long run, how does he stock up with detergents?

10. *Consumer Loyalty.* A housewife buys three kinds of cereal: A, B, C. She never buys the same cereal in successive weeks. If she buys Cereal A, then the next week she buys Cereal B. However, if she buys either B or C, then the next week she is three times as likely to buy A as the other brand. Find the transition matrix. In the long run, how often does she buy each of the three brands?

11. *Voting Loyalty.* In England, of the sons of members of the Conservative party, 70% vote Conservative and the rest vote Labor. Of the sons of Laborites, 50% vote Labor, 40% vote Conservative, and 10% vote Socialist. Of the sons of Socialists, 40% vote Socialist, 40% vote Labor, and 20% vote Conservative. What is the probability that the grandson of a Laborite will vote Socialist? What is the membership distribution in the long run?

12. If $[\frac{1}{3} \quad 0 \quad \frac{1}{3} \quad \frac{1}{3}]$ is a fixed probability vector of a matrix P, can P be regular?

13. *Family Traits.* The probabilities that a blonde mother will have a blonde, brunette, or redheaded daughter are .6, .2 and .2, respectively. The probabilities that a brunette mother will have a blonde, brunette, or redheaded daughter are .1, .7, and .2, respectively. And the probabilities that a redheaded mother will have a blonde, brunette, or redheaded daughter are .4, .2, and .4, respectively. What is the probability that a blonde

woman is the grandmother of a brunette? If the population of women is now 50% brunettes, 30% blondes, and the rest redheads, what will the distribution be:

(a)   After two generations?

(b)   In the long run?

14.   *Educational Trends.* Use the data given in the table and assume that the indicated trends continue in order to answer the questions below.

		Maximum Education Children Achieve		
		College	H.S.	E.S.
Highest educational level of parents	College	80%	18%	2%
	High school	40%	50%	10%
	Elementary school	20%	60%	20%

(a)   What is the transition matrix?

(b)   What is the probability that a grandchild of a college graduate is a college graduate?

(c)   What is the probability that the grandchild of a high school graduate only finishes elementary school?

(d)   If at present 30%, 40%, and 30% of the population are college, high school, and elementary school graduates, respectively, what will be the distribution of the grandchildren of the present population?

(e)   What will the long-run distribution be?

11.3 ABSORBING MARKOV CHAINS

ABSORBING STATES   □ GAMBLER'S RUIN PROBLEM   □ EXPECTED LENGTH OF STAY

We have already seen examples of transition matrices in our presentation of Markov chains in which there are states that are impossible to leave. Such states are called *absorbing.* For instance, in Problem 12 in Exercise 11.1, room 9 is absorbing since once room 9 is reached, the probability of leaving it and passing to some different room is 0. Similarly, rooms 6 and 7 are absorbing states since it is impossible to leave these rooms once they have been reached.

ABSORBING STATES

Absorbing State; Absorbing Chain   In a Markov chain, if p_{ij} denotes the probability of going from state E_i to state E_j, then E_i is called an *absorbing state* if $p_{ii} = 1$. A Markov chain is said to be an *absorbing chain* if and only if it contains at least one absorbing state and it is possible to go from *any* nonabsorbing state to an absorbing state in one or more stages.

Thus, an absorbing state will capture the process and will not allow any state to pass from it.

In general, chains described by stochastic matrices can oscillate indefinitely from state to state in such a way that they exhibit no long-term trend. One such example is a Markov process chain having the nonregular matrix

$$\begin{bmatrix} 0 & 1 \\ 1 & 0 \end{bmatrix}$$

as its transition matrix. The idea of introducing absorbing states is to reduce the degree of oscillation since when an absorbing state is reached, the process no longer changes. That is, absorbing chain matrices exhibit a long-term trend. Furthermore, we can determine this trend using a simple computational technique.

When working with an absorbing Markov chain, it is convenient to rearrange the states so that the absorbing states come first and then the nonabsorbing states follow.

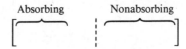

Once this rearrangement takes place, the transition matrix can be subdivided into four submatrices:

$$\begin{array}{cc} \overbrace{\quad\quad}^{\text{Absorbing}} & \overbrace{\quad\quad}^{\text{Nonabsorbing}} \\ \left[\begin{array}{c:c} I & \mathbf{0} \\ \hdashline S & Q \end{array} \right] \end{array}$$

Here, I is an identity matrix, $\mathbf{0}$ denotes a matrix having all 0 entries, and the matrices S and Q are the two submatrices corresponding to the absorbing and nonabsorbing states. For example, the absorbing transition matrix

$$
\begin{array}{c}
\begin{array}{ccccc} E_1 & E_2 & E_3 & E_4 & E_5 \end{array} \\
\begin{array}{c} E_1 \\ E_2 \\ E_3 \\ E_4 \\ E_5 \end{array}
\begin{bmatrix}
0 & .5 & 0 & 0 & .5 \\
0 & 0 & .9 & 0 & .1 \\
0 & 0 & 0 & .7 & .3 \\
0 & 0 & 0 & 1 & 0 \\
0 & 0 & 0 & 0 & 1
\end{bmatrix}
\end{array}
$$

is first rearranged to get

$$
\begin{array}{c}
\begin{array}{ccccc} E_4 & E_5 & E_1 & E_2 & E_3 \end{array} \\
\begin{array}{c} E_4 \\ E_5 \\ E_1 \\ E_2 \\ E_3 \end{array}
\begin{bmatrix}
1 & 0 & 0 & 0 & 0 \\
0 & 1 & 0 & 0 & 0 \\
0 & .5 & 0 & .5 & 0 \\
0 & .1 & 0 & 0 & .9 \\
.7 & .3 & 0 & 0 & 0
\end{bmatrix}
\end{array}
$$

Then the partitioned matrix is

$$
\left[
\begin{array}{cc:ccc}
1 & 0 & 0 & 0 & 0 \\
0 & 1 & 0 & 0 & 0 \\
\hdashline
0 & .5 & 0 & .5 & 0 \\
0 & .1 & 0 & 0 & .9 \\
.7 & .3 & 0 & 0 & 0
\end{array}
\right]
$$

Here,

$$
S = \begin{bmatrix} 0 & .5 \\ 0 & .1 \\ .7 & .3 \end{bmatrix} \qquad Q = \begin{bmatrix} 0 & .5 & 0 \\ 0 & 0 & .9 \\ 0 & 0 & 0 \end{bmatrix}
$$

□ **Example 1** Consider the Markov chains with P_1 and P_2 as their transition matrices:

$$
P_1 = \begin{array}{c} \\ E_1 \\ E_2 \\ E_3 \\ E_4 \end{array}
\begin{array}{c} \begin{array}{cccc} E_1 & E_2 & E_3 & E_4 \end{array} \\
\begin{bmatrix}
.4 & .2 & .4 & 0 \\
0 & 1 & 0 & 0 \\
.1 & 0 & .5 & .4 \\
.1 & 0 & .3 & .6
\end{bmatrix} \end{array}
\qquad
P_2 = \begin{array}{c} \\ E_1 \\ E_2 \\ E_3 \end{array}
\begin{array}{c} \begin{array}{ccc} E_1 & E_2 & E_3 \end{array} \\
\begin{bmatrix}
1 & 0 & 0 \\
0 & \frac{1}{4} & \frac{3}{4} \\
0 & \frac{1}{3} & \frac{2}{3}
\end{bmatrix} \end{array}
$$

Test to see whether either or both are absorbing chains.

Solution The chain having P_1 as its transition matrix is absorbing since the second state is an absorbing state and it is possible to pass from each of the other states to the second. Specifically, it is possible to pass from the first state directly to the second state and from either the third or the fourth state to the first state and then to the second. On the other hand, the matrix P_2 is an example of a nonabsorbing matrix since it is impossible to go from the nonabsorbing state E_2 to the absorbing state E_1. □

GAMBLER'S RUIN PROBLEM

Consider the following game involving two players, sometimes called the *gambler's ruin problem*. Player I has $3 and Player II has $2. They flip a fair coin; if it is a head, Player I pays Player II $1, and if it is a tail, Player II pays Player I $1. The total amount of money in the game is, of course, $5. We would like to know how long the game will last, that is, how long it will take for one of the players to go broke or win all the money. (This game can easily be generalized by assuming that Player I has M dollars and Player II has N dollars.)

In this experiment, how much money a player has after any given flip of the coin depends only on how much he had after the previous flip and will not depend (directly) on how much he had in the preceding stages of the game. This experiment can thus be represented by a Markov chain.

For the *gambler's ruin* problem, the game does not have to involve flipping a coin. That is, the probability that Player I wins may not equal the probability that Player II wins. Also, questions can be raised as to what happens if the stakes are doubled, how long the game can be expected to last, and so on.

Suppose the coin being flipped is fair so that a probability of $\frac{1}{2}$ is assigned to each event. The states are the amounts of money each player has at each stage of the game. Each player can increase or decrease the amount of money he has by only $1 at a time.

The transition matrix P is then of the following form:

$$P = \begin{array}{c} \\ 0 \\ 1 \\ 2 \\ 3 \\ 4 \\ 5 \end{array} \begin{array}{c} \begin{array}{cccccc} 0 & 1 & 2 & 3 & 4 & 5 \end{array} \\ \left[\begin{array}{cccccc} 1 & 0 & 0 & 0 & 0 & 0 \\ \frac{1}{2} & 0 & \frac{1}{2} & 0 & 0 & 0 \\ 0 & \frac{1}{2} & 0 & \frac{1}{2} & 0 & 0 \\ 0 & 0 & \frac{1}{2} & 0 & \frac{1}{2} & 0 \\ 0 & 0 & 0 & \frac{1}{2} & 0 & \frac{1}{2} \\ 0 & 0 & 0 & 0 & 0 & 1 \end{array} \right] \end{array}$$

Notice that p_{00} is the probability of having $0 given that a player has started with $0. This is a sure event, since, once a player is in state 0, he stays there forever, (he is broke). Similarly p_{55} represents the probability of having $5, given that a player started with $5, which is again a sure event (the player has won all the money).

With regard to this problem, the following questions are of interest:

(a) Given that one gambler is in a nonabsorbing state, what is the expected number of times that he will hold between $1 and $4 inclusive before the termination of the game? That is, on the average, how many times will the process be in nonabsorbing states?

(b) What is the expected length of the process (game)?

(c) What is the probability that an absorbing state is reached (that is, that one gambler will eventually be wiped out)?

To answer the above questions, let's look at the transition matrix P. Rearrange this matrix so that the two absorbing states will appear in the first 2 rows:

$$P = \begin{array}{c} \\ 0 \\ 5 \\ 1 \\ 2 \\ 3 \\ 4 \end{array} \begin{array}{c} \begin{array}{cccccc} 0 & 5 & 1 & 2 & 3 & 4 \end{array} \\ \left[\begin{array}{cc:cccc} 1 & 0 & 0 & 0 & 0 & 0 \\ 0 & 1 & 0 & 0 & 0 & 0 \\ \hdashline \frac{1}{2} & 0 & 0 & \frac{1}{2} & 0 & 0 \\ 0 & 0 & \frac{1}{2} & 0 & \frac{1}{2} & 0 \\ 0 & 0 & 0 & \frac{1}{2} & 0 & \frac{1}{2} \\ 0 & \frac{1}{2} & 0 & 0 & \frac{1}{2} & 0 \end{array} \right] \end{array}$$

If we let I_2, $\mathbf{0}$, S, and Q denote the matrices

$$I_2 = \begin{bmatrix} 1 & 0 \\ 0 & 1 \end{bmatrix} \qquad \mathbf{0} = \begin{bmatrix} 0 & 0 & 0 & 0 \\ 0 & 0 & 0 & 0 \end{bmatrix}$$

$$S = \begin{bmatrix} \frac{1}{2} & 0 \\ 0 & 0 \\ 0 & 0 \\ 0 & \frac{1}{2} \end{bmatrix} \qquad Q = \begin{bmatrix} 0 & \frac{1}{2} & 0 & 0 \\ \frac{1}{2} & 0 & \frac{1}{2} & 0 \\ 0 & \frac{1}{2} & 0 & \frac{1}{2} \\ 0 & 0 & \frac{1}{2} & 0 \end{bmatrix}.$$

we can write the matrix P in the form

$$P = \left[\begin{array}{c|c} I_2 & 0 \\ \hline S & Q \end{array}\right]$$

As we indicated earlier we can do this to any matrix representing an absorbing Markov chain. If r of the states are absorbing, the transition matrix P can be written as

$$P = \left[\begin{array}{c|c} I_r & 0 \\ \hline S & Q \end{array}\right]$$

where I_r is the $r \times r$ identity matrix, 0 is the zero matrix of dimension $r \times s$, S is of dimension $s \times r$, and Q is of dimension $s \times s$.

In order to answer the questions raised about the data of the gambler's ruin problem, we need the following result:

For an absorbing Markov chain that has a transition matrix P of the form

$$P = \left[\begin{array}{c|c} I_r & 0 \\ \hline S & Q \end{array}\right]$$

where S is of dimensions $s \times r$ and Q is of dimension $s \times s$, define the matrix T as

$$T = [I_s - Q]^{-1} \tag{1}$$

The entries of T give the expected number of times the process is in each nonabsorbing state, provided the process began in a nonabsorbing state.

Fundamental Matrix   The matrix T given in (1) is called the *fundamental matrix* of an absorbing Markov chain.

In the gambler's ruin problem, the fundamental matrix T is

$$T = \left[\begin{bmatrix} 1 & 0 & 0 & 0 \\ 0 & 1 & 0 & 0 \\ 0 & 0 & 1 & 0 \\ 0 & 0 & 0 & 1 \end{bmatrix} - \begin{bmatrix} 0 & \frac{1}{2} & 0 & 0 \\ \frac{1}{2} & 0 & \frac{1}{2} & 0 \\ 0 & \frac{1}{2} & 0 & \frac{1}{2} \\ 0 & 0 & \frac{1}{2} & 0 \end{bmatrix} \right]^{-1} = \begin{array}{c} 1 \\ 2 \\ 3 \\ 4 \end{array} \begin{array}{cccc} 1 & 2 & 3 & 4 \end{array} \atop \begin{bmatrix} 1.6 & 1.2 & .8 & .4 \\ 1.2 & 2.4 & 1.6 & .8 \\ .8 & 1.6 & 2.4 & 1.2 \\ .4 & .8 & 1.2 & 1.6 \end{bmatrix}$$

This provides the answers to question (a). The entry .8 in row 3, column 1, indicates that .8 is the expected number of times the player will have \$1 if he started with \$3. In the fundamental matrix T, the column headings indicate present money, while the row headings indicate money started with.

EXPECTED LENGTH OF STAY

The expected number of steps before absorption for each nonabsorbing state is found by adding the entries in the corresponding row of the fundamental matrix T.

So to answer question (b), we again look at the matrix T. The expected number of games before absorption (when one of the players wins or loses all the money) can be found by adding the entries in each row of T. Thus, if a player starts with $3, the expected number of games before absorption is

$$.8 + 1.6 + 2.4 + 1.2 = 6.0$$

If a player starts with $1, the expected number of games before absorption is

$$1.6 + 1.2 + .8 + .4 = 4.0$$

Our last result deals with the probabilities of being absorbed.

> The (i, j)th entry in the matrix product $T \cdot S$ gives the probability that, starting in nonabsorbing state i, we reach the absorbing state j.

Thus, to answer question (c), we find the product of the matrices T and S:

$$T \cdot S = \begin{bmatrix} 1.6 & 1.2 & .8 & .4 \\ 1.2 & 2.4 & 1.6 & .8 \\ .8 & 1.6 & 2.4 & 1.2 \\ .4 & .8 & 1.2 & 1.6 \end{bmatrix} \begin{bmatrix} \frac{1}{2} & 0 \\ 0 & 0 \\ 0 & 0 \\ 0 & \frac{1}{2} \end{bmatrix} = \begin{matrix} & \begin{matrix} 0 & 5 \end{matrix} \\ \begin{matrix} 1 \\ 2 \\ 3 \\ 4 \end{matrix} & \begin{bmatrix} .8 & .2 \\ .6 & .4 \\ .4 & .6 \\ .2 & .8 \end{bmatrix} \end{matrix}$$

The entry in row 3, column 2, indicates the probability is .6 that the player starting with $3 will win all the money. The entry in row 2, column 1, indicates the probability is .6 that a player starting with $2 will lose all his money.

The above techniques are applicable in general to any transition matrix P of an absorbing Markov chain.

In the gambler's ruin problem, we assumed Player I started with $3 and Player II with $2. Furthermore, we assumed the probability of Player I winning $1 was .5.

Table 3

Probability That Player I Wins	Amount of Units Player I Starts with	Amount of Units Player II Starts with	Probability That Player I Goes Broke	Expected Length of Game	Expected Gain of Player I
.50	9	1	.1	9	0
.50	90	10	.1	900	0
.50	900	100	.1	90,000	0
.50	8000	2000	.2	16,000,000	0
.45	9	1	.210	11	−1.1
.45	90	10	.866	765.6	−76.6
.45	99	1	.182	171.8	−17.2
.40	90	10	.983	441.3	−88.3
.40	99	1	.333	161.7	−32.3

Table 3 gives probabilities for ruin and expected length for other kinds of betting situations for which the bet is 1 unit.

Suppose, for example, that Player I starts with $90 and Player II with $10, with Player I having a probability of .45 of winning (the game being unfavorable to Player I). If at each trial, the stake is $1, Table 3 shows that the probability is .866 that Player I is ruined. If the same game is played with Player I having $9 to start and Player II having $1 to start, the probability that Player I is ruined drops to .210.

*MODEL: THE RISE AND FALL OF STOCK PRICES

This example from M. Dryden*, involves using Markov chains to analyze the movement of stock prices. The stocks (shares) were those whose daily progress was recorded by the London *Financial Times*. At any point in time a given stock was classified as being in one of three states: increase (I), decrease (D), or no change (N), depending on whether its price had risen, fallen, or remained the same compared to the previous trading day. The intent of the model was to study the long range movement of stocks through these states. Data reporting the past history of stock prices over a period of 1097 trading days were used to statistically fit a transition matrix to the model. The transition matrix used was

$$P = \begin{array}{c} \\ I \\ D \\ N \end{array} \begin{array}{ccc} I & D & N \\ \left[\begin{array}{ccc} .586 & .073 & .340 \\ .070 & .639 & .292 \\ .079 & .064 & .857 \end{array}\right] \end{array}$$

Thus, a share that increased one day would have probability .586 of also increasing the next day and a probability of .340 of registering no change the next day. Note that the tendency to remain in the same state is strongest for the no-change state, since p_{33} is the largest of the diagonal elements.

The fixed probability vector $\mathbf{t}$ for the transition matrix can be computed to be

$$\mathbf{t} = [.156 \quad .154 \quad .687]$$

Thus, in the long run, a stock will have increased its price 15.6% of the time, decreased its price 15.4% of the time, and remained unchanged 68.7% of the time.

How long will a stock increase before its price begins to fall? Or, in general, how long will a stock be in a given state before it moves to another one? These questions are highly reminiscent of those encountered while studying absorbing chains, yet here the transition matrix P is not absorbing. Thus the techniques used earlier do not apply. The way out is to engage in some wishful thinking.

Suppose we wanted to know on the average how long a stock would spend in states I or N before arriving in state D. We could then assume state D is an absorbing one

---

* Adapted from Myles M. Dryden, "Share Price Movements: A Markovian Approach," *Journal of Finance*, **24** (March 1969), pp. 49–60.

and replace the current probability p_{22} with 1 and make all other elements in the second row of P zero. The new matrix P' we have created is

$$
P' = \begin{array}{c} \\ I \\ D \\ N \end{array}
\begin{array}{c} \begin{array}{ccc} I & D & N \end{array} \\
\left[\begin{array}{ccc}
.586 & .073 & .340 \\
0 & 1 & 0 \\
.079 & .064 & .857
\end{array} \right]
\end{array}
$$

which is the matrix of an absorbing chain.

Partitioning this matrix, we obtain

$$
\begin{array}{c} \\ D \\ I \\ N \end{array}
\begin{array}{c} \begin{array}{ccc} D & I & N \end{array} \\
\left[\begin{array}{c:cc}
1 & 0 & 0 \\ \hdashline
.073 & .586 & .340 \\
.064 & .079 & .857
\end{array} \right]
\end{array}
$$

and recognize

$$
Q = \begin{array}{c} \\ I \\ N \end{array}
\begin{array}{c} \begin{array}{cc} I & N \end{array} \\
\left[\begin{array}{cc}
.586 & .340 \\
.079 & .857
\end{array} \right]
\end{array}
$$

as the fundamental matrix. Then

$$
(I - Q)^{-1} = \left[\begin{array}{cc}
.414 & -.340 \\
-.079 & .143
\end{array} \right]^{-1} = \begin{array}{c} \\ I \\ N \end{array}
\begin{array}{c} \begin{array}{cc} I & N \end{array} \\
\left[\begin{array}{cc}
4.42 & 10.51 \\
2.44 & 12.80
\end{array} \right]
\end{array}
$$

The entries of $(I - Q)^{-1}$ are interpreted as follows. The (i, j)th entry gives the average time spent in state j having started in state i before reaching the absorbing state D for the first time.

So, a stock currently increasing would spend an average of 4.4 days increasing and 10.5 days not changing before declining. Hence, a total of 14.9 days on the average would elapse before an increasing stock first began to decrease. Likewise, if a stock is currently exhibiting no change, the second row of the above matrix shows that an average of $2.44 + 12.80 = 15.24$ days would go by before it began to decrease.

Suppose a stock is increasing and then either levels off or declines. How long will it take before it starts rising again? In general, given we are in state i and leave, what is the average time that elapses before we return again to state i? The answer, which we state without proof, can be succinctly given:

> The average amount of time elapsed between visits to state i (called *mean recurrence time*) is given by the reciprocal of the ith component of the fixed probability vector **t**.

Here,

$$
\mathbf{t} = [.156 \quad .154 \quad .687]
$$

So we can then compute

State	Mean Recurrence Time (Days)
I	6.41
D	6.49
N	1.46

In this model, then, days on which a share's price fails to change follow each other fairly closely.

Exercise 11.3 *Answers to Odd-Numbered Problems begin on page* 630 .

In Problems 1–6 state which of the given matrices are absorbing Markov chains.

1. $\begin{bmatrix} 0 & 1 \\ \frac{1}{4} & \frac{3}{4} \end{bmatrix}$

2. $\begin{bmatrix} 1 & 0 \\ \frac{1}{3} & \frac{2}{3} \end{bmatrix}$

3. $\begin{bmatrix} 1 & 0 & 0 \\ \frac{1}{8} & \frac{5}{8} & \frac{2}{8} \\ 0 & 0 & 1 \end{bmatrix}$

4. $\begin{bmatrix} 0 & 0 & 1 \\ 1 & 0 & 0 \\ 0 & 1 & 0 \end{bmatrix}$

5. $\begin{bmatrix} 0 & 1 & 0 & 0 \\ 1 & 0 & 0 & 0 \\ 0 & 0 & 1 & 0 \\ \frac{1}{4} & 0 & \frac{3}{4} & 0 \end{bmatrix}$

6. $\begin{bmatrix} \frac{1}{3} & \frac{1}{3} & 0 & \frac{1}{3} \\ 0 & \frac{1}{4} & \frac{1}{4} & \frac{1}{2} \\ 0 & 0 & 1 & 0 \\ 0 & \frac{1}{2} & 0 & \frac{1}{2} \end{bmatrix}$

7. Find the fundamental matrix T of the absorbing Markov chain in Problem 3. Also, find S and $T \cdot S$.

8. Follow the directions of Problem 7 for the matrix in Problem 6.

9. Suppose that for a certain absorbing Markov chain the fundamental matrix T is found to be

$$
\begin{array}{c c c c}
 & \$1 & \$2 & \$3 \\
\begin{array}{c} \$1 \\ \$2 \\ \$3 \end{array} &
\begin{bmatrix} 1.5 & .5 & .8 \\ 1.2 & 2.3 & .6 \\ .3 & 1.8 & 2.1 \end{bmatrix}
\end{array}
$$

   (a) What is the expected number of times a person will have $3 given that he started with $1? With $2?

   (b) If a player starts with $3, how many games can he expect to play before absorption?

10. For the data in Problem 9, suppose that we are given the following matrix S:

$$
S = \begin{bmatrix} \frac{1}{2} & 0 \\ 0 & 0 \\ 0 & \frac{1}{2} \end{bmatrix}
$$

   What is the probability that the player will be absorbed if he started with $3?

11. *Gambler's Ruin Problem.* A person repeatedly bets $1 each day. If he wins, he wins $1 (he receives his bet of $1 plus winnings of $1). He stops playing when he goes broke, or when he accumulates $3. His probability of winning is .4 and of losing is .6. What is the probability of eventually accumulating $3 if he starts with $1? With $2?

12. The following data were obtained from the admissions office of a two-year junior college. Of the first-year class (F), 75% became sophomores (S) the next year and 25% dropped out (D). Of those who were sophomores during a particular year, 90% graduated (G) by the following year and 10% dropped out.

    (a)   Set up a Markov chain with states D, F, G, and S which describes the situation.

    (b)   How many are absorbing?

    (c)   Determine the matrix T.

    (d)   Determine the probability that an entering first-year student will eventually graduate.

13.   *Gambler's Ruin Problem.* Marsha wants to purchase a $4000 used car, but only has $1000 available. Not wishing to finance the purchase, she makes a series of wagers in which the winnings equal whatever is bet. The probability of winning is .4 and the probability of losing is .6. In a daring strategy Marsha decides to bet all her money or at least enough to obtain $4000 until she loses everything or has $4000. That is, if she has $1000, she bets $1000; if she has $2000, she bets $2000.

    (a)   What is the expected number of wagers placed before the game ends?

    (b)   What is the probability that Marsha is wiped out?

    (c)   What is the probability that Marsha wins the amount needed to purchase the car?

14.   Answer the questions in Problem 13 if the probability of winning is .5.

15.   Answer the questions in Problem 13 if the probability of winning is .6.

16.   Three armored cars, A, B, and C, are engaged in a three-way battle. Armored car A has probability $\frac{1}{3}$ of destroying its target, B has probability $\frac{1}{2}$ of destroying its target, and C has probability $\frac{1}{6}$ of destroying its target. The armored cars fire at the same time and each fires at the strongest opponent not yet destroyed. Using as states the surviving cars at any round, set up a Markov chain and answer the following questions:

    (a)   How many states are in this chain?

    (b)   How many are absorbing?

    (c)   Find the expected number of rounds fired.

    (d)   Find the probability that A survives.

17.   *Stock Price Model.* In the model, a stock currently showing no change would, on the average, stay how long in that state?

18.   *Stock Price Model.* By making state I an absorbing state compute the average number of days elapsed before a stock currently decreasing would start to increase again.

---

*11.4 AN APPLICATION TO GENETICS

Most of this section is based on the work of Gregor Mendel. The Mendelian theory of genetics states that many traits of an offspring are determined by the genes of the

---

* This section may be omitted without loss of continuity.
GREGOR JOHANN MENDEL (1822–1884), an Austrian monk, discovered the first laws of heredity and thereby laid the foundation for the science of genetics. For many years, Mendel taught science in the technical high school at Brunn, Austria, without a teacher's license. The reason—he failed the *biology* portion of the license examination!

parents. Each parent has a pair of genes and the basic assumption of Mendel's theory is that the offspring inherits one gene from each parent in a random, independent way.

Dominant
Recessive

In the most simple cases genes are of two types: *dominant,* denoted by *A,* and *recessive,* denoted by *a.* There are four possible pairings of the two types of genes: *AA, Aa, aA,* and *aa.* However, genetically, the two genotypes *Aa* and *aA* are the same. An individual having the genotype *AA* is called *dominant* or *homozygous;* an individual with the genotype *Aa* is called *hybrid* or *heterozygous;* and one with the genotype *aa* is called *recessive.*

Homozygous
Heterozygous

Let's consider some of the possibilities. If both parents are dominant (homozygous), their offspring must be dominant (homozygous); if both parents are recessive, their offspring are recessive; and if one parent is dominant (homozygous) and one recessive, their offspring are hybrid (heterozygous).

If one parent is dominant (*AA*) and the other is hybrid (*Aa*), the offspring must get a dominant gene *A* from the dominant parent and either a dominant gene *A* or a recessive gene *a* from the hybrid parent. In this case, the probability is $\frac{1}{2}$ that the offspring will be dominant (*AA*) and the probability is $\frac{1}{2}$ that the offspring will be hybrid (*Aa*).

Similarly, if one parent is recessive (*aa*) and the other is hybrid (*Aa*), the probability is $\frac{1}{2}$ that the offspring will be recessive (*aa*) and is $\frac{1}{2}$ that the offspring will be hybrid (*Aa*).

If both parents are hybrid (heterozygous), the offspring have equal probability of getting a dominant gene or recessive gene from each parent. Thus, the probability that the offspring will be dominant (homozygous) is $\frac{1}{4}$; recessive, $\frac{1}{4}$; and hybrid (heterozygous), $\frac{1}{2}$. See Figure 4.

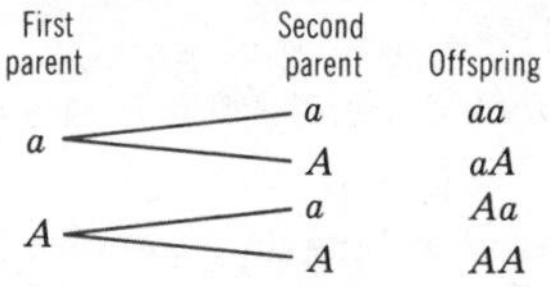

First parent   Second parent   Offspring

a ⟨ a → aa , A → aA

A ⟨ a → Aa , A → AA

Figure 4

□ **Example 1**   Suppose we start with one parent whose genotype is unknown and another whose genotype is known, say hybrid (heterozygous). Their offspring is mated with a person whose genotype is hybrid (heterozygous). This mating procedure is continued. In the long run, what is the genotype of the offspring?

Solution   Since the genotype of an offspring depends solely on the genotype of the parents, such a mating process is an example of a Markov chain. Label the possible states in the process by *D* (dominant), *H* (hybrid), and *R* (recessive). The transition matrix *P* is

$$P = \begin{array}{c} \\ D \\ H \\ R \end{array} \begin{array}{ccc} D & H & R \\ \left[\begin{array}{ccc} \frac{1}{2} & \frac{1}{2} & 0 \\ \frac{1}{4} & \frac{1}{2} & \frac{1}{4} \\ 0 & \frac{1}{2} & \frac{1}{2} \end{array}\right] \end{array} \tag{1}$$

The entries of *P* are obtained as follows: The first row $[\frac{1}{2} \ \frac{1}{2} \ 0]$ of *P* gives the probabilities that the offspring will be *D, H, R,* respectively, when the unknown parent is dominant (*AA*); the second row $[\frac{1}{4} \ \frac{1}{2} \ \frac{1}{4}]$ of *P* gives the probabilities that the offspring will be D, H, R, respectively, when the unknown parent is hybrid (Aa); the third row $[0 \quad \frac{1}{2} \quad \frac{1}{2}]$ of P gives probabilities that the offspring will be D, H, R, respectively when the unknown parent is recessive (aa).

Now, P is regular since the entries of P^2 are all positive:

$$P^2 = \begin{bmatrix} \frac{3}{8} & \frac{1}{2} & \frac{1}{8} \\ \frac{1}{4} & \frac{1}{2} & \frac{1}{4} \\ \frac{1}{8} & \frac{1}{2} & \frac{3}{8} \end{bmatrix}$$

The fixed probability vector of P is found to be

$$\mathbf{t} = [\tfrac{1}{4} \quad \tfrac{1}{2} \quad \tfrac{1}{4}] \tag{2}$$

Thus, in the long run, no matter what the genotype of the unknown parent, the probability that the genotype of the offspring will be dominant (homozygous) is $\frac{1}{4}$; hybrid (heterozygous), $\frac{1}{2}$; and recessive, $\frac{1}{4}$. □

□ **Example 2**

Brother – Sister
Mating Problem

In the so-called *brother – sister mating model,* two individuals are mated, and, from among their direct descendants, two individuals of opposite sex are selected at random. These are mated, and the process continues indefinitely. With three possible genotypes, AA, Aa, aa, for each parent, we have to distinguish six combinations of offspring as follows:

$$E_1: \quad AA \times AA \qquad E_2: \quad AA \times Aa \qquad E_3: \quad Aa \times Aa$$
$$E_4: \quad Aa \times aa \qquad E_5: \quad aa \times aa \qquad E_6: \quad AA \times aa$$

where, for example, E_4: $Aa \times aa$ indicates the mating of a hybrid (Aa) with a recessive (aa). The transition matrix for this experiment is

$$
\begin{array}{c c}
 & \begin{matrix} E_1 & E_2 & E_3 & E_4 & E_5 & E_6 \end{matrix} \\
\begin{matrix} E_1 \\ E_2 \\ E_3 \\ E_4 \\ E_5 \\ E_6 \end{matrix} &
\begin{bmatrix}
1 & 0 & 0 & 0 & 0 & 0 \\
\frac{1}{4} & \frac{1}{2} & \frac{1}{4} & 0 & 0 & 0 \\
\frac{1}{16} & \frac{1}{4} & \frac{1}{4} & \frac{1}{4} & \frac{1}{16} & \frac{1}{8} \\
0 & 0 & \frac{1}{4} & \frac{1}{2} & \frac{1}{4} & 0 \\
0 & 0 & 0 & 0 & 1 & 0 \\
0 & 0 & 1 & 0 & 0 & 0
\end{bmatrix}
\end{array} \tag{3}
$$

We obtain the entries in (3) using the following reasoning: States E_1 and E_5 both have 1 on the diagonal and 0 for all other elements in the same row, since crossing two dominants (homozygous) always yields a dominant (homozygous); likewise, crossing two recessives always yields a recessive. When the process is in one of the other states, say row E_3, we have

$$E_3: \quad Aa \times Aa \qquad P(AA) = \tfrac{1}{4} \qquad P(aA) = \tfrac{1}{2} \qquad P(aa) = \tfrac{1}{4}$$

$$E_1: \quad AA \times AA \qquad \tfrac{1}{4} \times \tfrac{1}{4} = \tfrac{1}{16}$$
$$E_2: \quad AA \times Aa \qquad 2 \times \tfrac{1}{4} \times \tfrac{1}{2} = \tfrac{1}{4}$$
$$E_3: \quad Aa \times Aa \qquad \tfrac{1}{2} \times \tfrac{1}{2} = \tfrac{1}{4}$$
$$E_4: \quad Aa \times aa \qquad 2 \times \tfrac{1}{2} \times \tfrac{1}{4} = \tfrac{1}{4}$$
$$E_5: \quad aa \times aa \qquad \tfrac{1}{4} \times \tfrac{1}{4} = \tfrac{1}{16}$$
$$E_6: \quad AA \times aa \qquad 2 \times \tfrac{1}{4} \times \tfrac{1}{4} = \tfrac{1}{8}$$

The process described above is an example of an absorbing Markov chain. The states E_1 and E_5 are absorbing states.

Now, let's perform the same calculations for the transition matrix in (3) as we did for the gambler's ruin problem in Section 11.3. The transition matrix P is rewritten as follows:

$$
P = \begin{array}{c} \\ E_1 \\ E_5 \\ E_2 \\ E_3 \\ E_4 \\ E_6 \end{array}
\begin{array}{c} \begin{array}{cccccc} E_1 & E_5 & E_2 & E_3 & E_4 & E_6 \end{array} \\
\left[\begin{array}{cc|cccc}
1 & 0 & 0 & 0 & 0 & 0 \\
0 & 1 & 0 & 0 & 0 & 0 \\ \hline
\frac{1}{4} & 0 & \frac{1}{2} & \frac{1}{4} & 0 & 0 \\
\frac{1}{16} & \frac{1}{16} & \frac{1}{4} & \frac{1}{4} & \frac{1}{4} & \frac{1}{8} \\
0 & \frac{1}{4} & 0 & \frac{1}{4} & \frac{1}{2} & 0 \\
0 & 0 & 0 & 1 & 0 & 0
\end{array} \right] \end{array} = \begin{bmatrix} I_2 & 0 \\ S & Q \end{bmatrix}
$$

where the matrices I_2, 0, S, and Q are

$$
I_2 = \begin{bmatrix} 1 & 0 \\ 0 & 1 \end{bmatrix} \qquad
0 = \begin{bmatrix} 0 & 0 & 0 & 0 \\ 0 & 0 & 0 & 0 \end{bmatrix}
$$

$$
S = \begin{bmatrix} \frac{1}{4} & 0 \\ \frac{1}{16} & \frac{1}{16} \\ 0 & \frac{1}{4} \\ 0 & 0 \end{bmatrix} \qquad
Q = \begin{bmatrix} \frac{1}{2} & \frac{1}{4} & 0 & 0 \\ \frac{1}{4} & \frac{1}{4} & \frac{1}{4} & \frac{1}{8} \\ 0 & \frac{1}{4} & \frac{1}{2} & 0 \\ 0 & 1 & 0 & 0 \end{bmatrix}
$$

The fundamental matrix T is

$$
T = [I_4 - Q]^{-1} = \begin{array}{c} \\ E_2 \\ E_3 \\ E_4 \\ E_6 \end{array}
\begin{array}{c} \begin{array}{cccc} E_2 & E_3 & E_4 & E_6 \end{array} \\
\begin{bmatrix}
\frac{8}{3} & \frac{4}{3} & \frac{2}{3} & \frac{1}{6} \\
\frac{4}{3} & \frac{8}{3} & \frac{4}{3} & \frac{1}{3} \\
\frac{2}{3} & \frac{4}{3} & \frac{8}{3} & \frac{1}{6} \\
\frac{4}{3} & \frac{8}{3} & \frac{4}{3} & \frac{4}{3}
\end{bmatrix} \end{array}
$$

The product of the fundamental matrix and S is

$$
T \cdot S = \begin{bmatrix}
\frac{8}{3} & \frac{4}{3} & \frac{2}{3} & \frac{1}{6} \\
\frac{4}{3} & \frac{8}{3} & \frac{4}{3} & \frac{1}{3} \\
\frac{2}{3} & \frac{4}{3} & \frac{8}{3} & \frac{1}{6} \\
\frac{4}{3} & \frac{8}{3} & \frac{4}{3} & \frac{4}{3}
\end{bmatrix}
\begin{bmatrix}
\frac{1}{4} & 0 \\
\frac{1}{16} & \frac{1}{16} \\
0 & \frac{1}{4} \\
0 & 0
\end{bmatrix}
= \begin{array}{c} \\ E_2 \\ E_3 \\ E_4 \\ E_6 \end{array}
\begin{array}{c} \begin{array}{cc} E_1 & E_5 \end{array} \\
\begin{bmatrix}
\frac{3}{4} & \frac{1}{4} \\
\frac{1}{2} & \frac{1}{2} \\
\frac{1}{4} & \frac{3}{4} \\
\frac{1}{2} & \frac{1}{2}
\end{bmatrix} \end{array}
$$

Genetically, the matrix $T \cdot S$ can be interpreted to mean that after a large number of inbred matings, a person is either in state E_1 or state E_5. That is, only pure genotypes remain, while the mixed genotype (hybrid heterozygous) will disappear. Notice also that if one starts in the state E_4: $Aa \times aa$, which has 3 recessive genes and 1 dominant gene, the probability for ending up in the state E_1: $AA \times AA$ is $\frac{1}{4}$, which is the ratio of dominant genes to total genes.

From the fundamental matrix, we can find the expected number of generations needed to pass from a nonabsorbing state to either absorbing state. Thus, the expected number of generations needed to pass from E_3 to either E_1 or E_5 is

$$
\frac{4}{3} + \frac{8}{3} + \frac{4}{3} + \frac{1}{3} = \frac{17}{3} = 5\frac{2}{3} \qquad \square
$$

Finally, consider a genetic experiment in which a large population is randomly mated. We assume that males and females have the same proportion of each genotype and that male and female offspring are equally likely to occur. It would seem a logical conclusion of Mendel's law that after a large number of matings, the recessive genotype must disappear. However, the mere fact that recessive genotypes continue to exist implies that this is not the case. This seeming discrepancy in the theory was resolved early in the twentieth century, by the famous mathematician G. H. Hardy who proved that the proportion of genotypes in a population stabilizes after one generation.*

Exercise 11.4   *Answers to Odd-Numbered Problems begin on page* 631 .

1. In Example 1, prove that the fixed probability vector **t** for the transition matrix P of (1) is given by (2).

2. *Mating Problem.* In Example 1, suppose the known genotype is dominant (homozygous) and each offspring is mated with a person having a dominant (homozygous) genotype.

   (a) Find the transition matrix P.
   (b) Find the fixed probability vector. Interpret the answer.
   (c) Find the fundamental matrix T.
   (d) What is the expected number of generations needed to pass from each nonabsorbing stage?

3. Answer the same questions given in Problem 2 if the known genotype is recessive.

CHAPTER REVIEW

Important Terms

Markov chain	transition probability	equilibrium distribution
initial state	probability vector	absorbing state
initial probability distribution	regular Markov chain	absorbing Markov chain
transition matrix	fixed probability vector	fundamental matrix
	equilibrium state	

True-False Questions

T F 1. The matrix $\begin{bmatrix} 1 & 0 \\ -1 & 1 \end{bmatrix}$ is a transition matrix for a Markov chain.

T F 2. The transition matrix $\begin{bmatrix} \frac{1}{2} & \frac{1}{2} \\ 0 & 1 \end{bmatrix}$ is regular.

G. H. HARDY (1877–1947), an English mathematician, is credited with the discovery in 1908 of the Hardy–Weinberg law in genetics. He published many brilliant articles in number theory as well.

*G. H. Hardy, "Mendelian Proportions in a Mixed Population," *Science,* N.S. **28** (1908), pp. 49–50.

T   F   3. The matrix $\begin{bmatrix} 0 & 1 \\ \frac{1}{3} & \frac{2}{3} \end{bmatrix}$ is an absorbing Markov chain.

T   F   4. If P is a transition matrix of a Markov chain, then P^2 gives the probability of moving from one state to another state in two stages.

Fill in the Blanks

1. In a Markov chain with m states, the initial probability distribution is a _____ row vector.

2. A probability vector is a vector whose entries are _____ and sum up to _____.

3. In a Markov chain with transition matrix P the probability distribution $v^{(k)}$ after k observations satisfies _____.

4. A Markov chain is said to be regular if for some power of its transition matrix P, all entries are _____.

Review Exercises

Answers to Odd-Numbered Problems begin on page 631.

1. Find the fixed probability vector of:

(a) $\begin{bmatrix} \frac{1}{4} & \frac{3}{4} \\ \frac{1}{2} & \frac{1}{2} \end{bmatrix}$ (b) $\begin{bmatrix} \frac{1}{3} & \frac{2}{3} \\ \frac{2}{3} & \frac{1}{3} \end{bmatrix}$

2. Define and explain in words the meaning of a *regular* transition matrix. Give an example of such a matrix and of a matrix that is not regular.

3. *Customer Loyalty.* Three beer distributors, A, B, and C, each presently holds $\frac{1}{3}$ of the beer market. Each wants to increase its share of the market, and to do so, each introduces a new brand. During the next year, it is learned that:

   (a) A keeps 50% of its business and loses 20% to B and 30% to C.
   (b) B keeps 40% of its business and loses 40% to A and 20% to C.
   (c) C keeps 25% of its business and loses 50% to A and 25% to B.

   Assuming this trend continues, after 2 years what share of the market does each distributor have? In the long run, what is each distributor's share?

4. If the current share of the market for each beer distributor A, B, and C in Problem 3 is A: 25%, B: 25%, C: 50%, and the market trend is the same, answer the same questions.

5. A representative of a book publishing company has to cover three universities, U_1, U_2, and U_3. She never sells at the same university in successive months. If she sells at University U_1, then the next month she sells at U_2. However, if she sells at either U_2 or U_3, then the next month she is three times as likely to sell at U_1 as at the other university. In the long run, how often does she sell at each of the universities?

6. *Family Traits:* Assume that the probability of a fat father having a fat son is .7 and that of a skinny father having a skinny son is .4. What is the probability of a fat father being the great grandfather of a fat great grandson? In the long run, what will be the distribution? Does it depend on the initial physical state of the fathers?

7. *Gambler's Ruin Problem.* Suppose a man has $2, which he is going to bet $1 at a time until he either loses all his money or he wins $5. Assume he wins with a probability of .45 and he loses with a probability of .55. Construct the transition probability for this game and answer the questions as stated on page 465 in Section 11.3. *Hint:* The fundamental matrix T of the transition matrix P is

$$T = \begin{bmatrix} 1.584282 & 1.062331 & .635281 & .285876 \\ 1.298405 & 2.360736 & 1.411736 & .635281 \\ .94899 & 1.725454 & 2.360736 & 1.062331 \\ .52194 & .949000 & 1.298405 & 1.584281 \end{bmatrix}$$

PART THREE

DISCRETE MATHEMATICS

LOGIC AND LOGIC CIRCUITS

12.1 PROPOSITIONS

PROPOSITIONS ☐ COMPOUND PROPOSITIONS ☐ EXCLUSIVE DISJUNCTION ☐ NEGATION; QUANTIFIERS

In this chapter, we survey many of the fundamental concepts found in the area of mathematics called *logic*. There are several reasons for studying logic. Two of the more important ones are *(1)* to gain proficiency in correct mathematical reasoning and *(2)* to apply the tool of logic to practical situations such as the design of *logic circuits* used in computers and other electronic devices.

In mathematics, the words "not," "or," "if . . . , then . . . ," "if and only if," and so on, are used extensively. A knowledge of the exact meaning of these words is necessary before we can make precise the laws of inference and deduction that are constantly used in mathematics. The study of logic will enable you to gain a basic understanding of what constitutes a mathematical argument. This will eliminate common errors made in mathematical, as well as nonmathematical, arguments.

We hope this chapter will give you some indication of the usefulness of logic in uncovering ambiguities and non-sequiturs. Furthermore, we hope this chapter offers evidence in favor of Church's remark that "the value of logic . . . is not that it supports a particular system, but that the process of logical organization of any system (empiricist or otherwise) serves to test its internal consistency, to verify its logical adequacy to its declared purpose, and to isolate and clarify the assumptions on which it rests." *

In the last two sections of this chapter, we apply the concepts of logic to a problem in the application of conflicting rules and to the design of electronic circuits.

PROPOSITIONS

English and similar languages are composed of various words and phrases with distinct functions which have a bearing on the meaning of the sentences in which they occur.

English sentences may be classified as *declarative, interrogative, exclamatory,* or *imperative.* In the study of logic, we assume that we are able to recognize a declarative sentence (or *statement*) and form an opinion as to whether it is true or false.

Proposition   A *proposition* is a declarative sentence that can be meaningfully classified as either true or false.

☐ **Example 1**   The price of an IBM-AT personal computer was $1800 on June 16, 1987.
This is a proposition, although few of us can say whether it is true or false.   ☐

BERTRAND RUSSELL (1872–1970) was a British philosopher and mathematician as well as a noted social reformer. In his principal work, he developed symbolic logic and applied it to mathematics and philosophy.

* Church, *Introduction to Mathematical Logic,* Vol. 1, Princeton University Press, Princeton, N.J., 1956, p. 55.

□ **Example 2**   The earth is round.

This sentence records a possible fact about reality and is a proposition. Some people would classify this proposition as true and others as false, depending on what the word *round* means to them. (Does it mean simply "curved," or "perfectly spherical?") Only in an ideal situation can we unequivocally state to which truth category a proposition belongs.   □

□ **Example 3**   What is the exchange rate from United States dollars to German marks?

This is not a proposition—it is an interrogative sentence.   □

□ **Example 4**   The prices of most stocks on the New York Stock Exchange rose during the period 1929–1931.

This is a proposition. It happens to be false.   □

In an ideal situation, a proposition could be easily and decisively classified as true or false. However, as Examples 1 and 2 illustrate, it is often difficult to classify propositions in this way, because of unclear meanings, ambiguous situations, differences of opinion, etc. In the mathematical treatment of logic, we avoid these difficulties by assuming "for the sake of argument" either the truth or the falsity of certain propositions to draw conclusions about other propositions, using *symbolic logic.*

COMPOUND PROPOSITIONS

Consider the proposition "Jones is handsome and Smith is selfish." This sentence is obtained by joining the two propositions "Jones is handsome," "Smith is selfish" by the word "and."

Compound Proposition; Connectives   A *compound proposition* is a proposition formed by connecting two or more propositions, or by negating a single proposition. The words and phrases (or symbols) used to form compound propositions are called *connectives.*

Some of the connectives used in English are: *or; either . . . or; and; but; if . . . , then; not.*

Conjunction   Let p and q denote propositions. The compound proposition p and q is called the *conjunction of p and q,* and is denoted symbolically by

$$p \wedge q$$

We define $p \wedge q$ to be true when both p and q are true and to be false otherwise.

□ **Example 5**   Consider the two statements

p: Washington, D.C., is the capital of the United States.

q: Hawaii is the fiftieth state of the United States.

The conjunction of p and q is

$p \wedge q$: Washington, D.C., is the capital of the United States and Hawaii is the fiftieth state of the United States.

Since both p and q are true statements, we conclude that the compound statement $p \wedge q$ is true.   □

□ **Example 6**   Consider the two statements

p: Washington, D.C., is the capital of the United States.

q: Vermont is the largest of the fifty states.

The compound proposition $p \wedge q$ is

$p \wedge q$: Washington, D.C., is the capital of the United States and Vermont is the largest of the fifty states.

Since the statement q is false, the compound statement $p \wedge q$ is false — even though p is true.   □

Inclusive Disjunction   Let p and q be any propositions. The compound proposition p *or q is called the* ***inclusive disjunction of p and q*** *and is denoted symbolically by*

$$p \vee q$$

We define $p \vee q$ to be true if *at least one* of the propositions p, q is true. That is, $p \vee q$ is true if both p and q are true, if p is true and q is false, or if p is false and q is true. It is false if both p and q are false.

□ **Example 7**   Consider the propositions

p: XYZ Company is the largest producer of nails in the world.

q: Mines. Ltd., has three uranium mines in Nevada.

The compound proposition $p \vee q$ is

$p \vee q$: XYZ Company is the largest producer of nails in the world or Mines. Ltd. has three uranium mines in Nevada.   □

EXCLUSIVE DISJUNCTION

The English word "or" can be used in two different ways — as an inclusive ("and/or") or exclusive ("either/or") disjunction. The correct meaning is usually inferred from the context in which the word is used. However, when it is important to be precise (as it often is in mathematics, business, science, etc.) we must carefully distinguish between the two meanings of "or."

Exclusive Disjunction   Let p and q be any proposition. The *exclusive disjunction of p and q,* read as *either p or q,* is denoted symbolically by

$$p \veebar q$$

We define $p \veebar q$ to be true if exactly one of the propositions p, q is true. That is, $p \veebar q$ is true if p is true and q is false, or if p is false and q is true. It is false if both p and q are false or if both p and q are true.

□ **Example 8**   Consider the propositions

> p: XYZ Company earned $3.20 per share in 1980.
>
> q: XYZ Company paid a dividend of $1.20 per share in 1980.

The inclusive disjunction of p and q is

> $p \vee q$:   XYZ Company earned $3.20 per share in 1980 or XYZ Company paid a dividend of $1.20 per share in 1980, or both.

The exclusive disjunction of p and q is

> $p \veebar q$:   XYZ Company earned $3.20 per share in 1980 or XYZ Company paid a dividend of $1.20 per share in 1980, but *not* both.   □

□ **Example 9**   Consider the compound proposition

> p: This weekend I will date Caryl or Mary.

The use of the connective "or" is not clear here. If the "or" means inclusive disjunction, then at least one and possibly both girls will be dated. If the "or" means exclusive disjunction, then only one girl will be dated.   □

NEGATION; QUANTIFIERS

Negation   If p is any proposition, the *negation of p,* denoted by

$$\sim p$$

and read as *not p,* is a proposition which is false when p is true and true when p is false.

The negation of p is sometimes called the *denial* of p. The symbol $\sim$ is called the

Negation Operator   *negation operator.*

The definition of $\sim p$ assumes that p and $\sim p$ cannot both be true. In classical logic,

Law of Contradiction   this assumption is known as the *law of contradiction.*

□ **Example 10**   Consider the proposition

> p: One share of XYZ stock is worth less than $85.

The negation of p is

> $\sim p$:   One share of XYZ stock is worth at least $85.

The sentence "A share of XYZ stock is worth more than $85" is *not* a correct statement of the negation of p.   □

Quantifier   A *quantifier* is a word or phrase telling how many (Latin *quantus*). English quantifiers include "all," "none," "some," "not all," etc. The quantifiers "all," "every," and "each" are interchangeable. The quantifiers "some," "there exist(s)," and "at least one" are also interchangeable.

□ **Example 11**   The following propositions all have the same meaning:

> p: All people are intelligent.
>
> q: Every person is intelligent.
>
> r: Each person is intelligent.
>
> s: Any person is intelligent.   □

□ **Example 12**   The negation of the proposition

> p: All students are intelligent.

is

> ~p: Some students are not intelligent.
>
> ~p: There exists a student who is not intelligent.
>
> ~p: There exist students who are not intelligent.
>
> ~p: At least one student is not intelligent.

The negation of

> q: No student is intelligent.

is

> ~q: Some students are intelligent.

Note that "No student is intelligent" is *not* the negation of *p*; "All students are intelligent" is *not* the negation of *q*.   □

Exercise 12.1   *Answers to Odd-Numbered Problems begin on page* 632 .

In Problems 1–8 determine which are propositions.

1. The cost of shell egg futures was up on June 18, 1980.
2. The gross national product exceeded one billion dollars in 1935.
3. What a portfolio!
4. Why did you buy XYZ Company stock?
5. The earnings of XYZ Company doubled last year.
6. Where is the new mine of Mines, Ltd?
7. Jones is guilty of murder in the first degree.
8. What a hit!

In Problems 9–16 negate each proposition.

9. A fox is an animal.
10. The outlook for bonds is not good.
11. I am buying stocks and bonds.

12. Mike is selling his apartment building and his business.

13. No one wants to buy my house.

14. Everyone has at least one television set.

15. Some people have no car.

16. Jones is permitted not to see that all votes are not counted.

In Problems 17–24 let p denote "John is an economics major" and let q denote "John is a sociology minor." State each proposition as a simple sentence.

17. $p \vee q$

18. $p \veebar q$

19. $p \wedge q$

20. $\sim p$

21. $\sim p \vee \sim q$

22. $\sim(\sim q)$

23. $\sim p \vee q$

24. $\sim p \wedge q$

12.2 TRUTH TABLES

TRUTH VALUES AND TRUTH TABLES ☐ LOGICAL EQUIVALENCE; THE LAWS OF LOGIC

TRUTH VALUES AND TRUTH TABLES

The *truth value* of a proposition is either *true* (denoted by T) or *false* (denoted by F). A *truth table* is a table that shows the truth value of a compound proposition for all possible cases.

For example, consider the conjunction of any two propositions p and q. Recall that $p \wedge q$ is false if either p is false or q is false, or if both p and q are false. There are four possible cases.

1. p is true and q is true.
2. p is true and q is false.
3. p is false and q is true.
4. p is false and q is false.

These four cases are listed in the first two columns of Table 1, which is the truth table for $p \wedge q$. For convenience, the cases for p and q will always be listed in this order.

The truth values of $\sim p$ are given in Table 2.

Using the previous definitions of inclusive disjunction and exclusive disjunction, we obtain truth tables for $p \vee q$ and $p \veebar q$. See Table 3.

Table 1

	p	q	$p \wedge q$
Case 1	T	T	T
Case 2	T	F	F
Case 3	F	T	F
Case 4	F	F	F

Table 2

p	$\sim p$
T	F
F	T

Table 3

p	q	$p \vee q$	$p \veebar q$
T	T	T	F
T	F	T	T
F	T	T	T
F	F	F	F

Besides using the connectives $\wedge$, $\vee$, $\underline{\vee}$, $\sim$ one at a time to form compound propositions, we can use them together to form more complex statements.

For example, Table 4 is the truth table for $(p \vee q) \underline{\vee} (\sim p)$. The parentheses are used to indicate that $\vee$ and $\sim$ are applied before $\underline{\vee}$.

Table 4

p	q	$p \vee q$	$\sim p$	$(p \vee q) \underline{\vee} (\sim p)$
T	T	T	F	T
T	F	T	F	T
F	T	T	T	F
F	F	F	T	T

Observe that the first columns of the table are for the component propositions p, q, . . . and that there are enough rows in the table to allow for all possible combinations of T and F. (For two components p and q, 4 rows are necessary; for three components p, q, and r, 8 rows would be necessary, and so on; for n statements, 2^n rows are needed.)

Table 4 has five columns, and each column corresponds to a stage in constructing the compound proposition, beginning with the simple components p, q, . . . At each stage, the components constructed in the previous stage are combined, until we obtain the final result in the last column.

We first outline the truth table for the given compound proposition:

p	q	$p \vee q$	$\sim p$	$(p \vee q) \underline{\vee} (\sim p)$
T	T			
T	F			
F	T			
F	F			

Each stage of the proposition is written on the top row, to the right of its intermediate stages; there is a column underneath each component or connective. Truth values are then entered in the truth table, one step at a time:

Stage 1

p	q	$p \vee q$	$\sim p$	$(p \vee q) \underline{\vee} (\sim p)$
T	T	T		
T	F	T		
F	T	T		
F	F	F		

Stage 2

p	q	$p \vee q$	$\sim p$	$(p \vee q) \underline{\vee} (\sim p)$
T	T	T	F	
T	F	T	F	
F	T	T	T	
F	F	F	T	

Stage 3

p	q	$p \vee q$	$\sim p$	$(p \vee q) \vee (\sim p)$
T	T	T	F	T
T	F	T	F	T
F	T	T	T	F
F	F	F	T	T

The truth table of the compound proposition then consists of the original columns under p and q and the fifth column entered into the table in the last stage.

☐ **Example 1** Construct the truth table for $(p \vee \sim q) \wedge p$. The component parts of this proposition are p, $\sim q$, and $p \vee \sim q$.

p	q	$\sim q$	$p \vee \sim q$	$(p \vee \sim q) \wedge p$
T	T	F	T	T
T	F	T	T	T
F	T	F	F	F
F	F	T	T	F

The parentheses are used to indicate that the $\vee$ is applied before $\wedge$ and the $\sim$ applies only to q. Notice that the truth table is the same as for p alone.   ☐

☐ **Example 2** Construct the truth table for $\sim (p \vee q) \vee (\sim p \wedge \sim q)$.

p	q	$\sim p$	$\sim q$	$p \vee q$	$\sim (p \vee q)$	$(\sim p \wedge \sim q)$	$\sim (p \vee q) \vee (\sim p \wedge \sim q)$
T	T	F	F	T	F	F	F
T	F	F	T	T	F	F	F
F	T	T	F	T	F	F	F
F	F	T	T	F	T	T	T

The parentheses indicate that the first $\sim$ symbol negates $p \vee q$ [not p alone and not $(p \vee q) \vee (\sim p \wedge \sim q)$]. Notice that the statements $\sim (p \vee q)$, $\sim p \wedge \sim q$, and $\sim (p \vee q) \vee (\sim p \wedge \sim q)$ all have the same truth table.   ☐

The next example is of a truth table involving three components, p, q, and r.

□ **Example 3**   Construct the truth table for $p \wedge (q \vee r)$.

p	q	r	$q \vee r$	$p \wedge (q \vee r)$
T	T	T	T	T
T	T	F	T	T
T	F	T	T	T
T	F	F	F	F
F	T	T	T	F
F	T	F	T	F
F	F	T	T	F
F	F	F	F	F

□

LOGICAL EQUIVALENCE; THE LAWS OF LOGIC

Very often, two propositions stated in different ways have the same meaning. For example, in law, "Jones agreed and is obligated to paint Smith's house" has the same meaning as "It was agreed and contracted by Jones that Jones would paint the house belonging to Smith and Jones is therefore required to paint the aforesaid house."

Logically Equivalent   **If two propositions a and b have the same truth values in every possible case, the propositions are called *logically equivalent*. This relationship is denoted by $a \equiv b$.**

□ **Example 4**   Show that $\sim(p \wedge q)$ is logically equivalent to $\sim p \vee \sim q$.

Solution   Construct the truth table as shown below.

1	2	3	4	5	6	7
p	q	$p \wedge q$	$\sim(p \wedge q)$	$\sim p$	$\sim q$	$\sim p \vee \sim q$
T	T	T	F	F	F	F
T	F	F	T	F	T	T
F	T	F	T	T	F	T
F	F	F	T	T	T	T

Since the entries in columns 4 and 7 of the truth table are the same, the two propositions are logically equivalent.   □

□ **Example 5**   Show that $\sim p \wedge \sim q$ is logically equivalent to $\sim(p \vee q)$.

Solution   Construct the truth table as shown. The entries under $\sim p \wedge \sim q$ and $\sim(p \vee q)$ are the same, so the two propositions are logically equivalent.

p	q	$p \vee q$	$\sim p$	$\sim q$	$\sim p \wedge \sim q$	$\sim(p \vee q)$
T	T	T	F	F	F	F
T	F	T	F	T	F	F
F	T	T	T	F	F	F
F	F	F	T	T	T	T

□

The following laws are especially useful in the study of logic circuits. They can be proved using truth tables.

Idempotent Laws   For any proposition p,

$$p \wedge p \equiv p \qquad p \vee p \equiv p$$

Here, $p \wedge p \equiv p$ since $p \wedge p$ is true when p is true and false when p is false. A similar argument shows that $p \vee p \equiv p$.

Commutative Laws   For any two propositions p and q,

$$p \wedge q \equiv q \wedge p \qquad p \vee q \equiv q \vee p$$

The Commutative Laws state that, if two or more propositions are combined using the connective *and,* changing the order in which the components are connected does not change the meaning of the compound proposition. The same is true of the connective *or.*

For example, if we consider the two statements

p: Mrs. Jones is attractive.

q: Mr. Jones is intelligent.

we see that the compound propositions

$p \wedge q$:   Mrs. Jones is attractive and Mr. Jones is intelligent.

$q \wedge p$:   Mr. Jones is intelligent and Mrs. Jones is attractive.

have the same meaning.

Associative Laws   For any three propositions p, q, r,

$$(p \wedge q) \wedge r \equiv p \wedge (q \wedge r) \qquad (p \vee q) \vee r \equiv p \vee (q \vee r)$$

Because of the Associative Laws, it is possible to omit the parentheses when using the same connective more than once. For instance, we can write

$$p \wedge q \wedge r \quad \text{for} \quad (p \wedge q) \wedge r$$

and

$$p \wedge q \wedge r \wedge s \quad \text{for} \quad [(p \wedge q) \wedge r] \wedge s$$

and similarly for $\vee$. Note, however, that the parentheses cannot be omitted when using $\wedge$ and $\vee$ together; see Problems 36 and 37.

> **Distributive Laws** For any three propositions p, q, r,
>
> $$p \vee (q \wedge r) \equiv (p \vee q) \wedge (p \vee r)$$
> $$p \wedge (r \vee q) \equiv (p \wedge r) \vee (p \wedge q)$$

Here, $p \vee (q \wedge r) \equiv (p \vee q) \wedge (p \vee r)$ means that p or (q and r) has the same meaning as (p or q) and (p or r). Also, $p \wedge (r \vee q) \equiv (p \wedge r) \vee (p \wedge q)$ means that the compound proposition p and (r or q) has the same meaning as (p and r) or (p and q).

□ **Example 6** Consider the three propositions

p: Betsy will do her homework.
q: Betsy will wash her car.
r: Betsy will read a book.

The first distributive law, namely,

$$p \vee (q \wedge r) \equiv (p \vee q) \wedge (p \vee r)$$

says that these two statements are logically equivalent:

1. Betsy will do her homework, or she will wash her car and read a book.
2. Betsy will do her homework or wash her car, and Betsy will do her homework or read a book. □

> **De Morgan's Laws** For any two propositions p and q,
>
> $$\sim(p \vee q) \equiv \sim p \wedge \sim q \qquad \sim(p \wedge q) \equiv \sim p \vee \sim q$$

That is, the compound proposition p or q is false only when p and q are both false. Similarly, p and q is false when either p or q (or both) is false. De Morgan's laws are proved using the truth tables in Examples 4 and 5.

□ **Example 7** Negate the compound statements:

(a) The first child is a girl and the second child is a boy.
(b) Tonight I will study or I will go bowling.

AUGUSTUS DE MORGAN (1806–1871), British mathematician and logician, was born in Madura, India, the son of a British army officer. He was graduated from Trinity College in Cambridge, England in 1827, but was denied a teaching position there for refusing to subscribe to religious tests. He was, however, appointed to a mathematics professorship at the newly opened University of London. He is best known for his work *Formal Logic,* which appeared in 1847. He also wrote papers on the foundations of algebra, philosophy of mathematical methods, and probability, as well as several successful elementary textbooks.

Solution   (a)   Let p and q represent the components:

p: The first child is a girl.

q: The second child is a boy.

To negate the statement $p \wedge q$ is to find $\sim(p \wedge q)$. By De Morgan's law,

$$\sim(p \wedge q) \equiv \sim p \vee \sim q$$

The negation can be stated as

The first child is not a girl or the second child is not a boy.

(b)   As above, we represent p and q as

p: I will study.

q: I will go bowling.

We want to negate the statement $p \vee q$. By De Morgan's law,

$$\sim(p \vee q) \equiv \sim p \wedge \sim q$$

The negation can be stated as

Tonight I will not study and I will not go bowling.   □

Absorption Laws   For any two propositions p and q,

$$p \vee (p \wedge q) \equiv p \qquad p \wedge (p \vee q) \equiv p$$

Here, $p \vee (p \wedge q) \equiv p$ means that p or (p and q) is logically equivalent to p. Similarly, $p \wedge (p \vee q) \equiv p$ means that p and (p or q) is logically equivalent to p.

□ **Example 8**   Use truth tables to prove the distributive law, $p \vee (q \wedge r) \equiv (p \vee q) \wedge (p \vee r)$.

Solution   Since the entries in the last two columns of the truth table below are the same, the two propositions are logically equivalent.

p	q	r	$q \wedge r$	$p \vee q$	$p \vee r$	$p \vee (q \wedge r)$	$(p \vee q) \wedge (p \vee r)$
T	T	T	T	T	T	T	T
T	T	F	F	T	T	T	T
T	F	T	F	T	T	T	T
T	F	F	F	T	T	T	T
F	T	T	T	T	T	T	T
F	T	F	F	T	F	F	F
F	F	T	F	F	T	F	F
F	F	F	F	F	F	F	F

□

□ **Example 9**   Use truth tables to prove the idempotent law, $p \wedge p \equiv p$.

Solution   The truth table is

p	$p \wedge p$
T	T
F	F

□

Exercise 12.2   *Answers to Odd-Numbered Problems begin on page* 632.

In Problems 1–16 construct a truth table for each compound proposition.

1. $p \vee \sim q$

2. $\sim p \vee \sim q$

3. $\sim p \wedge \sim q$

4. $\sim p \wedge q$

5. $\sim(\sim p \wedge q)$

6. $(p \vee \sim q) \wedge \sim p$

7. $\sim(\sim p \vee \sim q)$

8. $(p \vee \sim q) \wedge (q \wedge \sim p)$

9. $(p \vee \sim q) \wedge p$

10. $p \wedge (q \vee \sim q)$

11. $(p \underline{\vee} q) \wedge (p \wedge \sim q)$

12. $(p \wedge \sim q) \vee (q \wedge \sim p)$

13. $(p \wedge q) \vee (\sim p \wedge \sim q)$

14. $(p \wedge q) \vee (p \wedge r)$

15. $(p \wedge \sim q) \underline{\vee} r$

16. $(\sim p \vee q) \wedge \sim r$

In Problems 17–22 construct a truth table for each law.

17. Idempotent laws

18. Commutative laws

19. Associative laws

20. Distributive laws

21. Absorption laws

22. De Morgan's laws

In Problems 23–26 show that the given propositions are logically equivalent.

23. $p \wedge (\sim q \vee q)$ and p

24. $p \vee (q \wedge \sim q)$ and p

25. $\sim(\sim p)$ and p

26. $p \wedge q$ and $q \wedge p$

In Problems 27–30 construct a truth table for each proposition.

27. $p \wedge (q \wedge \sim p)$

28. $(p \wedge q) \vee p$

29. $[(p \wedge q) \vee (\sim p \wedge \sim q)] \wedge p$

30. $(\sim p \wedge \sim q \wedge r) \vee (p \wedge q \wedge r)$

In Problems 31–33 use the propositions

p: Smith is an exconvict.

q: Smith is rehabilitated.

to give examples, using English sentences, of each law.

31. Idempotent laws

32. Commutative laws

33. De Morgan's laws

34. Use the distributive and commutative laws to show that

$$(p \vee q) \wedge r \equiv (p \wedge r) \vee (q \wedge r)$$

35. Use the distributive and commutative laws to show that

$$(p \wedge q) \vee r \equiv (p \vee r) \wedge (q \vee r)$$

36. The statement

> The actor is intelligent or handsome and talented.

could be interpreted to mean either

> *a*:   The actor is intelligent, or he is handsome and talented;

or

> *b*:   The actor is intelligent or handsome, and he is talented.

Describe a case in which *a* is true and *b* is false.

37. The statement

> Michael will sell his car and buy a bicycle or rent a truck.

could be interpreted to mean either

> *a*:   Michael will sell his car, and he will buy a bicycle or rent a truck;

or

> *b*:   Michael will sell his car and buy a bicycle, or he will rent a truck.

Find a case in which *b* is true and *a* is false.

In Problems 38–40 use De Morgan's laws to negate each proposition.

38. Mike can hit the ball well and he can pitch strikes.

39. Katy is a good volleyball player and is not conceited.

40. The baby is crying or talking all the time.

12.3 IMPLICATIONS; THE BICONDITIONAL CONNECTIVE; TAUTOLOGIES

THE CONDITIONAL CONNECTIVE □ CONVERSE, CONTRAPOSITIVE, AND INVERSE
□ THE BICONDITIONAL CONNECTIVE □ TAUTOLOGIES □ BICONDITIONAL PROPOSITIONS
□ TAUTOLOGIES □ SUBSTITUTION

THE CONDITIONAL CONNECTIVE

Consider the following compound proposition: 'If I get an A in Math, then I will continue to study.'' The above sentence states a condition under which I shall continue to study.

Another example of such a proposition is: "If today is Sunday, then tomorrow is Monday."

Such propositions occur quite frequently in mathematics, and an understanding of their nature is extremely important.

Implication; Conditional Connective If p and q are any two propositions, then we call the proposition

If p, then q

an *implication* or *conditional statement* and the connective *if . . . , then* the *conditional connective.*

We denote the conditional connective symbolically by $\Rightarrow$ and the implication *If p, then q* by $p \Rightarrow q$. In the implication $p \Rightarrow q$, p is called the *hypothesis* and q is called the *conclusion.* The implication $p \Rightarrow q$ can also be read as follows:

Hypothesis
Conclusion

1. p implies q.
2. p is sufficient for q.
3. p only if q.
4. q is necessary for p.
5. q, if p.

In order to arrive at a truth table for implication we consider the following situation. Suppose we make the statement

If XYZ common stock reaches $90 per share, it will be sold.

When is the statement true and when is it false? Clearly, if XYZ stock reaches $90 per share and it is not sold, the implication is false. It is also clear that if XYZ stock reaches $90 per share and it is sold, the implication is true. In other words, if the hypothesis and conclusion are both true, the implication is true; if the hypothesis is true and the conclusion false, the implication is false.

But what happens when the hypothesis is false? In this case, we arbitrarily say that the implication is true (mainly because we cannot say it is false). The truth table for implication is given in Table 5.

Table 5

p	q	$p \Rightarrow q$
T	T	T
T	F	F
F	T	T
F	F	T

As in the previous section, we express a compound proposition symbolically by replacing each component statement and connective by an appropriate symbol.

For example, denoting "I study" and "I shall pass" by a and b, respectively, the proposition "If I study, then I shall pass," is written as $a \Rightarrow b$. This proposition can also be read as "A sufficient condition for passing is to study."

To understand "implication" better, look at an implication as a conditional promise. If the promise is broken, the implication is false; otherwise, it is true. For this reason, the only circumstance under which the implication $p \Rightarrow q$ is false is when p is true and q is false.

□ **Example 1**   Consider the implication

If you are a thief, then you will go to jail.

If you are a thief and you do go to jail, the implication is true. If you are a thief and you do not go to jail, the promise is broken; thus, the implication is false. If you are not a thief, we have no way of telling what would happen if you were a thief. Since the promise is not tested it is not broken; thus, the implication is true.   □

The word *then* in an implication merely serves to separate the conclusion from the hypothesis—it can be, and often is, omitted.

The implication $p \Rightarrow q$ can be expressed in the symbols defined previously. In fact, Table 6 shows that

$$\sim p \vee q \equiv p \Rightarrow q$$

Table 6

p	q	$\sim p$	$\sim p \vee q$	$p \Rightarrow q$
T	T	F	T	T
T	F	F	F	F
F	T	T	T	T
F	F	T	T	T

CONVERSE, CONTRAPOSITIVE, AND INVERSE

Suppose we start with the implication $p \Rightarrow q$ and then interchange the roles of p and q, obtaining the implication, "If q, then p."

Converse The implication *If q, then p* is called the *converse* of the implication *If p, then q*. That is, $q \Rightarrow p$ is the converse of $p \Rightarrow q$.

The truth tables for the implication $p \Rightarrow q$ and its converse $q \Rightarrow p$ are compared in Table 7.

Table 7

p	q	$p \Rightarrow q$	$q \Rightarrow p$
T	T	T	T
T	F	F	T
F	T	T	F
F	F	T	T

Notice that $p \Rightarrow q$ and $q \Rightarrow p$ are not equivalent. That is, the fact that an implication is true tells us nothing about the truth of its converse. As an illustration, consider the following example.

□ **Example 2**   Consider the statements

p: You are a thief.

q: You will go to jail.

The implication $p \Rightarrow q$ states that

If you are a thief, you will go to jail.

The converse of this implication, namely, $q \Rightarrow p$, states that

If you go to jail, you are a thief.

To say that thieves go to jail is not the same as saying that everyone who goes to jail is a thief.   □

This example illustrates that the truth of an implication does not imply the truth of its converse. Many common fallacies in thinking arise from confusing an implication with its converse.

Contrapositive   The implication *If not q, then not p,* written as $\sim q \Rightarrow \sim p$, is called the *contrapositive* of the implication $p \Rightarrow q$.

□ **Example 3**   Consider the statements

p: You are a thief.

q: You will go to jail.

The implication $p \Rightarrow q$ states "If you are a thief, then you will go to jail." The contrapositive, namely $\sim q \Rightarrow \sim p$, is "If you do not go to jail, then you are not a thief."   □

Inverse   The implication *If not p, then not q,* written as $\sim p \Rightarrow \sim q$, is called the *inverse* of the implication *If p, then q.*

□ **Example 4**   Consider the statements

p: You are a thief.

q: You will go to jail.

The implication $p \Rightarrow q$ states "If you are a thief, then you will go to jail." The inverse of $p \Rightarrow q$, namely $\sim p \Rightarrow \sim q$, is "If you are not a thief, then you will not go to jail."   □

□ **Example 5**   The truth tables for $p \Rightarrow q$, $q \Rightarrow p$, $\sim p \Rightarrow \sim q$, and $\sim q \Rightarrow \sim p$ are given in Table 8.

Table 8

State-ments		Implication	Converse			Inverse	Contrapositive
p	q	$p \Rightarrow q$	$q \Rightarrow p$	$\sim p$	$\sim q$	$\sim p \Rightarrow \sim q$	$\sim q \Rightarrow \sim p$
T	T	T	T	F	F	T	T
T	F	F	T	F	T	T	F
F	T	T	F	T	F	F	T
F	F	T	T	T	T	T	T

Notice that the entries under Implication and Contrapositive are the same; also, the entries under Converse and Inverse are the same. We conclude that

$$p \Rightarrow q \equiv \sim q \Rightarrow \sim p \qquad q \Rightarrow p \equiv \sim p \Rightarrow \sim q$$

Thus, we have shown that an implication and its contrapositive are logically equivalent. Also, the converse and inverse of an implication are logically equivalent.

□

THE BICONDITIONAL CONNECTIVE

The compound statement "p if and only if q" is another way of stating the conjunction of two implications: "if p, then q and if q, then p." For example, consider

p: Jill is happy.

q: Jack is attentive.

If we say "Jill is happy if, and only if, Jack is attentive," we mean that Jill is happy if Jack is attentive and Jill is not happy if Jack is not attentive; that is, if Jack is attentive then Jill is happy, but if Jack is not attentive then Jill is not happy. In symbols, we would write this as

$$(q \Rightarrow p) \wedge (\sim q \Rightarrow \sim p)$$

But the second implication in this conjunction is the contrapositive of the statement $p \Rightarrow q$; that is, "If Jill is happy then Jack is attentive." So we see that

$$p \text{ if and only if } q$$

is equivalent to

$$(q \Rightarrow p) \wedge (p \Rightarrow q)$$

or

$$(p \Rightarrow q) \wedge (q \Rightarrow p)$$

Biconditional Connective The connective *if and only if* is called the *biconditional connective* and is denoted by the symbol $\Leftrightarrow$. The compound proposition

$$p \Leftrightarrow q \qquad (p \text{ if and only if } q)$$

is equivalent to

$$(p \Rightarrow q) \wedge (q \Rightarrow p)$$

The statement $p \Leftrightarrow q$ may also be read as "*p* is necessary and sufficient for *q*," or as "*p* implies *q* and *q* implies *p*." (The abbreviation "iff" for "if and only if" is also sometimes used.)

We can restate the definition of the biconditional connective by its truth table (Table 9).

Table 9

p	q	$p \Rightarrow q$	$q \Rightarrow p$	$(p \Rightarrow q) \wedge (q \Rightarrow p)$	$p \Leftrightarrow q$
T	T	T	T	T	T
T	F	F	T	F	F
F	T	T	F	F	F
F	F	T	T	T	T

☐ **Example 6** Let p and q denote the statements

p: Betsy is happy.

q: Besty is not studying

Then "A necessary condition for Betsy to be happy is that Betsy is not studying" means "If Betsy is happy, she is not studying." Moreover, "A sufficient condition for Betsy to be happy is that Betsy is not studying" means "If Betsy is not studying, she is happy."

Thus, if both implications $(p \Rightarrow q, q \Rightarrow p)$ are true statements, then a necessary and sufficient condition for Betsy to be happy is that Betsy is not studying.

In other words, Betsy is happy if and only if she is not studying. ☐

TAUTOLOGIES

In Section 12.2 we saw how compound propositions can be obtained from simple propositions by using connectives. By using symbols of grouping (parentheses and brackets), we can form more complicated propositions. We denote by $P(p, q, \ldots)$ a compound proposition, where $p, q, \ldots$ are the components of the compound proposition. Some examples of such propositions are

$$\sim(p \wedge q) \qquad p \wedge \sim q \qquad (p \wedge \sim q) \qquad (\sim p \wedge q) \sim p \vee \sim(\sim q \wedge \sim r)$$

Ordinarily, when we write a compound proposition, we cannot be certain of the truth of that proposition unless we know the truth or falsity of the component propositions. But a compound proposition that is true regardless of the truth values of its components can be constructed. Propositions of this kind are called *tautologies*.

Tautology A *tautology* is a compound proposition $P(p, q, \ldots)$ that is true in every possible case.

Examples of tautologies are

$$p \vee \sim p \qquad p \Rightarrow (p \vee q)$$

Tables 10 and 11 show the truth tables of these tautologies.

Table 10

p	$\sim p$	$p \vee \sim p$
T	F	T
F	T	T

Table 11

p	q	$p \vee q$	$p \Rightarrow (p \vee q)$
T	T	T	T
T	F	T	T
F	T	T	T
F	F	F	T

Many other examples of tautologies are provided by the logical equivalences in Section 12.2. For instance, to say that

$$\sim(p \vee q) \equiv \sim p \wedge \sim q$$

is to say that the biconditional proposition

$$\sim(p \vee q) \Leftrightarrow \sim p \wedge \sim q$$

is a tautology.

SUBSTITUTION

Let $P(p, q, \ldots)$ be a compound proposition with p as one of its components. If we replace p with another proposition h, then we obtain a new compound proposition $P(h, q, \ldots)$. It should be clear that $P(p, q, \ldots)$ has the same truth value as $P(h, q, \ldots)$ whenever h has the same truth value as p. This leads to the following principle:

The Law of Substitution

Suppose p and h are propositions and $h \equiv p$. If h is substituted for p in the compound proposition $P(p, q, \ldots)$, a logically equivalent proposition is obtained:

$$P(p, q, \ldots) \equiv P(h, q, \ldots)$$

The Law of Substitution is often used to obtain new versions of existing tautologies. It is particularly useful in mathematics for constructing tautologies of a certain kind, known as *valid arguments* or *proofs*. This is the topic of Section 12.4.

Exercise 12.3   *Answers to Odd-Numbered Problems begin on page* 634 .

In Problems 1–10 write the converse, contrapositive, and inverse of each statement.

1. $\sim p \Rightarrow q$ **2.** $\sim p \Rightarrow \sim q$ **3.** $\sim q \Rightarrow \sim p$ **4.** $p \Rightarrow \sim q$

5. If it is raining, the grass is wet.

6. It is raining if it is cloudy.

7. It is raining or it is cloudy.

8. If it is not cloudy, then it is not raining.

9. Rain is sufficient for it to be cloudy.

10. Rain is necessary for it to be cloudy.

11. Give a verbal sentence that describes

    (a) $p \Rightarrow q$ (b) $q \Rightarrow p$ (c) $\sim p \Rightarrow q$

    using the components

                 p: Jack studies psychology.

                 q: Mary studies sociology.

12. Show that

$$p \Rightarrow q \equiv \sim q \Rightarrow \sim p$$

    using the fact that $p \Rightarrow q \equiv \sim p \lor q$.

13. Show that

$$p \Rightarrow (q \lor r) \equiv (p \land \sim q) \Rightarrow r$$

    (a) using a truth table; (b) using De Morgan's laws and the fact that $p \Rightarrow q \equiv \sim p \lor q$.

14. Show that

$$(p \land q) \Rightarrow r \equiv (p \land \sim r) \Rightarrow \sim q$$

    using the same two methods as in Problem 13.

In Problems 15–24 construct a truth table for each statement.

15. $\sim p \lor (p \land q)$ **16.** $\sim p \land (p \lor q)$

17. $p \lor (\sim p \land q)$ **18.** $(p \lor q) \land \sim q$

19. $\sim p \Rightarrow q$ **20.** $(p \lor q) \Rightarrow p$

21. $\sim p \lor p$ **22.** $p \land \sim p$

23. $p \land (p \Rightarrow q)$ **24.** $p \lor (p \Rightarrow q)$

In Problems 25–28 prove that the following only have truth value T.

25. $p \land (q \land r) \Leftrightarrow (p \land q) \land r$ **26.** $p \lor (q \lor r) \Leftrightarrow (p \lor q) \lor r$

27. $p \land (p \lor q) \Leftrightarrow p$ **28.** $p \lor (p \land q) \Leftrightarrow p$

In Problems 29 – 34 let p be "The examination is hard" and q be "The grades are low." Write each symbolically.

29. If the examination is hard, the grades are low.
30. The examination is not hard nor are the grades low.
31. The grades are not low, and the examination is not hard.
32. The examination is not hard and the grades are low.
33. The grades are low only if the examination is hard.
34. The grades are low if the examination is hard.

12.4 ARGUMENTS

VALID ARGUMENTS □ DIRECT AND INDIRECT PROOF □ MODEL: LIFE INSURANCE

VALID ARGUMENTS

In Section 12.3, we considered the implication $p \Rightarrow q$ as an abstract proposition whose hypothesis could be either true or false. Our point of view in this section is more practical; we will examine implications

$$H \Rightarrow C$$

where (1) the hypothesis H is a compound proposition, and (2) in every possible situation where H is true, the conclusion C is also true. In other words, $H \Rightarrow C$ is a tautology. (In such a case, we say that C is a *logical consequence* of H.)

Argument An *argument* or *proof* consists of a set of propositions $p, q, \ldots$ (called *premises* or *hypotheses*) assumed to be true, and another proposition (called the *conclusion*) which is claimed to be true. If the conclusion is a logical consequence of the conjunction of the premises, we say the argument is *valid*. If the argument is *invalid* (not valid), it is called a *fallacy*.

Thus, the conclusion of a valid argument is a true statement, provided that all of the premises are true. But it is important to realize that a valid argument may lead to a false conclusion if *one or more of the premises is false*. (This fact is sometimes used in mathematics as a form of indirect proof: If an argument is valid, and its conclusion known to be false, and all but one of the premises true, one concludes that the remaining premise is false.)

Similarly, if the conclusion of an argument is known to be true, this does not necessarily mean that the argument is valid. Sometimes a mathematics student will attempt a problem, make several mistakes, and leave out some steps, but eventually state the correct answer by luck, guessing, or prior knowledge. Even though the conclusion is true, the argument by which he or she arrives at this conclusion is not valid.

DIRECT AND INDIRECT PROOF

We shall limit our discussion to two types of argument: direct proof and indirect proof.

Direct Proof   In a *direct proof* we go through a chain of propositions, beginning with the hypotheses and leading to the desired conclusion.

□ **Example 1**   Suppose it is true that

> Either John obeys the law or John is punished.

and

> John was not punished.

Prove that

> John obeyed the law.

Solution   Direct proof: Let p and q denote the propositions

> p: John obeys the law.
>
> q: John is punished.

We can write the premise as

$$p \vee q   \text{and}   \sim q$$

Since $\sim q$ is true then, by the Law of Contradiction (see page 483), q is false. Since $p \vee q$ is true, either p is true or q is true. Thus, p must be true.   □

More examples of direct proof are given later, but before we look at them, let's discuss two laws of logic that are useful in direct proofs.

Law of Detachment   If the implication $p \Rightarrow q$ is true, and if p is true, then q must be true.

See Table 5, Section 12.3 for an illustration of this law.

Law of Syllogism   Let p, q, r be three propositions. If

$$p \Rightarrow q   \text{and}   q \Rightarrow r$$

are both true, then $p \Rightarrow r$ is true.

Table 12 illustrates this law.

Table 12

p	q	r	$p \Rightarrow q$	$q \Rightarrow r$	$p \Rightarrow r$	$(p \Rightarrow q) \wedge (q \Rightarrow r)$	$(p \Rightarrow q) \wedge (q \Rightarrow r) \Rightarrow (p \Rightarrow r)$
T	T	T	T	T	T	T	T
T	T	F	T	F	F	F	T
T	F	T	F	T	T	F	T
T	F	F	F	T	F	F	T
F	T	T	T	T	T	T	T
F	T	F	T	F	T	F	T
F	F	T	T	T	T	T	T
F	F	F	T	T	T	T	T

□ **Example 2**   Suppose it is true that

> It is snowing.

and

> If it is warm, then it is not snowing.

and

> If it is not warm, then I cannot go swimming.

Prove that

> I cannot go swimming.

Solution   Direct proof: Let p, q, r represent the statements

> p: It is snowing.
> q: It is warm.
> r: I can go swimming.

Our premises are the propositions

$$p \qquad q \Rightarrow \sim p \qquad \sim q \Rightarrow \sim r$$

We want to prove that

$$\sim r$$

is true. Since $q \Rightarrow \sim p$ is true, its contrapositive

$$p \Rightarrow \sim q$$

is also true. Using the law of syllogism, since $p \Rightarrow \sim q$ and $\sim q \Rightarrow \sim r$, we see that

$$p \Rightarrow \sim r$$

But we know p is true. By the law of detachment, $\sim r$ is true. That is, I cannot go swimming.

□ **Example 3**   Suppose it is true that

If Dan comes, so will Bill.

and

If Sandy will not come, then Bill will not come.

Show that

If Dan comes, then Sandy will come.

Solution   Let p, q, r denote the propositions

p: Dan comes.
q: Bill will come.
r: Sandy will come.

The premises are

$$p \Rightarrow q \qquad \text{and} \qquad \sim r \Rightarrow \sim q$$

If we assume $\sim r \Rightarrow \sim q$ is true, then the contrapositive $q \Rightarrow r$ is true also. Thus

$$p \Rightarrow q \qquad \text{and} \qquad q \Rightarrow r$$

By the law of syllogism it is true that

$$p \Rightarrow r$$

That is, if Dan comes, then Sandy will come.   □

□ **Example 4**   Suppose it is true that

If I enjoy studying, then I will study.

and

I will do my homework or I will not study.

and

I will not do my homework.

Show that

I do not enjoy studying.

Solution   Let p, q, r denote the three propositions

p: I enjoy studying.
q: I will study.
r: I will do my homework.

Then we know that

$$\sim r \qquad r \vee \sim q \qquad p \Rightarrow q$$

are true. We want to prove that $\sim p$ is true. Since $\sim r$ is true, then r is false. Also, either r or $\sim q$ is true. Thus, $\sim q$ is true. Since $p \Rightarrow q$, we have

$$\sim q \Rightarrow \sim p$$

is true. Hence, $\sim p$ must be true. □

In the examples of direct proof that we have just seen, one proceeds by the laws of logic from the premises to the conclusion.

Indirect Proof   In any valid proof, one shows that an implication $p \Rightarrow q$ is a tautology. To do this by the method of *indirect proof,* we tentatively suppose that q is false (equivalently, that $\sim q$ is true) and show that we are thereby led to a *contradiction*—that is, a logically impossible situation. This contradiction can be resolved only by abandoning the supposition that the conclusion is false. Therefore, it must be true.

An indirect proof is also called a *proof by contradiction.* The concept is illustrated in the next two examples.

□ **Example 5**   Prove the result of Example 1 using an indirect proof.

Solution   To prove that the conclusion p is true, we suppose instead that p is false, hoping to be able to show that this leads to a contradiction.

Thus we assume that

$$\sim p \qquad \sim q \qquad p \veebar q$$

all are true. Either p is true or q is true. But both p and q are false. This is impossible. Thus, we have reached a contradiction, which means that p must be true. □

□ **Example 6**   Suppose that

> If I am lazy, I do not study.

and

> I study or I enjoy myself.

and

> I do not enjoy myself.

Prove that

> I am not lazy.

Solution   Let p, q, r be the statements

p: I am lazy.

q: I study.

r: I enjoy myself.

Assume that

$$\sim r \qquad p \Rightarrow \sim q \qquad q \vee r$$

are true.

We want to show that $\sim p$, the conclusion, is true. In an indirect proof, we assume that $\sim p$ is false; that is, that p is true. If p and $p \Rightarrow \sim q$ are true, then $\sim q$ is true (by the law of detachment). That is, q is false. One of the premises is $\sim r$; thus, r is also false. But $q \vee r$ is true, which is impossible if q and r are both false. This contradiction tells us that we have falsely assumed that $\sim p$ is false. Thus, $\sim p$ is true.

MODEL: LIFE INSURANCE*

The following problem was first studied by Edmund C. Berkeley in 1936 and was solved by the use of principles of logic. His employer, the Prudential Life Insurance Company, had the procedure that when any policyholder requested a change in the schedule of premium payments, one of two rules was involved as company policy. The question was raised as to whether these two rules were logically equivalent. That is, did both rules give rise to the same payment arrangements or did the use of one rule over the other give different payment arrangements?

Berkeley was of the opinion that the two rules, in some instances, gave different directions to the policyholder. An example of a typical clause found in one of the rules was: If a policyholder was making premium payments several times a year with one of the payments falling due on the policy anniversary and if he requested the schedule be changed to one annual payment on the anniversary date, and if his payments were in full up to a date not the anniversary date and if he made this request more than 2 months after the issue date and if his request also came within 2 months after the policy anniversary date, then a certain action was to be taken!

Berkeley replaced this complicated part of one of the rules by the compound proposition

$$p \wedge q \wedge r \wedge s \wedge t \Rightarrow A$$

where p, q, r, s, t are the five statements and A is the action called for. By doing the same with all parts of both rules and by using the laws of logic, Berkeley was able to demonstrate an inconsistency of application of one rule over the other. In fact, there turned out to be four situations in which contradictory actions occurred.

As a result of Berkeley's effort, Prudential replaced the two cumbersome rules by a simple one.

Since this incident, similar situations involving a maze of if's, and's, but's, and implications, particularly in the areas of legal contracts between corporations, have been checked for accuracy and consistency (to eliminate loopholes, etc.) by the use of logic.

---

* John E. Pfeiffer, "Symbolic Logic," *Scientific American* (December 1960).

Exercise 12.4   *Answers to Odd-Numbered Problems begin on page* 635|.

Prove the statements in Problems 1–4 first by using a direct proof and then by using an indirect proof.

1. When it rains, John does not go to school. John is going to school. Show that it is not raining.
2. If I do not go to work, I will go fishing. I will not go fishing. Show that I shall go to work.
3. If Smith is elected president, Kuntz will be elected secretary. If Kuntz is elected secretary, then Brown will not be elected treasurer. Smith is elected president. Show that Brown is not elected treasurer.
4. Either Katy is a good girl or Mike is a good boy. If Danny cries, then Katy is not a good girl. Mike is not a good boy. Does Danny cry?

In Problems 5–7 determine whether the arguments are valid.

5. Hypothesis: When students study, they receive good grades.
   These students do not study.
   Conclusion: These students do not receive good grades.
6. Hypothesis: If Danny is affluent, he is either a snob or a hypocrite.
   Danny is a snob and is not a hypocrite.
   Conclusion: Danny is not affluent.
7. Hypothesis: If Tami studies, she will not fail this course.
   If she does not play with her dolls too often, she will study. Tami failed the course.
   Conclusion: She played with her dolls too often.

12.5 LOGIC CIRCUITS

CIRCUITS AND GATES □ REDESIGNING CIRCUITS □ NAND, NOR, AND XOR

CIRCUITS AND GATES

A *logic circuit* is a type of electrical circuit widely used in computers and other electronic devices (such as calculators, digital watches, and compact disc players). The simplest logic circuits, called *gates,* have the following properties.

1. Current flows to the circuit through one or two connectors called *input lines,* and from the circuit through a connector called the *output line.*
2. The current in any of the input or output lines may have either of two possible voltage levels. The higher level is denoted by 1 and the lower level by 0. (Level 1 is sometimes referred to as *On* or *True;* Level 0 may be referred to as *Off* or *False.*)

3. The voltage level of the output line depends on the voltage level(s) of the input line(s), according to rules of logic similar to the principles discussed in Section 12.3.

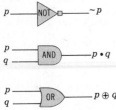

The three most basic types of gates are the *inverter* (or *Not gate*), the *AND gate,* and the *OR gate*. Three other types of gates, NAND, NOR, and XOR, are also frequently used.

The standard symbols for inverters, AND gates, and OR gates appear in Figure 1. In each case, the input lines appear at the left of the diagram and the output line at the right. The label on each line denotes the voltage level or *truth value* of that line; the symbols $\sim p$, pq (or $p \wedge q$), and $p \oplus q$ (or $p \vee q$) are defined by the output tables, in Tables 13, 14, and 15. Note that $\sim p = 1 - p$ and

Figure 1

$$p \vee q = \begin{cases} p & \text{if} & p \geq q \\ q & \text{if} & q > p \end{cases} = \max \{p, q\}$$

Table 13

p	$\sim p$
1	0
0	1

$(\sim p = 1 - p)$

Table 14

p	q	pq
1	1	1
1	0	0
0	1	0
0	0	0

Table 15

p	q	$p \oplus q$
1	1	1
1	0	1
0	1	1
0	0	0

Computer designers and electrical engineers frequently use one of the symbols $\tilde{p}$, $\bar{p}$, or p' in place of $\sim p$.

More complex logic circuits are constructed by connecting two or more gates.

□ **Example 1**   Construct a logic circuit whose inputs are p, q, r and whose output is $(pq) \oplus \sim r$. When is this output equal to 1?

Solution   Apparently, we need to connect an AND gate, an inverter, and an OR gate. Figure 2 shows how.

(Just as we write $ab + c$ for $(ab) + c$ in ordinary algebra, we write $pq \oplus r$ for $(pq) \oplus r$ and $pq \oplus \sim r$ for $(pq) \oplus (\sim r)$ in circuit algebra. Note that $p(q \oplus r) \neq pq \oplus r$.)

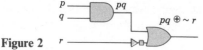

Figure 2

Table 16

p	q	r	pq	$\sim r$	$pq \oplus \sim r$
1	1	1	1	0	1
1	1	0	1	1	1
1	0	1	0	0	0
1	0	0	0	1	1
0	1	1	0	0	0
0	1	0	0	1	1
0	0	1	0	0	0
0	0	0	0	1	1

Table 16 is the output table for $pq \oplus \sim r$. This table confirms what we would expect: The output is 1 when $p = q = 1$ (regardless of whether r is 0 or 1) and when $r = 0$ (regardless of the values of p and q). ☐

REDESIGNING CIRCUITS

Since the output tables for circuits have the same form as the truth tables for propositions (with 1 and 0 corresponding to T and F, pq corresponding to $p \wedge q$, and $p \oplus q$ corresponding to $p \vee q$), the principles of logic formulated in Section 12.3 apply. We can translate these principles as follows:

1. Idempotent Laws

$$pp = p \qquad\qquad p \oplus p = p$$

2. Associative Laws

$$(pq)r = p(qr) \qquad\qquad (p \oplus q) \oplus r = p \oplus (q \oplus r)$$

3. Commutative Laws

$$pq = qp \qquad\qquad p \oplus q = q \oplus p$$

4. Distributive Laws

$$p \oplus qr = (p \oplus q)(p \oplus r) \qquad p(q \oplus r) = pq \oplus pr$$

5. De Morgan's Laws

$$\sim(p \oplus q) = (\sim p)(\sim q) \qquad \sim(pq) = \sim p \oplus \sim q$$

6. Absorption Laws

$$p \oplus pq = p \qquad\qquad p(p \oplus q) = p$$

These principles are often useful in simplifying the design of circuits. If two circuits perform the same function and one has fewer gates and connectors than the other, the simpler circuit is preferred because it is less expensive to manufacture or purchase, and also because it is less likely to fail due to overheating or physical stress. Very often it will also be more efficient in terms of power consumption and speed of operation.

☐ **Example 2**   Redesign the circuit of Example 1 so that $r = p$; simplify the circuit.

Solution   We can easily modify the circuit as in Figure 3. The solid dot is used in circuit

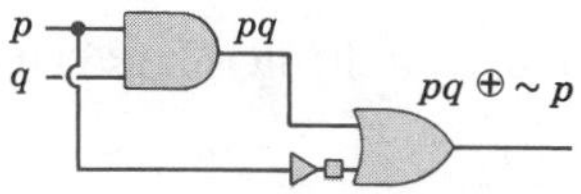

Figure 3

diagrams to show where a connector branches.
Using the distributive laws, we can simplify:

$$pq \oplus \sim p = (p \oplus \sim p)(q \oplus \sim p) = 1 \cdot (q \oplus \sim p) = q \oplus \sim p$$

(Recall that $\sim p = 1$ if $p = 0$, and vice versa.) The circuit can therefore be replaced with the one in Figure 4.   □

Figure 4

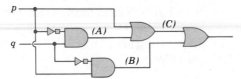

□ **Example 3**   Find the output of the circuit in Figure 5 and simplify its design.

Figure 5

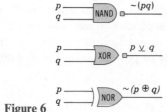

The output is $B \vee C$, where

$$A = (\sim p)q, \qquad B = p(\sim q), \qquad C = p \oplus A$$

Thus

$$C = p \oplus (\sim p)q = (p \oplus \sim p)(p \oplus q) = 1 \cdot (p \oplus q) = p \oplus q$$

and the output is

$$B \oplus C = p(\sim q) \oplus p \oplus q$$

This expression can be simplified to

$$p(\sim q) \oplus (p \oplus q) = [p(\sim q) \oplus p] \oplus q = p \oplus q$$

Thus the circuit can be replaced by a single OR gate.   □

NAND, NOR, AND XOR

The standard symbols for NAND, NOR, and XOR gates, and their outputs, are shown in Figure 6. (The names are abbreviations for NOT-AND, NOT-OR, and Exclusive-OR, respectively.) Table 17 is the output table for XOR.

Figure 6

Table 17

p	q	$p \vee q$
1	1	0
1	0	1
0	1	1
0	0	0

Exercise 12.7   *Answers to Odd-Numbered problems begin on page* 636.

In Problems 1–4 determine when the output of each circuit is 1; use a truth table if necessary.

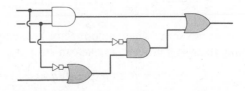

1.

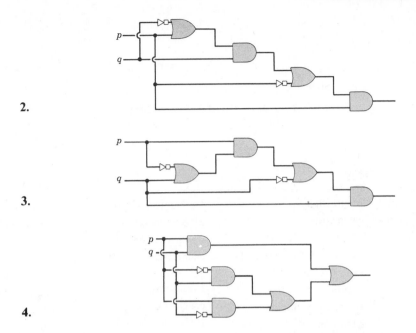

2.

3.

4.

In Problems 5–8 construct a circuit corresponding to each expression.

5. $(\sim p \oplus \sim q)(p \oplus q)$ **6.** $(p \oplus \sim q)(\sim p)$

7. $\sim(p \oplus q)(\sim p)$ **8.** $(\sim p \oplus q)[(\sim p)(\sim q)]$

9. Design simpler circuits having the same outputs as the circuits in Problems 3, 5, and 7.

10. Design simpler circuits having the same outputs as the circuits in Problems 2, 4, 6, and 8.

11. Design a logic circuit that can be turned On or Off from either of two switches. (That is, if the inputs are p and q, the output can be changed from 1 to 0 or from 0 to 1 by changing the level of either p or q, but not both.)

12. Design a circuit, consisting of at least two gates, whose output is always 1.

13. Design a circuit, consisting of at least two gates, whose output is always 0.

14. Using an OR gate, an AND gate, and an Inverter, design a circuit that will work as an XOR gate. [*Hint:* What combination of $\cdot$, $\oplus$, and $\sim$ has the same truth table as $\underline{\vee}$?]

15. Design a circuit that will work as an OR gate, using

    (a) two inverters and a NAND gate;

    (b) three NAND gates.

    [*Hint:* (a) Use De Morgan's laws. (b) How can a NAND gate be substituted for an Inverter?]

16. Design a circuit that will work as an AND gate using

    (a) two inverters and a NOR gate;

    (b) three NOR gates

*17. Show that a circuit whose output is

$$pq \oplus pr \oplus q(\sim r)$$

can be replaced by one whose output is

$$pr \oplus q(\sim r)$$

[*Hint:* $pq = pq(r \oplus \sim r) = pqr \oplus pq(\sim r)$]

18. Show that

    (a) $(p \oplus q)(p \oplus r)(q \oplus \sim r) = (p \oplus r)(q \oplus \sim r)$

    (b) $(p \oplus r)(q \oplus \sim r) = p(\sim r) \oplus qr$

CHAPTER REVIEW

Important Terms

proposition	De Morgan's laws	law of substitution
connective	absorption laws	argument
conjunction ($\wedge$)	implication ($\Rightarrow$)	fallacy
inclusive disjunction ($\vee$)	conditional connective	direct proof
exclusive disjunction ($\underline{\vee}$)	($\Rightarrow$)	law of detachment
negation	hypothesis	law of syllogisms
law of contradiction	conclusion	indirect proof
quantifier	sufficient condition	logic circuit
truth value	necessary condition	inverter
logically equivalent ($\equiv$)	converse	AND gate
idempotent laws	contrapositive	OR gate
associative laws	inverse	NAND gate
commutative laws	biconditional connective ($\Leftrightarrow$)	NOR gate
distributive laws	tautology	XOR gate

True-False Questions

T   F   1. The negation of the statement Some salesmen are intelligent is All salesmen are intelligent.

T   F   2. The statement $\sim(p \wedge q)$ is logically equivalent to $\sim p \vee \sim q$.

T   F   3. The statement $\sim(p \vee q)$ is logically equivalent to $\sim p \wedge \sim q$.

T   F   4. The statement $\sim p \Rightarrow q$ is logically equivalent to $q \Rightarrow p$.

T   F   5. The statement $p \Leftrightarrow q$ is logically equivalent to $(p \Rightarrow q) \wedge (\sim q \Rightarrow \sim p)$.

Fill in the Blanks

1. The compound proposition *p or q* is called the inclusive disjunction of p and q and is denoted by _____ .

2. The negation of p is denoted by _____ .

3. If two propositions have the same truth values in every possible case, the propositions are said to be _____ .

4. The two parts of an argument are the _____ and the _____.

5. The output of a logic circuit is either _____ or _____.

Review Exercises

Answers to Odd-Numbered Problems begin on page 637 .

In Problems 1–4 circle each correct answer; some questions may have more than one correct answer.

1. Which of the following negate the statement below?

    p: All people are rich.

    (a) Some people are rich.
    (b) Some people are poor.
    (c) Some people are not rich.
    (d) No person is rich.

2. Which of the following negate the statement below?

    p: It is either hot or humid.

    (a) It is neither hot nor humid.
    (b) Either it is not hot or it is not humid.
    (c) It is not hot and it is not humid.
    (d) It is hot, but not humid.

3. Which of the following statements are logically equivalent to the statement below?

    $$(\sim p \vee q) \wedge r$$

    (a) $(p \Rightarrow q) \wedge r$
    (b) $\sim p \vee (q \wedge r)$
    (c) $(\sim p \Rightarrow q) \wedge r$
    (d) $(\sim p \vee r) \wedge (q \wedge r)$

4. Which of the following statements are logically equivalent to the statement below?

    $$p \wedge \sim q$$

    (a) $\sim q \wedge p$
    (b) $p \vee q$
    (c) $\sim p \vee q$
    (d) $q \Rightarrow \sim p$

In Problems 5 to 8 negate each proposition.

5. Some people are rich.

6. All people are rich.

7. Danny is not tall and Mary is short.

8. Neither Mike nor Katy are big.

In Problems 9–12 construct a truth table for each compound proposition.

9. $(p \wedge q) \vee \sim p$

10. $(p \vee q) \wedge p$

11. $\sim p \vee (p \vee \sim q)$

12. $\sim p \Rightarrow (p \vee q)$

In Problems 13–15 let p stand for "I will pass the course" and let q stand for "I will do homework regularly." Put each statement into symbolic form.

13. I will pass the course, if I do homework regularly.

14. Passing this course is a sufficient condition for me to do homework regularly.

15. I will pass this course if and only if I do homework regularly.

16. Write the converse, contrapositive, and inverse of the statement

> If it is not sunny, it is cold.

17. Prove the following by the use of direct proof: If I do not paint the house, I will go bowling. I will not go bowling. Show that I will paint the house.

18. Using reasons from logic, give a valid argument to answer the question, "Is Katy a good girl?" Given that:

    (a)   Mike is a bad boy or Danny is crying.

    (b)   If Katy is a good girl, then Mike is not a bad boy.

    (c)   Danny is not crying.

19. Determine whether the following are logically equivalent:

$$\sim p \vee q \qquad p \Rightarrow q$$

20. Determine whether the two statements below are logically equivalent:

$$(p \Rightarrow q) \wedge (\sim q \vee p) \qquad p \Leftrightarrow q$$

21. Show that the output of an XOR gate is equal to

$$(p \oplus q)[\sim(pq)]$$

Use this fact to construct an XOR gate by connecting an OR gate, an AND gate, and a NAND gate.

22. Construct an XOR gate by connecting two NOR gates and an AND gate.

RELATIONS, FUNCTIONS, AND INDUCTION

13.1 RELATIONS

APPLICATIONS TO COMPUTER SCIENCE □ PROPERTIES OF RELATIONS

In this section we introduce relations, a concept fundamental in mathematics and its applications. The word relation is a common term used in mathematics to indicate a relationship between two objects. Relationships occur everywhere. Two people belonging to the same family may be related as father-and-son, mother-and-son, brother-and-sister, husband-and-wife, and so forth. In mathematics, two numbers may be related by being equal, or by one being greater than the other. Two sets may be related as one being a subset of the other, etc. These are only a few examples of relations. Later in this section, and in the exercises, we present more examples. Now let's give a formal definition.

Relation Let A and B be two nonempty sets. A *relation R* from A to B is a set R of ordered pairs (a,b) where $a \in A$ and $b \in B$. For every such ordered pair we write aRb, read "a is related to b by R." If the relation R is from the set A to itself we say R is a *relation on A.**

□ **Example 1**   Let $A = \{1,2,7\}$ and $B = \{2,5\}$. List the elements of each relation R defined below.

(a) $a \in A$ is related to $b \in B$, that is, aRb if, and only if, $a < b$.
(b) $a \in A$ is related to $b \in B$, that is, aRb if, and only if, a and b are both odd numbers.
(c) $a \in A$ is related to $b \in B$, that is, aRb if, and only if, $(a + b)$ is an even number.

Solution   (a)   Since $1 \in A$ is less than $2 \in B$, then $1R2$. Similarly $1R5$ and $2R5$. Therefore

$$R = \{(1,2), (1,5), (2,5)\}$$

Note that $7 \in A$ is not related to $5 \in B$, since $7 \not< 5$.

(b)   Since $1 \in A$ and $5 \in B$ are both odd then $1R5$. Similarly $7R5$. Therefore

$$R = \{(1,5), (7,5)\}$$

Note that $2 \in A$ is not related to $5 \in B$ since 2 is not odd.

(c)   Here, $1 \in A$ is related to $5 \in B$ since $1 + 5 = 6$ is even. Therefore, $1R5$. Similarly, $2R2$ and $7R5$. Therefore,

$$R = \{(1,5), (2,2), (7,5)\}$$

Note that $1 + 2 = 3$ is not even; thus $1 \in A$ is not related to $2 \in B$.   □

□ **Example 2**   Let A be the set of all integers. We define a relation R on A as follows: aRb if, and only if, a and b have the same remainder when divided by 2.†† Is $5R3$? Is $-1R1$? Is $7R4$?

Solution   Since both $5 \div 2$ and $3 \div 2$ give 1 as a remainder, then $5R3$. Since $-1 = -1 \cdot 2 + 1$ and $1 = 0 \cdot 2 + 1$, we conclude that both $-1 \div 2$ and $1 \div 2$ give 1 as a remainder; therefore, $-1R1$. Since $7 \div 2$ gives 1 as a remainder and $4 \div 2$ gives 0 as a remainder, 7 is not related to 4.   □

---

* R is sometimes called a *binary relation R* from A to B since the elements of the set R are ordered *pairs*.

†† This relation is called the "congruence modulo 2" relation and may be denoted by $a \equiv b \pmod 2$.

APPLICATIONS TO COMPUTER SCIENCE

Bits

Binary Word

Bytes

In computer science the binary digits 0 and 1 are called *bits*. An ordered collection of consecutive bits is called a *binary word*. Since computers store information in the form of binary words, they are important in the field of computer science. Of special importance are binary words of length 7, called *bytes,*† because a byte is the smallest addressable memory area in the computer, that is, the smallest unit that can be located in memory.

The sets S and S^* defined below are referred to in the exercises and in later sections of this chapter.

Let $S = \{0,1\}$. We use 0 and 1 to form binary words. Some binary words are 0, 00, 01, 11, 10, 000, 001, 010, 100, 110, 1101, 10011, 11000011, etc.

Now let S^* denote the set of all binary words. S^*, clearly, contains an infinite number of elements and hence makes its listing impractical. Next, for every word a in S^* let

$$\text{length } (a) = \text{the number of bits in } a$$

For example, if $a = 101011$, then length $(a) = 6$. With this in mind, we can define a relation R on S^* by considering the number of bits in each element in S^* as follows: For a and b in S^*, aRb if, and only if, length $(a) =$ length (b). Thus, for instance, $(000) R (111)$ since length $(000) =$ length $(111) = 3$, and $(1001) R (0110)$ since both 1001 and 0110 have length equal to 4.

☐ **Example 3**

Let the set S^* and the relation R be the ones defined above. Let 01 be in S^*. List all elements in S^* that are related to 01 under R.

Solution

01 is of length 2. The binary words in S^* related to 01 under R are also of length 2. The list of all such words is 00, 01, 10, 11.   ☐

☐ **Example 4**

During the execution of a program, the computer creates, among other things, a relation from the set of variables used in the program to the set of values assigned to these variables. A table, called the *symbol table,* is used to depict such a relation. For the following program segment, written in Pascal, construct a symbol table showing the variable name and its value.

$X := 2;$

$Y := X * X;$

WRITELN ('THE SQUARE OF', X, 'IS', Y);

FLAG := TRUE;

ANSWER := 'YES';

Solution

Variable Name	Value
X	2
Y	4
FLAG	TRUE
ANSWER	YES

☐

† On some computers, like the IBM computers, a byte is 8 bits long.

In the next example we consider the relation that exists between each character and its representation in the computer.

◻ **Example 5**

ASCII Code

Computers store data (or information) in the form of binary words. When a letter, a digit, or a symbol (that is, when a character) is entered into the computer, it is converted into a binary word. This is done by using a character code that is a relation R from the set of characters to the set of binary numbers. A common character code is the American Standard Code for Information Interchange, abbreviated ASCII. See Table 1. Using the ASCII code and the foregoing relation R, we can list some elements of R as follows:

$$\text{'\$'}R0100100,\ \text{'+'}R0101011,\ \text{'='}R0111101,\ \text{' '}R0100000,$$
$$\text{'A'}R1000001,\ \text{'b'}R1100010$$

In decimal representation, these elements of R are:

$$\text{'\$'}R36,\ \text{'+'}R43,\ \text{'='}R61,\ \text{' '}R32,\ \text{'A'}R65,\ \text{'b'}R98 \qquad ◻$$

Table 1

ASCII Code (Decimal)	ASCII Code (Binary)	Character†	ASCII Code (Decimal)	ASCII Code (Binary)	Character
32	0100000	space	80	1010000	P
33	0100001	!	81	1010001	Q
34	0100010	"	82	1010010	R
35	0100011	#	83	1010011	S
36	0100100	$	84	1010100	T
37	0100101	%	85	1010101	U
38	0100110	&	86	1010110	V
39	0100111	'	87	1010111	W
40	0101000	(	88	1011000	X
41	0101001	)	89	1011001	Y
42	0101010	*	90	1011010	Z
43	0101011	+	91	1011011	[
44	0101100	,	92	1011100	\
45	0101101	−	93	1011101	]
46	0101110	.	94	1011110	∧ (or ↑)
47	0101111	/	95	1011111	_ (or ←)
48	0110000	0	96	1100000	`
49	0110001	1	97	1100001	a
50	0110010	2	98	1100010	b
51	0110011	3	99	1100011	c
52	0110100	4	100	1100100	d
53	0110101	5	101	1100101	e
54	0110110	6	102	1100110	f
55	0110111	7	103	1100111	g
56	0111000	8	104	1101000	h
57	0111001	9	105	1101001	i
58	0111010	:	106	1101010	j
59	0111011	;	107	1101011	k

† Codes 0–31 and 127 (decimal) are nonprintable control characters.

Table 1 *(continued)*

ASCII Code (Decimal)	ASCII Code (Binary)	Character†	ASCII Code (Decimal)	ASCII Code (Binary)	Character
60	0111100	<	108	1101100	l
61	0111101	=	109	1101101	m
62	0111110	>	110	1101110	n
63	0111111	?	111	1101111	o
64	1000000	@	112	1110000	p
65	1000001	A	113	1110001	q
66	1000010	B	114	1110010	r
67	1000011	C	115	1110011	s
68	1000100	D	116	1110100	t
69	1000101	E	117	1110101	u
70	1000110	F	118	1110110	v
71	1000111	G	119	1110111	w
72	1001000	H	120	1111000	x
73	1001001	I	121	1111001	y
74	1001010	J	122	1111010	z
75	1001011	K	123	1111011	{
76	1001100	L	124	1111100	|
77	1001101	M	125	1111101	}
78	1001110	N	126	1111110	~
79	1001111	O	127	1111111	DEL

PROPERTIES OF RELATIONS

A relation R on a set A often satisfies certain properties. Three of these properties, reflexivity, symmetry, and transitivity, are defined as follows:

Reflexive   (i) R is *reflexive* if, for each element $a \in A$, we have aRa.

Symmetric   (ii) R is *symmetric* if, whenever aRb, we have bRa.

Transitive   (iii) R is *transitive* if, whenever aRb and bRc, we have aRc.

□ **Example 6**   Let R be a relation defined on the set $A = \{a,b,c\}$. For each definition of R given below determine whether R is reflexive, symmetric, or transitive.

(a) $R = \{(a,a), (a,b), (b,b), (c,c), (b,c)\}$.

(b) $R = \{(c,a), (a,c), (c,c), (c,b), (b,c)\}$.

(c) $R = \{(a,b), (b,a), (a,c), (c,a), (b,c), (c,b), (a,a), (b,b), (c,c)\}$.

Solution   (a)   Since (a,a), (b,b), and $(c,c) \in R$, then R is reflexive. Because $(a,b) \in R$, but $(b,a) \notin R$, then R is not symmetric. And because (a,b) and $(b,c) \in R$, but $(a,c) \notin R$, then R is not transitive.

(b)   This relation is not reflexive because $(a,a) \notin R$. It is not transitive because (a,c) and (c,a) are in R, but (a,a) is not. However, it is symmetric. (Why?).

(c) R is reflexive, symmetric and transitive. (Why?).   □

□ **Example 7** Let $A = \{1,2,3\}$ and let R be a relation defined on A. Suppose further that the ordered pairs $(1,1)$, $(1,2)$, and $(2,3)$ belong to R. What ordered pairs, besides the ones given above, must belong to R in order to make R

(a) reflexive.

(b) symmetric.

(c) transitive.

Solution (a) R will be reflexive if every element in A is related to itself. Since $(1,1) \in R$, then $(2,2)$ and $(3,3)$ must also belong to R to make it reflexive.

(b) R will be symmetric if whenever (a,b) is in R, so is (b,a). Obviously, $(1,1)$ satisfies this condition. Now since $(1,2) \in R$ then, for R to be symmetric, $(2,1)$ must also belong to R. Similarly, since $(2,3) \in R$ then, for R to be symmetric, $(3,2)$ must also belong to R.

(c) R will be transitive if whenever (a,b) and (b,c) are in R, so is (a,c). Now $(1,2)$ and $(2,3) \in R$ implies that, for R to be transitive, $(1,3)$ must also belong to R. □

Exercise 13.1 *Answers to Odd-Numbered Problems begin on page 638.*

1. Let $A = \{x,y,z\}$, $B = \{1,3,5\}$. A relation R from A to B is defined as

$$R = \{(x,5), (y,1), (z,3)\}$$

Answer true or false:

$xR5,$ $yR3,$ $zR3,$ $zR1,$ $yR1,$ $xR1,$ $xR3,$ $yR5,$ $zR5$

2. Let $A = \{1,2,3\}$, $B = \{a,b,c,d\}$. A relation R from A to B is defined as

$$R = \{(1,a), (1,c), (2,b), (3,a), (3,c)\}$$

Answer true or false:

$1Ra,$ $1Rb,$ $1Rc,$ $2Ra,$ $2Rb,$ $2Rc,$ $3Ra,$ $3Rb,$ $3Rc$

3. Let $A = \{2,3,5\}$, $B = \{2,4,6,10\}$. A relation R from A to B is given as follows:

$2R2,$ $2R4,$ $2R6,$ $2R10,$ $3R6,$ $5R10$

Write R as a set of ordered pairs.

4. Let $C = \{\text{Apple, TRS, IBM, Atari}\}$, $M = \{1000, 360, 370, 800, \text{II}\}$. Let R, the relation from C to M, be given as follows:

(Apple) R (II), (TRS) R (1000), (IBM) R (370), (Atari) R (800)

Write R as a set of ordered pairs.

5. Let $D = \{1,2,3,4,5\}$ and $C = \{1,4,9,16,25,36,49,64,81\}$. The relation R from D to C is defined as follows:

$$xRy \text{ means } y = x^2$$

Replace the "?" by the appropriate value:

$1R?,$ $2R?,$ $3R?,$ $4R?,$ $5R?,$ $?R4,$ $?R25$

6. Let $F = \{-2, -10, -1, 0, 1, 2\}$. The relation R on F is defined as follows:

$$aRb \text{ means } a \geq b$$

Answer true or false:

$$-2R-2, \quad -2R-1, \quad -1R-2, \quad -1R0, \quad 0R0, \quad 1R2, \quad 2R1$$

7. The *Cartesian product* of two nonempty sets A and B, denoted by $A \times B$, is the set consisting of all ordered pairs (a,b) with $a \in A$ and $b \in B$. That is,

$$A \times B = \{(a,b) \mid a \in A, b \in B\}$$

Let $A = \{1,2,5\}$ and $B = \{2,4,7\}$.

   (a) Find the cartesian product $A \times B$.
   (b) Now define the relation "less than," call it R, from the set A to the set B. Write R as a set of ordered pairs.
   (c) What can you say about the set R and $A \times B$?

8. Repeat Parts (b) and (c) of Problem 7, but now let R be the relation "greater than or equal to."

9. Let $S = \{a,b\}$ and S^2 = set of all words on S of length 2.

   (a) List all elements of S^2.
   (b) The relation L on S^2 is defined by: vLw means that the first letter in v is the same as the first letter in w where v and w are in S^2. Write L as a set of ordered pairs.

10. Repeat Problem 9(b) for L defined as follows: vLw means first letter of v is not the same as first letter of w.

11. Refer to the ASCII table, Table 1. Replace the "?" by the appropriate decimal value:

$$\text{`2'}R?, \quad \text{`a'}R?, \quad \text{`@'}R?, \quad \text{`P'}R?, \quad \text{`t'}R?, \quad \text{`n'}R?, \quad \text{`}\}\text{'}R?$$

12. Refer to the ASCII code table, Table 1. Replace the "?" by the appropriate character:

$$?R33, \quad ?R38, \quad ?R44, \quad ?R79, \quad ?R114, \quad ?R125$$

In Problems 13–22 write the set of ordered pairs in the relation R.

13. Let $A = \{1,2,3\}$, $B = \{2,4,6,8\}$. Define R to be the relation from the set A to the set B given by: aRb means a is a factor of b.

14. Let $A = \{1,2,3,4,5,6\}$. Let R be a relation on A given by: aRb means $a \equiv b \pmod{2}$ (see footnote page 516).

15. Let $A = \{1,2,3,4,5,6,7,8,9,10\}$; R is a relation on A given by: aRb means a and b are either both even or both odd.

16. Let $S = \{0,1\}$ and let G^2 = the set of all binary words of length at most 2. Define R on G^2 as follows: aRb means a and b have the same number of 1s.

17. Repeat Problem 16 for G^3 = the set of all binary words of length at most 3.

18. Let $S = \{0,1\}$ and G^3 be as defined in Problem 17. Define R on G^3 as: aRb means length (a) = length (b).

19. Let $A = \{0,1,2,3\}$ and R on A be defined as follows: aRb means $a \leq b$.

20. Let $A = \{1,2,3,4,5,9\}$ and R on A be defined as follows: aRb means $b = a + 2$.

21. Let $D = \{0,1,2,3,4,5,9,15,16\}$ and R on D be defined as follows: xRy means $x = \sqrt{y}$.

22. Let $I = \{-4,-2,-1,0,1,2,4\}$ and R on I be defined as: xRy means $x = y^2$.

For a relation R from the set A to the set B, the *inverse relation* of R, denoted R^{-1}, is a relation from B to A defined as follows:

$$bR^{-1}a \text{ means } aRb$$

For Problems 23–26 find R^{-1}.

23. $R = \{(1,1), (1,2), (2,5), (3,7)\}$.

24. $R = \{(a,a), (a,b), (b,a), (b,c)\}$.

25. $R = \{(*,42), (H,72), (/,47), (x,88)\}$.

26. R is the relation "$\leq$" on integers.

27. (Refer to Example 4). Construct the symbol table for the following program segment:

> PI := 3.14159;
>
> RADIUS := 10;
>
> RSQR := RADIUS * RADIUS;
>
> AREA := PI * RSQR;
>
> CIRCUM := 2 * PI * RADIUS;

28. Answer the question in Problem 27 for the following program segment:

> FOR N := 1 TO 5 DO
>
> B[N] := 10*N

In Problems 29–38 determine whether the given relation R on the set A is reflexive, symmetric, or transitive.

29. Let R on a set A of real numbers be defined as: aRb means $a = b$.

30. Let R on the set A of real numbers be defined as: aRb means $a < b$.

31. Let R be the relation of congruence modulo 2 on the set A of integers (see Example 2).

32. Let A be the set of integers and R a relation on A be defined as: aRb means a divides b (or a is a factor of b).

33. Let A be the set of all lines in the plane, and R be defined by: $l_1 R l_2$ means l_1 is a line parallel to l_2.

34. R means: if an arrow connects a point to another , then the 2 points are related. (See the figure.) That is,

$$R = \{(a,a), (a,b), (b,b), (b,a)\}$$

35. R means: if an arrow connects a point to another, then the 2 points are related. (See the figure.) That is,

$$R = \{(A,A), (A,B), (B,A), (B,B), (B,C), (C,B), (C,C), (A,C)\}$$

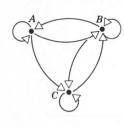

36. Let $A = \{1,2,3\}$ and $R = \{(2,2)\}$.

37. Let A be the set of variables that are declared type REAL in a Pascal program and let R be given as XRY means X and Y are both of type REAL.

38. Repeat Problem 37 for each of the following: A is the set of variables that are declared type:

   (i)   INTEGER

   (ii) BOOLEAN

   (iii) CHAR

39. Consider the set $A = \{t,u,v,w\}$ and the relation R on A defined as $R = \phi$. (That is, R is the empty relation. In other words, no relation exists between any pair of elements of A). Show that A is symmetric, transitive but not reflexive.

13.2 FUNCTIONS

SPECIAL TYPES OF FUNCTIONS

In this section we discuss one of the most important concepts in mathematics and its applications: the concept of a function. As we shall see, a function is a special kind of a relation.

Function Let A and B be two nonempty sets. A *function* f from A into B is a relation
Domain from A to B that relates every element in A to only one element in B. The set A is called
Image the *domain* of the function. For each element a in A, the corresponding element b in B,
Range related to a by f, is called the *image* of a. The set of all images of the elements of the domain is called the *range* of the function.

Since there may be elements in B that are the image of no a in A, it follows that the range of a function is a subset of B.

Functions are often denoted by letters such as f, F, g, G, etc. If f is a function from A into B, then for each element a in A the corresponding image in the set B, is designated by the symbol $f(a)$ and is read "f of a." Note that $f(a)$ does not mean f times a. We can think of a function f as associating elements in A to elements in B and visualize f by means of a simple diagram as we do in Figure 1.

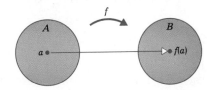

Figure 1

□ **Example 1** Let $A = \{1,3,5\}$ and $B = \{2,4\}$. Define the function f from A into B, as shown in Figure 2. Find $f(1)$, $f(3)$, $f(5)$, and the range of f.

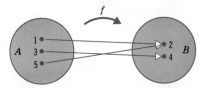

Figure 2

Solution Following the arrows, we have

$$f(1) = 2 \qquad f(3) = 4 \qquad f(5) = 2 \qquad \text{Range of } f = \{2,4\} \qquad \qquad □$$

□ **Example 2**   Let $A = \{1,2,3\}$ and $B = \{a,b,c,d,e\}$. Define the function f from A into B, as shown in Figure 3. Find $f(1)$, $f(2)$, $f(3)$, and the range of f.

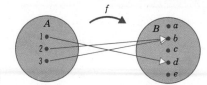

Figure 3

Solution   Following the arrows, we find

$$f(1) = d \qquad f(2) = b \qquad f(3) = b$$
$$\text{Range of } f = \{b,d\}$$

Because b and d are the only elements in B that are assigned to elements in A, we observe that the range of f is a proper subset of B.   □

□ **Example 3**   The diagrams in Figure 4 show a correspondence by which elements of $A = \{1,2,3\}$ are associated to elements in $B = \{w,x,y,z\}$. Which of these diagrams define a function from A into B?

Solution   In Figure 4(a) not all elements in A are associated with elements in B. For example, the element 3 in A has no image in B. This is indicated by the absence of an arrow going from 3 in A to an element in B. Thus (a) does not define a function from A into B. In Figure 4(b) every element in A is sent to a unique element in B. Thus Figure 4(b) defines a function. In Figure 4(c) the uniqueness of images is violated. For example,

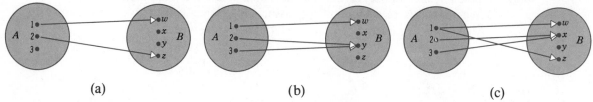

(a)   (b)   (c)

Figure 4

the element $1 \in A$ has two images. This is shown by the two arrows emanating from $1 \in A$ to w and to $z \in B$. Thus Figure 4(c) does not define a function.   □

When the sets A and B are infinite, a complete arrow diagram of a function f cannot be drawn. Because functions are sometimes defined by a formula, the images of f can then be found from the formula defining f.

□ **Example 4**   Let f be a function from the set of real numbers to itself defined by the formula

$$f(x) = 2x - 1$$

Find $f(0), f(0.5), f(-1), f(1), f(-10), f(100)$.

Solution $f(0)$ is obtained from substituting 0 for x in $2x - 1$. That is,

$$f(0) = 2(0) - 1 = -1$$

Similarly,

$$f(0.5) = 2(0.5) - 1 = 0$$
$$f(-1) = 2(-1) - 1 = -3$$
$$f(1) = 2(1) - 1 = 1$$
$$f(-10) = 2(-10) - 1 = -21$$
$$f(100) = 2(100) - 1 = 199 \qquad \square$$

□ Example 5
Pascal Function
CHR

Most programming languages provide several functions. In this example we discuss the Pascal function CHR. This function associates every 7-bit binary number or byte with its corresponding character based on the ASCII code. For instance,

$$CHR(1000001) = \text{'A'}$$
$$CHR(1011000) = \text{'X'}$$
$$CHR(1110110) = \text{'w'}$$
$$CHR(0100011) = \text{'\#'}$$

and so forth.

Referring to the ASCII code table, Table 1, page 518, we find that the domain of CHR is the set {0100000, 0100001, . . . , 1111111} and the range is the set of characters that appear in the table. Note that we are excluding the codes 0–31 (decimal), since they represent control characters. □

□ Example 6
Pascal Function
ORD

The Pascal function ORD associates every character that appears in the ASCII code table with its corresponding 7-bit binary number, or byte. For example,

$$ORD(\text{'A'}) = 1000001$$
$$ORD(\text{'X'}) = 1011000$$
$$ORD(\text{'w'}) = 1110110$$
$$ORD(\text{'\#'}) = 0100011$$

and so forth. □

□ Example 7
Hamming Distance
Function

In a branch of computer science, called *coding theory*, a function called the *Hamming distance function* is of importance. Refer to Section 8.2 Chapter 8. This function gives a measure of the difference between two binary words that have the same length. We define the Hamming distance function H as follows: Let (u,v) be a pair of binary words of the same length. We compare u and v position by position and define

$H(u,v)$ = the number of positions in which u and v have different bits

For example,

$$H(0101, 1010) = 4$$

because 0101 and 1010 differ in all 4 positions. On the other hand,

$$H(1110, 1010) = 1$$

because 1110 and 1010 differ only in one position, namely, the second position. □

SPECIAL TYPES OF FUNCTIONS

In Example 1 we notice that the two elements 1 and 5 in the domain A are assigned the same element 2 in the range B. And in Example 2 we notice that the range of f is not the entire set B. This shows that functions can be of different types. In the remainder of this section we introduce functions that have special properties. These functions are important in mathematics and its applications.

In the next four definitions we consider f to be a function from A into B.

One-to-One Function

One-to-One Function A function f from A into B is *one-to-one*, or *injective*, if for all elements a, b in A such that $a \neq b$ we have $f(a) \neq f(b)$. That is, if no two elements of A are assigned to the same element in B, or, equivalently, if each element of the range corresponds to exactly one element of the domain, then f is one-to-one.

☐ **Example 8** Let $A = \{1,2,3\}$, $B = \{a,b,c,d\}$, and let $f(1) = a$, $f(2) = d$, $f(3) = c$. Is f one-to-one?

Solution Yes, because the different elements 1, 2, 3, in A are assigned to the different elements a, d, c, respectively, in B. ☐

☐ **Example 9** Figure 5 defines a function f from the set $A = \{a,b\}$ into the set $B = \{x,y\}$. Is f one-to-one?

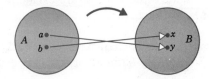

Figure 5

Solution Yes, because the two arrows show that a is assigned to y and that b, which is different from a, is assigned to x, which is different from y. ☐

☐ **Example 10** Let $f(x) = x^2$, x any real number. Show that f is not one-to-one.

Solution We need only show that two distinct numbers are assigned to the same number under f. Choose the distinct values $x_1 = 1$ and $x_2 = -1$. Now

$$f(x_1) = f(1) = (1)^2 = 1$$
$$f(x_2) = f(-1) = (-1)^2 = 1$$

Thus, we see that $f(1) = f(-1) = 1$. Therefore, f is not one-to-one. ☐

Onto Function

Onto A function f from A into B is *onto*, or *surjective* if every element of B is the image of some element in A, that is, if $B =$ range of f.

☐ **Example 11** The diagrams in Figure 6 define the functions f and g from the set $A = \{1,2,3,4\}$ into the set $B = \{a,b,c,d\}$. Which of these functions is onto?

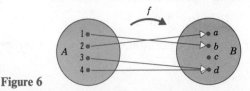
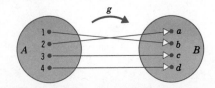

Figure 6

Solution   Under f, $c \in B$ is not the image of any element in A. Thus, f is not onto. Under g, every element in B is an image. Therefore, g is onto.   □

□ **Example 12**   Let $f(x) = x^2$, x any real number. Show that f is not onto.

Solution   Since we cannot find a real number whose square is negative, then the set of negative real numbers is not in the range. Thus f is not onto.   □

Bijective Function   **If a function f is both one-to-one and onto we say that f is *bijective*.**

   If a function f is bijective, then there will be another function g that will "undo" what f did. In a way, g will be the opposite of f as the following definition shows:

Inverse Function   **The function g from B to A is called the *inverse* of f if $g(b) = a$, where $f(a) = b$. g is usually denoted by f^{-1}, read "f inverse."**

   Note that if f is one-to-one and onto then the inverse g of f exists. Also, the range of f is the domain of g and the range of g is the domain of f.

□ **Example 13**   Let $A = \{1,2,3\}$, $B = \{a,b,c\}$. Define f from A into B as

$$f(1) = a, \qquad f(2) = b, \qquad f(3) = c$$

Since f is both one-to-one and onto, it is bijective. Therefore, f^{-1} from B into A exists and is defined as

$$f^{-1}(a) = 1, \qquad f^{-1}(b) = 2, \qquad f^{-1}(c) = 3 \qquad\qquad □$$

   In Problem 28 you are asked to show that the Pascal functions CHR and ORD are bijective. Thus they have inverses. Indeed they are the inverses of each other.

Exercise 13.2   *Answers to Odd-Numbered Problems begin on page* 639 .

1. Let $A = \{a,b,c\}$ and $B = \{1,2,3,4\}$. Let f be a function from A into B, as shown in the figure below. Find $f(a)$, $f(b)$, $f(c)$. Also find the range of f.

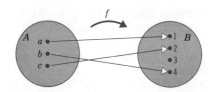

2. Let $A = \{0,1,2\}$ and $B = \{1,10,100\}$. Let f be a function from A into B, as shown in the figure below. Find $f(0)$, $f(1)$, $f(2)$. Also find the range of f.

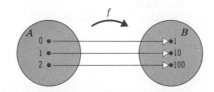

3. Let f be a function from the set of real numbers into itself defined by

$$f(x) = 5 - x$$

Find $f(0), f(5), f(-5), f(10), f(-10)$.

4. Let f be a function defined by

$$f(x) = \frac{-1}{x - 1},$$

where x is any real number and $x \neq 1$. Find $f(-2), f(-1), f(0), f(2)$.

In Problems 5–8, f assigns elements of $A = \{x,y,z\}$ into elements of $B = \{1,2,3,4\}$. State whether f defines a function. If it doesn't explain why.

5. $f(x) = 3, f(x) = 1, f(z) = 4$.

6. $f(x) = 1, f(y) = 2, f(z) = 3$.

7. $f(x) = 4, f(y) = 2, f(z) = 4$.

8. $f(y) = 2, f(y) = 3, f(z) = 1$.

In Problems 9–12, $A = \{0,1,2\}$ and $B = \{1,2,3,4\}$. Use the correspondence pictured in the accompanying figure to determine whether f is a function.

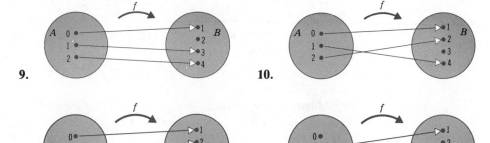

9. 10.

11. 12.

13. Consider the Pascal function CHR (see Example 5). Use the ASCII code table to find CHR(1000011), CHR(0111001), CHR(1100000), CHR(0101000), CHR(0111101).

14. Consider the Pascal function ORD (see Example 6). Use the ASCII code table to find ORD('B'), ORD(','), ORD('d'), ORD('*'), ORD('\'), ORD('2'), ORD('$'), ORD('@').

15. TRUNC is a Pascal function from the set of real numbers into the set of integers that deletes all the digits of a number to the right of the decimal point. For example, TRUNC(1.34) = 1, TRUNC(−3.1415) = −3, and so forth. Find TRUNC(0.05), TRUNC(100.25), TRUNC(−0.99), and TRUNC(−2.7182).

16. ROUND is a Pascal function from the set of real numbers into the set of integers that rounds off a given real number. For example, ROUND(2.43) = 2, ROUND(−6.731) = −7, ROUND(7.50) = 8, and so forth. Find ROUND(3.14159), ROUND(2.718), ROUND(−0.86), ROUND(−9.70), ROUND(−1.5), and ROUND(1641.415).

17. What is the value of ABSX obtained from the following program segment: (see Problem 16)

$$X := 126.752;$$
$$X1 := X * 100;$$
$$X2 := \text{ROUND}(X1);$$
$$ABSX := X2/100;$$

18. What is the value of TRNCX obtained from the following program segment: (see Problem 15)

$$X := 4321.9658;$$
$$X1 := X * 10;$$
$$X2 := \text{TRUNC}(X1);$$
$$TRNCX := X2/10$$

19. Let l be a relation from the set of all binary words into the set $M = \{0,1,2,3, \ldots\}$, defined by

$$l(w) = \text{length of } w$$

(see Section 13.1). Is l a function?

20. Let f be a relation that sends binary words into the set $\{0,1\}$ defined by:

$$f(w) = \begin{cases} 1, \text{ if } w \text{ contains an odd number of 0s} \\ 0, \text{ if } w \text{ contains an odd number of 1s} \end{cases}$$

Is f a function?

21. Let f be a relation that sends binary words into the set $M = \{0,1,2,3, \ldots\}$ defined by

$$f(w) = \text{number of 0s in } w$$

Is f a function?

22. Let H be the Hamming distance function. (See Example 7.) Find $H(1000, 0001)$, $H(1011, 1011)$, $H(10, 01)$, $H(101, 010)$, $H(1010101, 1010111)$.

In Problems 23–26, f is a function from A into B pictured in the accompanying figures. State whether f is one-to-one, onto, or bijective.

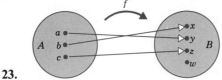

23.

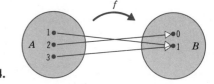

24.

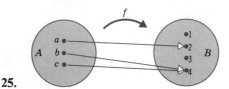

25.

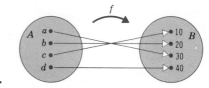

26.

27. Show that the Pascal functions TRUNC and ROUND (see Problems 15 and 16) are not one-to-one.

28. Show that the Pascal functions CHR and ORD are bijective.

29. Show that the Hamming distance function on the set of all pairs of binary words of length n is not one-to-one.

30. Show that the Hamming distance function on the set of all pairs of binary words of length n is not onto. [*Hint:* Can you find binary words u and v of length n such that $H(u,v) \geq n$?]

31. Let f be a function from the set of integers into the set of integers given by the formula $f(n) = 2n$. Is f onto?

32. Let f be the function from the set A into the set B given in the figure below. (a) Find $f(1)$, $f(2)$, $f(3)$. (b) Show that f is bijective.

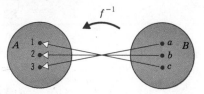

33. Refer to the figure of Problem 32. Find $f^{-1}(a)$, $f^{-1}(b)$, $f^{-1}(c)$.

34. Let f be a bijective function defined by

$$f(1) = 1, \qquad f(2) = 4, \qquad f(3) = 9, \qquad f(4) = 16$$

Find

$$f^{-1}(1), \qquad f^{-1}(4), \qquad f^{-1}(9), \qquad f^{-1}(16)$$

Composition of Functions

Let f be a function from A into B and let g be a function from B into C. The composition of f and g, denoted by $g \circ f$, read "g of f," results in a new function from A into C and is given by

$$(g \circ f)(a) = g(f(a))$$

where a is in A. That is, the function $g \circ f$ associates a in A to $f(a)$ in B first and then associates the element $f(a)$ in B to the element $g(f(a))$ in C. See the figure below.

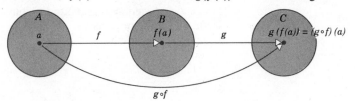

35. Use the figure below to find

$$(g \circ f)(1), \qquad (g \circ f)(2), \qquad (g \circ f)(3)$$

36. If f is a bijective function from A into B, then f has an inverse f^{-1} from B into A. This means that $f^{-1} \circ f$ is a function from A into A. Such a function has the property

$$(f^{-1} \circ f)(a) = a \text{ and } (f \circ f^{-1})(a) = a$$

Identity Function

We call this the *identity* function. Let $f(x) = x + 1$ be a function from the set of real numbers to the set of real numbers. If $f^{-1}(x) = x - 1$, show that $(f^{-1} \circ f)(x) = x$ and $(f \circ f^{-1})(x) = x$.

13.3 SEQUENCES

In this section we present a special type of function — one whose domain is the set of numbers $\{0,1,2,3, \ldots\}$. These functions are called *sequences*. Sequences are useful in both mathematics and computer science.

Let S be a set. A *sequence* is a function s from the set $\{0,1,2,3, \ldots\}$ into S. If S is the set of real numbers, then s is called a *sequence of reals*.

For every number n in the set $\{0,1,2,3, \ldots\}$, $s(n)$ will be the value assigned to n by the function s. We call $s(n)$ the nth term of the sequence and denote it by s_n [instead of $s(n)$]. We will also use the symbol (s_n) to denote the sequence itself.

□ **Example 1** Let the sequence (s_n) be given by

$$s_n = n^2$$

List the first four terms of (s_n).

Solution

$$s_0 = 0^2 = 0$$
$$s_1 = 1^2 = 1$$
$$s_2 = 2^2 = 4$$
$$s_3 = 3^2 = 9$$

□

□ **Example 2** Let $s_n = (-1)^n$. Write out the first four terms of (s_n).

Solution

$$s_0 = (-1)^0 = 1$$
$$s_1 = (-1)^1 = -1$$
$$s_2 = (-1)^2 = 1$$
$$s_3 = (-1)^3 = -1$$

Note that the range of s is $\{-1,1\}$.

□

☐ **Example 3**   Let (s_n) be a sequence given by $s_n = a$. List s_0, s_1, s_2, s_3, etc.

Solution $s_0 = a, s_1 = a, s_2 = a, s_3 = a$, etc.   ☐

☐ **Example 4**   For $(s_n) = \left(\dfrac{1}{n}\right)$, $n \neq 0$, write out the first four terms of s_n.

Solution $$s_1 = \frac{1}{1} = 1, \qquad s_2 = \frac{1}{2}, \qquad s_3 = \frac{1}{3}, \qquad s_4 = \frac{1}{4}$$ ☐

Sometimes values of a sequence may be matrices as the following example shows.

☐ **Example 5**   Let the matrix-values sequence (M_n) be given by

$$M_n = \begin{bmatrix} 1+n & -n \\ 0 & (-1)^n \end{bmatrix}$$

Write out the terms M_0, M_1, and M_2.

Solution

$$M_0 = \begin{bmatrix} 1+0 & 0 \\ 0 & (-1)^0 \end{bmatrix} = \begin{bmatrix} 1 & 0 \\ 0 & 1 \end{bmatrix}$$

$$M_1 = \begin{bmatrix} 1+1 & -1 \\ 0 & (-1)^1 \end{bmatrix} = \begin{bmatrix} 2 & -1 \\ 0 & -1 \end{bmatrix}$$

$$M_2 = \begin{bmatrix} 1+2 & -2 \\ 0 & (-1)^2 \end{bmatrix} = \begin{bmatrix} 3 & -2 \\ 0 & 1 \end{bmatrix}$$ ☐

Exercise 13.3   *Answers to Odd-Numbered Problems begin on page* 639.

1.   Suppose a sequence (s_n) is defined by $s_n = (-1)^n/n$, $n \neq 0$. Write out $s_1, s_2, s_3, s_4, s_{100}$.

2.   Answer the question in Problem 1 for $s_n = (-1)^{n+1}/n$.

3.   Consider a sequence (b_n) given by $b_n = n/(n+1)$

   (a)   List $b_0, b_1, b_2, b_3, b_4, b_5$
   (b)   Find $b_{n+1} - b_n$, for $n = 0, 1, 2$

4.   Answer the question in Problem 3 for $b_n = -n/(n+1)$.

5.   Find the first 8 terms of the sequence $a_k = 2^k$.

6.   Answer the question in Problem 5 for $a_k = 2^{-k}$.

7.   List the first 7 terms of the sequence $s_n = n!$.

8.   Let $A[N]$ be an array of type integer. What is the output of the following program segment?

$$\text{FOR N} := 0 \text{ TO } 9 \text{ DO}$$
$$A[N] := \text{SQR (N)} + 1;$$

9.   Let $P[J]$ be an array of type integer. What is the output of the following program segment?

$$\text{FOR J} := 1 \text{ TO } 100 \text{ DO}$$
$$P[J] := J/J;$$

10. Let $M_n = \begin{bmatrix} 1 & n^2 \\ n & 1 \end{bmatrix}$. Find M_0, M_1, M_2, and M_3.

11. Let $M_n = \begin{bmatrix} 1 & 1-n & 0 \\ 1-n & n & n-1 \\ 0 & n-1 & n+1 \end{bmatrix}$. Find M_0, M_1, M_2, and M_3.

12. Let $M_n = \begin{bmatrix} 1 & 0 \\ 0 & 1 \end{bmatrix}$. Find M_0, M_1, M_2, and M_{100}.

In Problems 13–18 write a formula for the nth term.

13. $1, -1, 1, -1, \ldots$

14. $2, 0, 2, 0, 2, 0, \ldots$

15. $1, 3, 5, 7, 9, \ldots$

16. $0, 5, 25, 125, \ldots$

17. $1, \dfrac{1}{2}, \dfrac{1}{3}, \dfrac{1}{4}, \dfrac{1}{5}, \ldots$

18. $1, \dfrac{1}{3}, \dfrac{1}{9}, \dfrac{1}{27}, \ldots$

19. *Towers of Hanoi.*[†] The number of moves required in solving the puzzle of the Towers of Hanoi for n disks is given by

$$(s_n) = 2^n - 1$$

Find s_0, s_1, s_2, s_3, s_4, s_5, s_6, s_7, and s_8.

20. Suppose we have a set of straight lines where none of the lines are parallel and no three of the lines go through the same point. The number of distinct regions that such a set of n lines divides the plane into is given by the nth term of the sequence

$$(s_n) = \binom{n+1}{2} + 1, \, n \geq 1$$

Find s_1, s_2, s_3, and s_4.

21. *A calculator problem.* The Fibonacci sequence§ is given by

$$(s_n) = \frac{1}{\sqrt{5}} \left[\left(\frac{1+\sqrt{5}}{2} \right)^{n+1} - \left(\frac{1-\sqrt{5}}{2} \right)^{n+1} \right]$$

Find s_0, s_1, s_2, s_3, s_4, s_5, s_6, s_7, and s_8.

13.4 ALGORITHMS

APPLICATION TO DIV AND MOD □ FLOWCHARTS

The technique of developing a program efficiently is a four-step process:

> **Step 1:** Defining the problem
> **Step 2:** Designing the solution
> **Step 3:** Writing the program
> **Step 4:** Executing the program

† See Example 3, Section 13.6.
§ See Example 2, Section 13.6.

In this section we discuss the second step, designing the solution. This involves developing a finite number of steps, or statements, stated clearly and listed in the order in which they are to be carried out. Such a collection of statements is called an *algorithm*.

An *algorithm* is a complete list of steps required to solve a problem.

All of our algorithms will begin with a statement displaying the name of the algorithm followed by the statements that solve the problem and finally an END statement that indicates the end of the algorithm. That is, our algorithm will have the following form:

Algorithm name

Steps that make up the algorithm body

An END statement

We will write our algorithms in pseudocode language, which is a narrative, Englishlike description. Pseudocode has several advantages over plain English. First, pseudocode language clearly resembles programming language, so that it is easy to translate into any desired programming language. Second, pseudocode does not require the punctuation and connectiveness of English sentences, so it gives an easy to follow outline. This makes it easy to modify pseudocodes.

□ **Example 1**   A family considers going on a picnic on a summer Sunday only if it does not rain. Otherwise, the family will stay home. Write an algorithm specifying this situation.

Solution

ALGORITHM PICNIC   (name of algorithm)

IF rain
THEN stay home   } (body of algorithm)
ELSE go picnicking

END of PICNIC   (END statement)   □

□ **Example 2**   The absolute value of a real number x is defined to be x, if x is positive or 0, and $-x$, if x is negative. Write an algorithm to find the absolute value of a real number x that we denote by ABSX.

Solution

ALGORITHM ABSOLUTE

Input x

IF x < 0

THEN ABSX := $-$x

ELSE ABSX := x

END of ABSOLUTE   □

APPLICATION TO DIV AND MOD

Some programming languages, such as Pascal, provide two built-in functions that operate on integers: the DIV and the MOD operators. For two integers A and B, B > 0, A DIV B equals the integer quotient obtained when A is divided by B; A MOD B equals the nonnegative integer remainder when A is divided by B. If A < 0 then A DIV B is negative. We illustrate the use of these two functions by the following example:

□ **Example 3**

$$3 \text{ DIV } 15 = 0 \qquad 3 \text{ MOD } 15 = 3$$
$$17 \text{ DIV } 5 = 3 \qquad 17 \text{ MOD } 5 = 2$$
$$-21 \text{ DIV } 10 = -3 \qquad -21 \text{ MOD } 10 = 9 \qquad \square$$

Next, we write an algorithm to implement these two functions, DIV and MOD, in a computer language that does not provide them as built-in functions. We restrict our algorithm to the case of positive integers.

□ **Example 4**   Write an algorithm to compute the DIV and MOD of two given positive integers.

Solution   We base our algorithm on the division algorithm, which states that for any two numbers A and B, $B > 0$, there are unique integers q and r such that

$$A = Bq + r \qquad \text{with } 0 \leq r < B$$

For our problem q is the DIV and r is the MOD.

ALGORITHM FUNCTIONS
Input A and B

10	MOD := A
20	DIV := 0
30	DoWhile (MOD ≥ B)
40	MOD := MOD − B
50	DIV := DIV + 1

End of while

END of FUNCTIONS   □

□ **Example 5**   Trace ALGORITHM FUNCTIONS in Example 4 for A = 17, B = 5. That is, execute every statement in ALGORITHM FUNCTIONS, in the given order, with A = 17 and B = 5.

Solution   By statement 10 in ALGORITHM FUNCTIONS we have MOD = 17. Statement 20 gives DIV = 0. Since $17 \geq 5$, then the condition in statement 40 gives MOD = 17 − 5 = 12, and by statement 50, DIV = 0 + 1 = 1. Since $12 \geq 5$, the while loop is executed again. For this execution, statement 40 gives MOD = 12 − 5 = 7 and statement 50 gives DIV = 1 + 1 = 2. Again, since $7 \geq 5$, the WHILE loop is executed one more time. This time MOD = 7 − 5 = 2 and DIV = 2 + 1 = 3. At this point the condition $2 \geq 5$ in statement 30 is false. This ends the while loop. The computed values are therefore

$$17 \text{ DIV } 5 = 3 \quad \text{and} \quad 17 \text{ MOD } 5 = 2 \qquad \square$$

FLOWCHARTS

A *flowchart* is a graphic representation in which symbols represent the logic used in a program. Because many algorithms are technical, describing them in ordinary English becomes less preferable than flowcharts. A standard set of flowchart symbols was established by the American National Standards Institute (ANSI). Some of the ANSI flowchart symbols are given below.

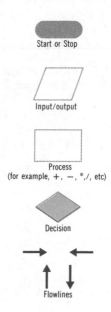

Start or Stop

Input/output

Process
(for example, +, −, *,/, etc)

Decision

Flowlines

To illustrate how flowcharts specify algorithms we give the algorithm in Example 2 as a flowchart.

□ **Example 6**   Represent the algorithm of Example 2 as a flowchart.

Solution   Using the ANSI flowchart symbols we have the following: □

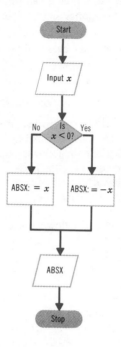

Exercise 13.4   *Answers to Odd-Numbered Problems begin on page* 639.

In Problems 1 and 2 what are the final values for x and y?

1. Algorithm ADD:

> $N := 5$
> $x := 0$
> $y := 0$
> Dowhile $(x < N)$
> > $x := x + 1$
> > $y := y + x$
>
> End of While
> End of ADD

2. Algorithm SQR:

> $N := 5$
> $x := N$
> $y := 1$
> Dowhile $(y \neq N)$
> > $x := x + N$
> > $y := y + 1$
>
> End of While
> End of SQR

In Problem 3–6, $N(1)$, $N(2)$, . . . , $N(m)$ is a list of m numbers. Write an algorithm that:

3. Computes the sum and average of the numbers.

4. Computes the sum of the squares of the numbers.

5. The product of the numbers.

6. The sum of the even numbers.

7. Suppose that a student with grade point average (GPA) greater than 3.5 is eligible for a scholarship. Write an algorithm that will read a list of 20 students' names; their GPA and output the names and GPA of those eligible.

8. Write an algorithm that reads a list of employees' names and hourly wages and prints out the names and wages of those with hourly wages that exceed $7.50.

9. Write an algorithm that will read in a student's grade average, an integer ranging from 0 to 100, and print out the student's name and letter grade according to the following scale

$$\text{A: } 90-100, \text{ B: } 80-89, \text{ C: } 70-79, \text{ D: } 60-69, \text{ F: } 0-59$$

10. Customers of a certain restaurant can find out about the *soup de jour* by entering the day into a computer terminal installed in the lobby. Write an algorithm that specifies this situation. Use the following information:
Monday: onion soup; Tuesday: split pea soup; Wednesday: lentil soup;
Thursday: liver dumpling soup; Friday: clam chowder soup;
Saturday: vegetable soup; Sunday: chicken noodle soup.

In Problems 11–14, a flowchart is given. Write the algorithm represented by each flowchart.

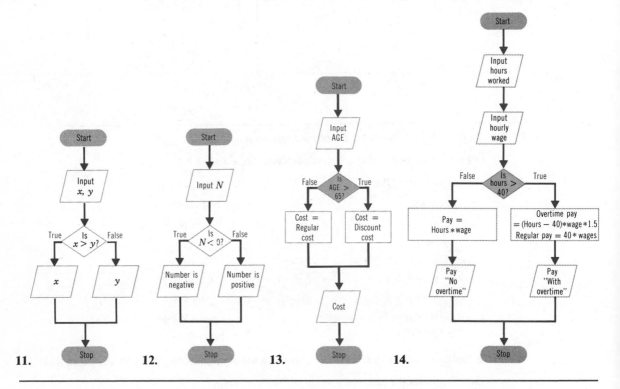

11.   12.   13.   14.

13.5 MATHEMATICAL INDUCTION

PRINCIPLE OF MATHEMATICAL INDUCTION □ APPLICATIONS TO COMPUTER SCIENCE

Mathematical induction is used to establish that mathematical statements involving positive integers are true for *all* positive integers. For example, we can use mathematical induction to prove that the following statement:

$$1 + 2 + 3 + \cdots + n = \frac{n(n+1)}{2} \tag{1}$$

holds for all positive integers n.

Mathematical induction is considered by some as the standard proof technique in computer science. For example, if we have a DO loop that computes the sum of the first 100 positive odd integers, then we can determine this sum by using a formula proven by mathematical induction (see Example 4). Or if we have a program that finds the square of a positive integer, mathematical induction can be used to show that the program always computes the square of a positive integer (see Example 5).

Before describing the method of mathematical induction, let us try to realize its power. To do this, we use equation (1) and substitute the various possible values of $n = 1, 2, 3, \ldots$ to construct the following table:

Value of n	Left-Hand Side of Equation (1)	Right-Hand Side of Equation (1)	Formula in Equation (1)
1	1	$\dfrac{1(1+1)}{2} = 1$	holds
2	$1 + 2 = 3$	$\dfrac{2(2+1)}{2} = 3$	holds
3	$1 + 2 + 3 = 6$	$\dfrac{3(3+1)}{2} = 6$	holds
4	$1 + 2 + 3 + 4 = 10$	$\dfrac{4(4+1)}{2} = 10$	holds
etc.			

We make two observations about this table:

1. It is impossible to substitute all possible values of n because there is an infinite number of them (as many as the number of positive integers). This means that our table can never be complete, and so equation (1) can never be proven by substituting all the various values of n.

2. Although the pattern of the right-hand side column suggests that $n(n+1)/2$ is valid, we can never be sure that equation (1) does not fail for some untried value of n.

By mathematical induction, however, we will prove that equation (1) holds for all positive integers n. We shall show this in Example 2.

In the remainder of this section we use $S(n)$ to denote the statement that we wish to prove is true.

□ **Example 1** Let $S(n)$ be the statement

$$1 + 2 + 3 + \cdots + n = \frac{n(n+1)}{2}$$

(a) Write $S(1)$. Is $S(1)$ true?
(b) Write $S(2)$. Is $S(2)$ true?
(c) Write $S(k)$. (k is a positive integer.)
(d) Write $S(k + 1)$.

Solution It is clear that $S(n)$ is the statement about the sum of the first n positive integers.

(a) $S(1)$ is the statement about the sum of the first positive integer. By formula (1), $S(1)$ is the statement

$$1 = \frac{1(1 + 1)}{2}$$

which is true.

(b) $S(2)$ is the statement about the sum of the first two positive integers. By formula (1), $S(2)$ is the statement

$$1 + 2 = \frac{2(2 + 1)}{2}$$

which is also true.

(c) $S(k)$ is the statement about the sum of the first k positive integers. By formula (1), $S(k)$ is the statement

$$1 + 2 + 3 + \cdots + k = \frac{k(k + 1)}{2}$$

(d) $S(k + 1)$ is the statement about the sum of the first $(k + 1)$ positive integers. This is obtained by substituting $k + 1$ for n in equation (1), to get

$$1 + 2 + 3 + \cdots + k + (k + 1) = \frac{(k + 1)[(k + 1) + 1]}{2} \tag{2}$$

□

We are now ready to state the principle of mathematical induction.

Principle of Mathematical Induction Let $S(n)$ be a statement that involves positive integers $n = 1, 2, 3, \ldots$. If we can show that the following two conditions are satisfied:

Condition I: The statement $S(1)$ is true

Condition II: Let k be any positive integer. If assuming $S(k)$ is true implies that $S(k + 1)$ is also true,

then $S(n)$ must be true for *all* positive integers.

□ **Example 2** Show that

$$1 + 2 + 3 + \cdots + n = \frac{n(n + 1)}{2} \tag{3}$$

is true for all positive integers n.

Solution We need to show first that $S(1)$ is true. Because $1 = 1(1 + 1)/2$, then Condition I is satisfied. To show that Condition II is true, we assume that formula (3) holds for some positive integer k. That is, we assume $S(k)$ is true for some positive integer k and, based on this assumption, we must show that $S(k + 1)$ is true. We look at the sum of the first $k + 1$ positive integers:

$$1 + 2 + 3 + \cdots + k + (k + 1) = [1 + 2 + 3 + \cdots + k] + (k + 1)$$

$$= \underset{\uparrow}{\frac{k(k + 1)}{2}} + (k + 1)$$

by our assumption that
$S(k)$ is true

$$= \frac{k(k + 1) + 2(k + 1)}{2}$$

$$= \underset{\uparrow}{\frac{(k + 1)[k + 2]}{2}}$$

Take $(k + 1)$ as a
common factor

$$= \frac{(k + 1)[(k + 1) + 1]}{2}$$

which is $S(k + 1)$. (See formula 2.) Thus, Condition II is also satisfied. And by the principle of mathematical induction, equation (3) is true for all positive integers n.

□

□ **Example 3** Let $S(n)$ be the following statement describing the sum of the first n positive odd integers:

$$1 + 3 + 5 + \cdots + (2n - 1) = n^2 \tag{4}$$

(a) Write $S(1)$ and show it is true.
(b) Write $S(2)$ and show it is true.
(c) Write $S(k)$.
(d) Write $S(k + 1)$.
(e) Show, using mathematical induction, that $S(n)$ is true for all positive integers n.

Solution (a) $S(1)$ describes the sum of the first positive odd integers; equation (4) gives $1 = 1^2$. This is true; therefore, $S(1)$ is true.

(b) $S(2)$ describes the sum of the first two positive odd integers; equation (4) gives $1 + 3 = 2^2$. Because both sides are equal to 4, then $S(2)$ is true.

(c) $S(k)$ describes the sum of the first k positive odd integers. Equation (4) gives $1 + 3 + 5 + \cdots + (2k - 1) = k^2$.

(d) $S(k + 1)$ describes the sum of the first $k + 1$ positive odd integers. Equation (4) gives

$$1 + 3 + 5 + \cdots + (2k - 1) + (2k + 1) = (k + 1)^2$$

(e) Since, from (a) above $S(1)$ is true, Condition I is satisfied. To show that Condition II is satisfied we assume that $S(k)$ is true [see (c) above] and we show that this implies $S(k + 1)$ [see (d) above] is true. So we consider the sum of the first $(k + 1)$ positive odd integers:

$$1 + 3 + 5 + \cdots + (2k - 1) + (2k + 1)$$
$$= \underbrace{[1 + 3 + 5 + \cdots + (2k - 1)]}_{\substack{= k^2 \text{ since we} \\ \text{assumed } S(k) \text{ holds}}} + (2k + 1)$$
$$= k^2 + 2k + 1$$
$$= (k + 1)^2$$

Thus, $S(k + 1)$ holds and so Condition II is satisfied, and formula (4) is true for all positive integers. □

APPLICATIONS TO COMPUTER PROGRAMMING

□ **Example 4** Consider the following Pascal program segment:

```
10   X := 0;
20   FOR I := 1 TO 100 DO
30   X := X + 2 * I − 1
40   END; {FOR}
50   WRITELN (X);
```

What value will be printed for X?

Solution To answer this question we go over the execution of the FOR loop for several values of I. That is, we trace the DO loop. We summarize this tracing in the following table:

I =	Instruction 30
1	X := 0 + 2 * 1 − 1 = 1
2	X := 1 + 2 * 2 − 1 = 1 + 3
3	X := 1 + 3 + 2 * 3 − 1 = 1 + 3 + 5
etc.	

This pattern tells us that when I = 100, instruction 30 makes X := 1 + 3 + 5 + · · · + 199. But according to formula (4) in Example 3, which we proved by mathematical induction, this sum equals $100^2 = 10{,}000$, and so the value printed will be 10,000. □

Mathematical induction is also used to prove that programs do what they claim to do.

□ **Example 5**   Consider the following Pascal function, where X is assumed to be an integer greater than or equal to zero.

FUNCTION SQX (X : INTEGER) : INTEGER;

VAR Y, Z : INTEGER;

BEGIN {SQX}

10   Y := 0;

20   Z := 0;

30   WHILE Z < > X DO

40   BEGIN {WHILE}

50   Y := Y + X;

60   Z := Z + 1;

70   END; {WHILE}

80   SQX := Y

END; {SQX}

(a)   Trace FUNCTION SQX for X equals 3 (see Example 5 in 13.4).

(b)   Using mathematical induction, prove that FUNCTION SQX computes the square of any positive integer.

Solution   (a)   Statement 10 makes Y = 0, and statement 20 makes Z = 0. X being 3 causes the WHILE loop in instruction 30 to execute. Instruction 50 makes Y = 0 + 3 = 3, and instruction 60 increases Z to 1. Because Z = 1 is not equal to X = 3, the WHILE loop is executed again; the result is Y = 3 + 3 = 6 (by instruction 50) and Z = 1 + 1 = 2 (by instruction 60). Z = 2 is still not equal to X = 3; therefore the WHILE loop executes one more time to give Y = 6 + 3 = 9 (by instruction 50), and Z = 2 + 1 = 3 (by instruction 60). Since now Z = 3 and X = 3 the loop execution terminates and by instruction 80, SQX = 9. Since $3^2 = 9$, SQX does indeed compute the square of 3.

(b)   The proof by mathematical induction is as follows: We observe that after passing through the WHILE loop n times X is added to itself n times, and at the same time Z will equal n. Let us denote this Z by Z_n. This says that the value of Y, denoted Y_n, after n times through the WHILE loop is

$$Y_n = X \cdot Z_n \tag{5}$$

Equation (5) will be our statement $S(n)$.

Now, $S(1)$ is $Y_1 = X \cdot Z_1 = X \cdot 1 = X$; thus Condition I is satisfied. To show that Condition II is also satisfied, we assume that $S(k)$, where k is a positive integer, is true. That is, we assume that after k times through the WHILE loop, $Y_k = X \cdot Z_k$. Show, based on this assumption, that $S(k + 1)$ is true. That is, show that after one more time through the WHILE loop $Y_{k+1} = X \cdot Z_{k+1}$. One more execution of the WHILE loop means

$$Y_{k+1} = Y_k + X, \text{ and } Z_{k+1} = Z_k + 1$$

That is,

$$Y_{k+1} = \underbrace{(X \cdot Z_k)}_{\substack{Y_k \text{ by our assumption} \\ \text{that } S(k) \text{ is true}}} + X$$

$$= X \cdot (Z_k + 1)$$
$$= X \cdot Z_{k+1}$$

Thus $S(k + 1)$ is true and Condition II is satisfied. To finish the proof we proceed as follows: When $Z = X$, the loop condition is false and therefore

$$Y = X \cdot Z = X \cdot X = X^2$$

This shows that FUNCTION SQX does compute the square of any positive integer. □

Exercise 13.5 *Answers to Odd-Numbered Problems begin on page* 641.

1. Let $S(n)$ be the statement

$$n < 2^n, \qquad n \text{ is a positive integer}$$

   (a) Write $S(1)$. Is $S(1)$ true?
   (b) Write $S(2)$. Is $S(2)$ true?
   (c) Write $S(k)$.
   (d) Write $S(k + 1)$.

2. Let $S(n)$ be the statement

$$1 \cdot 2 + 2 \cdot 3 + 3 \cdot 4 + \cdots + n \cdot (n + 1) = \frac{n(n + 1)(n + 2)}{3}$$

   (a) Write $S(1)$. Is $S(1)$ true?
   (b) Write $S(2)$. Is $S(2)$ true?
   (c) Write $S(k)$.
   (d) Write $S(k + 1)$.

3. Let $S(n)$ be the statement

$$1^2 + 2^2 + 3^2 + \cdots + n^2 = \frac{n(n + 1)(2n + 1)}{6}$$

   (a) Write $S(1)$. Is $S(1)$ true?
   (b) Write $S(5)$. Is $S(5)$ true?
   (c) Write $S(k)$.
   (d) Write $S(k + 1)$.

4. Let $S(n)$ be the statement

$$\frac{1}{1 \cdot 2} + \frac{1}{2 \cdot 3} + \frac{1}{3 \cdot 4} + \cdots + \frac{1}{n(n + 1)} = \frac{n}{n + 1}$$

(a) Write $S(1)$. Is $S(1)$ true?

(b) Write $S(3)$. Is $S(3)$ true?

(c) Write $S(k)$.

(d) Write $S(k+1)$.

5. Let $S(n)$ be the statement

$$1 + 2 + 2^2 + \cdots + 2^n = 2^{n+1} - 1$$

(a) Write $S(1)$. Is $S(1)$ true?

(b) Write $S(5)$. Is $S(5)$ true?

(c) Write $S(k)$.

(d) Write $S(k+1)$.

6. Let $S(n)$ be the statement

$$-1 + 1 - 1 + 1 - \cdots + (-1)^n = \frac{(-1)^n - 1}{2}$$

(a) Write $S(1)$. Is $S(1)$ true?

(b) Write $S(2)$. Is $S(2)$ true?

(c) Write $S(100)$. Is $S(100)$ true?

(d) Write $S(k)$.

(e) Write $S(k+1)$.

In Problems 7–12 prove by mathematical induction that the statement is true for all positive integers n.

7. $1 \cdot 2 + 2 \cdot 3 + 3 \cdot 4 + \cdots + n \cdot (n+1) = \dfrac{n(n+1)(n+2)}{3}$

8. $1^2 + 2^2 + 3^2 + \cdots + n^2 = \dfrac{n(n+1)(2n+1)}{6}$

9. $\dfrac{1}{1 \cdot 2} + \dfrac{1}{2 \cdot 3} + \dfrac{1}{3 \cdot 4} + \cdots + \dfrac{1}{n \cdot (n+1)} = \dfrac{n}{n+1}$

10. $2 + 4 + 6 + \cdots + 2n = n \cdot (n+1)$

11. $2 + 5 + 8 + \cdots + (3n - 1) = \dfrac{n(3n+1)}{2}$

12. $n < 2^n$

In Problems 13–18, determine the value printed for the variable X. (See the formulas in Example 2 and in Problems 7–10.)

13. X := 0;
     FOR I := 1 TO 100 DO
       FOR J := I TO 100 DO
         X := X + 1;
     WRITELN (X);

14. X := 0;
     FOR I := 1 TO 1000 DO
       FOR J := I TO 1000 DO
         X := X + 1;
     WRITELN (X);

15. X := 0;
    FOR I := 1 TO 1000 DO
        X := 2 + 2 * I;
    WRITELN (X);
16. X := 0;
    FOR I := 1 TO 99 DO
        X := X + 1/(I*(I + 1));
    WRITELN (X);
17. X := 0
    FOR I := 1 TO 1000 DO
        X := X + I *(I + 1);
    WRITELN (X);
18. X := 0
    FOR I := 1 TO 100 DO
        X := X + SQR (I);
    WRITELN (X);

13.6 RECURRENCE RELATIONS

Thus far we have defined a sequence by giving a general formula for its nth term or by writing a few of its terms. Often this approach is not possible. An alternative is to write the sequence by finding a relationship among its terms. Such a relationship is called a *recurrence relation.* Sequences defined this way normally arise when each term of the sequence depends upon the previous terms of the sequence. Defining a sequence recursively requires giving both the recurrence relation and specifying the first few terms of the sequence. Specifying the first few terms of the sequence is called setting *initial conditions.* An example will help clarify these concepts.

□ **Example 1**   Compute the first six terms of the sequence defined by the following recurrence relation and initial conditions:

(a)   Recurrence relation: $s_n = 2s_{n-1} + 1$,   for all integers $n \geq 1$
       Initial condition: $s_0 = 1$

(b)   Recurrence relation: $s_n = s_{n-1} + s_{n-2}$,   for all integers $n \geq 2$
       Initial conditions: $s_0 = 1$, $s_1 = 2$

(c)   Recurrence relation: $s_n = s_{n-1}^2 + ns_{n-2} + s_{n-3}$,   for all integers $n \geq 3$
       Initial conditions: $s_0 = 1$, $s_1 = 2$, $s_2 = -1$

Solution   (a)   Here the initial condition is given as $s_0 = 1$. Therefore we need to compute s_1, s_2, s_3, s_4, and s_5. Substituting $n = 1$ in the recurrence relation gives

$$s_1 = 2s_{1-1} + 1 = 2s_0 + 1 = 2(1) + 1 = 3$$
$$\uparrow$$
$$s_0 = 1$$

Similarly,

$$s_2 = 2s_{2-1} + 1 = 2s_1 + 1 = 2(3) + 1 = 7$$
$$\uparrow$$
$$s_1 = 3$$

$$s_3 = 2s_{3-1} + 1 = 2s_2 + 1 = 2(7) + 1 = 15$$
$$\uparrow$$
$$s_2 = 7$$

$$s_4 = 2s_{4-1} + 1 = 2s_3 + 1 = 2(15) + 1 = 31$$
$$\uparrow$$
$$s_3 = 15$$

and

$$s_5 = 2s_{5-1} + 1 = 2s_4 + 1 = 2(31) + 1 = 63$$
$$\uparrow$$
$$s_4 = 31$$

Thus the first six terms of this sequence are 1, 3, 7, 15, 31, 63.

(b) Here the initial conditions are given as $s_0 = 1$ and $s_1 = 2$; therefore, we need to compute s_2, s_3, s_4, and s_5. Substituting $n = 2$ in the recurrence relation gives

$$s_2 = s_{2-1} + s_{2-2} = s_1 + s_0 = 2 + 1 = 3$$
$$\uparrow$$
$$s_0 = 1 \text{ and } s_1 = 2$$

Similarly,

$$s_3 = s_{3-1} + s_{3-2} = s_2 + s_1 = 3 + 2 = 5$$
$$\uparrow$$
$$s_1 = 2 \text{ and } s_2 = 3$$

$$s_4 = s_{4-1} + s_{4-2} = s_3 + s_2 = 5 + 3 = 8$$
$$\uparrow$$
$$s_2 = 3 \text{ and } s_3 = 5$$

and

$$s_5 = s_{5-1} + s_{5-2} = s_4 + s_3 = 8 + 5 = 13$$
$$\uparrow$$
$$s_3 = 5 \text{ and } s_4 = 8$$

Thus the first six terms of this sequence are 1, 2, 3, 5, 8, 13.

(c) Here the initial conditions are given as $s_0 = 1$, $s_1 = 2$, and $s_2 = -1$; therefore, we need to compute s_3, s_4, and s_5. Substituting $n = 3$ in the recurrence relation gives

$$s_3 = s_{3-1}^2 + 3s_{3-2} + s_{3-3} = s_2^2 + 3s_1 + s_0 = (-1)^2 + 3(2) + 1 = 1 + 6 + 1 = 8$$
$$\uparrow$$
$$s_0 = 1, s_1 = 2, \text{ and } s_2 = -1$$

Similarly,

$$s_4 = s_{4-1}^2 + 4s_{4-2} + s_{4-3} = s_3^2 + 4s_2 + s_1 = 8^2 + 4(-1) + 2$$
$$\uparrow$$
$$s_1 = 2, s_2 = -1, \text{ and } s_3 = 8$$

$$= 64 - 4 + 2 = 62,$$

and

$$s_5 = s_{5-1}^2 + 5s_{5-2} + s_{5-3} = s_4^2 + 5s_3 + s_2 = (62)^2 + 5(8) - 1$$

$$s_2 = -1, s_3 = 8, \text{ and } s_4 = 62$$

$$= 3844 + 40 - 1 = 3883$$

Thus the first six terms of this sequence are $1, 2, -1, 8, 62, 3883$. ☐

These examples lead us to the following definition.

Recurrence Relation
Initial Condition

A *recurrence relation* for the sequence $s_0, s_1, s_2, s_3, \ldots$ is a formula that relates each term s_n to previous terms of the sequence. The *initial condition* for a recurrence relation is a set of values of the first few terms of the sequence.

The next two examples are two well known sequences that are defined recursively.

☐ **Example 2**   In 1202 A.D., a European mathematician named Leonardo Fibonacci posed the following problem:

Assume we start with a single pair of newborn rabbits and that each pair does not reproduce during its first month of life, but after its first month, it produces one new pair (a male and a female) at the end of every month. If we further assume that no rabbits die, how many pairs of rabbits will there be at the end of n months?

Solution   Let r_n denote the number of rabbit pairs at the end of the nth month. Since we started with one pair, then we have $r_0 = 1$. And, since this pair is not fertile during its first month, then at the end of the first month we will still have (this) one pair, that is, $r_1 = 1$. At the end of the second month this pair will produce another pair and so there will be two pairs, that is, $r_2 = r_0 + r_1 = 1 + 1 = 2$. At the end of the third month the one-month-old pair does not produce but the old pair does, the one we started with; thus there will be one newborn pair in addition to the previous two pairs, that is,

$$r_3 = r_2 + r_1 = 2 + 1 = 3$$

At the end of the fourth month there will be two pairs that are reproductive (as many as there was at the end of the second month, which is 2), which will produce two pairs, and the one-month-old pair that cannot produce. Thus,

$$r_4 = r_3 + r_2 = 3 + 2 = 5$$

Continuing in this manner we find that at the end of the nth month there will be r_{n-2} new pairs born plus r_{n-1} pairs (those include the one month olds). That is,

Recurrence relation $r_n = r_{n-1} + r_{n-2}$

Initial condition $r_0 = 1, \quad r_1 = 1$ ☐

Fibonacci numbers occur in many applications. For example, the number of binary words that do not contain the pattern 00, follows a Fibonacci sequence.

□ **Example 3**
The Towers of Hanoi

This is a puzzle about three poles and n disks of increasing sizes. Initially, all of the disks (all have holes at their centers) are placed on the first pole, as shown in Figure 7(a). We want to transfer all the disks from the first pole to the third, so that they appear as in Figure 7(b). If we can move only one disk at a time and if we are not allowed to place a larger disk on top of a smaller one, what is the minimum number of moves required to transfer a tower of n disks from the first pole to the third pole?

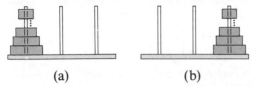

Figure 7   (a)   (b)

Solution

We begin by letting m_n be the minimum number of moves required to move the n disks from the first pole to the third. Obviously, $m_0 = 0$. $m_1 = 1$ because we can move one disk from the first pole to the third in one move. Notice that this is the minimum number of moves required to transfer one disk from the first pole to the third. To find m_2 we proceed as follows: First, we move the smaller disk from the first pole to the second leaving the larger one on the first pole (Figures 8a, 8b). Second, we move the larger disk from the first pole to the third (Figure 8c). Third, and last, we move the smaller disk from the second pole to the third (Figure 8d). Thus a minimum of three

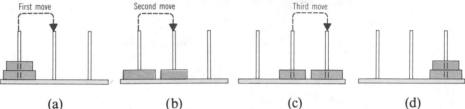

Figure 8   (a)   (b)   (c)   (d)

moves is needed to transfer two disks from the first pole to the third. This is the minimum number of moves because if we follow a different set of moves to transfer the two disks from the first pole to the third without violating the rules of the puzzle, we end up with more than three moves (Try it!). Thus m_2 requires the following: m_1 moves from the first pole to the second (moves for transferring the smaller disk from the first pole to the second), one move of the larger disk from the first pole to the third, and another m_1 moves from the second pole to the third (moves for transferring the smaller disk from the second pole to the third). Thus

$$m_2 = 2m_1 + 1 = 2 \cdot 1 + 1 = 3$$

For a tower of three disks the minimum number of moves m_3 required to transfer the three disks from the first pole to the third is computed as follows: m_2 moves are required to transfer the top two disks from the first pole to the second (Figures 9a, 9b), one move of the large disk from the first pole to the third (Figure 9c), and another m_2 moves of the smaller two disks from the second pole to the third (Figure 9d). Thus

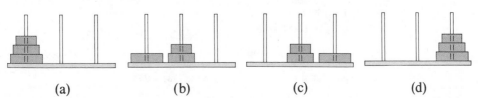

Figure 9   (a)   (b)   (c)   (d)

$$m_3 = 2m_2 + 1 = 2 \cdot 3 + 1 = 7$$

Continuing our reasoning† in this way, it can be shown that

Recurrence relation $\quad m_n = 2m_{n-1} + 1 \quad$ for all integers $n \geq 2$

Initial condition $\qquad m_0 = 0, \qquad m_1 = 1$ $\qquad\qquad$ □

More examples on recursively defined sequences are found in the exercises.

Exercise 13.6 *Answers to Odd-Numbered Problems begin on page* 641.

In Problems 1–14 a recurrence relation and an initial condition are given that define a sequence (s_n). Find the first six terms of (s_n).

1. $s_n = 2s_{n-1} \quad$ for all integers $n \geq 1$
   $s_0 = 1$

2. $s_n = s_{n-1} + n \quad$ for all integers $n \geq 1$
   $s_0 = 1$

3. $s_n = ns_{n-1} - 1 \quad$ for all integers $n \geq 1$
   $s_0 = 1$

4. $s_n = s_{n-1} + 2^n \quad$ for all integers $n \geq 1$
   $s_0 = -1$

5. $s_n = (n+1)s_{n-1} \quad$ for all integers $n \geq 1$
   $s_0 = 2$

6. $s_n = s_{n-1} + n^2 \quad$ for all integers $n \geq 1$
   $s_0 = 1$

7. $s_n = s_{n-2} + s_{n-1} + \binom{n}{2} \quad$ for all integers $n \geq 2$
   $s_0 = 1, s_1 = 1$

8. $s_n = 2s_{n-2} + s_{n-1}^2 \quad$ for all integers $n \geq 2$
   $s_0 = 1, s_1 = -1$

9. $s_n = s_{n-1}s_{n-2} \quad$ for all integers $n \geq 2$
   $s_0 = 1, s_1 = 2$

10. $s_n = (s_{n-1} + s_{n-2})^{1/2} \quad$ for all integers $n \geq 2$
    $s_0 = 3, s_1 = 6$

11. $s_n = s_{n-1} + s_{n-2} + s_{n-3} \quad$ for all integers $n \geq 3$
    $s_0 = 1, s_1 = 2, s_2 = 2$

12. $s_n = s_{n-1} + s_{n-2} - 2s_{n-3} \quad$ for all integers $n \geq 3$
    $s_0 = 2, s_1 = 1, s_2 = 1$

13. $s_n = ns_{n-1} + s_{n-2} - s_{n-3} \quad$ for all integers $n \geq 3$
    $s_0 = 1, s_1 = -1, s_2 = -1$

14. $s_n = (-1)^n s_{n-1} + ns_{n-2} + n^2 s_{n-3} \quad$ for all integers $n \geq 3$
    $s_0 = 1, s_1 = 1, s_2 = 1$

† A proof of this requires mathematical induction.

15. Use the recurrence relation and initial condition for the Fibonacci number sequence r_0, $r_1, r_2, r_3, \ldots$ defined in Example 2 to compute $r_{10}, r_{11}, r_{12}, r_{13}$, and r_{14}.

16. Use the recurrence relation and initial condition for the towers of Hanoi sequence m_0, $m_1, m_2, m_3, \ldots$ defined in Example 3 to compute m_6, m_7, m_8, and m_9.

17. (a) Write all binary words of lengths 0, 1, 2, 3, and 4 that do not contain the bit pattern 00.

    (b) For all integers $n \geq 2$, let $s_n =$ the number of binary words of length n that do not contain the pattern 00. Find a recurrence relation relating s_n to s_{n-1} and s_{n-2}.

18. Repeat Problem 17 for the binary words that do not contain the bit pattern 11.

19. *Compound Interest.* Suppose $1000 is invested in an account paying 10% interest compounded annually. Assume that no withdrawals are made, and let A_n be the amount in the account after n years.

    (a) Compute A_0, A_1, A_2, A_3, and A_4.

    (b) Find a recurrence relation relating A_n to A_{n-1} for all integers $n \geq 1$.

20. Repeat Problem 19 for $2000 with annually compound interest of 5.5%.

21. Consider a set of n lines in a plane no two of which are parallel and no three of which intersect at the same point. Let p_n denote the number of distinct regions formed by these lines. See the figure.

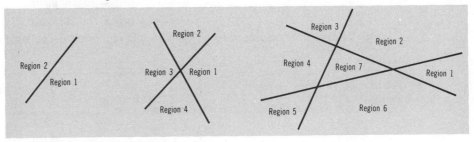

    (a) Find p_1, p_2, p_3, and p_4.

    (b) Find a recurrence relation relating p_n to p_{n-1} for all integers $n \geq 2$.

22. The high level programming language Pascal permits recursion. That is, it allows functions or procedures to call themselves. Consider the following Pascal function that uses recursion. Here the parameter N is zero or positive.

```
FUNCTION F (N : INTEGER) : INTEGER;
BEGIN
    IF N = 0 THEN
        F := 1
    ELSE
        F := N*F(N − 1)
END; {of FUNCTION F}
```

    (a) Trace FUNCTION F for N = 0, 1, 2, 3, 4, and 5.

    (b) In general, what does FUNCTION F compute?

CHAPTER REVIEW

Important Terms

relation	image	inverse function
bit	range	sequence
binary word	Pascal Function CHR	algorithm
byte	Pascal Function ORD	pseudocode
ASCII Code	one-to-one	MOD
reflexive	injective	DIV
symmetric	onto	flowchart
transitive	surjective	ANSI
inverse relation	bijective	mathematical induction
function	composition of functions	recurrence relation
domain	identity function	initial condition

True-False Questions

T   F   1. For all relations R from A to B and all $a \in A$, $b \in B$ if aRb, then bRa.

T   F   2. The range and the domain of all functions are the same.

T   F   3. A bijective function is both one-to-one and onto.

T   F   4. One way to define a sequence is to give a formula for its nth term.

T   F   5. Condition II of the principle of mathematical induction states that if the statement $S(k)$ is true for some positive integer k, then so is $S(k + 1)$.

T   F   6. Every recurrence relation must have some initial condition.

Fill in the Blanks

(Answers are on page 642)

1. A relation R from A to B is the set R of _____ _____ where $a \in A$ $b \in B$.

2. A _____ from the set X into the set Y is a relation that associates with each element of X exactly one element of Y.

3. A one-to-one and onto function is called _____ .

4. A sequence is a function whose domain is the set _____ _____ .

5. The _____ language is a narrative, Englishlike description.

6. _____ _____ is used to prove that a statement $S(n)$, which involves natural numbers, is true for all n.

7. A formula that relates each term of a sequence to previous terms is called a _____ _____ . Specifying the first few terms is giving the _____ _____ .

Review Exercises

Answers to Odd-Numbered Problems begin on page 642 .

1. Let $A = \{1,2,3,8,9,27\}$ and R be a relation on A defined by aRb if, and only if, a is the cube of b. Write R as a set of ordered pairs.

2. State the inverse relation R^{-1} of the relation R of Problem 1. Write R^{-1} as a set of ordered pairs.

3. Which of the following relations defines a function from $A = \{0,1,2\}$ to $B = \{0,1,2,3\}$?

   (a) $f(0) = 0, f(1) = 3, f(2) = 1$.
   (b) $g(0) = 1, g(1) = 1, g(2) = 1$.
   (c) $h(0) = 1, h(1) = 2$.
   (d) $F(0) = 3, F(1) = 2, F(0) = 1, F(2) = 3$.

4. Find the final values of A and B if the following sequence of instructions is followed.

$$A := 2;$$
$$B := 2 * A - 5;$$
$$A := B + 1;$$
$$A := A * A - 1;$$

5. Find the first 10 terms of the sequence

   (a) $a_k = (-1)^k + k$
   (b) $a_k = (-1)^k \cdot k$

6. Write an algorithm that will read in a person's age and determine whether the person is a minor, adult, or a senior citizen, depending on whether the age is less than 18, from 18 through 65, or above 65.

7. Draw the flowchart for the algorithm in Problem 6.

8. Suppose $S(n)$ is the statement $1 + 3 + 3^2 + 3^3 + \cdots + 3^n = \frac{1}{2}(3^n - 1)$.

   Find $S(1), S(2), S(3)$. Use mathematical induction to prove that $S(n)$ is true for all n.

9. What value will be printed for the variable N?

$$N := 0;$$
$$\text{FOR } I := 1 \text{ TO } 1000 \text{ DO}$$
$$N := N + 2 * I - 1;$$
$$\text{WRITELN } (N);$$

   [*Hint:* Use formula (4) in Example 3, Section 13.5.]

10. Find the first 5 terms of the sequence defined by the following recurrence relation and initial conditions:

$$s_n = (n-2)s_{n-2} + s_{n-1}, \qquad n \geq 2$$
$$s_0 = 1, \qquad s_1 = 0$$

11. Find the first 7 terms of the sequence defined by the following recurrence relation and initial conditions:

$$s_n = s_{n-3} \cdot (s_{n-2} + s_{n-3}), \qquad n \geq 3$$
$$s_0 = 2, \qquad s_1 = 2, \qquad s_2 = 1$$

12. Suppose that you start with a single pair of newborn rabbits and that each pair reproduces a new pair (a male and a female) every two months except the first two months of its life. If no rabbits die, how many rabbits will there be at the end of the

    (a) Fourth month?
    (b) Sixth month?
    (c) Tenth month?

14

GRAPHS AND TREES

14.1 GRAPHS

Many situations that occur in computer science, operations research, physical sciences, and economics, are of a combinatorial nature and can be analyzed by using techniques found in a relatively new area of mathematics called *graph theory*. In this chapter, we present a brief introduction and explain some of the more elementary results of graph theory and their applications.

Before giving a formal definition of a graph, we point out that the term *graph* has two quite different meanings. One definition of a graph is the one we studied in Chapter 1 and used when we graphed straight lines and linear inequalities.

Vertex
Edge

In this chapter a *graph* will mean a set of points (called *vertices*) with one or more curves or lines (called *edges*) connecting a point to itself or a pair of points. For a given pair of vertices, our concern is not what the edge looks like, but rather whether the two vertices have an edge joining them or not. For example, the two diagrams in Figure 1 represent the same graph: each has 4 vertices v_1, v_2, v_3, and v_4 and 8 edges e_1, e_2, e_3, e_4, e_5, e_6, e_7, and e_8. Note that the edges e_5 and e_6 intersect in the graph in Figure 1(a), but their intersection is not a vertex. Edges e_2 and e_7 connecting vertices v_2 and v_3 are

Parallel Edges
Loop

called *parallel edges* since they connect the same pair of vertices. Edge e_8 is called a *loop* because it connects a vertex, v_3, to itself.

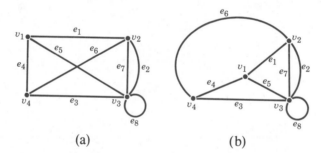

Figure 1   (a)   (b)

Graph   A *graph* G consists of the following two finite sets: (1) a nonempty set V of vertices and (2) a set E of edges, where each edge either connects two vertices or connects a vertex to itself.

Isolated Vertex

A vertex that is not connected to any other vertex or to itself is called an *isolated vertex*.

☐ **Example 1**   For the graph given in Figure 2

    (a)   Write the vertex set.

    (b)   Write the edge set.

    (c)   Find all isolated vertices.

    (d)   Find all loops.

    (e)   Find all parallel edges.

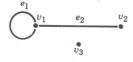 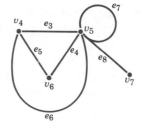

Figure 2

Solution (a) The vertex set is

$$V = \{v_1, v_2, v_3, v_4, v_5, v_6, v_7\}$$

(b) The edge set is

$$E = \{e_1, e_2, e_3, e_4, e_5, e_6, e_7, e_8\}$$

(c) v_3 is the only vertex that is isolated.

(d) e_1 and e_7 are the only loops.

(e) e_3 and e_6 are parallel edges since they both connect v_4 and v_5. ☐

Simple Graph **A graph with no parallel edges and no loops is called a *simple graph*.**

☐ **Example 2** Draw all simple graphs with 3 vertices.

Solution In Figure 3, we list all possible graphs having 3 vertices that are free of parallel edges and loops.

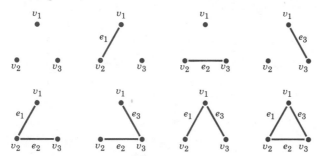

Figure 3 ☐

☐ **Example 3**

The Königsberg
Bridge Problem

This is one of the oldest problems involving graphs. The town of Königsberg (now Kaliningrad in the Soviet Union) is crossed by the Pregel river with two islands in the river. The islands are connected to each other by one bridge. The larger island is connected to each bank by two bridges. The smaller island is connected to each bank by one bridge. A total of seven bridges. See Figure 4. The townspeople wondered

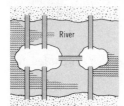

Figure 4

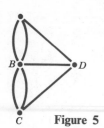

C   Figure 5

whether one can begin at one of the banks or islands, walk across each bridge exactly once, and return to the starting point. This problem is equivalent to the following: Let each mass of land be represented by a vertex and each bridge by an edge to obtain a graph as in Figure 5 where A and C are the river banks, B is the larger island, D is the smaller island, and the 7 edges represent the 7 bridges. Can one start at either one of the vertices A, B, C, or D, traverse each edge in Figure 5 exactly once and return to the starting vertex? A Swiss mathematician named Leonhard Euler (1707–1783) studied this problem and in 1736 was able to answer it. We give his answer in Section 14.3.

□

☐ **Example 4**
Communications
Lines Network

Computer, telephone, and transportation route networks (to name a few) can be represented by graphs. Inspecting or analyzing their graphs usually determines connecting edges for optimization purposes. Figure 6 shows a communication network.

Figure 6

□

☐ **Example 5**
Pascal Data Types

Relationships can be depicted by graphs. For example, the hierarchy of data types in the Pascal language is given in the graph in Figure 7.

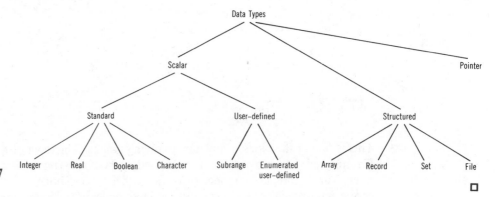

Figure 7

□

Examples 3, 4, and 5 show the usefulness of graphs. In the remainder of this section we discuss some definitions and results associated with a graph.

Degree of a Vertex

Let G be a graph and v a vertex of G. The *degree of v*, denoted deg(v), is the number of edges emanating from v. An edge that is a loop is counted twice.

Note that if v is an isolated vertex, then deg(v) = 0.

☐ **Example 6**   Find the degree of each vertex in the graph G shown in Figure 8.

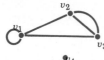

Figure 8

Solution   There are two edges connecting the vertex v_1 to the vertices v_2 and v_3, respectively, and there is a loop at the vertex v_1; thus $\deg(v_1) = 4$. Similarly, $\deg(v_2) = 3$; $\deg(v_3) = 3$; and $\deg(v_4) = 0$, since v_4 is not connected to any of the other vertices. ☐

It turns out that there is a connection between the number of edges in a graph and the sum of the degrees of the vertices in the graph. The following result gives this connection.

> Let G be a graph with vertices $v_1, v_2, \ldots, v_n$. Then the sum of the degrees of all the vertices of G equals twice the number of edges in G. That is,
>
> $$\deg(v_1) + \deg(v_2) + \cdots + \deg(v_n) = 2 \cdot (\text{the number of edges in } G) \quad (1)$$

Note that this theorem says that the sum of the degrees of the vertices is even.

☐ **Example 7**   Can we draw a graph G with 3 vertices v_1, v_2, and v_3 where

(a) $\deg(v_1) = 1$, $\deg(v_2) = 2$,   and $\deg(v_3) = 2$.
(b) $\deg(v_1) = 2$, $\deg(v_2) = 1$,   and $\deg(v_3) = 1$.
(c) $\deg(v_1) = 0$, $\deg(v_2) = 0$,   and $\deg(v_3) = 4$.

Justify your answers, and if yes, draw G.

Solution   (a)   No, since $\deg(v_1) + \deg(v_2) + \deg(v_3) = 1 + 2 + 2 = 5$, which is an odd number. Then, by the above theorem, such a graph does not exist.

(b)   Yes, $\deg(v_1) + \deg(v_2) + \deg(v_3) = 4$, which is an even number. Then, G can be either one of the two graphs shown in Figure 9. In each case

$$\deg(v_1) = 2, \qquad \deg(v_2) = 1, \qquad \text{and } \deg(v_3) = 1$$

Figure 9

(c)   Yes, $\deg(v_1) + \deg(v_2) + \deg(v_3) = 4$, which is an even number. Then G is the graph shown in Figure 10. Here $\deg(v_1) = 0$, $\deg(v_2) = 0$, and $\deg(v_3) = 4$. (Because of the two loops at v_3.)

Figure 10   ☐

Answers to Odd-Numbered Problems begin on page 643 .

In Problems 1 and 2 write the vertices and edges of each graph and find all loops, all isolated vertices, and all parallel edges.

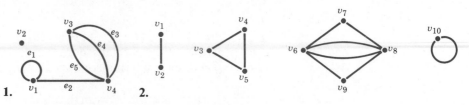

1.   **2.**

3. Draw all simple graphs that have two vertices.
4. Draw all simple graphs that have four vertices and six edges.
5. Find the degree of each vertex of the graphs in Problems 1–2.
6. Can we draw a graph with vertices v_1, v_2, v_3, v_4, v_5, v_6, v_7, and v_8 of degrees 2, 2, 3, 4, 5, 5, 6, and 8, respectively? Justify your answer.
7. Let G be a graph with vertices v_1, v_2, v_3, v_4, v_5, and v_6 of degrees 1, 2, 3, 3, 4, and 5, respectively. How many edges does G have? Justify your answer.
8. Can we draw a graph with vertices v_1, v_2, v_3, and v_4 of degrees:

    (a)   1, 2, 3, and 3, respectively?
    (b)   1, 1, 1, and 4, respectively?
    (c)   1, 2, 3, and 4, respectively?

    Justify your answers

9. Can we draw a simple graph with vertices v_1, v_2, v_3, and v_4 of degrees 1, 2, 3, and 4, respectively? Justify your answer.
10. Can we draw a simple graph with vertices v_1, v_2, v_3, v_4, and v_5 of degrees:

    (a)   2, 3, 3, 3, and 5, respectively?
    (b)   1, 1, 1, 2, and 3, respectively?

    Justify your answers.

11. Give an example of a simple graph (a) having no vertices of even degree (b) having no vertices of odd degree.

In Problems 12 and 13, use the following definition:

Complete Graph of Order n   The **complete graph of order n**, denoted by K_n, is the graph that has n vertices and every vertex is connected to every other vertex by exactly one edge.

12. Draw K_1, K_2, K_3, K_4, and K_5.
13. How many edges does K_6 have?

In Problems 14–15 use the following definition:

Subgraph   A graph G is called **subgraph** of a graph H if every vertex in G is also a vertex in H and every edge in G is also an edge in H.

14. Find five subgraphs of

15. Find three subgraphs that contain all vertices, of

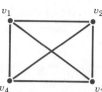

In Problems 16–18, use the following definition:

Complement **Let G be a simple graph. The *complement* of G is the simple graph $\overline{G}$ with the same vertices as G, but contains only those edges that are missing in G.**

16. Find the complement of

17. Find the complement of

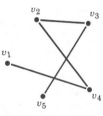

18. Find the complement of

14.2 PATHS AND CONNECTEDNESS

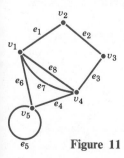

Figure 11

In this section we introduce some definitions and give some results regarding a special type of graph, the *connected graph*. Intuitively speaking, a graph is connected if it is possible to go from any vertex to any other vertex by traversing the edges of the graph. Many problems in graph theory involve the question of whether or not a graph is connected.

Going from a vertex to another in a graph amounts to following a sequence of neighboring edges. For example, in the graph in Figure 11 we can go from the vertex v_1 to the vertex v_3 by traversing the edges e_1 and e_2. This we write as an alternating sequence of adjacent vertices and edges: $v_1e_1v_2e_2v_3$. Or we can take a longer route as follows $v_1e_7v_4e_4v_5e_5v_5e_6v_1e_7v_4e_3v_3$. Obviously, there are several other routes that can also be followed to go from v_1 to v_3.

Path   **Let u and v be two vertices in a graph G. A *path* from u to v is an alternating sequence of adjacent vertices and edges of G. This sequence begins at u and ends in v.**

Trivial Path   If u and v are the same vertex (that is, $u = v$), then the path with no edges is *trivial* and is denoted by u or v.

Simple Path   A *simple path* from u to v is a path with no repeated vertices.

Circuit   A *circuit* (or *cycle*) is a path that begins and ends at the same vertex and has no repeated edges.

Simple Circuit   A *simple circuit* is a path with no repeated edges and no repeated vertices other than the first and the last.

□ **Example 1**   Consult the graph in Figure 12 to determine which of the following sequences are paths, simple paths, circuits, and simple circuits.

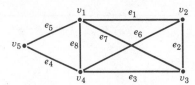

Figure 12

(a) $v_1e_1v_2e_6v_4e_3v_3e_2v_2$
(b) $v_1e_1v_2e_2v_3e_3v_4e_4v_5$
(c) $v_1e_8v_4e_3v_3e_7v_1e_8v_4$
(d) $v_5e_5v_1e_8v_4e_3v_3e_2v_2e_6v_4e_4v_5$
(e) $v_2e_2v_3e_3v_4e_4v_5e_5v_1e_1v_2$

Solution   (a)   This is a path from v_1 to v_2. Vertex v_2 repeats; therefore it is not a simple path. The first and the last vertices are different; therefore it is not a circuit.

(b)   This is a path from v_1 to v_5. No vertex repeats; therefore this is a simple path. (Note that a simple path is never a circuit.)

(c)   Here, edge e_8 repeats. Therefore this is just a path from v_1 to v_4.

(d)   This path starts and ends at v_5. It has no repeated edges. Vertex v_4 repeats; therefore, it is a circuit.

(e)   This path starts and ends at v_2. It has no repeated edges and no repeated vertices (other than v_2); therefore it is a simple circuit.   □

We are now ready to define a connected graph.

Connected Graph   Let G be a graph. Then G is said to be a *connected graph* if for every pair of distinct vertices u and v ($u \neq v$) in G, there is a path between u and v.

□ **Example 2** Let G_1, G_2, and G_3 be the graphs given in Figure 13. Determine which of these graphs is connected.

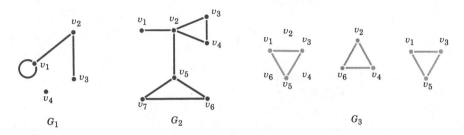

Figure 13

Solution   In G_1 there is no path from the vertex v_4 to any other vertex. Thus G_1 is not connected. In G_2 there is a path between every distinct pair of vertices. Thus G_2 is connected. For G_3, (a) and (b) in Figure 13 are the same graph. (b) shows that G_3 consists of two separate parts. That is, there is no path between, say, v_1 and v_2. Thus G_3 is not connected. You should not be misled by the graph of G_3 given in (a) which seems to show that G_3 is connected. (Recall that two edges may intersect but not necessarily at a vertex.)   □

We end this section by stating without proof two results, that may help in determining the connectedness of a given graph.

> **Theorem I.** Let G be a connected graph with n vertices. Then G must have at least $n - 1$ edges.

> **Theorem II.** Let G be a simple graph with n vertices (that is, G has no loops and no parallel edges). If G has more than $\binom{n-1}{2}$ edges, then it must be connected.

Exercise 14.2   *Answers to Odd-Numbered Problems begin on page* 643.

In Problems 1–4 a graph is given. Identify the specified paths as paths, not simple; simple paths; circuits; or simple circuits.

1. (a) $v_3 e_3 v_4 e_4 v_5 e_6 v_2 e_7 v_4$
    (b) $v_1 e_5 v_5 e_6 v_2 e_1 v_1 e_5 v_5$
    (c) $v_1 e_1 v_2 e_6 v_5 e_4 v_4 e_3 v_3$
    (d) $v_3 e_2 v_2 e_1 v_1 e_5 v_5 e_6 v_2 e_7 v_4 e_3 v_3$
    (e) $v_5 e_6 v_2 e_2 v_3 e_3 v_4 e_4 v_5$

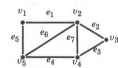

2. (a) $v_3 e_4 v_3$
    (b) $v_1 e_1 v_2 e_2 v_3$
    (c) $v_2 e_1 v_1 e_3 v_3 e_4 v_3 e_2 v_2$

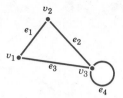

3. (a) $v_1 e_1 v_2 e_2 v_1$
    (b) $v_1 e_1 v_2 e_5 v_3 e_4 v_1$
    (c) $v_1 e_3 v_1$
    (d) $v_1 e_1 v_2 e_6 v_2 e_2 v_1 e_3 v_1$

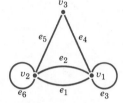

4. (a) $v_1 e_1 v_2 e_2 v_3 e_3 v_4 e_8 v_1$
    (b) $v_1 e_{10} v_6 e_6 v_2 e_2 v_3 e_7 v_1 e_1 v_2 e_6 v_6$

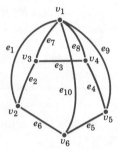

5. For the graph find:

    (a) Four different simple paths.
    (b) Four different circuits that are not simple.
    (c) Four different simple circuits.

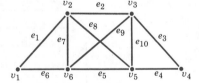

6. Find six simple paths from v_1 to v_4 in the graph.

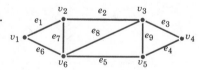

7. For the graph in Problem 6, find a circuit that is not simple, contains all vertices, and begins at v_1.

8. For the graph in Problem 6, how many simple circuits that contain all vertices and begin at v_1 are there?

9. Draw a simple circuit consisting of

    (a) Only one edge
    (b) Only two edges

10. Draw a graph that is connected, but removing one edge makes it disconnected.

11. Let G be a connected graph and let e be an edge. If removing e from G results in a disconnected graph, then e is called a *bridge*. Find all bridges for each of the following graphs.

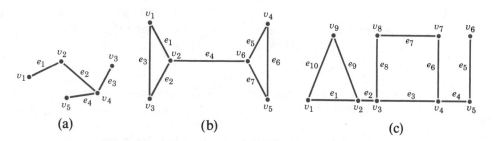

(a)　　　　　　　　(b)　　　　　　　　(c)

12. Can there be a connected graph G with n edges and n vertices where the deletion of one edge disconnects G? [*Hint:* Use Theorem (I).]

(Refer to Problem 14 of Section 14.1). A subgraph H of G is a *connected component* of G if and only if

　　1. H is connected.
　　2. G does not have a connected subgraph that contains H as its subgraph.

13. Find a connected component of the following graph.

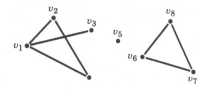

14. Repeat Problem 13 for the following graphs.

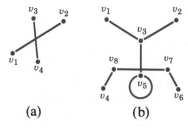

(a)　　　　　　　　(b)

15. If G is a simple graph with

　　(a)　6 vertices and 11 edges. Can G be disconnected? Why?
　　(b)　6 vertices and 10 edges. Can G be disconnected? Why?

14.3 EULERIAN AND HAMILTONIAN CIRCUITS

FLEURY'S ALGORITHM □ HAMILTONIAN CIRCUITS

In this section we present results that will help us solve the Königsberg bridge problem and problems similar to it. As noted in Section 14.1, Euler studied this problem and in 1736 published its solution. We begin with the following definition of an *Eulerian circuit.*

Eulerian Circuit **Let G be a graph. A circuit in G that contains every edge in G is called an *Eulerian circuit.***

Thus, an Eulerian circuit is a path that begins and ends at the same vertex, traverses every vertex at least once, and every edge exactly once.

□ **Example 1** Consider the graphs G_1 to G_6 given in Figure 14.

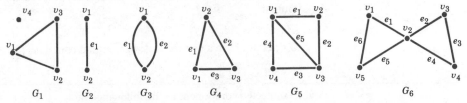

Figure 14　　G_1　　　G_2　　　G_3　　　G_4　　　　G_5　　　　　G_6

G_1 contains no Eulerian circuit because there is no edge connecting vertex v_4 to the rest of the graph; that is, because G_1 is not connected. G_2 contains no Eulerian circuit because any circuit will use e_1 twice. The circuit $v_1e_1v_2e_2v_1$ in G_3 is Eulerian. In G_4 the circuit $v_1e_1v_2e_2v_3e_3v_1$ is Eulerian. G_5 contains no Eulerian circuit (try it!). $v_1e_1v_2e_2v_3e_3v_4e_4v_2e_5v_5e_6v_1$ is an Eulerian circuit contained in G_6.　　□

We make the following observations regarding Example 1:

1. G_1 suggests that a disconnected graph cannot contain an Eulerian circuit.
2. G_2 and G_5, both of which contain no Eulerian circuit, have vertices of odd degree. Both vertices in G_2 are of degree 1. Vertices v_1 and v_3 in G_5 are of degree 3.
3. G_3 and G_6, which contain an Eulerian circuit, have all vertices of even degree. In G_3, v_1, and v_2 are of degree 2. In G_6, v_1, v_3, v_4, and v_5 are all of degree 2, and v_2 is of degree 4.

The above observations are not accidental. Indeed, there is a criterion for determining when a graph has an Eulerian circuit. We state this criterion without proving it. Later we will present an algorithm for finding an Eulerian circuit for those graphs that possess one.

Theorem I: Criterion for an Eulerian Circuit　Let G be a graph. G contains an Eulerian circuit if, and only if

1. G is connected,
2. Every vertex in G is of even degree.

☐ **Example 2**   Show that the graphs in Figure 15 contain no Eulerian circuit.

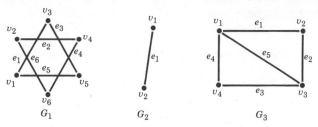

Figure 15 G_1 G_2 G_3

Solution G_1 is not connected. Therefore by Theorem I it cannot contain an Eulerian circuit. G_2 is connected, but vertices v_1 and v_2 are of degree 1, which is odd. Therefore, by Theorem I, G_2 cannot contain an Eulerian circuit.

G_3 is also connected but vertices v_1 and v_3 are each of degree 3, which is odd. Therefore, by Theorem I, G_3 cannot contain an Eulerian circuit.   ☐

We are ready, at this point, to give the solution to the Königsberg bridge problem outlined in Section 14.1, Example 3.

☐ **Example 3**   In Section 14.1, Example 3, it was pointed out that the town of Königsberg can be represented by a graph, such as graph G in Figure 16, where each vertex represents a mass of land and each edge represents a bridge. The problem can then be stated as follows: Is there a route that starts at a vertex, traverses every edge, exactly once, and returns to that vertex? In other words, does graph G contain an Eulerian circuit?

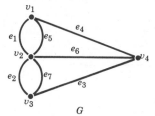

Figure 16 G

Solution   In the graph G in Figure 16, every vertex is of odd degree. Vertices v_1, v_4, and v_3 are of degree 3, and vertex v_2 is of degree 5. Therefore, by Theorem I, G does not contain an Eulerian circuit. That is, it is not possible to start at one of the banks or islands, cross every bridge exactly once, and return to the starting place.   ☐

Our discussion continues with an algorithm that gives a way to construct Eulerian circuits when they exist.

FLEURY'S ALGORITHM

If G is a graph that contains an Eulerian circuit, then this circuit can be obtained as follows.

1. Select any vertex in G as an initial vertex. From this initial vertex traverse edges in G, removing all edges that are traversed and all isolated vertices that are generated in the process.

2. If edge e is a bridge connecting vertices u and v (see Problem 11 section 14.2), then e can be selected only if the removal of e causes either u or v or both to become isolated.

We illustrate this procedure by applying it to a graph that contains an Eulerian circuit.

□ **Example 4**   Use Fleury's algorithm to find an Eulerian circuit of the graph G given in Figure 17.

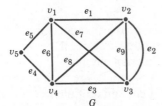

Figure 17

Solution G is connected and every vertex in G is of even degree. Therefore, by Theorem I, G contains an Eulerian circuit. To obtain this circuit we start at v_1 (we could start at any other vertex) and traverse edge, e_1, e_7, e_6, or e_5. We choose edge e_1 and, thus, remove it. Figure 18(a) shows edge e_1 removed. (We denote removed edges by dashed lines.) At v_2, there are three untraversed edges (e_2, e_8, and e_9; these are the solid lines at v_2 in Figure 18(a). We can choose to traverse any one of them. We choose e_8 and thus remove it. Figure 18(b) shows e_8 removed. Next, we traverse e_3 and remove it. Figure 18(c) shows e_3 removed. Note that we could equally choose e_4 or e_6. At this point we are at v_3 with edges e_2, e_9, and e_7 untraversed. Inspecting the remaining graph (Figure 18c), that is, the graph without the dashed (removed) edges, we find that e_7 is a bridge, which means that its removal disconnects the remaining graph. So, we do not choose

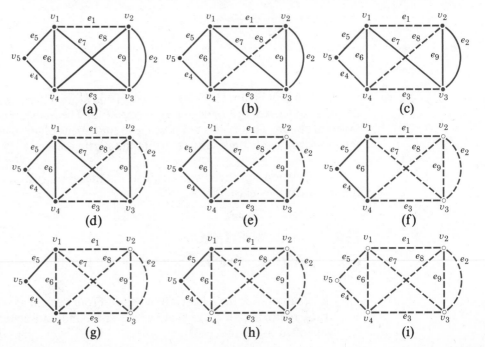

Figure 18

e_7 (unless we have no other choice). This means that we can only choose either edge e_9 or e_2. We select e_2, traverse, and remove it (Figure 18(d)). We are back at v_2. The only untraversed edge at this vertex is e_9. We traverse e_9 and remove it. This leaves v_2 isolated from the rest of the graph. In Figure 18(e) we draw v_2 as a blank circle to denote that it is a removed vertex. We proceed with our edge traversal in the following order: e_7, e_6, e_4, and e_5 as diagrammed in Figure 18(f) to 18(i). Thus the circuit that we obtain is

$$v_1 e_1 v_2 e_8 v_4 e_3 v_3 e_2 v_2 e_9 v_3 e_7 v_1 e_6 v_4 e_4 v_5 e_5 v_1$$

Remember that this is not the only Eulerian circuit in G. □

HAMILTONIAN CIRCUITS

Hamiltonian Circuit

A related problem to that of finding an Eulerian circuit, in which all edges of a graph appear exactly once, is that of finding a circuit in which all vertices of a graph appear exactly once. Such a circuit is called a *Hamiltonian circuit* honoring the Irish mathematician Sir William R. Hamilton (1805–1864) who introduced this problem in 1859 (see Problem 10). Note that a Hamiltonian circuit includes every vertex of a graph exactly once (except the first and last are the same), and may or may not include every edge.

□ **Example 5**   Which of the graphs given in Figure 19 has a Hamiltonian circuit. Give the circuits for the graphs that contain them.

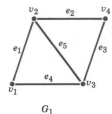

Figure 19 G_1 G_2

Solution

In G_1, we can start at v_1 and traverse edge e_1 to v_2, e_2 to v_4, e_3 to v_3, and then e_4 to v_1. Thus, G_1 has a Hamiltonian circuit given by $v_1 e_1 v_2 e_2 v_4 e_3 v_3 e_4 v_1$. Notice how all vertices appear in this circuit but not all edges. Edge e_5 is not used in this circuit.

For G_2 we argue as follows: If we start at v_1, v_2, v_3, or v_4 and visit every vertex, vertex v_5 will be visited twice. And if we start at v_5 itself, then in going from the vertices v_1 or v_4 to v_3 or v_2, respectively, or vice-versa, v_5 will be passed again (since we began at v_5). To complete the circuit we must come back to v_5, thus traversing it three times. All this means that G_2 has no Hamiltonian circuit. □

While there is a criterion for determining whether or not a graph contains an Eulerian circuit (Theorem I), a similar criterion does not exist for Hamiltonian circuits. There is, however, a procedure that can be used to determine that some graphs contain Hamiltonian circuits. We state this procedure without proof.

Theorem II   Let G be a connected graph with n vertices where $n \geq 3$. If the sum of the degrees of each pair of its nonadjacent vertices is greater than or equal to n, then G has a Hamiltonian circuit.

Note that Theorem II does *not* say that if a graph G with $n(\geq 3)$ vertices has a Hamiltonian circuit, then the sum of the degrees of each pair of its nonadjacent vertices *must* be greater than or equal to n. This is clear from the following example.

□ **Example 6** For the graph in Figure 20, $n = 5$ and the circuit $v_1 e_1 v_2 e_2 v_3 e_3 v_4 e_4 v_5 e_5 v_1$ is Hamiltonian. Yet the sum of the degrees of any two nonadjacent vertices is 4, which is not

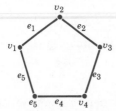

Figure 20

greater than or equal to 5. For instance, $\deg(v_1) + \deg(v_3) = 4$, $\deg(v_1) + \deg(v_4) = 4$ and so on.   □

Thus, Theorem II is a sufficient, but not a necessary, condition for a graph to possess a Hamiltonian circuit.

□ **Example 7** In the graph G_1 in Figure 19 page 569, the sum of the degrees of each pair of nonadjacent vertices is 4, $[\deg(v_1) + \deg(v_4)]$, which is equal to the number of vertices. Thus G_1 has a Hamiltonian circuit (see Example 5).   □

Exercise 14.3   *Answers to Odd-Numbered Problems begin on page* **644** .

1. Determine which of the following graphs contain an Eulerian circuit. If it does, then find an Eulerian circuit for the graph.

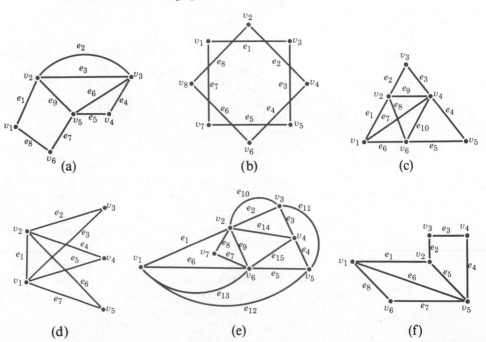

(a)

(b)

(c)

(d)

(e)

(f)

2. Does the complete graph K_4 (see Problem 12 in Exercise 14.1) contain an Eulerian circuit?

3. Does the complete graph K_5 contain an Eulerian circuit?

4. Does the complete graph K_n contain an Eulerian circuit? Explain.

5. A city consists of two land masses, situated on both banks of a river and three islands connected to each other and to the banks as shown in the figure. Is there a way to start at any point and make a round trip through all land masses crossing each bridge exactly once? If so, how can this be done?

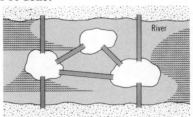

6. Give an example of a graph for which every vertex has an even degree but which does not contain an Eulerian circuit.

7. The following is a floor plan of a certain house. (A denotes the outside of the house.) Is it possible to start outside the house, or in any one of the rooms, take a tour through the house passing through each doorway, exactly once, and return to the starting place. [*Hint:* Represent the floor plan of the house with a graph where the outside and each room is represented by a vertex and each doorway by an edge.]

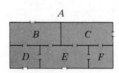

8. Repeat Problem 7 for the following floor plan.

9. Find a Hamiltonian circuit for each of the following graphs.

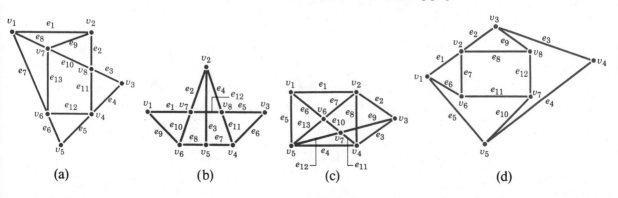

10. *Hamilton's Puzzle.* In 1859 Sir William Hamilton presented the following problem: Suppose each vertex in the graph represents a big international city and that each edge represents a transportation route. Can a salesperson make a round trip where he or she visits every city exactly once?

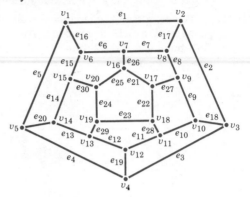

11. Show that the following graphs do not have a Hamiltonian circuit.

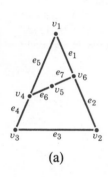

(a)

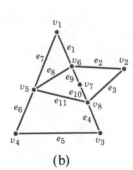

(b)

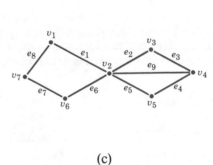

(c)

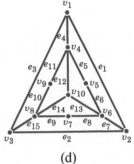

(d)

12. Determine whether or not the graph contains a Hamiltonian circuit. Find such a circuit for the graph that has one.

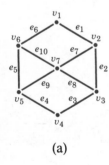

(a)

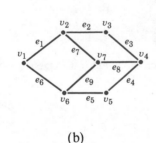

(b)

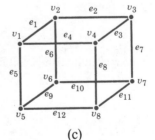

(c)

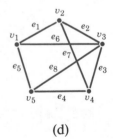

(d)

13. Give an example of a graph that contains both Eulerian and Hamiltonian circuits.

14. Give an example of a graph that contains an Eulerian circuit but does not contain a Hamiltonian circuit.

15. Give an example of a graph that contains a Hamiltonian circuit but does not contain an Eulerian circuit.

16. Which of the following complete graphs has a Hamiltonian circuit? (Refer to Problem 12, Exercise 14.1)

$$K_2, K_3, K_n \quad \text{where } n > 3$$

14.4 TREES

ROOTED TREE □ APPLICATIONS IN COMPUTER SCIENCE

Another class of graphs, called *trees,* are graphs that have no circuits (thus they cannot have parallel edges or loops). Trees arise frequently in computer science. In this section we present a brief exposure to the topic of trees.

Tree **Let T be a graph. T is called a *tree* if, and only if,**

(a) T is connected.
(b) T contains no circuits (except trivial ones).

Trivial Tree **T is called a *trivial tree* if it consists of a single vertex.**

□ **Example 1** Draw all distinct trees that have

(a) one vertex
(b) two vertices
(c) three vertices
(d) four vertices

Solution (a) A tree consisting of one vertex is the trivial tree T_1 shown in Figure 21(a).
(b) Figure 21(b) shows the tree T_2 that has two vertices.
(c) Figure 21(c) shows the tree T_3 with three vertices.
(d) Here, the tree may look like either one of the trees drawn in Figure 21(d). □

Figure 21 (a)   (b)   (c)   (d)

□ **Example 2** State why each graph in Figure 22 does not represent a tree.

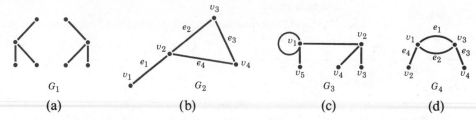

Figure 22   (a)   (b)   (c)   (d)

Solution   In Figure 22 the graph G_1 in (a) is not connected, so it is not a tree. The graph G_2 in (b) has the nontrivial circuit $v_2 e_2 v_3 e_3 v_4 e_4 v_2$. Therefore, it is not a tree. The graph G_3 in (c) contains a loop at v_1. Thus, it is not a tree. The graph G_4 in (d) has two edges e_1 and e_2 that are parallel. Hence, G_4 is not a tree.   □

The next theorem, which we present without a proof, is a useful way to characterize trees. In essence, it says that a tree is a connected graph with the fewest number of edges, meaning that if one edge is removed, then the graph becomes disconnected.

> **Theorem I** Let G be a connected graph that has n vertices. G is a tree if, and only if, it has exactly $n - 1$ edges.

ROOTED TREE

A special type of tree, called the *rooted tree,* is useful in computer science. We next give the definition of this tree and some terms related to it. Let T be a tree and let u, v, and w be vertices in T.

Root

1. If v is distinguished from the other vertices in T, then T is called a *rooted* tree and v is called a *root.*

Child
Left Child
Right Child

2. If u is adjacent to v (v need not necessarily be a root) but farther from the root than v, then u is called the *child* of v. If u and w are the only children of v with u located to the left of v and w to the right of v, then u and w are called, respectively, the *left* and the *right children* of v.

Binary Tree

3. If T is rooted and if every vertex in T has left and right children, either a left or a right child, or no children, then T is called a *binary tree.*

Leaf

4. If the vertex u has no children, then u is called a *leaf* (or a *terminal* vertex). If u has either one or two children, then u is called an *internal* vertex.

5. The *descendants* of the vertex u is the set consisting of all the children of u together with the descendants of those children.

□ **Example 3** Consider the rooted tree T in Figure 23.

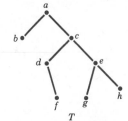

Figure 23 T

(a) What is the root of T?

(b) Is T a binary tree? If so, find the left and the right children of every vertex.

(c) Find the leaves and the internal vertices of T.

(d) Find the descendants of the vertices a and c.

Solution (a) Vertex a is distinguished as the only vertex located at the top of the tree. Therefore, a is the root.

(b) Yes, every vertex has two children, one child, or no children. The following table indicates the children of each vertex.

Vertex	Left Child	Right Child
a	b	c
b	None	None
c	d	e
d	None	f
e	g	h
f	None	None
g	None	None
h	None	None

(c) The leaves are those vertices that have no children. These are b, f, g, and h. The internal vertices are those that have either one child or two children. These are c, d, and e.

(d) The descendants of a are b, c, d, e, f, g, h. The descendants of c are d, e, f, g, h.

□

Let T be a binary tree, and let u and v be two vertices in T. The *subtree rooted at u* is the tree consisting of the root u, all its descendants, and all the edges connecting them. If u is the left child of v, then the subtree rooted at u is called the *left subtree of v rooted at u,* and if u is the right child of v, then the subtree rooted at u is called the *right subtree of v rooted at u.* If u is a leaf, then the subtree rooted at u is called a *trivial subtree.*

□ **Example 4** Consider the binary tree in Figure 24.

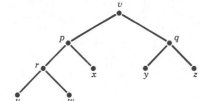

Figure 24

(a) Find the left and right subtrees of v.

(b) Find the subtree rooted at r.

Solution (a) The left subtree of v is given in Figure 25.

Figure 25

The right subtree of v is given in Figure 26.

Figure 26

(b) The subtree rooted at r is given in Figure 27.

Figure 27

☐

APPLICATIONS IN COMPUTER SCIENCE

Algebraic Expressions Binary trees are used to represent algebraic expressions. The vertices of the tree are labeled with the numbers, variables, or operations that make up the expression. The leaves of the tree can only be labeled with numbers or variables. Operations, such as addition, subtraction, multiplication, division, or exponentiation can only be assigned to internal vertices. The operation at each vertex operates on its left and right subtrees from left to right. The next two examples illustrate such uses of binary trees.

☐ **Example 5** Use a binary tree to represent the expression

(a) $x * y$ ("*" means multiplication)

(b) $(x + y)/z$ ("/" means division)

(c) $[(x - y) ** 2]/(x + y)$ ("**" means exponentiation)

Solution (a) In this expression the first term is x, the second term is y, and the operation is $*$. Therefore, our tree, shown in Figure 28, must be rooted at $*$ and must have two subtrees, one for each term.

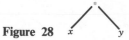

Figure 28

(b)   Here, we first add x and y and then divide by z. This means our tree must have /
as its root and two subtrees: a left subtree rooted at + that adds x to y and a right
subtree rooted at z. The tree is shown in Figure 29.

Figure 29

(c)   To get the first term, which is $(x - y)$ ** 2, we first subtract y from x, then
square. To get the second term, which is $x + y$, we add x to y. Finally, we divide
these two terms. This means our tree must be rooted at / and must have two
subtrees as shown in Figure 30.

Figure 30   □

The Binary Search Tree   Suppose we have a set of numbers. We will call them *keys*.
We are interested in two of the many operations that can be performed on this set:

1. Ordering (or sorting) the set.
2. Searching the ordered set to locate a certain key and, in the event of not finding
   the key in the set, adding it at the right position so that the ordering of the set is
   maintained.

In the next example we describe a method that uses trees to perform the operations
outlined above. This method involves storing the list in a tree where each element is
stored at a vertex.

□ **Example 4**   (a)   Use a binary tree to store the elements of the following list of numbers in an
increasing order: 7, 10, 21, 3, 24, 23.

(b)   Use the tree constructed in (a) to search for the number 19 in the list. If the
number is not found in the list, update the list by adding the number to it.

Solution   (a)   We begin by selecting any number from the list to be the root of our binary tree.
Say we select 10 to be this root. We draw the left and the right children of 10 as
shown in Figure 31(*a*).

Then, we pick another number from the list, say, 3. Now, 3 is less than 10, so we label the left child of 10 with 3 and then draw the left and the right children of 3, as Figure 31(*b*) shows.

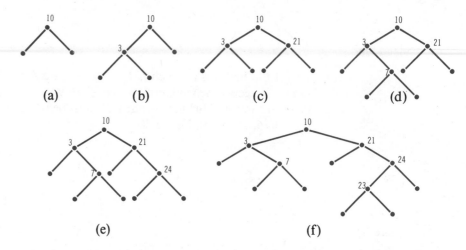

(a)　　　　　(b)　　　　　(c)　　　　　(d)

(e)　　　　　　　　　　(f)

Figure 31

Next, we pick another number from the list, say, 21. To position 21 on the tree, we start at the root 10 and compare it to 21. Since 21 is greater than 10, we move down to the right child of 10. This child is unlabeled, so we label it with 21 and then draw the left and the right children of this vertex. See Figure 31(*c*).

We continue in this fashion. We choose our next element from the list, say, 7. We again start at the root 10 and compare it to 7. Since 7 is less than 10 we move down to the left child of 10, which is the vertex labeled 3. We compare 7 to 3. Since 7 is greater than 3, then we move further down to the right child of 3. This child is unlabeled, so we label it with 7 and draw the left and the right children of 7. See Figure 31(*d*).

Say our next choice from the list is the number 24. Because 24 is greater than 10, we move down to the right child 21 of 10. Because 24 is greater than 21, we move further down to the right child of 21. This child is unlabeled. Therefore, we label it 21, and then draw the left and the right children of 24. See Figure 31(*e*).

Finally, the last number left in the list is 23. We start at the root 10. 23 is greater than 10, so we move down to the right child of 10, which is labeled 21. Since 23 is greater than 21, then we move further down to the right child of 21, which is labeled 24. Because 23 is less than 24, we move even further down to the left child of 24, which is unlabeled. So, we label it with 23 and then draw the right and the left children of 23. See Figure 31(*f*). Figure 31(*f*) is called a *binary search tree.*

Binary Search Tree

(b) To search for the number 19 in the order list, we begin at the root 10. Because 19 is greater than 10, we move down to the right child of 10, which is labeled 21. Because 19 is less than 21, we move down to the left child of 21, which is unlabeled. See Figure 31(*f*). Since we have reached an unlabeled vertex, we conclude that the number 19 is not found in the list, and we label this vertex 19 and draw the left and the right children of 19. See Figure 32. This adds the key 19 to the list while maintaining the increasing order of the numbers in the list.

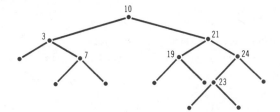

Figure 32   □

Exercise 14.4   *Answers to Odd-Numbered Problems begin on page* 645 .

1. Draw three distinct trees that have 5 vertices.

2. Draw three distinct binary trees that have 5 vertices.

3. Draw three distinct binary trees that have 7 vertices.

4. Draw three distinct binary trees that have 8 vertices.

In Problems 5–12 either draw a graph with the given properties or explain why such a graph cannot exist.

5. A tree that has 7 vertices and 7 edges.

6. A connected graph that has 7 vertices and 7 edges.

7. A tree that has 6 vertices with the sum of the degrees of the vertices being 10.

8. A tree that has (a) 6 vertices and 8 edges, (b) 6 edges and 8 vertices.

9. A tree with all vertices of degree 2.

10. A tree that has 10 vertices of degree 3, 3, 3, 3, 1, 1, 1, 1, 1, 1.

11. A connected graph that has 5 edges and 6 vertices and that is not a tree. (Theorem I!)

12. A tree that has 7 vertices.

13. Does a tree with 120 vertices and 119 edges exist? Explain.

14. Does a connected graph with 3 vertices and 1 edge exist? Explain.

15. Draw three distinct rooted trees that have 4 vertices.

16. Draw four distinct rooted trees that have 5 vertices.

In Problems 17 and 18, find all leaves (or terminal vertices) and internal vertices for the given graph.

17. 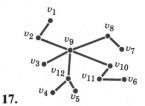   **18.**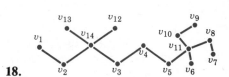

19. In a tree, can a leaf (or terminal vertex) be of degree 2? Explain.
20. In a tree, can an internal vertex be of degree 1? Explain.
21. Give an example of a nontrivial tree that has no internal vertices.

In Problems 22 and 23, given a tree T, find:

(a) All descendants of the vertices x and y.
(b) The left and the right subtrees of the vertices x and y.
(c) The subtree rooted at x.

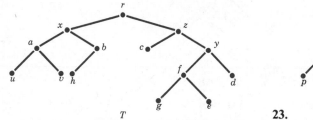

22.

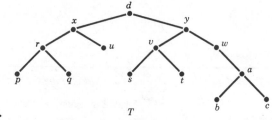

23.

24. Give an example of a binary tree that has neither a left nor a right subtree.

In Problems 25–28, a binary tree is given. Find the algebraic expression represented by the tree.

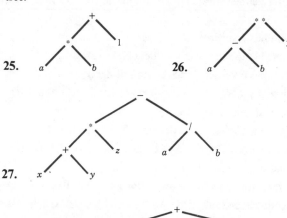

25.

26.

27.

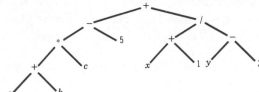

28.

In Problems 29 and 30, an algebraic expression is given. Use a binary tree to represent the expression.

29. $[(a + b)/c] + d$
30. $\{1/[(a + b) ** 2]\} - [(a + 1) * c] + b$

In Problems 31 and 32, a list is given. For this list:

(a) Construct a binary search tree that stores the set.
(b) Use the tree constructed in (a) to search for the given key. If the key is not found in the set, then add it to the set at the right location.

31. Bob, Mary, Peter, Frank, Michael, Sue, Angela. (The order must be alphabetic). Key is Paul.

32. 25, 99, 112, 56, 72, 65. (The order must be increasing.) Key is 132.

Use the definition below in Problems 33 and 34.

Spanning Tree *(Spanning Tree)* **Let *G* be a connected graph. If a subgraph *T* of *G* is a tree that contains all vertices of *G*, then *T* is called a *spanning tree* for *G*.**

33. (a) Is the tree (i)
  a spanning tree for the graph (ii)?
  (b) Is the tree (i)
  a spanning tree for the graph (ii)?

(i) (ii)

34. Find two spanning trees for the graph below.

(i) (ii)

14.5 DIRECTED GRAPHS

So far our discussion in this chapter has been about different types of graphs that are undirected, meaning that all edges have no directions; thus crossing an edge is possible in both directions, back and forth. In this section we discuss a new type of graph called a *directed graph*. In a directed graph every edge is assigned a certain direction, so that crossing an edge is possible only in the direction assigned. Directed graphs are used in many situations. For example, one-way streets are represented by directed graphs where the vertices are the intersections, and the edges are the streets. Flowcharts can be viewed as directed graphs where the vertices represent the instructions, and the edges represent the flow of control.

Directed Graph Let *D* be a graph. If every edge in *D* has a direction, then *D* is called a *directed graph* or *digraph* and its edges are called *arcs*. The vertex where an arc starts is called the *initial point* and the vertex where the arc ends is called the *terminal point*. When the directions of the edges in *D* are disregarded, the resulting graph obtained is called the *underlying graph* of *D*.

□ **Example 1**   Consider the digraph in Figure 33.

(a)   Give the initial and terminal points of each arc.

(b)   Draw the underlying graph.

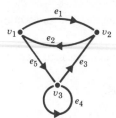

Figure 33

Solution   (a)   The following table gives all the arcs with their initial and terminal points.

Arc	Initial Point	Terminal Point
e_1	v_1	v_2
e_2	v_2	v_1
e_3	v_3	v_2
e_4	v_3	v_3
e_5	v_1	v_3

(b)   Figure 34 shows the underlying graph.   □

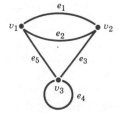

Figure 34

□ **Example 2**   Draw the digraph with the following specifications:

Arc	Initial Point	Terminal Point
e_1	v_1	v_2
e_2	v_3	v_2
e_3	v_3	v_4
e_4	v_4	v_1
e_5	v_2	v_4
e_6	v_4	v_2
e_7	v_3	v_3

Solution   Figure 35 shows the graph.   ☐

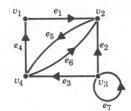

Figure 35

We mentioned that each vertex in a digraph has edges coming into it and (or) going out of it. This prompts us to define the following terms.

Indegree   **Let v be a vertex in the digraph D. The *indegree of v*, denoted by indeg(v), is the**
Outdegree   **number of arcs in D whose terminal point is v. The *outdegree of v*, denoted by outdeg(v), is the number of arcs in D whose initial point is v.**

☐ **Example 3**   In the digraph, in Figure 36, find the indegree and the outdegree of each vertex.

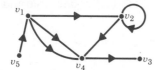

Figure 36

Solution   The answer is given in the following table:

Vertex	Indegree	Outdegree
v_1	1	3
v_2	2	2
v_3	1	0
v_4	3	1
v_5	0	1

Note that the loop at v_2 is counted as an arc coming out and going into v_2.   ☐

Directed Path   **A *directed path* in a digraph D is a sequence of vertices and edges such that the terminal point of one arc is the initial point of the next. If, in D, a directed path exists**
Reachable   **from the vertex u to the vertex v, then v is said to be *reachable* from u.**

☐ **Example 4**   Consider the graph in Figure 37.

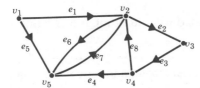

Figure 37

(a) Find three distinct directed paths from v_1 to v_5.

(b) Is v_1 reachable from v_4? Is v_1 reachable from v_5?

Solution

(a) One directed path from v_1 to v_5 is $v_1 e_1 v_2 e_6 v_5$. A second directed path is $v_1 e_1 v_2 e_2 v_3 e_3 v_4 e_4 v_5$. A third directed path is $v_1 e_1 v_2 e_2 v_3 e_3 v_4 e_8 v_2 e_6 v_5$.

(b) Since the indegree of v_1, is 0, then v_1 is not reachable from any other vertex. □

Digraphs where every vertex is reachable from any other vertex are important. We discuss them next.

Strongly Connected
Weakly Connected

Let D be a digraph. If every vertex in D is reachable from any other vertex in D, then D is called *strongly connected*. And if the underlying graph of D is connected, then D is said to be *weakly connected*.

□ **Example 5**

Which of the two digraphs in Figure 38 is strongly connected and which one is weakly connected.

Solution

In D_1, v_3 is not reachable from v_1 or v_2, and the underlying graph is connected. Therefore, D_1 is weakly connected. In D_2, every vertex is reachable from the others. Therefore, D_2 is strongly connected.

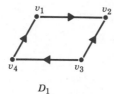

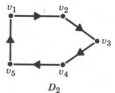

Figure 38 D_1 D_2 □

Suppose a graph represents a network of streets in a certain town where the vertices represent the intersections of the streets and the edges represent the streets connecting these intersections. An important question is whether or not the graph can be directed so that the streets can be made into one-way streets and still be able to get from any intersection to any other. That is, we want to determine whether or not the resulting digraph is strongly connected. We refer to this process of directing the edges of a graph as *orientation*.

Orientable Graph

Let G be a graph. If every edge in G can be given a direction such that the result is a strongly connected digraph, then G is said to be *orientable*.

The following theorem, stated without proof, is a criterion that characterizes an orientable graph.

Theorem I   A graph G is orientable if and only if it is connected and has no bridges.

Next, we present a procedure that produces an orientation for an orientable graph *G*. We remind you that a spanning tree of a graph *G* is a subgraph of *G* which is a tree that contains all the vertices of *G*. (See Problem 33, Section 14.4.)

Our procedure consists of the following steps.

Step 1: This step is referred to as a *depth-first search.* It involves the generation of a spanning tree *T* of the graph *G* as follows: We start at a vertex and search through the edges and vertices of *G* for a path. Then we extend this path as long as possible to a spanning tree. Because such a tree must include all vertices of *G*, if, during our search, a vertex is reached beyond which no new vertices can be reached, we back up along the path obtained, as far as necessary, to a vertex where branching to a new vertex is possible. We continue this process until a spanning tree of *G* is formed. During the search every vertex and edge encountered are numbered. Such numbering is called a *depth-first numbering* of *G*. Example 6 below explains further the process described in this step.

Step 2: We assign directions to the edges of *T* formed in Step 1 in the following way: Each edge of the tree *T* is directed from lower to higher depth-first number vertices.

Step 3: We direct all other vertices (not included in the tree *T*) from higher to lower depth-first number vertices.

We clarify this procedure by considering the following example.

□ **Example 6** Determine whether or not the graph drawn in Figure 39 is orientable. If it is, then use the above procedure to orient the edges so that the resulting graph is strongly connected.

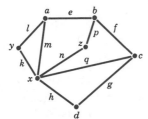

Figure 39

Solution Since the graph is connected and has no bridges, then it is orientable. To orient it we proceed as follows

Step 1: Our aim is to generate a spanning tree. So, we begin by selecting any vertex in the graph, we pick vertex *a* and label it v_1. Then we traverse edge *e* to vertex *b* labeling them e_1 and v_2, respectively. We continue in this fashion, avoiding all edges that will produce a circuit, to obtain the path $v_1 e_1 v_2 e_2 v_3 e_3 v_4 e_4 v_5$. See Figure 40(*a*), page 586. In this figure we denote the untraversed edges by dashed lines and the unvisited vertices by a blank circle. In this path, we stop at vertex *d* (labeled v_5) because we cannot go any further to reach a new vertex. Notice that if we continue the path from v_5 to the already visited vertex v_3 we would form the circuit whose vertices are v_3, v_4, and v_5 and thus no longer have a tree. Remember that trees are circuit-free connected graphs. Now, because no new vertices can be reached from v_5, we back up to vertex v_4 from which we can branch to either vertex y or vertex z. We choose to traverse edge k to vertex y and label them e_5 and v_6, respectively. See Figure 40(b).

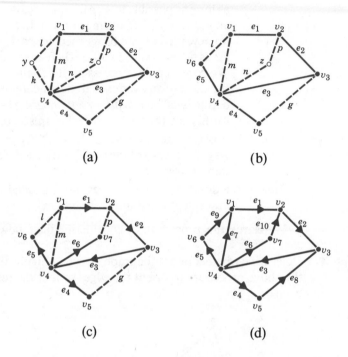

Figure 40

(a)   (b)

(c)   (d)

At v_6 no new vertices can be branched. So, here again we back up to v_4 from which we reach vertex z. We traverse edge n to this vertex and label them e_6 and v_7, respectively. See Figure 40(c).

This completes the generation of our spanning tree because the tree with vertices v_1, v_2, v_3, v_4, v_5, v_6, and v_7 and edges e_1, e_2, e_3, e_4, e_5, and e_6, which we just formed, is a subgraph of the given graph, connected, and contains all vertices of the given graph. Thus both our depth-first search and depth-first numbering are complete.

Step 2: We direct the edges of the generated spanning tree from lower to higher numbered vertices as shown in Figure 40(c). Note that no direction is assigned to the dashed lines at this point.

Step 3: We, finally, direct the edges that are not part of our spanning tree (formed in Step 1), that is, we direct the dashed lines in Figure 40(c) from higher to lower numbered vertices. See Figure 40(d).

The digraph thus produced is strongly connected because every vertex is reachable from any other vertex.   ◻

Exercise 14.5   *Answers to Odd-Numbered Problems begin on page* 646 .

In Problems 1 and 2 a digraph is given.

(a)   Find the initial and terminal points of each arc.

(b)   Find the indegrees and the outdegrees of all vertices.

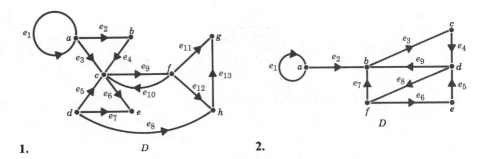

1.   *D*   **2.**

In Problems 3 and 4 draw the digraph with the given specifications.

3.   **4.**

Arc	Initial Point	Terminal Point
e_1	v_1	v_2
e_2	v_2	v_2
e_3	v_2	v_3
e_4	v_1	v_3
e_5	v_1	v_4
e_6	v_4	v_1

Arc	Initial Point	Terminal Point
e_1	v_2	v_1
e_2	v_3	v_2
e_3	v_3	v_4
e_4	v_4	v_1
e_5	v_1	v_3
e_6	v_3	v_1
e_7	v_4	v_2

In Problems 5 and 6 draw the digraph with the given specifications. (Note that the sum of the indegrees, or outdegrees, of all vertices is equal to the number of the arcs in the digraph.)

5.   **6.**

Vertex	Indegree	Outdegree
v_1	0	1
v_2	2	2
v_3	2	0
v_4	2	1
v_5	1	3
v_6	1	1

Vertex	Indegree	Outdegree
v_1	1	2
v_2	2	0
v_3	2	2
v_4	0	1

7.   Draw a digraph with three vertices where each vertex has indegree 2.

8.   Draw a digraph with three vertices where each vertex has outdegree 2.

In Problems 9 and 10 a digraph D is given.

(a) Is v_5 reachable from v_1?

(b) Is v_1 reachable from v_5?

Justify your answers.

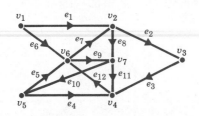

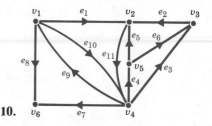

9.
10.

11. Find three distinct directed paths from v_1 to v_6 in the digraph in Problem 9.

12. Is the digraph in Problem 9 strongly connected? Justify your answer.

13. Is the digraph in Problem 10 strongly connected? Justify your answer.

14. A digraph D is called a *tournament* if it is loop-free and has exactly one arc between any two vertices. Thus, the vertices may represent contestants competing in a match, and an arc from vertex u to vertex v may mean u won over v. Given the following tournament:

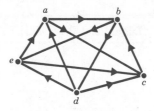

(a) What contestant won the greatest number of games?

(b) Find a path that does not start with the contestant in (a) and that contains all contestants.

15. Let $A = \{2,3,4,9,36\}$ and let R define the relation on A as follows: xRy if and only if x divides y. Draw a digraph D that represents R where the vertices of D are the elements of A and an arc from u to v in D means uRv.

16. Repeat Problem 15 for $A = \{1,2,5,8,9\}$ and R defined on A as follows: aRb if and only if a is less than b.

In Problems 17 to 20 determine whether or not the given graph is orientable, and if it is, then use the procedure given in this section to orient the edges so that the resulting graph is strongly connected.

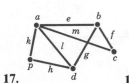

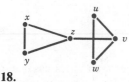

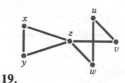

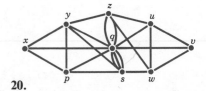

17.
18.
19.
20.

CHAPTER REVIEW

Important Terms			
	vertex	bridge	initial point
	edge	connected component	terminal point
	graph	Eulerian circuit	underlying graph
	parallel edges	Fleury's algorithm	indegree
	loop	Hamiltonian circuit	outdegree
	isolated vertex	tree	directed path
	simple graph	rooted tree	reachable
	degree	child	strongly connected
	complete graph	binary tree	weakly connected
	subgraph	leaf	orientable
	connected	internal vertex	depth first search
	path	descendants	depth first numbering
	simple path	subtree	tournament
	circuit	binary search tree	
	simple circuit	digraph	

True-False Questions *(Answers on page 647)*

T F 1. The sum of the degrees of the vertices of a graph may be any number.

T F 2. If a graph G has n vertices and $n - 1$ edges then G is necessarily connected.

T F 3. If the degree of every vertex in a graph G is even, then G must contain an Eulerian circuit.

T F 4. A Hamiltonian circuit need not include every edge.

T F 5. No tree can contain a circuit.

T F 6. In a strongly connected digraph D any vertex in D is reachable from any other vertex in D.

Fill in the Blanks *(Answers on page 647)*

1. A graph consists of a set V of _____ and a set E of _____.

2. G is a simple graph if G has no _____ and no _____ edges.

3. A circuit that contains every edge is said to be _____.

4. Trees are graphs that are _____-free.

5. In a digraph, every edge has a _____.

6. A graph G is orientable if its edges can be _____ in such a way that the resulting digraph is _____ _____.

**Review
Exercises**

Answers to Odd-Numbered Problems begin on page 647.

1. Can we draw a simple graph with vertices v_1, v_2, v_3, and v_4 of degrees 2, 2, 3, and 3 respectively? Justify your answer.

2. Draw the complete graph K_8.

3. Consult the Figure.
   Find

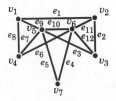

   (a) a simple path between v_1 and v_3 containing v_7.
   (b) a circuit starting at v_1 and containing v_7 and v_3.
   (c) a simple circuit starting at v_1 and containing v_7.

4. How many simple circuits, that contain all vertices, are there in K_4?

5. The Figure shows the outline of a city built on both banks of the river and on the three islands connected to the banks and to each other by the bridge shown. Can a tourist make a round trip through all land masses crossing each bridge once? Justify your answer.

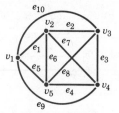

6. Does the graph in the Figure contain a Hamiltonian circuit? Justify your answer.

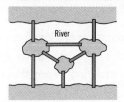

7. Use Fleury's algorithm to find an Eulerian circuit for the graph shown in the Figure.

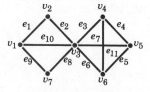

8. (a) Use a binary tree to store alphabetically the elements of the following list: one, two, three, four, five, six.

   (b) Use the tree in (a) to search for the word ten. If this word is not in the list, add it to the list at the right position without losing the alphabetical order.

9. Use a binary tree to represent the following algebraic expression

$$[(a - b)/d] + (d - 1)/a$$

10. Draw a rooted tree that has 3 internal vertices and 2 leaves.

11. Use the graph in the Figure to find two spanning trees.

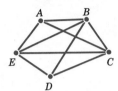

12. Draw a digraph with 5 vertices where each vertex has outdegree 2.

13. Is the digraph in the Figure strongly connected? Why or why not?

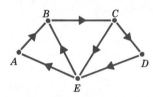

14. Determine whether or not the graph shown in the Figure is orientable. If it is, use the procedure of Section 14.5 to orient the edges in such a way that the resulting graph is strongly connected.

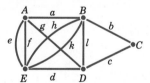

TABLES

Table 1
Amount of an Annuity

(a) Annual Compounding

No. of Periods	8% per annum		10% per annum		12% per annum	
n	A(n, i)	1/A(n, i)	A(n, i)	1/A(n, i)	A(n, i)	1/A(n, i)
1	1.00000000	1.00000000	1.00000000	1.00000000	1.00000000	1.00000000
2	2.08000000	.48076923	2.10000000	.47619048	2.12000000	.47169811
3	3.24640000	.30803351	3.31000000	.30211480	3.37440000	.29634898
4	4.50611200	.22192080	4.64100000	.21547080	4.77932800	.20923444
5	5.86660096	.17045645	6.10510000	.16379748	6.35284736	.15740973
6	7.33592904	.13631539	7.71561000	.12960738	8.11518904	.12322572
7	8.92280336	.11207240	9.48717100	.10540550	10.0890117	.09911774
8	10.6366276	.09401476	11.4358881	.08744402	12.2996931	.08130284
9	12.4875578	.08007971	13.5794769	.07364054	14.7756563	.06767889
10	14.4865625	.06902949	15.9374246	.06274539	17.5487351	.05698416
11	16.6454875	.06007634	18.5311671	.05396314	20.6545833	.04841540
12	18.9771265	.05269502	21.3842838	.04676332	24.1331333	.04143681
13	21.4952966	.04652181	24.5227121	.04077852	28.0291093	.03567720
14	24.2149203	.04129685	27.9749834	.03574622	32.3926024	.03087125
15	27.1521139	.03682954	31.7724817	.03147378	37.2797147	.02682424
16	30.3242830	.03297687	35.9497299	.02781662	42.7532804	.02339002
17	33.7502257	.02962943	40.5447029	.02466413	48.8836741	.02045673
18	37.4502437	.02670210	45.5991731	.02193022	55.7497150	.01793731
19	41.4462632	.02412763	51.1590904	.01954687	63.4396808	.01576300
20	45.7619643	.02185221	57.2749995	.01745962	72.0524424	.01387878
21	50.4229214	.01983225	64.0024994	.01562439	81.6987355	.01224009
22	55.4567552	.01803207	71.4027494	.01400506	92.5025838	.01081051
23	60.8932956	.01642217	79.5430243	.01257181	104.602894	.00955996
24	66.7647592	.01497796	88.4973268	.01129978	118.155241	.00846344
25	73.1059400	.01367878	98.3470594	.01016807	133.333870	.00749997
26	79.9544151	.01250713	109.181765	.00915904	150.333934	.00665186
27	87.3507684	.01144810	121.099942	.00825764	169.374007	.00590409
28	95.3388298	.01048891	134.209936	.00745101	190.698887	.00524387
29	103.965936	.00961854	148.630930	.00672807	214.582754	.00466021
30	113.283211	.00882743	164.494023	.00607925	241.332684	.00414366
31	123.345868	.00810728	181.943425	.00549621	271.292606	.00368606
32	134.213537	.00745081	201.137767	.00497172	304.847719	.00328033
33	145.950620	.00685163	222.251442	.00449941	342.429446	.00292031
34	158.626670	.00630411	245.476699	.00407371	384.520979	.00260064
35	172.316804	.00580326	271.024368	.00368971	431.663496	.00231662
36	187.102148	.00534467	299.126805	.00334306	484.463116	.00206414
37	203.070320	.00492440	330.039486	.00302994	543.598690	.00183959
38	220.315945	.00453894	364.043434	.00274692	609.830533	.00163980
39	238.941221	.00418513	401.447778	.00249098	684.010197	.00146197
40	259.056519	.00386016	442.592556	.00225941	767.091420	.00130363

Table 1 (continued)

(b) Monthly Compounding

No. of Periods n	8% per annum		10% per annum		12% per annum	
	A(n, i)	1/A(n, i)	A(n, i)	1/A(n, i)	A(n, i)	1/A(n, i)
12	12.4499260	.08032176	12.5655681	.07958255	12.6825030	.07884879
24	25.9331897	.03856062	26.4469154	.03781159	26.9734649	.03707347
36	40.5355577	.02466970	41.7818211	.02393385	43.0768784	.02321431
48	56.3499150	.01774626	58.7224919	.01702925	61.2226078	.01633384
60	73.4768562	.01360973	77.4370723	.01291371	81.6696699	.01224445
72	92.0253250	.01086657	98.1113137	.01019250	104.709931	.00955019
84	112.113307	.00891955	120.950418	.00826785	130.672274	.00765273
96	133.868583	.00747001	146.181076	.00684083	159.927293	.00625284
108	157.429535	.00635205	174.053713	.00574535	192.892579	.00518423
120	182.946035	.00546609	204.844979	.00488174	230.038689	.00434709
132	210.580392	.00474878	238.860493	.00418654	271.895856	.00367788
144	240.508386	.00415786	276.437876	.00361745	319.061559	.00313419
156	272.920390	.00366407	317.950103	.00314515	372.209054	.00268666
168	308.022573	.00324652	363.809201	.00274869	432.096982	.00231430
180	346.038221	.00288985	414.470347	.00241272	499.580198	.00200168
192	387.209149	.00258258	470.436376	.00212569	575.621974	.00173725
204	431.797243	.00231590	532.262781	.00187877	661.307751	.00151216
216	480.086127	.00208296	600.563217	.00166510	757.860630	.00131950
228	532.382965	.00187835	676.015602	00147926	866.658830	.00115386
240	589.020414	.00169773	759.368837	.00131688	989.255365	.00101086
252	650.358744	.00153761	851.450246	.00117447	1127.40021	.00088700
264	716.788125	.00139511	953.173781	.00104913	1283.06528	.00077938
276	788.731112	.00126786	1065.54910	.00093848	1458.47257	.00068565
288	866.645331	.00115387	1189.69158	.00084055	1656.12591	.00060382
300	951.026392	.00105150	1326.83341	.00075367	1878.84663	.00053224
312	1042.41104	.00095931	1478.33577	.00067644	2129.81391	.00046952
324	1141.38057	.00087613	1645.70241	.00060764	2412.61013	.00041449
336	1248.56452	.00080092	1830.59453	.00054627	2731.27198	.00036613
348	1364.64468	.00073279	2034.84726	.00049144	3090.34813	.00032359
360	1490.35944	.00067098	2260.48793	.00044238	3494.96413	.00028613

Table 2
Present Value of an Annuity
(a) Annual Compounding

No. of Periods	8% per annum		10% per annum		12% per annum	
n	$P(n, i)$	$1/P(n, i)$	$P(n, i)$	$1/P(n, i)$	$P(n, i)$	$1/P(n, i)$
1	0.92592593	1.08000000	.90909091	1.10000000	.89285714	1.12000000
2	1.78326475	.56076923	1.73553719	.57619048	1.69005102	.59169811
3	2.57709699	.38803351	2.48685199	.40211480	2.40183127	.41634898
4	3.31212684	.30192080	3.16986545	.31547080	3.03734935	.32923444
5	3.99271004	.25045645	3.79078677	.26379748	3.60477620	.27740973
6	4.62287966	.21631539	4.35526070	.22960738	4.11140732	.24322572
7	5.20637006	.19207240	4.86841882	.20540550	4.56375654	.21911774
8	5.74663894	.17401476	5.33492620	.18744402	4.96763977	.20130284
9	6.24688791	.16007971	5.75902382	.17364054	5.32824979	.18767889
10	6.71008140	.14902949	6.14456711	.16274539	5.65022303	.17698416
11	7.13896426	.14007634	6.49506101	.15396314	5.93769913	.16841540
12	7.53607802	.13269502	6.81369182	.14676332	6.19437423	.16143681
13	7.90377594	.12652181	7.10335620	.14077852	6.42354842	.15567720
14	8.24423698	.12129685	7.36668746	.13574622	6.62816823	.15087125
15	8.55947869	.11682954	7.60607951	.13147378	6.81086449	.14682424
16	8.85136916	.11297687	7.82370864	.12781662	6.97398615	.14339002
17	9.12163811	.10962943	8.02155331	.12466413	7.11963049	.14045673
18	9.37188714	.10670210	8.20141210	.12193022	7.24967008	.13793731
19	9.60359920	.10412763	8.36492009	.11954687	7.36577686	.13576300
20	9.81814741	.10185221	8.51356372	.11745962	7.46944362	.13387878
21	10.0168032	.09983225	8.64869429	.11562439	7.56200324	.13224009
22	10.2007437	.09803207	8.77154026	.11400506	7.64464575	.13081051
23	10.3710589	.09642217	8.88321842	.11257181	7.71843370	.12955997
24	10.5287583	.09497796	8.98474402	.11129978	7.78431581	.12846344
25	10.6747762	.09367878	9.07704002	.11016807	7.84313911	.12749997
26	10.8099780	.09250713	9.16094547	.10915904	7.89565992	.12665186
27	10.9351648	.09144810	9.23722316	.10825764	7.94255350	.12590409
28	11.0510785	.09048891	9.30656651	.10745101	7.98442277	.12524387
29	11.1584060	.08961854	9.36960591	.10672807	8.02180604	.12466021
30	11.2577833	.08882743	9.42691447	.10607925	8.05518397	.12414366
31	11.3497994	.08810728	9.47901315	.10549621	8.08498569	.12368606
32	11.4349994	.08745081	9.52637559	.10497172	8.11159436	.12328033
33	11.5138884	.08685163	9.56943236	.10449941	8.13535211	.12292031
34	11.5869337	.08630411	9.60857487	.10407371	8.15656438	.12260064
35	11.6545682	.08580326	9.64415897	.10368971	8.17550391	.12231662
36	11.7171928	.08534467	9.67650816	.10334306	8.19241421	.12206414
37	11.7751785	.08492440	9.70591651	.10302994	8.20751269	.12183959
38	11.8288690	.08453894	9.73265137	.10274692	8.22099347	.12163980
39	11.8785824	.08418513	9.75695579	.10249098	8.23302988	.12146197
40	11.9246133	.08386016	9.77905072	.10225941	8.24377668	.12130363

Table 2 (continued)

(b) Monthly Compounding

No. of Periods n	8% per annum		10% per annum		12% per annum	
	$P(n, i)$	$1/P(n, i)$	$P(n, i)$	$1/P(n, i)$	$P(n, i)$	$1/P(n, i)$
12	11.4957818	.08698843	11.3745084	.08791589	11.2550775	.08884879
24	22.1105436	.04522729	21.6708548	.04614493	21.2433873	.04707347
36	31.9118055	.03133637	30.9912356	.03226719	30.1075050	.03321431
48	40.9619129	.02441292	39.4281601	.02536258	37.9739595	.02633384
60	49.3184333	.02027639	47.0653691	.02124704	44.9550384	.02224445
72	57.0345221	.01753324	53.9786655	.01852584	51.1503915	.01955019
84	64.1592611	.01558621	60.2366674	.01660118	56.6484528	.01765273
96	70.7379704	.01413668	65.9014885	.01517416	61.5277030	.01625284
108	76.8124971	.01301871	71.0293549	.01407869	65.8577898	.01518423
120	82.4214808	.01213276	75.6711634	.01321507	69.7005220	.01434709
132	87.6006002	.01141545	79.8729861	.01251988	73.1107518	.01367788
144	92.3827995	.01082453	83.6765283	.01195078	76.1371575	.01313419
156	96.7984979	.01033074	87.1195419	.01147848	78.8229389	.01268666
168	100.875784	.00991318	90.2362006	.01108203	81.2064335	.01231430
180	104.640592	.00955652	93.0574389	.01074605	83.3216640	.01200168
192	108.116871	.00924925	95.6112588	.01045902	85.1988236	.01173725
204	111.326733	.00898257	97.9230083	.01021210	86.8647075	.01151216
216	114.290596	.00874963	100.015633	.00999843	88.3430948	.01131950
228	117.027313	.00854501	101.909902	.00981259	89.6550886	.01115386
240	119.554292	.00836400	103.624619	.00965022	90.8194164	.01101086
252	121.887607	.00820428	105.176801	.00950780	91.8526982	.01088700
264	124.042099	.00806178	106.581856	.00938246	92.7696833	.01077938
276	126.031475	.00793453	107.853730	.00927182	93.5834610	.01068565
288	127.868388	.00782054	109.005045	.00917389	94.0356475	.01060382
300	129.564523	.00771816	110.047230	.00908701	94.9465513	.01053224
312	131.130668	.00762598	110.990629	.00900977	95.5153208	.01046952
324	132.576786	.00754280	111.844605	.00894098	96.0200749	.01041449
336	133.912076	.00746759	112.617635	.00887960	96.4680186	.01036613
348	135.145031	.00739946	113.317392	.00882477	96.8655458	.01032359
360	136.283494	.00733765	113.950820	.00877572	97.2183311	.01028613

Table 3
Normal Curve Table
Z = Z-score

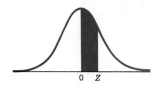

An entry in the table is the area under the curve between $Z = 0$ and a positive value of Z. Areas for negative values of Z are obtained by symmetry.

Z	0.00	0.01	0.02	0.03	0.04	0.05	0.06	0.07	0.08	0.09
0.0	0.0000	0.0040	0.0080	0.0120	0.0160	0.0199	0.0239	0.0279	0.0319	0.0359
0.1	0.0398	0.0438	0.0478	0.0517	0.0557	0.0596	0.0636	0.0675	0.0714	0.0753
0.2	0.0793	0.0832	0.0871	0.0910	0.0948	0.0987	0.1026	0.1064	0.1103	0.1141
0.3	0.1179	0.1217	0.1255	0.1293	0.1331	0.1368	0.1406	0.1433	0.1480	0.1517
0.4	0.1554	0.1591	0.1628	0.1664	0.1700	0.1736	0.1772	0.1808	0.1844	0.1879
0.5	0.1915	0.1950	0.1985	0.2019	0.2054	0.2088	0.2123	0.2157	0.2190	0.2224
0.6	0.2257	0.2291	0.2324	0.2357	0.2389	0.2422	0.2454	0.2486	0.2517	0.2549
0.7	0.2580	0.2611	0.2642	0.2673	0.2703	0.2734	0.2764	0.2794	0.2823	0.2852
0.8	0.2881	0.2910	0.2939	0.2967	0.2995	0.3023	0.3051	0.3078	0.3106	0.3133
0.9	0.3159	0.3186	0.3212	0.3238	0.3264	0.3289	0.3315	0.3340	0.3365	0.3389
1.0	0.3413	0.3438	0.3461	0.3485	0.3508	0.3531	0.3554	0.3577	0.3599	0.3621
1.1	0.3642	0.3665	0.3686	0.3708	0.3729	0.3749	0.3770	0.3790	0.3810	0.3830
1.2	0.3849	0.3869	0.3888	0.3907	0.3925	0.3944	0.3962	0.3980	0.3997	0.4015
1.3	0.4032	0.4049	0.4066	0.4082	0.4099	0.4115	0.4131	0.4147	0.4162	0.4177
1.4	0.4192	0.4207	0.4222	0.4236	0.4251	0.4265	0.4279	0.4292	0.4306	0.4319
1.5	0.4332	0.4345	0.4357	0.4370	0.4382	0.4394	0.4406	0.4418	0.4429	0.4441
1.6	0.4452	0.4463	0.4474	0.4484	0.4495	0.4505	0.4515	0.4525	0.4535	0.4545
1.7	0.4554	0.4564	0.4573	0.4582	0.4591	0.4599	0.4608	0.4616	0.4625	0.4633
1.8	0.4641	0.4649	0.4656	0.4664	0.4671	0.4678	0.4686	0.4693	0.4699	0.4706
1.9	0.4713	0.4719	0.4726	0.4732	0.4738	0.4744	0.4750	0.4756	0.4761	0.4767
2.0	0.4772	0.4778	0.4783	0.4788	0.4793	0.4798	0.4803	0.4808	0.4812	0.4817
2.1	0.4821	0.4826	0.4830	0.4834	0.4838	0.4842	0.4846	0.4850	0.4854	0.4857
2.2	0.4861	0.4864	0.4868	0.4871	0.4875	0.4878	0.4881	0.4884	0.4887	0.4890
2.3	0.4893	0.4896	0.4898	0.4901	0.4904	0.4906	0.4909	0.4911	0.4913	0.4916
2.4	0.4918	0.4920	0.4922	0.4925	0.4927	0.4929	0.4931	0.4932	0.4934	0.4936
2.5	0.4938	0.4940	0.4941	0.4943	0.4945	0.4946	0.4948	0.4949	0.4951	0.4952
2.6	0.4953	0.4955	0.4956	0.4957	0.4959	0.4960	0.4961	0.4962	0.4963	0.4964
2.7	0.4965	0.4966	0.4967	0.4968	0.4969	0.4970	0.4971	0.4972	0.4973	0.4974
2.8	0.4974	0.4975	0.4976	0.4977	0.4977	0.4978	0.4079	0.4979	0.4980	0.4981
2.9	0.4981	0.4982	0.4982	0.4983	0.4984	0.4984	0.4985	0.4985	0.4986	0.4986
3.0	0.4987	0.4987	0.4987	0.4988	0.4988	0.4989	0.4989	0.4989	0.4990	0.4990

ANSWERS TO ODD-NUMBERED PROBLEMS

CHAPTER 1

Exercise 1.1 (page 11)

1. 0.5 **3.** 1.625 **5.** 1.333 . . . **7.** 0.1666 . . . **9.** 45% **11.** 112% **13.** 6%
15. 0.25% **17.** 0.42 **19.** 0.002 **21.** 0.00001 **23.** 0.734 **25.** $\frac{1}{20}$ **27.** $\frac{3}{4}$ **29.** 150
31. 18 **33.** $x = 1$ **35.** $x = 6$ **37.** $x = -1$ **39.** $x = -4$ **41.** $x = 3$ **43.** $x = 1$
45. $x = 4$ or $x = -3$ **47.** $x = 3$ or $x = 2$ **49.** $x = 4$ or $x = -4$ **51.** $x = 9$ **53.** $x = \frac{1}{8}$
55. $x = -9$ **57.** $x = 2$ **59.** $x = 2$ **61.** $x = 5$ **63.** $\frac{1}{3} > 0.33$ ($\frac{1}{3} = 0.333 \ldots$) **65.** $3 = \sqrt{9}$
67. $x \le -1$ **69.** $x \ge -1$ **71.** $x \ge 1$ **73.** $x \le -4$
75. $x < 3$ ⟶ **77.** $x \le 5$ ⟶

Exercise 1.2 (page 15)

1. $A = (4, 2); B = (6, 2); C = (5, 3); D = (-2, 1); E = (-2, -3); F = (3, -2); G = (6, -2); H = (5, 0)$
3. 4 **5.** 1

7. $y = x - 3$

x	0	3	2	-2	4	-4
y	-3	0	-1	-5	1	-7

9. $2x - y = 6$

x	0	3	2	-2	4	-4
y	-6	0	-2	-10	2	-14

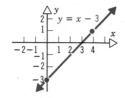

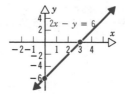

11.

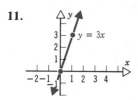

13.

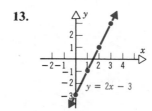

15.

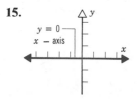

17.

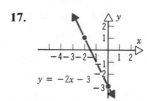

19.
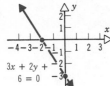
$3x + 2y + 6 = 0$

21.
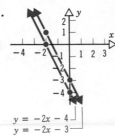
$y = -2x - 4$
$y = -2x - 3$

The lines are parallel.

Exercise 1.3 (page 23)
1. 1   **3.** 2   **5.** $\frac{37}{14}$ **7.** $2x - y + 7 = 0$ **9.** $2x + 3y + 1 = 0$ **11.** $x - 2y + 5 = 0$
13. $3x + y - 3 = 0$ **15.** $x - 2y - 2 = 0$ **17.** $x - 1 = 0$
19. Slope $\frac{3}{2}$, y-intercept -3 **21.** Slope $-\frac{1}{2}$, y-intercept 2   **23.** Slope undefined, no y-intercept

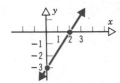
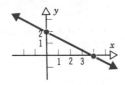
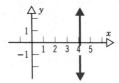

25. $x = 2y$ **27.** $x + y = 2$ **29.** $°F = \frac{9}{5}°C + 32$ or $°C = \frac{5}{9}(F - 32)$; $\frac{5}{9}(70 - 32) = \frac{190}{9} = 21.111 \ldots$

Exercise 1.4 (page 30)
1. $m_1 = m_2 = -1$ **3.** $m_1 = m_2 = \frac{2}{3}$ **5.** $(x, y) = (3, 2)$ **7.** $(x, y) = (9, \frac{13}{2})$ **9.** $(x, y) = (-\frac{1}{9}, \frac{7}{3})$
11. $(x, y) = (1, 2)$ **13.** $(x, y) = (0, 2)$ **15.** $(x, y) = (1, 3)$ **17.** $(x, y) = (-2, 0)$ **19.** No solution
21. Infinitely many solutions   **23.** One solution   **25.** No solution   **27.** $y = 2x$
29. 20 caramels, 30 creams; increase the number of caramels to increase profits.
31. \$31,250 in bonds; \$18,750 in savings certificates
33. 8 nickels   **35.** 30 cc of 15% acid; 70 cc of 5% acid   **37.** 3260 adults

Exercise 1.5 (page 38)
1. (a) $1000 + 180t$ (b) 1090   (c) 1180   (d) 1360
3. $x = 30$ **5.** $x = 500$ **7.** $x = 1200$ items

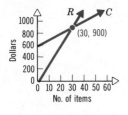
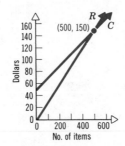
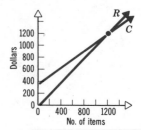

9. (a) \$80,000   (b) \$95,000   (c) \$105,000   (d) \$120,000

11. $p = \$1$ **13.** $p = \$10$ **15.** $p = 1$

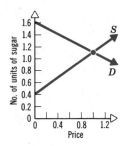

True–False Questions (page 40)
 1. F   **2.** T   **3.** T   **4.** F

Fill in the Blanks (page 40)
 1. x-coordinate, y-coordinate   **2.** Repeating, terminates   **3.** Undefined, zero   **4.** Negative
 5. Parallel

Review Exercises (page 40)
 1. $x = -7$ **3.** $x = -\frac{11}{3}$ **5.** $x = -11$ **7.** $x \leq 3$ **9.** $x \geq -1$
11. 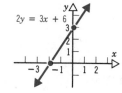   **13.**

15. $x + 2y - 5 = 0$ **17.** $3x + 2y = 0$ **19.** $2x - y + 2 = 0$ **21.** $x - y + 2 = 0$
23. Slope $= -\frac{9}{2}$ **25.** Slope $= -2$
 y-intercept $= 9$ y-intercept $= \frac{9}{2}$

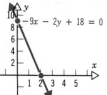

27. No solution   **29.** One solution   **31.** Infinitely many solutions
33. \$46,000 in bonds; \$44,000 in bank
35. (a)   (c) $y - 2800 = -200(x - 85)$
 (b)   (d) 2400

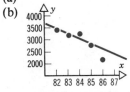

(Using only the last two digits of the date)

Mathematical Questions (page 42)
1. b 2. d 3. d 4. b 5. b 6. b 7. d 8. c 9. c 10. c 11. b 12. b

CHAPTER 2

Exercise 2.1 (page 54)

1. $\begin{bmatrix} 2 & -3 & | & 5 \\ 1 & -1 & | & 3 \end{bmatrix}$ 3. $\begin{bmatrix} 2 & 1 & | & -6 \\ 1 & 1 & | & -1 \end{bmatrix}$ 5. $\begin{bmatrix} 2 & -1 & -1 & | & 0 \\ 1 & -1 & -1 & | & 1 \\ 3 & -1 & 0 & | & 2 \end{bmatrix}$ 7. $\begin{bmatrix} 2 & -3 & 1 & | & 7 \\ 1 & 1 & -1 & | & 1 \\ 2 & 2 & -3 & | & -4 \end{bmatrix}$

9. $\begin{bmatrix} 4 & -1 & 2 & -1 & | & 4 \\ 1 & 1 & 0 & 0 & | & -6 \\ 0 & 2 & -1 & 1 & | & 5 \end{bmatrix}$ 11. $R_1 = r_2$ Interchange rows   13. $R_1 = 4r_1$ 15. $\begin{bmatrix} 1 & 0 & 2 \\ 0 & 1 & 4 \\ 3 & 6 & 9 \end{bmatrix}$
$R_2 = r_1$

17. $\begin{bmatrix} 0 & 6 & 3 \\ 0 & 1 & 4 \\ 1 & 0 & 2 \end{bmatrix}$ 19. $\begin{bmatrix} 3 & 6 & 9 \\ 1 & 3 & 7 \\ 1 & 0 & 2 \end{bmatrix}$ 21. $x = 2$ 23. $x = 2$ 25. $x = 2$ 27. $x = 2$
                                                             $y = 4$ $y = 1$ $y = 1$ $y = -3$

29. $x = \frac{1}{2}$ 31. $x = \frac{2}{3}$ 33. $x = 2$ 35. $x = \frac{2}{3}$ 37. $x = 1$ 39. $x = -1$ 41. $x = 2$
$y = \frac{1}{3}$ $y = \frac{2}{3}$ $y = 3$ $y = \frac{1}{3}$ $y = 4$ $y = 1$ $y = -1$
                                                                                     $z = 0$ $z = 2$ $z = 1$

43. $x = 0.5$ 45. $x = \frac{1}{3}$ 47. $x = 1$ 49. No solution
$y = 0.25$ $y = \frac{2}{3}$ $y = 2$
$z = 0.75$ $z = 1$ $z = 0$
                                         $w = 1$

51. Infinitely many solutions $(2x - 3y = 6)$ 53. No solution   55. Unique solution $(x = 1, y = 1)$
57. No solution $(3 \neq 0)$ 59. Infinitely many solutions $(x = 0, y = -6 + z)$
61. $1000 invested at 6%; $2200 invested at 7%; $1800 invested at 8%.

Exercise 2.2 (page 64)
1. Not in reduced row-echelon form   3. Not in reduced row-echelon form
5. Not in reduced row-echelon form   7. In reduced row-echelon form   9. In reduced row-echelon form
11. Infinitely many solutions   13. One solution   15. Infinitely many solutions
17. Infinitely many solutions   19. Infinitely many solutions   21. $x = 2, y = 1$ 23. $x = 1, y = -3$
25. $x_1 = 3, x_2 = 2$ 27. $x_1 = \frac{13}{4}, x_2 = -\frac{1}{2}$ 29. $x_1 = 3, x_2 = 2, x_3 = -4$
31. $x_1 = -17, x_2 = 24, x_3 = 33, x_4 = 14$
33. There are infinitely many solutions, and we can solve for x_1, x_2, and x_3 in terms of x_1:

$$x_1 = \frac{4}{3} + \frac{1}{3} x_4; \quad x_2 = \frac{14}{15} + \frac{11}{15} x_4; \quad x_3 = -\frac{16}{15} - \frac{4}{15} x_4.$$

35. The system is inconsistent.   37. The system is inconsistent.

39.

No. of Liters 10% Solution	No. of Liters 30% Solution	No. of Liters 50% Solution
55	15	30
50	25	25
45	35	20
40	45	15
35	55	10
30	65	5

Exercise 2.3 (page 73)
1. 2×2 3. 2×3 5. 2×1 7. 1×1
9. False. Two equal matrices must have the same dimensions.   11. True   13. True   15. True
17. $x = 4, z = 3$ 19. $x = 5, y = 1$ 21. $\begin{bmatrix} 3 & -5 & 4 \\ 5 & 3 & 3 \end{bmatrix}$ 23. $\begin{bmatrix} 13 & -6 & -7 \\ -6 & 1 & -7 \end{bmatrix}$ 25. $\begin{bmatrix} 9 & -5 & -6 \\ 1 & 1 & -3 \end{bmatrix}$

27. $\begin{bmatrix} -2 & -17 & 32 \\ 28 & 14 & 23 \end{bmatrix}$ 29. $\begin{bmatrix} 5 & -2 & 3 \\ -12 & 1 & -5 \end{bmatrix}$ 31. $x = 4, y = -11, z = 6$

33. (a) $\begin{bmatrix} \frac{5}{2} \\ -1 \\ 4 \end{bmatrix}$ (b) $\begin{bmatrix} \frac{3}{2} \\ -1 \\ 2 \end{bmatrix}$ (c) $\begin{bmatrix} \frac{5}{4} \\ -\frac{1}{2} \\ 2 \end{bmatrix}$ (d) $\begin{bmatrix} \frac{11}{2} \\ 6 \\ 4 \end{bmatrix}$ (e) $\begin{bmatrix} \frac{1}{2} \\ -2 \\ -1 \end{bmatrix}$ (f) $\begin{bmatrix} \frac{9}{8} \\ \frac{3}{4} \\ \frac{1}{2} \end{bmatrix}$

35.
$\frac{1}{2}''$ $1''$ $2''$
Steel $\begin{bmatrix} 25 & 45 & 35 \\ 13 & 20 & 23 \end{bmatrix}$
Aluminum
or
Steel Aluminum
$\frac{1}{2}''$ $\begin{bmatrix} 25 & 13 \\ 45 & 20 \\ 35 & 23 \end{bmatrix}$
$1''$
$2''$

37.
$<\$15,000$ $>\$15,000$
Dem $\begin{bmatrix} 351 & 203 \\ 271 & 215 \\ 73 & 55 \end{bmatrix}$
Rep
Ind
or
Dem Rep Ind
$<\$15,000$ $\begin{bmatrix} 351 & 271 & 73 \\ 203 & 215 & 55 \end{bmatrix}$
$>\$15,000$

39. $k(a_{ij} + b_{ij}) = ka_{ij} + kb_{ij}$

Exercise 2.4 (page 80)
1. Dimension $BA = 3 \times 4$ 3. AB is not defined.   5. $(BA)C$ is not defined.
7. $BA + A$ is defined. Dimension is 3×4 9. $DC + B$ is defined. Dimension is 3×3
11. $\begin{bmatrix} -1 & 10 & -1 \\ -4 & 16 & -8 \end{bmatrix}$ 13. $\begin{bmatrix} 11 & 5 \\ 13 & -9 \end{bmatrix}$ 15. $\begin{bmatrix} 6 & 10 \\ 8 & 2 \\ -4 & 5 \end{bmatrix}$ 17. $\begin{bmatrix} -6 & 42 & -9 \\ 1 & 20 & 6 \\ -7 & 4 & -18 \end{bmatrix}$ 19. $\begin{bmatrix} 3 & -1 \\ 4 & 2 \end{bmatrix}$

21. $\begin{bmatrix} 8 & 4 & 22 \\ 4 & 32 & 16 \end{bmatrix}$ 23. $\begin{bmatrix} -14 & 7 \\ -20 & -6 \end{bmatrix}$ 25. $\begin{bmatrix} 10 & 30 & 37 \\ 15 & 16 & 50 \\ -6 & 20 & -8 \end{bmatrix}$ 27. $AB = \begin{bmatrix} 4 & -2 \\ 6 & 4 \end{bmatrix}$ $BA = \begin{bmatrix} 7 & -3 \\ 7 & 1 \end{bmatrix}$

29. $A = \begin{bmatrix} 2 & 1 \\ -\frac{1}{2} & -\frac{1}{2} \end{bmatrix}$ 31. $\begin{bmatrix} 1 & 2 & 5 \\ 2 & 4 & 10 \\ -1 & -2 & -5 \end{bmatrix}\begin{bmatrix} 1 & 2 & 5 \\ 2 & 4 & 10 \\ -1 & -2 & -5 \end{bmatrix} = \begin{bmatrix} 0 & 0 & 0 \\ 0 & 0 & 0 \\ 0 & 0 & 0 \end{bmatrix}$

33. The possibilities are: $a = 0, b = 0; a = -1, b = 0; a = -\frac{1}{2}, b = \frac{1}{2}; a = -\frac{1}{2}, b = \frac{1}{2}.$ 35. $[\frac{1}{3}, \frac{2}{3}]$
37. (a) PQ represents the matrix of raw materials needed to fill order:
$PQ = [138 \quad 189 \quad 97 \quad 399]$
   (b) QC represents the matrix of costs to produce each product:
$QC = \begin{bmatrix} 311 \\ 653 \\ 614 \end{bmatrix}$
   (c) PQC represents the total cost to produce the order:
$PQC = 13,083$

Exercise 2.5 (page 90)
1. $\begin{bmatrix} 1 & 2 \\ 2 & 3 \end{bmatrix}\begin{bmatrix} -3 & 2 \\ 2 & -1 \end{bmatrix} = \begin{bmatrix} 1 & 0 \\ 0 & 1 \end{bmatrix} = I_2$ 3. $\begin{bmatrix} -1 & -2 \\ 3 & 4 \end{bmatrix}\begin{bmatrix} 2 & 1 \\ -\frac{3}{2} & -\frac{1}{2} \end{bmatrix} = \begin{bmatrix} 1 & 0 \\ 0 & 1 \end{bmatrix} = I_2$

5. $\begin{bmatrix} 1 & 2 & 3 \\ 2 & 3 & 4 \\ 1 & 2 & 1 \end{bmatrix}\begin{bmatrix} -\frac{5}{2} & 2 & -\frac{1}{2} \\ 1 & -1 & 1 \\ \frac{1}{2} & 0 & -\frac{1}{2} \end{bmatrix} = \begin{bmatrix} 1 & 0 & 0 \\ 0 & 1 & 0 \\ 0 & 0 & 1 \end{bmatrix} = I_3$ 7. $\begin{bmatrix} 3 & -5 \\ -1 & 2 \end{bmatrix}$ 9. $\begin{bmatrix} 4 & -1 \\ 3 & -1 \end{bmatrix}$

11. $\begin{bmatrix} 1.5 & -0.5 \\ -2 & 1 \end{bmatrix}$ **13.** $\begin{bmatrix} 0 & 0 & 1 \\ 0 & 1 & 0 \\ 1 & 0 & 0 \end{bmatrix}$ **15.** $\begin{bmatrix} \frac{4}{9} & \frac{1}{9} & \frac{1}{9} \\ \frac{4}{3} & -\frac{2}{3} & \frac{1}{3} \\ \frac{7}{9} & -\frac{5}{9} & \frac{4}{9} \end{bmatrix}$ **17.** $\begin{bmatrix} 1 & -1 & 2 \\ -1 & 2 & -3 \\ -1 & 1 & -1 \end{bmatrix}$

19. $\begin{bmatrix} 2 & -1 & -1 & -2 \\ -1 & 1 & 1 & 2 \\ -2 & 1 & 2 & 3 \\ -1 & 1 & 1 & 1 \end{bmatrix}$ **21.** $\begin{bmatrix} 4 & 6 & | & 1 & 0 \\ 2 & 3 & | & 0 & 1 \end{bmatrix} \rightarrow \begin{bmatrix} 4 & 6 & | & 1 & 0 \\ \boxed{0 & 0} & | & -\frac{1}{2} & 0 \end{bmatrix}$

23. $\begin{bmatrix} -8 & 4 & | & 1 & 0 \\ -4 & 2 & | & 0 & 1 \end{bmatrix} \rightarrow \begin{bmatrix} -8 & 4 & | & 1 & 0 \\ \boxed{0 & 0} & | & -\frac{1}{2} & 0 \end{bmatrix}$ **25.** $\begin{bmatrix} 1 & 1 & 1 & | & 1 & 0 & 0 \\ 3 & -4 & 2 & | & 0 & 1 & 0 \\ \boxed{0} & \boxed{0} & \boxed{0} & | & 0 & 0 & 1 \end{bmatrix}$ **27.** $\begin{bmatrix} 2 & -1 \\ -1 & 1 \end{bmatrix}$

29. $\begin{bmatrix} \frac{1}{3} & \frac{1}{3} \\ 0 & \frac{1}{2} \end{bmatrix}$ **31.** No inverse **33.** $x = 2, y = 4$ **35.** $x = 2, y = 1$ **37.** $x = \frac{1}{2}, y = \frac{1}{3}$

39. $x = 2, y = 3$ **41.** $x = 1, y = 4, z = 0$ **43.** $x = 2, y = -1, z = 1$ **45.** $x = \frac{1}{3}, y = \frac{2}{3}, z = 1$

47. $x = 1, y = 1$ **49.** $x = 2, y = 1$

51. $\begin{bmatrix} a & b \\ c & d \end{bmatrix}\begin{bmatrix} d & -b \\ -c & a \end{bmatrix} = \begin{bmatrix} ad - bc & 0 \\ 0 & -bc + ad \end{bmatrix} = \begin{bmatrix} \Delta & 0 \\ 0 & \Delta \end{bmatrix}$; thus, $\begin{bmatrix} a & b \\ c & d \end{bmatrix}\begin{bmatrix} \frac{d}{\Delta} & \frac{-b}{\Delta} \\ \frac{-c}{\Delta} & \frac{a}{\Delta} \end{bmatrix} = \begin{bmatrix} 1 & 0 \\ 0 & 1 \end{bmatrix}$

Exercise 2.6A (page 97)

1. $A = C = \$10,000, B = \frac{3}{4}C = \$7500$ **3.** $A = \frac{6}{15}C, B = \frac{11}{15}C$, where $C = \$10,000$ **5.** $\begin{bmatrix} 203 \\ 166.977 \\ 137.847 \end{bmatrix}$

7. $x_1 = 0.8x_4 = 8000, x_2 = 0.72x_4 = 7200, x_3 = 0.48x_4 = 4800, x_4 = \$10,000$ **9.** $x = \begin{bmatrix} 160 \\ 75.38 \end{bmatrix}$

Exercise 2.6C (page 106)

1. $\begin{bmatrix} 4 & 3 \\ 1 & 1 \\ 2 & 0 \end{bmatrix}$ **3.** $\begin{bmatrix} 1 & 0 & 1 \\ 11 & 12 & 4 \end{bmatrix}$ **5.** $[8 \ 6 \ 3]$ **7.** (a) $y = \frac{54}{33}x + \frac{27}{5}$ (b) 17.74

9. $y = \frac{334}{223}x + \frac{8058}{223}$ **11.** (2) is symmetric; yes

True–False Questions (page 112)
1. T **2.** F **3.** F **4.** T

Fill in the Blanks
1. 3×2 **2.** One, infinite **3.** Rows, columns

Review Exercises (page 112)

1. $\begin{bmatrix} -1 & 3 & 16 \\ 3 & 15 & 8 \\ 5 & 10 & 29 \end{bmatrix}$ **3.** $\begin{bmatrix} -3 & 9 & 48 \\ 9 & 45 & 24 \\ 15 & 30 & 87 \end{bmatrix}$ **5.** $\begin{bmatrix} -9 & -9 & -6 \\ -3 & 3 & -6 \\ -3 & -6 & 39 \end{bmatrix}$ **7.** $\begin{bmatrix} -20 & 0 & 70 \\ 10 & 80 & 30 \\ 20 & 40 & 210 \end{bmatrix}$

9. $\begin{bmatrix} -\frac{7}{2} & -\frac{3}{2} & \frac{25}{2} \\ 3 & \frac{9}{2} & \frac{11}{2} \\ -\frac{37}{2} & -10 & 19 \end{bmatrix}$ **11.** $\begin{bmatrix} 19 & 36 & 38 \\ 26 & 77 & 73 \\ 73 & 160 & 206 \end{bmatrix}$ **13.** $\begin{bmatrix} 16 & 32 & 27 \\ 16 & 10 & 19 \\ -104 & -80 & -113 \end{bmatrix}$ **15.** $\begin{bmatrix} \frac{1}{3} & 0 \\ \frac{2}{3} & 1 \end{bmatrix}$

17. $\begin{bmatrix} 1 & -3 & 2 \\ -3 & 3 & -1 \\ 2 & -1 & 0 \end{bmatrix}$ **19.** $\begin{bmatrix} \frac{1}{16} & \frac{1}{32} & \frac{1}{4} \\ \frac{3}{16} & \frac{3}{32} & -\frac{1}{4} \\ -\frac{3}{16} & \frac{13}{32} & \frac{1}{4} \end{bmatrix}$

21. $\left[\begin{array}{ccc|ccc} 1 & 2 & -3 & 1 & 0 & 0 \\ 0 & -2 & 14 & -4 & 1 & 0 \\ \hline 0 & 0 & 0 & 3 & 0 & 1 \end{array}\right]$ **23.** $\left[\begin{array}{ccc|c} 1 & 1 & -1 & 2 \\ 0 & 1 & -1 & 1 \\ \hline 0 & 0 & 0 & \frac{1}{2} \end{array}\right]$

The matrix has no inverse. There is no solution.

25. $x_1 = \frac{23}{16}, x_2 = -\frac{73}{32}, x_3 = -\frac{9}{4}$ **27.** $x_1 = 29, x_2 = 8, x_3 = -24$

29. $x_1 = \frac{10}{7} + \frac{3}{7}x_3, x_2 = -\frac{9}{7} + \frac{5}{7}x_3; x_1 = \frac{10}{7}, x_2 = -\frac{9}{7}, x_3 = 0; x_1 = \frac{13}{7}, x_2 = -\frac{4}{7}, x_3 = 1; x_1 = \frac{16}{7}, x_2 = \frac{1}{7}, x_3 = 2$

31. $x_1 = 1 - \frac{3}{5}x_3, x_2 = 2 + \frac{4}{5}x_3; x_1 = 1, x_2 = 2, x_3 = 0; x_1 = \frac{2}{5}, x_2 = \frac{14}{5}, x_3 = 1; x_1 = -\frac{1}{5}, x_2 = \frac{18}{5}, x_3 = 2$

33. $\left[\begin{array}{cc|c} 1 & 0 & 1 \\ 0 & 1 & \frac{1}{2} \\ \hline 0 & 0 & \frac{7}{2} \end{array}\right]$ There is no solution. **35.** $y = -z, x = w$ **35.** A correct answer.

CHAPTER 3

Exercise 3.2 (page 124)

1. $x \geq 0$

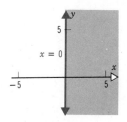

3. $x \geq 0, y \geq 0$

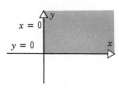

5. $2y - 3y \leq -6$

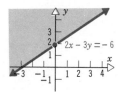

7. $5x + y \leq -10$

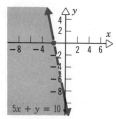

9. $x \geq 5$

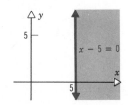

11. $x \geq 0, y \geq 0$ Bounded,
$x + y \leq 2$ Vertices: $(0, 0)$, $(0, 2)$, $(2, 0)$

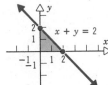

13. $x \geq 0, y \geq 0$ Bounded,
$x + y \geq 2$ Vertices: (0, 2),
$2x + 3y \leq 6$ (2, 0), (3, 0)

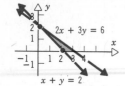

15. $x \geq 0, y \geq 0$ Bounded,
$2 \leq x + y, x + y \leq 8$ Vertices: (0, 2), (0, 8),
$2x + y \leq 10$ (2, 6), (5, 0), (2, 0)

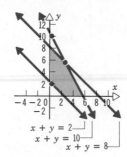

17. $x \geq 0, y \geq 0$
$x + y \geq 2, 2x + 3y \leq 12$
$3x + y < 12$
Bounded, Vertices:
$(0, 2), (0, 4), (\frac{22}{7}, \frac{12}{7}), (4, 0), (2, 0)$

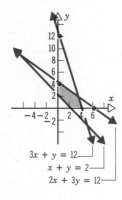

19. $x \geq 0, y \geq 0$
$1 \leq x + 2y, x + 2y \leq 10$
Bounded, Vertices: (0, 1),
(0, 5), (10, 0), (1, 0)

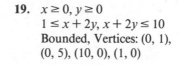
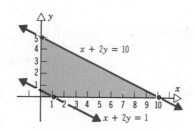

Exercise 3.3 (page 136)

1. The maximum is 38 at (7, 8).   **3.** The maximum is 71 at (7, 8).
  The minimum is 10 at (2, 2).   The minimum is 16 at (8, 1).

5. The maximum is 55 at (7, 8).
  The minimum is 14 at points on the line segment joining (2, 2) and (8, 1).

7. The maximum is 14 at (0, 2).   **9.** The maximum is 15 at (3, 0).   **11.** The maximum is 56 at (0, 8).

13. $z = 5x + 7y$ has no maximum under the conditions.   **15.** The minimum is 4 at (2, 0).

17. The minimum is 4 at (2, 0).   **19.** The minimum is $\frac{3}{2}$ at (0, $\frac{1}{2}$).

21. The minimum is $\frac{20}{3}$ at ($\frac{10}{3}$, $\frac{10}{3}$).
  The maximum is 10 at any point on the line segment between (0, 10) and (10, 0).

23. The minimum is 20 at (0, 10); the maximum is 50 at (10, 0).

25. The minimum is $\frac{70}{3}$ at ($\frac{10}{3}$, $\frac{10}{3}$); the maximum is 40 at (10, 0).

27. 90 packages of the low-grade mixture and 105 packages of the high-grade mixture.

29. 40 standard models and no deluxe models should be manufactured.

31. 15 units of the first product and 25 units of second product maximizes profit at $2100.

33. He should add 5 ounces of Supplement I and 1 ounce of Supplement II to each 100 ounces of feed.

35. 500 pounds of picnic patties and $83\frac{1}{3}$ pounds of hamburger should be made.
37. The price of the high-grade carpet should be between $520 and $620 per roll.

True–False Questions (page 140)
   1. T   **2.** F   **3.** T   **4.** T   **5.** T   **6.** F

Fill in the Blanks
   1. Half plane   **2.** Objective function   **3.** Feasible   **4.** Bounded   **5.** Vertex

Review Exercises (page 140)
   1. $x - 3y < 0$

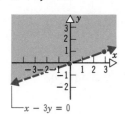

   3. $5x + y \geq 10$

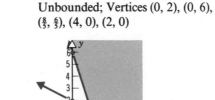

5. $x \geq 0$, $y \geq 0$, $3x + 2y \leq 12$, $x + y \geq 1$
   Bounded; Vertices $(0, 1)$,
   $(0, 6)$, $(4, 0)$, $(1, 0)$

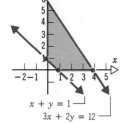

7. $x \geq 0$, $y \geq 0$, $x + 2y \geq 4$, $3x + y \geq 6$
   Unbounded; Vertices $(0, 2)$, $(0, 6)$,
   $(\frac{8}{5}, \frac{6}{5})$, $(4, 0)$, $(2, 0)$

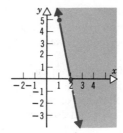

9. $x \geq 0$, $y \geq 0$, $3x + 2y \geq 6$, $3x + 2y \leq 12$, $x + 2y \leq 8$

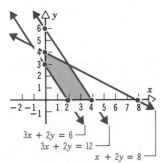

   Bounded; Vertices $(0, 3)$,
   $(2, 3)$, $(4, 0)$, $(2, 0)$

Problems 11–18 use the following graph:

$x \geq 0$, $y \geq 0$, $x + 2y \leq 40$, $x + y \geq 10$

The vertices are (0, 10), (0, 20), $(\frac{40}{3}, \frac{40}{3})$, (20, 0), (10, 0).

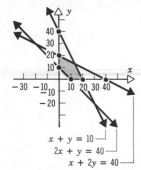

$x + y = 10$
$2x + y = 40$
$x + 2y = 40$

11. Maximum is $\frac{80}{3}$ at $(\frac{40}{3}, \frac{40}{3})$.   **13.**   Minimum is 20 at (0, 10).
15. Maximum is 40 at any point on the line segment between $(\frac{40}{3}, \frac{40}{3})$ and (20, 0).
17. Maximum is 20 at (10, 0).
19. Maximum is 235 at (5, 8); minimum is 60 at any point on the line segment between (0, 3) and (4, 0).
21. Maximum is 195 at (5, 6); minimum is 150 at (2, 6).
23. She should buy 7.5 pounds of A and 11.25 pounds of B.
25. Maximum profit of \$1760 with 8 downhill skis and 24 cross-country skies.

Mathematical Questions (page 141)
  1. b **2.** a **3.** c **4.** c **5.** d **6.** c

CHAPTER 4

Exercise 4.1 (page 156)
  1. Standard form   **3.** Not in standard form   **5.** Not in standard form   **7.** Not in standard form
  9. Standard form   **11.** Cannot be modified so as to be in standard form.
13. Cannot be modified so as to be in standard form.
15. Can be modified to:
Maximize $P = 2x_1 + x_2 + 3x_3$
Subject to the constraints

$x_1 - x_2 - x_3 \leq 6$ $x_1 \geq 0, x_2 \geq 0$
$-2x_1 + 3x_2 \leq 12$ $x_3 \geq 0$

17.
$$\begin{array}{cccccccc} & x_1 & x_2 & x_3 & s_1 & s_2 & s_3 & P \\ & 5 & 2 & 1 & 1 & 0 & 0 & 0 \,|\, 20 \\ & 6 & 1 & 4 & 0 & 1 & 0 & 0 \,|\, 24 \\ & 1 & 1 & 4 & 0 & 0 & 1 & 0 \,|\, 16 \\ \hline & -2 & -1 & -3 & 0 & 0 & 0 & 1 \,|\, 0 \end{array}$$

19.
$$\begin{array}{ccccccc} & x_1 & x_2 & s_1 & s_2 & s_3 & P \\ & 2.2 & -1.8 & 1 & 0 & 0 & 0 \,|\, 5 \\ & 0.8 & 1.2 & 0 & 1 & 0 & 0 \,|\, 2.5 \\ & 1 & 1 & 0 & 0 & 1 & 0 \,|\, 0.1 \\ \hline & -3 & -5 & 0 & 0 & 0 & 1 \,|\, 0 \end{array}$$

21.
$$\begin{array}{ccccccc} & x_1 & x_2 & x_3 & s_1 & s_2 & P \\ & 1 & 1 & 1 & 1 & 0 & 0 \,|\, 50 \\ & 3 & 2 & 1 & 0 & 1 & 0 \,|\, 10 \\ \hline & -2 & -3 & -1 & 0 & 0 & 1 \,|\, 0 \end{array}$$

23.
$$\begin{array}{cccccccc} & x_1 & x_2 & x_3 & s_1 & s_2 & s_3 & P \\ & 3 & 1 & 4 & 1 & 0 & 0 & 0 \,|\, 5 \\ & 1 & 1 & 0 & 0 & 1 & 0 & 0 \,|\, 5 \\ & 2 & -1 & 1 & 0 & 0 & 1 & 0 \,|\, 6 \\ \hline & -3 & -4 & -2 & 0 & 0 & 0 & 1 \,|\, 0 \end{array}$$

25. $s_1 = 300 - x_1 - 2x_2$
$s_2 = 480 - 3x_1 - 2x_2$
$P = x_1 + x_2$

$$\begin{bmatrix} \frac{1}{2} & 1 & \frac{1}{2} & 0 & 0 & | & 150 \\ 2 & 0 & -1 & 1 & 0 & | & 180 \\ \hline 0 & 0 & 1 & 0 & 1 & | & 300 \end{bmatrix}$$

$x_1 = 150 - \frac{1}{2}x_1 - \frac{1}{2}s_1$
$s_2 = 180 - 2x_1 + s_1$
$P = 300 - s_1$

27. $s_1 = 24 - x_1 - 2x_2 - 4x_3$
$s_2 = 32 - 2x_1 + x_2 - x_3$
$s_3 = 18 - 3x_1 - 2x_2 - 4x_3$
$P = x_1 + 2x_2 + 3x_3$

$$\begin{bmatrix} -2 & 0 & 0 & 1 & 0 & -1 & 0 & | & 6 \\ \frac{7}{2} & 0 & 3 & 0 & 1 & \frac{1}{2} & 0 & | & 41 \\ \frac{3}{2} & 1 & 2 & 0 & 0 & \frac{1}{2} & 0 & | & 9 \\ \hline 2 & 0 & 1 & 0 & 0 & 1 & 1 & | & 18 \end{bmatrix}$$

$s_1 = 6 + 2x_1 + s_3$
$s_2 = 41 - \frac{7}{2}x_1 - 3x_3 - \frac{1}{2}s_3$
$x_2 = 9 - \frac{3}{2}x_1 - 2x_3 - \frac{1}{2}s_3$
$P = 18 - 2x_1 - x_3 - s_3$

29. $s_1 = 20 + 3x_1 - x_3$
$s_2 = 24 - 2x_1 - x_4$
$s_3 = 28 + 3x_2 - x_3$
$s_4 = 24 + 3x_2 - x_4$
$P = x_1 + 2x_2 + 3x_3 + 4x_4$

$$\begin{bmatrix} 0 & 0 & 1 & \frac{3}{2} & 1 & \frac{3}{2} & 0 & 0 & 0 & | & 56 \\ 1 & 0 & 0 & \frac{1}{2} & 0 & \frac{1}{2} & 0 & 0 & 0 & | & 12 \\ 0 & -3 & 1 & 0 & 0 & 0 & 1 & 0 & 0 & | & 28 \\ 0 & -3 & 0 & 1 & 0 & 0 & 0 & 1 & 0 & | & 24 \\ \hline 0 & -2 & -3 & -\frac{7}{2} & 0 & \frac{1}{2} & 0 & 0 & 1 & | & 12 \end{bmatrix}$$

$s_1 = 56 - x_3 - \frac{3}{2}x_4 - s_2$
$x_1 = 12 - \frac{1}{2}x_4 - \frac{1}{2}s_2$
$s_3 = 28 - 3x_2 - x_3$
$s_4 = 24 + 3x_2 - x_4$
$P = 12 + 2x_2 + 3x_3 + \frac{7}{2}x_4 - \frac{1}{2}s_2$

Exercise 4.2 (page 170)

1. (b) Requires additional pivoting; the pivot element is in row 1, column 1.

3. (a) Final tableau; $P = \frac{256}{7}$, $x_1 = \frac{32}{7}$, $x_2 = 0$.

5. (c) No solution; all entries in the pivot column are negative.

7. $P = \frac{204}{7}$, $x_1 = \frac{24}{7}$, $x_2 = \frac{12}{7}$ **9.** $P = 8$, $x_1 = \frac{2}{3}$, $x_2 = \frac{2}{3}$ **11.** $P = 6$, $x_1 = 2$, $x_2 = 0$, $x_3 = 0$

13. No solution, since all the ratios for column two are negative.

15. $P = 30$, $x_1 = 0$, $x_2 = 0$, $x_3 = 10$ **17.** $P = 42$, $x_1 = 1$, $x_2 = 10$, $x_3 = 0$, $x_4 = 0$

19. $P = 40$, $x_1 = 20$, $x_2 = 0$, $x_3 = 0$ **21.** $P = 50$, $x_1 = 0$, $x_2 = 15$, $x_3 = 5$, $x_4 = 0$

23. $x_1 =$ number of cans of Can I; $x_2 =$ number of cans of Can III; $x_3 =$ number of cans of Can III; $P =$ maximum revenue. $P = 800$, $x_1 = 0$, $x_2 = 100$, $x_3 = 20$.

25. $12,000 is the maximum profit when there are 1200 television console cabinets, 0 stereo system cabinets, and 0 radio cabinets.

27. $30,000 is the maximum profit when 0 TVs are made in Chicago, 375 TVs are made in New York, and 0 TVs are made in Denver.

Exercise 4.3 (page 184)

1. Standard form   **3.** Not in standard form   **5.** Standard form

7. Maximize $P = 2y_1 + 6y_2$ subject to $y_1 + 2y_2 \leq 2$, $y_1 + 3y_2 \leq 3$, $y_1 \geq 0$, $y_2 \geq 0$.

9. Maximize $P = 5y_1 + 4y_2$ subject to $y_1 + 2y_2 \leq 3$, $y_1 + y_2 \leq 1$, $y_1 \leq 1$, $y_1 \geq 0$, $y_2 \geq 0$.
11. $C = 6$, $x_1 = 0$, $x_2 = 2$ 13. $C = 12$, $x_1 = 0$, $x_2 = 4$ 15. $C = \frac{21}{5}$, $x_1 = \frac{8}{5}$, $x_2 = 0$, $x_3 = \frac{13}{5}$
17. The minimum cost is $7.50. When there are 0 units of Food I, 7.5 units of Food II, and 0 units of Food III.

Exercise 4.4 (page 200)

1. $P = 44$, $x_1 = 4$, $x_2 = 8$ 3. $P = 27$, $x_1 = 9$, $x_2 = 0$, $x_3 = 0$ 5. $C = \frac{20}{3}$, $x_1 = 0$, $x_2 = 0$, $x_3 = \frac{20}{3}$
7. $P = 8$, $x_1 = 0$, $x_2 = 4$
9. The minimum cost is $70,000 when 0 units are shipped from M1 to A1, 300 units are shipped from M1 to A2, 200 units are shipped from M2 to A2, and 0 units are shipped from M2 to A2.

True–False Questions (page 202)

1. T   2. F   3. T   4. F   5. T

Fill in the Blanks (page 202)

1. Slack variables   2. Column   3. $\geq$ 4. Dual   5. Von Neuman duality principle

Review Exercises (page 202)

1. $P = 22,500$, $x = 0$, $y = 100$, $z = 50$ 3. $P = 352$, $x_1 = 0$, $x_2 = \frac{6}{5}$, $x_3 = \frac{28}{5}$ 5. $C = 7$, $x_1 = 3$, $x_2 = 1$
7. $C = 350$, $x_1 = 0$, $x_2 = 50$, $x_3 = 50$

Mathematical Questions (page 204)

1. *c*   2. *d*   3. *c*   4. *a*   5. *b*   6. *a*   7. *c*   8. *d*

CHAPTER 5

Exercise 5.1 (page 210)

1. $25   3. $45   5. $150   7. 10%   9. $33\frac{1}{3}$%   11. $13\frac{1}{3}$%   13. $1160   15. $1680
17. $A = $1263.16   19. $A = $1428.57   21. Simple discount rate of 9% better.

Exercise 5.2 (page 216)

1. $\approx$$1348.18   3. $545   5. $\approx$$854.36   7. $\approx$$95.14   9. $\approx$$456.97
11. $33\frac{1}{3}$% simple interest   13. Between 11 and 12 years (from Table 1)
15. The 10% compounded loan (b) results in less interest due.   17. $\approx$$1759.11   19. 5.35%
21. 6.82%   23. $6\frac{1}{4}$% compounded annually is better   25. 9% compounded monthly is better
27. $109,395.56

Exercise 5.3 (page 221)

1. $1593.74   3. $5073.00   5. $8356.36   7. 22192.08   9. As in Example 8, $\approx$ $205,368.

Exercise 5.4 (page 226)
1. $V = \$15495.62$ 3. $V = \$856.60$ 5. $V = \$85135.64$ 7. $V = \$34,054.26$ 9. $P = 470.73$
11. 5 years (20 years remaining): $18,699.94 10 years (15 years remaining): $24,493.23
13. $P = 2008.18$ 15. $A = \$25,906$
17. The principal of either loan is $95,000(= $120,000 - $25,000)$.

	Monthly Payment
8%, 240 months	($95,000)(0.008364) = $794.58
9%, 300 months	($95,000)(0.008392) = $797.24

The 9% loan requires the larger monthly payment. Since the payments are larger and there are more of them, the total amount of the payments, and therefore the total interest to be paid, is also larger.

	Equity After 10 Years
8%, 120 months remaining	$120,000 - ($794.58)(82.42148) = $54,509.54
9%, 180 months remaining	$120,000 - ($797.24)(98.5934) = $41,397.40

After 10 years, the equity from the 8%, 20 year loan is larger.
19. $335.46

Exercise 5.5 (page 230)
1. The corporation should lease the machine.
3. Since Machine B costs $160.53 more than it will save in labor costs, Machine A is preferable.
5. The price of the bond should be $1086.46.

Review Exercises (page 231)
1. $I = \$436$ 3. $A = \$125.12$ 5. (a) $I = \$1080$ (b) $A = \$1044.55$
7. The compound interest loan cost less $P = \$71.36$.   9. $P = \$378.12$
11. $545.22 monthly payments; total interest = $103,566; equity after 5 years ($n = 240$ months remaining): = $23,502.
13. $1049, $21,575.52   15. $p = \$119,432$ 17. $p = \$108,004$

Mathematical Questions (page 232)
1. b 2. c 3. b 4. b 5. d 6. a 7. c

CHAPTER 6

Exercise 6.1 (page 247)
1. None of these   3. None of these   5. $\subset, \subseteq$ 7. $\subset, \subseteq$ 9. $\subset, \subseteq$
11. $A \subseteq C$. This is called the *transitive law*.
13. $\{a, b, c, d\}, \{a, b, c\}, \{a, b, d\}, \{a, c, d\}, \{b, c, d\}, \{a, b\}, \{a, c\}, \{a, d\}, \{b, c\}, \{b, d\}, \{c, d\}, \{a\}, \{b\}, \{c\}, \{d\}, \varnothing$
15. $\{3\}$ 17. $\{1, 2, 3, 5, 7\}$ 19. $\{3, 5\}$ 21. $\{1, 2, 3, 4, 5, 6, 7\}$

23. (a) {0, 1, 2, 3, 5, 7, 8}   (b) {5}   (c) {5}   (d) {0, 1, 2, 3, 4, 6, 7, 8, 9}   (e) {4, 6, 9}
(f) {0, 1, 5, 7}   (g) ∅   (h) {5}

25. (a) {b, c, d, e, f, g}   (b) {c}   (c) {a, h, i, j, . . . , z}   (d) {a, b, d, e, f, . . . , z}

27. (a)   (b)   (c)   (d)

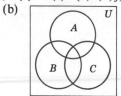
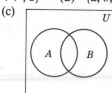
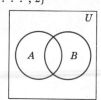

(e)   (f)   (g)   (h)

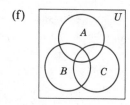
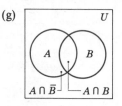
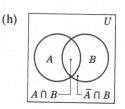

29. $A \cap E = \{x \mid x$ is a customer of IBM and is a member of the Board of Directors of IBM$\}$

31. $A \cup D = \{x \mid x$ is a customer of IBM or is a stockholder of IBM$\}$

33. $M \cap S = \{$All male college students who smoke$\}$

35. $\overline{M} \cap \overline{S} = \{$All female college students who do not smoke$\}$

37. 4   **39.** 10   **41.** 4   **43.** 0   **45.** 4   **47.** 4   **49.** $c[A \cap (B \cap C)] = c(\{8\}) = 1$

51. $c(A \cup B) = 5$ **53.** 2   **55.** 10   **57.** 452   **59.** 36   **61.** 46   **63.** 24   **65.** 3   **67.** 3

69.   109 = Number of male seniors who are not on the dean's list
97 = Number of female seniors who are not on the dean's list
369 = Number of female students who are not seniors and not on the dean's list
24 = Number of female seniors on the dean's list
73 = Number of female students on the dean's list who are not seniors
89 = Number of male students on the dean's list who are not seniors
347 = Number of male students who are not seniors and not on the dean's list
0 = Number of male seniors on the dean's list

71. (a) 42   (b) 9   (c) 5   (d) 2   (e) 44   (f) 31

73. Total for English, according to the diagram, is at least 303, whereas the staff member indicated that the total taking English was 281.

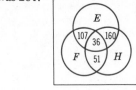

75. 68

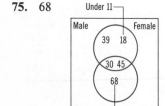

Exercise 6.2 (page 255)
1. 8   **3.** 24   **5.** 864   **7.** 36   **9.** 1320   **11.** 1200   **13.** 720, 40320   **15.** 360, 1296
17. 16   **19.** 5040   **21.** $2^{35} \simeq 3 \times 436 \times 10^{10}$
23. (a) 6,760,000   (b) 3,407,040   (c) 3,276,000   **25.** 120   **27.** 16

Exercise 6.3 (page 261)
1. 60   **3.** 120   **5.** 90   **7.** 9   **9.** 28   **11.** 42   **13.** 8   **15.** 1   **17.** 56   **19.** 1
21. (a) 720   (b) 120   (c) 24   **23.** 5040   **25.** 15120   **27.** 19,958,400   **29.** 3,368,253,000
31. 32,760   **33.** 90

Exercise 6.4 (page 265)
1. 15   **3.** 21   **5.** 5   **7.** 28   **9.** 56   **11.** 2380
13. If the 3 officers are of equal rank, the answer is $C(25, 3) = 2300$. If there are 3 distinct offices (e.g., president, vice-president, secretary), the answer is $P(25, 3) = 13,800$.
15. 15   **17.** 60
19. 26,046,720 (Order is not important if we assume that specific positions will be assigned to the 7 linemen after the team is formed.)
21. 10   **23.** 1,192,052,400   **25.** 75,287,520   **27.** 826   **29.** 128, 128   **31.** 1,217,566,350
33. 60   **35.** 10,626   **37.** $\dfrac{50!}{35!}$

True–False Questions (page 267)
1. T   **2.** T   **3.** F   **4.** F

Fill in the Blanks (page 267)
1. Disjoint   **2.** Permutation   **3.** Combination   **4.** Pascal   **5.** Binomial coefficients

Review Exercises (page 268)
1. None of these   **3.** None of these   **5.** None of these   **7.** ϵ **9.** $\subset$ **11.** None of these
13. $\subset, \subseteq$ **15.** None of these   **17.** (a) {3, 6, 8, 9}   (b) {6}   (c) {2, 3, 6, 7}   **19.** 3
21. (a) 45   (b) 33   (c) 50   **23.** 120   **25.** 10   **27.** 6   **29.** 72   **31.** Maximum: 12; 6
33. 218,400   **35.** (a) 525   (b) 1715   **37.** 12,441,600   **39.** 924 paths from A to B **41.** 240
43. 30   **45.** 24

CHAPTER 7

Exercise 7.2 (page 283)
1. (a) {H, T}   (b) {0, 1, 2}   (c) {M, D}   **3.** {$HHH, HHT, HTH, HTT, THH, THT, TTH, TTT$}
5. {$HH1, HH2, HH3, HH4, HH5, HH6, HT1, HT2, HT3, HT4, HT5, HT6, TH1, TH2, TH3, TH4, TH5,$
    $TH6, TT1, TT2, TT3, TT4, TT5, TT6$}
7. {RA, RB, RC, GA, GB, GC}   **9.** {RR, RG, GR, GG}

11. {$AA1, AA2, AA3, AA4, AB1, AB2, AB3, AB4, AC1, AC2, AC3, AC4, BA1, BA2, BA3, BA4, BB1, BB2, BB3, BB4, BC1, BC2, BC3, BC4, CA1, CA2, CA3, CA4, CB1, CB2, CB3, CB4, CC1, CC2, CC3, CC4$}

13. {$RA1, RA2, RA3, RA4, RB1, RB2, RB3, RB4, RC1, RC2, RC3, RC4, GA1, GA2, GA3, GA4, GB1, GB2, GB3, GB4, GC1, GC2, GC3, GC4$}

15. 16   **17.** 216   **19.** 1326   **21.** 1, 2, 3, and 6   **23.** 2   **25.** $\frac{1}{4}$ **27.** $\frac{1}{12}$

29. {$HHHH, HHHT, HHTH, HHTT, HTHH, HTHT, HTTH, HTTT, THHH, THHT, THTH, THTT, TTHH, TTHT, TTTH, TTTT$}; assign $\frac{1}{16}$ to each simple event.

31. {$HTTT, TTTT$}

33. {$HHHT, HHTH, HHTT, HTHH, HTHT, HTTH, THHH, THHT, THTH, TTHH$}   **35.** $P(A) = \frac{1}{18}$

37. $\frac{1}{9}$ **39.** $\frac{1}{6}$ **41.** $\frac{1}{2}$ **43.** $\frac{5}{6}$ **45.** $\frac{1}{2}$

47. (i) $P(E) = \frac{3}{4}$,   (ii) $P(E) = \frac{5}{9}$;   (i) $P(F) = \frac{1}{2}$,   (ii) $P(F) = \frac{4}{9}$;   (i) $P(G) = \frac{1}{4}$,   (ii) $P(G) = \frac{4}{9}$

49. {$RRR, RRL, RLR, RLL, LRR, LRL, LLR, LLL$}. Probability of each simple event is $\frac{1}{8}$. (We assume that the rat does not know left from right.)

     (a) $P(E) = \frac{3}{8}$ (b) $P(F) = \frac{1}{8}$ (c) $P(G) = \frac{1}{2}$ (d) $P(H) = \frac{1}{2}$

51. (a) The number on the red die is three times the number on the green die.

     (b) The number on the red die is 1 larger than the number on the green die.

     (c) The number on the red die is smaller than or equal to the number on the green die.

     (d) The sum of the numbers on the two dice is 8.

     (e) The number on the green die is the square of the number on the red die.

     (f) The numbers on the two dice are the same.

Exercise 7.3 (page 292)

1. .8   **3.** .5   **5.** .35

7. The events "Sum is 2" and "Sum is 12" are mutually exclusive. The probability of obtaining a 2 or a 12 is $\frac{1}{36} + \frac{1}{36} = \frac{1}{18}$.

9. .35   **11.** .2   **13.** (a) .7   (b) .4   (c) .2   (d) .3   **15.** (a) .68   (b) .58   (c) .32

17. (a) .57   (b) .95   (c) .83   (d) .38   (e) .29   (f) .05   (g) .78   (h) .71   **19.** $\frac{3}{4}$

21. $\frac{5}{12}$ **23.** $\frac{1}{2}$ **25.** The odds for E are 7 to 3; the odds against E are 3 to 7.

27. The odds for F are 4 to 1; the odds against F are 1 to 4.   **29.** 1 to 5; 1 to 17; 2 to 7

31. $\frac{11}{15}$. The odds are 11 to 4.

33. $P(A \cup B \cup C) = P(A \cup B) + P(C) - P[(A \cup B) \cap C]$

$= P(A) + P(B) - P(A \cap B) + P(C) - P[(A \cap C) \cup (B \cap C)]$

$= P(A) + P(B) + P(C) - P(A \cap B) - (P(A \cap C) + P(B \cap C) - P[(A \cap C) \cap (B \cap C)])$

$= P(A) + P(B) + P(C) - P(A \cap B) - (P(A \cap C) - P(B \cap C) + P(A \cap B \cap C)$

Exercise 7.4 (page 299)

1. $\frac{1}{52}$ **3.** $\frac{1}{4}$ **5.** $\frac{3}{13}$ **7.** $\frac{5}{13}$ **9.** $\frac{12}{13}$ **11.** $\frac{3}{23}$ **13.** $\frac{7}{23}$ **15.** $\frac{8}{23}$ **17.** $\frac{11}{23}$ **19.** $\frac{1}{6}$

21. $\frac{65}{150} \approx .433$ **23.** .236   **25.** .0298   **27.** Probability is greater than .99999.

29. Probability that all 5 are defective: $\approx .0000028$. Probability that at least 2 are defective: $\approx .103$.

31. (a) $\dfrac{1287}{2,598,960}$ (b) ≈ 0.0107 (c) ≈ 0.2743

33. (a) $\approx .0000015$ (b) $\approx .0000123$ (c) $\approx .00024$ (d) $\approx .0014$ (e) .0076

Exercise 7.5 (page 307)

1. .69   **3.** .9   **5.** 0   **7.** .40   **9.** .24   **11.** .10   **13.** .08   **15.** $\frac{5}{12}$ **17.** $\frac{1}{3}$ **19.** $\frac{1}{2}; \frac{1}{4}$

21. $\frac{1}{2}$ **23.** (a) $\frac{1}{26}$ (b) $\frac{1}{2}$ (c) $\frac{1}{13}$

25. (a) $\frac{5}{11}$ (b) $\frac{6}{23}$ (c) $\frac{5}{11}$ (d) $\frac{5}{12}$ (e) $\frac{14}{15}$ (f) $\frac{1}{4}$ **27.** $P(2 \text{ girls}|\text{1st girl}) = \frac{1}{2}$
29. $\frac{1}{16}$; yes $\frac{1}{8}$ **31.** $\frac{32}{75}$ **33.** $\frac{25}{204}$ **35.** $\frac{1}{13}$ **37.** .67 **39.** .5
41. $P(F) \cdot P(E|F) = P(E \cap F) = P(E) \cdot P(F|E)$
43. Since $F = (E \cap F) \cup (\overline{E} \cap F)$ and $(E \cap F) \cap (\overline{E} \cap F) = \varnothing$,

$$\frac{P(E \cap F)}{P(F)} + \frac{P(\overline{E} \cap F)}{P(F)} = \frac{P(E \cap F) + P(\overline{E} \cap F)}{P(F)} = \frac{P(F)}{P(F)} = 1$$

Exercise 7.6 (page 314)

1. .15 **3.** $\frac{1}{8}$ **5.** E and F are not independent. **7.** E and F are not independent.
9. E and F are independent. **11.** (a) $\frac{1}{4}$ (b) $\frac{13}{52} = \frac{1}{4}$ (c) $\frac{1}{16}$ **13.** E and F are not independent.
15. $P(A) = \frac{1}{4} + \frac{1}{4} = \frac{1}{2}$ $\quad A$ and B are independent;
$\quad\ \ P(B) = \frac{1}{4} + \frac{1}{4} = \frac{1}{2}$ $\quad A$ and C are independent;
$\quad\ \ P(C) = \frac{1}{4} + \frac{1}{4} = \frac{1}{2}$ $\quad B$ and C are independent;
$\quad\ \ P(A \cap B) = P(2) = \frac{1}{4} = P(A)P(B);$
$\quad\ \ P(A \cap C) = P(1) = \frac{1}{4} = P(A)P(C);$
$\quad\ \ P(B \cap C) = P(3) = \frac{1}{4} = P(B)P(C).$
17. Consider Problem 15.
$\quad$ (a) A and B are not mutually exclusive, but they are independent.
$\quad$ (b) Let $D = \{4\}$. Then: $P(D) = \frac{1}{12}$; $A \cap D = \varnothing$. Hence, they are mutually exclusive, but since $P(A \cap D) = P(\varnothing) = 0 \neq \frac{1}{12} \cdot \frac{1}{2}$, they are not independent.
$\quad$ (c) Let $E = \{1, 4\}$. Then: $A \cap E = \{1\}$; $P(E) = \frac{1}{4} + \frac{1}{12} = \frac{1}{3}$; $P(A \cap E) = P(1) = \frac{1}{4} \neq \frac{1}{2} \cdot \frac{1}{3}$. Thus, A and E are not independent and are not mutually exclusive.
19. $P(F) = 0.$
$\quad E \cap F \subset F$; hence, $P(E \cap F) \leq P(F) = 0$
$\quad$ Thus, $P(E \cap F) = 0$. But $P(E)P(F) = P(E) \cdot 0 = 0.$
$\quad$ Hence, E and F are independent.
21. If $E \cap F = \varnothing$, then $P(E \cap F) = P(\varnothing) = 0.$
$\quad$ But, by independence, $P(E \cap F) = P(E)P(F).$
$\quad$ Hence, $P(E)P(F) = 0$, which implies that $P(E) = 0$ or $P(F) = 0$—a contradiction. Thus, we have $E \cap F \neq \varnothing$.
23. (a) Let E = at least one ace, F = no ace.
$\quad\quad P(E) = 1 - P(F) = 1 - .4823 = .5177$
$\quad$ (b) Let G = at least one pair of aces, H = no pair of aces.
$\quad\quad P(G) = 1 - P(H) = 1 - .509 = .491$

Exercise 7.7 (page 324)

1. $\frac{12}{31}$ **3.** $\frac{7}{31}$ **5.** $\frac{12}{31}$ **7.** .017 **9.** .018 **11.** $P(A_1|E) = \frac{3}{17} \approx .176$ $P(A_2|E) = \frac{14}{17} \approx .824$
13. $P(A_1|E) = \frac{5}{18} \approx .278$ $P(A_2|E) = \frac{9}{18} = .500$ $P(A_3|E) = \frac{4}{18} \approx .222$
15. $P(A_1|E) = \frac{8}{29} \approx .276$ $P(A_2|E) = \frac{20}{29} \approx .690$ $P(A_3|E) = \frac{1}{29} \approx .034$
17. $P(A_2|E) = 0$; $P(A_3|E) = .065$; $P(A_4|E) = 0$; $P(A_5|E) = .065$
19. $P(U_\text{I}|E) = \frac{1}{3} \approx .333$ $P(U_\text{II}|E) = .20$ $P(U_\text{III}|E) = .467$ **21.** .80 **23.** $\approx .39, .21, .41$ **25.** .466, .343

True–False Questions (page 326)
1. T **2.** F **3.** F **4.** T

Fill in the Blanks (page 326)
1. For **2.** Equally likely **3.** Mutually exclusive **4.** Bayes' formula

Review Exercises (page 327)

1. $S = \{BB, BG, GB, GG\}$ 3. (a) $\frac{10}{91}$ (b) $\frac{45}{91}$ (c) $\frac{55}{91}$ 5. 0.2500

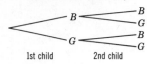

1st child   2nd child

7. (a) $\frac{1}{2}$ (b) $\frac{11}{24}$ (c) $\frac{13}{24}$ 9. $\frac{2}{3}$ 11. $\frac{7}{13}$ 13. (a) $\frac{1}{3}$ (b) $\frac{9}{38}$ (c) 0.56
15. (a) 0.0250   (b) 0.0625   (c) .4   17. 0.163

Mathematical Questions (page 329)

1. *b*   2. *e*   3. *c*   4. *d*   5. *c*   6. *d*   7. *b*   8. *a*   9. *c*   10. *b*

CHAPTER 8

Exercise 8.1 (page 339)

1. (a) 1024   (b) 210   (c) 56   (d) 968   3. (a) 120   (b) 63   (c) 35   (d) 1
5. 70   7. 1260   9. 4,989,600   11. 2100   13. (a) 280   (b) 280   (c) 640
15. $\dfrac{30!}{(6!)^5} \approx 1.37 \times 10^{18}$ 17. 93   19. $= .2051$ 21. $\approx .6907$ 23. $\frac{1}{19}$ 25. $\dfrac{1}{5!} = \dfrac{1}{120}$ 27. $\frac{1}{2}$

Exercise 8.2 (page 346)

1. $(x+y)^5 = x^5 + 5x^4y + 10x^3y^2 + 10x^2y^3 + 5xy^4 + y^5$

3. $(x+3y)^3 = x^3 + 3x^2(3y) + 3x(3y)^2 + (3y)^3 = x^3 + 9x^2y + 27xy^2 + 27y^3$

5. $(2x-y)^4 = (2x)^4 + 4(2x)^3(-y) + 6(2x)^2(-y)^2 + 4(2x)(-y)^3 + (-y)^4$

   $= 16x^4 - 32x^3y + 24x^2y^2 - 8xy^3 + y^4$

7. 10   9. 405   11. 32   13. 1023   15. 512

17. $\dbinom{10}{7} = \dbinom{9}{7} + \dbinom{9}{6} = \dbinom{8}{7} + \dbinom{8}{6} + \dbinom{9}{6} = \dbinom{7}{7} + \dbinom{7}{6} + \dbinom{8}{6} + \dbinom{9}{6} = \dbinom{6}{6} + \dbinom{7}{6} + \dbinom{8}{6} + \dbinom{9}{6}$

19. $\dbinom{12}{6}$ by Example 5 page 344.

Exercise 8.3 (page 354)

1. .0250   3. .0811   5. .0916   7. .2968   9. .22 . . .   11. $\approx .5787$ 13. $\approx .3292$
15. .0368   17. .2362   19. .0273   21. .03125   23. .3634   25. .1098   27. .0007
29. .1608   31. (a) .2793   (b) .0515   (c) .3366   (d) .9942   33. .3125

35. (a)

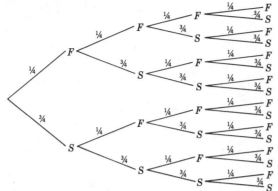

(b) .2109375
(c) .2109375

37. .6242 **39.** .6481 **41.** (a) .1094 (b) .4660 **43.** .9647 **45.** $341/12^5$
47. Investigate the binomial probabilities for $n = 5, 6, 7; k = 1, 2, 3;$ and $p = \frac{1}{3}$. When $n = 5$, there is a dual maximum for 1 or 2 successes. When $n = 7$, there is a single maximum at 2 successes. We are looking for the smallest n that has a single maximum at 2 successes. Thus, $n = 6$.

Exercise 8.4 (page 363)

1. 1.2 **3.** 44,560 **5.** She should pay $0.80 for a fair game.
7. He should pay $1.67 for a fair game. **9.** By 35¢ **11.** (a) $0.75 (b) No (c) Lose $2
13. It is not a fair bet.
15. The outcomes are **17.** $7
$e_1 =$ Heart not an ace, $p_1 = \frac{12}{52} = \frac{3}{13}$, $m_1 = .25$
$e_2 =$ Ace not ace of hearts, $p_2 = \frac{3}{52}$, $m_2 = .35$
$e_3 =$ Ace of hearts, $p_3 = \frac{1}{52}$, $m_3 = .75$
$e_4 =$ Neither an ace nor a heart, $p_4 = \frac{36}{52} = \frac{9}{13}$, $m_4 = -.15$
No, because her expected value is $-.012$.
19. The second site has a higher expected profit. **21.** $E = np = 2000(\frac{1}{6}) \approx 333.3$ **23.** 10 **25.** 1
27. 2.73 tosses
29. $E_1 = m_1 p_1 + m_2 p_2 + \cdots + m_n p_n$. Multiplying eack value by k we get:

$E_2 = km_1 p_1 + km_2 p_2 + \cdots + km_n p_n = k[m_1 p_1 + m_2 p_2 + \cdots + m_n p_n] = k \cdot E_1$

Thus, we can see that the expected value of the new experiment, E_2, is k times the original expected value E_1. Add to each outcome used in figuring E_1 the constant k. The new expected value is:

$E_3 = (m_1 + k)p_1 + (m_2 + k)p_2 + \cdots + (m_n + k)p_n = m_1 p_1 + kp_1 + m_2 p_2 + kp_2 + \cdots + m_n p_n + kp_n$
$\quad = m_1 p_1 + m_2 p_2 + \cdots + m_n p_n + kp_1 + kp_2 + \cdots + kp_n = E_1 + k(p_1 + p_2 + \cdots + p_n)$

Since $p_1 + p_2 + \cdots + p_n = 1$, we get $E_3 = E_1 + k$. Thus, we see that the expected value of the new experiment, E_3, is the expected value of the original experiment, E_1, plus k.

Exercise 8.5 (page 371)

1. The expected number of customers is 9. The optimal number of cars is 9. The expected daily profit is 48.40.

3.

Group Size	$p^n - \frac{1}{n}$
2	$(.95)^2 - .5 = .4025$
3	$(.95)^3 - .333 = .524$
4	$(.95)^4 - .25 = .565$
5	$(.95)^5 - .2 = .574$
6	$(.95)^6 - .167 = .568$

5. (a) $E(x) = 75,000 - 75,000(.05)^x - 500x.$ (b) Two divers should be used.   **7.** 1061.34

True–False Questions (page 372)
1. T   **2.** F   **3.** F   **4.** T

Fill in the Blanks (page 373)
1. Binomial theorem   **2.** (c) independent   (d) same   **3.** expected value

Review Exercises (page 373)
1. (a) 4845   (b) 5700   (c) 7805
3. $b(5, 0; .2) = .3277;\ b(5, 1; .2) = .4096;\ b(5, 2; .2) = .2048;\ b(5, 3; .2) = .0512;\ b(5, 4; .2) = .0064;$
   $b(5, 5; .2) = .0003$
5. (a) $\frac{1}{4096}$ (b) .3871   (c) 3871 to 6129   **7.** 29.52
9. (a) Expected value for five tickets is $0.90.   (b) She paid $0.35 extra.   **11.** $\frac{76}{7}$
13. Game is not fair, since $E = -\frac{1}{37}$ **15.** $1\frac{1}{2}$

Mathematical Questions (page 375)
1. *a*   **2.** *a*   **3.** *d*   **4.** *b*   **5.** *b*   **6.** *c*   **7.** *d*   **8.** *d*

CHAPTER 9

Exercise 9.1 (page 380)
1. A poll should be taken either door-to-door or by means of the telephone.
3. A poll should be taken door-to-door in which people are asked to fill out a questionnaire.
5. The data should be gathered from all different kinds of banks.
7. (a) Asking a group of children if they like candy to determine what percentage of people like candy.
   (b) Asking a group of people over 65 their opinion toward Medicare to determine the opinion of people in general about Medicare.
9. By taking a poll downtown, you would question mostly people who are either shopping or working downtown. For instance, you would question few students.

Exercise 9.2 (page 386)

1. (a) 250 (b) 249 (c) 275 (d) 50 (e) 33 (f) The 5th (g) 752 (h) Histogram
(i) Frequency polygon

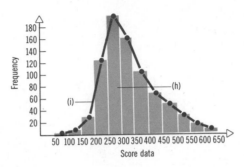

3. (a) Line chart

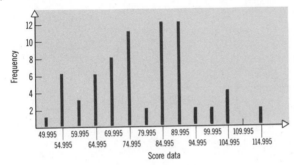

(b) Histogram (c) Frequency polygon (d) Cumulative frequency

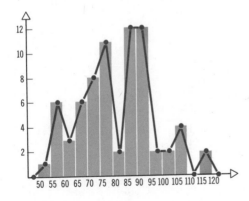

Class Interval	Tally	f	cf
114.995–119.995	||	2	71
109.995–114.995		0	69
104.995–109.995	||||	4	69
99.995–104.995	||	2	65
94.995–99.995	||	2	63
89.995–94.995	J̶H̶T̶ J̶H̶T̶ ||	12	61
84.995–89.995	J̶H̶T̶ J̶H̶T̶ ||	12	49
79.995–84.995	||	2	37
74.995–79.995	J̶H̶T̶ J̶H̶T̶ |	11	35
69.995–74.995	J̶H̶T̶ |||	8	24
64.995–69.995	J̶H̶T̶ |	6	16
59.995–64.995	|||	3	10
54.995–59.995	J̶H̶T̶ |	6	7
49.995–54.995	|	1	1

(e)   Cumulative frequency distribution

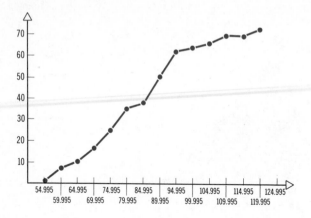

5.   (a)   Range $= 296 - 78 = 218$

Score	Tally	f	Score	Tally	f	Score	Tally	f
296	|	1	175	|	1	137	||	2
289	|	1	172	|	1	136	||	2
256	|	1	171	||	2	134	|	1
245	||	2	169	|||	3	132	||	2
240	|	1	166	||	2	131	||||	4
232	|	1	165	||	2	130	|	1
230	|	1	162	|	1	129	|||	3
224	||	2	161	||	2	128	||	2
222	|	1	158	|	1	127	|||	3
218	||	2	157	|	1	126	|	1
212	|	1	156	||	2	123	||	2
211	|	1	155	|	1	122	|	1
207	|	1	154	||	2	119	||	2
204	|	1	153	|||	3	116	|||	3
202	|	1	152	|	1	115	|	1
198	||	2	149	|	1	113	|	1
194	|	1	148	|	1	112	|	1
192	|	1	146	||	2	111	|	1
190	|||	3	145	||	2	110	|	1
188	|	1	144	||	2	108	|	1
185	|||	3	142	|	1	105	|	1
184	|	1	141	|	1	100	|	1
178	|	1	140	|	1	95	|	1
176	||	2	138	|	1	91	|	1
						78	|	1

(b) Line chart

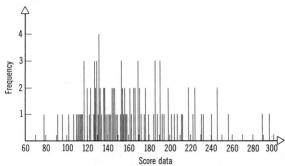

(c) Histogram   (d) Frequency polygon

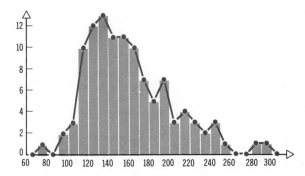

(e) Cumulative (less than) frequency

Class Interval	Tally	f	cf	Class Interval	Tally	f	cf
290.5 – 300.5	|	1	110	170.5 – 180.5	ⷭⷭ ||	7	80
280.5 – 290.5	|	1	109	160.5 – 170.5	ⷭⷭ ⷭⷭ	10	73
270.5 – 280.5		0	108	150.5 – 160.5	ⷭⷭ ⷭⷭ |	11	63
260.5 – 270.5		0	108	140.5 – 150.5	ⷭⷭ ⷭⷭ	10	52
250.5 – 260.5	|	1	108	130.5 – 140.5	ⷭⷭ ⷭⷭ |||	13	42
240.5 – 250.5	||	2	107	120.5 – 130.5	ⷭⷭ ⷭⷭ ||||	14	29
230.5 – 240.5	||	2	105	110.5 – 120.5	ⷭⷭ ||||	9	15
220.5 – 230.5	||||	4	103	100.5 – 110.5	|||	3	6
210.5 – 220.5	||||	4	99	90.5 – 100.5	||	2	3
200.5 – 210.5	|||	3	95	80.5 – 90.5		0	1
190.5 – 200.5	||||	4	92	70.5 – 80.5	|	1	1
180.5 – 190.5	ⷭⷭ |||	8	88				

(f)

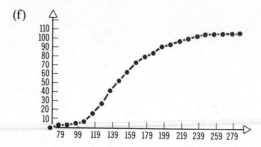

(g) Cumulative (more than) frequency

Class Interval	Tally	f	cf	Class Interval	Tally	f	cf
70.5 – 80.5	|	1	110	180.5 – 190.5	⧸⧸⧸⧸⧸ |||	8	30
80.5 – 90.5		0	109	190.5 – 200.5	||||	4	22
90.5 – 100.5	||	2	109	200.5 – 210.5	|||	3	18
100.5 – 110.5	|||	3	107	210.5 – 220.5	||||	4	15
110.5 – 120.5	⧸⧸⧸⧸⧸ ||||	9	104	220.5 – 230.5	||||	4	11
120.5 – 130.5	⧸⧸⧸⧸⧸ ⧸⧸⧸⧸⧸ ||||	14	95	230.5 – 240.5	||	2	7
130.5 – 140.5	⧸⧸⧸⧸⧸ ⧸⧸⧸⧸⧸ |||	13	81	240.5 – 250.5	||	2	5
140.5 – 150.5	⧸⧸⧸⧸⧸ ⧸⧸⧸⧸⧸	10	68	250.5 – 260.5	|	1	3
150.5 – 160.5	⧸⧸⧸⧸⧸ ⧸⧸⧸⧸⧸ |	11	58	260.5 – 270.5		0	2
160.5 – 170.5	⧸⧸⧸⧸⧸ ⧸⧸⧸⧸⧸	10	47	270.5 – 280.5		0	2
170.5 – 180.5	⧸⧸⧸⧸⧸ ||	7	37	280.5 – 290.5	|	1	2
				290.5 – 300.5	|	1	1

(h)

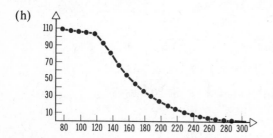

Exercise 9.3 (page 392)

1. Mean = 31.25; median = 30.5; no mode   3. Mean = 70.4; median = 70; mode = 55
5. Mean = 76.2; median = 75; no mode   7. Mean = $\overline{X}$ = 3.51; median = 3.45   9. 206.49
11. 19,300; median = 16,000. The median describes the situation more realistically, since it is closer to the salary of most of the faculty members in the sample.
13. Mean = \$162.61; median = \$160.52
15. For Table 5, $C_{75} \approx 91.77$, $C_{40} \approx 77.0$. For Table 6, $C_{75} \approx 93.03$, $C_{40} \approx 76.52$
17. Let 325 be the assumed mean; $n = 753$, $\Sigma fx' = -13$, $\overline{X} = 325 + \left(\dfrac{-13}{753}\right)(50) \approx 324.1$.

Exercise 9.4 (page 399)

1. (b)   **3.** ≈ 6.53 **5.** ≈ 5.196 **7.** ≈ 12.47 **9.** ≈ 66.68 **11.** ≈ 91.77

13. (a) 75%   (b) 64%   (c) $88\frac{8}{9}\%$ (d) 25%   (e) $11\frac{1}{9}\%$

Exercise 9.5 (page 407)

1. $\overline{X} = 8;\ \sigma = 1$ **3.** $\overline{X} = 18;\ \sigma = 1$

5. $Z = \dfrac{7 - 13.1}{9.3} \approx -0.6559,\quad Z = \dfrac{9 - 13.1}{9.3} \approx -0.4409,\quad Z = \dfrac{13 - 13.1}{9.3} \approx -0.0108$

$Z = \dfrac{15 - 13.1}{9.3} \approx 0.2043,\quad Z = \dfrac{29 - 13.1}{9.3} \approx 1.7097,\quad Z = \dfrac{37 - 13.1}{9.3} \approx 2.5699$

$Z = \dfrac{41 - 13.1}{9.3} = 3.0000$

7. 0.3085   **9.** 0.0688

11. (a) 0.3133 (b) 0.3642 (c) 0.4938 (d) 0.4987 (e) 0.2734 (f) 0.4896 (g) 0.2881 (h) 0.4988

13. $Z = \dfrac{x - \overline{X}}{\sigma};\ \overline{X} = 64,\ \sigma = 2.$ (a) 68.26% of the women are between 62 and 66 inches tall;

$(0.6826)(2000) = 1365.2 \approx 1365$ women   (b) ≈ 1909 women   (c) ≈ 1995 women

15. (a) 1.04%   (b) According to the table, Z must be close to 1.04 if the proportional area is 35% (≈ 0.3508). $(1.04)\sigma = (1.04)(5.2) \approx 5.4$ pounds. Thus, we expect 70% of the students to be within 5.4 pounds of the mean, or between 134.6 and 135.4 pounds.

17. The number of shoes he should expect to replace out of 1000 is 239.

19. Kathleen has the highest relative standing.

21. $b(15, 0; .3) \approx .0047$
$b(15, 1; .3) \approx .0305$
$b(15, 2; .3) \approx .0916$
$b(15, 3; .3) \approx .1700$
$b(15, 4; .3) \approx .2186$
$b(15, 5; .3) \approx .2061$
$b(15, 6; .3) \approx .1472$
$b(15, 7; .3) \approx .0811$
$b(15, 8; .3) \approx .0348$
$b(15, 9; .3) \approx .0116$
$b(15, 10; .3) \approx .0030$
$b(15, 11; .3) \approx .0006$
$b(15, 12; .3) \approx .0001$
$b(15, 13; .3) \approx .0000$
$b(15, 14; .3) \approx .0000$
$b(15, 15; .3) \approx .0000$

23. 0.7698   **25.** 0.5   **27.** 0.0287

True–False Questions (page 410)

1. F   **2.** T   **3.** F   **4.** T   **5.** T

Fill in the Blanks (page 410)

1. Mean, median, mode   **2.** Standard deviation   **3.** Bell shape   **4.** Z score
5. Random outcome lies between $\overline{X} + k$ and $\overline{X} - k$.

Review Exercises (page 410)

1. (a)

Score	Tally	Frequency	Score	Tally	Frequency
100	||	2	66	||	2
99	|	1	63	||	2
95	|	1	60	|	1
92	|	1	55	|	1
90	|	1	52	||	2
89	|	1	48	|	1
87	||	2	44	|	1
85	||	2	42	|	1
83	|	1	33	|	1
82	|	1	30	|	1
80	|||	3	26	|	1
78	||	2	21	|	1
77	|	1	20	|	1
75	|	1	19	|	1
74	|	1	17	|	1
73	||	2	14	||	2
72	||	2	12	|	1
70	|	1	10	|	1
69	|	1	8	|	1

Range $= 100 - 8 = 92$

(b) Line chart

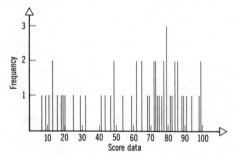

(c) Histogram

(d) Frequency polygon

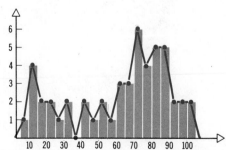

(e) Cumulative (more than) frequency

Class Interval	Tally	f	cf	Class Interval	Tally	f	cf
99.5–104.5	||	2	2	49.5–54.5	||	2	35
94.5–99.5	||	2	4	44.5–49.5	|	1	36
89.5–94.5	||	2	6	39.5–44.5	||	2	38
84.5–89.5	||||	5	11	34.5–39.5		0	38
79.5–84.5	|||||	5	16	29.5–34.5	||	2	40
74.5–79.5	||||	4	20	24.5–29.5	|	1	41
69.5–74.5	||||||	6	26	19.5–24.5	||	2	43
64.5–69.5	|||	3	29	14.5–19.5	||	2	45
59.5–64.5	|||	3	32	9.5–14.5	||||	4	49
54.5–59.5	|	1	33	4.5–9.5	|	1	50

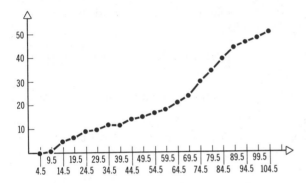

(f) Cumulative (less than) frequency

Class Interval	f	cf	Class Interval	f	cf
99.5–104.5	2	50	49.5–54.5	2	17
94.5–99.5	2	48	44.5–49.5	1	15
89.5–94.5	2	46	39.5–44.5	2	14
84.5–89.5	5	44	34.5–39.5	0	12
79.5–84.5	5	39	29.5–34.5	2	12
74.5–79.5	4	34	24.5–29.5	1	10
69.5–74.5	6	30	19.5–24.5	2	9
64.5–69.5	3	24	14.5–19.5	2	7
59.5–64.5	3	21	9.5–14.5	4	5
54.5–59.5	1	18	4.5–9.5	1	1

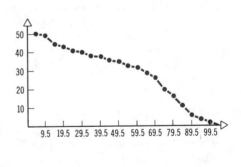

3. The mean is a poor measure in (b) because it gives too much importance to the extreme value 195.

5. $A = \{20, 15, 5, 0\}$; $B = \{12, 11, 10, 9, 8\}$: Both sets have a mean of 10. The standard deviation for the first set is $\sigma_1 = \sqrt{250/5} \approx 7.07$. The standard deviation for the second set is $\sigma_2 = \sqrt{10/5} \approx 1.41$.

7. ≈ 2.77

9. (a) $(0.6827)(600) = 409.62$ (b) $[(0.4987) - (0.3413)](600) = 94.44$ (c) $(0.4972)(600) = 298.32$

11. (a) $(0.4970) - (0.4115) = 0.0855$ (b) $(0.4599) - (0.3849) = 0.0750$ **13.** At least 0.75

Mathematical Questions (page 412)

1. *e*   **2.** *b*   **3.** *c*

CHAPTER 10

Exercise 10.1 (page 417)

1. Let the entries denote Tami's winnings in cents. Laura chooses columns and Tami chooses rows:

$$\text{Tami} \begin{array}{c} \text{I} \\ \text{II} \end{array} \begin{array}{cc} \text{I} & \text{II} \\ \begin{bmatrix} -10 & 10 \\ 10 & -10 \end{bmatrix} \end{array}$$

3. The entries denote Tami's winnings in cents.

$$\text{Tami} \begin{array}{c} 1 \\ 4 \\ 7 \end{array} \overset{\displaystyle \text{Laura}}{\begin{array}{ccc} 1 & 4 & 7 \\ \begin{bmatrix} -20 & 50 & -80 \\ 50 & -80 & 110 \\ -80 & 110 & -140 \end{bmatrix} \end{array}}$$

5. Strictly determined; value is -1.   **7.** Strictly determined; value is 2.   **9.** Not strictly determined.
11. Strictly determined; value is 2.   **13.** Not strictly determined.
15. $0 \le a \le 3$ (There is no saddle point in row 1, unless $a \le 3$; in row 2, unless $a \le -9$; in row 3, unless $a \le -5$; in column 1, unless $a \ge 0$; in column 2, unless $a \ge 8$; in column 3, unless $a \ge 5$. Thus, there is no saddle point unless $0 \le a \le 3$. But if $0 \le a \le 3$, then there is a saddle point in row 1, column 1.)

17. $a \le 0 \le b$ or $b \le 0 \le a$ (The matrix $\begin{bmatrix} a & 0 \\ 0 & b \end{bmatrix}$ is strictly determined if and only if there is a saddle point; a is a

saddle point if and only if $a = 0$; b is a saddle point if and only if $b = 0$. The 0 in row 1, column 2 is a saddle point if and only if $0 \le a$ and $0 \ge b$. The 0 in row 2, column 1 is a saddle point if and only if $0 \le b$ and $0 \ge a$.)

Exercise 10.2 (page 420)

1. $E = 1.42$ **3.** $E = \frac{9}{4}$ **5.** $E = \frac{19}{8}$ **7.** $E = \frac{17}{9}$ **9.** $E = \frac{1}{3}$.
11. The nonstrictly determined games are those without saddle points. If $a_{11} = a_{12}$ or $a_{21} = a_{22}$, then the game is strictly determined. (See Problem 16 in Exercise 10.1)
   (a) If $a_{11} > a_{12}$, then $a_{12} < a_{22}$ to prevent a_{12} from being a saddle point. This means that $a_{21} < a_{22}$ to prevent a_{22} from being a saddle point. Also, $a_{11} > a_{21}$ to prevent a_{21} from being a saddle point.
   (b) If $a_{11} < a_{12}$, then $a_{21} > a_{11}$ to prevent a_{11} from being a saddle point. This means that $a_{22} < a_{21}$ to prevent a_{21} from being a saddle point. Also, $a_{12} > a_{22}$ to prevent a_{22} from being a saddle point.

Exercise 10.3 (page 427)

1. The optimal strategy for Player I is [.75   .25].
The optimal strategy for Player II is [.25   .75].
The value of the game is

$E = 1.75$

3. The optimum strategy for Player I is [$\frac{1}{6}$ $\frac{5}{6}$].
The optimum strategy for Player II is [$\frac{1}{3}$ $\frac{2}{3}$].
The value of the game is

$E = PAQ = [\frac{1}{6} \;\; \frac{5}{6}] \begin{bmatrix} -3 & 2 \\ 1 & 0 \end{bmatrix} \begin{bmatrix} \frac{1}{3} \\ \frac{2}{3} \end{bmatrix} = \frac{1}{3}$

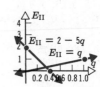

5. The optimum strategy for Player I is $[\frac{5}{8} \quad \frac{3}{8}]$.
    The optimum strategy for Player II is $[\frac{5}{8} \quad \frac{3}{8}]$.
    The value of the game is

$$E = PAQ = [\frac{5}{8} \quad \frac{3}{8}] \begin{bmatrix} 2 & -1 \\ -1 & 4 \end{bmatrix} \begin{bmatrix} \frac{5}{8} \\ \frac{3}{8} \end{bmatrix} = \frac{7}{8}$$

7. $p_1 = \frac{3}{8}; p_2 = \frac{5}{8};$
    $q_1 = \frac{1}{2}; q_2 = \frac{1}{2};$
    $V = 1.5$

    The game favors the Democrat.

9.   Opponent

		Deserted	Busy
Spy	Deserted	-100	30
	Busy	10	-2

    $p_1 = \frac{6}{71}; \quad p_2 = \frac{65}{71}; \quad q_1 = \frac{16}{71}; \quad q_2 = \frac{55}{71}$

    The value is $\frac{50}{71}$.

11. If $a_{11} + a_{22} - a_{12} - a_{21} = 0$, then the game is strictly determined. Otherwise, from Problem 11 is Exercise 10.2, we must have either:

    (a) $a_{11} - a_{12} > 0$ and $a_{22} - a_{21} > 0$; hence, $a_{11} + a_{22} - a_{12} - a_{21} > 0$, or
    (b) $a_{11} - a_{12} < 0$ and $a_{22} - a_{21} < 0$; hence, $a_{11} + a_{22} - a_{12} - a_{21} < 0$.

Exercise 10.4 (page 437)

1. Row 2 dominates row 3; the reduced matrix is $\begin{bmatrix} 8 & 3 & 8 \\ 6 & 5 & 4 \end{bmatrix}$.

    Column 2 dominates column 1; the reduced matrix is $\begin{bmatrix} 3 & 8 \\ 5 & 4 \end{bmatrix}$.

    $p_1 = \frac{1}{6} \quad q_1 = \frac{2}{3}$
    $p_2 = \frac{5}{6} \quad q_2 = \frac{1}{3}$
    $V = \frac{14}{3}$

3. Column 3 dominates columns 1 and 4; the reduced matrix is $\begin{bmatrix} 1 & 0 \\ -2 & 1 \end{bmatrix}$.

    $p_1 = \frac{3}{4} \quad q_1 = \frac{1}{4}$
    $p_2 = \frac{1}{4} \quad q_2 = \frac{3}{4}$
    $V = \frac{1}{4}$

5. Column 3 dominates column 1; column 2 dominates column 4; the reduced matrix is $\begin{bmatrix} -4 & 2 \\ 6 & -5 \end{bmatrix}$.

    $p_1 = \frac{11}{17} \quad q_1 = \frac{7}{17}$
    $p_2 = \frac{6}{17} \quad q_2 = \frac{10}{17}$
    $V = -\frac{8}{17}$

7. Row 1 dominates row 3; the reduced matrix is $\begin{bmatrix} 4 & -5 & 5 \\ -6 & 3 & 3 \end{bmatrix}$.

    Column 2 dominates column 3; the reduced matrix is $\begin{bmatrix} 4 & -5 \\ -6 & 3 \end{bmatrix}$.

    $p_1 = \frac{1}{2} \quad q_1 = \frac{4}{9}$
    $p_2 = \frac{1}{2} \quad q_2 = \frac{5}{9}$
    $V = -1$

9. Row 3 dominates rows 2 and 4; the reduced matrix is $\begin{bmatrix} 1 & 3 & 0 \\ 0 & 4 & 1 \end{bmatrix}$.

   Column 1 dominates column 2; the reduced matrix is $\begin{bmatrix} 1 & 0 \\ 0 & 1 \end{bmatrix}$.

   $p_1 = \frac{1}{2}$ $q_1 = \frac{1}{2}$
   $p_2 = \frac{1}{2}$ $q_2 = \frac{1}{2}$
   $V = \frac{1}{2}$

11. Row 2 dominates row 3; the reduced matrix is $\begin{bmatrix} 4 & 3 & -1 \\ 1 & 1 & 4 \end{bmatrix}$.

    Column 2 dominates column 1; the reduced matrix is $\begin{bmatrix} 3 & -1 \\ 1 & 4 \end{bmatrix}$.

    $p_1 = \frac{3}{7}$ $q_1 = \frac{5}{7}$
    $p_2 = \frac{4}{7}$ $q_2 = \frac{2}{7}$
    $V = \frac{13}{7}$

13. Let the thief be in area A with probability q_1. He is then in area B with probability $(1 - q_1)$. The detectives have six choices. The expected values for the probabilities for the detectives to find and arrest a thief for each of the six choices are:

    ① $E_1 = -.24q_1 + .75$
    ② $E_1 = .28q_1 + .36$
    ③ $E_1 = -.72q_1 + .91$
    ④ $E_1 = -.02q_1 + .60$
    ⑤ $E_1 = -.48q_1 + .85$
    ⑥ $E_1 = -.20q_1 + .76$

    The intersection of lines 2 and 6
    gives the optimum strategy of the thief.

    $q_1 = \frac{5}{6}$ $q_2 = 1 - q_1 = \frac{1}{6}$

    Eliminating rows 1, 3, 4, and 5, we get:

    $p_1 = \frac{5}{12}$ $p_2 = \frac{7}{12}$ $V = .5933 \ldots$

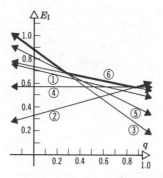

CHAPTER REVIEW

True–False Questions (page 441)
   1. T   **2.** T   **3.** T   **4.** F

Fill in the Blanks (page 441)
   1. Payoff   **2.** Value   **3.** Strictly determined, nonstrictly determined   **4.** Dominant

Review Exercises (page 441)
   1. (a) Not strictly determined.   (b) Strictly determined; value is 15.
       (c) Strictly determined; value is 50.   (d) Strictly determined; value is 9.
       (e) Strictly determined; value is 12.

3. Let's first examine the 2×2 matrix $\begin{bmatrix} a & b \\ c & d \end{bmatrix}$.

Let a be the saddle point. We know that $a \le b$ and $a \ge c$. If $d \le c$, then $b \ge d$ and row 1 dominates row 2. If $d \ge c$, then column 1 dominates column 2. Similar reasoning would have shown the desired result if we had chosen a saddle point other than a.

Now consider the matrix $\begin{bmatrix} a & b & c \\ d & e & f \end{bmatrix}$.

Let a be the saddle point. We know that $a \le b$, $a \le c$, and $a \ge d$. If $d \le e$, then column 1 dominates column 2. If $d \le f$, then column 1 dominates column 3. If $d \ge e$ and $d \ge f$, then row 1 dominates row 2. Similar reasoning would have shown the desired result if we had chosen a saddle point other than a.

5. (a) Column 1 dominates column 2; the reduced matrix is $\begin{bmatrix} 4 & 3 \\ 1 & 5 \end{bmatrix}$.

$p_1 = \frac{4}{5}$ $q_1 = \frac{2}{5}$
$p_2 = \frac{1}{5}$ $q_2 = \frac{3}{5}$
$V = \frac{17}{5}$

(b) Row 3 dominates row 2; the reduced matrix is $\begin{bmatrix} 1 & 6 \\ 7 & 4 \end{bmatrix}$.

$p_1 = \frac{3}{8}$ $q_1 = \frac{1}{4}$
$p_2 = \frac{5}{8}$ $q_2 = \frac{3}{4}$
$V = \frac{19}{4}$

(c) Row 3 dominates row 1; the reduced matrix is $\begin{bmatrix} 4 & 0 \\ 3 & 4 \end{bmatrix}$.

$p_1 = \frac{1}{5}$ $q_1 = \frac{4}{5}$
$p_2 = \frac{4}{5}$ $q_2 = \frac{1}{5}$
$V = \frac{16}{5}$

(d) Let Player I play row 1 with probability p. He then plays row 2 with probability $(1 - p)$. Player II has 3 choices. The expected earnings for Player I for each of the 3 choices are:

① $E_I = 0p + 4(1 - p) = 4 - 4p$
② $E_I = 3p + 2(1 - p) = 2 + p$
③ $E_I = 2p + 3(1 - p) = 3 - p$

By examining the graphs of these equations, we see that the intersection of lines 1 and 2 gives the optimum strategy for Player I: $p = \frac{2}{3}$, $1 - p = \frac{1}{3}$.

Eliminating column 3, we get $\begin{bmatrix} 0 & 3 \\ 4 & 2 \end{bmatrix}$.

$q_1 = \dfrac{2 - 3}{2 - 4 - 3} = \frac{1}{5}$ $q_2 = \frac{4}{5}$

Player I should select row 1 with probability $\frac{2}{3}$ and row 2 with probability $\frac{1}{3}$. Player II should select column 1 with probability $\frac{1}{5}$, column 2 with probability $\frac{4}{5}$, and never select column 3.

$V = \frac{12}{5}$

CHAPTER 11

Exercise 11.1 (page 450)

1. The sum of the entries in row 3 is not equal to 1; there is a negative entry in row 3, column 2.

3. (a) The probability of a change from state 1 to state 2 is $\frac{2}{3}$.

(b) $[\frac{1}{3} \quad \frac{2}{3}]$ (c) $[\frac{1}{4} \quad \frac{3}{4}]$

(d) $A^{(0)} = [0 \quad 1]$

$p_{21}^{(2)} = \frac{1}{4} \cdot \frac{1}{3} + \frac{3}{4} \cdot \frac{1}{4} = \frac{13}{48}$

$p_{22}^{(2)} = \frac{1}{4} \cdot \frac{2}{3} + \frac{3}{4} \cdot \frac{3}{4} = \frac{35}{48}$

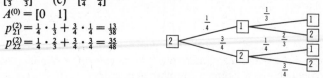

5. $[.3625 \quad .6375]$ **7.** $a = .4$ **9.** $[.5040 \quad .4960]$
                    $b = .2$
                    $c = 1$

11. (a) The probability that a Democratic candidate is elected depends only on whether the previous mayor was a Democrat or a Republican (and similarly for a Republican candidate).

(b) $\begin{array}{c} \\ D \\ R \end{array} \begin{array}{cc} D & R \\ \begin{bmatrix} .6 & .4 \\ .3 & .7 \end{bmatrix} \end{array}$ (c) $\begin{bmatrix} .48 & .52 \\ .39 & .61 \end{bmatrix}$; $\begin{bmatrix} .444 & .556 \\ .417 & .583 \end{bmatrix}$

13. 57% will drink brand X after 2 months.   **15.** $\begin{array}{c} \\ T \\ G \\ \text{Other} \end{array} \begin{array}{ccc} T & G & \text{Other} \\ \begin{bmatrix} .92 & .08 & 0 \\ .04 & .90 & .06 \\ .10 & .08 & .82 \end{bmatrix} \end{array} = P$; $[.45 \quad .30 \quad .25] = A^{(0)}$

(a) 77.7%

(b) 79.758%

17. $uA = [u_1 a_{11} + u_2 a_{21} \quad u_1 a_{12} + u_2 a_{22}]$

$(uA)_1 + (uA)_2 = (u_1 a_{11} + u_2 a_{21}) + (u_1 a_{12} + u_2 a_{22})$
$= u_1(a_{11} + a_{12}) + u_2(a_{21} + a_{22})$
$= u_1 + u_2 = 1$

Exercise 11.2 (page 461)

1. Regular: $[\frac{2}{3} \quad \frac{1}{3}]$ is the fixed vector.   **3.** Regular. $[t_1 \quad t_2] = [\frac{1}{2} \quad \frac{1}{2}]$ **5.** Not regular.

7. If $[t_1 \quad t_2] \begin{bmatrix} 1-p & p \\ p & 1-p \end{bmatrix} = [t_1 \quad t_2]$, then: $\begin{array}{l} (1-p)t_1 + pt_2 = t_1 \\ pt_1 + (1-p)t_2 = t_2 \end{array}$ $t_1 = t_2, \quad t_1 + t_2 = 1, \quad t_1 = \frac{1}{2}, \quad t_2 = \frac{1}{2}$

9. $P = \begin{array}{c} \\ A \\ B \\ C \end{array} \begin{array}{ccc} A & B & C \\ \begin{bmatrix} .7 & .15 & .15 \\ .1 & .8 & .1 \\ .2 & .2 & .6 \end{bmatrix} \end{array}$ He stocks Brand A 30.77% of the time, Brand B 46.15% of the time, Brand C 23.08% of the time.

11. The probability that the grandson of a Laborite will vote Socialist is .09.
The fixed probability vector is $[t_1 \quad t_2 \quad t_3] = [.5532 \quad .3830 \quad .0638]$.

13. 30%   (a) $[.377 \quad .375 \quad .248]$ (b) $[t_1 \quad t_2 \quad t_3] = [.35 \quad .40 \quad .25]$

Exercise 11.3 (page 470)

1. Nonabsorbing (no absorbing states)   **3.** Absorbing

5. Nonabsorbing (absorbing state 3 is not accessible to states 1 and 2).

7. $\begin{array}{c} \\ 1 \\ 3 \\ 2 \end{array} \begin{array}{ccc} 1 & 3 & 2 \\ \left[\begin{array}{cc|c} 1 & 0 & 0 \\ 0 & 1 & 0 \\ \hline \frac{1}{8} & \frac{2}{8} & \frac{5}{8} \end{array}\right] \end{array}$ $S = [\frac{1}{8} \quad \frac{2}{8}]$; $T \cdot S = [\frac{1}{3} \quad \frac{2}{3}]$ **9.** (a) $T_{13} = .8$; $T_{23} = .6$ (b) 4.2

11. With a stake of \$1, the probability is $\frac{4}{19}$. With \$2, the probability is $\frac{10}{19}$.
13. (a) Expected number of wagers is 1.4.
    (b) The probability that she is wiped out is .84.
    (c) The probability that she wins is .16.
15. (a) Expected number of wagers is 1.6.

    (b) $T \cdot S = \begin{bmatrix} .64 & .36 \\ .4 & .6 \end{bmatrix}$ The probability that she is wiped out is .64.

    (c) The probability that she wins is .36.
17. 12.80

Exercise 11.4 (page 475)

1. $\begin{bmatrix} \frac{1}{4} & \frac{1}{2} & \frac{1}{4} \end{bmatrix} \begin{bmatrix} \frac{1}{2} & \frac{1}{2} & 0 \\ \frac{1}{4} & \frac{1}{2} & \frac{1}{4} \\ 0 & \frac{1}{2} & \frac{1}{2} \end{bmatrix} = \begin{bmatrix} \frac{1}{4} & \frac{1}{2} & \frac{1}{4} \end{bmatrix}$

3. (a) $P = \begin{array}{c} \\ D \\ H \\ R \end{array} \begin{array}{c} \begin{array}{ccc} D & H & R \end{array} \\ \begin{bmatrix} 0 & 1 & 0 \\ 0 & \frac{1}{2} & \frac{1}{2} \\ 0 & 0 & 1 \end{bmatrix} \end{array}$

   (b) P is not regular, but a fixed probability vector does exist. It is [0 0 1]. This indicates that in the long run the unknown genotype will be R.

   (c) $\begin{array}{c} \\ R \\ H \\ D \end{array} \begin{array}{c} \begin{array}{ccc} R & H & D \end{array} \\ \left[\begin{array}{c|cc} 1 & 0 & 0 \\ \hline \frac{1}{2} & \frac{1}{2} & 0 \\ 0 & 1 & 0 \end{array} \right] \end{array}$ $T = \begin{array}{c} \\ H \\ D \end{array} \begin{array}{c} \begin{array}{cc} H & D \end{array} \\ \begin{bmatrix} 2 & 0 \\ 2 & 1 \end{bmatrix} \end{array}$

   (d) If the unknown is D to start, three stages are required.
       If the unknown is H to start, two stages are required.

CHAPTER REVIEW

True–False Questions (page 475)
   1. F   2. F   3. F   4. T

Fill in the Blanks (page 476)
   1. probability   2. $m \times m$ 3. non-negative, 1   4. $v^{(k)} = v^{(0)} P^k$ 5. positive

Review Exercises (page 476)
1. (a) $\begin{bmatrix} \frac{2}{3} & \frac{1}{3} \end{bmatrix}$ is the fixed vector.   (b) $\begin{bmatrix} \frac{1}{2} & \frac{1}{2} \end{bmatrix}$ is the fixed vector.
3. After 2 years [.4717 .2692 .2592]. In the long run, A's share is $\frac{80}{169}$, B's share is $\frac{45}{169}$, and C's share is $\frac{44}{169}$.
5. In the long run, she sells $\frac{11}{31}$ of the time at U_1, $\frac{16}{31}$ of the time at U_2, and $\frac{4}{31}$ of the time at U_3.
7. Transition matrix:

$$\begin{array}{c} \\ 0 \\ 1 \\ 2 \\ 3 \\ 4 \\ 5 \end{array} \begin{array}{c} \begin{array}{cccccc} 0 & 1 & 2 & 3 & 4 & 5 \end{array} \\ \begin{bmatrix} 1 & 0 & 0 & 0 & 0 & 0 \\ .55 & 0 & .45 & 0 & 0 & 0 \\ 0 & .55 & 0 & .45 & 0 & 0 \\ 0 & 0 & .55 & 0 & .45 & 0 \\ 0 & 0 & 0 & .55 & 0 & .45 \\ 0 & 0 & 0 & 0 & 0 & 1 \end{bmatrix} \end{array} \quad \text{or} \quad \begin{array}{c} \\ 0 \\ 5 \\ 1 \\ 2 \\ 3 \\ 4 \end{array} \begin{array}{c} \begin{array}{cccccc} 0 & 5 & 1 & 2 & 3 & 4 \end{array} \\ \left[\begin{array}{cc|cccc} 1 & 0 & 0 & 0 & 0 & 0 \\ 0 & 1 & 0 & 0 & 0 & 0 \\ \hline .55 & 0 & 0 & .45 & 0 & 0 \\ 0 & 0 & .55 & 0 & .45 & 0 \\ 0 & 0 & 0 & .55 & 0 & .45 \\ 0 & .45 & 0 & 0 & .55 & 0 \end{array} \right] \end{array}$$

The expected length of the game is 5.706158. The probability that he is wiped out is .7142275.

CHAPTER 12

Exercise 12.1 (page 484)

1. Proposition   3. Not a proposition   5. Proposition   7. Proposition
9. A fox is not an animal.   11. I am not buying stocks and bonds.
13. Someone wants to buy my house.   15. Every person has a car.
17. John is an economics major or a sociology major.
19. John is an economics major and a sociology major.
21. John is not an economics major or he is not a sociology major.
23. John is not an economics major or he is a sociology major.

Exercise 12.2 (page 492)

1.

p	q	$\sim q$	$p \vee \sim q$
T	T	F	T
T	F	T	T
F	T	F	F
F	F	T	T

3.

p	q	$\sim p$	$\sim q$	$\sim p \wedge \sim q$
T	T	F	F	F
T	F	F	T	F
F	T	T	F	F
F	F	T	T	T

5.

p	q	$\sim p$	$\sim p \wedge q$	$\sim(\sim p \wedge q)$
T	T	F	F	T
T	F	F	F	T
F	T	T	T	F
F	F	T	F	T

7.

p	q	$\sim p$	$\sim q$	$\sim p \vee \sim q$	$\sim(\sim p \vee \sim q)$
T	T	F	F	F	T
T	F	F	T	T	F
F	T	T	F	T	F
F	F	T	T	T	F

9.

p	q	$\sim q$	$p \vee \sim q$	$(p \vee \sim q) \wedge p$
T	T	F	T	T
T	F	T	T	T
F	T	F	F	F
F	F	T	T	F

11.

p	q	$\sim q$	$p \underline{\vee} q$	$p \wedge \sim q$	$(p \underline{\vee} q) \wedge (p \wedge \sim q)$
T	T	F	F	F	F
T	F	T	T	T	T
F	T	F	T	F	F
F	F	T	F	F	F

13.

p	q	$\sim p$	$\sim q$	$p \wedge q$	$\sim p \wedge \sim q$	$(p \wedge q) \vee (\sim p \wedge \sim q)$
T	T	F	F	T	F	T
T	F	F	T	F	F	F
F	T	T	F	F	F	F
F	F	T	T	F	T	T

15.

p	q	r	$\sim q$	$p \wedge \sim q$	$(p \wedge \sim q) \underline{\vee} r$
T	T	T	F	F	T
T	T	F	F	F	F
T	F	T	T	T	F
T	F	F	T	T	T
F	T	T	F	F	T
F	T	F	F	F	F
F	F	T	T	F	T
F	F	F	T	F	F

17.

p	$p \wedge p$	$p \vee p$
T	T	T
F	F	F

Since each column is the same,
$p \equiv p \wedge p \equiv p \vee p$

19.

p	q	r	$p \wedge q$	$q \wedge r$	$(p \wedge q) \wedge r$	$p \wedge (q \wedge r)$
T	T	T	T	T	T	T
T	T	F	T	F	F	F
T	F	T	F	F	F	F
T	F	F	F	F	F	F
F	T	T	F	T	F	F
F	T	F	F	F	F	F
F	F	T	F	F	F	F
F	F	F	F	F	F	F

The last two columns are the same, so
$(p \wedge q) \wedge r \equiv p \wedge (q \wedge r)$.

p	q	r	$p \vee q$	$q \vee r$	$(p \vee q) \vee r$	$p \vee (q \vee r)$
T	T	T	T	T	T	T
T	T	F	T	T	T	T
T	F	T	T	T	T	T
T	F	F	T	F	T	T
F	T	T	T	T	T	T
F	T	F	T	T	T	T
F	F	T	F	T	T	T
F	F	F	F	F	F	F

The last two columns are the same, so
$(p \vee q) \vee r \equiv p \vee (q \vee r)$.

21.

①	②	③	④	⑤	⑥
p	q	$p \vee q$	$p \wedge q$	$p \wedge (p \vee q)$	$p \vee (p \wedge q)$
T	T	T	T	T	T
T	F	T	F	T	T
F	T	T	F	F	F
F	F	F	F	F	F

Since columns 1 and 5 are the same, $p \equiv p \wedge (p \vee q)$.
Since columns 1 and 6 are the same, $p \equiv p \vee (p \wedge q)$.

23.

①	②	③	④	⑤
p	q	$\sim q$	$\sim q \vee q$	$p \wedge (\sim q \vee q)$
T	T	F	T	T
T	F	T	T	T
F	T	F	T	F
F	F	T	T	F

Since columns 1 and 5 are the same, $p \equiv p \wedge (\sim q \vee q)$.

25.

①	②	③
p	$\sim p$	$\sim(\sim p)$
T	F	T
F	T	F

Since columns 1 and 3 are the same, $p \equiv \sim(\sim p)$.

27.

p	q	$\sim p$	$q \wedge (\sim p)$	$p \wedge (q \wedge \sim p)$
T	T	F	F	F
T	F	F	F	F
F	T	T	T	F
F	F	T	F	F

29.

p	q	$\sim p$	$\sim q$	$p \wedge q$	$\sim p \wedge \sim q$	$(p \wedge q) \vee (\sim p \wedge \sim q)$	$[(p \wedge q) \vee (\sim p \wedge \sim q)] \wedge p$
T	T	F	F	T	F	T	T
T	F	F	T	F	F	F	F
F	T	T	F	F	F	F	F
F	F	T	T	F	T	T	F

31. Smith is an exconvict and he is an exconvict. $\equiv$ Smith is an exconvict or he is an exconvict. $\equiv$ Smith is an exconvict.

33. "It is not true that Smith is an exconvict or rehabilitated" means the same as the statement "Smith is not an exconvict and he is not rehabilitated." "It is not true that Smith is an exconvict and he is rehabilitated" means the same as "Smith is not an exconvict or he is not rehabilitated."

35. $(p \wedge q) \vee r \equiv r \vee (p \wedge q) \equiv (r \vee p) \wedge (r \vee q) \equiv (p \vee r) \wedge (r \vee q) \equiv (p \vee r) \wedge (q \vee r)$

37. Use a truth table to show that b is true and a is false if Michael rents a truck and does not sell his car.

39. Katy is not a good volleyball player or she is conceited.

Exercise 12.3 (page 500)

1. $\sim p \Rightarrow q$; Converse: $q \Rightarrow \sim p$; Contrapositive: $\sim q \Rightarrow p$; Inverse: $p \Rightarrow \sim q$.

3. $\sim q \Rightarrow \sim p$; Converse: $\sim p \Rightarrow \sim q$; Contrapositive: $p \Rightarrow q$; Inverse: $q \Rightarrow p$.

5. If it is raining, the grass is wet.
Converse: If the grass is wet, it is raining.
Contrapositive: If the grass is not wet, it is not raining.
Inverse: If it is not raining, the grass is not wet.

7. "It is raining or it is cloudy" is equivalent to "If it is not raining, it is cloudy,"
Converse: If it is cloudy, it is not raining.
Contrapositive: If it is not cloudy, it is raining.
Inverse: If it is raining, it is not cloudy.

9. If it is raining, it is cloudy.
Converse: If it is cloudy, it is raining.
Contrapositive: If it is not cloudy, it is not raining.
Inverse: If it is not raining, it is not cloudy.

11. (a) If Jack studies psychology, then Mary studies sociology.
(b) If Mary studies sociology, then Jack studies psychology.
(c) If Jack does not study psychology, then Mary studies sociology.

13. (a)

p	q	r	$q \vee r$	$p \Rightarrow (q \vee r)$	$p \wedge \sim q$	$(p \wedge \sim q) \Rightarrow r$
T	T	T	T	T	F	T
T	T	F	T	T	F	T
T	F	T	T	T	T	T
T	F	F	F	F	T	F
F	T	T	T	T	F	T
F	T	F	T	T	F	T
F	F	T	T	T	F	T
F	F	F	F	T	F	T

$$\uparrow \underline{\quad\quad\quad} \equiv \underline{\quad\quad\quad} \uparrow$$

(b) $\quad p \Rightarrow (q \vee r) \equiv \sim p \vee (q \vee r)$;
$(p \wedge \sim q) \Rightarrow r \equiv \sim(p \wedge \sim q) \vee r$
$$\equiv (\sim p \vee \sim(\sim q)) \vee r$$
$$\equiv (\sim p \vee q) \vee r$$
$$\equiv \sim p \vee (q \vee r)$$

15.

p	q	~p	p ∧ q	~p ∨ (p ∧ q)
T	T	F	T	T
T	F	F	F	F
F	T	T	F	T
F	F	T	F	T

17.

p	q	~p	~p ∧ q	p ∨ (~p ∧ q)
T	T	F	F	T
T	F	F	F	T
F	T	T	T	T
F	F	T	F	F

19.

p	q	~p	~p ⇒ q
T	T	F	T
T	F	F	T
F	T	T	T
F	F	T	F

21.

p	~p	~p ∨ p
T	F	T
F	T	T

23.

p	q	p ⇒ q	p ∧ (p ⇒ q)
T	T	T	T
T	F	F	F
F	T	T	F
F	F	T	F

25.

p	q	r	q ∧ r	p ∧ (q ∧ r)	p ∧ q	(p ∧ q) ∧ r	p ∧ (q ∧ r) ⇔ (p ∧ q) ∧ r
T	T	T	T	T	T	T	T
T	T	F	F	F	T	F	T
T	F	T	F	F	F	F	T
T	F	F	F	F	F	F	T
F	T	T	T	F	F	F	T
F	T	F	F	F	F	F	T
F	F	T	F	F	F	F	T
F	F	F	F	F	F	F	T

27.

p	q	p ∨ q	p ∧ (p ∨ q)	p ∧ (p ∨ q) ⇔ p
T	T	T	T	T
T	F	T	T	T
F	T	T	F	T
F	F	F	F	T

29. p ⇒ q   **31.** ~p ∧ ~q   **33.** q ⇒ p

Exercise 12.4 (page 507)

1. Let p and q be the statements, p: It is raining, q: John is going to school. Assume that p ⇒ ~q and q are true statements.

Prove: ~p is true.
Direct: p ⇒ ~q is true.
 Also, its contrapositive q ⇒ ~p is true and q is true.
 Thus, ~p is true by the law of detachment.
Indirect: Assume ~p is false.
 Then p is true; p ⇒ ~q is true.
 Thus, ~q is true by the law of detachment.
 But q is true, and we have a contradiction.
 The assumption is false and ~p is true.

3. Let p, q, and r be the statements, p: Smith is elected president; q: Kuntz is elected secretary; r: Brown is elected treasurer. Assume that p ⇒ q, q ⇒ ~r, and p are true statements.

Prove: ~r is true.
Direct: p ⇒ q and q ⇒ ~r are true.
 So p ⇒ ~r is true by the law of syllogism, and p is true.
 Thus, ~r is true by the law of detachment.

Indirect: Assume $\sim r$ is false.
 Then r is true; $p \Rightarrow q$ is true; $q \Rightarrow \sim r$ is true.
 So, $p \Rightarrow \sim r$ is true by the law of syllogism.
 $r \Rightarrow \sim p$, its contrapositive, is true.
 Thus, $\sim p$ is true by the law of detachment.
 But p is true, and we have a contradiction.
 The assumption is false and $\sim r$ is true.

5. Not valid **7.** Valid

Exercise 12.5 (page 510)

1.

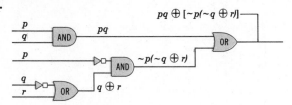

The output $pq[\sim p(\sim q \oplus r)]$ is 1 when

 1. $p = q = 1$
 2. $p = 0$ and $q = 0$
 3. $p = 0$ and $r = 1$

3. The output is $(\sim q \oplus [p(\sim p \oplus q)])q = (\sim q)q \oplus p(\sim p \oplus q)q = p(\sim p \oplus q)q = [p(\sim p) \oplus pq]q = pqq = pq$, which is 1 if and only if p and q are both 1.

5.

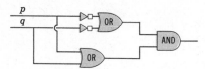

7.

9. (For Problem 3): $\dfrac{p}{q}$ AND

 (For Problem 5):

p	q	$\sim p \oplus \sim q$	$p \oplus q$	$(\sim p \oplus \sim q)(p \oplus q)$
1	1	0	1	0
1	0	1	1	1
0	1	1	1	1
0	0	1	0	0

$(\sim p \oplus \sim q)(p \oplus q) = [\sim (pq)](p \oplus q)$

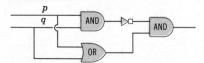

(For Problem 7): $\sim (p \oplus q) \sim p = \sim [(p \oplus q) \oplus p] = \sim [p \oplus q]$

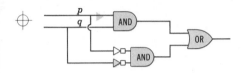

11. The truth table for this circuit is either

p	q	
1	1	1
1	0	0
0	1	0
0	0	1

or

p	q	
1	1	0
1	0	1
0	1	1
0	0	0

Thus two possible circuits are:

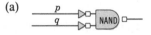

13.

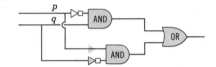

15. $p \vee q \equiv \sim (\sim p \sim q)$ (a)   (b)

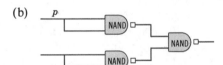

17. $pq \oplus pr \oplus q(\sim r) = pqr \oplus pq(\sim r) \oplus pr \oplus q(\sim r)$ $= pr(q \oplus 1) \oplus (p \oplus 1)[q(\sim r)] = pr(1) \oplus 1[q(\sim r)]$
              $= pqr \oplus pr \oplus pq(\sim r) \oplus q(\sim r)$ $= pr \oplus q(\sim r)$

CHAPTER REVIEW

True–False Questions (page 512)
  1. F   **2.** F   **3.** T   **4.** F   **5.** T

Fill in the Blanks (page 512)
  1. $p \vee q$ **2.** $\sim p$ **3.** logically equivalent   **4.** hypothesis, conclusive   **5.** 0, 1

Review Exercises (page 513)
  1. (c)   **3.** (a)   **5.** Nobody is rich.   **7.** Danny is tall or Mary is not short.

9.

p	q	$\sim p$	$p \wedge q$	$(p \wedge q) \vee \sim p$
T	T	F	T	T
T	F	F	F	F
F	T	T	F	T
F	F	T	F	T

11.

p	q	$\sim p$	$\sim q$	$p \vee \sim q$	$\sim p \vee (p \vee \sim q)$
T	T	F	F	T	T
T	F	F	T	T	T
F	T	T	F	F	T
F	F	T	T	T	T

13. $q \Rightarrow p$ **15.** $p \Leftrightarrow q$

17. Let p be the statement "I paint the house" and let q be the statement "I go bowling." Assume $\sim p \Rightarrow q$ and $\sim q$ are true.

Prove: p is true.

Since $\sim p \Rightarrow q$ is true, its contrapositive $\sim q \Rightarrow p$ is true. We have $\sim q$ is true and hence, by the law of detachment, p is true.

19.

p	q	$\sim p$	$\sim p \vee q$	$p \Rightarrow q$
T	T	F	T	T
T	F	F	F	F
F	T	T	T	T
F	F	T	T	T

$\sim p \vee q \equiv p \Rightarrow q$

21.

p	q	$(p \oplus q)[\sim(pq)]$	$p \veebar q$
1	1	0	0
1	0	1	1
0	1	1	1
0	0	0	0

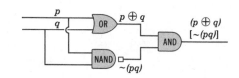

CHAPTER 13

Exercise 13.1 (page 520)

1. True, false, true, false, true, false, false, false, false.

3. $\{(2, 2), (2, 4), (2, 6), (2, 10), (3, 6), (5, 10)\}$. **5.** 1, 4, 9, 16, 25, 2, 5.

7. (a) $\{(1, 2), (1, 4), (1, 7), (2, 2), (2, 4), (2, 7), (5, 2), (5, 4), (5, 7)\}$.

(b) $\{(1, 2), (1, 4), (1, 7), (2, 4), (2, 7), (5, 7)\}$.

(c) R is a subset of $A \times B$.

9. (a) $\{aa, ab, ba, bb\}$ (b) $\{(aa, ab), (ab, aa), (ba, bb), (bb, ba)\}$. **11.** 50, 97, 64, 80, 116, 110, 125.

13. $\{(1, 2), (1, 4), (1, 6), (1, 8), (2, 2), (2, 4), (2, 6), (2, 8), (3, 6)\}$.

15. $\{(1, 1), (2, 2), (3, 3), (4, 4), (5, 5), (6, 6), (7, 7), (8, 8), (9, 9), (10, 10), (1, 3), (3, 1), (1, 5), (5, 1), (1, 7), (7, 1), (1, 9),$
$(9, 1), (2, 4), (4, 2), (2, 6), (6, 2), (2, 8), (8, 2), (2, 10), (10, 2), (3, 5), (5, 3), (3, 7), (7, 3), (3, 9), (9, 3), (4, 6), (6, 4),$
$(4, 8), (8, 4), (4, 10), (10, 4), (5, 7), (7, 5), (5, 9), (9, 5), (6, 8), (8, 6), (6, 10), (10, 6), (7, 9), (9, 7), (8, 10), (10, 8)\}$.

17. $\{(0, 0), (0, 00), (00, 0), (0, 000), (000, 0), (1, 1), (1, 01), (01, 1), (1, 10), (10, 1), (1, 001), (001, 1), (1, 010), (010, 1),$
$(1, 100), (100, 1), (00, 00), (00, 000), (000, 00), (01, 01), (10, 10), (01, 10), (10, 01), (01, 001), (001, 01),$
$(01, 010), (010, 01), (01, 100), (100, 01), (11, 11), (11, 011), (011, 11), (11, 101), (101, 11), (11, 110), (110, 11),$
$(000, 000), (001, 001), (001, 010), (010, 001), (001, 100), (100, 001), (010, 010), (010, 100), (100, 010),$
$(100, 100), (011, 011), (011, 101), (101, 011), (011, 110), (110, 011), (101, 101), (101, 110), (110, 110),$
$(111, 111)\}$.

19. $\{(0, 0), (0, 1), (0, 2), (0, 3), (1, 1), (1, 2), (1, 3), (2, 2), (2, 3), (3, 3)\}$.

21. $\{(0, 0), (1, 1), (2, 4), (3, 9), (4, 16)\}$. **23.** $\{(1, 1), (2, 1), (5, 2), (7, 3)\}$.

25. $\{(42, \text{'}*\text{'}), (72, \text{'H'}), (47, \text{'/'}), (88, \text{'x'})\}$.

27.

Variable Name	Value
PI	3.14159
RADIUS	10
RSQR	100
AREA	314.159
CIRCUM	628.318

29. Reflexive, symmetric, transitive. **31.** Reflexive, symmetric, transitive.

33. Reflexive, symmetric, transitive.

35. Reflexive. Not symmetric because $(A, C) \in R$ but $(C, A) \notin R$. Not transitive because $(C, B) \in R$ and (B, A), but $(C, A) \notin R$.

37. Reflexive, symmetric, transitive.

39. Since we cannot find a and b in A such that aRb; then R is symmetric. Similarly, since we cannot find a, b, and c in A such that aRb and bRc, then R is transitive. And since $(t, t) \notin R$, etc., then R is not reflexive.

Exercise 13.2 (page 527)

1. 1, 4, 2. Range = {1, 2, 4}. **3.** 5, 0, 10, -5, 15.

5. Does not define a function, because f assigns two different values (1 and 3) to x.

7. Yes, f defines a function. **9.** Yes, f is a function. **11.** No, f is not a function. Domain $\neq A$.

13. $C, 9, ', (, =$ **15.** 0, 100, 0, -2. **17.** X1 = 12675.2; X2 = 12675; ABSX = 126.75. **19.** Yes.

21. Yes. **23.** One-to-one not onto, therefore, not bijective.

25. Neither one-to-one nor onto, therefore not bijective.

27. For example, TRUNC(1.0) = 1 = TRUNC(1.1). And ROUND(2.7) = 3 = ROUND(3.1). Thus, TRUNC and ROUND are not one-to-one.

29. For example H(10, 10) = 0 = H(01, 01). Thus, H is not one-to-one.

31. No. Odd integers in the range are not associated with any integers in the domain.

33. 3, 2, 1. **35.** $(g \circ f)(1) = g[f(1)] = g(b) = z.$
$(g \circ f)(2) = g[f(2)] = g(a) = x.$
$(g \circ f)(3) = g[f(3)] = g(c) = y.$

Exercise 13.3 (page 532)

1. $-1, \frac{1}{2}, -\frac{1}{3}, \frac{1}{4}, \frac{1}{100}$.

3. (a) $0, \frac{1}{2}, \frac{2}{3}, \frac{3}{4}, \frac{4}{5}, \frac{5}{6}$.

(b) $n = 0, b_1 - b_0 = \frac{1}{2} - 0 = \frac{1}{2}.$
$n = 1, b_2 - b_1 = \frac{2}{3} - \frac{1}{2} = \frac{1}{6}.$
$n = 2, b_3 - b_2 = \frac{3}{4} - \frac{2}{3} = \frac{1}{12}$

5. 1, 2, 4, 8, 16, 32, 64, 128. **7.** 1, 1, 2, 6, 24, 120, 720. **9.** 1, 1, 1, 1, . . . , 1.

11. $M_0 = \begin{bmatrix} 1 & 1 & 0 \\ 1 & 0 & -1 \\ 0 & -1 & 1 \end{bmatrix}$

$M_1 = \begin{bmatrix} 1 & 0 & 0 \\ 0 & 1 & 0 \\ 0 & 0 & 2 \end{bmatrix}$

$M_2 = \begin{bmatrix} 1 & -1 & 0 \\ -1 & 2 & 1 \\ 0 & 1 & 3 \end{bmatrix}$

$M_3 = \begin{bmatrix} 1 & -2 & 0 \\ -2 & 3 & 2 \\ 0 & 2 & 4 \end{bmatrix}$

13. $(-1)^n, n = 0, 1, 2, \ldots.$ **15.** $2n + 1, n = 0, 1, 2, \ldots.$ **17.** $\dfrac{1}{n+1}, n = 0, 1, 2, \ldots.$

19. 0, 1, 3, 7, 15, 31, 63, 127. **21.** 1, 1, 2, 3, 5, 8, 13, 21, 34.

Exercise 13.4 (page 537)

1. $x = 5, y = 15$

3. Algorithm AVRG
    Sum := 0
    X := 1
    Do While (X ≤ M)
      Input N(X)
      Sum := Sum + N(X)
      X := X + 1
    End of While
    Average := Sum/M
  End of AVRG

5. Algorithm PRODUCT
    Prod := 1
    X := 1
    Do While (X ≤ M)
      Input N(X)
      Prod := Prod * N(X)
      X := X + 1
    End of While
  End of PRODUCT

7. Algorithm SCHOLARSHIP
    J := 1
    Do While (J ≤ 20)
      Input Name (J), GPA(J)
      If (GPA(J) > 3.5)
        Then Output Name (J), GPA(J)
      J := J + 1
    End of While
  End of SCHOLARSHIP

9. Algorithm GRADE
    Input name, score
    If (score ≤ 59)
      Then output name, 'Grade is F'
    Else if ((score > 59) and (score ≤ 69))
        Then output name, 'Grade is D'
      Else if ((score > 69) and (score ≤ 79))
        Then output name, 'Grade is C'
        Else if ((score > 79) and (score ≤ 89))
          Then output name, 'Grade is B'
          Else output name, 'Grade is A'
  End of GRADE

11. Algorithm GREATER
    Input x, y
    If $(x > y)$
      Then output x
    Else output y
  End of GREATER

13. Algorithm PRICE
 Input Age
 If (age > 65)
  Then cost is discounted
 Else cost is regular
 Output Cost
 End of PRICE

Exercise 13.5 (page 544)

1. (a) $1 < 2$. Yes. (b) $2 < 2^2$. Yes. (c) $k < 2^k$. (d) $(k+1) < 2^{k+1}$.

3. (a) $1^2 = \dfrac{1(1+1)(2+1)}{6}$. Yes.

 (b) $1^2 + 2^2 + 3^2 + 4^2 + 5^2 = \dfrac{5(5+1)(10+1)}{6}$. Yes.

 (c) $1^2 + 2^2 + 3^2 + \cdots + k^2 = \dfrac{k(k+1)(2k+1)}{6}$

 (d) $1^2 + 2^2 + 3^2 \cdots + k^2 + (k+1)^2 = \dfrac{(k+1)[(k+1)+1][2(k+1)+1]}{6} = \dfrac{(k+1)(k+2)(2k+3)}{6}$

5. (a) $1 + 2 = 2^2 - 1$. Yes.
 (b) $1 + 2 + 2^2 + 2^3 + 2^4 + 2^5 = 2^{5+1} - 1$. Yes.
 (c) $1 + 2 + 2^2 + \cdots + 2^k = 2^{k+1} - 1$
 (d) $1 + 2 + 2^2 + \cdots + 2^k + 2^{k+1} = 2^{(k+1)+1} - 1$

13. $100 + 99 + \cdots + 2 + 1 = 100\dfrac{(100+1)}{2} = 5050$

15. $2 + 2 + 2 + 4 + 2 + 6 + \cdots + 2 + 2000 = 2000 + 2 + 4 + 6 + \cdots + 2000 = 2000 + 1000(1001) = 100{,}300$

17. $1 \cdot 2 + 2 \cdot 3 + \cdots + 1000 \cdot 1001 = \dfrac{1000(1001)(1002)}{3} = 334{,}334{,}000$

Exercise 13.6 (page 550)

1. $1, 2, 4, 8, 16, 32$ 3. $1, 0, -1, -4, -17, -86$ 5. $2, 4, 12, 48, 240, 1440$ 7. $1, 1, 3, 7, 16, 33$
9. $1, 2, 2, 4, 8, 32$ 11. $1, 2, 2, 5, 9, 16$ 13. $1, -1, -1, -5, -20, -104$ 15. $89, 144, 233, 377, 610$
17. (a) The word that contains no bits is of length 0 that does not contain the bit pattern 00.
  The words 0 and 1 are of length 1 that do not contain the pattern 00.
  The words 01, 10, 11 are of length 2 that do not contain the pattern 00.
  The words 010, 101, 011, 110, 111 are of length 3 that do not contain the bit pattern 00.
  The words 1010, 1101, 1110, 1111, 0101, 1011, 0111, 0110 are of length 4 that do not contain the bit pattern 00.
 (b) Recurrence relation $s_n = s_{n-1} + s_{n-2}$ with $s_0 = 1$ $s_1 = 2$ as initial conditions.

19. (a) $1000, $1100, $1210, $1331, $1464.1.
    (b) $A_n = A_{n-1} + 0.1A_{n-1}$ (recurrence relations)
      $A_0 = 1,000$ (initial condition).

21. (a) 2, 4, 7, 11.
    (b) $p_n = p_{n-1} + n$ (recurrence relation)
      $p_1 = 2$ (initial condition)

CHAPTER REVIEW

True–False Questions (page 552)
  1. F   **2.** F   **3.** T   **4.** T   **5.** F   **6.** T

Fill in the Blanks (page 552)
  1. Relation   **2.** Function   **3.** Bijective   **4.** Natural numbers   **5.** Pseudocode
  6. Mathematical induction   **7.** Recurrence relation, initial condition

Review Exercises (page 552)
  1. {(1, 1), (8, 2), (27, 3)}   **3.** (a) and (b)
  5. (a) 1, 0, 3, 2, 5, 4, 7, 6, 9, 8   (b) 0, −1, 2, −3, 4, −5, 6, −7, 8, −9
  7.

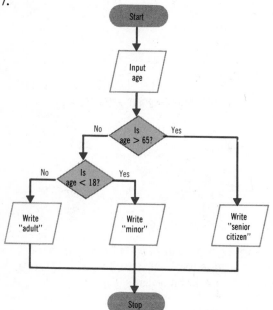

9. 1000,000   **11.** 2, 2, 1, 4, 12, 60, 960

CHAPTER 14

Exercise 14.1 (page 560)

1. Vertices: v_1, v_2, v_3, v_4. Edges: e_1, e_2, e_3, e_4, e_5. Loop: e_1. Isolated vertex: v_2. Parallel edges: e_3, e_4, e_5.

3. $v_1 \quad v_2$; $v_1 \qquad v_2$

5.
Vertex	Degree
v_1	3
v_2	0
v_3	3
v_4	4

Vertex	Degree
v_1	1
v_2	1
v_3	2
v_4	2
v_5	2
v_6	4
v_7	2
v_8	4
v_9	2
v_{10}	2

7. 9 as the following figure shows:

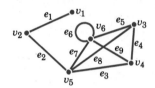

9. No, for $\deg(v_4) = 4$ there must be a loop.

11. (a) $v_1 \quad v_2$ (b)

13. 15

15.

17.

Exercise 14.2 (page 563)

1. (a) Path, not simple (b) Path, not simple (c) Simple path (d) Circuit (e) Simple circuit
3. (a) Simple circuit (b) Simple circuit (c) Simple circuit (d) Path, not simple

5. (a) $v_1 e_1 v_2$
   $v_5 e_5 v_6 e_9 v_3$
   $v_1 e_6 v_6 e_5 v_5 e_4 v_4$
   $v_2 e_2 v_3 e_3 v_4 e_4 v_5$

   (b) $v_1 e_1 v_2 e_7 v_6 e_5 v_5 e_{10} v_3 e_9 v_6 e_6 v_1$
   $v_1 e_1 v_2 e_8 v_5 e_5 v_6 e_9 v_3 e_2 v_2 e_7 v_6 e_6 v_1$
   $v_1 e_1 v_2 e_7 v_6 e_9 v_3 e_{10} v_5 e_5 v_6 e_6 v_1$
   $v_2 e_8 v_5 e_{10} v_3 e_3 v_4 e_4 v_5 e_5 v_6 e_9 v_3 e_2 v_2$

   (c) $v_1 e_1 v_2 e_7 v_6 e_6 v_1$
   $v_3 e_{10} v_5 e_4 v_4 e_3 v_3$
   $v_2 e_8 v_5 e_{10} v_3 e_9 v_6 e_7 v_2$
   $v_6 e_5 v_5 e_4 v_4 e_3 v_3 e_2 v_2 e_1 v_1 e_6 v_6$

7. $v_1 e_1 v_2 e_2 v_3 e_9 v_5 e_4 v_4 e_3 v_3 e_8 v_6 e_6 v_1$

9. (a) 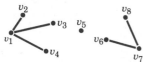   (b)

11. (a) e_1, e_2, e_3, e_4.   (b) e_4.   (c) e_2, e_4, e_5.

13.
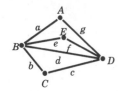

15. (a) No, because $11 > \binom{5}{2} = 10$ (Theorem II).
    (b) Yes, because $10 \not> \binom{5}{2} = 10$ (Theorem II).

Exercise 14.3 (page 570)

1. (a) Every vertex is of even degree. By Theorem 1 there is an Eulerian circuit.
   $v_1 e_1 v_2 e_2 v_3 e_4 v_4 e_5 v_5 e_6 v_3 e_3 v_2 e_9 v_5 e_7 v_6 e_8 v_1$ is an Eulerian circuit.
   (b) The graph is not connected, therefore, no Eulerian circuit.
   (c) Degree of $v_1 = 3$ is not even, therefore, no Eulerian circuit.
   (d) Every vertex is of even degree. Therefore the graph contains a Eulerian circuit. The circuit
   $v_1 e_1 v_2 e_2 v_3 e_3 v_1 e_5 v_4 e_4 v_2 e_6 v_5 e_7 v_1$ is Eulerian.
   (e) Every vertex is of even degree. Therefore the graph contains an Eulerian circuit. The circuit
   $v_1 e_1 v_2 e_{10} v_3 e_{11} v_5 e_{12} v_1 e_{13} v_6 e_5 v_5 e_4 v_4 e_3 v_3 e_2 v_2 e_{14} v_4 e_{15} v_6 e_9 v_2 e_8 v_7 e_7 v_6 e_6 v_1$ is Eulerian.
   (f) Degree of $v_1 = 3$ is not even. Therefore, the graph does not contain an Eulerian circuit.

3. Yes, each vertex is of even degree.

5.

Yes. Let A and C in the figure be the land masses; B, E, and D be the three islands; and $a, b, c, d, e, f,$ and g be the seven bridges. Note that each vertex has even degree. Therefore, the graph contains an Eulerian circuit. The following circuit is the desired round trip:

AaBbCcDdBeEfDgA.

7. No, the corresponding graph has vertex B (vertex representing room B) of degree, 3 which is not even.

9. (a) $v_1e_1v_2e_9v_7e_{10}v_8e_3v_3e_4v_4e_5v_5e_6v_6e_7v_1$
   (b) $v_1e_1v_7e_2v_2e_4v_8e_5v_3e_6v_4e_7v_5e_8v_6e_9v_1$
   (c) $v_1e_1v_2e_2v_3e_3v_4e_{11}v_7e_{10}v_6e_{13}v_5e_5v_1$
   (d) $v_4e_3v_3e_9v_8e_{12}v_7e_{11}v_6e_7v_2e_1v_1e_5v_5e_4v_4$

11. Use Theorem 2,
   (a) $\deg(v_1) + \deg(v_5) = 4 < 6$, number of vertices.
   (b) $\deg(v_2) + \deg(v_7) = 4 < 8$, number of vertices.
   (c) $\deg(v_1) + \deg(v_6) = 4 < 7$, number of vertices.
   (d) $\deg(v_5) + \deg(v_{10}) = 4 < 10$, number of vertices.

13.

15.

Exercise 14.4 (page 579)

1.

3.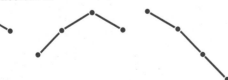

5. By Theorem 1, such a tree cannot exist.
7. Cannot exist. A graph with the given specifications must contain a circuit.
9. Cannot exist. Such a graph must contain a circuit.
11. Cannot exist. Such a graph *must* be a tree.
13. Yes. Use Theorem 1.

15.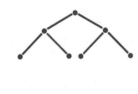

17. Leaves; v_1, v_3, v_4, v_5, v_6, v_7.
   Internal vertices: v_2, v_9, v_8, v_{10}, v_{11}, v_{12}.
19. No. By definition a leaf is connected to the rest of a tree by only one edge.

21.

23. (a) x: r, p, q, u
   y: v, s, t, w, a, b, c

(b)

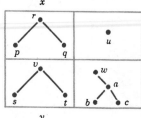

Vertex   Left subtree   Right subtree
     x

     y

(c)

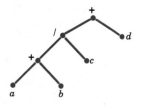

25. $a * b + 1$ **27.** $(x + y) * z - a/b$

29.

31.

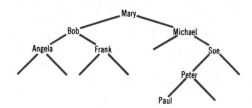

33. (a) Yes.   (b) Yes.

Exercise 14.5 (page 587)

1. (a)

Arc	Initial Point	Terminal Point
e_1	a	a
e_2	a	b
e_3	a	c
e_4	b	c
e_5	d	c
e_6	c	e
e_7	d	e
e_8	d	h
e_9	c	f
e_{10}	f	c
e_{11}	f	g
e_{12}	f	h
e_{13}	h	g

(b)

Vertex	Indegree	Outdegree
a	1	3
b	1	1
c	4	2
d	0	3
e	2	0
f	1	3
g	2	0
h	2	1

3.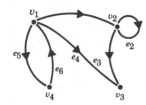

5.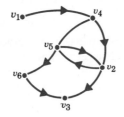

7.

9. (a) Yes. $v_1e_1v_2e_8v_7e_{10}v_5$ is a directed path from v_1 to v_5.
   (b) No. No arcs go into v_1, that is, indeg$(v_1) = 0$.

11. $v_1e_1v_2e_8v_7e_{10}v_5e_5v_6$; $v_1e_6v_6$; $v_1e_1v_2e_8v_7e_{11}v_4e_{12}v_6$

13. No. Since outdegree $(v_6) = 0$, then no other vertex is readable from v_6.

15.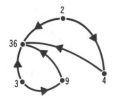

17. Graph is connected and contains no bridges. Therefore it is orientable. The digraph in the figure is the desired strongly connected digraph.

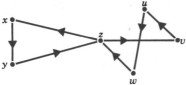

19. Graph is connected and contains no bridges. Therefore it is orientable. The desired strongly connected digraph is shown in the figure.

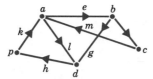

True–False Questions (page 589)
   1. F   **2.** F   **3.** T   **4.** T   **5.** T   **6.** T

Fill in the Blanks (page 589)
   1. Vertices, edges   **2.** Loop, parallel   **3.** Eulerian   **4.** Circuit   **5.** Direction
   6. Directed, strongly connected.

Review Exercises (page 590)
   1. No. Such a simple graph must at most have 6 edges.
   3. (a) $v_1e_9v_5e_5v_7e_4v_6e_{12}v_3$

(b) $v_1e_9v_5e_5v_7e_4v_6e_{12}v_3e_3v_5e_9v_1$

(c) $v_1e_9v_5e_5v_7e_4v_6e_{11}v_2e_1v_1$

5. No. The graph in the figure represents the city where the vertices A and B are the two banks, C, D, and E are the three islands and the edges are the bridges. Since $\deg(B) = 3$ which is odd, then the graph does not contain an Eulerian circuit.

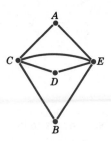

7. $v_1e_1v_2e_2v_3e_8v_5e_6v_2e_7v_4e_9v_1e_{10}v_3e_3v_4e_4v_5e_5v_1$ is an Eulerian circuit.

9.

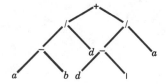

11.

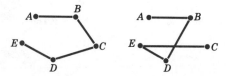

13. Yes. Every vertex is reachable from the others.

INDEX